THE
ROCKEFELLER
CENTURY

THE ROCKEFELLER CENTURY

JOHN ENSOR HARR

AND

PETER J. JOHNSON

CHARLES SCRIBNER'S SONS

NEW YORK

Charles Scribner's Sons
Macmillan Publishing Company
866 Third Avenue, New York, NY 10022
Collier Macmillan Canada, Inc.

Library of Congress Cataloging-in-Publication Data
Harr, John Ensor, 1926–
The Rockefeller century / John Ensor Harr and Peter J. Johnson.
p. cm.
Includes index.
ISBN 0-684-18936-4
1. Rockefeller family.   2. United States—Biography.   I. Johnson,
Peter J.   II. Title.
CT274.R59H37 1988
973.9′092′2—dcB
[19]
87-32437
CIP

Macmillan books are available at special discounts for bulk purchases for sales promotions, premiums, fund-raising, or educational use. For details, contact:

Special Sales Director
Macmillan Publishing Company
866 Third Avenue
New York, NY 10022

10 9 8 7 6 5 4 3 2 1

Designed by Jack Meserole

PRINTED IN THE UNITED STATES OF AMERICA

For Nancy and Dawn

CONTENTS

IV DEPRESSION AND WAR, 1929–1943

V THE TIES THAT BIND, 1944–1952

ILLUSTRATIONS

(All photographs courtesy of the Rockefeller Archive Center)

ix

PREFACE

This book is about three men with the same name—John D. Rockefeller.

For the sake of clarity in the pages that follow, we refer to them by names that were used frequently during their lifetimes by family members or associates. The original John D. (1839–1937), the one who created the Standard Oil trust, is "Senior." His only son, John D. Rockefeller, Jr. (1874–1960), is "Junior." And Junior's eldest son, John D. Rockefeller 3rd (1906–1978), is "John 3rd" in his youthful years and later "JDR 3rd" or, simply, "JDR."

Over three generations and the span of nearly a century, these three men were the leading philanthropists in the United States, the chief practitioners and bearers of a unique family tradition and dynasty that has no parallel in American history. That dynasty effectively ended with the death of JDR. Their careers thus form an important thread in the rich fabric of modern American history, both reflecting that history and in some ways helping to shape it.

As the best-known philanthropists in American history, the three John D.'s were indisputably men of social conscience, but the more interesting question is the motivation behind their exercise of conscience. Thus, we are concerned not only with *what* they attempted to do as philanthropists, but *why*, and also with the environment that shaped their careers—the events and historical currents of their times that stimulated them and the dynamics of their family life.

We thus hope that this book will be a contribution to the rapidly growing interest in the study of philanthropy as an important subject in American history. On that score, the comments of three scholars cited in the *New York Times* (November 18, 1986) are noteworthy. Professor John G. Simon of Yale characterized philanthropy "as the least understood aspect of our national life." Robert L. Payton, president of the Exxon Education Foundation, said: "There are all sorts of signs the nonprofit sector is awakening the intellectual interest of important scholars who have simply not paid attention until now." Professor Stanley Katz, president of the American Council of Learned Societies, cited the opening of the Rockefeller Archive Center in 1971 as "an important breakthrough." He said: "Until then,

xiii

it was virtually impossible to get access to the records of even one major foundation."

We begin this book by examining a decade of difficult transition for Senior, one in which he began to use his great fortune in a major way in philanthropic contributions that forged the family dynasty and formed so important an environment for his son's coming to manhood. We place a major emphasis on Junior, who was a towering figure in his time, clearly the pivotal figure in the family dynasty, yet one who has received much less adequate attention in the literature than his father. As for the third generation, we are concerned with all five Rockefeller brothers, but our main focus is on the last of the great philanthropists in this tradition, JDR, who has scarcely been written about at all.

Not long after JDR's death in 1978, Porter McKeever suggested that I write JDR's biography. Porter and I had been colleagues, two of the four people in JDR's office with the all-purpose Rockefeller title of "associate." I had worked for JDR for eleven years, Porter for five. In 1976 a fifth person, Peter Johnson, joined our ranks.

In planning the biography of JDR, I was happy to use Peter's skills as a trained historian. Over a period of about a year, the project took shape, with the approval and cooperation of JDR's immediate family and with Peter joining me as research associate.

Peter and I agreed that to do justice to JDR's life and career we had to broaden the focus. It would not be possible to understand JDR without knowing a great deal about his father, who was the most important influence on his life. And, of course, it is not possible to understand Junior without knowing something about *his* father. The task thus became a much more massive one—a history of the family philanthropic dynasty as well as a biography of JDR.

We made two decisions. One was to become coauthors in the fullest sense. I have done most of the writing and Peter most of the researching. This might seem to leave me free to claim any merits of the ultimate product, with Peter responsible for any errors. However, that is not the case. Each of us has participated extensively in the other's primary assignment in what we both feel has been an enjoyable and productive partnership and division of labor, sharing fully in any merits or demerits.

The second decision was to cover our subject in two volumes rather than in one very long one. After all, the material divided at a natural breakpoint—the early 1950s, when Junior retired and was transferring assets to his five sons, who were by then well launched in their careers. Thus, this book becomes a history of Rockefeller family philanthropy to that point. The second volume will continue the story of the lives of the five brothers, principally JDR, whose remarkable career, at times overshadowed in the public eye by the doings of several of his more famous brothers, is not well known or understood in its full scope and significance. Apart from the original purpose, the reason for the dominant interest in JDR is that it was he, among the five brothers, who clearly was the principal carrier of the family traditions.

The fact that we were actively associated with JDR, I for eleven years and Peter for two, carries with it both an asset and a potential liability. We did not know him intimately (almost no one did), but working with him and observing him over an extended period of time gave us insights into the man—how he thought, why he acted, and what he was trying to do—that no other writers, however skilled, could possibly obtain. It also gave us firsthand familiarity with family dynamics and history.

The potential liability that would cancel out the asset is that our association with JDR would lead us to engage in hagiography rather than objective history and biography. This danger is well illustrated by Raymond Fosdick's 1956 biography of Junior, *John D. Rockefeller, Jr.: A Portrait*. This book is so informative that it must be regarded as the only serious biography of Junior ever written. Yet it is badly flawed by the omission of material of the kind that Junior might have regarded as too sensitive or embarrassing. The result *is* a portrait of a saint. However, the neglected material *does* appear in our book.

Fosdick was associated with Junior for nearly forty years, thus giving him an unparalleled opportunity to know his subject. But this advantage was canceled by the omissions, which possibly occurred because Fosdick wrote the book while Junior was still living. In our case, we were associated with JDR for a much shorter time, much less intimately, and we began our work only after JDR's death.

Still, these differences do not necessarily relieve us of at least the prima facie suspicion of engaging in hagiography, not only because of our personal association with JDR, but also because our account of him is an "authorized" one in the sense that we enjoy the trust and candor of his survivors. When we began work, JDR's only son, Jay, told us to feel completely independent and objective and to "tell the true story, warts and all." He and his mother and three sisters played their part by being candid with us in interviews and refraining from attempts to censor or second-guess us.

Jay's advice may have been given in the comfortable knowledge that there are not many warts to be found in his father's life. Indeed, it is a challenging assignment to avoid a saintlike account of a man whom many regard as very nearly saintly. Yet there is much in JDR's life that, like his father, he conceivably might have wanted to gloss over as too embarrassing or sensitive if he had had the chance. But this is material that makes him intensely *human* rather than a cardboard character—and it makes his aspirations and accomplishments all the more remarkable. Thus, we have tried our best to follow Jay's injunction and our own desires and instincts to present an honest portrait.

The vast literature on the Rockefellers is overloaded with books biased in one of two directions—either too adulatory or hypercritical beyond any reasonable interpretation of the facts. From the foregoing, it is obvious that our intention has been to hew to the middle path of digging exhaustively into the primary and secondary sources, trying to be as objective as we can, and letting the facts speak for themselves.

At the same time, we recognize that no one can be totally objective. The next best thing is to be honest about one's biases. One of ours is the belief that Rockefeller philanthropy is a legitimate, interesting, and important facet of American history, one well worth exploring and understanding. Moreover, we believe that that philanthropy has preponderantly been well intentioned and good in its effects, and was generated primarily by praiseworthy motives rather than for reasons of personal ambition, political gain, or the expiation of guilt.

How well these views hold up, and, beyond them, how well we have done in our effort to be objective and definitive, are obviously matters for others to judge.

JOHN ENSOR HARR
Glen Ridge, New Jersey
January 1988

ACKNOWLEDGMENTS

After years of concentrated research, writing, and revising, authors may be forgiven the conceit that they alone are responsible for the words and ideas that finally remain on the printed page. Of course, this is rarely the case with any book and certainly not with this study. Our debts are many and varied. Intellectual influences are particularly difficult to acknowledge, or even to trace, in a collaborative effort. In many instances they began in crowded undergraduate lecture halls and have continued to have an impact through all the years of our professional lives. Thus, we recognize, without being any more explicit, the important role of both our mentors and those scholars whom we have never met but whose works have significantly influenced our thinking.

A number of individuals deserve special mention. Porter McKeever originally conceived the idea of a biography of John D. Rockefeller 3rd almost fifteen years ago. He has been a staunch supporter and a helpful critic of our efforts ever since. Datus C. Smith was also a strong advocate of the project and provided expert guidance into the publishing world. Blanchette Rockefeller made her husband's private papers available to us and gave freely of her time and knowledge. Her contribution to this book was subtle, but extremely important.

This book and its companion volume, to be published later, are based on extensive research in the papers of individual members of the Rockefeller Family and its affiliated organizations now housed at the Rockefeller Archive Center in Pocantico Hills, New York. Dr. Joseph W. Ernst, Rockefeller Family Archivist and Director Emeritus of the Archive Center, was exceptionally helpful in guiding us through this impressive and invaluable collection within the ground rules established for scholars, as was Dr. William Hess, the Associate Director. Two members of their staff, Claire Collier and Tom Rosenbaum, helped assemble the photographs included in this volume and tracked down many elusive files and references. Donal C. O'Brien, Jr., Marsha McLean, and Mary Jane Hesson of the Family Legal Office explained the significance and operation of the various trusts. David G. Fernald and members of the Room 5600 Accounting

Department, especially George Pipino and Dennis Ryan, provided access to the detailed financial information that distinguishes this work from all previous studies of the Rockefeller Family.

Other members of the Room 5600 Staff—George Taylor, Carmen Reyes, Dorothea Weissman, Maryetta Davis, and Patricia Sheehy— provided information on varied aspects of the Family's activities. Curtis J. Clow, formerly of the Archival Staff, supplied essential help at the outset. Gordon Jenkins and Ray Neugebauer, both unfortunately deceased, were unfailingly cooperative.

David Robarge and Randy Bergstrom, young historians of exceptional promise, added important historical information and sometimes painful intellectual criticism throughout the process. Kimberly Johnson paginated the original manuscript. Jacques Barzun improved this book through his immense erudition, literary style, and friendship.

Our thanks, as well, to our editor at Scribners, Susanne Kirk, for all her help and patience, and to friends who were kind enough to read draft chapters and offer their reactions—especially Anderson Clark, Jerry Zucker, Joe McLaughlin, and Ed Seymour.

Technological change has eliminated the need to thank a typist, but we are eternally grateful to "Tessie," the indomitable word processor.

Having assigned credit, we hereby absolve all of those mentioned above for any factual mistakes or errors of interpretation. We happily bear that burden ourselves.

PETER J. JOHNSON
Maspeth, New York
January 1988

THE
ROCKEFELLER
CENTURY

INTRODUCTION:
THE DYNASTY

In 1967 the National Institute of Social Sciences made an unusual decision—to grant its annual gold medal award for distinguished service not to one, but to five recipients. This set in motion a rare event, an appearance together in public of all five Rockefeller brothers.

The NISS is a venerable organization that traces its lineage back to the American Social Science Association, which was founded in the 1870s, the first organization of its kind. After giving birth to some of the professional societies in the social sciences that exist today, the association became the NISS, an organization of genteel amateurs, its members mostly older, successful New Yorkers of the kind people have in mind when they refer vaguely to "the establishment." Its program consisted of little more than giving its award to distinguished individuals at an annual banquet.

The NISS gold medal had been awarded in 1923 to John D. Rockefeller, the founder of the Standard Oil Company, who by that time had given nearly half a billion dollars to philanthropic causes. In 1929 the NISS award was given to his son, John D. Rockefeller, Jr., who carried on his father's work in philanthropy as a lifetime career. In 1967 the NISS had a good idea: continuing that tradition by giving the award to *his* sons, the five male members of the third generation, all of whom had made notable contributions in philanthropy or public service, or both. If they all appeared together, a successful awards banquet was guaranteed. To help ensure success, NISS policy decreed that the award would be given only if recipients appeared in person.

That stipulation gave the Rockefeller brothers some pause. They could not easily arrange their schedules so that all five could be together in the same place at the same time. Moreover, all of them had become adroit over the years in avoiding events or causes in which they did not have a personal interest. They also often declined awards or honorary degrees, having learned from experience that the purpose behind such honors often was to trade on the Rockefeller name or to establish a relationship to be used for some future request for financial assistance.

However, the NISS was not looking for money, and there was the precedent of the brothers' father and grandfather having received the award. Moreover, the five became intrigued with the idea of appearing together in public. They could not remember the last time that had happened. They were not clannish in the manner, say, of the Kennedy family, all rallying together to work in concerted fashion toward some great objective. There were always critics available to suggest that the brothers operated in a family conspiracy to control American political and economic life, a charge that does not square with the facts. The relationships among the brothers were generally good, in some cases close. They would often gather together at Christmas and meet socially at other times, and occasionally one would lend help to another on a project of mutual interest. But long ago they had decided that each should go his own way. That had happened when all had come of age, in meetings before and after World War II to talk about career intentions so that they would not find themselves directly competing with one another. This was the beginning of "brothers' meetings," random get-togethers in private to discuss family affairs. Rarely, in later years, would all five brothers be present.

On the evening of the NISS black-tie banquet, November 28, all five were there, seated on the dais to receive their awards and make brief acceptance remarks in order of seniority. First was John Davison Rockefeller 3rd, born in 1906, a tall, spare man with a craggy profile and twinkling eyes. As the oldest son, he had followed in the pattern set by his father—his full-time occupation was philanthropy. A very private person, he assiduously avoided publicity unless it was in the service of some worthwhile cause that he was promoting.

Next was Nelson Aldrich Rockefeller, born in 1908, the shortest of the brothers, stocky, with a big grin and a raspy voice. Charismatic and ebullient, Nelson was the quintessential politician. He was in his third term as governor of New York State, and, as usual, the brother most in the news. Everyone was speculating as to whether Nelson would make another try for the Republican nomination for president in 1968.

The middle brother was Laurance Spelman Rockefeller, born in 1910, a slender man thought by many to be the brother who most resembled the grandfather, and with the same keen intelligence and wry wit. Laurance was an active businessman, especially in high-technology fields, and was one of the most important American figures in the field of conservation. Also a private person, Laurance at times seemed to be vying with his brother John for the title of "least known" of the Rockefeller brothers.

The fourth brother was Winthrop Rockefeller, born in 1912, balding and somewhat overweight, very affable, the brother most with the common touch. For years he had been the "black sheep," unable to finish college, drifting from job to job and into an unfortunate first marriage, and engaged in a lifelong struggle with alcohol. But he had moved to Arkansas, pulled himself together, and performed the notable service of becoming an honest and reform-oriented governor of a state not previously well known for such leadership.

Last was David Rockefeller, born in 1915, genial, a bit overweight, possessed of a reedy voice, next to Nelson the best-known brother as the chairman of the Chase Manhattan Bank, highly active in philanthropic causes, and a man of intellectual prowess, having earned his Ph.D. at the University of Chicago.

The chairman of the NISS awards banquet, Frank Pace, began the proceedings by reading the citation for John 3rd's award, mentioning his most prominent accomplishments—development of Lincoln Center for the Performing Arts, the founding of the Asia Society and the reconstitution of the Japan Society, extensive work in Asia over many years in agriculture and the arts, leadership generally in philanthropy, establishment of the Rockefeller Public Service Awards, and others. But the chairman properly emphasized the field in which John 3rd was best known, his pioneering leadership for decades in efforts to combat the worldwide problem of overpopulation. So wide-ranging and intensive had his work in this field been that he became known in some circles as "Mr. Population."

John 3rd accepted the award and began to speak: "It is true, as Frank Pace has suggested, that the field of population and family planning has occupied much of my thought and energy for a number of years. But tonight's occasion makes me wonder." He paused and glanced at his brothers. "If my parents had been exposed to today's ideas of family planning, brothers Win and Dave might not have made it."

There was tentative laughter for a moment and then the audience burst into a roar of appreciation. Some of the audience members knew John 3rd personally, and all knew him by reputation. The prevailing image was one of a somewhat shy man, sensitive, retiring, and extremely serious about his work. He had never been known before to attempt humor in public. He continued in the same vein:

As I look at my fellow award winners, I feel myself to be in rather good company. There were times, long ago, when I used to worry a bit about these younger fellows, but I think they have all turned out very well. In fact, I am the only one of the five who is unemployed. One of my brothers works for the State of Arkansas, another for the State of New York, the third for a very large bank, and the fourth is an active businessman. I cannot be absolutely sure, but I don't think any of them is job-hunting.

There was another roar of appreciation for the last point, an obvious reference to all of the publicity about Nelson's political intentions. But it turned out that John 3rd was mistaken. Nelson did decide to go job-hunting, losing to Richard Nixon at the Republican convention in Miami the following year.

John 3rd then thanked the NISS, and quoted his grandfather's response when he was asked to account for his success: "He would say: 'My associates; I have been very fortunate in my associates.' I know I speak for my brothers as well as myself in saying that we, too, have been fortunate in being associated with outstanding men and women over the years."

The speaker then turned to the subject of the values that had been passed on to the brothers by their father and grandfather:

You honor them again through us, for they bequeathed to us not only our name and material resources, but also certain basic values. How well we have lived up to those values is for others to judge, but that they were instilled in us by our parents and grandparents there can be no doubt.

Several of these values have given shape and meaning to philanthropy to me. One of them is a sense of responsibility, of considering the resources passed on to us as a trust. Our task was to grow into this responsibility, to develop the ability to manage this trust in active efforts to promote human welfare.

Another value is the importance of being relevant to the problems and needs of one's time. One could be very busy as a philanthropist, and yet be relatively ineffectual. Thus, fifty years ago, the dominant concerns of philanthropy were health and welfare. Today, they are in such areas as over-population, urban decay, civil rights, conservation, the arts.

A third value is to give of one's self. We were taught that it is not enough to give only of one's name or material resources. One must also become involved personally, to contribute one's time and thought and energy. To me, this is the spirit of giving. And I know of no other way to stay relevant and be effective.

For a final comment, John 3rd spoke about the status of phi-lanthropy:

Philanthropy has been a unique social force in the United States; there is no real counterpart to it anywhere else. The resources of philanthropy have always been small in comparison to those of private enterprise and govern-ment, but they have been effective as venture capital in meeting social needs—sometimes in the role of catalyst, sometimes functioning as a balance wheel, other times as the cutting edge. Some may think that with the expansion of government services into many new areas, the need for philan-thropy is correspondingly lessened. I think precisely the opposite is true. The larger government becomes and the more varied its activities, the more philanthropy is important and needed. There are always things that govern-ment cannot do well, or should not do at all, or can best do in partnership with philanthropy. Moreover, the scope and complexity of social problems contin-ues to grow beyond the reach of either government or philanthropy, but hopefully not of both. Our task in philanthropy, and it is more difficult than ever before, is to be creative, to be venturesome, and to find effective methods of partnership with government and private enterprise.

He closed on a warm note: "Unlike old soldiers, philanthropists do not fade away. There really is no such thing as retirement in my chosen field. I hope to be active for many more years, especially with the warmth and encouragement that is evident here tonight."

He had spoken for only a few minutes, yet he had managed a humorous opening; a gracious expression of appreciation; a rather precise statement of family values; a concern for the relationships among government, private enterprise, and philanthropy that would dominate his thinking in the years ahead; and a warm closing.

Indicative of the way the brothers operated independently, they had not coordinated their remarks beforehand. Each had his own staff, and the staffs did not often interact, so John 3rd's brothers did not know what he was going to say as the lead-off speaker. The affair obviously was not meant as a competition, but inevitably comparisons would be made. As the oldest brother, John 3rd had the advantage of being the first speaker, but he was up against two experienced politicians and the best-known banker in the world. What happened was a rare triumph for him—the shy brother who shunned the spotlight was the hit of the evening. When he sat down, his brother Nelson, a much more experienced public speaker, leaned over to pay him a compliment: "Johnny, that was a ten-strike!" Winthrop chided him on the crack about "unemployment," wondering if John would like to trade places with him and be governor of Arkansas at the grand salary of $10,000 per year.

All of the Rockefeller brothers were well known in the specific areas and circles within which they worked, but only one of them was truly famous. Nelson was instantly recognizable almost everywhere, but probably not one American in a thousand could name all five brothers. Yet, collectively they were famous, permeating the consciousness of almost everyone as a sort of unique institution in American life, seemingly a permanent fixture.

That image ended when Winthrop died of cancer in 1973. On July 10, 1978, John 3rd tragically perished in an automobile accident at the age of seventy-two. A little over six months later, on January 26, 1979, Nelson died of a massive heart attack in the house on West 54th Street where John 3rd had been born.

In a very real sense, the death of the eldest brother, the one with *the* name, signaled the end of a unique dynasty in American life. With his grandfather and father before him, John 3rd had participated in a century-long story of a special brand of personal philanthropy; nothing like it will ever happen again.

To be sure, the family name continues to be associated with philanthropy through the Rockefeller Foundation and other institutions. The family fortune, which dwindled during the Depression and revived in the postwar boom only to dwindle again by the 1970s, is now reviving again in the mounting value in recent years of Rockefeller Center, now the main repository of family wealth. Two brothers survive and continue to be active. And there is the fourth generation, the surviving twenty-one sons and daughters of the five brothers and their older sister, the generation known as "the Cousins," ranging in age from the early twenties to the mid-fifties, many of whom are generous givers and active participants in worthy causes. And there are the next generations, now more than seventy young adults and children.

Significantly, the fourth John D. Rockefeller, John 3rd's only son, Jay, now a Democratic senator from West Virginia, has followed another tradition, that of public life, which has been prominent in the Rockefeller family but certainly not unique to it. The mere fact of the multiplicity of heirs suggests the end of the philanthropic dynasty, along with changing times, inheritance taxes, and the extensive distribution of the original fortune that has occurred over the past century. Because of these factors, the fourth John D. never really had the option of continuing the dynasty, of following in the footsteps of his father, grandfather, and great-grandfather as a full-time philanthropist. A wise saying of a taciturn man, the original John D. Rockefeller, was that "perpetuity is a long time." He did not expect nor did he intend that family wealth or the great philanthropic institutions he created would exist in perpetuity. They were meant to serve a purpose, to be of service, and not to exist in and of themselves.

The three John D. Rockefellers were the successive carriers of their family's traditions and responsibilities and principles. There are many famous families in American history, but none that can be compared to the Rockefellers in the sustained giving of wealth over three generations combined with the exercise of influence for what they perceived to be the public good. What the three John D. Rockefellers tried to accomplish, each in his own time, offers fascinating insights into American development and history over the span of nearly a century. One thread running through the lives of these three men is the theme of *conscience*—in this case, of course, "the Rockefeller conscience." That each of them exhibited a high degree of conscience in the sense of trying to do everything he could to use his wealth and influence for the betterment of others and of society in general there can be no doubt. The historical record speaks powerfully on this account, as we shall see. Conscience can be regarded as a neutral concept in the sense that it does not answer the question of motivation. Why did these three Rockefellers behave the way they did? The motivations behind philanthropy, behind the giving of one's self and one's resources in an attempt to help others, manifestly an important dimension of the human experience, is a subject that has never been adequately explored. In the case of people of wealth, why are some dedicated givers while others lead lives of self-indulgence and dissipation—particularly when the giver invites criticism, while American society has always reserved a kind of amused tolerance for the wealthy playboy?

There are the less palatable explanations—ego gratification, expiation of guilt, the quest for power or popularity, and the lugubrious Marxist interpretation of the Rockefellers—that they were predetermined and driven to be givers in order to control American life to their satisfaction. Then there are the "good" explanations. One, simply, would be having enough intelligence to perceive that a life devoted to giving is bound to be more satisfying in the long run than one of dissipation or lusting for power and fame. Others would include religious principles and a classical sense of civic duty. There is also the force of tradition, and of training and preconditioning in one's youth. There is no question that the idea of giving became a Rockefeller family tradition over three generations, so strong a tradition and so zealously acted out that it created its own mystique, with the result that Rockefeller prominence and influence lasted long after the family ceased to be the wealthiest in America.

Obviously, there can be no single or easy explanation of such a phenomenon. Understanding may come in part from the record of what the leaders of the family tried to do, and how and why they went about it. And deeper understanding may come from examining the dynamics of the family, the intensely human story of the Rockefellers as individuals and as family members. In this book, we are particularly interested in the formative years of the three John D. Rockefellers, in the father-son relationships, and the important influence of the Rockefeller wives. Major attention is paid to Junior as the pivotal figure in the family and to his career as a great liberal in public affairs and a staunch conservative in family matters. And equal attention is paid to the growth to manhood of his five sons and the launching of their careers, in particular that of John D. Rockefeller 3rd—the last of the great philanthropists in this tradition.

I

THE
ROCKEFELLER
LEGACY
1889–1918

1

THE FOUNDING
FATHER

THE TWO MEN stood in front of the brownstone at 4 West 54th Street in Manhattan, talking earnestly. It was May 17, 1889, a fine balmy day. Although the residential street was quiet, they could hear the distant rumble of a steam-drawn train on the new Sixth Avenue Elevated Line. An occasional hansom cab passed on the street and children hurried by on their way to school. The two men began strolling the short distance to Fifth Avenue. The younger and shorter of the two spoke vigorously and quickly, using his fingers to tick off his points. His companion gazed back impassively, nodding occasionally and asking a short question before turning to resume his stroll. Just as he reached the corner of Fifth Avenue, he seemed to have made up his mind and spoke briefly. The younger man could scarcely conceal his elation.[1]

On that street corner, John D. Rockefeller, president of the powerful and increasingly notorious Standard Oil Company, had finally agreed to help fund the creation of a new Baptist college that would rise in the city of Chicago. He had started the morning prepared to contribute $400,000 of the $1 million needed, contingent on the remainder being raised from among citizens of Chicago. But he agreed to raise his gift to $600,000, to put the effort more than halfway over the top, after listening to the pleas of the younger man, the Reverend Frederick T. Gates, secretary of the newly formed American Baptist Education Society.

The next morning, the first annual meeting of the society occurred at the Tremont Temple in Boston. Its main business was to consider a series of resolutions proposed by a special committee for the "founding of a well-equipped College in the City of Chicago." At the appropriate moment, Gates ascended the platform holding aloft a letter from "our great patron of education, Mr. John D. Rockefeller," which promised $600,000 "on the basis of the resolutions adopted by our Board." The minutes of the meeting described what happened next:

> The Secretary's remarks were interrupted at this point by tumultuous cheering and applause, accompanied by the waving of handkerchiefs and other evidences of enthusiasm.
> Order having been restored the entire assembly united in singing the doxology. "Praise God from whom all blessings flow."[2]

As a pious Baptist, Rockefeller was certainly not a person who would have identified himself with God. But he *was* by far the wealthiest Baptist in America. As such he had been pursued for years by his brethren to aid in the establishment of a new university. The decision he took on that morning in May was the turning point in a long series of discussions and negotiations, marked by a good measure of rivalry. The Northern Baptist Convention at that time was gifted with the presence of a number of talented and dynamic ministers. With a somewhat flamboyant style and boundless energy, Gates, at the age of thirty-six, was one of them. Another was Thomas W. Goodspeed of the Baptist Union Theological Seminary in Morgan Park on the South Side of Chicago. He had watched with sorrow the demise of the old University of Chicago. It had survived the great Chicago fire physically, but not financially. Some of the citizens who had pledged support were ruined, and the small university soon went bankrupt. It was Goodspeed in 1886 who first began writing to Rockefeller with the idea that he help in the creation of a new University of Chicago.

Another extraordinary Baptist minister was E. Benjamin Andrews, then at Cornell University. A friend of Rockefeller's, Andrews strongly supported Goodspeed's idea. Perhaps the most prominent Baptist of the time was Augustus H. Strong, president of the Rochester Theological Seminary. He had known Rockefeller for a long time, and his eldest son had wed Rockefeller's eldest daughter. Strong headed a group of ministers who had been putting pressure on Rockefeller for years to donate $20 million for the founding of a university in New York City, which Strong regarded "as the great strategic point for us Baptists to capture and master."[3] Still another group wanted the denomination to focus on building up Columbian University in Washington, D.C. (later renamed George Washington University). In addition to the grand vision of a great Baptist university being pressed by these three rival groups, Rockefeller was the constant recipient of pleas for aid from the presidents of a score of tiny and deficit-ridden Baptist colleges scattered throughout the East, Midwest, and South.

The Baptist minister who, along with Gates, finally tipped the scales in favor of Chicago was William Rainey Harper, only thirty-three years of age at the time Rockefeller made his first gift in 1889. Harper had been a colleague of Goodspeed's at the seminary in Chicago, where he taught Hebrew, but he had been lured away to Yale. He was a phenomenon, the "boy wonder" of the Baptist faith. He and Rockefeller came to admire each other deeply, despite the fact that their personalities could not have been more unlike. Gates described the differences well. Rockefeller was "temperamentally cool, reserved, cautious, circumspect, deliberate, amazingly patient, but in the end inflexible, adapting means to ends with long and accurate prevision." In contrast, Harper was "ardent, highly imaginative, with limitless capacity and insatiable eagerness for work, an undaunted optimist, minimizing difficulties, magnifying opportunities, rapid in conception, confiding, unsuspicious, bent on immediate results, willful, and impatient of opposition or delay."[4]

Rockefeller had come to envision the establishment of a college in Chicago that would grow in a slow and orderly way to the status of a university. Harper wanted a university immediately, complete with professional schools, one that would emphasize graduate education. He wanted to assemble the most brilliant faculty in the world by paying the unheard-of salary of $7,000 per year. He wanted to rival Oxford and Cambridge, the great German universities, and the best schools in the eastern United States. Although a scholar and visionary, not an administrator, Harper was the unanimous choice for president of the new institution among all those who favored the Chicago solution. But he agreed to take the post only after Rockefeller made a second gift a year later of $1 million.[5]

On that May morning, Rockefeller and Gates could not have known that their meeting would be the beginning of a close association between them that would last more than thirty years. And they could not have known that Rockefeller's gift of $600,000 would, over the next twenty-one years, escalate to a total of nearly $35 million. His support of the University of Chicago marked the largest philanthropic commitment to a single organization in American history up to that time.[6] More than this, he had embarked on a course that would gradually commit his fortune, and the lives of his son and grandsons, to the processes of change and reform in the United States. The initial gift to the University of Chicago was his first step on a journey that transformed his charitable giving into the organized, major philanthropy of the twentieth century.

The principal biographer of John D. Rockefeller, historian Allan Nevins, summed up his character and accomplishments in terms that echo the description by Gates:

His nature, for all its strength, was simple; his intellect, never clouded by emotion, was direct and analytical; his will, fixed on a few large purposes, was unwavering. With no great personal magnetism or versatility or breadth, he accomplished two epochal tasks: he set an original pattern in the efficient organization of industry, and an equally original pattern in the efficient superintendence of benefactions. He was not a mere arranger or manipulator of existing forces; he was a creator of new ideas and systems. By his clarity of thought, keenness of foresight, and strength of purpose, he made his life an important part of the nation's history.[7]

The character traits noted by Gates and Nevins were evident early. John Davison Rockefeller was born July 8, 1839, near Richford, New York. His mother, Eliza Davison Rockefeller, was a stern disciplinarian. She was intensely religious, shaped by her upbringing in the "burned-over district" of western New York State, so called because of the waves of evangelistic fervor that had repeatedly swept it during the early nineteenth century. From her the boy learned the values of piety, thrift, hard work, and sobriety. She taught him the strict tenets of her demanding Baptist faith. Drink, tobacco, card-playing, and dancing were sinful; a person's time should be devoted to self-improvement and service through work, prayer, and good deeds.

The father, William Avery Rockefeller, was a robust and magnetic man, a sometime salesman of herbal medicines and a small-time entrepreneur. From him the son learned something about affection, humor, and a zest for living. The father also seemed to have helped kindle ambition in the son as he taught him some of the rudimentary rules and practices of business. Yet the father was prone to long and mysterious absences from home, which engendered hints of scandalous behavior. These absences had the effect of placing an unusual burden on John as the oldest son, and he responded to this extremely well. The father also had several mysterious brushes with the law, causing the family to move progressively westward until, in 1853, they settled in the vicinity of Cleveland, Ohio, a bustling city of 30,000 people.

John attended high school for two years and a commercial college for three months, and at the age of sixteen in 1855 he was ready to seek his first job. He wanted one that would provide good experience to lead to "something big," and he found it as a bookkeeper and clerk with a small commission merchant's firm.[8] Within a few years, he had established a reputation among Cleveland businessmen as an uncommonly hardworking, honest, and competent young man. As a result of this and the business boom caused by the Civil War, John prospered after he took a partner and started his own commission firm.

From the day he was employed, earning about twenty-three dollars a month at the age of sixteen, young John showed a consistent trait that was often overlooked in later criticisms of him—he was a giving man, one who gave generously and regularly, as the handwritten entries in his famous personal ledger ("Ledger A") show.[9] Although most of his giving centered on his church, the Erie Street Baptist Church, he early showed another characteristic that would be important later on—an occasional willingness to give to other denominations and causes. As Nevins pointed out:

During the war, disregarding lines of faith, race, and nationality, he gave to a Catholic orphanage, a colored mute and blind society, an industrial school, and a Swedish mission in Illinois. In 1864, his gifts suddenly swelled to $671.86, and in 1865 went above the thousand-dollar mark. He had not waited to become rich before he became generous.[10]

But he soon became rich as well. In 1859 Colonel Edwin Drake had drilled the first successful oil well near Titusville in western Pennsylvania. A fervor akin to a gold rush soon seized the region, and young Rockefeller, handling barrels of petroleum among the other commodities on which he earned a commission, watched men become rich and go broke with equal rapidity. The "age of illumination" had dawned as uses were found for the many distillates of petroleum—naphtha, benzine, paraffin, other chemical derivatives, lubricating oils, and the most prized of all, kerosene for illumination. The only distillate for which no one had found a practical use was gasoline. Rockefeller and his partners listened to the ideas of a young technical expert, Samuel Andrews, about making kerosene from crude oil, and in 1863 they built a refinery in Cleveland, the first in that city to produce kerosene on a commercial scale. With Rockefeller's good credit lines and his organizing, managerial, and cost-cutting skills, the refinery soon became the largest in Cleveland and, within a few years, the largest in the world.

Rockefeller was on his way to becoming a very wealthy man. He was also a devoted and happy family man. In 1864 he had married Laura Celestia Spelman, a pretty, vivacious, and deeply religious young lady of his own age whom he had first met in high school in Cleveland. Their family grew, but the children seemed destined to be all girls—first Bessie, then Alice (who died in infancy), then Alta and Edith. Finally, on January 29, 1874, a son and heir was born. Nevins described the reaction:

> The father was inexpressibly happy. On the morning his son was born he burst into the office to tell his associates the news, and [they] affectionately put their arms about him, while the room rang with their congratulations, and tears of joy stood in Rockefeller's eyes.[11]

The baby was named John Davison Rockefeller, Jr., and thereafter became known almost universally as "Junior" to differentiate him from his father. For the same reason, the father became known within the family as "Senior."

By the time the son was born, Senior was committed to the goal of bringing order out of the chaos of the oil industry through the building of the great Standard Oil trust. For several decades after Drake's success at Titusville, everyone involved in the industry endured chronic uncertainty, sharp price fluctuations, and, in many cases, financial disaster. Intense competition resulted in overproduction, which glutted the slowly growing market and drove prices and profits down. Out of this depressed situation a variety of schemes for achieving stability emerged—producers' associations, refiners' associations, various types of pooling arrangements, and solemn compacts to limit production. One of the more notorious of these attempts was the "South Improvement Company," wrongly attributed to Senior by his later critics. All of these efforts failed, except in certain limited areas, as among the Cleveland refiners, because they were essentially voluntary associations of competitors; it was too tempting for a participant in an arrangement sooner or later to find a secret way to gain an edge on his competitors.

In 1870 Standard Oil was incorporated, consisting of the Cleveland refinery and a number of other installations and businesses that Senior and his partners had either started or acquired. Within a dozen years, it had become the Standard Oil trust, a near-monopoly of the oil industry in the United States, a giant combine of scores of companies in many states. How this was accomplished is obviously a long and very complicated story.[12] Some of the essential factors can be cited:

managerial skill; aggressive use of the growing power of Standard, especially in exacting favorable rates from the railroads; the strategy of staying out of the individualistic chaos of the oil-producing fields in favor of concentrating on refining, distribution, and marketing; a long string of acquisitions, mergers, and lease arrangements; massive entry into the export market, which was considerably stronger than the domestic market (this was a specialty of Senior's younger brother, William); and the assembling of a formidable group of executives, the Standard Oil "associates."

These were the years when the American industrial revolution was at the height of its transforming force, a tumultuous and chaotic period marked by cycles of boom and bust and ruinous competition, as well as by impressive growth. Senior's goal was to overcome waste and disorder by building a new kind of industrial organization, one that stressed careful planning, large volume, efficient organization, and market control. Standard's operations were always adequately capitalized, profits were plowed back into the company to finance further expansion, and technological innovations were quickly adopted to improve products and lower costs. On the question of why Standard prospered so much, Senior could only say, many years later, that it was "because it has managed its affairs well and economically and with great vigour."[13] His biographer elaborated the point:

The story offers the picture of a vigorous, realistic, superbly-led organization, rising swiftly to a power greater than any other American corporation had won. This organization zealously pursued its interests in a new, ill-organized, chaotic field, sometimes allying itself with and sometimes combating the yet unregulated railroads, whose practices were unstandardized and frequently unscrupulous. The Standard Oil by 1879 held a position new in economic history. It had attained monopolistic power in a great industrial field by its own efforts, and not by state grant, patent rights, exclusive control of raw materials, or special geographic position.[14]

The story is as controversial as it is complicated. A great age of reform was coming, a widespread revulsion against the excesses of the unbridled laissez-faire system of nineteenth-century America. Standard Oil was to become a prime target of the muckrakers and reformers. And, by the first decade of the new century, Senior was to emerge indelibly in the public mind as the very model of the robber baron. Why this happened and the profound impact it had on his only son will be examined in Chapter 3. For the present, suffice it to say that the legacy of criticism has spawned an enduring school of thought that remains deeply suspicious of Rockefeller wealth and power.[15]

As far as Standard Oil itself is concerned, however, the more dispassionate and objective judgment of modern scholarship, from the perspective of nearly a century later, is that by the rules of its time Standard was one of the more scrupulous operators in American business. Many of the charges levied by the muckrakers have been shown to be exaggerations, mistakes, or fabrications. Standard did not engage in the corrupt practices that were so rife then, such as bribery of state legislatures and the watering of stock. Many of its acquisitions were the luck of circumstance, the product of the fact that Standard was strong enough to survive economic hard times and thus be in a position to acquire companies from those eager to sell. For a time during the Panic of 1873, it seemed that Standard was the only American oil company that would not go bankrupt. Exacting rebates from the railroads was more a matter of survival than chicanery. As Nevins observed, if Rockefeller and his associates sometimes employed ruthless methods, "they to a great extent acted according to the economic ethics of the time; if they had not used those weapons, still more ruthless men would have used them against the Standard organizers."[16]

None of this gainsays the truth that Standard was highly aggressive in using its power and fully earned the criticism that came its way by the overwhelming fact of achieving a near-monopoly in its industry. The accumulation of great wealth and economic power in the hands of a few could not continue endlessly in the face of widespread social injustice, poverty, and inhumane working conditions. Massive criticism and change were inevitable. The Interstate Commerce Act was passed in 1887, followed by the Sherman Antitrust Act in 1890. Although it would be a number of years before court decisions and other legislative actions would put teeth into these laws, they were harbingers of what was to come. The prevailing ethic would change and Standard would be forced to change with it.

Senior professed to remain untroubled throughout all the years of attack on Standard and on him personally. He firmly believed that great benefits had accrued to society through the process of industrial combination and corporate management he had helped to develop. Even his most effective critic, Ida Tarbell, agreed that Senior and Standard had simply performed better than their competitors. In a chapter entitled "The Legitimate Greatness of Standard Oil," the influential muckraker grudgingly concluded:

> . . . this huge bulk, blackened by commercial sin, has always been strong in all great business qualities—in energy, intelligence, in dauntlessness. It

has always been rich in youth as well as greed, in brains as well as unscrupulousness. If it has played its great game with contemptuous indifference to fair play, and to nice legal points of view, it has played it with consummate ability, daring, and address.[17]

Tarbell went on to enumerate the reasons for the company's success, stressing its administrative centralization, excellent organizational structure, strong financial condition, ability to take infinite pains with minor details, and the abilities of the men Senior had surrounded himself with. In this Tarbell was echoing the sentiments of more friendly observers of the contemporary scene. William H. Vanderbilt, himself the son of a powerful and tenacious empire builder, noted of the Standard Oil group that he "never came into contact with any class of men as smart and able as they are in their business, and I think that a great deal of their advantage is to be attributed to that. They never could have got in the position they are in now without a good deal of ability, and one man could hardly have been able to do it. It is a combination of men."[18]

Senior's pursuit of business success might seem to suggest that he was among the most materialistic of men. But the accumulation of great wealth beyond his own needs was never his goal. It was an accidental by-product of the joy of work and accomplishment, of playing the "Great Game" of business as he called it: "That's the thing— accomplishment, playing the game. . . . Yet some say that because a man is successful and accumulates wealth, all he is after is to get wealth and oppress. How blind!"[19] His life was centered on his family, his church, and his business, and he continued to live in a relatively simple and unostentatious way.

But by the time he met with Frederick T. Gates to commit himself to supporting the founding of the University of Chicago, the fact of great wealth was beginning very nearly to overwhelm him. He had largely accomplished his business goals, and was already beginning to think of retirement, though he was only forty-nine years of age. As the leader of the Standard Oil group, he was the largest single stockholder, and Standard continued to pay hefty dividends. In addition, he had followed the practice of his associates, though not as flamboyantly as some of them, of investing a portion of his growing wealth in other business ventures, and these required a share of his time and attention. As early as 1872, during a time of depression in the oil industry, he had written his wife to reassure her: "You know we are independently rich outside of investments in oil."[20] Year by year his wealth grew, accelerating with a momentum of its own, until it reached staggering proportions. By the turn of the century, Senior's net worth was $200 million, second in America only to that of steel magnate Andrew Carnegie, whose fortune at the same time was $425 million. But that represented the peak of Carnegie's wealth while Rockefeller's began to increase even more rapidly in the early years of the new century as the demand for petroleum products expanded with the steadily increasing use of the internal combustion engine. Senior's wealth peaked in 1913 at just under $1 billion.[21]

One reason Senior's great wealth began to seem overwhelming to him was that it was making his charitable giving unmanageable. The financial records for the quarter century 1865–1890 show that he continued to be a giving man, but, paradoxically, the percentage of his income that he gave to church and charity declined as his income grew; during this period his giving did not average much more than 5 percent a year. The reason was not some sudden meanness of spirit or retreat from principles, but the simple logistical fact that he could not keep up. Most of Senior's gifts were relatively small. Few exceeded $1,000; most were in the $50-to-$500 range. If his income in a given year were, say, $5 million (it far exceeded that by the 1890s) and he were to try to give away 10 percent—$500,000—in $50 to $500 sums, the number of gifts and amount of work would be immense.

Because he believed his good fortune was God-given, he saw himself as a steward of the wealth, with a duty to handle it responsibly for good purposes. This meant that he could not give money away frivolously; he must satisfy himself that requests for money were genuine and served worthwhile causes. But the scale was beginning to make this impossible. During one trip to Europe, so much mail requesting donations had been forwarded to Senior that it required two steamer trunks to pack it for the trip home. He had long since learned what every serious giver learns—that to give money away responsibly is often harder than earning it in the first place. By the time Senior made his commitment to the University of Chicago, he was already dismayed by the fact that he was spending nearly as much time trying to deal with the tide of requests for contributions as he was in managing Standard Oil and his personal investments. And he realized it was likely to get worse, that he was fighting a losing battle.

One answer might be to make a small number of large gifts instead of a large number of small ones. Presumably, much less time and thought was required for Senior to make his $600,000 gift to create the

University of Chicago than if he had made six hundred $1,000 gifts. But this was not an easy answer for him either, although the time would come when he would essentially solve his problem by making a series of very large gifts. By nature, he was a cautious and conservative man, and he lacked experience in outside interests that would give him confidence in any particular field of activity. He had made the University of Chicago commitment only after years of hearing about the need from his Baptist brethren. At the least, the strong opinions voiced consistently by men he respected gave him confidence that the gift was worthwhile. But even here he soon learned that large gifts carried with them a special kind of responsibility and ongoing involvement. By the time he made the Chicago commitment, it seems clear that he was thinking about ways to apply the principles of organization and efficiency that he had developed in business to what he came to call "this business of benevolence."

Andrew Carnegie was thinking along the same lines. It is a fascinating historical fact that these two great entrepreneurs, the two richest men in America, who were so different in personality and temperament and interests, independently came to the same conclusion at about the same time. The conclusion was that men of wealth had a responsibility to put their surplus wealth to good purposes during their lifetimes, and that this would require a concerted and organized effort. Carnegie first projected his views in an essay entitled "Wealth," perhaps the most famous single piece of writing on the subject of philanthropy, which appeared in the *North American Review* of June 1889, only a month after Rockefeller had made his Chicago commitment.

Merely the idea of writing an essay to publicize one's views is enough to suggest the radical difference between Carnegie and Rockefeller. The latter was a very private person who shunned the spotlight, public commentary, and any involvement in politics. Not until later in life would he publish anything, and then only nostalgic reminiscences.[22] In contrast, Carnegie was a political activist, heavy campaign contributor, and avid publicity seeker. He was vain, outgoing, gruff, hearty, and likable. For years the free public libraries were his highest priority, always, of course, with the Carnegie name on them.

Motivation marked perhaps the most significant difference between the two men. There is no question that Rockefeller's exclusive motivation for giving was his religious conviction and the old-fashioned concept of stewardship, not the expiation of guilt or the buying of public favor. This is abundantly clear from the consistency of his habits and principles throughout his long life. As a historian of philanthropy, Robert H. Bremner, observed:

According to popular legend John D. Rockefeller, alarmed by muckraking attacks such as Ida M. Tarbell's . . . employed a public relations counselor, Ivy Lee, who advised him to increase his benefactions in order to buy public favor. Actually, Lee did not become associated with Rockefeller until 1914, more than twenty years after Rockefeller had become a wholesale philanthropist.[23]

In contrast, Carnegie specifically disavowed any religious motivation, classifying himself as a "scientific humanist." His philosophy bespoke the rugged individualist and self-made man, and was infused with the Social Darwinism of his friend Herbert Spencer. As a result, his giving at times could be erratic or quixotic, alongside some brilliant endeavors and the great institutions he was to create.[24] Carnegie's essay "Wealth" was directed to millionaires, advising them that it was a disgrace to die rich and that the wealthy man should administer his fortune as a public trust instead of bequeathing vast sums to heirs who had not earned them and might dissipate them frivolously. An English clergyman, nettled by the brash and self-assured tone of Carnegie's article and the absence of any religious context, sarcastically called it "the gospel of wealth" to distinguish it from the gospel of Christianity. Carnegie cheerfully accepted the amendment and continued to write and talk about his views.

Although there was little contact between Carnegie and Rockefeller, the latter in 1896 was moved to write a letter of reassurance and support to the steel king. In it he said:

I am pleased with the sentiments you give expression to. I would that more men of wealth were doing as you are doing with your money; but be assured, your example will bear fruits, and the time will come when men of wealth will more generally be willing to use it for the good of others.[25]

The fact that two such different men with different motivations were heading in the same direction suggests that some natural evolution was occurring—an idea whose time had come. As Carnegie's biographer observed, organization was "as natural a development in the field of philanthropy as Standard Oil and United States Steel were in manufacturing."[26]

The difference in motivation is interesting when seen from the perspective of Max Weber's ideas, particularly in *The Protestant*

Ethic and the Spirit of Capitalism.[27] The great sociologist of religion developed the thesis that Protestant doctrine, as it evolved from the time of John Calvin, was partly responsible for the rise of modern capitalism. Pure Calvinism had nothing to do with any idea of expanding or intensifying business activity, but two of its most important tenets served to encourage it—the sanctioning of secular activity (in contrast to the "otherworldy" emphasis of Catholicism) and asceticism (discipline and the renunciation of immediate satisfactions). In Weber's terms, the "ideal type" of the successful businessman became the sober, thrifty, hardworking Protestant. Moreover, evolving Protestant doctrine soon adopted good works in this life as signs of grace and then as a path to salvation.

In the New World, Protestantism continued to evolve in ways uniquely suited to indigenous needs—the frontier spirit, westward expansion, economic growth, correct behavior and good works as signs of grace, and social reform. The great revivalists brought a simple and powerful message to thousands of souls like Eliza Davison Rockefeller: before accepting Christ as the Savior, man is shackled by sin; acceptance of Christ means freedom from bondage; salvation must come through conversion consciously experienced at a definite time and place. This is a far cry from Martin Luther's doctrine of justification by faith alone or John Calvin's emphasis on predestination. Moreover, the idea took firm root that the aggregation of correct forms of behavior brought about by conversion or acceptance of Christ would hasten the arrival of the millennium, or "Christian Commonwealth." This made the line between individual spiritual rebirth and social reform very easy to cross.

Evidence of Christian conversion would be manifested not only by a life of hard work, thrift, and tithing the church, but also avoidance of wordly snares such as gambling, dancing, the theater, and, most particularly, "Demon Rum." An individual's concern about the effect of these evils would often spill over into social and political action, which helps explain the great crusades to abolish slavery, prohibit the manufacture and sale of alcoholic beverages, secure women's rights, and put an end to many forms of luxury and self-indulgence.

All this suggests that John D. Rockefeller was the living prototype of Weberian theory and that Andrew Carnegie's ideas and actions were drawn directly from the spirit of American Protestantism, despite his disavowal.

It also suggests that ideas spawned by American Protestantism were gradually producing a doctrine of social action that would become secularized and persist long after its religious roots became obscure. Rockefeller and Carnegie, especially the latter, were transitional figures in this, quite apart from their two great contributions of applying the systematic methods of business to philanthropy and donating enormous wealth. We will see this transition from religious to social doctrine very clearly in Junior's education at Brown University, in his life's work, and in the development and careers of his five sons.

One of Senior's problems in trying to manage his triple work load was that he had no personal staff outside the Standard Oil office. He reasoned that if he hired someone as a personal assistant to help him in his charitable giving, this would ease the pressure enough so that he could handle his other two responsibilities—Standard Oil and personal investments. One day in March 1891, Gates, who had moved to Chicago to assist in the launching of the university, came to see Senior on university business. He was astonished to find that he was being offered a job. Senior began the meeting by saying: "Mr. Gates, I am in trouble." Gates described the problem as Senior presented it to him:

. . . he told me that the pressure of appeals for philanthropic causes on his time and strength had become too great to be borne; that he was so constituted as to be unable to give away money with satisfaction without inquiry as to the worthiness of the cause; that these inquiries were now consuming more of his time and energy than his business and indeed injuring his health, and that either he must shift the burden to other shoulders, or he must cease giving entirely. He invited me to come to New York and assist him in his benevolent work by taking the interviews and inquiries and reporting results for his action.[28]

Inasmuch as most of Senior's giving was still to Baptist causes, Gates was certainly a reasonable choice. Moreover, Gates' own experience as a fund-raiser equipped him to cast a discerning eye on the importunings of others. Senior soon learned what an excellent choice he had made. Gates showed himself to be a man not only of intelligence and dedication, but also one with a sense of vision and considerable entrepreneurial flair. When he arrived on the scene in September 1891, Gates discovered that Senior "was constantly hunted, stalked, and hounded almost like a wild animal. . . . Neither in the privacy of his home nor at his table, nor in the aisles of his church, nor during his business hours, nor anywhere else, was Mr. Rockefeller secure from insistent appeal." After a careful examination of the financial records, interviews of previous recipients of Senior's largesse, and perusal of the many letters that inundated his office every day asking for assistance, Gates "found not a few of Mr. Rockefeller's habitual charities to be worthless and practically fraudulent." The former Baptist minister discovered, to his horror one suspects, that Baptists were among the sinners. The "numberless" letters from pastors and church members "begging" for all manner of gifts were "unworthy" in Gates' view, many of them consisting of requests that had been turned down by responsible local bodies. Senior, formerly having no real way of checking on the validity of these requests, but desiring to contribute to the comfort and security of his coreligionists and assuming that a Baptist connection was evidence of worthiness, had developed the habit of responding with small gifts, ranging from $50 to $500.[29]

Gates' response to the limitless demand for a limited supply of goods was to develop a system of "scientific" giving that gradually moved Senior out of the area of "retail" giving into the realm of "wholesale" philanthropy—channeling funds through reputable groups and organizations instead of responding to individual requests. This required researching each eligible request to see if a genuine need existed and applying accountancy principles to determine if it seemed likely that the gift could accomplish the objective sought. This procedure eliminated entire categories of requests immediately, in particular "begging" letters from individuals for "pianos, wedding trousseaux, a musical or art education" or from individuals who wanted "to be set up in business, or have a troublesome mortgage removed." Also excluded were requests from local churches and charities. Gifts of this sort amounted to traditional alms-giving, and Gates planned to go beyond this level completely.

In line with the move to "wholesale" giving, Gates encouraged the development of large, comprehensive denominational and charitable agencies by contributing funds to them for their operating budgets or designated projects. This was particularly true for varied educational and missionary activities of the Northern Baptist Convention. Substantial funds soon began to flow to the American Baptist Home Missionary Society, American Baptist Missionary Union, the American Baptist Education Society, and the Baptist state conventions in a number of northern states. Gates also funneled money for work in urban areas through the Cleveland and New York City Baptist

Missionary Societies, which provided funds for church support and proselytizing of the poor.

Rather than innovation, Gates' work in the 1890s on behalf of Senior's philanthropy was concerned with the application of systematic methods and the consolidation of giving in the direction of organized groups, largely within the Baptist framework. The great advances toward new purposes, new institutions, and efforts to get at the roots of problems rather than dealing with their symptoms, which all became hallmarks of Rockefeller philanthropy, did not begin until after the turn of the century. There were three reasons for this.

One was that Senior's giving for some years was dominated by his commitment to the University of Chicago, with which Gates was very much in accord. Senior had displayed his innate caution by making his initial contribution conditional on the support of others, in effect a "matching grant," a staple of philanthropic endeavor ever since, although this terminology did not come into vogue until later. But nevertheless he had the proverbial tiger by the tail in the ebullient William Rainey Harper. Senior and Gates never doubted the magnificence of Harper's visions, but they were left with the practical questions of how long Senior could continue to finance them and how well they were being executed from an administrative point of view. It was an important experience that permeated Rockefeller philanthropy from that time forth, including awareness of the danger that once a Rockefeller becomes involved there is a tendency for everyone else to step aside.

Senior found himself in the position of meeting mounting annual deficits as Harper proceeded exuberantly to build a university the way it should be built—his way. For years the Gothic buildings spread along the north edge of the Midway Plaisance, first on property donated by Marshall Field and then on many adjacent plots that Senior bought and donated. Harper succeeded in attracting an extraordinary faculty and a large and impressive student body, and in establishing important innovations in higher education. But it was all threatened by slipshod financial and administrative practices and seemingly endless dependence on one major source of funding. Finally, the problem was brought to a head in the years following the turn of the century. Major efforts toward a solution came from the Rockefeller side—hard work, pressure on the trustees resulting in administrative reforms, and a final grant of $10 million in 1910. This also was to be a staple of philanthropy—the "terminal"grant, usually a generous one with some conditions attached and meant to end a long relationship of dependency. In this case, it did so in the sense of ending basic support, but there were to be many more instances of Rockefeller contributions to the university for specific purposes. The other factor was the momentum of Harper's vision itself. By the early years of the twentieth century, he had largely succeeded—a great university had come into being, now well established, an enormous boon to its region and capable of attracting diverse support.[30]

The second reason that Senior's philanthropy did not become more venturesome during the 1890s is that he and Gates found themselves preoccupied with business affairs. The Panic of 1893 drew Senior into what would be his last intensive period of activity as the head of Standard Oil. This and a sudden bout of poor health left him without the time and energy to give adequate attention to his personal business investments. Although Gates initially had been hired to work on philanthropy, Senior now turned to him to manage the investments, a measure of the confidence and faith he had come to place in his new personal secretary. This is where Gates showed a surprising talent for business affairs, delving into the investment problems with apparent zest, and giving ample evidence that Senior's confidence was not misplaced.

The investments were wide-ranging and complicated, and had not been organized or monitored closely. As Senior's fortune grew, there were new ventures to be undertaken and old ones to be discarded. Some of the investments were profitable, but others were in trouble. Too often Senior had taken a minority position in enterprises mounted by men who seemed competent, but who turned out to be incompetent or worse. He then faced the choice of taking a loss or pouring more money in and assuming control or management of the venture. It was in several such cases of converting disastrous investments into stunning successes that Gates showed his brilliance, as for example in constituting the profitable Everett Timber and Investment Company out of the shambles of a series of Senior's investments in the Pacific Northwest.

His greatest success came in Senior's extraordinary involvement in the iron-ore business in the 1890s, which became so strategically valuable that Senior for a time seemed to be rivaling the great steel magnates, including Andrew Carnegie. In the beginning, the investment had been so dubious, and rapidly became so complicated and troublesome, that some observers thought Senior had lost his touch. But with the shrewd assistance of Gates, he ended up controlling the great Mesabi iron-ore range in northern Minnesota, the railroad to transport the ore to dockside, and the Bessemer Steamship Company, by far the largest ore fleet on the Great Lakes. However, Senior had no plan to take over the steel industry, as some feared he intended, nor did Andrew Carnegie. Both men wanted to retire and concentrate on philanthropy. Both eventually sold their interests to the imperious J. P. Morgan in separate transactions in 1901 in the forming of United States Steel. The price for Senior's holdings was $88.5 million, giving him a profit conservatively estimated at $50 million from an involvement that he had at first shunned.[31]

Beyond the preoccupation with the problems of the University of Chicago and the personal investments, there was a third reason why Senior's philanthropy in the 1890s did not venture much beyond the basic organizing work that Gates had done. In an important sense, the two men were not yet ready to explore new purposes for philanthropy. They were men of their time whose assumptions concerning the nature of society and the meaning of reform differed from the younger men who were coming of age amid the devastating labor struggles, social upheaval, and intellectual ferment in the years surrounding the turn of the century.

Like Senior, Gates subscribed without question to the traditional Baptist viewpoint, which emphasized individual responsibility and distrusted the state, and like good capitalists they vehemently opposed labor unions. In his philanthropic work, Gates placed his faith primarily in the various Baptist denominational organizations, some of which he had helped to create. His goal was a Baptist, or at least a Christian, commonwealth, and throughout his life he "continued to believe that the love and good-will exemplified in the Spirit of Jesus are the secret of human well-being, and that in this Spirit lies the hope of mankind."[32] Gates was to display rare insight and vision in important secular projects yet to come, but in the 1890s he was still learning to adjust to the experts and professionals who were rapidly crowding into the fields of reform and philanthropy.

Senior and Gates needed help—a younger man, one more conversant with the intellectual ferment of the times, a contemporary of the new leaders in ideas and reform. That help soon arrived in the person of John D. Rockefeller, Jr. Although Junior was to undergo a difficult adjustment and apprenticeship of his own, he was to be uniquely important as a link for his father and older colleague to new ideas in the early years of the twentieth century.

Overburdened as Senior was by his business and philanthropic commitments, the 1890s had been a difficult time for him. Gates had provided invaluable help, but the burden was still such that Senior suffered a nervous collapse for a time.[33] He developed persistent digestive problems and then a case of generalized alopecia, a rare disease that causes serious discomfort and the loss of all bodily hair. He wanted desperately to retire from Standard Oil. He was able to taper off by 1896, and in 1897 he retired at the age of fifty-eight. Characteristically, Senior did not announce his retirement publicly, and so much litigation affecting Standard Oil was pending that he agreed with his associates that he would retain the title of "president" for the time being. As a result, Senior was widely thought to be still running the great trust for nearly a decade afterward.

But the retirement was genuine, even if it was not entirely recognized as such—understandably so—by critics, reformers, and the general public. Senior was rarely seen again in the company offices at 26 Broadway after 1897, ironically the same year that his only son graduated from college and joined Gates in managing Senior's interests. For years the elder Rockefeller had eagerly anticipated the time when his son, whom he trusted and loved deeply, would come of age and be able to take over the management of family affairs.

2

ы

THE NEW MAN

THE FOUNDING of the University of Chicago was overshadowed for a
time in 1893 by another momentous event taking place on the South
Side of Chicago—the World's Columbian Exposition, a world's fair to
commemorate four centuries of progress since the discovery of the
New World in 1492.[1]

The leaders of Chicago, still regarded by most Americans as a
"western city," had won the competition for the rights to the fair with
their ingenious plan for building it on a network of parks, the result of
the "South Park system" designed by Frederick Law Olmsted in 1871.
His plan linked Jackson Park on the lakefront to Washington Park,
several miles inland, by means of a broad stretch of greensward
known as the Midway Plaisance. In both parks and on the Midway,
the buildings, exhibits, and sideshows of the fair were erected, all
painted a dazzling white, and so garishly illuminated at night by the
new wonder of electric lights that the fair became known as "White
City" in contrast to "Gray City," the university, which was being built
on property along the northern edge of the Midway.[2]

The fair was an outstanding success, drawing some 21 million
visitors from May to October, and, rare for such events, showing a
profit at the end. The visitors marveled at the great buildings designed
by America's leading architects,[3] most of them classical in design and
leading to a revival of that style of architecture. They toured the
exhibits, rode the giant Ferris wheel, attended conferences, colloquia,
and religious services, and watched "Little Egypt" shimmying in her
sideshow tent. Amid the hubbub along the Midway, they might have
heard the saws and hammers at the nearby construction sites of the
university or the sounds from the playing field where Coach Amos
Alonzo Stagg was holding his first football scrimmages.

In many ways, the city, the fair, and the university all stood as symbols of the radical transition taking place in American life, the clash between the values and institutions of an older agricultural order and those of the new industrialism and scientific thought that were inexorably transforming the nation. The fair combined in one place and time all of these contradictory impulses and tendencies, seemingly forcing a temporary unity upon them that did not deter thoughtful observers from pondering their meaning and ultimate direction, the sweeping changes that were occurring and would still occur.

There was one young man in attendance at the fair that summer who was to have a profound influence on the future of America for the next half century, perhaps more so than anyone else among the millions of visitors—John D. Rockefeller, Jr. It was his first extended visit to Chicago.[4] Junior turned nineteen in January 1893, and was to begin his college career at Brown University in the fall. It was a time of personal transition for him, moving from a narrow and sheltered upbringing to a setting where he would be exposed to some of the realities of the world, and to the massive changes and intellectual crosscurrents of the time.

He saw impressive evidence of the physical changes at the fair, the telephones, electric lights, giant turbines, self-propelled automobiles, and modern agricultural implements that testified to the impact of the industrial mode of production and its potentialities for the future. To many proud observers, these were proof of the maturation of the United States. But, if the fair and the city that sheltered it revealed much that was positive, optimistic, and dynamic about America, there was also much that was somber and unsettling. The same week that the fair opened its gates to the public, a financial panic was emerging that would lead to three hard years of economic recession. From the top of the Ferris wheel one could see the areas of Chicago that would bear the brunt of this latest downturn in the seemingly unalterable cycle of boom and bust, the hundreds of mean and squalid blocks stretching away to the horizon. Here dwelled the growing underclass of immigrants from Europe and distant prairie provinces, a dispossessed and landless peasantry laboring under appalling conditions in the city's factories and stockyards.

These were the people who had risen at Haymarket Square in 1886 and who would rise again in 1894 during the great Pullman strike to protest the conditions under which they worked and lived, only to be ground into submission by the forces of order. One of these men, driven to the limits of despair, assassinated the mayor of Chicago on the fairgrounds, another in a long list of anarchic acts that so alarmed the upper classes during the hard years of the 1890s.

The promoters of the exposition had not included the demands of the working class or the critiques of its more articulate supporters among the educational displays that dotted the fairgrounds, but they were present nonetheless. The threat of industrial unrest and the growing possibility of class warfare hovered over the crowded Midway as surely as the odor from the nearby stockyards, suggesting a darker side to the future of the United States.

More important than the transitory phenomenon of the Columbian Exposition itself were the ideas it seemed to generate about the changing American scene, especially those of two visitors, Frederick Jackson Turner and Henry Adams.

Turner appeared on the fairgrounds in July before the World's Congress of Historians to read his essay on "The Significance of the Frontier in American History." The young historian believed that "the existence of an area of free land, its continuous recession, and the advance of American settlement westward" could be used "to explain American development." In the repeated renewal of civilization as settlement moved west, Turner saw a process of social evolution that had endowed the nation with the values, institutions, and characteristics needed to adapt to the American environment. On the frontier, the European became an American and instinctively developed the methods and institutions of democracy in a natural setting. Now was a time of great transition: "And now, four centuries from the discovery of America, at the end of a hundred years of life under the Constitution, the frontier has gone, and with its going has closed the first period of American history."[5]

The restless mind of Henry Adams, always searching for integration and order in a world he saw as inherently disintegrative, was stimulated by the exhibits and machines assembled in Chicago. In them the great historian, critic, and scholar read the triumph of a new social order "which had ruthlessly stamped out the life into which [he] had been born." The pessimistic grandson of John Quincy Adams saw the end of a century-long struggle between "two forces, one simply industrial, the other capitalistic, centralizing, and mechanical." Adams believed that in 1893 the American people had decided once and for all "in favor of the capitalistic system with all its necessary machinery" and the men who had created the corporate "monopolies capable of controlling the new energies that America adopted." With a noticeable lack of enthusiasm, he concluded:

A capitalistic system had been adopted, and if it were to be run at all, it must be run by capital and capitalistic methods; for nothing could surpass the nonsensity of trying to run so complex and so concentrated a machine by Southern and Western farmers in grotesque alliance with city day laborers as had been tried in 1800 and 1828, and had failed even under simple conditions.[6]

Although Adams was sure that capitalists would run the new order, he was not at all certain that this new economic oligarchy would be capable of arresting the social degeneration and moral decay he saw all about him. Rather, he thought that the "acceleration of knowledge" about nature and man was outstripping society's ability to comprehend, integrate, and devise a stable intellectual system to contain it. However, Adams did modify his pessimism enough to allow that the new economic elite might at least bring a more concentrated energy to bear on the solution of the most prominent symptoms of social disintegration. He said that an enlightened leadership might emerge from the clash of conflicting interests and ideals, and that "the new man could only be a child born of contact between the new and the old energies."[7]

There is no evidence that any such deep thoughts occupied the mind of John D. Rockefeller, Jr., as he toured the fair. In fact, only one comment of his on the fair is on record, saying that he developed "a very good general idea of its vastness and immensity."[8] He came to Chicago from Cleveland in a private railroad car with his mother and three sisters, Senior having remained in New York to cope with business problems brought on by the Panic of 1983. The group arrived in time for the big fireworks extravaganza at the fairgrounds on the Fourth of July. During their visit, the family stayed with Nettie Fowler McCormick, widow of Cyrus McCormick, at her mansion on Rush Street. A romance was in progress between her son Harold and Junior's youngest sister, Edith. For the visitors, tours of the fair alternated with attendance at prayer meetings organized by evangelist Dwight L. Moody, who had received financial support for his revivals from both the Rockefeller and McCormick families.[9]

Despite his own cautious reaction to the fair, the image of the younger Rockefeller standing before the same exhibits that alarmed and amazed Adams and moved Turner to celebrate American individualism and adaptability is a striking one. In his own person and birthright, Junior was an exemplar of the forces and tendencies, hopes and fears, to which the two historians had devoted so much thought. His family background reflected both the individualism and adaptability of the American character and the increasing concentration of wealth and centralized direction of the economy that unbridled individualism seemed to engender. A member of the new capitalist class that was moving rapidly to a position of dominance in American life, Junior had been raised to revere the traditional religious and social truths. If the Columbian Exposition captured the United States in mid-passage, offering a rich and varied mosaic of America's past and present as well as intimations of future possibilities, one finds John D. Rockefeller, Jr., poised at a similar point between his own adolescence and manhood. The transition from one to the other would be painful in both cases. Junior, in the years that lay ahead of him, would become deeply involved in the development and reform of American institutions, in trying to reconcile the past and the future. His career in the decades ahead would make him seem the ideal type of the "new man" that Henry Adams prophesied would emerge.

During his earliest years, Junior's environment was Cleveland and the family homestead, Forest Hill. But then the family moved gradually into a split existence as Senior was forced to spend more and more time in New York City for business reasons. Not wishing to be separated, Senior began, in 1877, the practice of having his family spend some of the winter months with him at the Buckingham Hotel, located at 49th Street and Fifth Avenue. The length of these winter stays gradually increased, meaning that for Junior schooling began to consist of private tutoring, arranged both at Forest Hill and in New York. For quite a few years, Forest Hill was still "home" to the family, even as it tended to become only a summer residence and even as Senior bought the first family home in New York in 1884. He negotiated the purchase of the four-story brownstone at 4 West 54th Street, including several adjacent lots, from the notorious Arabella Worsham, the "unofficial" wife of the wealthy railroad financier Collis P. Huntington.[10]

The choice of a home in what was then the periphery of Manhattan reflected both the values of the Rockefellers and their subordinate position in the city's well-defined social hierarchy. They were, after all, new to the city, only part-time residents for a number of years, and largely unknown. They were certainly "nouveau riche" in the literal sense, but not in the pejorative sense of being pretentious and socially ambitious. Very private people, they were simply not interested in the social ladder.

The aristocratic heart of the city was then centered on lower Fifth Avenue between Washington and Madison squares. It was in these precincts that the core of old New York society—the Schermerhorns, Stuyvesants, Brevoorts, Roosevelts, Astors, Goelets, and Stewarts—lived and dictated who and what were acceptable. Not included were the representatives of the newer commercial and industrial wealth, by reason of background, occupation, and, in some cases, ethnic heritage. This is why the men who had made their fortunes in oil, railroads, iron and steel, and in the newer areas of the retail field, men like Andrew Carnegie, Henry Clay Frick, Cornelius Vanderbilt, Collis P. Huntington, E. H. Harriman, John Archbold, William Rockefeller, and John D. Rockefeller, all made their homes along what came to be known as "upper Fifth Avenue," the area between the Croton Reservoir and Central Park. For the even less palatable reason of ethnicity, the same was true of the representatives of the great German-Jewish banking, brokerage, and mercantile houses—the Schiffs, Seligmans, Warburgs, Guggenheims, and others.[11]

This kind of elite discrimination meant a great deal to some of the newly wealthy, as witness the titanic battles between Mrs. William Astor and Mrs. Cornelius Vanderbilt for leadership within the Four Hundred, but it had little or no impact on the Rockefellers, who did not appear in the Social Register until the mid-1890s. Their concerns were of a different nature, centering on family, home, church, and business. The physical axis of their lives ran from the house on West 54th to the Fifth Avenue Baptist Church on West 46th Street, and 26 Broadway, the headquarters of Standard Oil.

With the family settled in New York during the school year, Junior finally began regular schooling in 1884, first at the New York School of Languages and then in a small school operated by C. N. Douglass, each for one year, and then two years at the Cutler School, with one year out for illness. Junior's biographer, his longtime associate Raymond B. Fosdick, noted that Junior's classmates at the Cutler School included Albert Milbank, whose law firm represented his family in later years, Cornelius Bliss, Arthur Choate, Cornelius Vanderbilt, Jr., and James Hazen Hyde, all sons of the new industrial elite and the professional classes that began to serve them.[12]

Junior completed his preparatory work at the Browning School, from 1889 until June 1893. This school had started as a tutorial operation for Junior, his cousin Percy Rockefeller, Stanley and Harold McCormick, and John's close friend, Everett Colby. It functioned in a small brownstone owned by the Rockefellers on West 55th Street. At the beginning, the sole teacher was John A. Browning, but gradually other staff members were added. Junior became close to Browning, and felt he was the only precollege teacher who had an enduring effect on him: "He was a gifted teacher, who inspired interest in learning. . . . I wasn't much of a scholar, but I always tried hard, and I didn't like to be reproached. Just the same, I was very fond of him."[13]

Despite Junior's enthusiasm for Browning, the course of study at his school and the others he attended was constrained by the classical-ism that dominated American education prior to the Deweyan revolu-tion of the succeeding decade. Like most of his contemporaries, Junior slogged through a deadening series of Greek and Latin translations every term. He also took courses in French, German, arithmetic, chemistry, geography, bookkeeping, English and Ameri-can history, and English composition. In all of this, there is no evidence that any of his studies were brought to bear on the social and economic problems around him. English history was an examination of each of the dynastic lines, and American history concentrated on the Constitution and the Civil War. With the emphasis on classical languages as a prerequisite for college entrance, there was little time left for the study of current issues.

In these years, Junior comes through as a smallish boy (not yet stocky), handsome, serious, bright, and extremely conscientious. He consistently received high grades and a place on the honor roll. Though the youngest child in his family, he was the only boy, and so obedient and dependable that he took on relatively mature roles early. Years later, he commented:

I took responsibility early and like my parents I was serious. Although I was the youngest, my parents turned to me for advice on many questions, including my sisters, particularly their love affairs, and because I was close to my sisters I was able to understand their point of view, which in turn I could translate to my parents. Whether it was because I was the only boy in the family or whether it was because I naturally took to responsibility, I do not know.[14]

The most important influence on Junior during his formative years was not school, but religion as it was brought to him by his mother and father, supported by the church. As Raymond Fosdick noted:

What he did, where he went, with whom he went—all such decisions were inextricably bound up with this central purpose [to become a good Christian] which sprang from a deeply ingrained religious faith. In this case it was the Baptist faith as it existed in nineteenth-century, midwestern America;

and no understanding of the background of John's boyhood is possible outside the context of his Baptist church environment.[15]

From his earliest years, Junior's devout father and exceptionally pious mother inculcated values of thrift, sobriety, aloofness from worldly temptations, and individual responsibility for salvation. Aside from the prominence given the ordinance of baptism itself, the Baptist faith did not differ significantly in basic beliefs from most other Protestant denominations, but was notable for its severity and simplicity and its identification with rural and frontier America. Baptists cared little for theological nuance, placing their greatest emphasis on outward behavior as a sign of inward grace. On a practical level, this meant a complete abjuration of all worldly vices—card-playing, dancing, opera, the theater, smoking, and particularly, drinking.

Deep convictions such as these often led to broader reform activities. Laura Spelman Rockefeller was an early supporter of the temperance movement in Cleveland, and Senior made the support of "dry" groups one of his earliest and most consistent philanthropies.[16] His son and daughters joined the Loyal Legion Temperance Society in New York, Junior signing the pledge to abstain from "tobacco, profanity and the drinking of any intoxicating beverages" when he was ten years old.

The lives of the Rockefellers were focused on their religion, and many of their waking hours were devoted to prayers, church services, Sunday school, and meetings of temperance and missionary societies. In a speech he made years later, Junior still vividly recalled the structure of the family's week:

In [our] home, family prayers before breakfast had always been the custom, each one taking part, either reading from the Bible in turn or reciting a verse of scripture, many of which were thus learned and retained vividly throughout life. The blessing was asked before each meal. On Sunday the parents and children went together to church and Sunday school. . . . Friday night was prayer meeting night; the whole family always attended the meeting. At an early age the children were encouraged by their mother to take part like the older people, either in a brief prayer or a word of personal experience.

Sunday was invariably observed as a day of rest; only necessary duties were performed. A cold dinner was the rule, that work might be reduced to a minimum. No studying was allowed or games of any kind, while the reading of the Bible and Sunday books only was permitted. If the children had done wrong during the week, their mother would point out earnestly to them how they had sinned against God, whose forgiveness she would lead them to seek in prayer.[17]

Dreary as this ritual might seem to the modern mind, one can also appreciate how it could serve to strengthen family bonds. In the same speech, Junior alluded to this, asserting that Sunday "was a happy day, for it was a family day."

The mother was the primary influence in matters of behavior and morality for her children. She was protective of her only son and dedicated to the task of guarding him from life's pitfalls and guiding him onto paths of righteousness that would "exemplify the life of Christ." She set strict standards and constantly instructed her children about duty and matters of right and wrong. This was never done harshly. Laura was a gentle and pious person; her influence radiated throughout the household.

One result, however, was that Junior, though intelligent and mature in some ways, was extremely inhibited in social matters. "The trouble was that I never had any social experience as a child," Junior recalled years later. He contrasted this with the experience of the children of the William Rockefellers, who lived only a few doors away on Fifth Avenue: "They had much more expensive presents and they had a gay kind of social life, packed with parties, etc., which we used to wish we could have." A childhood centered on family and church, perpetually concerned with introspective soul-searching and striving to perfect one's conduct, left Junior with both a lifetime creed and an initial fear of normal social contact. Junior said that his upbringing "had its limitations" and was "narrow and confining." His mother's "intense religious feeling" had served to produce a young man who "was very diffident and socially awkward." When he was ready to go to college, Junior "didn't know what to say to a girl or how to talk to her. The thought of making a speech frightened me and I was ill at ease in company."[18]

These observations did not signify any rejection of his mother. Junior loved her deeply, respected her, remained devoted to her, and frequently consulted her before even minor decisions. Rather, he was talking objectively from the perspective of later life. Because of her extreme piety, Junior had to undergo a painful process of socialization as he left home. But in return she had given him a kind of moral armor that stood him in good stead his entire life.

To some extent, the father was a leavening influence, offering his son some glimpses of the world beyond. There is no evidence that the elder Rockefellers ever disagreed about the upbringing of the children. But Senior had a different temperament and personality, and, unlike Laura, he had to function in the world of affairs as well as the cocoon of the home. In contrast to the portrait soon to be drawn in the popular press by the muckrakers of a humorless, ruthless, money-making machine, with his mouth full of Christian pieties even as he gained a rapacious business reputation, Junior saw a father full of humor and energy, a devout man who valued time with his family and introduced his son patiently to the wonders of the world. Senior was a man of simple pleasures, with a highly organized mind and great self-discipline. He was able to wear his Baptist faith easily, having no difficulty in living simultaneously within its strictures and in the world of practical affairs.

Junior spoke of his father as a "beloved companion," saying that he had "always adored him." The reason is not hard to find. Senior never insisted on "discipline of any kind. He never told us what not to do. He was one with us." Senior engaged enthusiastically in the children's games: "He taught us everything—how to skate, swim, ride, drive horses, and we were never so happy as when we were with him." He admired blood horses, and kept a number of pairs with him in the city. After work or on Saturday, he enjoyed driving with his children around the fashionable circuit "up the west side of Central Park and then up Seventh Avenue . . . to McCombs Dam Bridge." Quite often, Senior would engage his brother William or another Standard Oil associate in a spontaneous, spirited race for part of the way.[19]

Senior also made sure that his son saw something of the world at a fairly young age. The elder Rockefeller took his family on trips to the Rockies and the West Coast, renting a private train for the purpose. And, during the summers of 1887 and 1889, the family toured Europe. Also of importance for Junior's future development were the trips downtown to visit his father's office in Lower Manhattan. Here he could look out onto the bustling scene below him from the windows of the Standard Oil Building at 26 Broadway. From this vantage point, a dynamic panorama of the city opened up. To the south, he could see the United States Custom House, the offices of the great shipping firms, the immigrant depot at Castle Garden, the incredible congestion of the port with ships jostling each other to disgorge or take on their cargo, and in the distance the new and majestic presence of the Statue of Liberty. On a clear day, he would be able to discern the outline of the Jersey Standard oil refinery in Bayonne along the shore of the Kill Van Kull and perhaps the Brooklyn Bridge to the east. To the north, by stretching out the window, his eye could meet the spire of Trinity Church in the heart of the financial district, nestling among the great banking and brokerage houses.[20]

During these visits to 26 Broadway, Junior's horizons might also

have been widened by meeting the Standard Oil associates of his
father, that group of men whom W. H. Vanderbilt had lauded in such
superlative terms. He was also exposed to some of the great reformers
of the day who came to plead their special causes and ask for financial
assistance, as did politicians and religious workers. Both at his father's
office and in the family drawing room at home, Junior gradually
became aware of the seamy side of life in the great metropolis as
discussions were held about the evils of prostitution, police involvement in gambling and brothels, the machinations of Tammany bosses,
and the exploits of heroic reformers. On occasion, this would occur at
the breakfast table as well when Senior would read letters that
requested assistance and ask members of the family for their advice on
the proper response. It was at times like these that Junior learned the
reasons for his father's contribution of a thousand dollars to Theodore
Roosevelt's mayoral campaign in 1886 (fear of the single-taxer, Henry
George) and his support for the Lexow investigation and the reform
candidacy of William L. Strong for mayor in 1894 (the opportunity to
drive Tammany Hall from power).[21]

These discussions were seen by the parents as a natural part of
Junior's education. They were couched in language that was biblical
in tone, seeing problems through the simplifying lens of Protestant
morality, the stark contrast between good and evil. Thus, they
reinforced the lessons his mother sought so assiduously to teach him.

The purpose of these discussions went beyond drawing moral
lessons for the children; they also served to help guide the philanthropy of the Rockefellers. Just as everything seemed to be in
transition in the decade of the 1890s, so it was with philanthropy. One
issue was the extent to which the individual and the church had a
responsibility to go beyond conventional charity—giving alms to the
poor—to a more active role in trying to solve the ills of society. A
cautious view prevailed at the Fifth Avenue Baptist Church. The
young minister, W. H. P. Faunce, a graduate of Brown University and
the Andover Theological Seminary, was a liberal in theology, but
conservative when it came to social action. He was aware of the
challenges to the church posed by scientific thought, the industrial
revolution, and the reform impulses of the day, but his response was a
limited one. He did take the lead in establishing a settlement house
on 43rd Street just north of the infamous Tenderloin district, called
Armitage House after his predecessor in the Fifth Avenue pulpit. But
Faunce believed that Christians should be careful about mixing
religion with politics and economics: "I am sorry for Christian

ministers, usually of a tender age, who rush into the market place with a sociological poultice for all the ills that the body politic is heir to, and thus would commit a Christianity of nineteen centuries to a philosophy not yet out of the cradle."[22]

Another issue was the emergence of new thinking about the causes of social ills. The conservative view still dominated, ascribing poverty and its attendant evils to individual failure rather than underlying social and economic factors. According to this view, pauperization, addiction to vice in its many forms, unemployment, political corruption, even the prevalence of disease in many parts of the city, could best be explained by the laziness and moral decay of the poor, just as their opposites, health, wealth, personal purity, and civic virtue, stemmed from the superior intelligence, industry, and Christian faith of the righteous. "Demon Rum" was still identified as the primary social evil, and involvement in efforts to restrict or prohibit its use was one of the most enduring of American reform activities. The drunkard and the saloon were viewed as central elements in a causal chain linking all the social ills of the city. Participation in the temperance cause emerged as a fight of good against evil, and proponents saw themselves as not only following God's law personally, but also as working toward the salvation and redemption of society.

Senior was already beginning to broaden his philanthropy beyond these traditional limits. Most of his giving was still church-related, but the variety of purposes it served was expanding—for example, his continued support of the University of Chicago even as it grew beyond its Baptist origins to become a great secular citadel of scientific learning and progressive thinking.

But the time was still some years away before criticism of the prevailing social order would burst into a storm, before Senior would begin applying the organizational genius that created Standard Oil to the field of philanthropy, and before his son would dedicate his life to that end and carry it to lengths never before imagined. For the present, there was no evidence that Junior experienced any anxiety over the conflicting images that gradually filled his mind—comfortable wealth on upper Fifth Avenue, dire poverty in Five Points and Hell's Kitchen; order and efficiency at 26 Broadway, corruption and mismanagement at City Hall; individual redemption and moral perfection at the Fifth Avenue Baptist Church, prostitution and drunkenness at the "sporting houses" of the Tenderloin; skyscrapers and dumbbell tenements; the Brooklyn Bridge and outdoor privies; respectable businessmen in frock coats and the ragged garments of immigrants. At the age of nineteen, ensconced in his rooms on the fourth floor of his parents' home, Junior was secure in his Baptist faith and the reassuring interpretation of the world that it presented. His overriding objectives were to "help his father" and live a Christian life. As he grew older, he would find that the achievement of these laudatory goals would prove much more difficult and complex than he had ever imagined. The next step on that journey, his years away at college, would prepare him well by opening his mind to new ideas and experiences.

During his third year at the Browning School, Junior passed preliminary examinations to qualify for admission to Yale University. But he decided to spend a fourth year at the Browning School, perhaps because he did not feel adequately prepared—he had missed several months of the school year due to illness. Then he began to have second thoughts about Yale, concerned that he might be a stranger and out of place as a freshman at such a large school. He began to consider Brown University in Providence, Rhode Island, encouraged by the fact that several of his best friends and classmates intended to go there. He sought the advice of two Baptist ministers, Harper of the University of Chicago and Faunce of the Fifth Avenue Church. Both men recommended another Baptist minister—President Elisha Benjamin Andrews of Brown. Harper wrote:

> After all it is not the *Institution* but the men with whom you come in contact at the Institution. I may say to you frankly, though confidentially, that there are no men today at Yale of preeminent character as Instructors. Most of us as we look back in our lives find that we owe practically everything to intellectual stimulus which we have received from one or two men. Mr. Andrews is a man, who more than any other man in my acquaintance has it in him to stimulate in the best way the men with whom he comes into relationship.[23]

Faunce's reasons for favoring Brown over Yale included a more "healthful" climate, the presence of a certain "fast set" at Yale, Brown's semidenominational status, and Andrews: "You would be under the constant inspiration of Pres. Andrews, who is one of the most stimulating minds of this country."[24]

It would be difficult to imagine a more successful college career than Junior's four years at Brown (1893 to 1897), judging from the social and intellectual transformation it worked on him. So important was this in preparing him for his remarkable life's work that it bears close examination.

The process of Junior's socialization is a story with a good deal of human interest, which may explain why his biographer emphasized it to the relative neglect of the academic-intellectual stimulation Junior underwent. Fosdick tells in detail the story of how Junior gradually began to come out of his shell and conquer his shyness. It was a painful process for a considerable time, but by the end of his sophomore year he had come to enjoy dancing, parties, the theater, dating, and people in general. He helped himself by joining the Alpha Delta Phi fraternity, an experience he remembered all his life. He faced frontally his fear of speaking in public, seeking every opportunity to do so, and gradually came to feel more comfortable. Junior's growing social ease and acceptance by his contemporaries was evidenced by his election as junior class president, his selection to the Cammarian Society, his service as football manager, and his tentative courtship, during his senior year, of a "gay, popular Providence belle," Miss Abby Aldrich, daughter of Senator Nelson W. Aldrich of Rhode Island. He was affectionately nicknamed "Johnny Rock" by his classmates, who learned to tolerate his religious scruples, frugal habits, and temperance views, just as he learned to accept their absence in many of them. Junior made lifelong friendships at Brown, and always looked back on his college years as a happy time.[25]

Probably more profound in shaping Junior's career was his intellectual awakening at Brown. From a limited and conventional view of the world, the product of his economic class and sheltered upbringing, he emerged as a "new man"—exposed to new ideas and insights, aware that there was much to criticize and change in the society about him, and with a sense of responsibility to participate actively in that. Just as Harper and Faunce had suggested, the major intellectual influence was President Andrews, directly in courses Junior took that were taught by Andrews and indirectly in the environment of the institution, so strongly shaped and dominated by its president. Andrews was one of those nineteenth-century characters who seem larger than life. He fought in the Union Army during the Peninsula and Wilderness campaigns, and lost an eye at the battle of the Crater during the siege of Petersburg. After the war, he graduated from Brown and was ordained a Baptist minister after study at the Newton Theological Seminary in Massachusetts. He became president of Denison University in Ohio, and then taught homiletics at Newton and history and political economy at Brown and Cornell. The historian of Brown University commented on Andrews' first years at his alma mater: "It was felt at once that a great power had come into the university. His robust, magnetic personality thrilled and stimulated the students both in and out of his classes, and hero-worship became a popular cult."[26]

A leading economist and a man committed to applying scientific knowledge to the solution of economic and social problems, Andrews joined with Richard T. Ely, E. J. James, Simon Patten, E. R. A. Seligman, Francis Amasa Walker, Henry C. Adams, and other progressive economists in establishing the American Economics Association in 1885. These men articulated the need for new ways to understand society, questioned the efficacy of laissez-faire doctrine, and asserted that they regarded "the state as an educational and ethical agency whose positive aid is an indispensable condition of human progress."[27]

Andrews exposed Junior to new ideas about the role of business in society, the role of government in the economy, and perhaps more importantly, the strong belief that individuals and institutions had a duty to work ceaselessly for the improvement of society and the common good. Given Junior's later career, the most lasting insight he gained during his college years may well have been Andrews' philosophy of social action combined with scientific analysis. In a speech entitled "The Duty of a Public Spirit," Andrews summarized this philosophy: "Just as the appearance of the power of abstract thought marked a turning-point in evolution in general, so now, in social evolution, we are at a turning-point, which is characterized by the application of conscious thought to the direction of society." Holding that "idle trust in God and the so-called natural laws of social growth" were no longer safe, Andrews said, "More than ever manifest in our day is the need of a conscious human guidance to society in its evolution." As population increased and "angry problems" arose, Andrews saw no easy solutions, but called for a frankly experimental approach: "If given efforts to reform, shape, and manage society suffer shipwreck, the proper inference is not that a let-alone policy is best, but that we need in the field deeper study and a more consummate art."[28]

Andrews increasingly came to be seen by many businessmen, especially alumni and trustees of Brown, as a man with dangerous ideas—basically antibusiness and threatening to the social order.[29] Andrews clearly was not antibusiness. He held that "in all economic activity the presumption is in favor of individual liberty and free competition" and that the growth of trusts and combinations was a reasonable response to the uncertainty of the economic order. In fact, Andrews even conceded that economic combinations might be socially beneficial because they rationalized the system through centralized control, kept employment steady, and produced goods at lower cost. However, Andrews believed that society had the right to ensure that these benefits were distributed widely, and he urged experimentation with different forms of regulation and control, including price- and profit-fixing.[30]

As the decade of the 1890s wore on, Andrews took other positions that angered many businessmen, first advocating bimetallism, then the free and unlimited coinage of silver, and finally coming out for William Jennings Bryan in the election of 1896. This made Andrews' tenure during Junior's years at Brown a stormy one indeed. Pressed by the trustees to retract his statements "for the good of the University," Andrews refused and submitted his resignation instead. After a series of bitter trustees' meetings and a newspaper campaign by his supporters focused on the issue of academic freedom, the board relented and asked Andrews to withdraw his resignation. However, his effectiveness had been eroded, and he left the university for good a year after Junior had graduated.[31] Junior always remembered him as a "man of enormous courage" who "was of great influence on my life."[32]

In line with his views about public service and social responsibility, Andrews had revised the Brown curriculum, instituting a prelaw program, expanding the offerings in engineering, and adding courses in political economy, economics, and social science. He also brought in young, like-minded faculty members in the latter fields. Junior became close to one of them, Henry B. Gardner, a Johns Hopkins Ph.D. and disciple of Richard T. Ely. It was during his upper-class years, after being freed from most required courses, that Junior's intellectual horizons broadened. He was being weaned away from the complacent moralisms of his youth and toward an awareness of the complexity of the modern world. The essays he wrote in his classes displayed progress from conventional attitudes to a more open and questioning mind.

Junior took nearly a dozen courses in the social sciences; the concept of a "major" was not in practice then, but if it had been, his major would have been political economy. He took Gardner's year-long introductory course in this field, and then another, entitled "Practical Economic Questions," which discussed the "main elements of strength and weakness in the existing economic system and some of the more important propositions for modifying it." While Gardner praised the dominant capitalistic system for its energy, inventiveness, and productivity, he also pointed out its inherent wastefulness, brutality, and inability to provide a decent standard of living for a substantial portion of the population. He had his students read Charles Booth's study of the East London poor and compare its findings with conditions in American cities. Junior noted one of Gardner's conclusions: "Whereas in certain directions, progress has been marvelous, the results of this progress have certainly been very unevenly distributed and had not reached at all a considerable number of the population. Many people are so badly off that they have derived no gain from the industrial progress of the last 100 years." Junior styled his work in this course as an examination of the "individualistic" and "socialist" theories, and noted that the latter was "more in harmony with Christian thought."[33]

During his senior year, Junior took another course from Gardner described in the Brown University catalog of the time as a "study of Karl Marx's *Capital*." There is irony in the image of the son of one of the richest men in the world and the epitome of capitalist concentration dutifully thumbing the pages of this enduring critique of capitalism. It is interesting to note, too, that a full course on Marx was being offered at an American university less than a decade after *Das Kapital* had first been translated into English. Marx's analysis of labor value, surplus value, and the dominance of capitalism through its concentration of economic resources and the expropriation of the tools of the workers was carefully read, and important points and definitions recorded by Junior in his notebook or on the margins of his copy of the book.[34]

In Gardner's courses, Junior was exposed to the ideas that formed the core of the radical critique and spirit of reformism soon to burst on the American scene. He heard a call to action and personal involvement in courses offered by another young faculty member, George Wilson, and by President Andrews. Wilson's courses on social institutions, from the perspective of "Anthropology and Ethnology," examined the family, marriage, divorce, pauperism, charity, intemperance, and social legislation, and presented statistical analyses of a number of social problems. Wilson, who later went on to a distinguished career as a scholar of international relations, stressed the need for "intelligent giving" and "charity organization" as a solution to the problems of social disorganization and disintegration.

Andrews' course on "Practical Ethics," offered through the Philosophy Department, was in many ways the culmination of Junior's college career. Andrews, who had been on sabbatical leave in Europe for part of the school year, returned specifically to teach the course to graduating seniors. He was also in the middle of his long struggle with the board, so his lectures carried an additional layer of meaning. Andrews spoke to his students about alarming increases in all indices of social disorder, and attributed these not to individual moral failings but to the essential inequities of the social and economic system. Convinced of the basic importance of individual initiative, he was equally convinced that unbridled individualism had failed in important respects, and he saw the answer in a combination of government action to restrain monopoly, a moral reformation of all classes in society, and a program of voluntary population control that would reduce pressures on social institutions and natural resources. He foresaw a somber future unless such programs were undertaken soon.

Alone among contemporary economists, Andrews considered rapid population growth, through both natural increase and immigration, as a serious threat. He based his argument on Malthus' original proposition, holding that the operation of his law had been delayed by "fuller division of labor, improved technology and methods, and the availability of virgin land." However, the strength of these factors was eroding under the impact of unprecedented population growth. As a consequence, "three hard facts confront us. One is that the earth's stock of substances capable of sustaining human life is, after all, limited. Another, that many of these are passing hopelessly beyond man's reach. The third is that such utilization of plant nutrition as is intrinsically possible must forever increase in cost."

Andrews might have been speaking directly to Junior when he informed his students that it was their duty as Christians and men of substance and ability to involve themselves in the solution of these problems: "The world painfully needs two more classes of missionaries still—social missionaries to the rich and political missionaries. Where are the young men and women of means and leisure who will duly study the social problems of our time and help to their solution?"

In some respects, Andrews was ahead of his time. But the power of his words and example, and to a lesser extent those of Gardner and Wilson, stayed with Junior, permanently altering his perception of the world he lived in and the role he was to play in it. He had entered Brown in 1893 as a socially inhibited young man with little understanding of the realities of the world and the sweeping changes taking place. When he left college in 1897, at the age of twenty-three, he was socially at ease, though he remained a courteous man who would never lose an air of formality and reserve in his interactions with others. And he left with a mind opened to new ideas. He had not been radicalized, nor had his moral principles and religious beliefs been compromised in any way. But he was curious, sensitive to what others thought, and anxious to be of service to his society. He was to undergo some painful experiences and adjustments before finally settling on his life's course. But he had been well prepared.

3

THE APPRENTICE

ON THE MORNING of October 1, 1897, Junior arrived at 26 Broadway for his first day of work. He was fresh from a two-month tour of Europe with college friend Willard Richardson and a two-week visit with Abby Aldrich at her father's summer home on Warwick Neck, Rhode Island. From there, he traveled to New York City on the midnight sleeper. Ideas of going to law school or taking a world tour had vanished before the realities of Junior's sense of duty to his father and the existence of the great Rockefeller fortune. Seemingly everything in his life up to this point had been directed toward seating him behind a desk at 26 Broadway. When he awoke in the morning, with the train pulling slowly into Grand Central Depot, he shaved and dressed hurriedly, sent his luggage home to 4 West 54th Street, and made his way to his father's office.

A profound change had taken place in that office in 1897. Father was no longer there. As noted, he had been ill, and was tired. He was quite serious about retiring. Nearing sixty years of age, he could not have known that he would live for nearly forty more years. His youngest child and only son was a great joy; he had complete confidence in Junior, and vested in him all his hopes for the future conduct of family affairs.

Nevertheless, the absence of the father at the very time the son entered the family office created a curious sort of vacuum for Junior. Not only did Senior not lecture, exhort, or second-guess his son, but he gave him no instructions at all about his new job. In 1920, Junior commented on this: "Father never said a word to me about what I was to do in the office before I began to work there, nor has he since. Moreover, he did not say anything on the subject to anyone else in the office, so far as I have ever learned. Apparently he intended that I should make my own way."[1]

Nor was there any automatic sinecure with Standard Oil. Its structure at that time was complicated, and knowledge of modern corporate forms is of little help in understanding it.[2] Senior certainly had been "first among equals" within the oligarchy that ran the giant trust, and he was by far the major stockholder—but he was no longer in command. It was not a family business to be passed on from father to son automatically. In due course, the Standard Oil associates, led by John D. Archbold, took increasing note of Junior and his obvious abilities. Believing that having a Rockefeller actively in the trust would be an asset, they made him a vice president and director in 1901. Given these facts and his father's status, there is little doubt that Junior could have done very well at Standard, perhaps working his way to the top—if that is what he had really wanted.

But Junior's salary was paid by his father, not Standard Oil—$6,000 a year to start, with a raise to $7,200 within a year—a princely sum in those days, especially for a young bachelor living with his parents. And Junior went to work not in the offices where the associates were located, but in a dingy set of three rooms on the ninth floor, where a small staff worked on his father's own business affairs (as distinct from those of Standard Oil) and philanthropic interests. This was the origin of what would become known decades later as "Room 5600," the Rockefeller family offices with a staff numbered in the hundreds. In 1897, with the addition of Junior and his secretary, Charles O. Heydt, the family office had a staff of eight.

It was presided over by Frederick T. Gates, that formidable combination of missionary and entrepreneur to whom Senior had entrusted the management of his personal business and philanthropic affairs. The remaining staff included Gates' secretary; Senior's personal secretary, George Rogers; E. C. Cary, a bookkeeper and accountant; J. Alva Jenkins, who acted as purchasing agent and manager for the various Rockefeller homes; and a Mrs. Tuttle, the telegrapher who linked the office with 4 West 54th and Forest Hill in Cleveland.

Under the guidance of Gates, Junior began to learn what his father's far-flung concerns were all about; he pored over account books, made long business trips with Gates, took over the management of household accounts, and held seats on the boards of a score of companies and institutions in which his father had major interests. In particular, he worked on real estate matters, selling off dozens of holdings in the Cleveland area and acquiring others in Westchester County and Manhattan, as well as in Chicago for the benefit of the university. Despite the herculean efforts of Gates to clean up and rationalize Senior's business affairs, it was still a jumbled, chaotic, and growing empire. Senior gave Gates and Junior considerable leeway, but still made the key decisions, especially those involving any substantial commitment of funds. Because Senior rarely came to 26 Broadway, Gates communicated with him in written reports and Junior in oral presentations made at home.

It was a peculiar situation for Gates and Junior. Gates, the hired hand, was in charge, and Junior, the son and heir, was the apprentice. Gates must have known that Junior would gradually assume power as he grew older and became more experienced. And Junior had to be patient during the apprenticeship, finding his way and often deferring to the older man's tutelage. One can imagine all sorts of frictions and problems that could have arisen in this relationship. The fact that they did not says a great deal about the character of the two men.

By the time Junior had fully assumed the leadership role, Gates had come to regard him as too liberal, as we shall see. But their close association for approximately fifteen years was a productive one. Both men spoke warmly of each other in later reminiscences. Junior said: "Never shall I forget the patient, painstaking way in which he inducted me into the business world, and the problems of our office. . . . No father could have been more kindly or helpful to his own son than was Mr. Gates to me." And for his part, Gates wrote that Junior came into his father's office "endowed with great energy" and "a large capacity for work." He said that by 1901 Junior "may fairly be said to have completed a postgraduate course in business and benevolence."[3]

There was an interesting difference in the working styles of father and son. Senior had always been a member of a group, a team player. The conditions of Junior's work and life, and perhaps elements of his character, made him much more of a "loner." There was the cultural shock of moving from the easy camaraderie of college to the loneliness of 26 Broadway and 4 West 54th where there were only Gates and his family to relate to. Public awareness of the huge and growing Rockefeller fortune had been mounting for years, resulting in constant publicity. In this situation, one had to build defenses, and they fortified the style of the loner. It became difficult for Junior to know if a contact with another human being was truly divorced from some "hidden agenda" related to his father's wealth. This was not a matter of being able to trust no one, but rather that it made friendships hard to make and sustain.

Moreover, as the only son in these circumstances, Junior was troubled in several ways. He had no way of knowing his true value to the enterprise. He even envied the secretaries in this regard, because they were paid according to some measure of their value, while his pay was an arbitrary figure. Because he had had no specific preparation for his work, he felt he was being overpaid. He tried to make up for it by diligence, overwork, and becoming extremely meticulous in everything he did. He was never to earn money or meet a payroll in any normal sense, nor to feel the stimulus of competition. As he told his biographer many years later: "In my father's office I wasn't in a race with anybody. I didn't have to worry that somebody would get my job. I was the only one and there wasn't anybody else. I really was in a race with myself and my own conscience."[4]

One day at lunch with a college friend, Henry Cooper, Junior let down his guard and talked about his concerns, the burden of work, and his lack of experience. Cooper then wrote him a warm letter, citing Junior's strong points, but concluding:

> You are altogether too grumpy, too morose, and gloomy, John. And I'll tell you what the cause is: you are allowing such things as you spoke to me about at lunch to weigh upon your mind; you are thinking too much of yourself not selfishly, you understand, but introspectively. . . . I truly think it would do you good, for instance, to take up smoking an occasional cigarette, or something of that sort. I am not joking. Just try being a shade more reckless or careless as to whether or not you reach perfection within five years, and see if you don't find more happiness.[5]

Junior found taking the larger dose of advice to be rather difficult, but a few days after this lecture he carefully noted in his ledger, "pack of cigarettes—10¢." He never smoked again, nor did he ever drink. But this minor transgression illustrates how Junior, on occasion, could move away from some of the more strict fundamentalist constraints, as he already had in his great love for dancing. This did not alter his deep religious faith. The Fifth Avenue Baptist Church occupied an important place in his life. He attended services regularly, helped out at the Armitage House, and budgeted 10 percent of his income for church-related benevolences, usually exceeding this by a substantial amount. He participated actively in the Men's Bible Class, and soon took over its leadership from no less a personage than Charles Evans Hughes. This meant that he had to spend two or three evenings every week preparing his Sunday talk.

There were compensations for the rigors of office and church work. New York then was perhaps the most dynamic city in the world, as well as a crucible for all the social ills and human conflicts imaginable in a time of rapid growth, and Junior found it ever more fascinating. His closest companionship was with those who shared his unique status problems—his sisters—especially Alta, with whom he would spend time going to museums, riding, or just talking. And he began to build a social life with frequent notations in his personal ledger for tickets to dances, plays, musicales, and the opera. He occasionally squired young ladies, as the entries "flowers for Miss Swift" and "dinner—Miss Hunt" attest.

Always in the background, however, was his attraction to Abby Aldrich. They corresponded regularly, and Junior saw her whenever she and her mother came to New York on shopping trips. He demonstrated his devotion by frequently taking a late afternoon train to Providence, spending a few hours with Abby in the Aldrich home at 110 Benevolent Street, and catching the midnight sleeper back to New York. But there was no explicit understanding between them, so the popular Abby naturally was seeing other young men, causing Junior to feel the pangs of jealousy more than once.

His somewhat tentative courtship of Abby proceeded in this fashion for four years, including brief vacations under heavy chaperonage and a romantic trip to Cuba in the spring of 1900 aboard President McKinley's yacht, in the company of Senators Aldrich, Teller, Allison, Spooner, and Beveridge to investigate conditions in the wake of the Spanish-American War. Despite his deep affection for Abby and the obvious dynastic implications of the match, Junior hesitated to propose marriage. His innate caution and "dread of marrying someone and finding out later that I loved someone else more" held him back. He told his biographer that he prayed every night for four years for guidance in this crucial matter.

Finally, the young couple agreed "not to see each other or write to each other for six months to determine whether we would get over it or whether we wouldn't." A few months of isolation in New York and a number of conversations with his mother convinced Junior of the proper course. Discussing the situation with her one evening, he recalled that she "laughed and said, 'Of course you love Miss Aldrich. Why don't you go and get her?'" He wrote immediately and then left for Providence the next day. Determined to do things properly, Junior formally asked Senator Aldrich for his daughter's hand in marriage. Standing before the powerful politician in the drawing room of his yacht in Newport Harbor, the young Rockefeller began to explain his financial prospects. The Senator quickly interrupted to say: "I am only interested in what will make my daughter happy."[6]

The young couple exchanged vows on October 9, 1901, in a ceremony held at the Aldrich summer home at Warwick Neck. On the lawn sloping down to the waters of Narragansett Bay, they pledged their eternal devotion before approximately a thousand guests. The alliance between great wealth and great political power symbolized by the wedding kept the nation enthralled and entertained for weeks. Every scrap of information about the couple, their parents, the ceremony, the bride's trousseau, and the honeymoon was seized upon, savored, and digested by the ravenous press. Immediately after the reception, the Rockefellers left for a four-week honeymoon on one of the properties that Junior and his father had been quietly buying up near the tiny village of Pocantico Hills in Westchester County. They then began their long life together by staying for a few weeks with the elder Rockefellers at 4 West 54th until their rented house across the street (No. 13) was ready for them.

As Gates suggested, it is quite appropriate to view Junior's first four years in his father's office, up to the time of his marriage, as a "postgraduate course in business and benevolence." His work under Gates continued on through the first decade of the century, a remarkably productive period for the two men during which Junior functioned on the whole with growing confidence, now that he had four years of experience under his belt and had settled the question of his life's partner. He was now to grapple with another important decision—the particular direction and emphasis his own career would take. His father had three careers—Standard Oil, personal business investments, and philanthropy. In taking his father's place, Junior faced the question of whether he would continue to function in all three of these careers or in only two of them or only one. There was severe personal trauma in store for him until he made his choice at the end of the decade.

He made his share of mistakes in business and benevolence but began to have successes as well. To his chagrin and embarrassment, he learned an important lesson when he was swindled and lost one million dollars in a speculative stock venture. On the other hand, he scored a personal triumph in refusing to be cowed by the formidable J. P. Morgan when negotiating the sale of his father's holdings in the Mesabi iron-ore range (in connection with Morgan's assembling of the Carnegie and other interests to create United States Steel). On the first, he received no reproaches from his father, who merely said, "All right, John, don't worry. I will see you through." On the second, Senior exclaimed to Laura, "Great Caesar, but John is a trump!"[7]

But it became increasingly clear that it was philanthropy that drew Junior's deepest interest and showed his talents plainly. He brought in new associates, expanded the fields of interest, sought to apply the insights he had gained at Brown, and, together with Gates, undertook innovations that brought about an enduring change in the nature of American philanthropy.

These developments, as well as Junior's personal trauma and decisions, cannot be understood outside the context of the times. Historians unanimously regard the two decades flanking the turn of the century as one of the periods of most profound change in two centuries of American life. The latter part of the period has come to be known as the "Progressive era," a label not to be confused with, but certainly related to, the forming of the Progressive Party in 1912 by dissident Republicans, chiefly Senator Robert M. La Follette of Wisconsin and former President Theodore Roosevelt. The Progressive era presents a vast and bewildering sea of change, not a neat sequence of events that can be dissected in terms of cause and effect. It had its powerful antecedents in the 1890s when the populist tide reached its peak, fueled by economic discontent, the bitter complaints of western farmers and city workers, radical critiques of the prevailing order, and strong reform impulses. The American entry onto the world scene, marked by the Spanish-American War and the brief sortie into imperialism, seemed a diversion, but was actually symptomatic of the ferment of the times.

The effect of the Progressive movement was to readjust the nation's political institutions to the needs of the modern world and to further democratize the political process. One historian has characterized it "as a popular effort, which began convulsively in the 1890s, to insure the survival of democracy in the United States by the enlargement of governmental power to control and offset the power of private economic groups over the nation's institutions and life." The Progressive reformers never existed as a unified movement "with common goals and a machinery geared to achieve them," but as an uneasy and shifting coalition of feminists, businessmen, liberal clergy, social workers, municipal reformers, farmers, labor union members, and Prohibitionists.[8]

One prominent strand of the Progressive movement was the phenomenon of the muckrakers, which left an indelible mark on Junior. These crusading journalists were given this pejorative label by President Roosevelt (in a speech on April 14, 1906), even as TR himself was fast becoming the most prominent muckraker of all. He likened them to a character in Bunyan's *Pilgrim's Progress,* "the Man with the Muckrake . . . who could look no way but downward." But the label became a badge of honor for some of those involved, such as Upton Sinclair, Samuel Hopkins Adams, Ray Stannard Baker, Lincoln Steffens, Ida Tarbell, and others who elevated social protest into an enduring literary form, detailing the operations of the bloated plutocracy, the horrors of life in the factories, workshops, and slums, and the very real threat posed to the survival of American institutions by the alliance between greedy businessmen and corrupt politicians.

Others, however, were not so reputable, sensing political or commercial advantage in the rising storm of criticism, and exploiting it to the fullest. Prominent among them was William Randolph Hearst. Having failed to advance his political career materially by fomenting a war, the publisher saw another opportunity in the protest movement, and also a chance to upstage his rival Joseph Pulitzer in the bitter New York press war of the time. His eye on the White House, the colorful, shrewd, and demagogic Hearst pushed exposé journalism well beyond any reputable standards. He had already served two terms in Congress as a Tammany Democrat, accepted the nomination of his own Civil Alliance Party for the mayoralty *against* Tammany in 1905, and finally ran, *with* Tammany's support, for the governorship of New York in 1906 (losing to the Republican Charles Evans Hughes). Throughout the decade, the Rockefellers and Standard Oil served as constant targets for Hearst's political ambitions.

The first major attack on Standard Oil was *Wealth Against Commonwealth* by William Demarest Lloyd, published in 1894. Criticized by responsible journals at the time and discredited later by historians, Lloyd's book nevertheless had its impact on the public and set the style for the muckrakers to come. A similar exercise occurred when *Frenzied Finance* was published in 1905 by Thomas W. Lawson, himself one of the most frenzied of financiers. In between, as noted, came one of the great books of the period and a telling blow, Ida M. Tarbell's *History of the Standard Oil Company,* published in two volumes in 1904, after being serialized since 1902 in *McClure's.* Although one-sided, much of the work was based on voluminous research and was so confident and straightforward in tone that it constituted a damning indictment in the eyes of the public and the press.

As a result of these books and the assenting chorus of the "yellow" press, Senior emerged as the single greatest villain in all that was wrong with the prevailing economic system.[9] Such a convenient symbol could not escape the shrewd political eye of President Roosevelt. Genuinely fearing that the reform movement could become so radicalized that it could put the country on the path toward socialism, TR's very astute response was to stay one step ahead, containing the movement by joining it and becoming, with typical gusto, one of the most vociferous critics of all. For years he engaged in personal attacks on Senior, as late as 1908 excoriating a man who had retired eleven years earlier, nearly five years before TR became president.[10]

Given the fact that other wealthy business leaders were truly corrupt or lived much more extravagant lives than Senior did, or both, why did he emerge as the arch-villain of the time? The answer probably lies in a combination of Standard Oil's unmatched success, Senior's great and growing wealth, and his remoteness and indifference to public opinion. Standard was not yet the largest of the great trusts, but it was the most nearly perfect one. Senior had achieved his business goals—bringing order out of chaos in his industry, innovating a new pattern of industrial organization, improving the quality of products, and selling them at low cost. But in the course of doing so, he and his associates had been more efficient in eliminating competition than any other leaders of industry.

Some of Senior's qualities, which otherwise might seem admirable, were made to order for criticism. Once he had been singled out, they helped to heighten that criticism until it reached gigantic proportions. His policy was never to engage in public controversy, so he remained silent when attacked, which made the substance of the attacks seem all the more true. Senior's continued silence under mounting attacks made him seem cold and remote. This, in turn, made his religious piety a special irritant to many; it seemed a clear case of sanctimonious hypocrisy. His philanthropies came to be seen as his means of expiating guilt—few knew or bothered to point out that he had always been a giving man.

Also, because Senior did not announce his retirement publicly, he continued to be seen for more than a decade afterward as the evil genius behind the growing power of Standard Oil. He had few defenders, and their voices were lost in the chorus of criticism. Because he was not politically active, Senior's personal campaign contributions were modest, apt to be seen by needy politicians as niggardly, nearly an insult, considering his wealth.

It was an agonizing ordeal for Junior to witness the constant attacks on his father. He, of course, saw his father as a warm and loving family man, a generous giver to worthy causes, a man of deep religious conviction, and one who remained calm and cheerful at the worst of times. There is no evidence that Senior ever felt any guilt. His advice to his son was to keep on doing what he thought was right and "let the world wag." But Junior chafed under what he regarded as the injustice of the attacks on his father, and it left him permanently wary of the press. To his credit, however, he did not let this turn him into a bitter reactionary. One of the ironies in the emergence of Senior as the arch-villain of the times was the fact that both father and son, especially the latter, were liberals in their attitudes toward many of the current problems of society, in some ways as close to the spirit of progressivism as many of its avowed leaders.

These liberal and reformist tendencies became manifest at the beginning of the first decade of the century and grew steadily thereafter. The fact that Senior was now interested mainly in philanthropy, combined with the explosive growth of his fortune, meant that philanthropy would become very big business indeed. The founding of the University of Chicago was only the beginning of large-scale giving. Within the next half-century, Rockefeller gifts would total over $1 billion.

As Allan Nevins commented, it would have been "intolerable to the systematic and conscientious Rockefeller" to give money away on the basis of "whims and casual impulses. . . . He knew that he was only a tenant or trustee of his wealth, which in the main was an historical accident. He had a high conception of a trustee's duty. Fortunate it was that as he made philanthropy his main pursuit, he found two such aides as his son and Frederick T. Gates." The three men made a unique team, sharing basic principles, but each bringing special qualities to the task:

Rockefeller had sharp limitations of education and outlook; he was not well read, not much interested in literature, science, or art, not expertly equipped to work with leaders in education and social welfare. But Gates and John D. Rockefeller, Jr., were able to help him plan his benefactions with sweep and imagination, to open epochal new undertakings, and to use his wealth in broad national and international channels. Like Rockefeller, they were able to create bold new designs. Like him, they were ready to put an unresting energy into making an unconventional and creative activity a success. Like him, they delighted in pioneering ventures; and they encouraged him to invest large sums in supporting new ideas, fresh patterns of action, and courageous leaders.[11]

Although most of Gates' ideas remained cast within the Baptist framework, he was still a visionary, capable of brilliant bursts of insight. But Junior was the workhorse, the one who made the ideas into realities and contributed many of his own, the "new man" who was ready for the challenges of the twentieth century and the full flowering of the Progressive era.

Junior was applying beliefs he had gained both at Brown and in his growing acquaintance with civic leaders and professional men in the city, beliefs that were intrinsically part of the Progressive movement. Chief among them was the conviction that social problems could be solved by bringing intelligence, good organization, careful management, and scientific thinking to bear upon them. He was more interested in problem-solving than palliatives, in devising new approaches in place of the classic maintenance functions of charity. He recognized that there were no single causes for difficult problems, that one always encountered a complex web of causative factors requiring a comprehensive scheme. His orientation was toward basic support for efforts to modernize governmental administration, eliminate poverty and disease, reconcile capital and labor, and improve education at all levels. In his efforts, he became adept at seeking out men of high competence and character, the leading experts in their fields.

New men were added to the staff. One of these was Henry Cooper, Junior's college friend, who worked mainly on investments. Another was Starr J. Murphy, an able attorney and committed reformer who originally had been used by Gates to do research on an idea for a new medical institute. Junior made Murphy a permanent member of the staff, and he became a close and trusted aide, by the end of the decade the de facto head of philanthropic activities under Junior as Gates grew less active.

Rockefeller gifts during the first decade of the century totaled $130.3 million, more than ten times the amount given in the previous decade. In the 1890s, the University of Chicago absorbed almost two-thirds of the gifts; during the next decade, this shrank to less than 10 percent, even while the total amount going to the university actually increased. There were gifts to other universities as well, totaling $4.2 million, with substantial sums going to Yale, Harvard, Johns Hopkins, Columbia, and Cornell. Giving to Baptist missionary societies and churches was consolidated and stabilized at a relatively small percentage of the total.

More impressive than the amount of money were the new directions that the giving took. An important shift occurred in support for groups involved with the poor in New York City. Under Gates, most of the money had been channeled through Baptist organizations, concerned mainly with church projects and subsidies in areas overwhelmed by the immigrant tide. Under the influence of Junior and Murphy, this giving was largely diverted to such professional and nonsectarian organizations as the Children's Aid Society, the Charity Organization Society, the New York Association for Improving the Condition of the Poor, and the YMCA. In addition, the office began to support innovative groups that were attempting to deal with causes rather than symptoms—the University Settlement, the Jacob Riis Settlement, the Henry Street Settlement, Whittier House in Newark, the Social Halls Association, the Tenement House Commission, the National Child Labor Committee, and the Bureau of Municipal Research.[12]

The notable breakthrough of the decade was the creation of the first great foundations. In the case of the Rockefellers, these were the Rockefeller Institute for Medical Research (1901), the General Education Board (1903), the Rockefeller Sanitary Commission (1909), and the beginning of the effort to create the Rockefeller Foundation in 1906 (not finally consummated until 1913). Two noteworthy foundations created by others during this period were the Milbank Memorial Fund (1905) and the Russell Sage Foundation (1907). Andrew Carnegie was busy also, creating the Carnegie Institution of Washington (1904), the Carnegie Foundation for the Advancement of Teaching (1905), and the Carnegie Corporation of New York (1911).

Historian Robert Bremner sees the significance of this spate of development in the "boldness of the enterprise" to which the new institutions were committed:

Most earlier charitable trusts had been established for some narrowly defined purpose. The smaller Carnegie funds, designed to promote the donor's particular philanthropic interests, continued in this tradition. The major trusts founded by Carnegie and Rockefeller, however, were limited only to the advancement of knowledge and human welfare. Relieving the needy was not their objective. They would attack misery at its source through the weapon of research. . . . Rockefeller's and Carnegie's chief contribution to philanthropy was to found institutions capable of distributing private wealth with greater intelligence and vision than the donors themselves could hope to possess. The great philanthropic trusts they established climaxed the long effort to put large-scale giving on a businesslike basis.[13]

In part, the creation of the foundations was a natural result of the trends then sweeping America, in particular the penchant for organization and efficiency. All over the nation, individuals and groups were combining in organizations to become more effective and wield greater influence. Businessmen had been the first to perceive the advantages, but now they were being followed by people in every line of endeavor. This phenomenon was so marked that the years around the turn of the century can be said to have constituted the watershed between the "age of the individual" and the "age of organization." It should be remembered that *Looking Backward,* Edward Bellamy's utopian novel of a future society safely anchored by technology and efficient organization (first published in 1888), was the runaway best-seller of this period, with more than a million copies sold by 1900. Economy, efficiency, organization, professionalism, and a somewhat naive belief in the efficacy of science became the symbols of progress into the future for millions of people. A popular view of the history of the period may tend to focus on the technological innovations—the telephone, the sewing machine, electricity, the internal-combustion engine, and a host of others. But underlying all of these was the massive and steady movement of the American people toward the anticipated benefits of organization and efficiency.[14]

The prominence of Rockefeller and Carnegie in creating philanthropic organizations caused the press to perceive a "race" between the two wealthiest Americans. Both were amused by this, especially Carnegie, because the press invariably saw him as ahead. But if anyone had actually declared a race, the Rockefellers would have ended up the clear winners. For one thing, Carnegie soon dropped out. As his biographer noted, by 1906 "Carnegie was tired of the game, and by 1910 he was desperately sick of it." His act of creating the Carnegie Corporation of New York and putting the bulk of his remaining fortune ($150 million) into it was an act of surrender. With that he ceased his active participation.[15]

An important difference between the Rockefeller and Carnegie organizations, therefore, was the nature of personal involvement by the founders. Carnegie not only dropped out, but also had no son to follow through. The result, despite some early notable achievements, was that the Carnegie Corporation, for example, did not earn its justly deserved reputation for excellence in philanthropy until after World War II. But the organizations developed by the Rockefellers early in the century made significant contributions almost immediately, and proceeded steadily to build towering reputations for leadership and quality. There were doubtless many reasons for this, but two important ones were the specific contributions of Junior. One was personal involvement. It became an article of faith for Junior that it was not enough to give money—one must also give one's personal leadership and time and energy, a belief that he passed on to his sons. The personal involvement of a donor (or representative of a donor) in a philanthropic organization can be a sensitive issue. Whether or not it works well depends on the character, ability, and intentions of the donor. The right kind of involvement can infuse an organization with a sense of mission and keep it true to its purposes. The wrong kind, obviously, can be disastrous.

Here Junior's second important contribution comes into play—the ability to work effectively with experts. Senior was a practical man who wanted to see results. He was cautious and reticent, aware that he was not well equipped to work with experts in fields other than business. But he also knew that experts would be needed to effect the grand designs of Gates in philanthropy. For this he had the two men he trusted most in the world—Gates and Junior. Gates was the man of purpose who kept pressing his ideas with almost biblical fervor. But it was the quiet, moderate Junior who was the doer, the one who soon displayed a talent for finding experts, placing them in positions of responsibility, trusting them, working with them closely, and backing them strongly. In contrast, Andrew Carnegie tended to distrust experts, and he had no trusted agents to act as a countervailing influence. He placed mainly businessmen on the boards of the organizations he created, and for a long time the organizations suffered for it.

Junior was also a practical man who was eager to see tangible results. He recognized that it was just as wrong to put blind faith in experts as it was to distrust them in the first place. He was to learn that the relationship between a lay leader and an expert was never an easy or simple one, that it required good faith and constant attention on both sides to be successful. There would always be problems to be worked out and policy issues to be settled. Achieving the delicate balance of knowing when to restrain his own impatience and when to exert influence was to be a constant concern throughout Junior's career and that of his eldest son. But Junior's approach to problems and needs, stemming from both instinct and his own excellent education, was always to seek the best people available and then find ways to work with them effectively—coming full circle to the need for personal involvement.

Junior and Gates were a remarkably effective team. But nothing would have happened without the basic commitment of Senior. He sounded the keynote for what was to be done as early as 1899 in a speech he delivered at the tenth anniversary of the founding of the University of Chicago: "Let us erect a foundation, a trust, and engage directors who will make it a life work to manage, with our personal co-operation, this business of benevolence properly and effectively."[16] He spoke in the singular, and the Rockefeller Foundation, the most difficult of the organizations to bring into being, was to fit his prescription most closely. But, in the meantime, there were other organizations to create.

4

⚓

THE INSTITUTION BUILDERS

THE FIRST GREAT ADVENTURE, the establishment of the Rockefeller Institute for Medical Research in 1901, was the inspiration of Gates. The idea came to him during his summer vacation in 1897 while reading William Osler's somber account of the state of medical knowledge and education, *Principles and Practice of Medicine*. He proposed to Senior that "an institution for scientific medical research on the general lines of the work of Koch in Berlin and the Pasteur Institute in Paris" be established in the United States.[1]

Senior's reaction was revealing of the man—he was cautiously receptive even though his own view of medicine was decidedly old-fashioned. He was following a personal regimen that he had developed over the years. His personal physician and frequent traveling companion was Dr. H. F. Biggar, a homeopath devoted to the nostrums and practices of the nineteenth century. As late as the 1930s, Senior continued to refuse the ministrations of modern medicine. One evening he told his son: "The doctor came to see me today. He wouldn't give me the medicine I wanted, and I wouldn't take the medicine he prescribed, but we had a lovely talk."[2]

Senior wanted to see a thorough study done before any funds were committed for the founding of a medical research institute. At first, he and Gates explored the possibility of locating it at the University of Chicago and then at Harvard, but neither plan worked. Gates recruited his Montclair, New Jersey, neighbor, lawyer Starr Murphy, to do a survey in Europe and elsewhere in the United States while Junior began a series of interviews with leading medical authorities in New York City. It was slow going at first with Murphy and Junior encountering a great deal of skepticism as to whether it was possible to create a first-rate medical research institute in the United States, whether there were sufficient men of stature to man it, and, if there were, whether they could be attracted to an organization not affiliated with a university.

Gates was the fiery champion of the cause. Some years later, after the Institute for Medical Research was established, Biggar criticized it to Senior, who sent Biggar's letter to Gates. Gates responded with four letters to Senior roundly criticizing Biggar—for his old-fashioned medical views, not his worth as a friend and traveling companion.[3] Senior remained unperturbed, continuing both his use of Biggar and his support of the institute.

This episode was typical of the outspoken Gates, who was decidedly not a "yes man." Gates' view was that if Senior did not want a frank expression of views he could buy himself a machine and talk into it "and by turning the crank get back his own words and thoughts accurately expressed." Gates saw his role as quite different:

I was there to present my own views with courtesy indeed but with absolute and undeviating frankness and truth. This therefore I always did. I usually came to clear and fortified judgments which I sometimes expressed strongly. I have no doubt that at times I irritated him. If so, he had great skill in concealing it. He was indeed very patient and very considerate. On the other hand, his deliberation was sometimes extreme . . .[4]

Here the invaluable role of Junior came into play, as he later described how the cause was advanced:

Gates was the brilliant dreamer and creator. I was the salesman—the go-between with Father at the opportune moment. Gates and I were Father's lieutenants, each of us with a different task, but acting in perfect harmony. Gates did the heavy thinking, and my part was to sell his ideas to Father. Of course, I was in a unique position. I could talk with Father at the strategic moment. It might be a relaxed mood after dinner, or while we were driving together. Consequently I could often get his approval of ideas which others couldn't have secured because the moment wasn't right.

Junior also used the technique of sending key letters and reports to his mother with the suggestion that she might find it interesting to read them—and also find an opportunity to read them aloud to Senior.[5]

Junior's role in the creation and success of the institute was to be much greater than the initial salesmanship with his father. By 1901 the project finally was ready to move forward. Senior was prepared to make a commitment on the basis of Murphy's reports and the results of Junior's consultations with medical authorities. The decisive meeting took place when Junior invited seven of these men to the

Rockefeller residence at 4 West 54th Street one evening early in the year. Senior was not present. Junior announced that his father had agreed to the suggestion of providing $20,000 a year for ten years for research grants and the launching of an institute. This was merely an opening wedge, as evidenced a year later when Senior made available $1 million for the purchase of property near the East River at 66th Street and the building of a research laboratory.[6] In the meantime, the seven men Junior had worked with agreed to form an active group and then became the directors of the institute when it was incorporated under the laws of New York State on June 14, 1901. All seven were men of remarkable stature and accomplishments, though only one of them, Dr. William H. Welch, was over forty years of age. Welch was the dean of the Johns Hopkins Medical School and probably the foremost figure in American medicine at the time; some of the others had been his students. Under the leadership of these directors, with Welch as chairman, one of the greatest success stories in the history of American philanthropy unfolded with remarkable rapidity. One of the original seven, Dr. Simon Flexner, agreed to become director of the new laboratory, and he proceeded to recruit a staff of experts in pathology, biological chemistry, physiology, and pharmacology who began work in temporary quarters on Lexington Avenue.

With this, Junior's education in working with experts began in earnest. He and Gates were hoping for immediate attention to the diseases that were ravaging the world in recurring epidemics, many of them virulent in New York City, including influenza, diphtheria, cholera, typhus, dysentery, meningitis, scarlet fever, and tuberculosis. Many families, including the Rockefellers, had lost members to one or another of these diseases. Dr. Flexner and his colleagues were just as anxious as anyone else to see these maladies conquered, but their vision of the institute was more open-ended, more concerned with "pure" research than "applied" research. They wanted to pursue any problem in biological science that might have a bearing on medicine, believing that adding to knowledge of the underlying chemical and biological structure of life was a more effective way in the long run to solve specific problems. Gates and Junior argued that there were times when problems demanded immediate attention and could not await the slow and careful analysis of the scientist. There was some tension over such issues for a while.[7]

The tension was productive, however. It soon became clear that each side heard the other and that both purposes would be served. One of the first research grants given by the Rockefeller Institute, in collaboration with the New York City Department of Health, was $7,000 for a study of the city's milk supply. The finding that it was contaminated regularly by germs of dysentery and tuberculosis was emblazoned in the tabloid headlines, resulting in a public outcry. This led quickly to new regulations and enforcement that solved the problem, and to the promotion of Dr. Hermann Biggs, one of the original seven and a member of the institute's board, to be chief medical officer of the Department of Health in the reform administration of Mayor Seth Low, a post that Biggs used to introduce other important public health measures.[8]

Only a few years later came the next great "practical" development—an effective serum for cerebrospinal meningitis developed by Simon Flexner. An epidemic of the disease in New York City in 1905 had focused his attention on the problem, and by 1907 the serum was proved effective and made available around the world. With accomplishments such as these, the institute quickly earned a reputation for excellence that has endured to this day. By 1907 it was clear that the founders had come to accept fully the emphasis on pure research that Flexner and his colleagues wanted. As the historian of the institute put it:

It is very much to the credit of the founding group, and particularly the two Rockefellers and Gates, who were not scientists, that they saw the need for fundamental principles as gradually revealed to them by the work of the laboratory staff, and that they gave their unquestioning support to scientific research.[9]

One measure of this was the fact that Junior shifted his interest in specific public health improvements to other Rockefeller organizations—the Rockefeller Sanitary Commission, the Bureau of Social Hygiene (created by him in 1913), and, most especially, the Rockefeller Foundation. Another measure was the fact that Rockefeller support of the institute became unstinting. In 1907 Senior provided a $2.5 million endowment fund and in 1908 he gave funds for a hospital where patients with diseases being studied by the institute were treated free of charge. Numerous other gifts followed, including a farm in New Jersey for animal and plant pathology studies.

By the 1920s, Simon Flexner had forgotten the early pressure and could speak of the relationship with the institute's donors only in the most glowing terms. "We never asked Mr. Rockefeller's representatives for anything," he said. "They always came to us and asked, 'Suppose you had more money, what would you do with it?'" Flexner wrote:

The Institute . . . has been expected to explore, to dream. Our founder and his advisers have said to us again and again, in effect: "Don't be in a hurry to produce anything. Don't worry about making good. We have faith that you will make good, and if you don't, the next fellow will. . . . This thing may go on for generations; then suddenly somebody will give us a practical result."[10]

In the decades that followed, the institute became the leading research organization of its kind in the world. Merely listing its research accomplishments would require one long book. In all, Senior's contributions totaled some $61 million. Support was continued by Junior, by various Rockefeller philanthropic organizations, and by the Rockefeller brothers, with David taking a particular interest. Today the institute is known as Rockefeller University, probably the most unique university in the United States, offering only the Ph.D. and concentrating overwhelmingly on research.

The second great institution created by Senior was the General Education Board (GEB), chartered by act of Congress and incorporated on January 12, 1903. It would be difficult to overstate the value of the work the GEB did in the ensuing half century. Ironically, it seems largely forgotten today, perhaps because of the prosaic name or the fact that, unlike other Rockefeller institutions, it no longer exists.[11] Another factor may be the varying missions the GEB undertook, with the result that it is not an easy organization to categorize except under the very general rubric of "education."

To understand the GEB, one must see it as an agency of change, one of such remarkable accomplishments that it is scarcely an exaggeration to refer to its work as revolutionary. In succession, it was chiefly responsible for (1) generating the movement toward public high school education in the South for blacks (referred to at the time as "colored" or "Negroes") and poor whites; (2) substantially upgrading black higher education in the South; (3) eliminating the devastating hookworm parasite that plagued the South (through its "spin-off" organization, the Rockefeller Sanitary Commission) and introducing professional public health administration and practice throughout the region; (4) introducing (and partly administering) agricultural experimentation and farm demonstration work to the entire South; (5) reforming college administration and developing professional standards for graduate education throughout the United States; and (6) modernizing the teaching and practice of medicine throughout the country.

The work of the GEB had a streak of missionary fervor to it, not surprising considering that its founders and some of its leaders were devout Baptists. But this was missionary fervor with a difference. The organization's proseletyzing had nothing to do with religion, but was done in the service of its objectives in education, agriculture, and public health. And the work was done very quietly, with great circumspection and skill, for the good reason that, like any agent of change, the GEB was up against some form of established opposition in each of its successive missions, whether it be prideful southerners, still very mindful of the Civil War, who resented any intrusions of northerners for any purpose, or the established leadership in higher education and medicine in the United States generally. Because the GEB was trying to change prevailing ways, its work was constantly tinged with controversy. Its board and staff were largely successful in controlling controversy by working behind the scenes, involving local leaders wherever possible, creating opportunities for others to act instead of trying to impose change, and avoiding too much publicity or the taking of too much credit themselves.

Perhaps the most surprising contribution of the GEB is that it provided the model for American overseas financial and technical assistance programs after World War II. The relationship of the South to the North was analogous to that between the former colonies and the Western powers after World War II, in terms of colonial heritage, economic underdevelopment, and the need for capital transfer and technical assistance. Even before the Civil War, the rural South stood in a colonial relationship to the industrial North, in economic terms at least; after the war, the South was prostrate, impoverished, stagnant, and ridden with disease, illiteracy, and economic hardship. Northern philanthropists began the process of financial and technical assistance, with the GEB as by far the major vehicle. The analogy comes across strikingly in C. Vann Woodward's classic study, *Origins of the New South: 1877–1913*, especially in the chapters entitled "The Colonial Economy" and "Philanthropy and the Forgotten Man."[12]

As we shall see in later chapters, the GEB experience was more than a model. A direct link to American technical assistance programs was provided by Junior's two oldest sons, John 3rd and Nelson, especially the latter, who probably deserves more credit than any other individual for originating American overseas aid programs. Both men were brought up in a family with a strong interest in missionary work, and both were knowledgeable about the GEB, especially John, who served as GEB chairman during its latter years. John had all the right ideas at an early date and became a much more consistent and proficient operator overseas than Nelson; moreover, his programs were among the "purest" to be found in the sense of devotion to the problems at hand rather than power politics. But for a variety of reasons, John did not begin his overseas work until the early 1950s. Nelson was involved much earlier, even before World War II, and he was a key figure in official Washington in formulating the policies that led to the assistance efforts.

All this began with the interest of Senior in doing something to assist education for blacks in a more organized and effective way than the random gifts he had been making to black institutions over all the years since his contribution in 1862 to a "colored mute and blind society." Senior's interest had been stimulated by his wife's parents, Harvey Buel Spelman and Lucy Henry Spelman, both of Massachusetts birth and staunch abolitionists. They had participated in the "Underground Railroad" to help escaped slaves and helped to found Spelman College in Atlanta. Junior had been brought up in this atmosphere. As a boy, he had heard often from his maternal grandmother about the plight of the blacks, and he wrote to her from Brown about the "three colored men" in his class and about the time he led the service at a "colored church." His parents had taken him on visits to Spelman College (named after his grandmother) and to the Hampton Institute, where they purchased a scholarship in Junior's name.

Senior's interest was stirring at a propitious time. For more than a decade, the South had been undergoing another wrenching transition, this time away from the chaos and excesses of the Reconstruction period. The first stirrings of the "New South" saw the emergence of a number of enlightened moderates seeking economic development and the general improvement of the region. On the dark side, there was a move toward segregation, eliminating the gains some blacks thought they had made, and a wave of terror and the rise of the Ku Klux Klan. In 1897 segregation had become the law of the land with the *Plessy* v. *Ferguson* decision ("separate but equal") of the Supreme Court.

The turmoil of the times served to renew the interest of northern philanthropists in southern education. In the words of C. Vann Woodward, southern schools were "miserably supported, poorly attended, wretchedly taught, and wholly inadequate for the education of the people."[13] If the schools were bad for white students, they were abysmal for blacks. The tradition of tax-supported public education had never taken root in the South as it had in the North. There were only a few hundred free public schools in a few states. Only Kentucky among southern states had a compulsory school attendance law at the turn of the century, whereas all northern states except two had such laws. Most schooling was done in private academies, some of them fairly good for the sons and daughters of the well-to-do, but the great majority of them squalid one-room hovels in a region whose population was 85 percent rural. The term "poor whites" was not only a pejorative label, but a reality. Most whites were little better off than the blacks who were at the bottom of the ladder.

Northern help began soon after the Civil War, by missionary bodies and the Massachusetts-born London banker George Peabody, who in 1869 established the Peabody Fund to aid education in the South. In 1882 Connecticut textile manufacturer John F. Slater created the $1 million Slater Fund to aid black education in the region. Over the years, these funds and the missionary societies had been able to do little more than prop up some of the private schools in the South. The ferment around the turn of the century energized a number of individual leaders in both the North and the South.

There were two prime movers who collaborated in organizing a series of annual conferences on southern education, beginning in 1898. One was J. L. M. Curry of Alabama, a Confederate veteran and former congressman and college professor who had become field agent for both the Peabody and Slater funds. The establishment of free public education in the South had become his life's goal. The other leader was Robert C. Ogden, an urbane New York businessman associated with John Wanamaker. Through his church work, Ogden had long been interested in black education and had been a member of the group that founded the Hampton Institute, the first of the black industrial schools in the South. Curry and Ogden had interested a number of other men in their conferences, including Charles W. Dabney, president of the University of Tennessee; Edwin A. Alderman, president of Tulane University (later the brilliant president of the University of Virginia); two influential New York magazine editors, Albert Shaw and Walter Hines Page (the latter a North Carolinian); the venerable New York banker Morris K. Jesup; William H. Baldwin, president of the Long Island Railroad; Daniel Coit Gilman, president of Johns Hopkins; and another New York banker, the Georgia-born George Foster Peabody (no relation to the founder of the Peabody Fund).

Trying to advance the cause, Ogden in 1901 conceived a flashy idea that turned out to be a phenomenal success in that it led to the creation of the GEB. His idea was to hire a special Pennsylvania Railroad train to take fifty prominent people to the South for a conference and a visit to several of the black colleges and elementary and secondary schools. The guests included some of the men mentioned above; another person who accepted the invitation was John D. Rockefeller, Jr. Having listened to his father talk about helping black education in the South, Junior thought the excursion would be a convenient way to find out more about the problem.

Derisively called "the millionaires' special" by southern newspapers, the trip, as Junior later told his biographer, turned out to be "one of the outstanding events of my life." He and his father had talked about creating a new fund for Negro education in the South. But as a result of participating in Ogden's special trip, Junior came to realize at first hand not only the urgency and scope of the problem, but also gained the important insight that the only way to help black education in the South effectively was to help white education. This point was made forcefully by one of the travelers, Henry St. George Tucker, president of Washington and Lee University, in a talk to the group on the homeward-bound trip. As reported in the *New York World* of April 25, 1901, Tucker said:

> If it is your idea to educate the Negro, you must have the white of the South with you. If the poor white sees the son of a Negro neighbor enjoying through your munificence benefits denied to his boy, it raises in him a feeling that will render futile all your work. You must lift up the "poor white" and the Negro together if you would approach success.

Back home, Junior was eager to move forward with a major project based on what he had learned. But it was a busy time for him. He was preoccupied with the creation of the Rockefeller Institute and with his courtship of Abby and the consequent marriage. They set up their own household in the attractive townhouse at 13 West 54th Street, diagonally across the street from Senior's residence. During this period, Junior found time for conversations with this father and Gates about the southern education problem, and he stayed in touch with several of the men he had traveled with on the Ogden trip. Most of all, he consulted with Wallace Buttrick, secretary of the Baptist Home Mission Society, who had traveled extensively in the South in connection with the society's assistance to church-supported private schools. Buttrick emphatically endorsed Henry St. George Tucker's advice that the only effective way to help black education was to help education generally. This was one reason why the resulting organization was named the *General* Education Board instead of the Negro Education Board, as Junior had first contemplated.

The plan was developed further in a dinner meeting at Morris Jesup's house on January 15, 1902. Aside from Jesup, those present were Junior, Ogden, Curry, Peabody, Baldwin, and Buttrick. On February 27, the newlywed Rockefellers hosted this group for dinner at 13 West 54th, and invited several others as well—Page, Shaw, Gilman, and lawyer Edward M. Shepard, a friend of Peabody's. In his written report to his father, Junior noted: "Abby was the only woman present." Shepard presented a charter he had drawn up for the new organization, using the name Junior and Buttrick had agreed upon, and, according to their instructions, making no mention of the South or of blacks. The charter stated the broad purpose of the GEB as "the promotion of education within the United States without distinction of race, sex or creed." This familiar phrase, much-used since then, might seem to suggest that the group was contemplating integrated education as it is known today; however, such a notion was impossible eighty-five years ago—segregated education was the law of the land.

One of the wise decisions made that evening was the appointment of Wallace Buttrick as secretary of the GEB, a title that in those days was the equivalent of "executive director" today. With this title, and subsequently as president and chairman, Buttrick, an overweight, jovial, totally dedicated man, did more than any other individual over the next twenty-three years to make the dreams of the founders of the GEB come true.

Another reason why "general" was used in the name of the GEB was the hope that wealthy northerners other than the Rockefellers could be persuaded to contribute. The first one approached, J. P. Morgan, brusquely refused. Andrew Carnegie was persuaded to become a trustee of the GEB, but resigned after four months without contributing anything. It was all up to the Rockefellers. By the end of the first decade, Senior's original $1 million commitment had grown to more than $33 million in gifts. His lifetime contributions to the GEB totaled $129 million. Most of the rest of the $188 million received by the GEB came from the Rockefeller Foundation. The GEB was meant to spend itself out of existence in completing its missions. By the time it did so in 1960, it had expended the amazing total of $324 million—all of its principal and the income earned from it.

This is not the place to attempt more than a description of the essence of the GEB's major contributions. The first approach was a seemingly logical one—to assist elementary schools and then advance through each higher level of education. But Buttrick soon realized that this was hopeless. The reason: there was no supply of teachers for elementary schools. The point of entry became high schools—for years the only source of teachers for elementary schools would have to be high school graduates. The next realization was that J. L. M. Curry's lifelong goal was the only answer to the massive problem— free, tax-supported public schools for both blacks and whites. No private philanthropy, however large, could possibly fund all of the schools needed in the South. Even if it could, it would have been wrong—the schools could survive only if community interest and support existed.

A brilliant strategy was developed. Public persuasion—in essence, a public relations or propaganda campaign in support of the goal—was taken on by the Southern Education Board (SEB), an organization created a few months earlier than the GEB with a $30,000 grant from George Foster Peabody. Meanwhile, the GEB began working quietly to fill the demand being stirred up by the SEB (which was later subsumed within the GEB). The breakthrough came with a simple and ingenious idea. The GEB persuaded each of the state universities in the South to appoint a full-time professor of education whose job was to sell the public school idea in his state. All salaries and expenses were provided by the GEB. The story of the dedicated and sometimes dangerous work of these "missionary-professors" (as they came to be called) is fascinating. First, they lobbied for enabling legislation at the state capitol. As soon as that was accomplished, they moved out to persuade counties and municipalities to vote the local taxes needed to build public schools. These men were "circuit riders," traveling their states incessantly by horse and buggy, Model T, and railroad, con- stantly urged "to get out in the field" by Buttrick. A measure of their success is that by the 1920s public schools in the South were numbered in the thousands compared to only a few hundred in 1900.

The work of these "state agents" cost the GEB slightly less than $1 million. In addition, the GEB funded "rural school agents" and provided grants to professionalize state departments of education. For these and other purposes—fellowships, scholarships, normal schools, summer training institutes, conferences, and demonstration projects—the GEB spent some $26 million fostering public schools in the South, $10 million for white schools and $16 million for black. Moving on to the next level, the GEB over the years contributed $41.2 million to upgrade black colleges in the South.

The early realization that significant tax dollars were going to be hard to come by in an impoverished region led the GEB into economic development. In an area that was overwhelmingly agricultural, the primary need was to improve the lot of farmers, most of whom were so poor and debt-ridden that they lived in virtual peonage. This problem seemed at least as difficult to overcome as the educational one, but again Buttrick not only found a breakthrough, but one that fitted under the general mandate of education. Spurred by Gates, Buttrick in 1905 went on an eight-month fact-finding tour in search of methods of teaching modern techniques to farmers. This led him to Texas for a meeting with the legendary Seaman A. Knapp, an imposing figure of seventy with huge white sideburns to compensate for his bald pate. With several successful careers already behind him, Knapp was then in the process of inventing the farm demonstration and county agent system that would revolutionize American farming, ultimately under the auspices of the U.S. Department of Agriculture. Knapp disdained the printed material emanating from the USDA and the land-grant colleges. In the South, most farmers could not read. The "Knapp system" was to go right to the soil and show the farmer how to do it—speaking his language and exercising some tact in order not to wound his pride. In Texas Knapp's method had worked wonders. Buttrick and Knapp were both of rural origins in upstate New York; they hit it off, and Knapp agreed to come to work for the GEB.

Spurred by the boll weevil infestation in Texas and Arkansas, Congress had appropriated $40,000 to extend Knapp's demonstration work to affected counties. Gates, Buttrick, and Knapp went to Washington to call on the Secretary of Agriculture to find out if federal assistance could extend Knapp's work to all southern states. But the USDA was authorized to spend money only where the boll weevil was an interstate menace. Within a few weeks, Buttrick had worked out a unique agreement with the USDA in which it would finance demonstration work in weevil-infested areas and the GEB would cover the remaining states. The GEB started in Mississippi and then moved on to other states as the boll weevil marched eastward and the USDA took over the GEB program in affected states. At one point, the GEB was paying the salaries and expenses of county agents in five southern states.

The movement spread rapidly as the agents were put in place and Knapp picked up on the imaginative idea of a county school superintendent in Mississippi who had created a "corn club" for boys. Soon the GEB was sponsoring "corn clubs" in a number of areas and then "tomato clubs" for girls. This led eventually to the creation of the 4-H Clubs in farm areas across the nation. One technique was to have each boy responsible for planting corn on one acre of his father's farm. In a typical case of using the new methods, a boy would produce eighty-five bushels on his acre while his astonished father was averaging sixteen on each of the other acres.

By 1914 the GEB was able to withdraw entirely from agricultural work, turning its programs over to the USDA, which had received new enabling legislation to carry on farm demonstration projects nationally. The recruiting of Seaman Knapp and the agricultural work of the GEB had resulted in another stunning success—all for an expenditure of only $1.2 million.

Just as the GEB had to enter the agricultural field in order to help the progress of education, so it had to enter the public health field. In 1902 a zoologist of the U.S. Public Health Service, Dr. Charles W. Stiles, had identified the cause of the chronic weakness and indolence that afflicted so many southerners and millions of others in the warm climates of the world. It was the tiny hookworm parasite that entered the human body through the soles of bare feet and multiplied rapidly. Army doctors in Puerto Rico discovered a simple cure—doses of thymol and Epsom salts. Stiles verified this cure and began trying to generate interest in a large-scale campaign to eradicate the pest that northern newspapers had dubbed "the germ of laziness." He had no success until 1908 when he told the story to journalist Walter Hines Page, who knew where to turn for help—he talked to Wallace Buttrick. By this time, it had become clear that poor southerners were being ravaged by this disease. It was a formidable barrier to any efforts to improve education and the economy in the South. Buttrick consulted with Gates, Junior, Stiles, and William Welch and Simon Flexner of the Rockefeller Institute. After hearing the story, Senior donated $1 million for a ten-year war on hookworm. The group decided to create a separate organization, named the Rockefeller Sanitary Commission, to carry on this specialized task. At the same time, the GEB spent more than $400,000 for grants and fellowships to upgrade the administration of public health in the South.

Chosen to head the commission was Wickliffe Rose, a former professor of philosophy at Peabody College in Nashville who had been working with the GEB for several years. Rose was another of the remarkable men associated with the GEB who were to have brilliant careers ahead of them in various Rockefeller philanthropies. Under his direction, the commission controlled the hookworm menace in five years, curing more than 500,000 southerners. The president of Harvard, Charles W. Eliot, called this "the most effective campaign against a wide-spreading disease which medical science and philanthropy have ever combined to conduct." Having completed its work by 1914, the commission was absorbed by the Rockefeller Foundation, forming the basis for its long-term program of promoting public health throughout the world.[14]

Over its fifty-seven-year history, the bulk of the GEB's funds, some $208 million, went for the support of higher education generally throughout the United States, based on meeting a series of needs that were perceived and on the early lesson learned in the South that "education is indivisible."[15] In addition to Gates and Buttrick, there were two key figures in the early stages of assistance to higher education, two more men who were to be important advisers to Junior and participants in Rockefeller philanthropies. One was Jerome D. Greene, a man with a keen analytical mind who had been secretary to President Eliot of Harvard and secretary of the Harvard Corporation before becoming general manager of the Rockefeller Institute in 1910. The other was Abraham Flexner, a distinguished educator and brother of Simon Flexner, who joined the GEB staff in 1913.

The first goal was the improvement of college administration, particularly financial administration. Field surveys by Gates and Buttrick revealed that the situation generally was chaotic, with the great majority of colleges and universities poorly administered and in bad financial shape. The result was a program of grants with many strings attached—usually requiring that the recipient college raise other funds equivalent to several times the initial grant, that the college free itself of debt before the grant would be approved, and that other administrative reforms be introduced. There was considerable acrimony over the tough terms of this program, but the result was a gradual and substantial upgrading of administrative practices in higher education generally. By the 1920s, the GEB relaxed its requirements and began operating on a more subtle basis, confident that its point had been made and that institutions were mindful of what it would take to have a grant request approved.

A special campaign within the program developed soon after World War I, a cause eloquently argued by Jerome Greene and another leader, George E. Vincent (who became president of the Rockefeller Foundation in 1917). The cause was raising faculty salaries, which always lagged and now were far behind because of postwar inflation. The result was a $50 million "Christmas" gift from Senior to the GEB in December 1919. Over a five-year period, this sum was disbursed to 170 colleges and universities, which raised $83 million in matching funds to help raise salaries.

Perhaps the most famous of the GEB efforts in higher education was the campaign to reform medical schools based on the seminal studies Abraham Flexner had done for the Carnegie Foundation for the Advancement of Teaching, *Medical Education in the United States and Canada* (1910) and *Medical Education in Europe* (1912). Flexner's succinct conclusion after completing the two studies was that the best medical school in the United States was much worse than the worst medical school in Germany. It was clear that Andrew Carnegie was not willing to do anything more than sponsor the studies; in fact, Flexner found it necessary to carry with him on his research trips a letter dispelling the notion that any financial help would be forthcoming for those he was studying.

Gates, however, still mindful of his reading of Osler in 1897 and appalled by Flexner's findings, was the prime mover in having the GEB follow through, strongly supported by Junior and Buttrick. Beginning in 1914, the GEB disbursed $94 million to twenty-five medical schools. The result was a thorough revamping of admissions standards, curriculum, internship and residency requirements, and the commitment of physicians to teaching. The last was the most controversial issue, running up against the fact that physicians teaching clinical studies (as contrasted to those in research institutions) were far more interested in their private practices than their part-time teaching. Flexner believed strongly that teaching should be full-time as it was in Europe, even though this was considerably more expensive. He did not win the battle in his lifetime, though he moved the profession a considerable distance toward acceptance of full-time faculties.

Although twenty-five schools benefited, the GEB concentrated on building up a few select schools to the highest caliber, in line with a view often expressed by Jerome Greene and Wickliffe Rose that in any field of activity it made sense to emphasize a few "centers of excellence" when resources were limited, confident that the example and a ripple effect would in time benefit the field and the society generally. The medical schools chosen by the GEB for special attention were those of Vanderbilt University ($17.5 million), the University of Chicago ($14.4 million), and Johns Hopkins ($11.1

million). Other major grants for medical schools were made to Cornell University ($8.2 million), Tulane University ($3.4 million), the University of Rochester ($5.8 million), Washington University in St. Louis ($7.3 million), Yale University ($6.9 million), and one black institution, Meharry Medical College ($8.7 million).

In addition to all of the major accomplishments of the GEB, there were other endeavors—funds given for the study of child psychology and development, the science of education, the introduction of intelligence testing, the creation of an experimental secondary school in New York (the Lincoln School), and a special post–World War II effort to upgrade graduate education in the South (at Vanderbilt, Emory, and Tulane).[16]

Despite the impressive record of involvement and achievement, the question has been raised whether the actions of the Rockefellers and their associates did enough to change the basic social structure of the South; in particular the system of school segregation that buttressed white supremacy. Raymond Fosdick dealt candidly with this issue, writing at a time (1962) when the modern civil rights movement was reaching a peak and when the events of the "Second Reconstruction," to use the insightful phrase of C. Vann Woodward, were about to unfold. Fosdick felt compelled to address unspecified criticisms of the GEB for "gradualism" and serving to perpetuate segregation by aiding education in the South. He stated that some of the early supporters, particularly J. L. M. Curry and Baldwin of the Long Island Railroad, were avowed white supremacists even though they were committed to aiding black education, and he recounts the agonizing of Buttrick and others over the slow pace of change necessitated by their unbending policy of working carefully within the existing mores and laws of the South. Fosdick correctly argues that using the values and beliefs of the 1960s to criticize the actions of men fifty years earlier is "a misuse of historical analysis." Their choice was to help education within the prevailing pattern or do nothing, and the record of what they accomplished is there to be examined. His final point is that the GEB may well have hastened the days of desegregation and the civil rights movement by making possible the emergence of educated men and women to serve as leaders and a more educated South generally to adapt to inevitable change.

Junior's commitment to black aspirations was not limited to the GEB, but extended in many directions, including years of dedicated service to the United Negro College Fund. The most succinct expression of Junior's views came in an address he made to a UNCF dinner in New York in May 1949. He said "there are potentialities in the Negro race which, if given adequate opportunities for development, will make for the broad enrichment of the country, but which if suppressed will inevitably lead to national embitterment." The goal was that these "fellow citizens be vouchsafed in reality the same right to life, liberty, and the pursuit of happiness that our country professedly offers to all its citizens."

Yet Junior unmistakably was a man of his times and a gradualist. As we will see in a later chapter, he was not willing to accede to his oldest son's request and break the prevailing law in Virginia by opening the guest facilities of Colonial Williamsburg to blacks in the early 1950s. All his life, he had carefully observed the laws and customs wherever he functioned, and he was not going to change that practice.

The first decade of the century saw a vast outpouring of Senior's wealth for philanthropic causes—some $130.3 million not counting a commitment of $100 million to launch the Rockefeller Foundation. As we have seen, the chief goad to Senior was Frederick T. Gates and the effective salesman was Junior. Gates is said to have shouted once to Senior: "Your fortune is rolling up, rolling up like an avalanche! You must keep up with it! You must distribute it faster than it grows! If you do not, it will crush you and your children and your children's children!"[17] In a more sober if no less direct tone, Gates made this point to Senior in a letter on June 3, 1905, that was to have far-reaching consequences:

I have lived with this great fortune of yours daily for fifteen years. To it, and especially its uses, I have given every thought. It has been impossible for me to ignore the great question of what is to be the end of all this wealth. . . .

Two courses seem to me to be open. One is that you and your children, while living, should make final disposition of this great fortune in the form of permanent corporate philanthropies for the good of mankind . . . or at the close of a few lives now in being it must simply pass into the unknown, like some other great fortunes, with unmeasured and perhaps sinister possibilities.

Gates argued strongly for the first course, terming any other "morally indefensible." He wrote: "If you and Mr. John Jr. are to discharge this trust while you live there is only one thing possible to be done, and that is to provide legally incorporated endowment funds under competent management. . . ." Gates had plenty of ideas for what these funds might do—promote higher education, medical research, the fine arts, scientific agriculture, "Christian ethics and Christian civilization throughout the world," and "intelligent citizenship and civic virtue in the United States." On June 21, Junior followed with a letter to his father: "Mr. Gates' letter to you seems to me a powerful and unanswerable argument . . . and I endorse it most heartily."

Fosdick thinks this one-two punch was done by prearrangement between Gates and Junior. In any case, the mutual plea to Senior had the desired effect. He very shortly began making his gifts in the tens of millions in support of the Rockefeller Institute and the GEB. And the vision Senior had presented in 1899 at the University of Chicago for a great philanthropic trust was rekindled. The three men began earnest discussions about the steps involved in creating the foundation that was to overshadow all the others in scope and resources—the Rockefeller Foundation.

Senior had several thoughts to contribute. One was that the orientation of the Foundation should be primarily international. Because Standard Oil's principal earnings for many years had come from overseas, he felt that a major share of his giving should not be restricted by national boundaries. His second request was that a congressional charter be sought for the new organization. There was no requirement to do this, but it seems that in those days such a charter was thought desirable for nonprofit trusts of broad scope. It also added a measure of prestige for the endeavor and underscored the irrevocability of the commitment. Andrew Carnegie had obtained congressional charters for several of the trusts he created. Because the Rockefeller Institute was an institution to be located in New York City, there seemed no need to go to Congress, but the Rockefellers did so in the case of the GEB because it was to operate nationally. The bill to charter the GEB was introduced by Junior's father-in-law, the powerful Senator Nelson W. Aldrich, and it passed with no opposition.

It was 1908 before the planning for the Foundation was completed. Senior was prepared to launch it with a gift of $100 million in securities, and Senator Aldrich once again was asked to introduce a bill for a congressional charter. However, this time opposition was voiced and the session ended without the bill being passed. Aldrich reported back that it would be necessary to agree to a number of conditions that had been expressed and to make a more tangible commitment. Senior agreed and appointed three interim trustees,

Gates, Junior, and son-in-law Harold McCormick, and he made $50 million in Standard Oil securities available to them for creating the Foundation. Aldrich reintroduced the bill on June 29, 1909. This time the opposition was vehement.

The problem was that criticism of the Standard Oil trust and the Rockefellers was reaching a fever pitch. In 1907 Judge Kenesaw Mountain Landis had made his "grandstand play" of slapping a $30 million fine on Standard of Indiana. Although this was quickly overturned by a superior court, which termed the fine "an abuse of judicial discretion," the pulse of criticism and lawsuits that would lead to the dissolution of Standard was intensifying.[18] It was not a good time for a Rockefeller to go to Congress for anything, but Senior persisted in seeking a charter—with the result that there was to be a substantial delay before the grand design was initiated.

It was an exhilarating decade of personal growth and exciting activity for Junior—but also one of severe personal tension. He chafed over what he fervently believed was the unfairness of the attacks on his father. A classic example occurred in 1905 when Senior made a $100,000 gift to the Congregational Board of Foreign Ministers. Instead of being praised for making such a substantial gift across denominational lines, Senior was attacked. One of the most prominent Congregationalist ministers, Dr. Washington Gladden, publicly demanded that the gift be returned and called it "tainted money," a phrase that caught on and created a national storm. True to his policy, Senior remained silent. The gift was not returned. When it came out several months later that the board had actually solicited the gift in the first place, Gladden and others apologized, but this went almost unnoticed compared to the furor caused by Gladden's "deathless phrase," as Gates termed it.

Junior began to feel the sting of public criticism himself when he took over the Men's Bible Class at the Fifth Avenue Church. The combination of wealth and righteousness in the person of this particular young man was too much for the penny press to resist. Reporters took to dropping in on the class, and Junior occasionally was subjected to public ridicule in the newspapers for his weekly efforts.

In 1902 he made a speech on "Christianity in Business" before the Brown University YMCA, and he used a metaphor that would have been scarcely noticed if it had been uttered by anyone but Junior or his father. Most of the speech stressed the need for Christian virtue and ethics in business, but Junior also felt the need to defend business consolidation, and so he said: "The American Beauty Rose can be produced in its splendor and fragrance only by sacrificing the early buds which grow up around it." All else in the speech was forgotten as this unfortunate bit of Social Darwinism met with immediate and vitriolic denunciations. As late as 1909, Junior was still being condemned in the pulpit for his "American Beauty Rose" speech.[19]

In 1904 Junior suffered a nervous collapse. In a conversation with his biographer almost half a century later, Junior minimized his illness, attributing it to overwork and exhaustion. But this was probably a case of the common human tendency to suppress something painful in one's past, because it clearly was more severe than that. To recover, Junior took his wife and baby daughter (born in 1903) to the south of France, intending to stay for a month. The month lengthened into six, with Junior wandering through country towns of the Languedoc or staring at the blue Mediterranean from the balustrades of the Promenade des Anglais in Nice. Returning to New York in early 1905, Junior stayed quietly at home for another few months before returning to the office on a part-time basis.

For a man as addicted to work as Junior was, such a prolonged absence indicates that something much more than exhaustion was bothering him. One can only speculate as to what it was. Undoubtedly, anguish over the incessant public attacks on his father and himself played a part. But, judging from the basic decision Junior eventually made, it seems likely that he had been undergoing an identity crisis having to do with the question of how he would spend the rest of his life.[20]

One indication of the change that was taking place came when Junior declared his independence from his father's policy of silence when attacked. The *New York American,* a Hearst paper, ran a story on December 17, 1908, about terrible working conditions at the Corn Products Refining Company in Chicago, including a "peonage stockade" for keeping "hobo workers" on the job, which, it alleged, Junior had organized. The story wrongly said that Corn Products was a Standard Oil concern. The charges were false. Junior sued for libel and won the case.

When Senior had had his nervous collapse a decade earlier, the cause was not the press of business, feelings of guilt, or the public attacks on him. It was the problems associated with philanthropy, the frustration of trying to deal with the requests for financial assistance that came in, literally, by the thousands. For Junior, it seems to have been the opposite. He found philanthropy to be a fulfilling challenge. It was the world of business and the questionable ethics of many businessmen that made him increasingly uncomfortable. "I came out of college something of an idealist and I was immediately thrust into the tough give-and-take of the business world. I really wasn't ready for it," Junior revealed in a conversation with Raymond Fosdick many years later. In particular, he was disturbed by the political activities and secret campaign contributions of Standard Oil under John Archbold's direction. Junior said that he was "sickened" by the importuning of political leaders such as Mark Hanna and Cornelius Bliss who were always at 26 Broadway, "at the back door, hat in hand," at campaign time. This feeling was fortified when Junior learned of the connections between Archbold and Senator Foraker of Ohio (a Hearst exposé in 1907, for once an accurate one). Junior's conclusion was that he "could never be happy in this business atmosphere."[21]

Junior wanted to withdraw from business altogether, other than the normal superintending of his personal investments. This meant severing his relationship with Standard Oil, resigning his directorships with other companies, and forgoing the managerial role that Gates had flourished in. Junior had thrived on the philanthropic institution–building of the previous few years, and there were great challenges to come, especially the creation and development of the Rockefeller Foundation. Junior's strong endorsement of Gates' letter to Senior was a clear indication of where he wanted to spend his energies.

There is no record of a precise date on which Junior made his decision. He apparently agonized over it for several years. He had become aware that Archbold believed that Junior's resignation from his Standard Oil posts would be taken by the press and public as showing a lack of faith in the trust and its leadership, another blow to an already tarnished image. He certainly would have feared that he would hurt his father, seeming to turn his back on the source of his family's fame and fortune, from both of which Junior benefited. He discussed his dilemma with his father, and Senior apparently put his son's concerns to rest because Junior gradually began resigning his directorships—with Standard Oil, the American Linseed Oil Company, United States Steel, the National City Bank, and other companies. In one of those small acts that often can play havoc with a man's future, he neglected to resign from the Colorado Fuel and Iron Company, a mining and smelting operation headquartered in the town of Pueblo in southern Colorado. It would come back to haunt him.

By 1910 Junior had made his transition away from active participation in the business world. Then thirty-six years of age, he prepared to embark on a life's work that would embody the lessons of his college years and the decade of experience with business and philanthropy. His goal was somehow to assist in the creation of a new unity and order out of the disparate elements of Christianity, industrial capitalism, and modern reformism. The vehicle he chose to produce this new synthesis was philanthropy, and its primary instrument was science.

His motives for the decision he made would appear to be more complex than the religious beliefs and sense of stewardship that guided his father. As we have seen, the popular idea that Senior gave money away to expiate his guilt must be dismissed as nonsense. Perhaps not quite so with Junior. We know that he agonized over the attacks on his father so that the expiation of guilt, subconsciously at least, may have been a factor. One book holds that Junior's career was a lifelong conspiracy to cleanse the family name and control the destiny of America, to the point that the Rockefeller century of philanthropy is seen as synonymous with "the American century."[22] Leaving aside the obvious exaggerations, there is a germ of truth in this. Junior certainly would have wanted to see the attacks cease and his family come to be regarded with respect, and a lifelong dedication to good works would not be an unreasonable choice in hoping to achieve this. And there must have been an exhilarating sense of power in finding out, as Junior already had, that the application of his abilities in the use of his father's money could achieve great ends.

Clearly, one must not discount Junior's religious upbringing. Although he was to come to have a much more ecumenical outlook than his father, he was indisputably a deeply religious man, consequently one with firm moral principles and a strong sense of duty. He also had a well-developed sense of civic virtue, instilled not only by religion and family upbringing, but also by what he had learned in his upper-class years at Brown. There were problems and needs in society, and Junior had the resources and abilities to do something about them. There could be no question that he would try to do what he could.

Finally, there is the ultimately indefinable phenomenon of character. Whatever hereditary and environmental factors produced it, Junior clearly was a temperate, moderate, and intelligent man. He could perceive alternatives and consequences, and weigh and balance them with a keen mind. He could understand that a life of solving problems and helping others would be infinitely more satisfying than one devoted to power for its own sake or to conspiracy or dissipation.

Whatever the complex mix of motives, one thing is clear. Having gone through his identity crisis, Junior was not confused or immobilized. From 1909 on, his course was firm and undeviating, and he was to play it out with consummate skill.

5

♯

THE THIRD GENERATION

WHEN Junior and Abby had their first child, they might have wondered if they were due to repeat the experience of the senior Rockefellers—having a succession of daughters and not knowing for a long time whether they would ever have a son. But in fact the family balance was to be almost exactly the reverse.

The first child and only daughter, born November 9, 1903, was named Abby, and soon became known as "Babs" to differentiate her from her mother. There followed that remarkable string of sons who later in the century gained fame collectively as "the Rockefeller brothers."

Following the custom in those days, Abby bore her first two children at home, in her own bedroom at 13 West 54th Street. John Davison Rockefeller 3rd was born on the first day of spring, March 21, in 1906. Abby was about a week overdue, and when labor began, her physician, Dr. Allen M. Thomas, also a resident of West 54th Street, came quickly. The baby, weighing approximately eleven pounds, was born at 9:30 P.M., and, as was the case with all of Abby's births, both mother and child were fine.[1]

JDR 3rd came into the world at a time when the notoriety of the Rockefeller family was at its peak, with constant attacks on Standard Oil, the family wealth imagined as limitless, and Senior depicted as a merciless monster of greed. Nor was the maternal side of JDR 3rd's lineage spared. Leading senators of the time were regarded by the muckrakers and reformers as the eager abettors of the robber barons, with Senator Aldrich of Rhode Island always a favorite target. A good example is a series by David Graham Phillips on "The Treason of the Senate," which was appearing in Hearst's *Cosmopolitan* at the very time when John 3rd was born. It vilified his maternal grandfather (as well as the Rockefellers' 54th Street neighbor, Senator Chauncey

Depew) as particularly corrupt and subservient to big business. These men were characterized as the agents of "interests as hostile to the American people as any invading army could be, and vastly more dangerous; interests that manipulate the prosperity produced by all, so that it heaps up riches for a few; interests whose growth and power can only mean the degradation of the people, of the educated into sycophants, of the masses toward serfdom."[2]

It was this series more than any other that led President Roosevelt to repudiate the muckrakers and urge a more responsible form of journalism, although his own trust-busting zeal and denunciations of the elder Rockefeller continued as strong as ever. It seemed nothing could stem the attacks on Standard Oil and on the Rockefeller and Aldrich families. The antitrust suits that eventually led to the dissolution of Standard were pending in 1906. Senior, retired, in ill health at the time, and resting at his golfing lodge in Lakewood, New Jersey, was being pursued by process servers. And Junior, at the age of thirty-two, was struggling to adjust to a world that seemed hostile at every turn.

With all this going on, it is small wonder that the birth of a Rockefeller heir was regarded by the newspapers as a noteworthy event. The lead in the Hearst evening paper, the *New York Journal*, of March 22, was typical: "John D. Rockefeller 3rd, heir in direct male line to the most colossal hoard of gold that has been piled up since the days of the profligate sovereigns of ancient history, was born last night, and today his grandfather, the wealthiest man in the world, a prisoner in his villa at Lakewood, is forced to put a curb upon his eagerness to view his grandson for fear of process servers, who lurk in wait for his advent in the State of New York."[3]

The *New York Telegram* reported that the birth was the chief topic of gossip in downtown financial circles, with brokers speculating whether it would "buoy the market or merely hold it steady." Under the headline "Richest Baby in History," the story in the *Boston Post* said: "At the present rate of growth of the Rockefeller fortunes it is almost impossible to estimate the amount of the fortune which the baby will come into when he grows to be a man." Nevertheless, the *Post* made an estimate—$4 billion—and claimed that JDR 3rd would be "the richest man on earth since the days of Adam." The story continued with other predictions: "He will be the most powerful man financially, and all other men of wealth must bow to his will. He will be able to control all the markets of the world; he will be able to control every big industry."

The Hearst morning paper, the *New York American,* one of the most persistent critics of Standard Oil, featured both a cartoon and a poem on the birth of JDR 3rd. The cartoon showed "John D. No. 1" holding a baby ("John D. No. 3") on his lap with the public represented by a bird, and the baby pointing to the bird and telling his grandfather that he wanted it. The first verse of the poem, by one James J. Montague, provides the flavor:

> You little dimpling dumpling, well
>   may you bill and coo!
> Old Uncle Henry Rogers shall dance
>   a jig for you;
> And if that doesn't please you, he'll
>   tap grandfather's till,
> And wave before your wondering eyes
>   a billion-dollar bill.
> So lie there in your cradle, and laugh,
>   and glug, and play,
> And think of all the rebates that shall
>   be yours some day.[4]

With this kind of publicity, Junior and Abby obviously faced problems in rearing a family. They might well fear that their children would become arrogant snobs, wastrels, insensitive to the realities of the world, or unable to bear the burdens of family responsibilities and traditions; or, rebel against them in the classic fashion of the "black sheep." In the inescapable grip of great wealth, how could these parents instill in their children the healthy attitude about money and material things that they themselves possessed? How could the children be made to understand the notoriety of the family without becoming insensitive to criticism or, at the other extreme, becoming ridden with guilt? Notoriety was bad enough, but the reformism of the times increasingly came to have a violent edge to it, and Junior began to receive the threatening letters that were to be a fact of life for all the Rockefellers.[5] How could the children be protected from danger as well as from worldly temptations, and still grow to be as self-reliant and sensible as any parents would wish?

That Junior had been well aware of this burden was suggested by a comment he made years later in a speech: "To have given the world one clean, honest, God-fearing son, with an active sense of his obligations, is about as large a contribution to our day as any father can hope to make."[6] Yet he would face the challenge of raising five sons—as well as a daughter who was to have quite a willful spirit of her own.

Junior and Abby had no easy formula for meeting that challenge. They could find the answer only in their own characters and personalities, their beliefs, and their relationship. In these respects, they were well equipped for the task. Their differences as individuals were, as a couple, complementary rather than divisive, and firmly anchored in a common bond of love and respect.

Love, high ideals, and seriousness of purpose all come through clearly in Junior's frequent letters to Abby when they were apart. Here is an example, written October 19, 1906, six months after JDR's birth, while Junior was on one of his horseback-riding expeditions in upstate New York in his continuing effort to build up his health in the wake of his breakdown in 1905:

> My darling little girl. I have this evening received your sweet letter and it has made me very, very happy. I was so happy to have a letter from you that I kissed it several times on the way from the Postoffice. . . . The high ideal which you have of me is an inspiration and a help to right living. I am not what you think me to be as you look at me through those dear eyes blinded by love, but I want to be all that you think me to be, and with God's help I shall always try to live up to your ideal. I am glad to have you say that above all you place my faith in God. I feel more and more that that is the only sure basis of right living and yet the tendency of life is so much, so increasingly toward worldliness and absorption in the mere detail of living and of pleasure. That we will always have to contend against, and it seems to me that we need constantly to enlist the help of those things which lead our minds and thoughts toward the realities of life, the things of value and supreme importance. I feel for myself constant need of moral tonic. . . . I think, dear little woman, that you and I must always plan to be engaged in some Christian work because if for nothing else of its influence and helpfulness in our own lives. You see your letter fills me with a sweet seriousness. It is so womanly, so tender and trustful. What would I be, darling, without your love and trust in me? . . . I would come back tomorrow, dear, if I did not feel that everyone of these health-giving days which I can appropriate it is my duty to embrace. I must get stronger each month and I must keep well. Otherwise I will be a drag on those who ought always to feel that they can lean on me. . . . My love to the children, a great deal of it; also to the family. And for yourself, dear one, I have nothing better than myself with a heart filled to overflowing with tenderest affection. God bless and keep you is my prayer tonight.
>
> Devotedly, John

What also comes through in this letter is the fact that Junior was a driven man, mortally afraid that he would fall into sin and error—

doubtless the effect of his mother's intense religiosity. We recall how Junior prayed for four years before proposing to Abby, so fearful was he of making a mistake. He also feared that his children would err in life. In his extreme self-discipline, Junior was most demanding of himself; next came his children. To the outside world, he was a pleasant, polite, and generous man; within the family circle, he was the classic authoritarian father. His role was to set standards for his children, teach them the right way to live, and discipline them, not to be their friend and playmate. He was serious to a fault, cautious, logical, demanding, not to say puritanical and perfectionist. He was the kind of person who commanded respect and obedience not so much because he was harsh and punitive, but because he was so conscientious, meticulous, and highly principled that he engendered in those around him a fear of disappointing him. He was, for the most part, a courteous and thoughtful man, but also a very formidable one.

He was also a man of intellectual endowments, with a much greater breadth of interests than his father. But he lacked his father's sense of humor, his ability to relax and let the burdens down for a while and simply be playful. It would be hard to imagine a more loving and mutually fulfilling father-son relationship than that which existed between the first and second John D. Rockefellers, but they never displayed this in any emotional way. There was always reserve and formality. So it was with Junior and his family. He was loving, yet reserved; caring, yet stern and constantly burdened with a sense of mission and great responsibilities.

His role as father figure would not have worked without Abby's support and influence; it can definitely be said that Junior married very well. She was a striking person physically, though her nose was too long and her chin too firm for her to be regarded as beautiful. Her wedding picture is a classic portrait of the full-figured woman thought highly attractive at the turn of the century. Nothing about Abby was forbidding. She was relaxed and warm, with a zest for life, a love of surprises, parties, and people. Early in their married life, she gave her husband to understand in no uncertain terms that she had a mind of her own.[7] Junior loved her for it and remained captivated by her through their long married life together. With her independent spirit thus established, Abby became an extraordinary wife and mother. She could carry on a spirited discussion with her husband without acrimony. She was intelligent, compassionate, supportive, a peace-maker, and thus the privotal figure in the family, the leavening influence on Junior's stern and serious demeanor.

How this combination worked is suggested by Junior and Abby's practice of each having a special room near the entrance hall in their several homes. On the right as one entered was Mother's sitting room, feminine and frilly, where cookies and milk were always available in the afternoon. Here the children invariably stopped after school, not because they were asked or ordered to, but because it was the place for cookies and milk, and, more important, Mother was there, always ready to laugh at a joke, read a portion of a book, explain away a taunt or insult a child might have endured that day at school.

Across the foyer was Father's study. Here the children trooped dutifully one by one on Saturday mornings not because they wanted to, but because they were expected. The purpose: to check their account books with Father. Senior had kept a ledger since he was sixteen, and Junior had also kept meticulous accounts from early boyhood. He abhorred waste and firmly believed that the only way to learn the value and proper use of money and to know where it went was to keep accounts. He also believed that as long as he gave his children money, he had a right to know what they did with it. As Junior later commented: "I was always so afraid that money would spoil my children and I wanted them to know its value and not waste it or throw it away on things that weren't worthwhile. That was why I insisted that my children keep accounts just the way I did and I think the effect has been good."[8] Allowances were kept modest so that the children would retain the incentive to earn by performing chores. For years the boys eagerly sought ways to earn an extra nickel or dime by doing anything from picking fruit to shining shoes.

In addition to the strength of their own relationship in raising their children, Junior and Abby had the great asset of their religious faith. Again, they had different backgrounds. The Aldriches were Congregationalists, and though church was important to them, it did not dominate the family. As with the William Rockefellers, theirs was a relaxed, cosmopolitan existence. As we have seen, the religious upbringing of Junior was in marked contrast, so strict that he felt awkward as a young man, lacking in social graces. The one tacit concession he obtained from the strong fundamentalist views of his mother was social dancing—"round" dancing as opposed to "square" dancing. Like his father, Junior was not a narrow sectarian. As he grew older, he took a broad interest in interdenominational affairs, and these became for him a significant field of activity.

Yet, Junior was strict enough, and Abby supported him for the most part. He was against smoking, drinking, and gambling, and he disapproved of work or play on the Sabbath. For the children, there were prayers every morning at family breakfast, Sunday school at eight o'clock every Sunday morning, followed by church, and hymn-singing in the evening. All this suggests a formidable bluenose, yet Junior cannot fairly be said to have been one. He did not try to proselytize, and he was generally tolerant of the views and habits of others. His strictness was for himself and his immediate family, and in spite of it, for example, he allowed his children to play nongambling forms of cards (his own mother prohibited card-playing of any kind). And, when the children were older, Junior allowed tennis to be played on Sunday afternoons, responding to the urgings of Abby and the opinion expressed by the renowned minister and personal friend, Harry Emerson Fosdick.

Junior firmly believed the adage that a sound body is a prerequi-site to a sound mind. He loved the outdoors, and he took exercise in horseback-riding and chopping wood. He liked to play squash; though he tried, he could never take to his father's favorite game—golf. Throughout his life he enjoyed dancing, so much so that in later years Arthur Murray instructors were known to visit the Rockefeller house occasionally to teach the latest steps to Junior and Abby, she being considerably less enthusiastic than her husband. Both parents encour-aged their children to be physically active and to develop skills and interests such as woodworking, cooking, music, French, and dancing. From time to time, there were tutors and special classes for these purposes.

One can often learn a great deal about the life of a family by knowing something about the surroundings it chooses and how it makes use of them. In perhaps the greatest period of conspicuous consumption by the wealthy in American history, the Rockefellers were not particu-larly ostentatious. They certainly lived very well, with servants, nurses, tutors, multiple dwellings, and so forth—and Junior was so fascinated with construction that he tended to get carried away at times. But Senior's utilitarian attitude toward man-made structures was a restraining influence. While other industrial magnates were building great mansions at Newport and elsewhere, he and Laura lived quietly for a long time in the brownstone at 4 West 54th.[9] It seemed extraordinarily modest compared to some of the palatial residences soon to be built nearby. Only in 1901, several years after he had retired, did Senior buy his place in Lakewood, and then only because he could play golf almost ten months of the year in Ocean County, New Jersey. Not until 1918 did he buy his house in Ormond Beach, Florida. He came to appreciate the beauty of Westchester County when visiting the estate of his brother William, and in 1893 Senior purchased his first tract of land in the area known as Pocantico Hills, north of Tarrytown. Joined later by Junior, he kept acquiring parcels of land, some with residences on them, until by 1908 he owned more than three thousand acres.[10]

Although this acquisition of land might be regarded as an extravagance, the fact remains that the Rockefellers did not use it to build great baronial mansions. For both father and son the fascination of Pocantico was the natural beauty of the area, the gently rolling hills and broken country with its outcroppings of rock, its meadows and forests, the occasional stream and distant view of the Hudson near the river's widest point, Tappan Zee. It was not by accident that conservation became one of the great passions of Junior's life.

Senior abhorred ostentatiousness of the kind displayed by his brother William on his estate, which neighbored Pocantico. William had purchased the estate in 1884 for $150,000, naming it Rockwood Hall. But he spent $3 million enlarging and decorating the main house on the property until it grew to 204 rooms, the largest mansion on the Hudson. In contrast, Senior and Laura divided their time among three modest dwellings—No. 4 West 54th, Lakewood, and the simple frame house on the Pocantico estate known as the Parsons-Wentworth house. Another indication of Senior's penchant for modest living was that, like No. 4, he had purchased the Parsons-Wentworth house furnished and simply used the existing furniture instead of redecorating.

He briefly contemplated building a new house about three hundred yards northwest of the Parsons-Wentworth house on a rocky crag known as Kykuit, a Dutch word meaning "lookout," but he dropped the idea. Even after the Parsons-Wentworth house burned to the ground in September 1902, he simply moved to another modest frame dwelling on the Pocantico property, the Kent house. Junior then proposed that he supervise the planning and building of a more suitable residence for his father, on Kykuit Hill. It took several years of urging before Senior finally acceded to his son's request, and construction began in 1906. This was Junior's first major experience in supervising construction, another lifelong preoccupation—he became known for always carrying a four-foot rule and a notebook with him.

In view of Junior's breakdown in 1905, it may well be that Senior found it difficult to turn down something his son wanted very much to do. Building Kykuit thus was a form of therapy for Junior, just as were his horseback treks in upstate New York. However, owing to his father's repeated remonstrance, Junior kept the dimensions of Kykuit relatively modest, only forty by ninety feet, though with touches of elegance in the stonework and detail. But he did not restrain himself when it came to the extensive gardens and landscaping on the slopes around the building. The house, including architect's fee and interior decorating, cost Senior $702,555, the landscaping more than $600,000, including a beautiful Japanese garden and teahouse.

Senior and Laura occupied Kykuit in late October 1908, having had little to do with the project. Despite Junior's filial effort, they were disappointed. Laura did not like the steep roof, dormers, and small guest rooms on the third floor. Both of the elder Rockefellers were also unhappy with the location and operation of some of the amenities— elevator, plumbing, delivery entrance, and poor chimney drafts. This led to extensive remodeling begun in 1911 and completed in July 1913, involving the addition of a fourth story, elimination of the dormers and the steep pitch of the roof, rearrangement of the facade, and construction of a long delivery tunnel to eliminate noise and dirt. The reconstruction cost Senior an additional $400,000.[11]

Junior eventually was to become the master of Kykuit himself, but in the meantime he and Abby used another Pocantico structure, the Weeks house, as their country place and summer residence. It was a stuccoed house in the Hudson Valley Dutch style, with dormered windows and awnings. Junior renovated and enlarged it as his family grew, and soon renamed it Abeyton Lodge.

Home, when the first children were born, was in Manhattan in the house at 13 West 54th Street, with its graceful facade, a bookend match to No. 15 next door.[12] From the time Junior and Abby occupied it early in December 1901, Senior paid the rent, at first $9,600 a year and then $12,000. In the spring of 1906, shortly after the birth of JDR 3rd, Senior bought the house from Mrs. Jessie L. Neilsen for $192,000, including the furniture and fixtures (the house had been electrified in the meantime), and then conveyed the property to Junior for "one dollar and other valuable considerations."[13] It was a four-story house with cellar built on a standard New York City lot (25 feet × 100 feet 5 inches), standing just west of the University Club, which had been built on the grounds of St. Luke's Hospital in 1900. As soon as he became the owner, Junior installed an Otis elevator and a central vacuum-cleaning system (at a cost of $2,500).

Raymond Fosdick remembered this house as "a very homey place, with a big lion's skin rug on the floor as you came in the door."[14] But with two children already born and more anticipated, the Rockefellers began to feel cramped. Junior added another floor to accommodate a playroom and rooms for the nurses, building also a double-hipped mansard roof. There is a report, perhaps typical of the times, about the attempt of a certain "Superintendent Murphy" in the New York Buildings Department to secure a bit of graft.[15] The building code called for strengthening the supporting walls by some eight inches to allow for the added floor. This was both expensive to do and structurally unnecessary. If the contract went to his firm, Murphy said he would forget about the reinforcing and promised that no building inspector would ever report the violation. Needless to say, Junior chose the expense of strengthening the walls.

In 1908 Abby was expecting her third child, and she and Junior decided to spend the summer in Seal Harbor, Maine, near the Aldrich family. In the cottage they rented, Nelson Aldrich Rockefeller was born on July 8. Once again, Junior became enchanted with the physical beauty of an area and in 1910 made his first purchase of Maine real estate, the sixteen-acre "Clarke property" with a huge, rambling house known as the Eyrie. The price was $26,500. His penchant for construction began to show immediately. In the ensuing years, he expanded the number of rooms in the Eyrie from 65 to 107, and added new outbuildings (including a "playhouse") and gardens and acreage. The house eventually had 2,280 windows, 44 fireplaces, and 22 bathrooms. All this cost Junior ten times the original purchase price.

With the advent in 1910 of the fourth child, Laurance, Junior realized he would have to seek a larger house in Manhattan. In 1911 Senior purchased for him the house at 10 West 54th from Mrs. Janetta McCook for $200,000. He already owned the land between No. 4 and No. 10, part of which he had had cemented over for a skating rink. On this site, Junior planned his new home with the aid of the architect William Welles Bosworth, who had done the landscaping for Kykuit. Work began in 1912 with the tearing down of the McCook house and the erection of a new nine-story house for the Rockefellers. With the children now numbering five after the birth of Winthrop, the family spent its first night at No. 10 on September 23, 1913.

Although the new place cost $518,000, Junior wrote to Senior that he viewed it as temporary; he and Abby were happy to remain near his parents for a time, but eventually wanted to move to upper Park Avenue. This was symptomatic of the changing neighborhood. As noted before, Senior was one of the early representatives of the new class of industrial magnates and Jewish bankers and merchants who came to live in the "upper Fifth Avenue" area, while the older patrician families of New York remained further downtown. But just as a section of upper Fifth Avenue became known as "Millionaire's Row," it was already beginning to change. This was due generally to the explosive growth of Manhattan around the turn of the century and specifically to rapid transit provided by the Sixth Avenue Elevated, the first such line in New York. At the start in 1889, it used steam locomotives, but was now electrified. This enabled ordinary working people to commute to downtown jobs. Cheaper housing and neighborhood saloons and shops began to appear along Sixth Avenue and west on the numbered side streets. One by one, the wealthy families began to leave, the William Rockefellers, the Vanderbilts, Whitneys, Depews, some of the Standard Oil associates who lived around the corner on Fifth Avenue, the great Jewish families such as the Schiffs and Seligmans. By 1922, the Fifth Avenue Baptist Church itself was to move uptown, from West 46th Street to the corner of 64th and Park Avenue. But Senior seemed unperturbed by all of this, possibly because he spent so little time at No. 4. And so the younger Rockefellers stayed, too, not moving to Park Avenue until 1936 when their youngest child had turned twenty-one.

The reason that "temporary" became twenty-two years was no doubt that No. 10 turned out to be an excellent home for such a large family: with the birth of David in 1915, the family now had its full complement of six children. Although its exterior lacked architectural distinction, the house had bedrooms for every member of the family, guest suites, ample quarters for the servants, a rooftop playground with a squash court, a gymnasium, an infirmary, two drawing rooms, an art gallery, and a music room. No. 10 was also an excellent location for the active social life of the parents. During Junior's boyhood at No. 4, most guests had been associated with the Fifth Avenue Baptist Church. With Junior's wider-ranging interests and Abby's outgoing nature, the Rockefeller children at No. 10 were exposed to a more cosmopolitan stream of interesting and important people.

They were also exposed to art, which made a mark on the lives of all of them. Despite his art courses at Brown, Junior's upbringing had been Spartan, whereas Abby had grown up in a cultured environment. She loved paintings, while his tastes ran to more "practical" items such as porcelains and tapestries; his feeling for beauty came principally from his love of music and nature. Originally interested in primitives and old masters, Abby gradually developed a taste for modern art, much to the puzzlement of Junior. This interest became pronounced, and Abby became a collector and a leading force in the creation of the Museum of Modern Art in New York City.[16]

Before World War I, city life for the Rockefellers tended to be somewhat formal, with the older boys often appearing in Eton suits with stiff collars and knickers, Junior somberly dressed and wearing a silk top hat if he ventured outdoors, and Abby in ankle-length silk gowns. But during the weekends spent "in the country" at Pocantico or the summers at Seal Harbor, the atmosphere was informal, which may explain why these two venues tended to remain more vivid in the memories of the children. They relished freedom from lessons and tutors and confining clothes. Although for a long time there were no swimming pools or tennis courts, there were the barns and craft shops to explore, ponies to ride, woods to hike in, secret hideouts to build, games to invent.

As the Pocantico estate grew and the farms and outbuildings were developed, it became a favored place, a retreat from busy Manhattan to another world, although in the heat of the summer the family was glad to escape to Seal Harbor. Only the central portion of Pocantico, about 250 acres including Kykuit and Abeyton Lodge and known as the Park, was cleared and fenced in. Except for some farming areas, the rest of the more than three thousand acres was left in its natural state.[17] It was at Kykuit that the children most often saw their grandfather, and came to enjoy the old man and his droll stories at the frequent Sunday dinners. But the visits were almost always scheduled and limited in time; Senior was approaching eighty before the first of Junior's children became teenagers.

It was also at Pocantico or Seal Harbor that the children most often saw their very busy father; in the city, he rarely had time to spend with them. The fact that Junior was serious and introspective and set such high standards did not mean that family life was dour by any means. He was one focus around which the family revolved, but not the only one. Abby's cheerful nature amid a houseful of children made life happy and boisterous at times. Junior's nature affected his children in different ways. It was most difficult for Babs, John 3rd, and Winthrop; Babs and Winthrop because they never felt they could live up to his expectations, and John perhaps because he tried too hard for much of his life. Nelson, Laurance, and David seemed to have much less difficulty in adjusting; they experienced life with Father without noticeable blunting of their own personalities.

As regards discipline, Junior and Abby were intelligent enough to know that lecturing children had limited value. The difference was that she could resist it; he could not. Abby's style was to give advice in a suggestive and thoughtful way, almost never hectoring, as her letters to her sons show. Junior had never been lectured by *his* father. Senior had always set a good example and his son had responded. That was the way it should be. Junior said that his father "had a genius with children, was lovely with them—kind, generous and gracious. No discipline of any kind. He never told us what not to do." It was his mother who "talked to us constantly about duty, and displeasing the Lord, and paining your parents. She instilled a personal conscious-ness of right and wrong, training our wills and getting us to do the things we ought to do." To an extent, Junior and Abby reversed these roles. Junior often found that his children were not responding as he thought they should to the good examples set, and so he did what came naturally to a man of strong opinions. Hard as he tried to avoid it, he lectured. He could also be cutting and sarcastic in disciplining his children. His reactions could be so serious and literal that he often deflated childish excitement and enthusiasm. Yet at other times he engaged in good-natured debates with his boys, and the children enjoyed sociability and parties of the kind he had never had as a child.[18]

Junior had never been spanked, and so he tried to avoid corporal punishment in his own household as well, but again without complete success. There were too many boys who got into too many fights, and he was driven to administer an occasional spanking, especially to the more mischievous, Nelson and Laurance. He admitted spanking Babs once, at Seal Harbor, and told Raymond Fosdick that she was the most difficult of the children to bring up.[19] This father-daughter relation-ship was a poignant one, almost guaranteed to be so because of his puritanical nature and her rebellious one. Babs matured early, an attractive young lady and a free spirit. Her father was too stiff and formal to communicate any love for his daughter and she feared him too much to show love in return. She defied him by taking up smoking at age fifteen and keeping careless accounts.

The gulf between Junior and his daughter emerges clearly in an interview of Babs conducted in 1973 by her niece Laura Chasin, Laurance's oldest daughter:

She mentioned that her way of rebelling against her father had been to do badly in school. . . . She deeply resented [his] overinvolvement in her schoolwork. She recalled that at one point he called up the school for weekly reports on her progress. On the one hand, he told her that she was smarter than he was, and then he would get his report card for the comparable grade and compare the marks he had gotten with hers and speculate as to why she wasn't doing better. The impression that she gave of her father was of a man whose intentions were good, but who expressed his concern in such a way that she felt torn down by it. . . .

I cannot convey the tone of bitterness that crept into her speech. . . . She constantly said that [her father] meant well and expressed her admiration for [him], and yet it is clear that she hated and feared him. He never got angry in the sense of raising his voice or losing his temper. When he got angry, he would get very sarcastic as she recalled. She viewed him as a man who was incapable of enjoying himself. . . .

She responded to her father primarily negatively, with anger and fear, and felt threatened by him. The other pole of feeling was not her mother but her Aunt Lucy, who, as she said, "built me up.". . . She described her mother as a "grande dame" in the good sense of the word. She said their relationship was not particularly close, but there was no difficulty. . . .

She recalled that every morning at seven-thirty they would read the Bible with their father. And her main memory of the prayers that were said was "the fannies waving" that she saw when she looked up and down the row of kneeling people. . . . She said she had never refused to go to church as long as she was living with her family, but that she had never gone since she got married.[20]

John 3rd's way of coping with his father's domineering style was at the opposite extreme. Babs told Laura Chasin that "John was always good and compliant and never tried to rebel as she had." From the beginning, he was a serious and sensitive child, so dutiful and obedient that his parents would wonder at times if their training was working *too* well. Being the two oldest, Babs and John were somehow set apart from the others. Babs found that her serious younger brother was a person she could confide in and rely upon, and he always did his best to take care of "Sis." She was affectionate toward him and was the one who most often called him "Demy" (as in demijohn), while to the others he was "Johnny." Tall and thin, he had the spare physique of his grandfather, but with the Aldrich nose and chin. Although he grew to be a handsome boy, he became extremely self-conscious about the angular jaw on the right side of his face, which he thought was somehow deformed.[21] He spent many hours in later years seeing doctors to find out if there was an operation that could correct it. But he was not a complainer. As Junior commented years later: "He is such a taciturn boy that it is difficult always to know from him just what his physical condition is."[22]

There were more childhood diseases for parents to fear in those days than now, and the health of the six children was a constant worry.

No subject was more prevalent in the voluminous correspondence between Abby and the nurses over the years than the illness of the moment besetting one or more of the children, usually nothing more than a cold. The two most frail children seemed to be John and Laurance, both of whom were ill enough to give their parents very serious concern.

To a considerable extent in his boyhood, John 3rd seems to have been lonely in a crowd. This, of course, was due mainly to his own quiet, shy, and introspective nature. He was so well behaved that he demanded little special attention from his parents. But it was probably due also in part to his position in the hierarchy of birth. His sister was two and a half years older, and thus their relationship, although good, was necessarily limited. And he was almost two and a half years older than the next child, Nelson. The younger boys seemed instinctively to respect his quiet nature, leaving him pretty much alone. In time, he came to occupy a position somewhere between parental and sibling roles, a source of stability to the younger boys, a sometime bridge to Father, and a good friend-in-need, especially to Nelson during their young manhood and to Winthrop in later years.

It would be difficult to imagine two brothers more different in personality than John and Nelson. Physically, Nelson resembled his father, the shortest of the brothers and with a stocky frame, but he was completely unlike him otherwise. He had the impish nature of his grandfather and the extroverted personality of his mother. He never seems to have had a self-conscious moment. With a hearty appetite for life, he loved pranks and the rough-and-tumble of boyhood; he was "all boy," and, it seems likely, the secret favorite of both his mother and father. Although he exasperated them at times, his antics were so good-natured and he took his punishment so cheerfully that no one could stay angry at him for long.

Nelson had difficulty reading, as did John to a lesser extent. Much later in life, Nelson's problem was diagnosed as dyslexia; it seems likely that John 3rd also suffered from a milder form. This, of course, has nothing to do with intelligence, and both boys learned to compensate in their own characteristic ways, John by sheer dogged hard work and Nelson by mustering the energy for sporadic bursts of concentration when he really had to or wanted to. For example, he tired at being consistently beaten at chess by his younger brother, Laurance, and so he forced himself to concentrate to the point where he could win about half the time. Nelson also learned to compensate by becoming observant and learning through social interaction with other people, a natural way for one with such an ebullient personality; this also became a distinct talent of John's in later life as he came out of his shell more. Of course, in the early part of the century, no one knew anything about dyslexia, and so its effects were simply seen as part of each boy's nature; John was something of a drone and Nelson's mind was always elsewhere.

Nelson and Laurance were the closest of the children in birth, less than two years apart, and they early formed a lifelong alliance that was based on a rare and deep kind of brotherly love. They were "partners in crime" as boys, as Laurance expressed it in one of his letters. Although Nelson was usually the leader in pranks, in ideas for a boyhood business or experiment, Laurance was the perfect foil to him, and also the one who could most easily deflate his ego and bring him back to earth. All of the Rockefeller children were poor spellers (an Aldrich trait, their mother said), but Laurance was easily the champion. As a result of this and his mordant wit, his boyhood letters to his brother John were hilarious.

As time passed and children kept coming, Junior's severity in dealing with them lessened. Babs and John were the most constrained, and Nelson, for example, was forced by Junior away from his natural left-handedness. But when Winthrop and David were also born left-handed, Junior didn't even try to convert them. Yet, it was the next to youngest child, Winthrop, who had the most problems in growing up and adjusting to family norms and traditions. As a young man, his transgressions were of such a nature that, had they been John 3rd's, they would have been a scandal within the family. One reason for Winthrop's troubles may have been that he was something of the "odd man out" among the children. Although he grew to be a handsome young man, he was bulky and somewhat clumsy as a child. He was thus the natural butt of much of the teasing and mischief of the fast-moving team of Nelson and Laurance. If was as if those two were the same age and Winthrop the younger brother who was never quite admitted to their camaraderie. And when Winthrop looked down the line, all he could see was David, more than three years his junior and thus too young to be a playmate.

Aside from being the occasional target of Winthrop's frustration, David seems to have cruised through childhood serenely, though feeling lonely and left out much of the time. He was the baby of the family, too far removed from the other children to be considered anything more than that for a long time. He was bright, precocious, self-reliant, and lovable, and on the whole seems to have had a happy childhood.

In some early photographs of the boys, their personalities seem to leap out at the observer: John with a serious, almost haunted, demeanor; Nelson ready to perform some act of mischief; Laurance observing everything with sardonic humor; Winthrop in a state of frustration; and David in a state of serenity. Their different natures and rivalries were natural for a large family, but they grew to have a great deal of affection for each other.

In the end, the one who bore the greatest burden was John 3rd—as the firstborn son, the one with *the* name. Although Nelson's confident and happy nature was undoubtedly inborn, it is also true that he had a great deal of room and freedom to express it because John 3rd was there, bearing the weight of family expectations. The earliest written expression of that burden on record came to John 3rd when he was fifteen years old, in a Christmas letter from his grandfather. Senior was not given to lecturing and advising others. But he loved his son so much, and so feared the toll his responsibilities might take, that he was moved to write to his grandson: "We look to you for great and good and valiant service, walking in the footsteps of your dear father. So equip yourself for this service and quit you like a man."[23]

6

THE PROGRESSIVE

ONE CAN IMAGINE the scene as it might be written by a Hollywood scriptwriter:

A grim-faced man stands at the top of a staircase and breathes the dank air of the early morning city. Through the wooden doors behind him, he hears the tinkling chords of ragtime piano and the shrill laughter of whores in counterpoint to the guttural tones of their male companions. His clothes reek of cigar smoke and cheap whiskey. The street in front of him is lit by the eerie glow of gaslights and filled with hundreds of men crowding into saloons, gambling parlors, and "sporting palaces." Farther down the street, he sees a policeman in his distinctive blue uniform and conical hat emerge from a well-known "spa," billy club tucked under his arm, carefully counting a sheaf of bills. Young boys accost inebriated men, pressing handbills on them advertising the delights offered by various establishments. Cabdrivers fight their way through the crowds or wait patiently at curbside for customers in need of expert assistance in choosing their entertainment. The man descends the stairs and heads toward Times Square, nodding to a few acquaintances, including the policeman, as he walks along. He has only a few hours to sleep and to prepare his report before his breakfast meeting with his employer.

The man was an undercover detective, a Chicago attorney named Clifford G. Roe, who had been making a virtual career of undercover investigation in the field of vice. He had served in a similar role for the Chicago Vice Commission. His employer was none other than John D. Rockefeller, Jr.

At eight o'clock in the morning, Roe entered the dining room of the prestigious City Club on West 44th Street. Junior was already there conversing with two other men, Charles E. Whitman, district attorney of New York, and his assistant, James Bronson Reynolds, former head of the University Settlement House. The three men ushered the detective to a seat and listened intently as he described the latest findings in the course of his two-month investigation of New York's "social evil"—prostitution. He had compiled lists of more than three hundred "resorts" that he and his assistants had visited during that period, dividing them into the "dollar houses" below 41st Street and the "swell houses" between 42nd and 63rd streets on the West Side, where up to fifty dollars was charged for acts of prostitution. Roe outlined the close and profitable links between the madams who ran the houses, the local saloonkeepers who referred customers, and the cabdrivers who steered prospects to specific houses and also worked to procure young girls to serve in them, for a fee and a share of the profits.

In general, the information provided by Roe came as no surprise to his listeners. The prevalence of the "social evil" in New York was notorious. What the listeners were seeking was specific information—documented evidence and witnesses who would be willing to testify. The most interesting part of Roe's report, therefore, was the information that Anne Falcone, a seventeen-year-old prostitute in a "swell house" operated by a madam named May Livingston, had agreed to give evidence against both the madam and a cabdriver, "English Red," who had lured Anne into the business when she was fifteen years old and a recent arrival in New York City. Armed with this information, Whitman and Reynolds left to prepare indictments.[1]

What was going on here? Why was Junior involved in such a strange affair? When he had made his decision to withdraw from an active role in business, he surely did not envision that his newly liberated energies and self-conscious dedication to philanthropy and social reform would be immediately occupied in investigations into the nether world of New York City. He probably assumed he would be the arbiter of his own fate, concerned mainly with the philanthropic trusts that he and Gates had helped his father to create, and others yet to come. Indeed, there were to be two major organizations endowed by Senior during the second decade of the century, the Rockefeller Foundation and the Laura Spelman Rockefeller Memorial. But other events over which Junior had little or no control were to shape his life for the next few years. The first of these was his selection as foreman of the so-called White Slave Grand Jury in January 1910, which led him eventually to hire Clifford Roe and to create his first philanthropic organization on his own, the Bureau of Social Hygiene. The second event was the final dissolution of the Standard Oil trust on May 15, 1911. The third was the famous "Ludlow massacre" of April 20, 1914.

In the simplified view of the world that often accompanies moral fervor, drunkenness was regarded by many social reformers at the turn of the century as the primary evil; for it was thought to be the cause of other vices. But it was prostitution and the luring of young girls to a "life of shame"—the so-called white slave trade—that brought reform protests to the level of fury. The modern history of the campaign against prostitution began with the Reverend Charles Parkhurst's sermons on the subject in February 1892. From the pulpit of the Madison Square Presbyterian Church, Parkhurst delivered his searing attacks on Tammany Hall and the New York Police Department, and their role in protecting vice in the city for their own gain. Haled before a Tammany-dominated grand jury, Parkhurst was unable to prove his charges. He then set out on a series of nocturnal excursions to gather evidence of official complicity in prostitution. In a subsequent sermon, Parkhurst declared the municipal administration to be "essentially corrupt, interiorly rotten, and in all its combined tendency and effect to stand in diametric resistance to all that Christ and a loyally Christian pulpit represent in the world."[2]

Parkhurst's charges created such a storm of criticism that an independent grand jury was impaneled and a state legislative investigation began. This investigatory group, called the Lexow Committee after its chairman, substantiated most of Parkhurst's charges in a lengthy report based on the testimony of scores of witnesses. A pervasive pattern was revealed of criminality, mismanagement, and performance of the police function for individual gain and political control. The going payoff for a liquor license was $10,000, and madams paid a weekly "tax" that might enrich a police captain by as much as $30,000 before he was transferred, so as to allow another captain to preside over a lucrative district. The staff of the Lexow Committee found that the graft secured by the police—principally payoffs from madams and saloonkeepers—totaled many times more than the regular annual appropriations for the department. In return for their share of this largesse, the police worked hard to keep cooperative politicians in office through their formal role in the electoral process and in other ways.[3]

The Lexow Report initiated a fifteen-year battle by reformers to clean up a city that was indeed "interiorly rotten" as Parkhurst had charged. It was a colorful period, featuring a series of investigatory commissions; periodic outbursts of moral fervor from the pulpit and the press in attacking Tammany, the "social evil," and other forms of corruption; and the spectacle of Police Commissioner Theodore Roosevelt emulating Parkhurst in making nocturnal sweeps through the high crime districts. Twice the reformers elected their candidate as mayor—William L. Stong in 1894 and Seth Low in 1901. Each made good efforts to clean up some of the more obvious forms of corruption, but these soon faded in the face of the entrenched power of Tammany and the police. New Yorkers quietly gravitated back to Tammany's way of doing things, "as an inveterate drunkard returns to his liquor."[4]

When it became obvious that nothing had really changed, the moral fervor would build up again for another round in the seemingly endless struggle. Tammany's strategy for blunting reformist pressure was to select respectable and moderate men as its candidates for mayor, knowing that they could do little so long as Tammany controlled other political offices, as well as the bureaucracy, the police, and the wards. So it required some sensational revelation of police involvement in corruption for the reformers to win an electoral triumph. During the election of 1909, the sensationalism was provided by the coining of the term "white slavery" to denote the alleged existence of an organized traffic in women and young girls. The result was sobering to Tammany. Although its candidate, a moderate named William J. Gaynor, was elected mayor, other key offices (including all five borough presidencies) went to "fusionist" (reform) candidates. Something had to be done to dampen the continuing outcries, and this is why a special grand jury was called to investigate the "white slavery" allegations.

On January 3, 1910, Judge Thomas C. O'Sullivan impaneled twenty-three men for the jury and named John D. Rockefeller, Jr., as foreman. Junior went to see the judge in chambers to protest his appointment, saying that the judge could not have picked a man more ignorant of the subject. Junior said that "most men did at least know from private experience about the thing, but [I] had not even had the private experience." The judge would not relent, and Junior had to respond to his civic duty. In the opinion of Junior's biographer, Raymond Fosdick, the grand jury was a "Tammany trick" designed to quiet the public clamor without actually accomplishing anything. A favorite Tammany ploy, harking back to its origins over a century earlier in seizing political control from the aristocrats and monied classes, was to find an apparently ineffectual member of those classes to serve as a figurehead for such inquiries. The bosses thought they had their man in Junior. They were soon disabused of that notion.[5]

There is no reason to doubt that Junior was truthful in saying that he lacked "private experience," but he was being less than candid in claiming ignorance of the subject. Since boyhood he had heard about the evils of prostitution, and for the previous decade he had quietly supported a host of reform groups that were prominent in the attacks on organized vice. It is important to note that the campaign against prostitution was more than a reflexive spasm of Victorian morality. It was the most vitriolic issue in a much broader effort to secure a safer, healthier, and more responsible city government, an effort that enlisted the talents of a wide range of New Yorkers. Junior's reluctance to become so directly involved was probably due to a combination of his tendency to avoid public exposure and a conviction that he had more productive uses for his time. But once reconciled, he threw himself into the effort with characteristic thoroughness, commenting later to Fosdick that he had "never worked harder in my life." He read much of the literature in the field, consulted experts on public health, immigration, police administration, and tenement house reform, and secured the testimony of prostitutes, pimps, settlement house workers, and policemen. After the normal one-month term was up, Junior refused to terminate the grand jury. Only after another five months of work did he feel that he was ready.

One key finding was that while a traffic in "white slavery" did indeed exist, it was not an organized conspiracy, but rather the product of numerous individuals working on their own. The grand jury had accumulated an impressive body of evidence on prostitution and related criminal activities, and it indicted fifty-four individuals on charges ranging from rape to maintaining disorderly houses. When Judge O'Sullivan at first refused to accept the presentment, the foreman of the grand jury argued heatedly with him in open court. This caused the press to take Junior seriously, attracted by the spectacle of a wealthy young man working hard in a worthy cause. He was tackling Tammany when, in the popular imagination, he could have been living the life of ease. When Junior argued with the judge, he became something of an overnight hero.

After weeks of delay, Judge O'Sullivan finally accepted the presentment, but not in open court. Most of those indicted were acquitted. Mayor Gaynor also "accepted" the findings of the grand jury, but did nothing significant to implement them. In particular, Junior had been hoping for action on what he considered the most important recommendation—the appointment of a special commission "to make a careful study of the laws relating to and the methods of dealing with the social evil in the leading cities of this country and of Europe, with a view to devising the most effective means of minimizing the evil in this city."

The publicity gradually died down, and the Tammany bosses breathed easier. But Junior was like a terrier—once he got his teeth into something, he wouldn't let go. By the end of 1910, when it was clear that no official action was forthcoming, Junior decided to proceed on his own. He gained the cooperation of Jacob Schiff and Paul Warburg, two leading philanthropists, in an informal "Committee of Three." Because Schiff wanted to stay behind the scenes, the actual threesome consisted of Warburg, Junior, and Starr Murphy. This was an example of the distinctive new "establishment" in New York City. Boston had its "Brahmins" and Philadelphia its "Main Line," but the peculiar circumstances of New York, including its prominence as the port of immigration, meant that civic responsibility frequently relied on alliances between wealthy and socially responsible Jews and Christians. The Warburgs, a merchant banking family, and the Rockefellers remained particularly close for many decades.

Aside from retaining Clifford Roe as investigator, the Committee of Three sponsored activities among the Jewish immigrant population of the Lower East Side in cooperation with Julia Richman and Lillian Wald. Schiff and Warburg were alarmed over the vulnerability of young immigrant girls to the temptations of the procurers and madams. The committee was also concerned about what happened to the "white slaves," the young women who were the real victims of the prostitution racket. This led to an interest in the work of Katherine B. Davis, a Vassar graduate and holder of the Ph.D. in economics from the University of Chicago, who was building a reputation as an enlightened and innovative administrator in running the experimental Bedford Reformatory for Women in Westchester County. In 1912 Junior gave $91,000 in support of her rehabilitation work. On other projects, the Committee of Three contributed approximately $45,000 in a series of small grants over a two-and-a-half-year period, most of the funds coming from Junior and the rest from Schiff, Warburg, and the New York Foundation.

These activities were both a follow-up to the White Slave Grand Jury and a precursor of an organized and more permanent effort to deal with the many aspects of the vice problem in New York. From his participation in reform efforts and keen observation of them, Junior drew the conclusion that one could not rely on public outrage and the occasional electoral victory to achieve lasting reform. He recognized that moral fervor could not be sustained at a high pitch indefinitely. Everything about Junior's education and experience thus far led him to conclude that better results would come from a more indirect approach—carefully and quietly examining the actual administration of government agencies and finding and promoting better ways to do things.

In short, Junior wanted to institutionalize the ideas and commitment of the Committee of Three in the field of vice control. A model for what he had in mind already existed in the Bureau of Municipal Research (BMR), a pioneering organization that had evolved from the Citizen's Union and the Bureau of Civic Betterment in 1906. Its purpose was the study of public administration and the promotion of more systematic methods. The BMR, under the leadership of William Allen, Henry Bruere, and Frederick Cleaveland, was a seminal force in advancing public administration as a recognized discipline, a need that had first been argued persuasively in the United States in 1887 by Woodrow Wilson in his famous essay "The Study of Administration."

The principal thrust of the BMR was budgetary reform. At the time, no level of government in the United States had adopted the systematic budgeting procedures that were becoming commonplace in Europe. The reformers saw systematic budgeting as an instrument of orderly planning and program and fiscal control. Much of the impetus came from the example of business, where, under the influence of the writings of Frederick Winslow Taylor, the father of "Scientific Management," organization and efficiency were much more advanced than in government administration. Taylor's work in eliminating duplication and waste and promoting economy and efficiency in industry seemed ripe for application to the chaos and corruption of the public sector. As one scholar comments: "The drive for budgetary reform . . . begins historically at the point at which the ideas of 'efficiency and economy' of business join with the search of Progressivism for more adequate popular control of the 'people's business.' Budget reform has typically been advanced as simultaneously promoting both efficiency and democracy." A giant step forward was made by President Taft's Commission on Economy and

Efficiency, organized in 1910 under the chairmanship of Frederick Cleaveland. One of its studies, "The Need for a National Budget," published in 1912, was the precursor of the Budget and Accounting Act of 1921, the legislative base for creation of the Bureau of the Budget and the General Accounting Office. But the work of the BMR led to the adoption of a modern budgeting system by New York City in 1913, the first of its kind and soon emulated by municipalities all across the nation.[6]

As one of the chief financial supporters of the BMR, contributing about 40 percent of its annual funding needs, Junior was well acquainted with its work. He resolved to create a similar organization to study a series of problems made prominent by the original concern over prostitution and to propose reforms. In his meticulous fashion, he began with a round of consultations with men who were known to be both reform-oriented and knowledgeable about municipal administration.[7] He had heard good things about a young man named Raymond B. Fosdick, then serving as assistant to John Purroy Mitchel, who was the commissioner of accounts in the administration of Mayor George B. McClellan, son of the Civil War general. The purpose of this office was to investigate graft and corruption in city administration, and Mitchel and Fosdick were zealous in their work.

The meeting of Junior and Fosdick was to have an important impact on the careers of both men. Fosdick, the son of a high school principal in Buffalo, had started college at Colgate and finished at Princeton, where he also took a master's degree. He had worked for a year at the Henry Street Settlement with Lillian Wald and was attending night classes at the New York Law School. His city job had resulted from a suggestion by McClellan, a Princeton man who had known Fosdick as a student. Fosdick was to become intimately involved in many of Junior's wide-ranging activities in the years ahead, finally serving as president of the Rockefeller Foundation and as Junior's biographer. His older brother, the Reverend Harry Emerson Fosdick, already gaining recognition as a reform-oriented minister in Montclair, New Jersey, was also to become closely associated with Junior.

Based on his research, Junior incorporated the Bureau of Social Hygiene (BSH) under the laws of New York State on May 19, 1913. The members of the Committee of Three—Junior, Paul Warburg, and Starr Murphy—were named trustees, along with Katherine Davis and Charles Heydt, Junior's office assistant. For the next few years, the BSH operated on funding provided by Junior at the level of about

$50,000 per year, with Junior and Heydt administering the program. Not until after World War I did the BSH get its own staff and larger appropriations. Even before incorporation of the BSH, Junior had initiated its first project, a study by Abraham Flexner of how prostitution was regulated in Europe. The resulting book, *Prostitution in Europe*, became a classic in its field. A companion study soon followed, *Commercialized Prostitution in New York City* by Katherine Davis and George J. Kneeland. Flexner's principal finding was that any hope of controlling prostitution rested on an honest and efficient police system. So Junior asked Raymond Fosdick to study police systems in Europe. Fosdick had succeeded Mitchel as commissioner of accounts, and then had left that post to work on Woodrow Wilson's election campaign. After the election, he embarked on a two-year study, which resulted in his book *European Police Systems*. He followed that with another study and book, *American Police Systems*. Central to Fosdick's thinking was the need to get the police to concentrate on police work on the most modern basis, and to eliminate their role in other administrative duties, including electoral supervision, which New York police had traditionally performed.[8]

There was a favorable milieu for the work of the BSH because in 1913 John Purroy Mitchel was elected to a four-year term as mayor, at thirty-four the youngest man ever elected to that office and perhaps the most progressive. Mitchel appointed Katherine Davis as commissioner of corrections, and his commissioner of police was Colonel Arthur Woods, a former Groton faculty member, an able administrator, and a committed reformer. After Mitchel was defeated in his bid for reelection in 1917, Junior hired Woods as director of the BSH and Davis as general secretary. The BSH continued its pressure on police reform and became the first organization to make a serious study of the traffic in narcotics. It made numerous studies in penology and rehabilitation, and funded the establishment of diagnostic clinics for venereal disease. In the 1920s, it became a major force in supporting birth control clinics and research.

The BSH was Junior's first large-scale effort in philanthropy all on his own. As its sole supporter, he was to give it $5.4 million over the next two decades. Its style of operation and objectives reflected his own vision of reform—careful scientific study, use of the best people he could find, due attention to the interrelatedness of social problems, and persistent follow-through. Both the BMR and the BSH demonstrated that massive amounts of money were not always needed—a

THE PROGRESSIVE   115

thorough study by a competent person might cost only a few thousand dollars, yet it could result in important changes.

Interestingly, neither of the two bureaus has ever had much scholarly attention, even though the Bureau of Municipal Research was influential in the development of the discipline of public administration and the Bureau of Social Hygiene played a pioneering role in many areas, including the modern field of population studies. The work of the two bureaus was instrumental in modernizing municipal administration in New York City in ways that set standards for hundreds of communities across the nation. The fact that the BSH was entirely supported by Junior and the BMR heavily supported by him indicates an attitude toward government that he held firmly and passed on to his sons. It was not antigovernment, not an attempt to replace government by private activity, but rather a positive view of the citizen's duty to help improve government for the benefit of all. From a sea of corruption, New York City in two decades became a laboratory for leadership and effectiveness in municipal reform, and this ultimately led to the downfall of Tammany Hall.

For Junior it had all started with the frustrations he had encountered as foreman of the White Slave Grand Jury. The bosses had picked the wrong man as the "fall guy" for that assignment.

Although the press was beginning to see Junior in a new and favorable light as a result of his work on the grand jury and his philanthropic activities, this was dwarfed by the continuing unfavorable attention focused on the Rockefeller family and Standard Oil. Revelations about the somewhat scandalous life of old "Bill" Rockefeller (Senior's long-dead father) and the Archbold-Foraker letters shared space with news accounts about the numerous court cases involving the great trust and the ill-fated efforts to secure a congressional charter for the Rockefeller Foundation. Both these last two matters involved the question of the family's wealth: in the one, its endless growth; in the other, what to do with it.

After a long series of lawsuits in many states, the matter of the Standard Oil trust finally came to rest before the Supreme Court. The final decision, handed down May 15, 1911, set forth the "rule of reason." The decision found that Standard had violated the first two sections of the Sherman Antitrust Act and had to divest itself of its subsidiaries within six months. The impact on the Rockefeller fortune was immediate and profound, but not in the way that those critical of the Rockefellers had anticipated. At the time of this dissolution order, Senior owned 244,500 of the outstanding 983,383 shares of stock of the Standard Oil Company of New Jersey, almost exactly 25 percent. Two weeks before the expiration of the dissolution deadline, Senior and all other stockholders received a proportionate number of shares in each of the thirty-four companies that emerged from the death of the parent company.

To give some idea of what happened, within one year twenty-six of the thirty-four new companies paid dividends amounting to 53 percent of the *value* of the capital stock of the old New Jersey company and were to continue to pay dividends regularly. Moreover, the value of the securities of most of the new companies appreciated at an impressive rate owing to the new commercial and industrial applications of petroleum and the potential for growth produced by the dissolution. For instance, the value of Standard of New York's stock rose from a range of $260–$275 per share in January 1912 to $560–$580 in October of the same year; Atlantic Refining from $260–$300 to $610–$620; and Standard of Indiana from $3,500 in January to $5,400 in March. Simply by holding on to his shares of stock in these companies as the old trust was cracked like a petroleum molecule, Senior's net worth doubled in a very short time. And, of course, his income from his many other investments over the years in stock and real estate continued. Long second to Andrew Carnegie, he had now become the wealthiest man in America.[9]

As we have seen, long before this windfall Senior had concerned himself with the question of the ultimate disposition of his wealth. There were two possible answers. One was to put the money into philanthropic trusts, as Gates and Junior had urged in 1905. In addition to the several organizations already created, the primary vehicle for this was to be the Rockefeller Foundation.

The other answer was to pass the remainder of his wealth (apart from the portion that went to philanthropic organizations) to his heirs. Although not as dogmatically against this as Carnegie, Senior did not want to pass a huge fortune on blindly, without assurance that it would be used for worthy purposes. It would be one thing to leave his heirs comfortably well off for life, but quite another to give them stewardship of hundreds of millions of dollars beyond their personal needs. The obvious candidate for the role of steward of the wealth was Junior. We have seen that Senior had always taken a special delight in his only son; their relationship was a close one. Senior and Laura had raised a son who was honorable, moral, upright, and intelligent. He had done very well in school. He had chosen to enter the family office where, with no particular guidance from his father, he had worked hard and turned in an excellent performance. He had chosen philanthropy as his major interest in life. He had married well and was raising a fine family. Everything about Junior suggested that he was the perfect heir and successor to his father. Yet Senior hesitated and waited for years before taking steps that would actually put his son in control of the vast fortune.

Senior did not begin to transfer substantial wealth to his son until 1916, a year in which he turned seventy-seven years of age and Junior forty-two. From his original $6,000 salary in 1897, Junior in 1909 was being paid $19,000 a year plus a like amount for living expenses. During the same year, Senior revised his will, reaffirming Laura as the beneficiary of the bulk of his estate. At the same time, he was transferring to Junior some assets—small gifts of stock as well as real estate, including 13 West 54th. One reason for this was so that Junior would not have to "come to father" every time he wanted to do something beyond the ordinary. It was this modest wealth that enabled Junior to increase his philanthropic giving, for example in establishing the Bureau of Social Hygiene.

A second reason was to place Junior in a position of responsibility to superintend some of Senior's investments, particularly those that were not doing too well. Thus, on March 8, 1909, Senior gave his son his entire holdings in the American Linseed Oil Company, with a book value of $2.7 million. No dividends had been paid for a long time. In the letter of gift, Senior said:

I have been thinking for some time to give you my entire interest in the Linseed business with the understanding that I would not lessen my attention to the business. I desire very much that we shall work out the problem and save the investment.[10]

When Junior made his decision to devote his major interest to philanthropy, he clearly forsook an entrepreneurial role in business, but this did not extend to the more routine function of superintending some of his father's investments. American Linseed Oil fell into this category, as did Colorado Fuel and Iron. Junior sat on the CFI board, representing the family investment; interestingly, Senior did not transfer any holdings in CFI to Junior in 1909. He was to do this several years later under much more extraordinary circumstances.

Records are spotty, but, all things considered, Junior's net worth by the time of the Standard Oil dissolution was probably on the order of $4 million to $5 million. The majority of his holdings did not yield income, as in the case of American Linseed Oil. Therefore, his annual income from real estate rentals, stocks and bonds that were paying dividends, and his salary and allowance probably did not exceed several hundred thousand dollars.

This changed dramatically in 1916 when Senior gave his son $23 million in Standard of Indiana stock. Over the new few years, there followed a deluge of wealth passed from father to son until by the early 1920s Senior completed the final disposition of his fortune, transferring slightly less than half a billion dollars *each* to philanthropic trusts and to Junior.

Latter-day feminists may chafe at this concentration on the son to the neglect of the daughters, but the historical context is sufficient explanation. The Rockefellers were not alone in thinking dynastically only of the male line. The one daughter who seemed to have a head for business, Bessie, died in 1906 at the age of forty. Alta and Edith were not good at figures or managing affairs, and Junior took care of their holdings from an early age. The surviving daughters, of course, were left comfortably well off, but clearly it was Junior who was to be solely in command of the family's affairs.

But why did Senior wait to make this decision until he was nearing eighty years of age and Junior was past forty? And, having waited so long, why did Senior suddenly begin the process of transferring significant wealth in 1916? There is no definitive statement in the documentary record to answer these questions, but a number of factors that conditioned Senior's actions can be cited. One, certainly, was his own innate caution. We have ample testimony from those who knew him and those who studied his life that he was an amazingly calm, patient, and methodical man, accustomed to allowing matters to develop over a long period of time before taking action. This suggests that he might have wanted to see his son fully matured and having passed a series of tests before entrusting such stupendous wealth to him. But it is difficult to imagine what more Senior might have expected of his son by the time, say, of the Standard Oil dissolution in 1911. Junior had already passed a great many "tests." He had strongly seconded Gates' 1905 admonition to Senior to put his fortune securely to good works in philanthropic trusts. There is no evidence that Senior's failure to pass on significant wealth to Junior had caused any resentment or friction. And Junior's performance on the White Slave

Grand Jury was convincing evidence of his own methodical and determined nature. True, there were still important accomplishments to come for Junior—bringing the Rockefeller Foundation to life, his war relief work, and surmounting the trauma of the bloody Colorado mine strike, in which the family became involved because of its holdings in Colorado Fuel and Iron (see next chapter). But, by the beginning of the second decade of the century, Junior, quite simply, had done everything right from Senior's point of view, the major exception being Junior's nervous breakdown at the end of 1904.

Raymond Fosdick's failure to mention the breakdown in his biography of Junior skews his portrait of Junior's development, presenting a neat and linear pattern in which everything is wonderful, instead of the reality of serious setbacks and concern. The breakdown in fact was traumatic and extremely important in Senior's attitude toward his son. After a prolonged absence from work, Junior was able to return only on a part-time basis for many months. It was years before he felt himself fully recovered. He continued to have concern for his health and his recurring respiratory problems and headaches that only later would become known as migraine. He continued his regimen of diet, frequent rest, and long horseback outings with his cousins William and Percy to rebuild his health.

From Senior's perspective, the dominant reaction would not have been a loss of confidence in his son, but very deep concern for his health. Senior had thrived on business competition, but had come very close to a breakdown himself over the pressures of philanthropic giving. He was convinced that giving money away responsibly was more difficult than earning it. Now Junior had decided to devote his life to philanthropy. Senior might well have feared that giving his son a huge fortune to pursue that interest would be more of a burden than a blessing in the light of Junior's breakdown. He would want to be absolutely convinced that Junior could handle that burden without destroying his health. Even after having made the decision to endow Junior, Senior continued to worry about his son's health and looked forward to the day when his grandsons would be able to help their father.

Senior's act of confirming Laura as his chief beneficiary in 1909 must be regarded as a temporary measure. He would not want to burden his pious, otherworldly wife with a huge fortune any more than he would burden a son whose health was uncertain. She would remain his beneficiary until he put the bulk of his remaining money into philanthropic trusts or designated Junior as his successor. From

1912 to 1914, Senior added securities and real estate worth $3.2 million to Junior's portfolio. By that time, he had given $100 million to endow the Rockefeller Foundation. Laura's death in 1915 and Senior's own advancing age finally moved him to the point of decision in 1916 with the beginning of his major transfers to Junior, a process that took five years to complete.

With this decision made, the reasons become clear why Senior created a family dynasty in philanthropy and Andrew Carnegie did not. One was simply that Carnegie had no sons while Senior had one. Another is that by any standard the son was a remarkable individual, fully prepared and committed to the challenge he was in the process of inheriting. In his plea to Senior, Gates had not thought beyond the two generations. But Junior, in turn, had five sons whom he raised in the family tradition of civic responsibility, and each in his own way accepted that responsibility and tried to meet it.

For several years, the effort to obtain a congressional charter for the Rockefeller Foundation limped along as restrictive clauses were added by Senator Aldrich to his bill in order to meet objections. But as we saw, the tide of opinion was against it, given Senior's image as a robber baron and the publicity over the dissolution of Standard Oil. Public criticism of Senior and Standard Oil had reached a new peak with speeches on the floor of Congress and newspaper headlines featuring such phrases as "tainted money," the "kiss of Judas Iscariot," and "the Trojan Horse." The final blow was the opposition of the Taft administration. President Taft called Aldrich's bill the "proposed act to incorporate John D. Rockefeller." Attorney General George Wickersham called it "a scheme for perpetuating vast wealth" and intimated that the Foundation "might be in the highest degree corrupt in its influence." Although there was criticism of "hordes" of Rockefeller lobbyists, Starr Murphy and Jerome Greene were the only representatives of the Rockefellers to testify on behalf of the bill. In vain both tried to explain the donor's intentions. Greene stated:

The motive actuating the incorporation of the Rockefeller Foundation and expressed in its charter, is the desire to make this munificent gift directly to the whole American people, and forever subject to the control of their elected representatives. This provision not only possesses a sentimental advantage which the charter of a single state would not afford, but it expresses an implicit confidence in the stability of our national life and in the will of the people to deal justly now and forever with the high purposes of the proposed foundation.

The sincerity of this intention gradually permeated the press, if not the Congress. Editorial opinion began to shift to a favorable view. The *Washington Times* said: "Generations yet undreamed of will profit by the work of this Foundation, and no man is possessed of vision so clear as to even glimpse the possibilities of its service." The *Philadelphia Inquirer* commented: "Much of the criticism is simply because of [Rockefeller's] success, and much more of it is through an attempt to apply modern business ethics to a time when they did not exist or were not recognized. In any event, the public ought to welcome whatever good the money can produce."

Jerome Greene's final plea to Congress stated: "To defeat the present bill will not prevent the establishment of the Foundation. It will merely prevent Congress from exercising any control over it." But the cause was lost, and after Congress ended its session, the Rockefellers turned to New York State. A bill was passed by the state legislature on May 14, 1913, to charter the Rockefeller Foundation. The restrictive clauses were dropped, and the purpose of the Foundation was summed up in one glowing phrase coined by Gates: "To promote the well-being of mankind throughout the world."

Senior rapidly fulfilled his pledge to endow the Foundation with $100 million, providing nearly $35 million in 1913 and more than $65 million in 1914. He subsequently added another $82.8 million, all the major gifts completed by 1919. Aside from the two Rockefellers, the original trustees of the Foundation were Greene, Gates, Starr Murphy, Charles Heydt, President Harry Pratt Judson of the University of Chicago, Dr. Simon Flexner, Wickliffe Rose, Charles Eliot of Harvard, and A. Barton Hepburn of the Chase National Bank. At the first meeting, Junior was named president and Greene secretary, the actual administrative head. The operation was small at first, with the office consisting of one secretary and one four-drawer file cabinet, as Jerome Greene later reminisced. But the international interest was manifested immediately in support for programs of international public health and medical education in China. Having completed its mission in the South, the Rockefeller Sanitary Commission was rechristened the International Health Commission and merged with the Rockefeller Foundation. It remained virtually autonomous, with its own trustees and Wickliffe Rose as director, but with funding supplied by the Foundation.

The medical program in China was constituted in the same autonomous fashion. Its origins lay in Junior's interest in the work of the missionary societies in the Far East. In 1909 he had financed a study of conditions in China by the Oriental Education Commission, headed by Dr. Ernest Dewitt Burton of the University of Chicago. Gates had been the instigator of this, having in mind a repeat of the University of Chicago experience—creating a great Western-style university in China. The six-volume report of the Burton Commission, a vast blueprint of educational opportunities in China, dispelled this idea. There were two problems. One was that the missionary societies were against it, believing that a nonsectarian university in China would "tend toward infidelity." The second was the instability of China and the prevalence of graft and corruption. A university could be built only under Chinese control, and results could not be guaranteed.

Gates' thinking then moved to the field that had become the great passion of his life—medicine. He thought there was a chance that work in this more specialized field could progress under foreign control until the time that enough Chinese were trained to take it over. He was strongly supported in this approach by Charles Eliot. Therefore, one of the first acts of the new Rockefeller Foundation was to dispatch another commission to China, this one under Dr. Judson's leadership, to see if this seemed possible. Within a year, its favorable report led to creation of the China Medical Board, which began a program of small grants to assist medicine throughout China, but put its main energies into construction of the Peking Union Medical College. Wallace Buttrick agreed to take temporary command of the China Medical Board in addition to his duties as head of the General Education Board.[11]

With these two semiautonomous programs having their own staffs, Jerome Greene had little in the way of operational duties to perform until war relief became a prominent activity for the Foundation. In the meantime, he busied himself making speeches about the intentions of the Foundation in an effort to counteract all the negative publicity generated by the attempt to secure a congressional charter. Greene's first task, however, was an attempt to define a set of operating principles. With much assistance from Gates, Greene prepared and submitted a memorandum to the board late in 1913. The six principal points were:

(1) that the Foundation should avoid individual charities; (2) that it should exclude purely local enterprises except those intended to serve as models; (3) that it should make any grants to communities or groups in a way that would generate community cooperation and use of local resources; (4) that it should assume no permanent share in the expenses of any institution or undertaking which it did not control; (5) that it should "not hamper the trustees of other institutions by gifts in perpetuity narrowly limited to particular uses"; and (6)

that it should give preference to "objects . . . which go to the root of individual or social ill-being and misery" as against those that are palliative in nature.[12]

Some of the lessons already learned by the Rockefellers and their advisers are evident in these principles. For example, the fourth one suggests the University of Chicago experience of avoiding long-term dependency. A consciousness of the limitation of resources is evident in the third and sixth principles, possibly benefiting from the General Education Board's early recognition that no philanthropic organization could possibly support all of the schools in the South and that the objective had to be sought by indirect means involving ingenuity, leadership, and example. George Vincent, who would later serve the Foundation as president from 1917 to 1929, was fond of making this point with various ingenious comparisons, such as pointing out that the entire resources of the Foundation would cover the costs of the federal government for only four days or all charitable gifts in the entire nation for eleven days.

There were other lessons to be learned and principles to be added as experience was gained. It should be remembered that all of this was virgin territory—the foundation in a modern sense was only then in the process of being pioneered. Among the most sensitive lessons were those dealing with the proper relationship between a donor and his family and the philanthropic organization they created. This involves such matters as the degree of influence exercised by the donors, whether any use of the foundation's resources can be construed as of personal benefit, and the degree to which the board of trustees can be regarded as impartial and public in character. Decades later, as the income tax laws increasingly came to have an important bearing on philanthropy, numerous detailed provisions were added to the Internal Revenue Code affecting the relationship between donors and tax-exempt organizations they created. The all-purpose phrase summing up the intent of these provisions is "dealing at arm's length."

In 1913 all of this was an open book. But if the tax laws were not yet a factor, public opinion in general nevertheless was important in shaping the proper relationship between donors and organizations they created. This was only dimly understood at the time, but very shortly the Rockefellers were to learn some important lessons in this regard.

With the launching of the Foundation, Junior might well have looked upon his future as bright and promising. He had a happy family life, improved health, the prospect of great wealth and a number of organizations through which to pursue his philanthropic interests, and an impressive and growing body of associates and advisers. But a wrenching shock was in store for him—an incident that plunged him once again into the painful notoriety he thought had been left behind. It was to embroil the Rockefeller Foundation and bring upon Junior's head public criticism more harsh and menacing than anything his father had endured.

7

SOME LESSONS
LEARNED

On September 23, 1913, miners employed by some thirty companies in southern Colorado went on strike. They were demanding wage increases, the eight-hour day, enforcement of safety regulations, abolition of company scrip, the right to choose their own checkweighmen, and the right to choose where they would live. The mine owners had made limited concessions or offered compromises on some of these issues. A major sticking point was the demand for union recognition. The western section of the United Mine Workers was behind the attempt to organize the Colorado miners, an objective pursued so aggressively that eventually even the UMW International was forced to disassociate itself from the strike. The mine owners and managers were adamantly opposed to unionization and used every conceivable measure to thwart the union.

The inevitable result was that violence broke out between the workers and the strikebreakers brought in by the managers, steadily worsening to the point that Governor Elias Ammons was forced to call out the National Guard to restore peace. After several months of a tenuous truce, violence broke out again as it became clear to the workers that the effect of the presence of the militia was to keep production going while they made no progress toward a settlement to their liking. The incident that electrified the nation occurred on April 20, 1914, at the tiny hamlet of Ludlow. It was here that units of the National Guard, during a day-long battle with strikers, most of them Colorado Fuel and Iron Company (CFI) workers, burned a miners' encampment to the ground. A number of men were killed on both sides, but what converted the incident into the famous "Ludlow massacre" was the inadvertent deaths of two women and eleven children who sought refuge in a cellar and were suffocated when a tent above it was set afire. This brought the enraged miners to open warfare, as they seized and dynamited mines, ambushed strike-breakers and policemen, and took de facto control of most of southern Colorado. On April 28, President Wilson sent in six troops of U.S. Cavalry to restore order.[1]

The Rockefellers became involved in these tragic events through their control of CFI. At the urging of Gates, Senior had purchased 40 percent of the stock in 1902. Although the largest of the thirty companies involved in the Colorado strike, the CFI was not particularly profitable. Senior had earned some of his $34 million investment back through the CFI's interest-bearing bonds, but the company had not paid dividends for years. In an attempt to improve performance, Senior had followed Gates' advice and installed new management in 1907. The man placed in charge as board chairman was none other than Gates' uncle, L. M. Bowers, the hard-driving businessman of the old school who had done such an excellent job in building and running Senior's Great Lakes ore fleet. Other new executives were brought in—J. F. Welborn as president and E. H. Weitzel as mining superintendent. Representing the Rockefeller family's controlling interest on the CFI board of directors was Junior, though he did not own any CFI stock himself at the time. As noted, this was a role that Junior was playing in regard to a number of investments. Because of his dominant interest in philanthropy, the task of superintending certain family investments was a comparatively minor part of his life, almost routine—until the "Ludlow massacre" brought the public eye to bear on him.

The operation of the Colorado mining companies was paternalistic in the extreme. The low wages were paid in company scrip that was redeemable only at company stores and as rent for company housing. Managers took the position that they had to protect their workers, almost entirely immigrant Italians, Greeks, and Bulgarians, from all sorts of bad influences. Of course, they regarded the union organizer as the worst influence of all. Bowers called the organizers "disreputable agitators, socialists, and anarchists." Weitzel "hated unions with all his heart." Gates was vociferous in support of his uncle's views, holding that the strikers were engaged in an "organized and deliberate war on society." He believed that the CFI officers were "standing between the country and chaos, anarchy, proscription and confiscation, and in so doing are worthy of the support of every man who loves his country."[2]

Opposition to unions was very nearly universal among business owners and managers early in the century, and the Rockefellers were no exception. But Junior had also become concerned about industrial peace and fairness to workers. The clash between labor and management had been a prominent national issue for a long time, with incidents of violence increasing in the years immediately before Ludlow. Late in 1912, Congress established the U.S. Commission on Industrial Relations with a limited term to conduct an inquiry and find "the underlying causes of dissatisfaction in the industrial situation." It fell to incoming President Woodrow Wilson to appoint the nine members representing employers and employees, and he named Frank P. Walsh, a crusading liberal attorney from Kansas City, as chairman.[3]

Earlier, Junior had been engaged in an effort to set up a new organization in the private sector to conduct research and educational activities in an effort to find peaceful and cooperative solutions to labor-management problems. His approach was similar to that which led to the Bureau of Social Hygiene, based again on the model of the Bureau of Municipal Research: when an important and enduring problem area becomes evident, consult with experts, form an organization, and begin to apply scientific thinking to the problem. For some time, Junior had aided kindred organizations—the National Child Labor Committee, the American Association for Labor Legislation, the National Civic Federation, and the League for Social Service. But he had come to feel that these efforts were piecemeal and that a more concerted approach was needed. In mid-1912, he and Jerome Greene carried on discussions with J. P. Morgan, Theodore Vail of American Telephone and Telegraph, and William K. Vanderbilt, with an eye to raising $1 million to underwrite the proposed organization for five years. But Vail and Morgan were interested only in a propaganda campaign. Junior and Greene pressed for a research and educational program. When the two sides could not agree, the idea was put aside.[4]

This background shows how much thought Junior had given to the labor-management problem, but it was all cerebral, far removed from the reality of managerial problems and any real comprehension of the working man's life and conditions of work. Personal involvement came to him with a vengeance when public clamor arose over the Colorado strike. It focused on Junior when it became known that he, not his father, was responsible for the family's CFI holdings by virtue of holding a seat on the board. All during this period, the only source of information on the events in Colorado that Junior considered reliable was the CFI managers. His stubborn adherence to their point of view constituted a rare case of ineptitude and misplaced loyalty on Junior's part.

A few weeks before Ludlow, Junior testified before a subcommittee of the House Committee on Mines and Mining and said, "All we can do is keep in touch with the officers whom we trust, whom we believe will do absolutely what is right and fair, and the moment we believe they are not doing what is right, . . . it will be our next and immediate duty to take the matter up with them." The chairman of the subcommittee, Representative Martin Foster, repeatedly pressed Junior to go to Colorado personally to see if he could find some way to settle things instead of letting violence go on. Junior kept dodging this on the grounds that competent managers were on the scene and that he was in touch with them. On the strike itself, he presented a picture drawn straight from Bowers: the cause of the strike was the UMW and its agitators, 90 percent of the men were nonunion and did not want to strike, and the central issue was to keep an open shop.

A passage from the record shows how Foster's persistence led Junior to make statements that he later would regret. On April 6, 1914, the following exchange occurred:

FOSTER: You are willing to let these killings take place rather than to go there and do something to settle conditions.
JUNIOR: There is just one thing that can be done to settle this strike and that is to unionize the camp and our interest in labor is so profound and we believe so sincerely that the interest demands that the camps be open camps, that we expect to stand by the officers at any cost.
FOSTER: And you will do that if it costs all your property and kills all your employees?
JUNIOR: It is a great principle.[5]

Junior's testimony was both widely criticized and widely acclaimed. Although some of his statements would be damaging to him later, he had remained steadfast under fire. His parents were jubilant and Senior presented him with a not very wise gift—10,000 shares of CFI stock.

Two weeks later, on April 20, the crisis was reached with the massacre at Ludlow, changing everyone's perceptions overnight. There was a national firestorm of criticism, with Junior at the eye. There were mass rallies; Junior was picketed wherever he went; he was publicly threatened with murder; and he was the target of several unsuccessful bomb attempts. The shock wave of Ludlow made Junior begin to doubt the veracity of Bowers and to suspect that what was happening in Colorado could not be explained by union agitation alone. He began to see some justice in the charge that he was negligent as a board member in having no independent or direct information on working conditions and the course of the strike in Colorado.

Junior recognized that he would have to become actively involved and find some way to redress the situation. He made two decisions. One was to find a labor expert to work with him in devising a plan that would settle the grievances of the CFI miners. The second was to find a person versed in the mysteries of public opinion who could devise an informational program. The result was that two extraordinary men entered Junior's life—W. L. Mackenzie King of Canada and Ivy Ledbetter Lee of Georgia.

The decision to retain a public relations man was not as radical a departure for the Rockefellers as it might seem. It will be recalled that Junior had signaled a break from his father's strict policy of silence when attacked by successfully suing the Hearst newspaper chain for libel over the Corn Products Refining Company allegations in 1908. Standard Oil had hired a public relations man, one Joseph I. C. Clark, in 1907 as the antitrust pressure intensified. One of Clark's projects had been to try to get a biography of Senior written, but two attempts were so amateurish that they were abandoned. But the Rockefellers themselves had never hired a public relations man. Junior was moved to do so now because he felt a great deal of misinformation was coming out of Colorado and that management's side of the story was not being communicated adequately.

He was led to Ivy Lee by the advice of a journalist he knew in New York City. The son of a Methodist minister, Lee was a tall, slender man who walked with a slight limp. He was possessed of charm, fine manners, a keen mind, and considerable writing and editing skill, having worked his way through Princeton before taking a job as a newspaperman in New York City. Lee soon developed a set of ideas and embarked on a career that in time would earn him the label of "the father of public relations." With business so much on the defensive against the attacks of the muckrakers and other critics, Lee perceived that businessmen generally had no understanding of public opinion and little skill in communicating effectively with the press and the public. Lee disdained the press agents of the time who would use any influence or trick to get a story on their clients printed, regardless of the truth or merits of the matter at hand. He set high standards of honesty and openness in dealing with the press, and he was as concerned about the wisdom of the policies of his clients as he was in communicating them. It was these characteristics of Lee's work with a wide range of clients over the years that began to distinguish "public relations" from "publicity" or "press agentry."

When Junior called, Lee was committed to aiding the Pennsylvania Railroad in its bid to win a rate increase. Samuel Rea, president of the railroad, told Junior that he could not release Lee, but that he had no objection to Lee helping the Rockefellers "in his spare time." Lee went to New York for a meeting with Junior. As Lee's biographer described the result:

> "Tell the truth," Lee told Rockefeller, "because sooner or later the public will find it out anyway. And if the public doesn't like what you are doing, change your policies and bring them into line with what the people want." That was the essence of his advice. It was disarmingly simple and proved to be effective. It was so artless yet so efficacious that a generation of cynical critics suspected Ivy Lee of sinister machinations and callous manipulation. John D. Rockefeller, Jr., however, liked Lee's point of view and took his word.
>
> The result was that the Rockefellers opened their books, told their side of the story, and changed many of their policies, the most important being in management-employee relations.[6]

In June 1914, only six weeks after Ludlow, Lee began producing an occasional "bulletin" on behalf of the Colorado mineowners, sending it to a list of opinion leaders he had compiled. He was embarrassed on several occasions when information supplied to him by the CFI managers turned out to be erroneous, and so, with Junior's concurrence, he decided to make an investigatory trip. After touring the mines, he reported to Junior that the reality indeed was at variance with much of what Bowers had been saying. He wrote: "It is of the greatest importance that as early as possible some comprehensive plan be devised to provide machinery to redress grievances."[7]

Junior, of course, was already moving in this direction. Months before Ludlow, he had wanted to activate his economic research idea of several years earlier by creating a "bureau of economic research" within the Rockefeller Foundation. This had been recommended by a consulting group of economists he had formed, led by Edwin F. Gay of Harvard. The Colorado strike was not the stimulus; Junior's idea was to study and develop ways of achieving labor-management cooperation and harmony on a broad scale within the United States and overseas. The idea was still in the talking stage when Ludlow occurred and gave it some specificity and urgency. Junior recognized that before creating any organizational unit he needed to find the right man to develop and head it.

Charles Eliot and Jerome Greene had a man to recommend whom they had known at Harvard—W. L. Mackenzie King. With Junior's concurrence, they both sent telegrams to King inviting him to New York to discuss the matter. The grandson of the great Canadian patriot William Lyon Mackenzie, King was superbly qualified for the potential assignment. He was a graduate of both the University of Chicago and Harvard, where he had taken his doctorate in economics. He had become prominent in Canadian politics, having served in Parliament and as minister of labor until his Liberal Party lost the 1911 election and King lost his seat. He had authored the innovative Industrial Disputes Investigation Act and had been instrumental in having labor affairs organized as a separate department of the Canadian government.[8]

A full record exists of King's involvement with the Rockefellers because he kept a detailed diary and because of a fascinating book by F. A. McGregor, who had been King's secretary at the Ministry of Labor and became his sole staff aide at the Rockefeller Foundation. Entitled *The Fall and Rise of Mackenzie King*, McGregor's book covers only the years that King was out of office, 1911 to 1921, and hence deals prominently with his experience at the Foundation.[9]

On Saturday, June 6, 1914, King met with Junior, Greene, and Starr Murphy at 13 West 54th Street. During the day, King also met Senior and chatted with him. King had traveled to New York not entirely certain why he had been asked to come. Junior explained the idea of instituting a broad inquiry into improved industrial relations methods under the auspices of the Foundation, and King suggested the names of some individuals he thought qualified to head such a project. The matter of the Colorado strike came up, with Junior asking whether King had any plan or suggestion that might be helpful in such a situation. King recorded his response in his diary:

I . . . told him that my experience in personally intervening in industrial disputes had led me to believe that purely economic questions were easily adjusted, that it was the personal antagonisms and matters arising out of prejudice and bitterness and individual antipathies which were the ones which caused most concern.[10]

Junior later confided to King that he had thought of the first meeting only as a one-day consultation to get King's advice on the

Colorado situation and the broader inquiry, but that by the time the day was over he had made up his mind to ask King to head up the work himself. In fact, Junior acted quickly after King returned to Canada. Three days later, Jerome Greene telegraphed and wrote to King making a definite proposal. He wrote that the Foundation had in mind

an investigation of the great problem of industrial relations, with a special view to the discovery of some organization or union, or at any rate of some mutual relationship of capital and labor which would afford to labor the protection it needs against oppression and exploitation, while at the same time promoting its efficiency as an instrument of economic production.[11]

Despite all the reserve and formality of that first meeting, there had been instantaneous rapport between Junior and King, the beginning of an association that was to ripen into lifelong friendship. "Seldom have I been so impressed by a man at first appearance," Junior later told Raymond Fosdick; in Fosdick's opinion, King became the closest friend Junior ever had.[12] Less than eight months after the first meeting, Junior paid King such a warm compliment that King was momentarily embarrassed. Junior said: "I feel I have found in you the brother I have never had and have always wished to have." Some months later, he wrote to King's parents to convey his "deep regard for the mother and father of the man whom so unreservedly I respect and admire, and for whom I entertain feelings akin to those of a brother."[13]

The warmth was fully reciprocated by King, at first somewhat to his own astonishment. He had come to New York for that first encounter harboring deep suspicions about the Rockefellers. King had once flirted with socialism; although he had rejected it, his politics throughout his career remained definitely left of center—he was a liberal as well as a Liberal. His instinctive sympathies were with disadvantaged people and the working man. He tended to distrust capitalists, and confessed in his diary that he had a particular bias against millionaires. In addition to his early identification with labor, King had worked against monopolies and combines in Canada. He had had no reason to discount the widespread negative view of the Rockefellers, particularly the image of Senior as a robber baron. As he came to know them, however, King began to change his mind. After one evening's long conversation, in which Junior and King touched on religion among other subjects, King wrote in his diary: "I feel a perfect sympathy in all things as we talk together and have felt it since we first met; it is the more extraordinary as it is the last thing I should have expected to experience. Clearly, there is a spiritual or psychic power that has attracted and that attracts and holds." To a friend in England, King wrote:

I have found in Mr. John D. Rockefeller, Jr., one of the best of men and most welcome of friends. . . . Whatever his father may have done or is, that man I have found to be almost without exception the truest follower of Christ. . . . His humility, his sincerity, his fearlessness, his simple faith, his fidelity to principle—so far as he has horizon at all his one purpose is to serve his fellowmen.

That sentiment shows that King continued to hold some reservations regarding Senior. Aware of this, Junior told him simply, "You will see." After a number of informal meetings with Senior over a period of months, King wrote:

Far from being the kind of man he is pictured to be by the press, he seemed to be the very opposite. In appearance, he is not unlike pictures one sees of the old popes. In manner he is singularly simple and natural and genuinely kindly. He spoke in the most natural way of his boyhood and life on a farm and of some of his early experiences. . . . I had the feeling I was talking with a man of exceptionally alert mind and great discernment of character. He is a good deal of a mimic, and in telling of people and his own feelings is apt to imitate the expression of the person or the attitude he is representing. He is full of humor, particularly in conveying a shrewd knowledge of situations and men. His whole nature is a gentle one and a sweet one.

The gap he perceived between the image and the reality motivated King to speak frankly to the Rockefellers about a belief he strongly held—that an open attitude was far more beneficial and productive than a policy of silence and remoteness. F. A. McGregor recounts the exchange that occurred after King voiced this view and told Senior that that was how he would counsel his son:

Rockefeller was touched by these words and commented: "I wish I had had you the thirty or forty years I was in business to advise me on policies." Mackenzie King long remembered this remark and his son's rejoinder: "I am glad you didn't, because I would be prevented then from having Mr. King for the next thirty or forty years."[14]

As this passage suggests, Senior was not too old to learn. Because Ivy Lee also was a firm believer in a policy of openness, he and King became natural allies in counseling the Rockefellers. In time, their views made a considerable difference in the stance the father and son took toward the press and the public.

Obviously, King and Junior each filled a need for the other. King was a lonely man, and he needed a friend not involved in Canadian politics to whom he could unburden himself. Junior's view of King as fulfilling the qualities of a brother speaks for itself. He might have seen him as a twin, for the two were alike to an uncanny degree. They were the same age; both were introspective and thoughtful, yet charming in company, with a mutual passion for social dancing. They were even similar in appearance. Both were very religious men, highly idealistic, and yet with a strong streak of pragmatism that enabled them to operate effectively in daily affairs. Both venerated their parents, with Junior especially close to his father and King revering his mother.

Significant differences existed as well, of course, with family background and economic circumstances among the more obvious. Junior and King did not agree on everything, and their relationship, although strong, was not always smooth. One inescapable fact was that for a number of years Junior was the employer and King the employee.

Another difference was that Junior was happily married and raising a family while King was still a bachelor. King had avoided any liaisons up to the time he lost his seat in Parliament, but as he neared forty he began to worry about his prospect of finding the right woman to share his life. After 1911 his diary records a series of attempts that were unsuccessful for one reason or another.

The offer to take charge of a new industrial relations program at the Rockefeller Foundation threw King into a quandary. He feared what accepting it might do to his political career, but there were other factors that made it extremely attractive, so much so that he later referred to it in his diary as a "heaven-sent deliverance." He had been somewhat at loose ends ever since his party went out of power. He had no independent means, and was subsisting on his savings and occasional fees for writing and speaking. King had a mystical faith that some day he would be prime minister of Canada. Not wishing to endanger his independence and political standing, he had refused several offers of employment from Canadian business firms, despite the added financial burden of having to care for his aging parents and a chronically ill brother. His political career, to which he was so deeply committed, seemed as bleak as his financial situation. His political mentor was Sir Wilfred Laurier, a pivotal figure in Canadian history as the first French-Canadian prime minister (1896 to 1911), who had done much to bridge the gulf between the English-speaking and

French-speaking regions through his political skill, anticlerical position, and great ability as an orator in both languages. King's relationship with Sir Wilfred was complex, at times seemingly close, at other
times remote; King was never quite sure where he stood in the
Liberal Party leader's plans. The solid strength of the party was in
Quebec; support in other regions was critical to the party's chances for
success, but not easy to obtain. This created a dilemma for a non-
French member such as King—to find a "safe" district for a parlia-
mentary seat in an English-speaking area was difficult; to take one in
Quebec was a confession of weakness. For years King had been
searching for a safe seat in Ontario with, in his view, insufficient help
from Sir Wilfred.

When the offer came from New York, King agonized over it for
nearly two months and asked numerous friends for advice. The first
person he talked to was Sir Wilfred, who said he admired the younger
Mr. Rockefeller but was reluctant to give advice; the decision would
have to be King's alone. King's brother, residing in Denver for his
health, wrote that he feared the association would cause labor to brand
King forever "as a tool of the Rockefellers." Some friends urged
acceptance. In his diary, King wrote: "I felt that once associated in any
way with the Rockefeller concern, my future in politics would be
jeopardized. . . . [I] would have rejected it utterly had the offer come
to enter the service of the Standard Oil industry and not to work under
a foundation where money was held in trust." King finally accepted,
subject to some conditions, and later explained his decision to Junior:

. . . in accepting I had had to consider that I was prejudicing my political
future for all time to come, that my battles henceforth would not be with the
political issues but against the Rockefeller prejudice, that I would not be
harangued against as a Liberal politician but as a "Standard Oil man." Still I
felt I was not going to be governed by prejudice, and had decided on this
basis.

King stipulated that he retain his Canadian citizenship and residence in Ottawa, that the term of the agreement be five years, and that
he be free at any time to take leave of absence if political or public
service duties in Canada called. In answer to a query, he proposed an
annual salary of $15,000 plus expenses. Although Junior readily
accepted all of the conditions, on the matter of salary he said he had
never thought of a figure of less than $10,000, but that the policy of the
Foundation was to pay salaries higher than the academic field and less
than business. He proposed a compromise of $12,000, adding: "If after

further and mature reflection you feel that $15,000 is the proper figure, it is our disposition to be guided by your wishes in the matter." Pleased that there was no problem about pursuing political opportunities in Canada if they arose, King accepted the compromise "in the light of a financial sacrifice for the sake of opportunity of independent public service."[15]

King was not able to arrive in New York to take up his new post until October 1; with his arrival, the "industrial relations section" of the Rockefeller Foundation finally came into existence. It was not a formal division, however, because King did not want elaborate staff or offices. He worked mainly out of his room at the Harvard Club. As for help, he wanted only F. A. McGregor and the ability to let an occasional contract for a specific task. For a time, King worked quietly, reading, thinking, and making elaborate charts of his ideas. It seemed there was nothing that could be done immediately about the Colorado situation. Junior had dismissed the intransigent L. M. Bowers and was hoping that C. F. Welborn could be persuaded to take a more enlightened attitude. Opinion was virtually unanimous that the strike should not be settled by recognizing the western section of the United Mine Workers. This attitude was taken not only by the owners and managers, but also by the congressional committees that had investigated the strike, as well as by other investigative bodies and the governor of Colorado. Even the UMW international organization, led by President John White and Secretary William Green, had disavowed the organizers for their tactics. Junior had been urging Welborn to develop proposals for settling grievances on a fair basis, but Welborn's ideas were dismissed by King as "a patch-work job."

And then, suddenly, the strike was over. In early December 1914, the men filed back to work, beaten by the intransigence of the owners and the exhaustion of strike funds. The owners were perfectly free to do nothing about conditions at the mines. But just as Junior had persevered in the wake of the White Slave Grand Jury, he was determined now to work out a fair and just settlement for the CFI workers and pursue the larger design in industrial relations that had brought Mackenzie King to the Rockefeller Foundation. Moreover, with the strike settled it was now possible for King to go to Colorado to study the problem at first hand and devise a solution to present to the CFI managers and workers.

However, another problem arose when the U.S. Commission on Industrial Relations scheduled hearings on the Colorado situation. The freewheeling chairman, Frank P. Walsh, announced the hearings as soon as he heard of the new Foundation program in industrial relations. He was suspicious that Rockefeller millions now would be spent in an antilabor campaign, and he resented the appointment of a foreign-born expert to head the program. Walsh clearly was hostile; as Raymond Fosdick commented: "Already convinced that JDR Jr. was chiefly responsible for the events in Colorado, Walsh was determined to extract a confession of guilt. His methods were those of a prosecutor rather than an investigator. . . ."[16] Junior, King, and Jerome Greene were subpoenaed to appear before the commission. Among Junior's advisers, the two most supportive of King's approach were Ivy Lee and Starr Murphy. Together with King, they began working with Junior to prepare him for the hearings. But it was King who clearly was the leader, and it was during this period that he and Junior began to be extremely close. King's biggest challenge was to bring Junior out of the antiunion background in which he had grown up, to get him to see that an industrial relations plan such as he was working on for the CFI was a legitimate alternative, but not a substitute for unions in general.

The hearings were held in New York City, and not until January 25, 1915, was Junior called. Under King's tutelage, Junior survived three days of merciless grilling by Chairman Walsh very well. His basic defense was still the somewhat lame one he had had since the troubles began—that as a shareholder and director he was far removed from the scene and that policy had been the responsibility of company management in Colorado. Junior conceded that the experience had taught him something about the responsibilities of a director, and he said he favored organized labor "most heartily" when its purpose "is to promote the well being of the employees, having always due regard for the just interests of the employer and the public." King breathed easier when Junior said that it was "just as proper and advantageous for labor to associate itself into organized groups for the advancement of its legitimate interests, as for capital to combine for the same effect." Junior also announced that he would go to Colorado personally to study the problems there with an eye to resolving them.[17]

Junior's calm manner and sincerity converted the ordeal into a personal triumph. Senior was just as pleased as he had been when his son had opposed unions almost a year earlier before the House subcommittee, suggesting that King's advice was rubbing off on him as well. He gave Junior 80,000 shares of CFI stock, a move that King interpreted as positive: "I think . . . the old gentleman had in mind giving [his son] a freer hand to work out his policy in regard to Colorado." Having predicted that Junior would win applause at the conclusion of his testimony, King rejoiced at the outcome. He wrote:

That prophecy was literally and absolutely fulfilled. . . . He has the admiration of the Commission, of the press, of the labour men, and even of many of the Socialists and I.W.W. workers who were most bitter in their hatred against him. . . . Altogether, in his replies, he has shown wonderful political sense and sagacity. He has great tact and really would, if he permitted himself to undertake it, make a splendid public man. He has all the qualities which count to make a true statesman.

King also saw a larger meaning to what had happened:

It makes one shudder to think what an opposite course, or one of indifference or antagonism to the Commission might have meant, not merely for Mr. R. personally, but for capital generally in the United States, and for the welfare of the industrial classes. It may be that his attitude . . . has helped to save millions of dollars to capital, has helped to prevent even industrial revolution. . . .

My own feeling is that, not only has Mr. R. given himself a new start with the American public, and particularly with labour, but he has also helped to make an epoch in the industrial history of the country itself. Students will go back to his evidence . . . in indicating the period of transition from indifference on the part of directors to the assuming of obligation by them. . . . I look forward to seeing Mr. R. ultimately get a great reception from the workingmen of Colorado.[18]

These first hearings over, events began to move rapidly, with Mackenzie King busily orchestrating them. Junior had never conversed with a union leader, and King set about changing that, arranging meetings with William Green of the UMW and A. B. Garretson, a labor member of the commission and president of the Order of Railway Conductors. After a long session with Garretson, Junior commented to King, "What a splendid man that is: I wish very much my father could meet him." A dramatic moment occurred during the hearings when King introduced Junior to "Mother" Jones, an eighty-three-year-old native of Ireland who was venerated by the miners and had often been thrown in jail as a labor organizer. She had railed against the Rockefellers when working as an organizer in Colorado. In a subsequent meeting in Junior's office, as reported by King, "Mother" Jones told Junior:

She had thought Mr. R. was a man with a thin, hard jaw, who kept his teeth and mouth firmly compressed and his hands clutching out for money all the time. She imitated as she spoke. "When I saw you going on the stand, and listened to the evidence, and saw the kind of man you are, I was filled with remorse. I felt I had done you a great injustice." She went on to say that she would now strive to remove the false impressions she had given; that if he did not do anything, she would, of course, feel free to fight him; but that if he did all that she felt he would, she would do all she could to remove these false impressions.[19]

Junior and King scheduled their trip to Colorado in March. Senior was concerned and urged that Junior's secretary, Charles Heydt, act as a bodyguard and carry a pistol. King said this would not be necessary, and Junior agreed. Before they could depart, however, family sorrow intervened—Junior's mother died on March 12 at age seventy-five. A month later, Senator Nelson Aldrich died suddenly. Junior spent a great deal of his time with his lonely and bereaved father and with his wife, Abby, who was in an advanced state of pregnancy when her father died. On June 12, Abby bore her last child, David. The year had taken a toll on her, and she needed prolonged rest and recovery.

For these reasons, Junior had to postpone his visit, but King decided to go ahead on his own for a preliminary investigation. Before leaving, he acted on reports of desperate economic conditions among the Colorado miners by proposing to the trustees of the Rockefeller Foundation that they make a $100,000 grant for relief. Junior was reluctant for fear that the grant would be seen as an attempt to "buy" the goodwill of the miners, but the trustees acquiesced when King said it would all be arranged under the auspices of the public authorities in Colorado. He then had the novel experience of writing a letter to the governor of Colorado and, in effect, answering it himself. When he arrived in Denver, King explained the circumstances to the governor, who happily agreed to set up an emergency relief fund. King helped him work out the details and draft his response to King's initial letter. In the months ahead, the Foundation grant and other monies raised helped avert starvation among miners and their families who had been left destitute by the prolonged strike.

King then toured the CFI mines, talked with workers, and began to hone his ideas for an industrial representation plan. One of his goals on this trip was to educate the company president, J. F. Welborn, whose support would be crucial for its own sake, but also in helping to convert the middle-level supervisors and pit bosses who were accustomed to having completely arbitrary authority over the men. Accordingly, King spent several weekends at Welborn's ranch riding horses and playing with his children. Welborn's wife turned out to be an intelligent woman who was entranced with the friendly and worldly Canadian visitor. King's charm worked, and Welborn gradually became an enthusiastic student of his ideas.

After his Colorado trip, King had to face the prospect of testifying before the Walsh Commission, which announced another round of hearings in April and May of 1915 in Washington. Junior was also called again, as were Ivy Lee, Starr Murphy, and Jerome Greene. All of the witnesses did well, but it was King who battled the most with the chairman. Recognizing that he was in a delicate position, King nevertheless resolved to speak his mind rather than take the course of a "moral coward" by adopting a "quiet and conciliatory manner." This led to a number of angry exchanges between King and Walsh, with King writing in his diary about Walsh's "contemptible insinuations and perversions of truths." He was particularly incensed over Walsh's repeated efforts to pin him down as saying that what John D. Rockefeller, Jr., did in Colorado was more important than American public opinion. The *New York Times* editorialized:

It is obvious that Mr. King's words did not justify the interpretation that was placed on them . . . that he thought the younger Rockefeller more powerful than the American people. His intention, of course, was to emphasize the efficiency of one man whom he credited with high and sincere conscientiousness to do a particular thing at a particular time and place.[20]

Walsh had subpoenaed Junior's earlier correspondence and triumphantly probed the record of his stout support of the antiunion stand taken by the CFI management. During another three-day ordeal of sharp questioning, Junior calmly reiterated that he had learned a lesson about the responsibilities of a director, that he now supported the right of workers to organize, and that the only thing he opposed was the closed shop. Walsh's attacks were blunted by the fact that the correspondence in question was more than a year old, by Junior's frank admission that he had learned much since then, and by the chairman's habit of ranging far afield into unrelated elements of Junior's background, a habit that alienated much of the press and many observers. Once again, Junior had fared well under pressure. With its term nearly up, the commission split on the issues, and its report had little effect.[21]

Despite his dislike for Walsh's manner, King thought that on balance the commission had a good effect by keeping the issues open and forcing consideration of them. He took his greatest pleasure in the conduct of his star pupil:

. . . the progress which has been made by him towards a modern, progressive outlook is remarkable indeed. What is particularly satisfying . . . is that every bit of it has been based on conviction. He has said absolutely nothing that he does not with his whole heart and mind believe. . . .[22]

The summer was spent in refining the plan, and in September Welborn came to New York to meet with Junior, King, Lee, and Murphy. Welborn showed signs of backsliding, saying that the plan was just not practical in his environment in Colorado. But he could not muster a convincing argument against any of the provisions as the group reviewed them. With some minor modifications made, Junior and King were finally ready for their joint trip to Colorado. Looking somewhat out of place in bib overalls and miner's hats, they spent two weeks touring eighteen CFI coal mines and numerous working camps, meeting with hundreds of workers individually and in evening group sessions, and visiting their homes, trailed all the while by a group of journalists. The social highlight occurred toward the end of the visit at the Cameron camp when Junior suggested a dance. The floor was cleared and he managed to dance with every woman present.

The climax of the trip came in Pueblo on October 2, a "red-letter day" in Junior's life, as he termed it.[23] He appeared before 200 workers representing all of the company's locations and delivered a humorous lecture on economics. Junior divided a pile of coins on a table to show where the company's income went. By the time coins were allocated to workers, supervisors, and directors, there were none left for the owners. Senior's $34 million investment in CFI had never yielded any dividends. King then orally presented the industrial relations plan. Printed in thirteen languages, the plan was distributed to all CFI workers for a secret ballot. It won their approval by a margin of 85 percent.

The central feature of the plan was representation, with employees electing delegates from their own ranks, one for every 150 workers and organized into district councils. There were elaborate procedures for resolving grievances, including quarterly conferences, employee-management committees on various issues, a provision for arbitration, and a troubleshooter reporting directly to the president who traveled throughout the company facilities. In addition, numerous concessions were made, including posting a scale of wages, paying in cash, permitting employees to shop and live where they chose, practicing no discrimination against union members, and fully implementing the eight-hour day.[24]

The success of the "industrial representation plan" at CFI made Junior eager to get on with the larger design for developing the methods further and applying them to other industrial situations. For King it introduced a period of worry and exhaustion nearly to the point of a nervous breakdown. He spent the balance of 1915 caring for his ailing mother. In December she died, "the saddest day [King] was ever to know," wrote his biographer.[25]

For weeks King was under the care of doctors recommended by Simon Flexner. As his health returned, he began working on a book, his idea of the most productive next step in furthering the cause. To be entitled *Industry and Humanity*, it was to be part philosophy and part practical advice, using the Colorado plan as a model. The central thesis was that industry should be subservient to humanity rather than the reverse, and King probed questions of how to achieve industrial peace, productivity, and fair treatment from the point of view of each of four "parties" to industry—capital, labor, management, and the community. It was a laborious task, and King worked at it intermittently for the better part of three years, with Junior and the Foundation trustees growing uneasy over the lack of concrete action in the industrial relations program.

In 1917 unfortunate circumstances brought about a general election in Canada despite the fact that the country was in the midst of a war. The Canadians had done their part in the war effort through voluntary enlistments, but with heavy losses in France it now seemed that conscription was necessary. Opinion was against it in Quebec, and Sir Wilfred, who had strongly supported the war effort, had no choice but to take an anticonscription position. This led to the desertion of many of the English-speaking Liberals. King was one of the few who remained loyal, as he took leave from the Foundation to run for Parliament in North York. He and his party went down to a crushing defeat at the polls.

His political career seemingly in shambles, King returned to New York to resume working on his book, and began seriously to consider whether his future might best be that of an industrial relations counselor in the United States. Hoping for this, Junior proposed a new arrangement—terminating the Foundation program and placing King on his staff to work actively in the industrial relations field. Earning a salary plus fees for consultation, King's financial worries ended as his income rose handsomely. He found he was in demand as he worked successfully with a number of clients throughout 1918—Consolidation

(Above, left) John D. Rocke-feller, c. 1890. The founder of the dynasty posed for this photograph when he was at the height of his power as president of the Standard Oil Company. *(Above, right)* William Avery ("Big Bill") Rockefeller, pictured here on one of his rare visits to New York in the late 1880s.

Another view of John D. Rocke-feller, the famous Eastman Johnson portrait of 1895

This rare photograph captured a trip by Senior's family and friends to Colorado in the summer of 1875. Posed against a backdrop in an artist's studio are *(left to right)* Bessie, Aunt Lucy Spelman, Laura Spelman Rockefeller with John, Jr., on her lap, Mr. and Mrs. Robert Hopkins, Edith and Alta, and Charles Norris.

John D. Rockefeller at the age of twenty with his brothers and sisters in 1859. *Left to right:* John, Lucy, Mary, Frank, and William.

Junior and his sisters, late 1880s. *Left to right:* Bessie, Alta, Edith, and Junior.

Sexton Building, housing the offices of Rockefeller and Andrews, Commission Merchants, on the lakefront in Cleveland, Ohio, 1865. Senior began his involvement in the petroleum industry from these premises.

"The most famous address in the world": the private office of John D. Rockefeller and John D. Rockefeller, Jr., in the Standard Oil Building at 26 Broadway, New York City, 1920

Kykuit, John D. and Laura Rockefeller's home in Pocantico Hills, Westchester County, New York, as it appeared soon after its reconstruction in 1914

Junior *(right)* with Willard S. Richardson in York during their bicycle trip through England in the summer of 1896

College days. Junior *(center)* as an undergraduate at Brown, with his close friends Lefferts Dashiell *(left)* and Everett Colby.

Abby Greene Aldrich, in her engagement photograph, 1901. She was the eldest daughter of the powerful Republican senator from Rhode Island, Nelson W. Aldrich.

Abby Aldrich Rockefeller on her wedding day, October 10, 1901

The Rockefeller homes on West 54th Street, New York City, 1920. Senior's house, Number 4, is in the foreground. Number 10, home of Junior and Abby and their growing family, towers over it in the rear. This is now the site of the Sculpture Garden of the Museum of Modern Art.

Abeyton Lodge at Pocantico, Junior and Abby's country home from 1903 to 1937

The Eyrie, overlooking the Atlantic at Seal Harbor, Maine, purchased in 1912 as a summer home. Junior added to it substantially over the years.

Coal Company, Bethlehem Steel, General Electric, International Harvester, and others. At the end of 1918, *Industry and Humanity* was finally published. It sold well and enhanced King's reputation, leading to important speaking engagements in Canada, the United States, and England.

The warmth Junior and Abby felt for King extended to counseling marriage, and they tried matchmaking by introducing him to a lady of quality whom King referred to in his diary as "Miss X." King was smitten, writing that she was "all that I most wish to find in a woman." A successful courtship would have done more than anything else to keep King in New York, although his biographer avers that Junior and Abby "had no such ulterior motive."[26] However, King's ardent pursuit was unavailing, and he was to remain a bachelor the rest of his long life.

Another enticement to stay in New York came at the end of 1918 from Mr. and Mrs. Andrew Carnegie. King knew them socially. One afternoon at tea at their East 91st Street residence, the aging Scot and his charming wife made King the astounding offer of taking charge of all the Carnegie philanthropic organizations, some six of them, including the Carnegie Corporation of New York with its $130 million endowment. A salary of as much as $100,000 per year was hinted. King was overwhelmed. He wrote: "To accept such an offer is a great responsibility, to reject it is an equally great responsibility." The prospect conjured up an ecstatic view of the future:

Here is the promise of a life full of great opportunity and free from anxieties and harassments of every kind. It would mean going to live in New York, being able to have a comfortable house and library there, to meet the best people of the world, to be in touch in a commanding way with the affairs of the world on the subjects which I have most at heart, industrial peace, international peace, social well-being. It would mean fine opportunity of study and rest and enjoyment, a life of the highest kind of intellectual enjoyment and spiritual enjoyment as well, since the opportunity of helping others is what it is.[27]

Junior was miffed and jealous when he heard of the offer. "He seemed quite depressed when I told him of what had transpired," King wrote. Among others, King consulted Sir Wilfred Laurier, whose advice this time was that King's real future lay in Canadian politics. Sir Wilfred, who was to live only a few more months, said that King was his personal choice to succeed him as head of the Liberal Party. It was the moment of truth for Mackenzie King, and he remained true to himself by declining the Carnegie offer.

King resumed his counseling work in New York to Junior's deep satisfaction. But King's opportunity finally came at the Liberal Party convention in Ottawa in August 1919. Although Sir Wilfred died without making public his choice of a successor, King's enhanced reputation and his loyalty in 1917 paid off among the party members. It was a stiffly fought contest among half a dozen men, but King won and became the new leader.

Junior much preferred that King return to politics than take the Carnegie offer. He lost King as an associate, but gained him as a lifelong friend. For his part, King regarded his work with Junior as a turning point in his life, one that opened new horizons, refreshed and restored him, and enabled him to return to his first love better equipped than before. In 1921 he fulfilled his dream by becoming prime minister and served an unprecedented twenty-one years out of the next twenty-four, through to the end of World War II. One is left to speculate about the course of Canadian history if "Miss X" had yielded to him or he had yielded to the Carnegie offer.

Several of the important lessons that Junior learned during the second decade of the century led to a heightened sensitivity on his part as to the propriety of the Rockefeller Foundation's governance and his family's relationship to it. This in turn led to a reorganization of the Foundation that began in 1916 and culminated in 1917. The main stimulus was a barrage of criticism over the creation of an "industrial relations program" within the Foundation and the hiring of Mackenzie King. What Junior learned was that public perceptions could be just as important as private realities. He knew in his own mind that his intention was honorable, that he had contemplated taking such a step long before the Colorado strike, and that his plan was to work toward industrial peace far beyond the immediate problem of the Colorado strike and the "Ludlow massacre." But these niceties were all lost in the public perception, which was that the Rockefellers were using monies placed in trust to bail themselves out of a personal problem. In a sense, this criticism was a continuation of the controversy that attended the effort to obtain a congressional charter for the Foundation and seemed to confirm some of the suspicions that had been voiced then.

Junior had a stubborn streak, and once he realized the public perception of what he had done, he was not about to abruptly cave in to it and change the arrangement—particularly in view of the fact that it was important to Mackenzie King to come to New York under the auspices of the Foundation and not of the Rockefellers personally. But King's departure for the 1917 election created an opportunity to make a fresh start. Moreover, the Colorado problem was over and the criticism of the Foundation had died down, so Junior could make a change without seeming to kowtow to pressure—and King was amenable to the change.

The lesson for Junior was that never again would he ask the Foundation to become involved in an activity that had anything to do with a personal or family problem, or for that matter with any highly personal preference of his own as to where money should go. An ameliorating factor was that Junior was now wealthy enough to do these things on his own anyway—in the future he would be highly active personally as a philanthropist in addition to serving as a trustee of philanthropic organizations.

A related action taken by Senior served further to distance the Foundation from the family. When Senior made his second large gift to complete the $100 million initial funding of the Foundation, he attached a condition referred to as "founder's designations." His letter said:

> It is a condition of this gift that from the income of the Foundation the sum of Two Million Dollars ($2,000,000) annually, or so much thereof as I shall designate, shall be applied during my lifetime to such specific objects within the corporate purposes of the Foundation as I may from time to time direct.[28]

This seemed like a perfectly reasonable idea to Senior at the time. After all, he had contributed all the money in the first place; all he was asking was that a share of the income from it be used for his personal giving. This would free him from worrying about that altogether for the rest of his life, which at the age of seventy-five he might have thought would last only a few more years, but in fact extended for another twenty-three. He would simply refer supplicants to the Foundation and would not have to have a secretary or any kind of staff assistance. His designations included one for $2,550,000 to the Rockefeller Institute, which the Foundation honored even though it exceeded Senior's self-imposed annual limitation.

As exaggerated as the criticism had been when the Foundation was being created, the central valid point became more clear at the time of the Colorado hearings. Senior's arrangement was not a proper one in relationship to an organization that held monies in trust. Junior spoke with him, making a subtle argument that was reflected in Senior's letter of July 19, 1917, which rescinded the arrangement:

In view of the increasing demand upon the funds of the Foundation, especially those arising in connection with the great war for human freedom in which our country is now engaged, which have led the Foundation to appropriate a part of its principal, as well as all of its income, I hereby release the conditions.

Junior's new concern for the propriety of the family's relationship to the Foundation required a revamping of the board and staff as well. Gates had always had a high conception of the governance of the organizations he had urged Senior to create. In his 1905 letter to Senior, he wrote

that to become a trustee of one of them would be to make a man at once a public character. They should be so large that their administration would be as much a matter of public concern and public inquiry and public criticism as any of the functions of the government are now. They should be so large as to attract the attention of the entire civilized world, their administration become the subject of the most intelligent criticism of the world, and to their administration should be addressed both directly and indirectly the highest talent in those particular spheres of every generation through which the funds would go. . . .

Although Gates had not dwelled specifically on the point, the import of his words was something Junior now realized—the majority of the Foundation's trustees should have public stature independently of any hold over them by the Rockefeller family, either real or perceived. However, the fact was that most of the original trustees of the Rockefeller Foundation were either family members or men beholden to the family—Senior, Junior, Gates, Jerome Greene, Starr Murphy, Wickliffe Rose, Simon Flexner, and Charles Heydt. There were only three "independent" members—A. Barton Hepburn, Charles Eliot, and Harry Pratt Judson. And the independence of the last named, as president of the University of Chicago, could be challenged,. given the indebtedness of the university to the Rockefeller family.

For this reason, an infusion of new talent on the board became the central feature of the reorganization. Added to the board were Harry Emerson Fosdick; Frederick Strauss of New York; Charles Evans Hughes, who had lost as Republican candidate in the presidential election of 1916 against Woodrow Wilson; two noted Chicago philanthropists and business leaders, Julius Rosenwald of Sears, Roebuck and Martin Ryerson of Inland Steel; and George Vincent, former president of the University of Minnesota. Also added was a man who did not fit into the "independent" category, but was highly esteemed by everyone—Wallace Buttrick of the General Education Board.

Righting the balance on the board was not something Junior expected to achieve in one stroke—that would have required excusing some of the eminent men related to the family. Junior was not about to ask such men as Gates or Murphy or Rose to leave the board. However, there was no problem asking Charles Heydt to step down. As Junior's secretary, he had merely been holding a place. Also, Junior knew that some of the elderly men would be retiring soon in any event, as Eliot did late in 1917, Gates in 1923, and Senior in 1922 (without ever having attended a board meeting). Filling these vacancies with independent leaders would achieve a board of unimpeachable stature. This was accomplished by the early 1920s, and from that point on, the Rockefeller Foundation board could be compared favorably at any time with the Cabinet of the U.S. president—and indeed many trustees later served as Cabinet members.

As part of the reorganization, Junior decided that the Foundation needed a full-time president, a man with special qualities of leadership. Junior would then move up from president to become chairman. The search began in mid-1916 and by August Junior had his man— George E. Vincent. An established scholar, though not known for original research, Vincent had earned his B.A. at Yale and his doctorate at the University of Chicago, where he served as dean of the faculties of art, literature, and science until 1911, when he became president of the University of Minnesota. But Vincent was perhaps best known as one of the great public speakers of the time, having served (1907–1915) as president of the Chautauqua Institution, of which his father had been a cofounder.[29] Vincent also was a man of likable personality and good sense of humor, with a strong measure of skeptical common sense.

The Vincent appointment was a blow to Jerome Greene, who had been serving as chief executive of the Foundation in his post as secretary. A man of brilliant intellect, Greene was tough-minded and had a somewhat abrasive personality. It is likely that Junior thought that Vincent's reputation and oratorical skill would be helpful in improving the public image of the Foundation. Vincent summarized his understanding of the situation in a letter to Junior on July 5: "You lack confidence in Mr. Greene as chief executive, but you have a high regard for him personally and would be glad to have him continue in some relation to the Foundation."

However, Greene played the good soldier and made way for his successor. Not having learned of the Vincent appointment until it was all arranged, he stayed at his post until January 1917 when Vincent was able to come to New York. Greene maintained a connection with the family, however, by remaining on the General Education Board, and he returned to the Foundation board in 1928 after building a successful career in investment banking and becoming an active leader in several international organizations.

One can perceive the irony that reforming the Rockefeller Foundation in order to distance it from real or apparent family control required that Junior exercise very direct control himself for a period of time. All the foregoing changes were the result of his direct involvement and influence. Another change is evident—Frederick Gates had faded almost completely out of the picture. In part, this was the natural result of Gates' own advancing age. But it also resulted from the gulf between Junior and Gates on policy toward the Colorado strike and the fact that Junior was now definitely his own man with his own agenda and sense of direction. That Senior approved of his son's assertiveness is made manifest by the fact that the old man now was steadily transferring his wealth to him.

The changes affecting the governance of the Rockefeller Foundation were also timely in preparing for a broadening of the Foundation's program. It had not developed much beyond the early commitments in international health, medical education in China, and industrial relations. The great preoccupation now was the World War. The Foundation spent more than $22 million over a five-year span, including Belgian relief during the German occupation; assistance to the Balkan countries before America's entry into the war; substantial donations for the war relief work of the American Red Cross, the International Red Cross, the YMCA, and the YWCA; and postwar relief in Russia and China.

Junior also was involved personally in wartime work. Aside from buying Liberty Bonds and contributing substantially to relief activities, his main effort was serving as Greater New York chairman for the United War Work campaign, raising $35 million for a coalition of seven relief agencies. In 1918 Junior also worked to activate one of his father's last great acts as a philanthropist—the creation of the Laura Spelman Rockefeller Memorial in memory of Senior's deceased wife, with an endowment of $74 million. Although it was incorporated with a general charter, Senior's original intent was that the Memorial would be active in areas that had been of interest to Laura, chiefly projects in aid of women and children. Junior placed his college classmate Willard Richardson in charge temporarily. At first, the work of the Memorial was limited to small-scale grants, but within a few years it was to find its own remarkable and unique mission.

In a very real sense, the events of the second decade of the century completed Junior's education, building on what he had learned at Brown, in his apprenticeship with Gates, through the years of institution-building and the personal trauma that led to his decision to devote his life to philanthropy. He had emerged with strengthened character and principles from such life-forming experiences as the White Slave Grand Jury and the "Ludlow massacre." He had continued to show skill in finding and enlisting men of great talent, and he had learned much from them. Now fully in charge of family affairs, he was confident and prepared for the beckoning postwar world—with a personal fortune of half a billion dollars, a key role to play in a whole set of major philanthropic organizations, a growing circle of trusted and talented advisers, and goals and interests that would lead him to perform as a philanthropist over the next decade, both overseas and at home, on a wide-ranging scale never before seen and never since equaled.

II

THE LIBERAL
VISION
1918–1929

8

THE INTERNATIONALIST

THE GREAT CREATIVE PERIOD of Junior's philanthropy was the decade of the 1920s. These postwar years were marked by a surge of optimism and hope and idealism. To Junior and many other Americans, there seemed to be no limit to what human intelligence and goodwill and faith could accomplish. He entered this period in his mid-forties, fully prepared to play a leading role by virtue of his experience and education, his moral values and deep faith, his spirit of progressivism, and his unique position as a man in command of an impressive range of financial, organizational, and intellectual resources.

More than this, he had a vision, a great liberal vision of how human society could function at its best. This provided a unifying thread for the extremely wide range of his philanthropic activity, preventing it from becoming merely the random and sporadic spending of a wealthy man to appease his latest whims (although there was a touch of this at times). Junior articulated his world view in pursuing some of his major objectives, such as unifying the Protestant churches and achieving harmony in industrial relations; it was clearly reflected in others, as in his love of art and nature and his penchant for idealizing the past in his support of restorations. And it was nowhere more evident than in his many projects overseas; in an era supposedly dominated by isolationist thinking, he was a leader among the many Americans who had a strongly internationalist outlook.

Junior believed that reason firmly based in faith could conquer the problems of the world—problems of war, disease, ignorance, vice, poverty, factional squabbling—that these in time could be overtaken by a spirit of cooperation, peace, and harmony. In this he was certainly an optimist and an idealist; yet, he was no Pollyanna. He had been through enough to know that it was never easy to accomplish anything worthwhile. And so the streak of pragmatism was there, too. He set no timetables. He experienced setbacks without discouraging easily. He was patient in the face of obstinacy and wrongheadedness.

Yet he could not have been prepared—as no one was—for the harsh blows that the realities of the world would deal to idealism of every sort at the end of the decade.

After a decade marked by domestic reform and global warfare, the United States entered the 1920s with its citizens seemingly more interested in stability and preservation than in change. The ratification of the Prohibition amendment, the rejection of the League of Nations, the election of Warren G. Harding in 1920, and the drive to restrict immigration all indicated a popular mood predominantly conservative concerning domestic issues and isolationist in regard to the rest of the world.

Yet the world *had* changed. The economies of the most powerful trading nations, Britain, France, and Germany, were in disarray after four years of total war. The great dynasties of central and eastern Europe, the Hohenzollerns, Hapsburgs, and Romanovs, were gone. The 1920s were an attempt at an illusory "return to normalcy," peace and prosperity, before the seismic shocks of the World War manifested themselves in further changes with the most profound consequences.

Historians and political scientists have seen Woodrow Wilson's failure to gain U.S. entry into the League of Nations as the great event that signified a return to the isolationist posture that had been the dominant motif of American foreign policy since George Washington's Neutrality Proclamation of 1793. There is, of course, a broad truth in this view, but it is also simplistic. It obscures the remarkable vigor with which many leading Americans, both in the private sector and in government, pursued foreign interests, particularly in the economic sphere.

Despite the rebuff to Wilson, these interests combined under the banner of the Wilsonian ideal of a "new diplomacy" in Europe and renewed pursuit of the "Open Door" policy for China, first enunciated by Secretary of State John Hay in 1899. This was not merely an exercise in idealistic sentiment, but an attempt to harness ideals to practical purposes. Virtually unscathed by the Great War, the United States emerged as an economic power of the first rank. The need seen by some American leaders was for a new system of international relations to contain and modify the power politics and imperialism of Britain, France, and Japan, thus allowing for American economic penetration around the world, which now seemed possible. This intention was quickly manifested in a variety of initiatives toward Europe and the Far East, culminating in the Washington Conference of 1921–1922 in which Harding's secretary of state, Charles Evans Hughes, worked to maximize American interests. Although begun as a conference on naval disarmament, the gathering soon became oriented toward a Far Eastern realignment in pursuit of the long-standing American goal of a China progressively more unified and less subject to the imperialism of the Anglo-Japanese alliance.[1]

Such a foreign policy was rightly thought to have implications for domestic policy. Expansion of foreign trade would increase employment, particularly with radically curtailed immigration, and it would help ease the class and ethnic tensions that had been so pronounced in previous decades. Moreover, efforts to achieve domestic reform worked best in a situation of economic growth. It was typical of the optimism of the early 1920s that success along all these lines was expected to lead to peace and prosperity and the further vindication of voluntarism and a limited role for government, which had stood at the center of American political thought for well more than a century.

This postwar climate was also conducive to new American cultural, educational, missionary, and philanthropic initiatives on the world scene, a prospect that appealed strongly to John D. Rockefeller, Jr. As a Republican, Junior was no supporter of Wilson, but he was a moderate in foreign affairs unlike his fellow philanthropists Andrew Mellon and Henry C. Frick, who financed the propaganda campaign of the hard-line opponents of American entry into the League.[2] Junior came to accept the idea of the League of Nations and made significant financial contributions to its activities as the decade wore on.

Isolationist sentiment was strong in the vast American heartland; it was along the eastern seaboard that the internationalist outlook flourished, especially in New York City, among intellectuals, journalists, professional men, and members of affluent families. Party affiliation was not a distinguishing factor; easterners avidly interested in foreign affairs included both Republicans and Democrats. This phenomenon gradually gave rise to the notion of an "eastern liberal establishment," a term prominent in American political jargon for the next half century and always particularly identified with foreign affairs. Junior, predisposed by his education and upbringing to a wide-ranging interest in the world, was a prime mover in this group.

A tangible indication of eastern internationalism in a time supposedly dominated by isolationist thinking was the rise of several organizations devoted to a world outlook. Prominent among them was the Council on Foreign Relations, soon to be identified, along with the Rockefeller Foundation, as a bastion of the "establishment." The council had its genesis in the dissatisfactions felt by a number of American and British members of the delegations to the Paris Peace Conference at the end of the World War. These men strongly believed that the conference was in danger of missing a glorious opportunity to achieve a lasting peace by opting for revenge on the defeated Central Powers. On May 30, 1919, they founded the Institute of International Affairs. Some time after the conference ended, the group split, the British reconstituting themselves as the Royal Institute of International Affairs, familiarly known as Chatham House. The Americans were preoccupied by the debate over American entry into the League of Nations, and when that failed, they saw a vital need for an organization that would help make the public aware of the role they believed the United States should play in world affairs. In 1921 they incorporated the Council on Foreign Relations, adopting the name and some of the members of an informal group of New Yorkers who had held occasional dinner meetings during the war to discuss American policy.[3]

Among the approximately one hundred original members of the council were John Foster Dulles, Herbert Lehman, Henry Stimson, Elihu Root, Jerome Greene, and Ivy Lee. The council's journal, *Foreign Affairs,* began publication in 1922, with Hamilton Fish Armstrong as managing editor. By this time, the council had grown to five hundred members. Junior rarely joined organizations, but he manifested his support of the council by contributing $1,500 a year, and in 1929 made a gift of $50,000 toward its new headquarters on East 65th Street. All of his sons joined the council as they came of age.

Another internationalist organization, the Foreign Policy Association (FPA), came into existence in 1918, founded by a group of "editors, publicists, and students of international relations" with the motto: "For a liberal and constructive American foreign policy." While the Council on Foreign Relations served an elite clientele in the East and tried to influence U.S. foreign policy, the FPA had a more wide-ranging educational mission aimed at the hinterlands. Although headquartered in New York, the FPA soon established local chapters in some fifteen cities across the country, and it distributed information and articles on foreign affairs to newspapers, many of which lacked a consistently good source of such material.

The chairman of the FPA, a full-time paid position, was James G. McDonald, a native of Ohio who had earned his M.A. at Indiana University and worked toward a Ph.D. at Harvard before teaching history at Indiana. As FPA chairman, McDonald traveled abroad every year to gather material for his bylined articles in newspapers and magazines and his radio talks on foreign affairs. Junior's wife, Abby, became interested in the FPA and thought highly of McDonald, so it was not surprising that Junior began supporting the organization with grants totaling more than $100,000 from 1925 through 1930. Judging by the fact that Junior made a rare exception and joined the FPA in 1924, he seems to have been more comfortable with this organization than with the Council on Foreign Relations. Despite its motto, the FPA carefully avoided taking positions on foreign policy issues, concentrating on straightforward nonpartisan education.

Still a third organization emerged, in 1925, this time oriented to the Far East—the Institute for Pacific Relations. It was born at a YMCA conference in Hawaii. One of the three principal organizers was Ray Lyman Wilbur, president of Stanford University, who had become a Rockefeller Foundation trustee in 1923. The structural design of the IPR called for privately supported "councils" to be created within nations having an interest in the Pacific Basin and to be federated under the leadership of a "Pacific Council" composed of delegates appointed by each of the national groups. Headed by a secretary-general, the Pacific Council had its office in Honolulu and functioned as the organization's secretariat.

By the time of the second conference in Honolulu in 1927, six national councils existed, and five more were added within a few years. The American Council (later called the American Institute for Pacific Relations) was the largest and best funded of the national councils, and thus exerted a strong influence within the IPR. One of the organizers of the American Council was Jerome Greene, who had a lifetime interest in the Far East, stemming from his background as the son of missionary parents—he was born in Yokohama in 1874. Junior also had a deep interest in the Far East, and he became an important financial supporter of the IPR, contributing $70,000 over a four-year period in the late 1920s.

Junior's full-time work as a philanthropist was about evenly divided between his personal giving and the role he played in the organizations he had helped his father to create, as well as the smaller Bureau of Social Hygiene that he had created himself. By 1921 Senior was almost entirely out of the picture, having completed the disposition of his vast fortune and taken every step he could to prepare his son for his life's work. In the period 1917–1921, Senior made his last significant charitable gifts, about $200 million worth, on top of the hundreds of millions he had already given. These last gifts included the $74 million to endow the Laura Spelman Rockefeller Memorial, large gifts to the other three Rockefeller organizations (the Foundation, the Institute for Medical Research, and the General Education Board), and terminal grants to the many Baptist organizations Senior had supported faithfully throughout his life.

This left Senior with some $500 million to distribute to his heirs (after reserving a relatively small amount for himself). In these personal transfers, the preeminence of Junior in his father's mind was emphatically clear—the son received $465 million of the half billion available. These transfers were made through a series of laconic notes from father to son, rarely exceeding one sentence in length, as for example:

February 17, 1920

Dear Son:

I am this day giving you $65,000,000 par value of United States Government First Liberty Loan 3½% bonds.

Affectionately,
Father

During the five-year span 1917–1921, Senior gave his only son and primary heir an incredible portfolio of stocks, bonds, and commercial paper. Included among the gifts were 241,000 shares of Standard of California, 186,000 shares of Standard of New York, 113,000 shares of Standard of New Jersey, 110,000 shares of the Consolidation Coal Company, and smaller amounts in Standard of Indiana, Vacuum Oil, Prairie Oil and Gas, Chase National Bank, Bankers Trust, the Equitable Trust, and the New York Central, as well as bonds of the United States, New York State, and New York City. Also transferred were real estate holdings in New York, Ohio, and Florida, and $5.2 million in cash, which came to Junior in the form of checks in a rapid series of installments over a three-week period in 1920. In this fashion, Junior's net worth increased from about $20 million in January 1917 to about $500 million by the beginning of 1922.[4]

These holdings steadily increased in value throughout the 1920s, with Junior's net worth peaking at slightly less than a billion dollars ($994.7 million) in 1928. Junior achieved this not by functioning as an active trader or entrepreneur, but in the main simply by holding on to his blue-chip petroleum stocks. His fortune yielded an income ranging from a low of $14 million in 1920 to a high of $50 million in 1928. Because federal and state income taxes were relatively low after the war—his annual payments ranging from $3.2 to $6.3 million—Junior had plenty of income available for his personal expenses and philanthropy without touching principal.[5] (See Appendix A.)

In the postwar years, managerial and coordinating needs expanded due to the scale of Junior's personal giving, his key role in so many philanthropic organizations, and the superintending of his fortune and property. The office at 26 Broadway had grown slowly through all the years since Junior had entered it in 1897. Departments specializing in accounting, investments, real estate, and office services had been added, and the staff increased correspondingly. Among the mainstays in the 1920s were three old-timers, Charles Heydt, Bertram Cutler, and Willard Richardson. Heydt had graduated from his earlier status as Junior's secretary to become the office expert on real estate. Robert Gumbel joined the staff as property manager and general factotum.

However, there were losses among senior advisers. Mackenzie King, of course, had gone off to his political career in Canada. Starr Murphy died in 1921 and Wallace Buttrick retired in 1923. Gates in effect had been lost some years before. There had been no open breach, but as noted he and Junior had drifted apart over their differences of opinion on the Colorado strike. The first blow had been Junior's action in firing Gates' uncle, L. M. Bowers. Then Junior's changing attitudes under the tutelage of King had been regarded as much too liberal by Gates. He no longer had a role in the family office, but was active as a trustee on several of the Rockefeller boards until his retirement in 1923.

Ivy Lee had been on the family payroll for only one year, 1915, and then had formed his own firm. He numbered the Rockefellers among his prominent clients, probably spending more time working with Senior than on the occasional public relations assignment from Junior. Contrary to legend, it was not Lee who suggested to Senior that he hand out shiny new dimes to youngsters. That was entirely Senior's idea, but Lee encouraged it and was able to persuade the amiable old gentleman to be available occasionally for "photo opportunities." At

Junior's behest, Lee worked for quite a long time trying to find the right person to write Senior's biography.[6]

It took Junior a few years to solve the problem of finding new senior advisers. One certain need was to have a full-time legal adviser to replace Murphy, as well as retaining outside counsel. Charles Evans Hughes performed the latter service from the time of his narrow defeat in the 1916 presidential election until he became secretary of state in 1921. Then the function was taken over by Raymond B. Fosdick, who had set up his own law firm in 1921 with Junior as his first client. Not until 1924 did Junior find the right man to come on his staff as general counsel. He was the urbane Thomas M. Debevoise, who was born the same year as Junior and belonged to the same fraternity, Alpha Delta Phi, though at Yale rather than Brown. A resident of Montclair, New Jersey, Debevoise knew Gates and Murphy well. Also serving as general counsel of the Foundation, the Institute for Medical Research, and the General Education Board, Debevoise was to be a prominent person in the family office until after World War II.

In addition to Raymond Fosdick, Colonel Arthur Woods joined the triumvirate of senior advisers along with Debevoise. When John Purroy Mitchel was defeated in his reelection bid in the 1917 New York City mayoralty race, Woods left his post as police commissioner and was recruited by Junior to serve as the head of the Bureau of Social Hygiene. His performance in that role soon confirmed to Junior that Woods was a man of sound judgment and a very competent administrator, and as the 1920s passed, he gradually assumed increasing responsibility to become, in effect, the chief administrator of Junior's office.

The man who came the nearest to taking the place of Mackenzie King, not so much as an intimate personal friend, but as Junior's closest and most trusted adviser, was Raymond Fosdick. It will be recalled that Fosdick had undertaken studies of police administration in Europe and the United States at the request of Junior. The expertise he gained in these projects, plus the fact that he was well known to the Wilson administration (having worked on Wilson's first campaign and then as comptroller of the finance committee of the Democratic National Committee in 1916), led Fosdick to an interesting series of assignments over the next five years. First, he was asked by the newly appointed secretary of war, Newton D. Baker, to study the National Guard training camps strung out along the Mexican border as a result of the raids into American territory by Pancho Villa during his insurrection.

In turn, this led to a similar assignment when the United States entered the World War. Baker created a Commission on Training Camp Activities and named Fosdick chairman. Camps sprang up all over the country, and many of them were little better than sinkholes, surrounded by brothels and bars. All of them had problems of idleness and lack of healthy activities for the men. Fosdick labored for two years to correct these conditions. In one aspect of the work, coordinating the programs of private agencies, he was frequently in touch with Junior. Fosdick created a "law enforcement division" and a "social hygiene division," built scores of post exchanges and "Liberty theaters," and installed athletic directors at each camp.

During the latter months of the war and throughout 1919, the locus of Fosdick's work shifted to the many American Army and Navy posts in France and England. Attached to General Pershing's staff, Fosdick was thus in Europe during the exhilarating period of victory parades and peace negotiations. On one of his trips abroad, Fosdick was assigned to the same ocean liner that carried the American peace delegation to Paris, and he had several private talks with President Wilson. He records him as saying, "If we can create a League of Nations, we will at last do something that the world has been dreaming about for generations." Wilson seemed to have intimations of troubles to come:

At another time [Fosdick wrote], I found him concerned about the spread of Bolshevism—a "poison" he called it. Its absolutism repelled him, and he quoted Jefferson's pledge of "eternal hostility against any form of tyranny over the mind of man." Wilson called himself a liberal, but liberalism must be more liberal than ever before, if civilization is to survive, he said. Conservatism he defined as the policy of "make no change and consult your grandmother when in doubt." "Those who argue for the *status quo ante bellum,*" he added, "or any other *status quo,* are like so many vain kings sitting by the sea and commanding the tide not to rise."[7]

With demobilization, Fosdick's training camp work ended, but he was back in New York only two days before he learned that Wilson had appointed him to the senior post reserved for an American in the League of Nations administration. The plan called for a British secretary general and two under secretaries, one American and one French. Sir Eric Drummond became secretary general, and Jean

Monnet was the French appointee. Fosdick's account of his stay in Paris throughout 1920 offers an insight into the pioneering work that had to be done to create the first world organization in the midst of many handicaps, the greatest one being Wilson's losing battle to win American acceptance of the League. Fosdick rejects the prevailing view that Wilson lost because he refused to compromise with the demands of the "irreconcilables." Although he candidly analyzes Wilson's weaknesses and faults, Fosdick argues that compromise was never a viable alternative. Several of the demands would have emasculated the League, and if Wilson had accepted them, the opposition would merely have added still another and more intransigent demand.[8]

The latter period of Fosdick's tenure in his job was grim as he experienced the change in European public opinion from a passion for America to deep distrust and resentment over the efforts of Wilson's opponents to "Americanize" the League and disenchantment with Wilson himself. Fosdick came to Washington to be available for consultation and testimony, and then quietly resigned before the Treaty of Versailles was voted down by the Senate in order to remove the anomaly of a high-level American appointee to the League as an issue in the debate. He then set up his New York law firm with Chauncey Belknap and James C. Curtis, and began his long association with Junior.

Several times Junior suggested that Fosdick join his staff full-time as an associate, but Fosdick declined, wanting to retain his independence. However, it is likely that as much as 80 percent of his time was spent on Junior's projects. Some of them were even operated out of Fosdick's law office for a time, such as the ongoing work on industrial relations (see next chapter). Fosdick gradually became a board and executive committee member of every one of the philanthropic organizations with which Junior was concerned.

Fosdick demonstrated the reason he wanted his independence by starting up the "League of Nations News Bureau" in his office and supporting it himself during three difficult years in which the Harding administration disappointed League supporters, including many prominent Republicans, by taking a cold attitude toward the nascent organization despite campaign promises to the contrary. During this period, Fosdick became somewhat controversial as a fiery champion of the League and other international activities, stumping the country, writing articles, and even engaging in a bitter series of exchanges in print with Secretary of State Charles Evans Hughes, an internationalist with moderate views. In a sense, Fosdick and others of a like mind won their battle—the mood changed during the Coolidge and Hoover administrations; there was a good deal of tacit American cooperation with the League, including the dispatching of unofficial American representatives to work on various international projects. In 1929 when Hughes rejoined the Rockefeller Foundation board (only to leave it again a year later when he returned to the Supreme Court, this time as President Hoover's choice as chief justice), he greeted Fosdick with a smile and an extended hand and asked: "Friends or enemies?" Fosdick records that he never served with an abler trustee.[9]

In many ways Fosdick reinforced and extended the liberalizing influence on Junior that Mackenzie King had exercised. Lest one think there was a liberal cabal ensnaring Junior, however, the underlying and most interesting fact is that Junior was drawn to these men, sought them out, and brought them to his side only with some difficulty. Fosdick writes of the differing points of view and backgrounds that he and Junior had, but says that their relationship was always characterized by the utmost frankness:

He was . . . a person of great sincerity and integrity, with a lively sense of social responsibility. Combined with this was a modesty of spirit rare in one brought up in his circumstances. There was nothing dogmatic or opinionated about him. His position in the world of finance gave him no feeling of power or even of assurance. He hated the hollow deference paid to wealth and the obsequiousness of timid minds. He wanted to be convinced, not deferred to. "The only way you can help me," he said to me at our first interview, "is to tell me at all times exactly what you think."[10]

The loss from the Rockefeller Foundation board in the early 1920s of Senior, Gates, Murphy, Buttrick, Hughes, H. E. Fosdick, and A. Barton Hepburn (who stepped in front of a streetcar in 1922) meant a considerable turnover once again and a chance to complete the process of making the board predominantly composed of independent men. In addition to Raymond Fosdick, the new trustees included: John G. Agar, prominent New York lawyer; John W. Davis, the defeated Democratic candidate in the 1924 presidential election; Vernon L. Kellogg, zoologist and author of important studies on evolution; William Allen White, famed editor of the *Emporia* (Kansas) *Gazette;* and Ray Lyman Wilbur, president of Stanford University.

With these additions, the board attained the high level of prestige and quality that has characterized it ever since. No one had a more elevated notion of the responsibilities of a Rockefeller Foundation trustee than Frederick Gates. Raymond Fosdick vividly recalls Gates' farewell address to his fellow trustees in 1923 when "with a voice that thundered out of Sinai" he shook "his fist at a somewhat startled but respectfully attentive Board" and said:

When you die and come to approach the judgment of Almighty God, what do you think He will demand of you? Do you for an instant presume to believe that He will inquire into your petty failures or your trivial virtues? No! He will ask just one question: *"What did you do as a trustee of the Rockefeller Foundation?"*[11]

Junior did not express himself in such colorful language, but he unquestionably believed in open discussion and independent thinking. He commented on the independence of the boards to Allan Nevins:

The philanthropic boards which my father established usually began in a small way and developed gradually. . . . it was only natural that, generally speaking, they should have been manned at the outset by members of our "official family" and those with whom we had been working along similar lines. However, as rapidly as capable and interested men were found outside this group they were added to the boards, in which members of the "official family" gradually and properly became a minority.

Obviously, no one had more real and potential influence vis-à-vis these boards than Junior, but the evidence shows that he exercised it circumspectly and with great regard for due process. One result was that he was frequently outvoted. Junior added this wry statement to his comment to Nevins: "It is significant that with at least some of the officers and directors my interest in a project has been more apt to prejudice its favorable consideration than to forward it, so wholly independent of the founder and his so-called 'official family' have they been." Nevins adds this passage on Junior's conduct as a trustee:

. . . if the younger Rockefeller had the power to dominate, he never exercised it. "Time and again," writes one observer, "Mr. Rockefeller, Jr., has been outvoted on the boards of his father's donations." His colleagues gave striking instances of this; for he always insisted that they treat him precisely as they treated each other. . . . Moreover, as a sharp critic of foundations remarks, the younger Rockefeller was "a man of such catholic and impersonal interests and of such statesmanlike qualities" that his influence always proved strongly beneficial.[12]

Junior's influence as chairman varied according to the conditions of each of the boards. The two oldest, the Rockefeller Institute and the

General Education Board, had long since carved out their special missions and had able staffs and trustees. The Foundation now was in good shape as far as staff and trustees were concerned. The result was that in these three cases Junior could play the circumspect role that he thought was proper. The Laura Spelman Rockefeller Memorial was new and needed shepherding, so Junior naturally exercised more direct influence until he found the right person to lead it off on its unique mission—Beardsley Ruml, a young man with a brilliant and creative mind (see Chapter 9). The Bureau of Social Hygiene differed from the rest in that it had no endowment, but functioned solely on the money Junior gave it each year. It was what today would be called an "operating" foundation, really an extension of Junior's personal giving and thus guided by his policy direction.

The danger of program duplication among these organizations called for some sort of coordinative mechanism. For example, three of them were heavily involved in medical education—the Rockefeller Institute, the Foundation, and the General Education Board. One step Junior took was to begin a "Monday luncheon group" composed of the executive heads of the organizations. This was reminiscent of Senior's practice at Standard Oil in which the heads of the operating divisions met daily at lunch to coordinate their activities. It was a collegial group with no one person dominating, and the same was true of the "Monday luncheon group."

In another move to improve coordination, Junior in 1919 established a "Committee on Benevolences," which, as the name suggests, was for the purpose of advising him on his personal giving, and thus became known more informally as the Advisory Committee. The key initial members were Woods and Richardson, and others joined the committee as they became advisers to Junior, including Fosdick, Debevoise, and Ruml. Junior almost never attended a meeting; the normal procedure was for the committee to meet and pass its recommendations to him for decision. In time, this became a useful coordinative group as well.

Having this kind of apparatus was not surprising because, in a sense, Junior could be regarded as a foundation with assets of more than $500 million—greater than the four major philanthropic institutions put together. One part of the committee's work was essentially reactive; it dealt with the routine giving that any prominent citizen is likely to engage in annually. This particular prominent citizen, of course, was the target for an enormous number of requests for relatively small amounts from church groups, service groups, charity fund drives, and so on. The screening process of the Advisory Committee relieved Junior of much of the burden of this "citizenship giving," as it came to be called, a staff function in the Rockefeller family office ever since.

The other part of the work was more generative; it dealt with new and innovative giving, sometimes involving quite substantial sums. Much of this activity pertained to projects having to do with social change, and thus often required close cooperation with the Bureau of Social Hygiene and the Laura Spelman Rockefeller Memorial, which was made easy by the presence of Woods, Fosdick, and Ruml on the committee. This more elevated form of philanthropic counseling also became an ongoing staff function in the Rockefeller family office. In Junior's case, it by no means accounted for all of his personal philanthropy. He was quite capable of going off in major new directions all on his own, as we shall see.

Junior pursued projects overseas in three ways—through his own efforts, through the four major foundations, and by creating a new institution, the International Education Board. There were also projects in international relations carried on in the United States. For example, Junior provided funding for International Houses to be created at three universities, Columbia, the University of Chicago, and the University of California at Berkeley (and later also at the University of Paris). Known informally as "I Houses," these were all similar and became a distinctive new institution, serving as a residence and social center for foreign students, most of whom found themselves barred from joining American fraternities and sororities. In fact, it was the loneliness of foreign students that motivated Junior to finance the "I Houses," particularly after he learned of the work of Harry Edmonds, YMCA secretary for metropolitan New York, who had become aware of the problem years earlier and had dedicated himself to providing hospitality for young people from other countries.[13] Also, the Rockefellers frequently entertained foreign students at their home. It was not unusual for the Rockefeller boys to arrive from school to find forty Chinese students having tea at No. 10.

How much of an internationalist Junior had become was illustrated when he spoke to foreign students from many countries at the New York "I House" on November 8, 1924. He used words and images that foreshadowed such different figures as as Wendell Willkie and Martin Luther King, Jr.:

We are standing tonight on the mountain top, with the world spread out at our feet—your country, your country, my country—all about us. . . . We are above the divisive things of life. We do not see the things which separate men and women, but rather the things they have in common. From this pinnacle of idealism there is no distinction of race, color, or creed. . . . So it may come to pass that some day, some day, the people of all nations will stand on the mountain top together, and no one will speak of "my country," but all will speak of "our world."

During the 1920s, the Rockefeller Foundation did not branch out to new fields in its overseas work, but its growth in the original areas of public health and medical education was impressive, once the war had ended. Funded by the Foundation, the China Medical Board engaged in training a whole generation of Chinese doctors with the opening of the "Johns Hopkins of China"—the Peking Union Medical College—and sponsored numerous activities elsewhere in that vast country, particularly in the training of premedical students. Rapid progress was made toward the goal of increasing the number of Chinese doctors and administrators at the college to the maximum extent possible. When the college opened in 1921, 25 percent of the staff were Chinese, most of them trained in Europe and the United States. By 1927 the proportion had risen to 67 percent, including many trained in China. Grim times were ahead for China with the Japanese invasion, World War II, and the Communist takeover in 1949. By the time that termination of the program was forced, the Rockefeller Foundation had spent $45 million in China.[14]

The story of the International Health Division (known first as a "commission" and then as a "board" before becoming a "division") of the Rockefeller Foundation, like that of the General Education Board, verges on an incredible saga. One wry measurement of success is that its work over a span of forty years unquestionably was more responsible than any other such agency, and probably more than all others combined, in bringing about the worldwide reduction in death rates that inadvertently led to what became known in the 1950s as "the population explosion." It did this in two ways: first, by conquering or finding means to control a whole series of ravaging diseases, through extensive research, experimentation, and field work; and second, by institutionalizing the profession of public health in scores of countries around the globe, especially in Latin America, Africa, and Asia.

Wickliffe Rose had both of these goals clearly in mind when he took over the new International Health Board of the Foundation in 1913, having profited from the experience of administering the

Rockefeller Sanitary Commission. There Rose had learned that finding a cure for a particular disease was a necessary but not sufficient condition for solving a problem. The cure also had to be made available and applied in timely fashion. More than this, it was vital to take measures to prevent the outbreak of disease, and this in turn required surveillance of sanitary conditions in many aspects of living. In short, each country needed public health professionals, government support, and an infrastructure of public health facilities. Rose was able to get off to a quick start because of the Sanitary Commission's success in combating hookworm in the American South. The disease continued to ravage people in other warm climate zones around the globe. The medical treatment was simple and lent itself to basic public health demonstration and training about preventive measures, so the control of hookworm worldwide became the first major effort of the international health program. There was rapid success, which paved the way for broadening the program.

In the course of its existence, the International Health Division did battle against a host of diseases: malaria, tuberculosis, typhus, scarlet fever, influenza, dengue fever, yaws, rabies, schistosomiasis, undulant fever, oroya fever, syphilis, anemia, amoebic dysentery, and yellow fever. In all cases, much was learned about the epidemiology of the diseases and either a cure or an effective program of control was worked out. The most epic battle was against yellow fever, one that was waged for twenty-five years, taking its toll of laboratory and field workers through illness or death. For many years, the focus was on controlling the carrier of yellow fever in the field, based on the success of General W. C. Gorgas in controlling the disease in the building of the Panama Canal. On two occasions, all of the evidence suggested complete success, only to have the disease pop up again somewhere in the world with a different type of carrier. The breakthrough finally came with the development of a vaccine that protects against yellow fever as successfully as vaccines protect against smallpox and typhoid. The solution came in time for the Rockefeller Foundation to manufacture and distribute without cost 34 million doses of the vaccine to the Allied armed forces and civilian population in susceptible areas throughout World War II.

Equally impressive, though less spectacular, was the progress in building up the profession of public health in scores of countries through grants to schools, special training programs, fellowships, and the involvement of local personnel in field work. By the 1950s, the International Health Division had operated in ninety-three countries around the globe and spent more than $94 million.[15]

Junior's largest single gift during the 1920s was $28 million to establish the International Education Board, intended to be the international counterpart to the General Education Board. This came about when Wickliffe Rose was asked to leave the International Health Division of the Rockefeller Foundation in order to take charge of the GEB upon the retirement of Wallace Buttrick in 1923. Rose demurred at first—he enjoyed working in the international arena and wanted to continue doing so. Then he convinced Junior that a program supporting education on a global scale was required, given the devastation of the World War and the increasing need for the exchange of knowledge across international borders. In line with this reasoning, Rose said that such a program should be a "bird of passage"—expending both income and principal as quickly and effectively as possible. Rose might have thought that the "passage" should last about five years—he was due to retire himself in 1928 when he would become sixty-five. The simplest course might have been to create a new division within the Rockefeller Foundation, but Junior decided against attempting this. The due process of the Foundation board would require months of deliberation, and most of the initiative would have to come from him, a practice he had come to avoid as much as possible. Moreover, there was a personal touch in Rose's idea, so Junior decided to fund it himself. A new organization was necessary because the congressional charter of the GEB limited its work to the United States—so Rose became head of both the GEB and the IEB.

At the core of the welter of activity that followed was a coherent plan. Rose saw the natural sciences as fundamental: "Promotion of the development of science in a country is germinal. It affects the entire system of education and carries with it the remaking of a civilization." Important centers of scientific learning existed; the problem was to extend their knowledge and capability beyond relatively few countries so that the entire world could benefit. Rose's strategy was to identify scientists and institutions of great quality that would agree to be "centers of inspiration and training" for an "international migration of select students" who would agree to return to their home countries and serve as nuclei of scientific learning there.[16]

The IEB began making major grants to select institutions such as the University of Copenhagen with its Institute of Theoretical Physics headed by Niels Bohr; the mathematics faculties of the Universities of Göttingen and Paris; and the laboratories of botany, zoology, agriculture, and physiology at Cambridge. It funded new biology laboratories at a dozen European universities. Hundreds of fellowships were provided for graduate and postdoctoral students from a host of countries. An indication of how effective this was in one field, atomic physics, is suggested by the fact that these fellows included Enrico Fermi, Robert Oppenheimer, Isidor Rabi, and Werner Heisenberg.

Even though the GEB was carrying out major projects in the United States under Rose's guidance, he considered his home country to be a part of the international scene as far as the IEB was concerned. Among the projects financed in the United States were a new biological laboratory at Harvard and the most ambitious undertaking of all—$6 million to the California Institute of Technology for the new 200-inch reflecting telescope at Mount Palomar.

So much confidence did Junior have in Rose that he watched from a distance as his $28 million was rapidly spent—he never attempted to influence any of Rose's decisions.

In his personal giving overseas, Junior was careful to avoid duplicating anything that the various boards were doing as he took up projects that piqued his interest. His giving was not totally random—in fact, with a few notable exceptions he tended to concentrate in the areas of restoration, preservation, and antiquities. He showed a similar marked interest in his domestic projects (see Chapter 10).

Junior and Abby took a trip to France in 1923 and became aware of the run-down condition of some of the country's greatest edifices—the Palace of Versailles, court of the Sun King; Fontainebleau, the magnificent Renaissance chateau built by Francis I; and especially the war-damaged Rheims Cathedral, where all of France's kings had been crowned. All three were in a sad state, with weather damage continuing through leaky roofs. Efforts to halt the damage had lagged seriously because the French government was forced to accord a higher priority to other postwar reconstruction. Sensitive to Gallic pride, Junior's offer to help was a masterpiece of diplomacy. In his letter to Premier Raymond Poincaré he wrote:

I realize that this situation is only temporary and will eventually right itself as the people of France are able to turn from other and more pressing tasks and resume that scrupulous maintenance of their public monuments for which they have established so enviable a reputation. In the meantime, I should count it a privilege to be allowed to help toward that end, and shall be happy to contribute one million dollars, its expenditure to be entrusted to a small committee of Frenchmen and Americans.[17]

The premier promptly accepted the offer and appointed a committee headed by the French ambassador to the United States, Jean Jusserand. A year later, Junior again visited the monuments and was delighted to see how much progress had been made. He also could see how much more had to be done, so he decided on a second gift, this time of 40 million francs ($1,850,000), tendered in similar gracious language. Responding to the gift, Ambassador Jusserand wrote to him:

> Your new gift, so ample that it will allow all the chief work of reconstruction or defence against time to be perfected, is accepted with deep emotion. The whole of France now and later will bless the name of one who, unasked and simply for having seen the danger, came to the rescue at the hour when it was most needed and when we could do the least for ourselves.[18]

The work continued until, as Raymond Fosdick expressed it, "an incredible rebirth had taken place."[19] At Versailles twenty-five *acres* of roof had been replaced. The restoration extended to many of the priceless works of art within Versailles and Fontainebleau. From a battered hulk, the Rheims Cathedral was brought to its former glory as a Gothic masterpiece.

Junior's interest in ancient civilizations was stirred by a brilliant and charismatic scholar, Dr. James H. Breasted, who had become the first professor of Egyptology in the United States (in 1895 at the University of Chicago). Breasted had become a protégé of William Rainey Harper after studying Semitic languages under him at Yale. Through the Harper-Gates connection, Breasted received a $50,000 grant from Senior in 1902 for archaeological exploration and research in the Near East. No more was forthcoming, however, until after the World War when the political settlement opened new areas for field work in the Near East. Breasted had used his "exile," as he called it, to produce two best-selling textbooks, which made him the best-known American scholar of ancient civilizations. When he came to know Junior in 1919, Breasted's lifelong dream became a reality—the Oriental Institute at the University of Chicago. The beginning was modest, with Junior committing to only $10,000 a year, but this soon grew to $50,000 a year and then more, to the point that Junior contributed a total of nearly $1 million in support of the Oriental Institute over the span of a decade. This led to another $10 million in support from the various Rockefeller boards as the institute grew under Breasted's inspired leadership to become world-famous in its field.

Junior also supported specific projects, such as providing $275,000 in two grants for the excavation of the ancient fortified city of Megiddo in Palestine. The greatest project came to naught—a plan for rebuilding the Cairo Museum. Under Breasted's guidance, Junior became aware of the deteriorated condition of the existing museum, with priceless relics constantly in danger from Nile floods. He set aside $10 million to fund a new museum and offered this to King Fuad with his usual diplomatic letter. But Fuad was out of sorts and began raising objections to facets of the plan. News of the offer leaked and was received with jubilation by the Egyptian press and public opinion. Nevertheless, Fuad remained obstinate even after changes were made to please him, and after a year of fruitless negotiation Junior reluctantly abandoned the idea.

A bit gun-shy after this episode, Junior warned Breasted that there was not one chance in a thousand that he would take up the scholar's next suggestion—funding a new museum in Jerusalem where priceless objects from the days of Christ and before were gradually being destroyed by time and weather because there was no adequate facility to house them. But after investigating, Junior did provide $2 million for construction of the Palestine Archaeological Museum, standing at the northeast corner of the Old City of Jerusalem, and termed by Fosdick "one of the finest buildings in the Near East."[20]

Meanwhile, Junior had also taken an interest in the Greek and Roman civilizations, making small grants in support of the American Academy in Rome and the American School of Classical Studies in Athens. A major project developed when Abraham Flexner drew his attention to the fact that a long-cherished goal of the Greek government—excavating the Agora, the ancient center of Athenian political, commercial, and social life—had made no progress because of the lack of funding. The site was covered by centuries of debris and a modern-day slum. In desperation, the Greeks had asked the American School of Classical Studies to take over the project, but the school also had no success in raising money up to the time Junior entered the picture. In a series of grants over the period of a decade, he contributed nearly a million dollars for what turned out to be archaeological work of first-rank importance. So pleased with it was Junior that he wrote to Flexner in 1932: "It was you who brought this opportunity for cooperation in Athens to my attention. I shall always owe you a debt of gratitude for having done so."[21]

Junior was also fascinated by the ancient wonders and art of the Far East. During his visit to Peking in 1921, he was depressed by the sadly run-down condition of the Forbidden City. But restoration was not a priority for the war lords in control of sections of China, and no responsible local group existed to take on a major project. Junior contented himself by giving $5,000 to a committee for restoration of four ancient temples within the Forbidden City.

He did make an important contribution in Japan, however. In fact, the reason he did so was that so much Rockefeller support had gone to China (for the China Medical Board) that "it seemed desirable that something significant should be done for Japan."[22] The suggestion came to Junior from Colonel Arthur Woods, who told him of the complete destruction of the library of the Imperial University in Tokyo in the earthquake of 1923. Junior provided $1.5 million to rebuild the library, writing to the president of the university: "I quite realize that in time the Japanese people will themselves accomplish the complete restoration of their cities and institutions which have been destroyed. However, I shall regard it as a great privilege to hasten the day when your University, which stands among the foremost institutions of learning in the world, will again be provided with adequate library facilities."[23]

Junior was sowing some goodwill for himself, his family, *and* the United States in these overseas gifts. There were many more smaller ones, particularly to universities such as Lingnan University in southern China, Louvain University in Belgium, the University of Geneva in Switzerland, Acadia University in Canada. One other area of Junior's personal philanthropy overseas bears mentioning—his support of the League of Nations, an interesting one for a Republican who had opposed Woodrow Wilson. Over the years, Junior gave numerous small grants in support of League activities such as investigations into the narcotics trade and the traffic in women and children, various League conferences and publications, and so on. His major gift was $2 million to build and endow a library for the League with stacks for 1 million books. This library functioned throughout World War II and remains today a resource for documentation and research for the United States.

9

RELIGION, INDUSTRY,
AND SCIENCE

JUNIOR drew his moral values from his religious faith; at the same time, he believed the church itself was in dire need of reform if his vision of a world governed by cooperation and brotherhood was to be achieved. How far he had moved from the Baptist orthodoxy of his upbringing to become an apostle of modernism in religion can be seen in a speech he made on December 11, 1917, at a dinner of the Baptist Social Union. Entitled "The Christian Church—What of Its Future?" the speech was subsequently printed in the *Saturday Evening Post*. With the fervor of a missionary, Junior called for a reborn church:

It would pronounce ordinance, ritual, creed, all non-essential for admission into the Kingdom of God, or His Church.

A life, not a creed, would be its test; what a man does, not what he professes; what he is, not what he has.

Its object would be to promote applied religion, not theoretical religion. This would involve its sympathetic interest in all the great problems of human life; in social and moral problems, those of industry and business, the civic and educational problems; in all such as touch the life of man.

It would be the church of all people, . . . the church of the rich and the poor, the wise and the ignorant, the high and the low—a true democracy.

Its ministers would be trained not only in the seminary, but quite as much in life, with the supreme emphasis on life.[1]

With this speech, Junior placed himself firmly in the camp of the liberals whose challenge to the conservatives rocked the mainline Protestant denominations—Baptists, Methodists, Presbyterians, Episcopalians—during the first three decades of the century. It was only the latest in the long series of disputes, controversies, debates, and wars that seemingly had characterized Christianity since moments after the crucifixion of Christ. But it was highly relevant to its time and the issue of reconciling the findings of modern science and the dogmas of ancient religion. It was characterized by H. Richard Niebuhr as "the engagement of the Christian mind with the emergent scientific mind" in which "the conflict of religion with science disappears; dogma and sacraments lose in authority, but gain in richness, adaptability and strength to survive."[2] The liberals accepted the findings of science, including Darwinian evolution, as explanations of how God had ordered the universe. They accepted much of the biblical criticism of recent decades that stressed the humanity of Christ and showed that much of doctrine and ritual were man-made, the products of history rather than divinity. From this it was an easy step to see Protestant sectarianism as needlessly divisive and wasteful, and to adopt the goal of a simplified and unified Protestantism. On their side, the conservatives rejected all of this as heresy, and reaffirmed the word of Scripture as literal and pure truth.

Junior was far from alone in his views, and his conversion from orthodoxy was not quite as sudden and inexplicable as it seemed. It is likely that he waited until after his mother's death to proclaim his views in public, but the thinking that led to them had been going on for a long time. His father's views did not constrain Junior; although a faithful Baptist, Senior was also a more tolerant one than his wife, as evidenced by his giving across denominational lines since the time of the Civil War. The seeds of Junior's conversion to liberalism were probably sown at Brown under the influence of E. Benjamin Andrews. They were nurtured by the ministers of the Fifth Avenue Baptist Church. Though he had been disdainful of what he regarded as trendy sociology, W. H. P. Faunce was a decided liberal in theology. When he went off to take the presidency of Brown (succeeding Andrews), Faunce's successors in the Fifth Avenue pulpit, especially Cornelius Woelfkin, were also liberals.

Surprisingly, Frederick T. Gates was an important liberalizing influence. For all his social conservatism, antiunionism, and faith in free-market capitalism, Gates had become an extreme liberal, if not radical, when it came to issues of church polity and doctrine. His growing fascination with science and scientific method probably accounted for Gates' own conversion from a pious parish minister to a vehement advocate of evolution and "applied religion." In his autobiography, he wrote about how he had become convinced that

Christ had neither founded nor intended to found the Baptist church, nor any church; that neither he nor his disciples during his lifetime had baptized; that the communion was not conceived by Christ as a church ordinance, and that the whole Baptist fabric was built up on texts which had no authority, and on ecclesiastical conceptions wholly foreign to the mind of Christ.[3]

Gates was equally blunt in denouncing sectarianism. While some viewed the proliferation of Protestant sects as the logical culmination of the freedom and democratization of religion, Gates saw it as the result of narrow thinking and the hairsplitting of doctrine and ritual. He conveyed his views to Junior in a letter dated October 19, 1911:

Sectarianism is the curse of religion at home and abroad; a blight upon religion, whether viewed from an economic, intellectual or spiritual standpoint. The union of evangelistic denominations would solve more problems of human progress than any other single reform. It is needed abroad, but needed still more at home. The multitudes of men and the millions of money wasted on sectarianism in Protestant countries are sufficient, if these wastes could be saved by union, to evangelize the whole world, so far as the world is capable of being evangelized by human effort.

Junior plunged wholeheartedly into the first major opportunity after the war to pursue his ecumenical views—the Interchurch World Movement. Initiated by the Presbyterians, this was a massive and overambitious effort spurred by the unprecedented success of the wartime fund-raising campaign on behalf of the seven major service organizations, in which Junior had played a part. If the concerted effort by these seven groups, which included Catholic, Jewish, and Protestant charities, could yield $202 million, so the reasoning went, then the combined effort of the Protestant denominations should be able to do even better. Some thirty-one denominations joined the campaign to raise a third of a billion dollars for the stated purpose: "To present a unified program of Christian service and to unite the Protestant churches of North America in the performance of their common task."[4] Junior accepted an invitation to be on the hundred-member general committee for the movement, and overcame the last remnants of his shyness and reticence over speaking in public by participating in a cross-country tour on behalf of the effort, sleeping fourteen consecutive nights in a Pullman berth and making dozens of platform appearances.

Although $170 million was raised, the Interchurch World Movement turned out to be a fiasco as far as Protestant unity was concerned. In reality, there were thirty-one simultaneous fund-raising drives, with each denomination taking its share and leaving only $3 million for the central body, which had borne most of the costs and had run up obligations of nearly $13 million. Liquidation was the only answer, and Raymond Fosdick performed the legal work and served as receiver in bankruptcy. He said that "no adequate method of solving the problem could have been found" were it not for Junior's "generous support."[5]

Because no "unified program" or "common task" had survived the Interchurch World Movement, Junior and other wealthy lay leaders funded a low-key successor organization, the Institute of Social and Religious Research. The idea was to apply scientific methods to the study of religious institutions. In its fourteen-year existence, the institute studied church-oriented problems and increasingly moved toward broader sociological inquiries, including the famous *Middletown* study by Helen and Robert Lynd.

Meanwhile, Junior continued giving substantial sums in grants every year to a wide range of Protestant institutions, from a low total of $698,000 in 1922 to a high of $5,585,000 in 1929. Invariably, he was gently trying to push his ecumenical approach with the theological seminaries, missionary bodies, and Baptist organizations that were the recipients of his gifts. Since 1910 he had been contributing to the Federal Council of Churches, and in the 1920s his annual gifts ranged up to $50,000. He was a generous giver to the churches with which he had a personal tie (in Seal Harbor, Pocantico, Manhattan, and Cleveland). In 1925 he contributed over $1 million to the Union Theological Seminary on Morningside Heights, the bastion of Protestant Liberalism. In the same year, he donated $500,000 to the building fund for the Cathedral of St. John the Divine in Manhattan because he liked the ecumenical sentiments voiced by Episcopal Bishop William T. Manning. But Bishop Manning resisted Junior's suggestion that it might be appropriate to include a few representatives of "sister churches" on the governing body of the cathedral.

In 1922 the Fifth Avenue Baptist Church became the Park Avenue Baptist Church when the congregation moved into its new building. Its aging pastor, Cornelius Woelfkin, was ready to retire. The ideal man to succeed him, in the view of Junior and his friends in the dominant liberal faction of the congregation, was Harry Emerson Fosdick, who had emerged as one of the most prominent liberal theologians in the United States. Indeed, as early as 1912, when Woelfkin became pastor, Junior and others in the congregation had been interested in the young and then little-known Fosdick. Now, from his posts at Union Theological Seminary and "Old First" (the First Presbyterian Church, still standing at Fifth Avenue and 12th

Street, and at the time the most prestigious pulpit in New York City), Fosdick issued a steady stream of pamphlets and articles advancing the liberal position and attacking the fundamentalists. The struggle between factions reached a peak in 1922 when Fosdick delivered his most powerful sermon, "Shall the Fundamentalists Prevail?" This brought him into stormy confrontation with Presbyterian conservatives, including the most prominent one of all, William Jennings Bryan, with the result that Fosdick's ministry at "Old First" became untenable.[6]

It was at this opportune time that Junior broached the idea of his coming to the Fifth Avenue Baptist Church, but Fosdick declined on several grounds. The first was that he could not conduct a pastorate in a church where baptism by immersion was required for full membership. Junior said that should be changed. Then Fosdick said he did not want to be, in effect, a "private chaplain" to a relatively small group of wealthy people in a church in "the swankiest residential area of the city." Junior's answer was that another larger church could be built that would serve the entire metropolitan area. Somewhat astonished by this notion, Fosdick still declined. When Junior asked why, Fosdick said, "Because you are too wealthy, and I do not want to be known as the pastor of the richest man in the country." There was dead silence until Junior broke it with a witty comeback that made Fosdick roar with laughter. Junior said, "I like your frankness, but do you think more people will criticize you because of my wealth than will criticize me on account of your theology?"[7]

From Fosdick's account, one might assume that all of this occurred at a single luncheon session, but the wooing process actually extended over a period of several years. Nor did Junior toss out the idea that would lead to the building of Riverside Church merely as an inducement for Fosdick. He had been thinking about this for some time, and it appears that, with or without Fosdick, he would have gone ahead with his dream of building a great interdenominational Christian church designed to serve the entire community. It should also be noted that Junior was not acting unilaterally, although of course he did have great influence within the congregation. Opinion varied as in any congregation, but this one had a substantial liberal majority, not surprising for a church that had had a succession of liberal pastors for nearly a half a century.

At the same time, it is also true that Fosdick was very important to Junior's dream. If he had learned anything, it was that great ventures required great leadership—and Fosdick not only was a star, the most dynamic and talented minister of his time, but also one with all the right ideas as far as Junior was concerned. Like Mackenzie King, Fosdick was decidedly his own man and hard to get; but again like King, he was in the end attracted by Junior's sincerity and faith.

The building of Riverside took nearly six years and more than $10 million of Junior's money. There were other contributors among the well-to-do congregation, of course, and the sale of the Park Avenue building to the Presbyterians helped, but Junior bore by far the greatest share of the burden.

The result is an imposing edifice on the high ground of Morningside Heights, dominating the northern end of Manhattan Island. The conception is Gothic, the principal architects (Charles Collens, and Henry C. Pelton) having traveled to Europe to study the great cathedrals for inspiration. They drew the most from Chartres Cathedral, but Riverside is no mere replica. Its square Gothic tower, for example, is the only functional one in the world, providing twenty-four floors of space for offices and church activities. Use of the Gothic style has been criticized, but defenders hold that the blending of tradition with modernist theology is singularly appropriate. It is the interior that strikingly reflects the ecumenism of the founders. In addition to the figures of Christ and the traditional Christian saints, the iconography includes Confucius, Buddha, Muhammad, and Moses. There are physicians (Pasteur), teachers (Socrates), prophets (Savonarola), humanitarians (Booker T. Washington), missionaries (Augustine), artists (Bach), and reformers (Luther). There are scientists and philosophers as well—Darwin, Einstein, Kant, Hegel. The church has three great organs and one of the most notable carillons in the world, with seventy-four bells ranging in size from ten pounds to twenty tons.

It is a beautiful and inspiring place, in fact so overwhelmingly perfect in its physical dimensions that Fosdick began to worry about whether this particular house would ever become a home, a place imbued with vitality and life and meaning. He worked very hard to make it so, and clearly Riverside has been a great church under his ministry and those of his successors—Robert J. McCracken, Ernest T. Campbell, and William Sloane Coffin, Jr. It has been liberal not only in theology, but in every other sphere as well, a center of pro–civil rights and antiwar sentiment. It has been a powerful force for social service, not only in its own community, but in many other parts of the world.

There were to be more projects and policy decisions for Junior in the field of religion, but certainly none that surpassed Riverside as an expression of his belief in Protestant unity, both as a symbol and as a tangible effort to advance the cause. Indeed, the cause *was* advanced, with many examples of cooperation among the denominations that could be cited. Yet there also were some unwelcome and unantici- pated results. Somewhere along the way, one suspects Junior must have recognized that the goal was utopian, and even more so the larger vision of a peaceful and harmonious world for which he believed Protestant unity was a necessary condition. If so, he never commented on this, nor did he express any bitterness, cynicism, or regrets, as if to suggest he knew that all he could do was to make his best effort, and beyond that the world would have its way.

So liberal and modernist were the views of Junior, Fosdick, and the many like-minded people of their time that it is important to emphasize that it was all based on a deep and profound belief and faith in Christ and Christianity. Their approach to religion was certainly humanistic, but not secular. This point seems necessary in light of the irony that the liberal surge of the 1920s and thereafter probably was an important cause (doubtless among others) of the decline in churchgoing that became so marked by the 1950s, and then of the resurgence of fundamentalism in the 1970s and 1980s. If dogma and ritual and sacrament are downplayed as much as they were by the modernists, it is not a very large step to conclude that it is not essential to be in a particular place at a particular time—a church—to be a religious person. Junior's own children and most of his grandchildren were among the millions who gradually ceased to be churchgoers without regarding themselves as irreligious. They strayed from the church despite Junior's best efforts to keep them in the fold, including peppering them with a steady stream of homilies and moralisms.

The assessment of Junior's role by Fosdick's biographer, Robert Moats Miller, seems apt. He says that Junior's approach to religion can be criticized for its "rationalism, emphasis on bureaucratic values, and Taylorization of the Church," but adds, "John D. Rockefeller, Jr., was a considerate, generous, self-effacing, kind, loyal, courageous, and above all caring human being."[8]

Of all of Junior's other activities, the one that most resembled the quest for Protestant unity in having the earmarks of a crusade was his industrial relations program. In fact, he often explicitly related the two, as in a draft of a twenty-page article he wrote entitled "Why I Am a Church Member." In it he said:

In no field of human relationships is the spirit of brotherhood on which the church was founded more profoundly needed than in industrial relations. . . . The men in the Colorado coal fields who some years ago had been on strike for many months and in whose minds the most intense bitterness had grown up, responded to the genuine spirit of brotherhood when it was made manifest among them, while personal contact and the rubbing of elbows soon dispelled hatred and bitterness and established mutual confidence and good will.[9]

The significance of the work that Junior and Mackenzie King had started must be seen within the larger context of what scholars have termed "welfare capitalism," which was an effort by more enlightened employers to correct the harsh and exploitive labor practices of the late nineteenth century. There were some early examples—the model town built by George Pullman near Chicago and the profitsharing plan introduced by Proctor & Gamble in 1886. But the movement did not begin to spread until some powerful incentives appeared after the turn of the century—the exposés of the muckrakers, the force of public opinion, and growing labor unrest. Soon another incentive appeared in the "scientific management" approach of Frederick W. Taylor and the emerging school of industrial psychology, which held that how a worker was treated had a lot to do with how he performed. A man working eight hours a day could equal or exceed the production of one working twelve hours a day because he was healthier and felt better about his job and his company.

For many businessmen, welfare capitalism was attractive as a means of staving off further legislation, regulation, labor unrest, and unionism. But it had its higher motivations and positive aspects, and ranks as an important phase in the development of labor-management relations in the United States. The specific contribution of Junior and King was to introduce and legitimize the theme of employee representation. One scholar terms this "the most celebrated labor experiment of the decade," an idea that had "found a small group of advocates before World War I, above all, in John D. Rockefeller, Jr."[10] King had always warned against positioning the employee representation plan as antiunion in character. In his mind, the important thing was to create conditions in which collective bargaining was a reality. This could occur when a company had either an employee representation plan or a union or both. In fact, an employee representation plan could be seen as a step on the way to eventual unionism within a company, which is why the UMW International office supported the solution at Colorado Fuel and Iron. Some employers accepted representation plans in hope of preventing unionism; others, such as Judge Elbert Gary of United States Steel, rejected such plans because they thought they were "an opening wedge" to unionism and collective bargaining.[11]

Junior seems to have accepted King's viewpoint fully by the time he participated in a special industrial relations conference convened by President Wilson in late 1919. There were forty-five appointees in all, equally divided among representatives of labor, management, and the public. Junior was one of the fifteen public members. At one dramatic point, he made a stirring speech in defense of employee representation, likening it to "the principle upon which the democratic government of our country is founded." He said there was "sure to come a progressive evolution from single autocratic control, whether by capital, labor, or the state, to democratic cooperative control by all three." *Survey* magazine commented: "The incident closed with the labor group clapping, as he sat down, the man they had damned from one end of the country to the other five years ago."[12]

However, the labor delegates told Junior they could not vote for a resolution based on his speech because the form of representation would be determined by all of the parties instead of the workers themselves. Junior thereupon modified his position, but lost the support of the employer group who now thought his words were too prounion. Finally, the conference voted on a resolution introduced by Samuel Gompers, which read:

The right of wage earners to organize, without discrimination, to bargain collectively, to be represented by representatives of their own choosing in negotiations and adjustments with employers in respect to wages, hours of labor and relations and conditions of employment is recognized.[13]

Junior voted for this, as did all of the public and labor delegates, but the employer group voted against it. Under the rules, which required a majority of all three groups to pass a resolution, the conference was deadlocked.

With Mackenzie King gone, Junior forged on alone, seeking to convince union leaders, businessmen, and the general public that a middle way existed between the extremes of militant unionism and business paternalism. The operative phrase in his effort was "community of interest." He summarized his philosophy in a speech to the Babson Institute: "I believe that labor and capital are partners, not enemies, that their interests are common, not opposed, and that neither can attain the fullest measure of prosperity at the expense of the other, but only in association with the other."[14]

However, Junior found that his attention had to be directed mainly to employers, who generally were slow to make positive moves. When a coal mine strike occurred in Maryland, he came out quickly on the side of the strikers. He criticized Standard Oil of Indiana for adhering to the twelve-hour-day and seven-day-week policy at its Wyoming installations, publicly terming this policy "unnecessary, uneconomic and unjustifiable." He said it "should no longer be tolerated in industry, either from the point of view of public policy or of industrial efficiency." He supported an Interchurch World Movement study of the steel industry, which called for cutting the workday from twelve to eight hours. Junior called several times on Henry Frick and Judge Elbert Gary to argue the point, and found the two United States Steel leaders to be cordial but unyielding. According to Raymond Fosdick, Junior sold his U.S. Steel stock in protest.[15]

When Raymond Fosdick established his law firm and took on Junior as a client, he proposed a plan for making Junior's industrial relations interest more programmatic. The two men met with Mackenzie King at Seal Harbor in 1921 to discuss the idea, and King enthusiastically endorsed it. The program was set up in Fosdick's office with several staff aides working under a succession of business executives who had become advocates of the industrial relations approach—George J. Anderson of the New York Employing Printers Association, Arthur H. Young of International Harvester, and Clarence J. Hicks of Standard Oil of New Jersey. The value of the industrial relations work that Hicks had performed at the New Jersey company under enlightened management might be gauged by the fact that the company remained strike-free for the next forty years.

The work of these men was so successful that in 1926 Junior decided to formalize the effort by incorporating Industrial Relations Counselors (IRC) as a consulting firm, agreeing to subsidize its expenses until it earned sufficient income from clients. One of IRC's goals was to establish industrial relations as a recognized academic discipline by giving grants for fellowships, research centers, development of academic courses, and industrial relations libraries, first at Princeton and then at other universities. In all, Junior provided $1.4 million to IRC for these and other activities.

Within a few years, the industrial relations movement was well established, with some 317 companies introducing employee representation plans. It was a favorable time, with the economy booming and the emergence of a number of industrial statesmen who championed the movement, including Charles M. Schwab of Bethlehem

Steel, E. K. Hall of American Telephone and Telegraph, and Owen D. Young and Gerard Swope of General Electric. Judge Gary began uttering favorable comments, even though he had been virtually forced to accede to the eight-hour day by the intervention of President Harding and Secretary of Commerce Herbert Hoover.

In the course of his campaign for better treatment of workers, Junior repeatedly stressed the need for high ethical standards in business. When a case of unethical behavior developed close to home, he felt compelled to go to extraordinary lengths to combat it. The culprit was Colonel Robert W. Stewart, chairman of the Standard Oil Company of Indiana. Stewart and several other businessmen had set up a trading company that, in a complicated series of hidden transactions, contracted to purchase more than 33 million barrels of oil at $1.50 a barrel, then sold them (to Standard of Indiana among others) at $1.75 a barrel, thus gaining an illegal profit of more than $8 million. The deal, of couse, was secret, but Senator Thomas J. Walsh, chairman of the Senate Committee on Public Lands and Surveys, came across some clues from evidence compiled in investigations of the Teapot Dome scandal. It took several years for the story to emerge, and by 1925 Colonel Stewart was traveling on long trips abroad to dodge subpoenas.

As a major stockholder of Standard of Indiana, Junior had not been pleased with the company in any case because its concessions in labor policy always seemed begrudging in contrast to the New Jersey company. But he gave Stewart every fair chance to tell his side before cooperating with Senator Walsh to bring pressure to bear on Stewart to appear before the committee. Incensed by Stewart's recalcitrance, Junior himself testified before the committee in 1928 in support of the investigation, and appeared on a nationwide radio hookup to speak on the need for "high standards of business ethics." Stewart finally appeared twice before the committee and was subsequently indicted for perjury, but in two ensuing court cases he was acquitted on technical grounds, so Junior decided to wage a proxy fight with a limited objective—to oust Stewart, not take over the company himself.

Junior and his two sisters controlled less than 10 percent of the stock. In order to win the battle, they had to persuade many of the 58,000 shareholders that their cause was right. But Stewart as chairman was in a strong position; at one point he declared a 50 percent stock dividend to keep shareholders in line. Junior's strategy committee, which met daily during the struggle, included Fosdick, Ivy Lee, and

Charles Evans Hughes as special counsel. In the end, publicity won the battle—the American press was almost unanimous in support of Junior, giving the story strong coverage for weeks on end. When the votes were counted at the annual meeting on March 29, 1929, Junior's side won 57 percent, and Stewart was through.

National acclaim poured in for Junior after this victory for ethics in business,[16] but in that same year the death knell was sounded for "welfare capitalism" by the onset of the Great Depression. Industrial leaders like Schwab and Swope struggled for years into the Depression to continue enlightened policies, trying to avoid layoffs and parceling available work out among as many men as possible even when hard business facts dictated otherwise. But as labor historian David Brody points out, "welfare capitalism could not sustain the management-dominated system of labor relations. The failure was not inherent in its functioning in the 1920s, but sprang rather from an extraordinary downturn in the business cycle." Brody argues that it is mistaken to see welfare capitalism merely as "a passing and aberrant phase of American industrialism." It might well have taken deep root and grown were it not for the Depression—an interesting thought given the modern-day strength of Japan's economy under a much more highly developed form of welfare capitalism.[17]

However, industrial relations survived as a profession, a discipline, and a permanent feature of the American industrial scene. The vacuum created by the crisis allowed labor unions to gradually build up strength, aided by New Deal legislation. In fact, the specific type of employee representation plan forged by King and Junior in Colorado was outlawed by the Wagner Labor Relations Act of 1935. But IRC had long since established a reputation as a professional and neutral source of expertise, numbering unions among its clients as well as business firms, and it continued to function until World War II.

In pursuing his vision of a peaceful and harmonious world, Junior could feel satisfied that action was being taken in a number of areas—religion, industrial relations, education at home and abroad, public health, medical research. But other fields also required attention if overall progress were to be made toward the goal. Prominent among them was the need to find solutions to difficult social problems.

The Bureau of Social Hygiene (BSH), of course, was already at work in this field. As we have seen, the BSH since its inception in 1913 had been conducting research and giving grants on a small scale in such areas as public administration, police administration, prostitution, penology, and narcotics control. An obvious step was to expand what the BSH was doing, and Junior proceeded to do this by increasing his annual allocation to the organization, confident that it was in able hands with its staff of Colonel Arthur Woods, Dr. Katherine B. Davis, and several assistants.

There was another organization also working in social welfare, but with a decided difference. This was the Laura Spelman Rockefeller Memorial, which was referred to in the Rockefeller office simply as "the Memorial." The difference was that the Memorial, even though it had distributed some $9 million in grants in the years 1919 to 1922, was functioning more like an old-fashioned charity than a typical Rockefeller organization—meaning one that was research-oriented and dedicated to making significant advances in its field of operations instead of serving as a palliative. In their study of the Memorial, Martin and Joan Bulmer characterize its program during this period as "unremarkable" and having no connection "with either the advancement of learning nor with the analysis of the social problems with which it was concerned. Its objectives were charitable, with particular attention to women and children and a bias toward projects in New York City. . . . The programme was lacking in direction and was undistinguished."[18]

With its large endowment, the Memorial offered obvious potential if the right mission and leadership could be found. When Raymond Fosdick became available as senior adviser, Junior was able to turn his mind to the question of what to do about the Memorial. In late 1921, Fosdick began searching for the right person to head it, and after reviewing some forty applicants he found his man. When Junior approved the choice, another extraordinary individual entered the circle of his associates. He was Beardsley Ruml, an overweight, cigar-smoking, garrulous young man of twenty-seven with a brilliantly creative mind. He was to become noted later in life as the chairman of R. H. Macy (the large New York retailing firm), chairman of the New York District of the Federal Reserve, a New Deal adviser, and inventor of the "pay as you go" income tax plan. The son of an immigrant Czech laborer, Ruml was born in Cedar Rapids, Iowa, in 1894. His brilliance earned him scholarships to complete his education, at Dartmouth and then at the University of Chicago, where he completed his Ph.D. in psychology as a protégé of the chairman of the department, James Rowland Angell, who went on to become head of the Carnegie Corporation and then president of Yale. Ruml distinguished himself in Washington during the war in devising tests for personnel classification for the War Department, one of the first instances of applied social science in the United States.[19] He then went to work for Angell at the Carnegie Corporation. It was Angell and Abraham Flexner who brought Ruml to Fosdick's attention. When Ruml was offered the post of director of the Memorial, Angell wrote to him: "I hate to lose you from CC [the Carnegie Corporation], especially in the present drastic state of things, but if you must go, I am relieved to have so fine an opening come to you. Rockefeller salaries are apt to be low, but you will have all sorts of chances to give and make good."[20]

Angell was right on all counts—Ruml's salary was $7,500, and he had an extraordinary opportunity, which he proceeded to make the most of. There is almost no documentary record of the understanding that Ruml had with Junior and Fosdick when he took over the Memorial, but it seems clear that the mission was a bold one—to stimulate and upgrade the study, teaching, and application of the social sciences generally. The background is interesting—the idea had already been suggested of merging the Memorial with the Rockefeller Foundation, which then would have a program in the social sciences. But Frederick Gates, who had a low opinion of the social sciences, was adamantly against this, and he influenced several of the older trustees. As Fosdick noted, "by 1920 the Foundation had to all intents and purposes been captured by the doctors."[21] He and Junior decided that pressing the social sciences at that time would have been unnecessarily divisive for the Foundation. Ironically, Gates' opposition resulted in a much more dynamic program by the Memorial than probably would have occurred had a merger taken place.

Because of this, however, Ruml sensed that he had a limited period of time in which to work. There is no record that anyone characterized the Memorial as "a bird of passage," the phrase Wickliffe Rose used to describe the International Education Board, meaning spending both principal and income over a relatively few years in order to make a decisive impact and difference. But this is the direction that Ruml took, thinking in terms of a decade of activity or less.

Coming on board in May 1922, Ruml wrote a comprehensive "Memorandum" outlining the rules, policies, and strategy for the Memorial's program, a document termed by the Bulmers as "one of the most important statements about the financial support of the social sciences in the United States in the first half of the twentieth century."[22]

In a single paragraph, Ruml summarized the rationale for his intent to make a leap from charitable support of social welfare agencies to a program of upgrading basic social science:

An examination of the operations of organizations in the field of social welfare shows as a primary need the development of the social sciences and the production of a body of substantiated and widely accepted generalizations as to human capacities and motives and as to behavior of human beings as individuals and in groups. All who work toward the general end of social welfare are embarrassed by the lack of that knowledge which the social sciences must provide.

The goal clearly was social welfare. Repeatedly, Ruml stressed a humanistic approach, the need to solve problems, and the practical application of new knowledge. He thought that much was at stake, as he articulated in the following prescient passage:

It is becoming more and more clearly recognized that unless means are found of meeting the complex social problems that are so rapidly developing, our increasing control of physical forces may prove increasingly destructive of human values. To be sure, social knowledge is not a substitute for social righteousness; but unless we are ready to admit that the situation is utterly hopeless, we must believe that knowledge is a far greater aid to righteousness than is ignorance.

Ruml's thesis was that the only meaningful way in the long run to solve social problems and serve human welfare was through development of the social sciences, not charitable giving to ease the effects of social problems. He saw the social sciences as weak and much more difficult to develop than the physical sciences because the subject matter was only marginally susceptible to controlled experimentation. There was little rigor in the disciplines and almost no significant support for research. As a result, the social science research product from universities was "largely deductive and speculative, on the basis of second-hand observations, documentary evidence and anecdotal material." Ruml's goal was to see research steadily increasing in all of the relevant disciplines on the basis of field work, firsthand empirical observation, and the use of testing and survey data.

Ruml's paper was approved by the Memorial's trustees, including Junior, Fosdick, and Colonel Woods, in October 1922, and he was off and running. In less than six years, he expended $41 million in pursuit of his goals. He did this by making multiyear grants to some twenty-five universities and other institutions and the social science departments within them for enlarging social science faculties, giving large numbers of graduate fellowships, and sponsoring research. Five institutions accounted for more than half the total—the University of Chicago, Columbia, the Brookings Institution, the London School of Economics, and Harvard. Others that received substantial sums included Yale, Minnesota, Iowa State, Vanderbilt, North Carolina, California, Stanford, and Texas. Ruml also collaborated with a close friend and adviser, political scientist Charles Merriam of the University of Chicago, in creating and funding the Social Science Research Council. The disciplines Ruml listed in his original paper were "sociology, ethnology, anthropology, and psychology, and certain aspects of economics, history, political science and biology." But he added others as he went along, and he showed a marked interest in interdisciplinary studies.

There were also special projects from time to time. Encouragement of the public administration profession offers a case in point. This was a "certain aspect" of political science that interested both Ruml and Merriam deeply. At the time, few universities other than Columbia, Wisconsin, and California offered courses in public management or accounting. Only one organization had a full program with a reputation for excellence, the National Institute for Public Administration (the new name given the Bureau of Municipal Research in 1919) in New York City. In 1924, with the assistance of Fosdick, Ruml encouraged the NIPA to detach its educational arm (the Training School for Public Service) from its research apparatus. The Training School was moved *in toto* to Syracuse University, where it was reconstituted as the Maxwell School of Citizenship and Public Affairs, the first full-fledged school of public administration in the country. The director of the Training School, Dr. William Mosher, also moved to Syracuse to become the first director of the Maxwell School. Much of the research component was transferred to Washington, D.C., where it became one of the elements that formed the Brookings Institution. At Syracuse most of the funding was provided by a Boston patent lawyer and millionaire, George Maxwell; at Brookings it came from Ruml and the Memorial.

Progress in the social sciences, of course, is notoriously difficult to measure, but that notable advances were made in the 1920s cannot be doubted. Chancellor Robert M. Hutchins of the University of Chicago later remarked about Ruml's tenure: "The Laura Spelman Rockefeller Memorial in its brief but brilliant career did more than any other agency to promote the social sciences in the United States."[23]

Although Ruml never made the mistake of seeing the social sciences as totally neutral and value-free, he did emphasize the need for as much objectivity as possible and avoidance of the political partisanship and controversy that frequently had plagued the field. Yet he was working for a man who wanted to see difficult and controversial social problems attacked. It was the existence of the Bureau of Social Hygiene that made it possible for Ruml to stick to his pure path. He spoke directly to the division of labor in a memorandum to Fosdick on September 29, 1925:

> My feeling has been that the Bureau of Social Hygiene should be used as the instrument for our participation in most of these programs for social reform in contradistinction to the scientific and educational program of the Memorial. It seems to me that the Bureau might be an aggressive instrument in these matters, and be quite prepared to face, as it has in the past, such public criticism and public ridicule as might follow.

With this understanding in place, Ruml continued to have a free hand, with no interference from Junior. Such coordination as was needed was made easy by the fact that Colonel Woods served as president of both the Memorial and the BSH, and both Woods and Ruml were members of Junior's Advisory Committee.

During the 1920s, Junior's annual allocations to the BSH often exceeded $400,000. Some of the money went for the research of its own small staff, but most was given for research, publications, and educational work by other organizations concerned with the problems of interest to the BSH, which might be lumped together under the heading of "crime and sex." The most important and innovative work of the BSH in the 1920s was in the areas of human sexual behavior and birth control, two highly controversial subjects. They were of primary interest to the general secretary of the organization, Katherine B. Davis, who had pursued her own research on sexual behavior among women, culminating in the publication of *Factors in the Sex Lives of Twenty-two Hundred Women* in 1919. Her interest was shared by Junior, Fosdick, and Woods.

As we have seen, Junior first became aware of the potential problems associated with population growth and distribution when he listened to the prescient lectures of E. Benjamin Andrews at Brown University in 1897. Then he began to be concerned about problems associated with human sexual behavior during his experience on the White Slave Grand Jury and its aftermath.

Not until after the war did the BSH begin to expand its support of studies of population and sexual behavior. In 1920 it made a five-year grant to the National Research Council to establish and operate a Committee for Research in Problems of Sex. For many years afterward, this committee spurred the development in American universities of endocrinology, the study of the body's hormonal regulatory system, a prerequisite to understanding human sexual physiology.

About this time, the issue of birth control was coming to the fore, pressed by a number of new groups. Junior's attention was drawn to the movement by Raymond Fosdick, who had served briefly as the general counsel of the American Birth Control League. In a letter to Junior on June 13, 1924, Fosdick noted that a number of requests "in connection with projects dealing with birth control" had come before both the BSH and the Advisory Committee. Dr. Davis had studied the field in depth and had advised support. Fosdick agreed with her recommendation, concluding:

Personally, I believe that the problem of population constitutes one of the great perils of the future and if something is not done along the lines that these people are suggesting, we shall hand down to our children a world in which the scramble for food and the means of subsistence will be far more bitter than anything we have at present.

Junior immediately authorized grants to Margaret Sanger's Birth Control Clinical Research Bureau and Dr. Robert L. Dickinson's newly formed National Committee on Maternal Health. Numerous grants to a variety of organizations followed in the succeeding years, including many in support of Margaret Sanger's activities. Militant feminist, suffragette, organizer for the International Workers of the World during the famous Lawrence textile strike of 1912, Sanger would seem an unlikely candidate for the philanthropic largesse of the Rockefellers. But Junior and his colleagues were impressed with the lady and her ideas and convinced that she represented a positive force in a field of fundamental importance. An interesting note is that birth control was a bit too controversial for Junior to associate himself with publicly. The grants of the BSH and Junior's personal grants to Sanger and others were made anonymously. The "heat" was taken by those working in the field, like Margaret Sanger, who found herself in jail on several occasions. Nevertheless, the financial support was crucial, and this activity marked the beginning of more than half a century of involvement of the Rockefeller family in population studies and related issues. In all these, Junior's oldest son, John 3rd, took the prominent role.[24]

The BSH lasted into the 1930s, but the Memorial ceased to exist in 1928. The specific reason was a major reorganization centered on the Rockefeller Foundation. There are intimations that discontent with Ruml was a cause; Fosdick in particular seems to have become concerned about Ruml's energy and "lavish" spending.[25] Certainly, it is true that Ruml cut quite a distinctive figure in the staid Rockefeller setting, but the fact is that he participated in planning the reorganization and supported it.

Moreover, Ruml was able to make one last grant, his largest one, $10 million to endow a newly created organization, the Spelman Fund. The specialized mission of the Spelman Fund was to continue promotion of the field of public administration, which it proceeded to do with zest, ultimately spending not only its $10 million, but also another $3 million that later came to it from the Rockefeller Foundation. The fund operated under the guidance of Ruml, Merriam, and Guy Moffet, and involved such key figures in the field as Herbert Emmerich, Louis Brownlow, and Luther Gulick. Among its notable contributions was creation of the famous "1313" of public administration lore—the Public Administration Clearing House at 1313 East 60th Street in Chicago, associated with the University of Chicago. This became the headquarters for twenty-one professional associations in subfields of public administration, covering everything from city managers to personnel to public works. Another significant achievement was support of President Roosevelt's Committee on Administrative Management (the Brownlow Committee), whose recommendations brought about important changes in administration of the Executive Branch, including, for better or worse, the White House staff system.

Much more was afoot in the reorganization of 1928 than anyone's possible disenchantment with Ruml. As noted, there were intimations of a reorganization as early as 1920, before Ruml took over the Memorial. The reorganization had two major objectives. One was to build more rationality and symmetry into Rockefeller philanthropy as a whole by consolidating duplicating and overlapping functions into one organization. The second was to break the near-monopoly of medicine and public health in the Foundation's program and turn it into the more comprehensive organization that had been originally envisioned. As long as other Rockefeller boards functioned in such fields as education and social science, the Foundation's professional staff and older trustees had a reasonable basis for opposing any broadening of the program. This was the problem Fosdick was referring to when he wrote of the Foundation being "captured" by the doctors. There may well have been another agenda item in the minds of Junior and Fosdick—to gradually increase the power and prominence of Fosdick.

Active discussion of reorganization possibilities began in 1925 among the attendees of the Monday luncheon group and between Junior and Fosdick. That Junior discussed the matter with his father is evident in a letter he received the following year in which Senior commented: "If the whole thing were to be done today, you have rightly understood me as feeling that it should be done and could be done through a single organization."[26]

The reorganization planning was mainly the work of Fosdick, strongly supported by Junior and Woods.[27] With the retirement of Gates, the principal opponent was Wickliffe Rose. The International Health Division had flourished during the years that he had been its director. When he resigned the post in 1923 to become president of both the General Education Board (GEB) and the new International Education Board (IEB), Rose remained a Foundation trustee, where he worked hard to see to it that public health and medical education continued as the major programs of the Foundation. As the president of two organizations that conceivably could be subsumed within the Foundation in a reorganization scheme, Rose opposed the tendency toward consolidation. Though not nearly as hidebound as Gates on the subject, Rose had serious misgivings about Ruml's activities in the social sciences. He was a firm advocate of the "hard" sciences, believing that the accumulation of knowledge in mathematics, physics, and chemistry would, in due time, permeate all other areas of man's knowledge and endeavor to good effect.

When, late in 1925, Fosdick reported to Junior that there was sentiment among members of the Monday luncheon group to form an "interboard committee" to study ways to improve the operations of the institutions, with an eye to possible reorganization planning, Junior responded strongly in the affirmative:

As you know, this whole matter has long been very much on my mind. . . . It is not necessary for me to tell you that there is nothing sacred or inviolate about any type of organization. Machinery and personnel are merely the instruments by which objectives are reached, and unless we keep ourselves clear-eyed and fresh and keep the machinery elastic, we run the risk of dry rot.

If these Foundations are going to fulfill the high purposes that the Founder had in mind for them—indeed, if they are to escape the decay which seems eventually to attach itself to all human institutions—they must be subjected to constant, critical scrutiny, and their directors and officers must be ready at all times to redefine their aims, reorganize their technique, and scrap existing machinery in favor of something that is better.

I hope you will take occasion to say at the next meeting of the Monday luncheon group how profoundly interested I am in this whole question, and with what keenness and confidence I shall follow the work of the new committees to be set up.[28]

The Interboard Committee on Reorganization was established, and Fosdick began to press his views, encountering the opposition of Rose. However, Rose was due to retire in 1928 when he would become sixty-five years old. In 1927, Fosdick reported on progress to Junior:

I confess that I am not very happy about the situation in the Foundations. As far as our reorganization plans are concerned, things are at a stand-still, pending the selection of a successor for Rose. It is more or less of a vicious circle. We can not very well go ahead with our plans until we know who is going to succeed Rose, and we can not easily pick a successor to Rose without knowing something about what the new organization is to be.[29]

The more difficult problem was that the GEB, with its federal charter, could not be taken over by the Foundation without going to Congress for permission. The solution was to adopt some of its programs and staff, leaving the GEB in existence with a narrower focus on its original mandate in education. When Rose retired in 1928, the English-born Trevor Arnett, an expert on college finance and a University of Chicago graduate, replaced him. Arnett had been a key staff member of the GEB for a decade. The IEB had expended almost all of its money, so its programs and small staff were assimilated and the organization was soon liquidated. Similarly, the program and some of the staff members of the Memorial were taken by the Foundation and the Memorial ceased to exist as an organization.

At the same time, the China Medical Board was taken out of the Foundation and reconstituted with a separate board. Ownership of the lands and buildings in Peking were transferred to it, and it was given an endowment fund of $12 million by the Foundation. Although it was recognized at the time that the Foundation would have to provide financial support of the China program in the future, the hope—a vain one—was that separate status might help in attracting other sources of support, including Chinese sources. Another reason for the separation was that the China Medical Board, like the Spelman Fund, was regarded as a specialized and operational program that did not fit within Fosdick's organizing principle for the Foundation, which was that all Rockefeller philanthropies concerned with "the advance of human knowledge" should be gathered within the Foundation and operational programs kept out of it.[30]

The logic was somewhat strained inasmuch as the Rockefeller Institute for Medical Research was never considered as a candidate for merger—and it could hardly be said that the institute was *not* concerned with "the advance of human knowledge." However, it *was* too big and too well established—and perhaps too operational in a sense—to be taken over.

Fosdick's design organized the Foundation into five divisions—international health, medical sciences, natural sciences, social sciences, and humanities. Only the International Health Division continued as before, under Dr. Frederick F. Russell, who had succeeded Rose in 1923. One of his associates in international health, Dr. Richard M. Pearce, became the head of the new Medical Sciences Division, which took over former GEB and IEB programs. The Social Sciences Division, of course, continued the work of the Memorial, under Harvard economist Edmund E. Day, who had been associated with Ruml. The smallest and weakest division was humanities, under classicist Edward Capps. For years it did not venture much beyond the classical and antiquarian fields that had so fascinated Junior overseas.

The arrangement for the Natural Sciences Division, which also took over GEB and IEB activities, was a special one. It was headed by Max Mason, a mathematical physicist who left the presidency of the University of Chicago to join the Foundation. The reason was that he was slated to become president of the Foundation in 1929 when George Vincent retired.

There was new blood on the board as well as the staff. A number of vacancies had been accumulated with the death of Wallace Buttrick and the retirements of Rose, John G. Agar, Martin Ryerson, Harry Pratt Judson, and Charles Evans Hughes. Other retirements were imminent—Vincent, Simon Flexner, Julius Rosenwald, Frederick Strauss. Aside from Arnett and Mason, new board members included Owen D. Young, chairman of General Electric; David L. Edsall, dean of the Harvard Medical School; Ernest M. Hopkins, president of

Dartmouth; James R. Angell, president of Yale; Charles P. Howland, prominent New York attorney; Anson Phelps Stokes, clergyman and educator, an active person in black education as president of the Phelps Stokes Fund; George H. Whipple, prominent bacteriologist and pathologist; and H. Spencer Hadley, former trust-busting district attorney in Missouri and president of Washington University in St. Louis.[31] Another addition was Jerome Greene, coming back to the board not as a Rockefeller minion, but as a successful man in his own right in investment banking and as a leader in private-sector international organizations.

The reorganization of 1928, extensive as it was, marked only a beginning. Old habits were hard to break—public health and medicine still dominated. As president, Max Mason was most at home with the natural sciences and tended to favor them to the neglect of the social sciences and humanities. The organization of the Foundation into five broad branches of human knowledge, reminiscent of a university, began to introduce some rigidity and make it difficult for the board to cope with the experts representing the divisions. All of this led to another major review, in 1934, which turned out to be the final step to Fosdick's ascendancy to the presidency of the Foundation in 1936.

10

◆

ON THE SIDE OF PLEASURE

ALL OF JUNIOR'S ACTIVITIES in the 1920s discussed up to now would seem to have been enough to keep any person fully occupied. But for him, there was much more. In this same decade he began major commitments in conservation, historical restoration, and the arts and humanities.

A love of nature, a reverence for history, and a sense of aesthetics were all congruent with his vision of a peaceful and harmonious world. Yet there was a difference—Junior found deep personal satisfaction and pleasure in these pursuits, whereas his other fields, such as religion, industrial relations, and the efforts to solve social problems were suffused with morality and civic duty. There was the element of tangibility, too, which seemed to become increasingly important to Junior. One could see and touch and smell a new park, a restored building, a work of art, a new museum.

When his idealistic vision of the world was destroyed by the harsh reality of the Great Depression, Junior did not abruptly abandon any of the efforts he had started. But he attempted no great new projects, and he seemed to lose himself more and more in his growing passion for nature, history, and art. Long after he had given up trying to solve the problems of the world, he continued to find satisfaction in these fields.

Shortly before the stock market crash of 1929, Junior made a commitment to a new project that combined civic betterment with aid to the arts. By comparison to many of his other activities, it seemed at first to be a relatively minor commitment. But the strange circumstances of the Depression converted it into the building of Rockefeller Center. Very shortly, as the full force of the Depression hit, this became a massive financial burden. But serendipity was at work. The building of Rockefeller Center turned out to be a positive economic factor amid the gloom of the Depression, a giant step forward for New York City, a remarkable innovation in urban development, a source of pleasure for Junior, and ultimately, in an entirely unexpected way, the salvation of the Rockefeller family fortune.

Enjoyment of nature was part of growing up for Junior, learned from his father and experienced in family trips out West and in the life he and his family led in the beautiful Westchester County countryside around the Pocantico estate. Raymond Fosdick records Junior's reminiscences:

> I think perhaps I have always had an eye for nature. I remember as a boy loving sunsets. I remember the sunsets from my bedroom window at 4 West Fifty-fourth Street, which looked west. I remember what the sycamore trees looked like and the maple trees. Every time I ride through the woods today, the smell of the trees—particularly when a branch has just been cut and the sap is running—takes me back to my early impressions in the woods.[1]

Nevertheless, it was not until after the World War, when Junior's personal fortune increased so dramatically, that he entered the field of conservation in a major way. Very shortly, he became a towering figure, the greatest ally the National Park Service ever had. And yet his assistance in many national park projects was but a portion of his conservation work. He was uniquely equipped to play this role, with his keen judgment, his ability to act quickly and decisively, his great flexibility in finding ways to help. He could draw on his own funds and often on the appropriate sections of the Rockefeller institutions. When the wheels of government turned slowly, he could buy a valuable piece of land that might otherwise be lost forever to timber or other development interests and add to it and hold on to it, in one case for several decades, until the government finally was able to accept it.

It would take a good-sized book to fully tell the story of Junior's involvement in conservation. Many of the projects were extremely complicated; no two were alike. Invariably, one had to work with private groups, local citizens, and some combination of federal, state, and local authorities. Some of the projects Junior adopted had beginnings early in the century. Others, begun in the 1920s, did not reach fruition for many years. But the joy he felt in helping to preserve the beauty of nature for future generations overrode all of the inevitable frustrations; he was infinitely patient and tireless in pursuing that goal.

Junior's first major involvement came close to home—his summer home at Seal Harbor on Mount Desert Island in Maine. This was becoming a popular summer spot by the time Junior purchased his property there early in the century. Some longtime summer residents, led by Charles Eliot of Harvard and conservationist George B. Dorr, had already become concerned about overdevelopment and were buying up property to preserve as much of the natural beauty of the island as possible. Junior became an important contributor to the association they had formed, which had the goal of donating the land to the federal government in return for its being designated a national park. Every year the group petitioned the Department of the Interior to act on this proposal. Finally, in 1916 when some 5,000 acres had been accumulated, President Wilson acted under the executive authority provided by the Antiquities Act of 1906. His executive proclamation accepted the land and designated it "Sieur de Monts National Monument." This was a first step, preserving the land and allowing time to get the bill through Congress to make it a national park. In 1919 Wilson signed the bill converting the national monument into Lafayette National Park, with George Dorr as the first superintendent. It was the first national park east of the Mississippi River and the only one ever to be created entirely by private donations.

At this point, Junior went to work in earnest. Over the following decade he purchased and donated more than 11,000 additional acres, paid for surveys to position park buildings, and built a whole network of carriage trails to provide access to the most beautiful sights in what was soon rechristened as Acadia National Park. The value of his contributions exceeded $3 million.[2]

Road-building became a passion for Junior, as it had been for his father in Pocantico. He personally designed and supervised much of the construction of the carriage trails, which were so well built that they served as an excellent base for roads when, inevitably, the automobile had to be admitted to the park.

In several ways, this first major involvement of Junior's set the pattern for his subsequent efforts. First was the remarkable exercise of public-private cooperation in conserving areas of natural beauty, of which Acadia Park was one of the first great examples. The National Park Service was always to be in a relatively weak position in securing congressional authorizations and appropriations; it very much needed private-sector support, and Junior became by far the leader in providing it. Also, the Acadia experience clearly indicates that Junior's motivation went much deeper than a mere desire to protect the beauty of an area in which his secluded summer residence was located, as was true of others involved in the effort, such as Charles Eliot, who had become the first president of the National Conservation Association in 1909. Such a narrow purpose would not have accounted for Junior's devotion of time and money to nurture Acadia along as nearly as possible to his vision of an ideal park long after the area had become protected by law. Nor would it account for his simultaneous involvement in dozens of other conservation projects all over the nation.

Junior's devotion to conservation is another indication of how much his attitudes were in consonance with the Progressive era; the subject was prominent on the Progressive agenda ever since President Roosevelt's White House Conference on Conservation in 1901. The idea was to overcome rampant waste, inefficiency, and the squandering of natural resources by application of careful planning, scientific methods, and efficient management.[3]

Then, as now, the conservation movement covered many shades of opinion. The mainstream, led by Theodore Roosevelt and Gifford Pinchot, was concerned with protecting virgin lands from wasteful exploitation through a "best use" policy, frequently requiring a delicate balancing of interests. Within this broad middle ground, opinion ranged on a spectrum from highly utilitarian to highly protectionist stances. Even so, mainstream opinion often was wrongly condemned as a "no use" policy by those seeking riches through tourist development or in securing timber, water, mineral, or grazing rights. Over on the other side, the mainstream view was opposed by purists such as John Muir, who wanted to preserve virgin lands in a pristine state, meaning not only no economic use whatsoever, but often little or no opportunity for public enjoyment of areas of natural beauty. Junior clearly belonged to the "best use" school. In aiding the development of tourist facilities and carriage roads at Acadia, his purpose was to bring the public in to enjoy the park under proper conditions that would preserve its beauty, not to create a protected haven for the exclusive use of wealthy summer residents. This concern for public participation and enjoyment was a prominent feature of all his conservation activities.

The creation of Acadia National Park went smoothly; in contrast, the fruition of another of Junior's major efforts, as one observer described it, "may have been the most difficult in conservation history."[4] The project was the expansion and completion of Grand Teton National Park in northwest Wyoming, just to the south of Yellowstone Park. Today many observers believe that the Grand Teton Park is the "gem" of the National Park Service—but achieving it in its present form involved an incredible saga of delay, obstructionism, petty self-interest, bureaucratic rivalry, and political ambition.

In the company of his three oldest sons, Junior had his first good look at the Grand Tetons during a summer trip in 1924. Like many another tourist, he was awed by the saw-toothed mountains, with some of the peaks nearing 14,000 feet, and felt that it was the most strikingly beautiful range he had ever seen. It was obvious to him, as it had been to other visitors since the late nineteenth century, that the mountains and the Jackson Hole Valley to the east should become a national park. As early as 1883, General Philip Sheridan of Civil War fame brought President Chester Arthur to see the Grand Tetons and proposed that the region be added to Yellowstone Park. Later proponents urged that the mountains and the valley be constituted as a separate park.

Always, the valley was considered a crucial part of any prospective park. Bisected by the Snake River, it forms a sort of natural arena, providing access to the area and by far the best view of the mountains. Between the river and the mountains, the valley includes a number of exquisite piedmont lakes, rolling grassland, and scattered stands of virgin forest. To the east of the Snake River, the familiar western sagebrush takes over as the land begins to rise toward the Absaroka Mountain Range. The valley also serves as a natural sanctuary and grazing ground for migratory elk and other wildlife of the entire Yellowstone area.

The Department of the Interior had legal jurisdiction over the national parks, while the U.S. Forest Service belonged to the Department of Agriculture. The groundswell of interest in conservation generated by the Progressive era strengthened Interior's role by raising the parks function to agency status in the National Park Service Act of 1916. The first director of the new service, Stephen Mather, took an immediate interest in the Grand Tetons, as did his new assistant, twenty-five-year-old Horace Albright, who was assigned to research the Jackson Hole–Grand Teton area with an eye to possible park status. He saw immediately that the valley was vulnerable to various forms of development that could ruin it for park purposes. He was appalled by what the Bureau of Reclamation had already done in damming up Jackson Lake, the largest one in the valley, converting it into a reservoir. Working with conservation-minded residents and politicians in the region, Albright helped fashion a bill to incorporate the mountains and the valley into Yellowstone Park. It nearly passed Congress in 1918, but was killed at the last minute by the intervention of Idaho Senator John Nugent on behalf of a handful of sheep ranchers in his state.

The opportunity was gone: interest waned and support was lacking when another attempt was made to pass the bill in 1919. The Forest Service had not opposed the 1918 effort, but quietly lobbied against the bill in 1919.[5] The Park Service and the Forest Service share a basic interest in conservation, but for different purposes that often put the two agencies at odds. The "best use" for the Park Service is for recreation and tourism; once it takes jurisdiction of land, economic development is ruled out. The mission of the Forest Service includes the judicious assigning of timber, water, mineral, and grazing rights. It had jurisdiction over some 600,000 acres of timberland located to the north, east, and south of Jackson Hole Valley, as well as some portions of the valley itself. The Park Service's plan for a Grand Teton park would require the inclusion of substantial portions of lands under Forest Service control; this provided the basis for an enduring bureaucratic struggle.

The Forest Service can be a formidable bureaucratic foe because it usually can muster vociferous and politically persuasive allies among those interested in economic development. In fact, it was only by accident that the Park Service was able to compete at all once the 1918 bill failed. At the point when it was assumed that the bill would pass, President Wilson issued an executive order barring the Forest Service holdings in the Grand Teton area from any development or disposal without Park Service concurrence. Although the bill failed, the executive order stayed in effect, thus giving the Park Service a kind of "veto power" over any development plans. But it was a tenuous power; the executive order could be rescinded at any time by the president.

In 1919 Horace Albright became superintendent of Yellowstone, and proceeded to make the saving of the Grand Teton–Jackson Hole area the guiding mission of his life. He quietly sought allies in the area, and in 1923 a notable meeting occurred in a log cabin owned by Maud Noble, an avid supporter of the proposed park. The group agreed that the Grand Tetons and the Jackson Hole Valley should be constituted as a national park separate from Yellowstone. The group's best idea for achieving the goal was to persuade wealthy individuals to buy up as much privately held land in the area as possible and then hold it until it was politically feasible to create the park. They would then turn the land over to the government and be recompensed for it. Accordingly, two members of the group journeyed to New York to call on the Whitneys, the Morgans, and the Vanderbilts. They were rebuffed, and Albright reluctantly gave up on this scheme as impractical.

One is immediately struck by the failure to call on the Rockefellers for support. There was a very good reason. By this time, Junior had emerged as the leading patron of the Park Service, and its leadership was quite perceptive in understanding his personality and method of operating. He liked to make up his own mind; he did not want to be pushed or cajoled. Therefore, the strict policy was to treat Junior circumspectly, to let nature take its course, and to avoid importuning him. It was not that the Park Service refrained from informing Junior of needs or opportunities from time to time, but a request would be made only once and never with any show of aggressive salesmanship. Thus, Albright had to restrain his missionary zeal for the Grand Teton park idea when Junior made his next trip to the area in 1926, accompanied by his wife, Abby, and their three youngest sons. Fosdick quotes Albright as recalling that he had been specifically warned by his superiors not to discuss any projects with Junior, but to let him enjoy his trip "as a regular visitor."[6]

One can imagine Albright's frustration. He had made countless speeches and escorted scores of influential visitors through the Jackson Hole Valley in an effort to sell the park idea, but now he could not mention the subject. However, Abby helped him out. Albright could see that the beauty of the area was working its magic on her. On the main road through the valley, the group encountered the local eyesores—gas stations, a dance hall, flimsy tourist traps, and abandoned farm buildings. Abby was agitated by this, and Albright's responses to her stream of questions gradually described the kind of park that the group that met in Maud Noble's cabin wanted to see created. Junior did not react to this and Albright dutifully did not press the idea.

However, a letter from Junior soon arrived asking if Albright could send him a map detailed enough to show the location of the offensive buildings, together with an estimate of the cost of acquiring the land. This was the response that Albright and his superiors were hoping their low-key approach would bring. But Albright was not certain whether Junior was interested only in clearing away the eyesores or in some larger purchase. What Junior had done (and was still doing) for the Acadia Park had become a legend in Park Service circles. Would he be willing to do this again, but for a project that ideally required the purchase of more than three times as much land? Albright did not have the temerity to talk about the entire valley, but he took a chance by outlining on a map the piedmont area lying between the west bank of the Snake River and the Grand Tetons—some 14,000 acres.

Map in hand, Albright showed up in New York to see Junior, fervently hoping that he was not suggesting too much. On the contrary, he found he had not asked enough. Junior was disappointed—he wanted maps showing *all* the privately held land in the valley, *both* west and east of the Snake River. He explained that he could not enter such a project with halfway measures, that he was interested only in the "ideal" project that Albright's group had in mind.[7] The euphoric Albright learned that Junior not only wanted to buy all the private land in the valley, but also intended to give it to the federal government for the proposed park with no thought of recompense, just as he had with Acadia.

Junior assigned his trusted executive Colonel Arthur Woods to the operation. Based on Albright's information, the goal was to acquire in excess of 30,000 acres at a projected cost of $1.5 million. To avoid driving up prices, it was clear that the Rockefeller name should be kept out of the project as long as possible. In 1927 Woods incorporated the Snake River Land Company in Salt Lake City under Utah law. His two chief assistants were New York attorney Vanderbilt Webb and Kenneth Chorley, a naturalized American of English birth who had joined Junior's staff to assist on conservation projects. Within two years, most of the desired land purchases had been made.

It was fortunate that this was the case because at the same time events were moving rapidly to establish a park that did *not* include the Jackson Hole Valley. The bill, introduced by Senator John Kendrick of Wyoming, quickly passed and was signed into law by President Coolidge in February 1929. It had been warmly supported by the Forest Service and development interests because the new Grand Teton National Park did not include any significant portion of Forest Service lands and left the valley wide open for development. The Park Service leaders reluctantly had concluded that they could not be in the position of opposing the bill, that half a loaf was better than none—for the present at least. In the words of historian Robert Righter, the result "was only half a park . . . a Pyrrhic victory," a park that was not even one-twentieth the size of Yellowstone.[8] Because of their ruggedness, the mountains were never vulnerable to despoliation, but the valley was. The Park Service veto over development of Forest Service land and Junior's ownership of private land could forestall the worst of it, but for how long? Unless the park was expanded to include the valley, sooner or later there would be development along the shores of the lakes and the Snake River and alongside the roads through the area.

The forces for and against the enlargement of Grand Teton National Park were not evenly balanced. Supporters included a relatively small number of residents who were conservationists and an even smaller number with the foresight to realize that the most promising economic future for the valley lay in recreation and tourism. A number of dude ranches had sprung up, and the owners generally favored anything that would not ruin the valley. Few political figures were in favor, with the notable exception of Wyoming Governor Leslie Miller, whose defeat in 1938 probably was due to his support of park expansion.

Prominent among the opponents were timber and cattle interests, even though the valley land was not especially good for either purpose. Quite apart from those with specific development interests, there was the widespread bias in the region in favor of the "multiuse" Forest Service and against what was regarded as the "no-use" Park Service. More than this, there was a kind of rugged individualism prevalent among westerners. Many resented any outside influence, all the more if it came from the East or had anything to do with the federal government. Hardest to take were the divided opinions among conservationists themselves. There were purists who objected to the inclusion of Jackson Lake on the grounds that it would set a precedent for having reservoirs in other national parks. Others wanted the sagebrush area excluded because it was not unique, even though it formed an integral part of the valley. An especially difficult issue was the potential removal of almost 90 percent of the land in Teton County from the local tax rolls. And always ready to capitalize on any form of local opposition was the U.S. Forest Service.

In this milieu, the policies and practices of the Snake River Land Company were not helpful. As Kenneth Chorley later observed, the company was very good at land acquisition, but not so good at public relations.[9] For one thing, the local agent selected for the land transactions was an influential banker who personally was adamantly opposed to park expansion but was unaware that he was helping to accumulate land for exactly that purpose. When he later learned the truth, of course, he was enraged. The policy of secrecy was generally a problem; suspicion and rumors intensified as the land program progressed. Vague assurances that the ultimate purposes were recreation and conservation were of little help. There were no illegalities and fair market value was always paid, but some of the tactics bordered on pressure and manipulation. Junior's agents drew heavily on Park Service manpower for detailed information. The General Land Office cooperated by withdrawing public lands in the area that had been earmarked for homesteading, and those who had not "proved up" their existing claims within the allotted five years lost them instead of getting extensions. As Robert Righter commented:

This collusion between the Snake River Land Company, the National Park Service and the General Land Office was, of course, totally within the letter, but perhaps not the spirit, of the law. Their actions were legal, but not always just or equitable.[10]

By 1930 the point had come when the policy of secrecy had to be ended. Several newspapermen were on the verge of learning the facts in any case. Accordingly, a press release was issued explaining that the "client" involved was John D. Rockefeller, Jr., and that the land was being purchased for the future use of the National Park Service in extending Grand Teton Park. This had the effect of mobilizing the opposition, and the politically ambitious junior senator from Wyoming, Robert D. Carey, sensed an opportunity. He became the most vociferous critic of all and threatened a congressional investigation. He then tried to arrange a personal meeting with Junior, seeking to use the threat of the investigation as a lever to force a compromise solution to his liking.

Junior did not agree to meet Carey. He had some experience with congressional investigations, and he was not worried about this one. In fact, he thought it would be a good idea to get all the facts out. Kenneth Chorley later summarized the matter succinctly: Carey could investigate Mr. Rockefeller or have lunch with him—but not both.[11] Carey was infuriated and became even more intemperate in his charges, alleging that the Snake River Land Company was engaging in illegal practices on the scale of Teapot Dome. The hearings were held in the town of Jackson in August 1933 before a subcommittee of the Senate Committee on Public Lands and Surveys. Reporters from major newspapers were on hand. The chairman, Senator Gerald Nye of North Dakota, was a populist and corporation baiter, but he was scrupulously fair in conducting the hearings. Despite the best efforts of the subcommittee counsel, who was Carey's man, all of the charges against the Park Service and the Snake River Land Company were dismissed as groundless.

It was an impressive victory. Newspaper editorials warmly praised Junior and the Park Service. Senator Peter Norbeck of South Dakota publicly criticized the "outrageous expenditure" of public funds to investigate such insubstantial charges, and said the park extension plan had become a "political football." Chairman Nye vowed to go to Washington to see Interior Secretary Harold Ickes and President Roosevelt "with the primary thought in mind of settling down on the Forest Service. They still block the way to proper settlement."[12]

With this dramatic change in public opinion, the opponents suddenly were willing to settle. Meetings were held with all parties represented and a new bill was drafted. The Park Service, satisfied that the desired boundaries of the extension would be intact, agreed to a number of minor concessions. Introduced by Carey, the bill breezed through the Senate, and once again it looked as if the long-cherished dream was about to come true. But in the House the bill was killed by the Bureau of the Budget. The issue was a provision for the government to pay to Teton County the equivalent of the taxes on the Rockefeller land for another twenty years. The bureau feared that this would set a precedent for other public lands. There was a hint that perhaps Junior might consider paying the future taxes. Although the sum involved was relatively small, Junior did not take the hint, feeling that it was unjust to expect him to do this after he had bought the land, paid taxes on it as long as he owned it, and was ready to give it to the government free. In retrospect, this bit of principled stubbornness was unfortunate, because Junior found himself paying the taxes anyway for the next fifteen years.

With the bill dead and the whole issue now out of the public eye, the fragile coalition fell apart and the opposition dug in its heels again. All subsequent attempts to get legislation for a park extension were beaten back.

A complication arose in 1937 involving the JY Ranch, the most scenic dude ranch in the Jackson Hole area. The 3,000-acre property had been acquired in 1932 at a cost of $90,000. The headquarters of the Snake River Land Company were transferred there. Junior began using the ranch for vacations, and he and his family fell in love with it. Laurance honeymooned there in 1934, as did his brother David in 1940. Junior wrote to Arno Cammerer, Park Service director, saying, "My children are greatly interested in this ranch and are anxious that I retain it, for the present at least, for the general use of the family."[13] The ranch was located near the southern edge of the proposed park extension area. Junior queried Cammerer on the question of "exclusivity"—should the ranch stay within the future Park Service area or should the line be redrawn to exclude it? The advantage of the former was that no congressional action would be required when the Rockefeller family eventually decided to give the JY Ranch to the Park Service. As much as the Park Service disliked "in-holdings," Cammerer opted to keep the line where it was. He further reasoned, very shrewdly and correctly as it turned out, that as long as the Rockefellers kept the JY Ranch, they would maintain a strong interest in the welfare of Grand Teton National Park.

The years rolled by with no chance of favorable action by the Congress. Finally, Junior decided to try to force the issue. In 1942 he wrote Interior Secretary Ickes to say that if the government did not want the land or was unable to accept it within the following year "it will be my thought to make some other disposition of it or, failing in that, to sell it in the market to satisfactory buyers."[14] Ickes responded:

This great conservation project which you have made possible would have been accepted long ago if it had been within my power to do so. You know the selfish local interests that have prevented the final consummation of your praiseworthy plans.

I have marveled at your patience in this matter. . . . There is not even the slightest obligation upon you to continue to offer what so far has failed of acceptance. I suspect that I would have withdrawn the offer long ago if it had been mine. Notwithstanding, as a public servant intimately concerned, I appreciate your further generous attitude and within the year which you have allowed, I will do everything within my power to bring about the acceptance of your gift as an addition to the national park system.[15]

Action was soon forthcoming. On March 14, 1943, President Roosevelt signed an executive proclamation creating the "Jackson Hole National Monument," which comprehended all of the land desired by the Park Service and more. Junior and Ickes exchanged jubilant letters, but FDR's move brought forth a storm of criticism. The acid pen of Hearst columnist Westbrook Pegler compared Roosevelt's "annexation" of land in Wyoming to "Adolph Hitler's seizure of Austria."[16] Wyoming Senator Edward V. Robertson called it "a foul, sneaking Pearl Harbor blow."[17] Thomas E. Dewey, whom the Rockefellers had supported politically, was reflexively opposed to almost anything FDR did, and in his ignorance of the real story described the transaction as "characteristic of the deviousness of the New Deal and its lack of responsibility for the rights and opinions of the people affected."[18] Western senators and congressmen quickly introduced a bill to abolish the monument, and it was passed by Congress in December 1944. FDR promptly vetoed it.

The action taken by Ickes and FDR, as obscure as it may be today, must rank as one of the most clever and courageous maneuvers in the history of American public administration. It was all the more remarkable considering that FDR obviously was preoccupied with World War II, but of course it was his status as wartime leader that enabled him largely to ignore and survive the tidal wave of criticism that greeted his action and the frenzied efforts over the next several years to overturn it.

As noted, the power to create a national monument comes from the Antiquities Act of 1906, which was designed to protect sites of archaeological, scientific, or historical interest on federal lands. The crucial point is that this can be done by executive proclamation while a national park can be created only by an act of Congress. The use of the term "monument" has led to some confusion, but the act has been used numerous times for its original purpose and also as the first stage of creating such national parks as Acadia, Grand Canyon, Bryce Canyon, and Zion. Nevertheless, it seems that the anti–park extension forces who were aware of this possibility were confident that the adamant congressional opposition would make such an end-run around Congress politically unfeasible.[19]

Junior's letter to Ickes triggered the maneuver, and Robert Righter raises an interesting question: did Junior act on his own volition or on the advice of his staff or in collusion with Secretary Ickes? Neither the documentary record nor the recollections of participants still alive yields an answer. Righter's conclusion is that the most likely scenario was that Junior and Ickes were acting in concert.[20] He is almost certainly correct. It is not remotely conceivable that after fourteen years of persevering in the effort Junior would suddenly give up and be prepared to sell off the land. Everything about his character and style of operating suggests that he would have been ready to "hang in" for another fifty years if it was necessary to achieve his goal. His letter merely provided the tool that Ickes wanted to help persuade President Roosevelt that quick action was essential.

For one thing, Junior and Ickes were in frequent touch and came to be warm admirers of each other. Junior had been comfortable during the Hoover administration with Ray Lyman Wilbur, a Rockefeller Foundation trustee, serving as secretary of the interior. But nothing was lost when the Democrats came to power. FDR was conservation-minded and Ickes quickly became a staunch supporter of the park extension plan. Ickes thought the Forest Service should report to him as the Park Service already did, and he publicly argued the matter with Agriculture Secretary Henry Wallace. In classic Rooseveltian fashion, the two were left to fight it out with no resolution coming from the White House. The result was that any time Ickes could help the Park Service win a struggle with the Forest Service he was delighted to do so. Moreover, Ickes was well aware of the national monument option. The idea had been much discussed between the Rockefeller interests and the Park Service long before Junior wrote his letter. The Park Service had created a draft of a proposed presidential proclamation for Ickes as early as 1939.

A step taken by Junior in 1941 offers more evidence that he was planning to act in concert with Ickes. Junior created the Jackson Hole Preserve, Inc., as a nonprofit corporation, which took over most of his Jackson Valley land as the Snake River Land Company was dissolved. It seems clear that this was a preparatory step to passing the land to the government. Another reason was that Junior found it necessary to get into the tourism and transportation businesses to help accommodate the growing number of visitors to the Grand Teton region. The Jackson Hole Preserve took over operations of the Grand Teton Lodge and a local bus line. It became the agency for continuing Rockefeller aid to the park, as well as a foundation with broader interests in the conservation field. It was in connection with the preserve and the JY Ranch that Laurance Rockefeller first manifested his lifelong interest in conservation and resort development.

Ickes met twice with President Roosevelt to argue the case for the executive order. On the second occasion, he warned his chief about the prospects of dire political fallout. FDR went ahead anyway.[21] The Jackson Hole National Monument authorized by his proclamation included the following: 99,345 acres of Forest Service land, 31,640 acres of water surface (the area of all of the lakes in the valley), 39,323 acres of withdrawn public lands, 1,406 acres of state lands, and 49,896 acres of private land (32,117 from the Jackson Hole Preserve)— 221,610 acres in all.

The bitter opposition to FDR's move died out within the next few years. By 1950 the next and final step was possible—the incorporation of the Jackson Hole Monument into an enlarged Grand Teton National Park. Wyoming Senator Joseph O'Mahoney's bill to this effect was passed by Congress and signed into law by President Truman on September 14. O'Mahoney could not resist one little dig—the bill included a provision banning the creation of national monuments in Wyoming without the consent of Congress. Thus ended the president's power under the Antiquities Act of 1906—but only in the state of Wyoming! The Bureau of the Budget's opposition on the local tax issue was overruled. The bill authorized the federal government to pay the taxes on the private land for four years and then for another twenty at a decreasing rate of 5 percent a year.

It was a total victory for Junior, Albright, and all those who had fought the battle for more than two decades. For those who might feel that the method employed was a bit undemocratic, as many did at the time, there are several persuasive counterarguments. Perhaps the most convincing is that the result clearly has been wise public policy. Scores of former opponents of the park have readily conceded this. One of the most beautiful wilderness areas in the world has been preserved for all the public, and the region has prospered. Its economic future clearly *was* in recreation and tourism. The park has been amazingly successful, drawing more visitors than Yellowstone—3.5 million a year by the 1970s. Regarding those visitors, the *Jackson Hole News* commented on the occasion of the twenty-fifth anniversary of the expanded park in September 1975: "They don't know this land was once a battleground."[22]

Given the intensity and duration of the struggle, one could forgive Junior if he had never wished to hear of Jackson Hole again. But, apparently, the harder the battle, the sweeter the victory. In the years after 1950, Junior continued his support of Grand Teton National Park, donating more land and building extensive tourist facilities. In all, his contributions totaled approximately $13 million. In 1972 a fitting testimonial was authorized by the Congress—the transfer of 24,000 acres of Forest Service land for the John D. Rockefeller, Jr., National Memorial Parkway connecting Yellowstone and Grand Teton national parks.

The drama of the Jackson Hole story should not obscure the fact that all during this time Junior was extensively engaged in other conservation projects. He became aware of the threat to the California redwoods in 1919 when the Save-the-Redwoods League was created by Henry Fairfield Osborn, president of the Museum of Natural History in New York; Madison Grant, president of the New York

Zoological Society; and others. Redwoods are not only the most majestic trees in the world, but also among the best for providing lumber. At the rate they were being cut, Osborn estimated that the finest stands that were reasonably accessible to the public would be gone within a decade. In 1923 Junior pledged $1 million, and the league raised a like amount from other private sources. When Junior learned that the state of California would match funds raised by the league, he contributed another $1 million, bringing the league's resources up to $6 million. This enabled the preservation of a number of stands of coastal redwoods, including two of the most beautiful in existence, at Bull Creek Flat and neighboring Dyerville Flats. These purchases barely evaded the woodsman's ax—cutting had already started at Dyerville Flats.

In 1928 the league advised Junior that the Sierra Nevada redwoods were now endangered, particularly those in the pine forests that provided a magnificent entrance to Yosemite Valley. Junior contacted the Park Service and offered to help. As a result, Congress authorized the secretary of the interior to match any private funds raised. Junior contributed more than $1.5 million; this and the government funds were used to preserve 15,000 acres of forest leading to Yosemite Valley. Junior was not yet finished with California's big trees. Some years later, using Jackson Hole Preserve, Inc., as a conduit, he contributed $1 million to save the last great unprotected stand in an area known as the South Calaveras Grove. Combined with adjacent federal lands, this created a small park of 5,000 acres.

Junior regularly contributed relatively small sums for specific needs at many of the national parks. For example, he gave up to $15,000 for several years for clean-up and repair work at Yellowstone. Junior's concern for the visitor was evident at Mesa Verde National Park where he realized that tourists had little opportunity to understand the fascinating prehistoric culture of the Indians who had inhabited the area. He gave money to help build a museum. He made similar contributions at other parks until the Park Service itself was finally authorized to undertake interpretive development through its annual appropriations.

The movement to create more national parks east of the Mississippi was eagerly supported by Junior. He pledged one-fifth of the funds needed to purchase land for Shenandoah National Park in Virginia and Great Smoky Mountains National Park in Tennessee and North Carolina when the two parks were authorized by Congress in 1926. The burden of raising funds fell on the states, and the breakthrough for the Great Smoky Park came when, at Junior's suggestion, the Laura Spelman Rockefeller Memorial made one of its terminal grants in 1929 in the amount of $5 million for purchasing land for the park. When the two Appalachian parks were created, a plan emerged for linking them via the projected five-hundred-mile Blue Ridge Parkway. One tract, the Linville Falls property in North Carolina, stood in the way, and Junior offered to donate one-half the purchase price. When the Park Service was unable to provide the rest, Junior gave the entire amount.

Junior did not neglect his home city—he was largely responsible for two important park developments in the heavily urbanized New York City area. One, Fort Tryon Park, was entirely his doing. Fort Tryon originally was the site of the northern earthworks of Fort Washington, where the Continental Army suffered a major defeat at the hands of the British in 1776. The location is the rugged heights at the northern tip of Manhattan Island. As early as 1916, Junior had his eye on this site as a worthy addition to the New York City park system. The following year, with the aid of $1 million provided by his father, he was able to purchase the sixty-acre Fort Tryon property from the C. K. Billings estate, plus surrounding acreage. Twice his offer of the property was turned down by the city. Junior realized that the reason was lack of funds for developing and landscaping the park and installing access roads. So he hired the Olmsted brothers for overall design and landscaping. In 1930 he offered the site again to Mayor James J. Walker in a letter in which he said he would also provide funds for all the developmental work. This time the offer was accepted and the park opened in 1935. In all, the cost to Junior was slightly less than $6 million.

Across the Hudson River from Fort Tryon, the majestic Palisades of the Hudson begin at Fort Lee, New Jersey, and run for some fourteen miles north to the New York border and beyond. These towering cliffs are a remarkable work of nature, having served, for example, as a source of inspiration for the Hudson River school of painting that flourished in the nineteenth century. Toward the end of that century, the Palisades became threatened by rock quarrying and other development. In 1901 the Palisades Interstate Park Commission was created by the two states, and private groups began raising funds to purchase the face of the cliffs and the shoreline. Senior gave $500,000, and other generous contributors included J. Pierpont Morgan and Mrs. E. H. Harriman. Over the years, the Rockefeller Foundation gave $1 million, and three gifts came from the Laura

Spelman Rockefeller Memorial for land purchase and park development.

In the 1920s, it became apparent that the purpose of the whole project was threatened by development on land along the top of the cliffs. This would have ruined the skyline, cut off access to the public, and aborted a proposal by the Regional Plan Association to create a scenic parkway. In another secret land-buying operation, Junior began acquiring parcels along the top of the Palisades in a strip deep enough to protect the skyline and make a parkway possible. In 1933 he made a gift of seven hundred acres to the commission, and the purpose behind the land acquisition became known publicly. Junior continued acquiring and donating land until the entire fourteen-mile stretch was in the hands of the commission. Today the Palisades have been preserved, the skyline is unmarred, and the parkway exists. Junior's contributions totaled more than $17 million.[23]

Closely allied to Junior's love of nature was his reverence for history and what it could teach current and future generations in building the harmonious world he envisioned. His way of giving tangible expression to this was to engage in historical restorations. We have seen his receptivity to opportunities to preserve and restore ancient sites and antiquities overseas. Domestically, he funneled his energies into one great restoration project that became one of the most widely known of all his activities—Colonial Williamsburg. Junior heard the basic idea of the project described at a Phi Beta Kappa dinner in New York City in the autumn of 1924. The speaker was Dr. William A. R. Goodwin, both professor of sacred literature and ethics and endowment officer of the College of William and Mary, as well as rector of Bruton Parish Church in Williamsburg. He had been invited to explain the fund-raising campaign for the restoration of the Christopher Wren Building for the sesquicentennial of Phi Beta Kappa in 1926. Junior had agreed to serve as the national chairman of the campaign. Goodwin took the opportunity to move beyond the Wren Building and the needs of William and Mary and outlined his vision of a small Tidewater town, stripped of its modern excrescences and restored to the historical condition of the mid-eighteenth century, when Williamsburg was the capital of Colonial Virginia. Junior did not react to this speech or to repeated personal pleas by Goodwin to help fund his project.

Two years later, in the early spring of 1926, Junior planned a vacation tour of Virginia to coincide with a speech at Hampton

Institute. Rarely able to avoid mixing business with pleasure, he arranged to visit William and Mary to inspect the progress of the reconstruction of the Wren Building. Goodwin seized on this chance to escort the family through the Wren Building *and* the other areas of town that he had in mind for restoration—Bruton Parish Church, the Wythe House, and the Governor's Palace. Junior thanked him for his kindness and said nothing more. The group then drove on to Richmond where they spent a few days as the guests of Governor Harry F. Byrd at the Executive Mansion.

Previous treatments of the origins of the Colonial Williamsburg project have failed to note the important connection between Junior and Byrd, then early in his first term as governor. The two men, so diverse in their backgrounds, had much in common. Both strongly supported Prohibition and efforts to promote enforcement on the local level. Both believed in the need to rationalize government through measures to encourage economy and efficiency; Byrd had made the reform of the machinery of state government the central element of his campaign and would later hire the Bureau of Municipal Research (heavily funded by Junior and the Memorial) to advise him on the process. More to the point, Byrd was committed to the economic rejuvenation of Virginia by attracting industry and promoting tourism. The means for achieving this end was the Virginia State Commission on Conservation and Development, established on March 13, 1926, and headed by Will Carson, Byrd's campaign manager and a prominent businessman. Carson, with Byrd's enthusiastic support, sought "to develop Virginia by conserving it—using the state's historic wonders to attract tourists and, indirectly, industry."[24]

Over the next decade, Carson worked closely with Horace Albright of the National Park Service and Kenneth Chorley of Junior's office on two principal projects: the creation of Shenandoah National Park and the building of the Colonial National Parkway that would link the Yorktown Battlefield with Jamestown and Colonial Williamsburg. Both projects were completed eventually through quiet cooperation between the federal government, the state of Virginia, and the private sector, represented by the Rockefeller Office.

A belief in the importance of economic development, in this case, the potential role of tourism and recreation in rescuing a state from economic stagnation, needs to be added as a motivating factor in Junior's participation in the restoration of Colonial Williamsburg. However, the reverence of history and belief that it had some very important lessons to teach the contemporary world was at the core of

Junior's response to Goodwin's vision. Soon after he returned to New York in April 1926, he wrote to the rector and indicated that he would pay for preliminary surveys and architectural drawings. He also insisted on total anonymity as the price of his continued involvement.

In November 1927, after viewing a more complete set of plans from the architectural firm of Perry, Shaw, and Hepburn, walking over the ground again with Goodwin, and consulting with his closest advisers on legal and real estate implications, Junior decided to proceed with the next phases of the project. He pledged $5 million for the purchase of property, the hiring of expert staff, and the preservation and restoration work. "It is my desire and purpose," he wrote in a memorandum to Woods, "to carry out this enterprise completely and entirely. . . . The purpose of this undertaking is to restore Williamsburg, as far as that may be possible, to what it was in the old colonial days and to make it a great centre for historical study and inspiration."

In time, the Williamsburg project became the real passion of Junior's life, as Fosdick observed:

> From the beginning the restoration was for Mr. Rockefeller a personal experience. He underwent all the pleasures and pangs of creation and as the plans began to materialize he proudly watched each advancement. No building was restored or reconstructed without his knowledge, and he followed every detail of the project with characteristic meticulousness. . . . Of all the things he ever undertook, Williamsburg seemed to reward him with the greatest satisfaction.[25]

Over the following decades, an army of architects, draftsmen, archaeologists, historians, landscapers, craftsmen, and construction workers toiled on the project, lovingly restoring and recreating the entire colonial town. With his usual meticulous care for visitors, Junior helped plan inns, lodges, taverns, an interpretive center, and other tourist facilities. For many years, the architect in charge of the careful historical redesign work was Thomas Mott Shaw of the Boston firm. The chief landscape architect was Arthur Shurcliff, also of Boston, no mean task, since the work had to be historically exact.

In time, Colonial Williamsburg became world-famous, a habitual stop on the itineraries planned for visiting foreign leaders by the State Department. Throughout his lifetime, Junior spent some $55 million on the restoration of Williamsburg. Knowing that in a sense the restoration would never be finished and would need responsible leadership after his death, Junior tried to pass on full authority to his oldest son, John 3rd, but could never quite do it. A misunderstanding over policy for Williamsburg led to a dispute between father and son and very nearly a serious breach. Ironically, it was a turning point in John 3rd's life, one that finally enabled him to liberate himself from his unconsciously domineering father (see Chapter 25).

Junior and Abby became great collectors of art, by itself not at all surprising for a couple of such wealth. But their interest took some unique turns that ultimately were to be of great value to the public— and the love of art they instilled in their children was to amplify that value manyfold.

Abby was probably responsible for the beginnings of art-collecting by the young couple soon after they were married; as noted, Junior's upbringing had been on the puritanical side while Abby's home environment had emphasized cultivation of the arts. And, of course, an interest in art was practically *de rigueur* for a well-educated and socially prominent couple of wealth.

They began acquiring paintings for their home, primarily old masters. And then their interests went off in markedly different directions. Junior was a traditionalist and developed a love for tangible three-dimensional objects—ceramics, classical sculpture, medieval architecture and tapestries. While Abby could appreciate these, her great passion became modern art. Junior could not reciprocate the favor—he was totally puzzled by modern art, disliked most of its genres, and was mystified by his wife's interest in it. Out of deference to this, she kept the objects she collected in the former children's playroom on the top floor of the house at 10 West 54th—now her "art gallery." Apart from a few Impressionist paintings, the art displayed in the rest of the house consisted of things he liked.

Abby's interest was probably stirred by the famous Armory Show of 1913, considered to be the event that introduced modern art to the American public. Among the organizers of the show were American artists anxious to stimulate greater public appreciation of modern art. In the end, they were frustrated by the generally negative reaction and by the fact that, to the extent there was acclaim, it was reserved for the European works that dominated the show.

The idea that led to creation of the Museum of Modern Art (MOMA) was developed in 1928 by Abby and two friends, Miss Lillie P. Bliss and Mrs. Cornelius J. Sullivan. This trio, variously called "the Ladies," "the daring ladies," and "the adamantine ladies" by the historian of MOMA, Russell Lynes, was intent on establishing not just a gallery for public exhibitions, but a full-fledged museum that would have a permanent collection.[26] The ladies moved quickly to establish a committee, including A. Conger Goodyear, one of the most prominent collectors of modern art at the time; Professor Paul J. Sachs of the Fogg Art Museum at Harvard; Frank Crowninshield, editor of *Vanity Fair;* and Mrs. W. Murray Crane, another of Abby's wealthy friends. The group obtained a temporary charter from the Regents of the State University of New York and rented space for the new museum on the twelfth floor of the Heckscher Building at the corner of Fifth Avenue and 57th Street. On the recommendation of Sachs, they took a chance on a young instructor of art history at Wellesley College, Alfred H. Barr, Jr., as the first director of the museum. Barr's distinguished career as head of MOMA was to last thirty-seven years.

MOMA opened to the public on November 1, 1929, just ten days after the stock market crash that ushered in the Great Depression. Despite the unfortunate timing, the museum eventually was to flourish to the point that it became one of the most unique and successful in the world. This was signaled by the success of its first loan exhibition in November 1929, displaying paintings by van Gogh, Gauguin, Cezanne, and Seurat. Writing in *The Nation* of December 4, 1929, art critic Lloyd Goodrich said: "Just as the Armory Show of 1913 was the opening gun in the long bitter struggle for modern art in this country, so the foundation of the new museum marks the final apotheosis of modernism and its acceptance by respectable society."

The accepters did not include Junior. Abby's involvement was entirely on her own—at first. Even the drafting of legal papers was done by Mrs. Sullivan's husband, not by a lawyer furnished by Junior. His uneasy tolerance of his wife's interest is well captured in Frank Crowninshield's account of what happened in 1938 at a dinner given by the Rockefellers for fifty guests in honor of Henri Matisse. After coffee Matisse turned to Junior and "began, half seriously, to plead" the cause of modern art. It was an "inspired lecture" in which Matisse developed the thesis that modern artists were serving the same aesthetic goals that were evident in the traditional works of art surrounding the dinner guests and throughout the Rockefeller home. Crowninshield chronicled Junior's response:

But the philanthropist, who had listened very politely, regretted, quite as politely, and in the most polished French, that he must still appear adamant. Then, with an engaging burst of confidence, he added that Mr. Matisse must not altogether despair because though he might still seem to be of stone, he suspected that Mrs. Rockefeller, thanks to her very special gifts of persuasion, would eventually wear him down to the consistency of jelly.[27]

In this engaging response, Junior already seemed on the verge of surrendering, but it was to take a number of years before he gradually emerged as one of the major financial supporters of MOMA. He loved his wife very much and respected her judgment. Despite his dislike of modern art, he was objective enough to realize that it was an important cultural phenomenon that deserved support. He was perhaps also motivated by the fact that his second son, Nelson, so avidly followed his mother's interest in modern art that he succeeded to the presidency of MOMA in 1939. David also became a devotee of modern art and a staunch supporter of the museum. Junior's gifts to MOMA, valued at more than $6 million, included grants for its endowment and some of the property that now forms the MOMA site.

Strong financial support of MOMA was continued by members of the third generation of Rockefellers and by various institutions associated with the family, such as the Rockefeller Foundation and the Rockefeller Brothers Fund. This level of personal involvement and financial support lends substance to Russell Lynes' view that MOMA has "since the beginning been a Rockefeller responsibility, a protectorate, one might almost say. . . ."[28]

By this time, of course, Junior's own particular interests in art had become a lifelong avocation, a never-ending source of pleasure for him. His love of Chinese porcelains was kindled in 1913 when he first bought a pair of small vases. He began acquiring more, particularly pieces from the seventeenth-century Ming dynasty. An unprecedented opportunity arose in 1915 when J. P. Morgan's great collection, on loan to the Metropolitan Museum, became available for purchase upon the owner's death. The renowned art dealer Joseph Duveen, with whom Junior was to engage in many transactions, made the young man aware of the opportunity. Junior selected pieces that would cost him more than $1 million to acquire. He didn't have the money available, so he asked his father for a loan. Senior demurred, being a very practical man who could not understand the passion for collecting art. Junior then wrote a letter to him that is interesting in itself, but also because it exhibits a rather formal pattern of discourse between father and son that Junior came to expect of his own sons. Instead of arguing with one's father when there is a disagreement, one should carefully write a letter that presents the case in as logical and appealing a way as possible. This is only fair because it gives the father all the information he needs in playing his role as judge. If the father still decides against the request, the son never mentions it again. Junior's sons soon learned the technique. In part, Junior's letter read:

I have never squandered money on horses, yachts, automobiles or other foolish extravagances. A fondness for these porcelains is my only hobby—the only thing on which I have cared to spend money. I have found their study a great recreation and diversion, and I have become very fond of them. This hobby, while a costly one, is quiet and unostentatious and not sensational. . . . The money put into these porcelains is not lost or squandered. It is all there, and while not income-producing, . . . a sale under ordinary circumstances would certainly realize their full cost value, and, as the years go by, more. . . .

Is it unwise for me to gratify a desire for beautiful things, which will be a constant joy to my friends and to my children as they grow to appreciate them, as well as to myself, when it is done in so quiet and unostentatious a manner?

Much as I want to do this thing—and I think you do not realize how much I should like to do it, for you do not know the beauty and charm of these works of art—I want more to do what you fully approve, so I have ventured to write this long letter, hoping that perhaps this fuller statement of the situation may lead you to see it in a somewhat different light.[29]

Senior made the money available, not as a loan but as a gift. Junior rejoiced in the "extraordinary breadth of mind and unprecedented generosity" of a father who could be "so ready to reverse his decision in the light of the facts presented." In later years, Junior would be prepared to act in such a manner toward sons who observed the proper ritual of presenting the "facts" in this manner. Senior's acquiescence surely was based on a realization of how important the matter was to his beloved son, not on any thought that a profit could be made on the collection. And this certainly was never Junior's real intention, as indicated by his reflections years later, after he had amassed a huge collection, on the question of whether he was being merely self-indulgent. He arrived at the final justification, as he told his biographer: "I came to the conclusion that a man could buy this kind of thing for himself without jeopardizing other causes, and that he was justified in spending at least a portion of his money on beautiful objects, particularly when they would in time probably come into public possession through their ownership by museums. In the end, therefore, beauty would be preserved for a wider audience."[30]

As if to give substance to this conclusion, Junior did much to aid art museums during his lifetime, not only MOMA, but also substantial gifts to the Fogg Museum and the Metropolitan Museum among others. But his greatest project was the building of the Cloisters in Fort Tryon Park, a magnificent gem of a museum that houses much of the medieval collection of the Metropolitan. This project was a manifestation of Junior's love of medieval art—sculpture, tombs, chalices, frescoes, stained glass, architectural fragments, and, above all, tapestries.

Junior's imaginative idea of combining his love of medieval art with Fort Tryon Park and the Metropolitan Museum was born after he met an extraordinary character, sculptor George Grey Barnard, who had been retained by the architect William Welles Bosworth to create three statues for the gardens of Kykuit. Barnard's great passion in life was scouring the European countryside to acquire neglected pieces of medieval sculpture and stonework. After twenty years of collecting, he had enough to open a museum in 1914 at 190th Street and Fort Washington Avenue in Manhattan, which he called the Cloisters. Containing parts of four French cloisters and a diverse array of other items, the Barnard Cloisters had the only important collection of Romanesque and Gothic sculpture in the United States aside from Fenway Court in Boston. Barnard held options on a number of Gothic pieces that he could not afford to buy, and he tried to enlist Junior's aid.[31]

Bosworth strongly endorsed the idea of rescuing Gothic sculpture that was "being sacrificed among the heaps of ruins all over Northern France and Belgium," but he later advised Junior against a direct partnership with the eccentric artist.[32] But when Barnard retired in 1925 and put his collection up for sale, Junior funded the purchase of it ($600,000) by the Metropolitan Museum of Art and added $400,000 for maintenance and additional purchases. With this the Metropolitan opened its own "Cloisters" on Barnard's property in May 1926. In the meantime, with the assistance of Barnard, Junior had amassed his own collection of 102 stone and wooden Gothic pieces, most of them stored in the long delivery tunnels at Kykuit. Eventually, he gave sixty-two of these pieces to the Cloisters, most of the rest going to the Cleveland Museum of Art. In the late 1920s, he developed the idea of creating a proper museum of medieval art, instructing the architects who were laying out the plan for the land that would become Fort Tryon Park to set aside four acres at the highest point for the new museum.

Once the deal was set for the city to accept Fort Tryon Park, work began on the new museum and Junior began giving substantial grants to the Metropolitan to help build its medieval collection. Junior stayed close to the project, lavishing on it the same care and attention he devoted to the reconstruction of Williamsburg and the building of Rockefeller Center. Though basically modern in design, the museum was acclaimed by architectural critics for harmonizing with the medieval works it housed and for the air of peace and serenity it projected. At the time of the opening of the museum in 1938, 90 percent of the Metropolitan's medieval collection had been donated or paid for by Junior.

The architect, Charles Collens, and James J. Rorimer, the curator of the collection, cunningly included an area called the Tapestry Hall in the building. The Metropolitan had no suitable tapestries and Junior had not breathed a word about his own. But the power of suggestion was there. Tapestries and fine Oriental rugs were a special passion for Junior. He had built a collection of Polonaise rugs (Persian silk rugs woven of gold and silver thread). But his most cherished possessions were two sets of tapestries known as *The Months of Lucas* and *The Hunt of the Unicorn*. Junior had purchased the building at 12 West 54th Street, next door to the family home, primarily to handle the overflow of art. Here the two sets of tapestries, seventeen in all, were hung on the walls, covering doors and windows in some cases. This became Junior's favorite retreat, and he delighted in bringing friends there to see for the first time the dazzling beauty and gorgeous color, particularly of the Unicorn Tapestries. It was a difficult decision, but when Junior and Abby moved from No. 10 to a triplex Park Avenue apartment, he made it—the rugs and the tapestries went to the Metropolitan, the latter to hang in the Cloisters.

Still, Junior was not finished. He financed the painstaking restoration of the Nine Heroes Tapestries from ninety-seven fragments that had been used as curtains. It gave him immense satisfaction when this magnificent fourteenth-century work was finally exhibited in a room adjacent to the Unicorn Tapestries in the Cloisters. Having spent some $15 million on Fort Tryon, the Cloisters, and the medieval art housed there, Junior in 1952 made a final grant of $10 million to the Metropolitan "for the enrichment of the Cloisters in the broadest sense of the term and for the preservation, housing and presentation of its collection." The *New York Herald Tribune* commented editorially: "It represents a sort of philanthropy which is all too rare. . . . The Cloisters is a museum blessed with breath of life."[33]

Junior could certainly look back on the decade of the 1920s with a great sense of accomplishment—assuming he allowed himself that unaccustomed pleasure. He had worked tirelessly for rational social reform, improved industrial relations, and Christian unity. He had managed the family fortune and foundations with imagination and skill, drawing around himself an incomparable group of experts on many aspects of modern life. He had initiated a project to restore the glory of colonial America, helped to preserve some of civilization's greatest treasures, and enabled a portion of his country's natural heritage to be saved for future generations. For these and many other acts of leadership and initiative, he had become an immensely respected national leader.

But, not one to rest on his laurels, Junior had another item on his agenda as the decade drew to a close. The Metropolitan Opera Company was badly in need of a new home, and the idea emerged of using the need as the occasion for redeveloping the area in midtown Manhattan bounded by 48th and 51st streets and Fifth and Sixth avenues. It was virtually a slum, filled with bars, pawnshops, dilapidated buildings, and fleabag hotels. The project could not go forward without an overall sponsor, and Junior agreed to play this role, entering into a twenty-four-year lease with the owner of the land, Columbia University, in December 1928. Early in 1929, work on tenant relocation and demolition of vacant buildings began. The plan called for the Met to purchase part of the property to build its new home, with Junior to donate the land in front of the new opera house as an open plaza. The viability of the project depended on lining up business corporations to lease the remaining plots to erect new headquarters buildings. Several real estate experts assured Junior that the project was sound and that the entire development would be completed in three or four years.

The sudden collapse of the stock market in October caused everyone to back out of the project except Junior, who was stuck with a yearly obligation of $3.3 million to Columbia and only about 10 percent of that amount coming back in existing rentals. Junior faced a dilemma—whether to swallow the loss annually or attempt development by himself. Given the magnitude of Junior's wealth, he was never to be in dire financial straits. Nevertheless, it was a difficult decision as the Depression began to make deep inroads into Junior's net worth and annual income.

Though no one quite realized it, an era had passed quickly and irretrievably. The "Roaring Twenties" were gone, and, as it seemed, only bleak prospects lay ahead for the 1930s. The world in which Junior had been raised, the values he had been taught to cherish and had in turn taught his children, would no longer work with the same force and validity. As Junior contemplated the unwanted lease and other problems in trying to chart a course through the unfamiliar terrain of the 1930s, there was one exciting prospect for him. His eldest sons were coming of age and would soon be available to help him carry his immense responsibilities.

III

THE THIRD
ROCKEFELLER
1912–1929

11

⚜

THE ELDEST SON

DURING the second decade of the century—a very busy period for Junior and one clouded by painful notoriety—he and Abby turned their attention to the education of their children. How could wholesome results be secured? Babs was sent to the Brearley School in New York City and later to its sister institution, the Chapin School. In part, Babs' rebellion consisted of not caring much about school; she never graduated. It was very important that the boys do much better.

At the age of six, John 3rd was enrolled in the Roger Ascham School, which had been founded a few years earlier by one Anne Winsor. The school was named after a sixteenth-century English classical scholar and author of *The Schoolmaster*, known for his innovative views on education. The school—small, private, and coeducational—was on East 79th Street. It was limited to the kindergarten and early grades. John 3rd attended for three years and Nelson and Laurance followed him.

One morning in July 1915, while strolling on Sixth Avenue, Junior encountered John A. Browning, headmaster of the school that he had attended for so many years. The two men had a warm feeling of mutual admiration and respect. Browning volunteered to advise Junior on the education of the boys irrespective of what schools they would attend. Later that summer, Junior wrote to inquire if a place in the Browning School could be found for his son John, supposing he could qualify, commenting that John "is developing rapidly" and needs "the companionship of boys of his age, while those in his present class are all younger." He characterized his son as follows:

John is in temperament a good deal like his father; conscientious, desirous of learning, interested in his work where the work is made interesting, and with, I should say, a fair degree of application. He is perhaps timid rather than aggressive among boys of his own age, at the same time he is fond of games and activity.[1]

Browning was delighted, and in his response exclaimed that Junior's request had "stirred happy memories of twenty-five years ago!" He wrote:

Although our classes for younger boys are completed, I have on several occasions in the past felt justified in breaking the old rule of "six in a class" in the case of sons of former pupils or brothers of existing ones. If, therefore, you approve, I shall be glad to "tuck away" your boy as an "extra" in whatever group he may be qualified to join.

Browning described the regimen at the school as follows:

Our boys of nine are usually fitted to do the work of what is generally understood to be the Fourth Grade, i.e. they read fluently in a "Third" Reader, write fairly well, and have done Arithmetic as far as, or through, simple Short Division. . . . During the first two years the daily session is from 9 a.m. til 12:45. The boys may return in the afternoon about 2:30 for play in the Park under the supervision of two or three of the masters. On rainy days they play at the school, but generally devote a part of the afternoon to work in the shop or some kind of hand work in the classroom. My experience has fully convinced me that the average boy needs the companionship of his mates just as much as the scholastic exercises of the regular school session; with the majority of very young boys organized play is the most significant part in their educational development.[2]

The result was pleasing for both Browning and Junior, and, judging by comments in Junior's letters to Browning, it worked well for the boy as well. On one occasion, Junior wrote:

Again may I express our pleasure and satisfaction with John's work and his attitude toward school, his teachers and his companions. It has been a source of great happiness to me that you and he have developed such a sympathetic relationship.[3]

The education offered by the Browning School, as it had evolved over the years, appealed to Junior's own ideas. Like many parents and educators of the time, he had come to doubt the value of the formal atmosphere and emphasis on classical studies that characterized many private schools. Although the Browning School included Latin in its curriculum, as well as English, mathematics, geography, history, and rudimentary science, it also emphasized the manual arts and outdoor activities. Junior was seeking a difficult combination: progressive education of high quality, protection from unwanted influences and possible danger, and yet a certain democratic and competitive spirit that would prepare his boys to deal with the real world. Although it was very exclusive, the Browning School clearly was striving to meet such a prescription for its privileged students. Junior's care in selecting schools reflected a perennial concern both for himself and his sons as they grew up: how to live out lives of inescapable privilege, very much in the public eye, without insulating themselves totally from the realities of life or becoming warped or spoiled.

The emphasis on a "democratic" spirit was particularly interesting. Such a thought never entered the heads of many wealthy people of the time, but for others, including the Rockefellers, it was very important. In Junior, this was the natural product of all the attitudes and motivations that led him to devote his life to philanthropy, particularly his acute social consciousness. No sacrifice in one's living standards was required, but the "democratic" spirit did call for avoiding any flaunting of one's wealth, for cultivating a sense of humility instead of self-importance. With considerable success, Junior and Abby worked hard to inculcate these values in their children. In due course, Junior was to be praised frequently in the press for his own "democratic" spirit.

For four years, John attended the conveniently located Browning School (on West 55th Street, just one block from the Rockefellers). Yet Junior enrolled Nelson and Laurance not in the Browning School, but in the Lincoln School, which first opened its doors in the fall of 1917. And, he withdrew John from the Browning School in June 1919. The reasons for these moves seem to be the imminent retirement of the headmaster and the excitement of the times over new ideas of progressive education. Browning was elderly and not in good health; it was clear he would be retiring soon, as indeed he did in 1920. Junior was dubious about those who would replace the man who had a "profound influence" on his life.[4]

Just as his father and uncle had participated in the founding of the Browning School in 1888, so Junior had a hand in the creation of the Lincoln School. It was initially funded by the General Education Board, principally at the initiative of Abraham Flexner, and it operated in rented quarters at 646 Park Avenue under the supervision of Teachers College of Columbia University. A report to Junior on the school said that "the controlling theories of education behind this experiment are those of the 'new' 'scientific' and 'social' movements" that could be identified with such reformers as Charles W. Eliot, president emeritus of Harvard University, and Professor John Dewey of Columbia University: "In general it can be said that the school attempts to reproduce actual community life on a democratic basis, to establish social habits and attitudes and in particular the habits of scientific thinking."[5]

All four of the younger boys attended the Lincoln School. The development plan for the school called for offering six elementary grades and six secondary grades to reach a total of about 350 pupils. Nelson finished his precollege education there, Laurance all but one year, Winthrop all but three years, and David all twelve grades. In 1920 the Lincoln School moved to its own building at 123rd Street, not far from Amsterdam Avenue. This Manhattan location meant that all four of the younger Rockefeller boys were day students throughout almost all their schooling; they lived at home, 10 West 54th Street. For the eldest son, it was to be different.

In the fall of 1919, John 3rd was transferred to the Harvey School in Hawthorne, New York, a private day school less than two miles from the family estate in Pocantico Hills. This interim measure was taken for good reasons besides the imminent retirement of Browning. Young John completed the equivalent of seventh grade in June 1919, and his parents likely felt that he was too far along to adapt readily to the Lincoln School, with its completely revised curriculum and experimental approach. They also might have felt that he needed a less competitive environment. He had lagged a bit in school, and in fact was to require two years more to be ready for prep school. Physical frailty may have been a contributing cause. John suffered from a steady succession of colds, sore throats, stomachaches, and headaches that often kept him out of school. He had poor teeth, and had to visit the dentist often—for fillings, for having his bands adjusted, and later for braces, which he wore through most of his prep school years. Abby and Junior may well have thought it wise to keep so frail a boy "in the country," especially during the influenza pandemic of 1919. Besides, scarlet fever and polio were continual scares for parents. A final reason was that 1919 was a year of exceptional violence in the labor movement, and the number of "crank" letters received by the Rockefellers increased in proportion. Although all of the children were vulnerable to kidnapping or other violence, the one most vulnerable was obviously the one with the famous name.

John 3rd thus had to endure a lonely year at the Harvey School, living at Abeyton Lodge on the Pocantico estate with no one but servants for company, except on weekends and holidays. Then his brothers would come up, and less frequently his parents, or he would be taken to the city to stay with the family at 10 West 54th.

His most frequent companion at Abeyton Lodge was the highly trusted and warmhearted nurse-governess, Florence M. Scales. She seems to have been the perfect stand-in for the parents when they traveled, as they did frequently. Because John 3rd was away from the family, but not in a boarding school, Miss Scales was deputed to be with him much of the school year.

One of her tasks was to keep Abby informed, and Miss Scales did it very well; she wrote virtually every day when Abby was on her travels, giving detailed accounts of what the children were doing. The flavor of the war years comes through in these letters, as she describes the gardens the older boys were keeping, or a trip to Central Park to hear Marshal Joseph Joffre, the former commander in chief of the French army, speak, or an automobile tour through Manhattan during the Armistice celebration. She wrote of the boys' pet rabbits, their riding the ponies, playing baseball, collecting fruit, making a hideaway in the woods; likewise of John dutifully practicing the violin and Nelson and Laurance making "peat" by soaking rolled-up newspapers in water. She was no tattletale, so there was no mention of fights among the boys, except when an incident could be told humorously and with a happy ending. The big subject always was health. Hardly a day passed when one or the other of the boys was not suffering from some minor ailment. But these accounts invariably ended with a cheerful prognosis.

Miss Scales clearly was affectionate toward all of the children, but the one who really amused her was Nelson. She wrote with an air of tolerant exasperation about how he would continually stray from his studies, but when she pinned him down, he always knew the lesson. One day Nelson was denied dessert because of his antics at dinner, but he sat there amiably chewing on a piece of meat gristle, pretending he was having dessert. On another occasion she described how he looked when he returned from summer camp—radiant, husky, and tanned, with shocks of hair sticking out all over and bleached white at the tips by the sun. One year he was determined to start his garden although it was much too early, but, as she wrote, there was no way to convince him of that.

In that lonely year 1919–1920, John 3rd began his diary-writing habit, which he maintained, literally, until the day of his death.[6] He also began to develop his formidable letter-writing power, possibly benefiting from the example of the redoubtable Miss Scales. Of course, in those days the writing of letters was a social necessity, an obligation taken for granted by everybody. John 3rd soon excelled and became the champion correspondent among all the Rockefellers. This accomplishment included an accurate memory of all birthdays, anniversaries, holidays, and other special occasions; John 3rd was always the first with a telegram, a letter, or a gift. Before long, his less organized brothers often would begin their letters to him with an apology for not having responded sooner.

The forming of these habits was perhaps a symptom of loneliness, as were the less permanent hobbies John 3rd adopted at the same time—stamp-collecting and autograph-collecting (not in person, but through correspondence). In his first diary entries, he confided no intimate feelings, limiting himself to such entries as "Went to school, coasted there," "Went to school, had a snowball fight there," "Went to school, rained hard," It is only from a few references in Florence Scales' letters to Abby that we have intimations of his loneliness and dislike of the Harvey School. For example, one day he had a sore arm and couldn't play baseball after school. She urged him to have some "quiet play" with the boys at school, but she reports: "But no, he was quite content to come home and be alone. He certainly doesn't care much for the boys in that school." In fairness, one must add that the real problem was John's peculiar situation that year. For the greater part of each week, he had neither the companionship of a boarding school nor of a family.

But there was to be a marvelous release from loneliness that summer. Junior and Abby decided to take their older children on a western trip, the first major trip they would have together as a family. On May 26, 1920, John 3rd entered in his diary: "Went to school and to the city (for good). Packed my trunk and suitcase for the trip." From the day of departure (May 29) on, his diary takes on the color of life: every page is crammed full of information and description. What is more, John kept a larger travel log, with full-page accounts of each day's activities—another habit he was to follow when he made extensive trips in the future.

Besides the parents and the four oldest children, the expedition included a medical doctor from the Rockefeller Institute, an associate from the office to help Junior in business matters, a French maid to assist Abby, and a young Englishwoman to chaperone sixteen-year-old Babs. Left behind at Abeyton Lodge for the summer were Winthrop, who came down with measles before departure, and David. Being left behind with the "baby" apparently was a traumatic experience for Winthrop.[7]

The trip was to be made in style, aboard a private railroad car, the Pioneer. John drew a diagram of the car in his log: it shows a dining room, observation room, porch, five staterooms (John and Nelson sharing one), and quarters for the three "very nice colored men," a cook, a porter, and a waiter ("We had awfully good food on our car. John Reed is an excellent cook"). The Pioneer was always attached to the rear of the train ("which was nice") and at every station stop the boys jumped out to play ball ("which was good exercise"). The first stop for the family was Cleveland, to visit the site of Junior's boyhood, Forest Hill, and "the cemetery where Grandmother Rockefeller is buried" and the "monument there which Father designed." The next stop was Chicago ("much nicer than I expected"), where the family dined with the president of the University of Chicago, and then on to Omaha, where the president of the Union Pacific Railroad attached his private car to the train. He invited the family to dinner on his car, and the next day allowed the boys to ride in the engine ("It nearly deafened us every time the whistle blew") before detaching his car from the train in Julesburg, Colorado ("We walked around the cunning little town after supper").

There followed sixty-five more days, along the circular route through the Rockies, up and down the state of California, to the Pacific Northwest, back eastward through Canada, with side trips at many points, before arriving at Bangor, Maine, and then to Seal Harbor (August 4) for the rest of the summer.

The measles did not stay home with Winthrop: Babs, Nelson, and Laurance all came down at once. Only John was immune, from an earlier bout, which brought an unexpected bonus. He was the only one able to accompany his father on a three-day motor trip through the Rockies, to the Colorado Fuel and Iron Company works at Trinidad, and to Pueblo, Crested Butte, the Continental Divide, an Indian reservation, and several small mountain towns. John wrote: "I thought my trip with Father through the Rockies was great. The only trouble was it wasn't long enough to suit me."

The thrill of travel for these boys, who as adults were to become globe-trotters, consisted of new sights and fresh adventures—their first time west of the Mississippi, their first view of the Pacific Ocean, their first visit to Canada. They shot the rapids with Indians in canoes and rode horseback through mountains on overnight camping expeditions. John's enthusiasm increased his descriptive powers, and his log accordingly becomes highly readable and interesting for one written by a boy recently turned fourteen. He comments on seeing so many

American bald eagles on one camping trip, and is critical of how logs were "snaked" at a Weyerhaeuser lumber mill: "The process of 'snaking' is very ruenous because it kills all the little trees that are to small to use thus leaving a barren wast."[8]

It was on this trip that he also learned about the power, persistence, and fallibility of the press: "All along on our trip newspaper photographers were after us trying to take pictures of us, and reporters were after Father trying to get interviews of him." On another occasion, he wrote: "There were lots of very funny things put in the papers about us and lots of very untrue things. The newspaper reporters were after poor Father most of the time."

On the long haul back across Canada, childhood illness stalked the Pioneer once again. All the children came down with what John described in his diary as "some form of intergestion." But when the trip was finally over, he called it "the nicest most interesting and instructive trip I have ever had." But: "Our chief annoyanse was the news paper reporters and the camera men."

Once back in Seal Harbor, amid the rain and fog, there were the usual activities—riding ponies into the woods, John and Nelson building a log cabin, playing tennis, sailing, meeting and playing with the children of other well-to-do families who summered there. The big question for John was how to use the coming school year to prepare himself for prep school. Junior had become aware of an interesting school located near his father's golfing lodge in Lakewood, New Jersey, the Pine Lodge School, run by a Mr. and Mrs. Olmstead (and hence also "the Olmstead School"). It was very small, accommodating exactly ten boys; what made it special was the pronounced emphasis on a physically healthy environment. It was a country school in the full sense of the word—no electricity, just gas lamps and candles for light in the evenings. It was bedtime every night at eight-thirty and up in the morning at dawn. There was a rigorous program of outdoor activities and exercise and a work schedule. The school had its own stable, and the boys went riding virtually every day. All this activity was, of course, in addition to the usual classroom subjects, which were taught every morning except Sunday. With so few boys of varied ages, much of the work amounted to individual tutoring.

There had been a polio scare in Maine that summer, with several cases occurring on a vacation island near Seal Harbor. To Junior and Abby, the Olmstead School seemed the perfect place to send not only John, but also the other son who was prone to illness. So Laurance was taken out of the Lincoln School, and he and John began at the Olmsteads' early in October 1920. One of their eight fellow students was Douglas Dillon, who was to become a prominent public figure and a lifelong friend of both John and Laurance.

For the most part, judging from his diary, it was a happy year for John: "Went riding." "Played socker." "Did some shooting in the afternoon which I liked." "Played tennes. Beet Mr. Olmsted." "Played the finals of the tennis tournament which I beat." Olmstead took the boys on trips to Princeton football games, to the site of the Battle of Monmouth, to the big dirigible hangar at Lakewood, to Trenton and Philadelphia. For John and Laurance, there were occasional Sunday dinners with Grandfather at his nearby villa. Several times during the school year, Junior and Abby came to visit. Abby described the first visit in a letter to her sister Lucy, who was on a trip to China with Babs:

We arrived to the school at four o'clock in time to see the boys return from their ride. They came galloping up the road with Laurance in the lead beside Mr. Olmsted. Both boys seemed so cheerful and happy. John looks extremely well. I am sure that he has gained in weight and his color is better too. . . . My one fear is that John being a little older than the others and being able to beat them in most of the sports may not be entirely good for him, but there are one or two bright boys in the school who will probably give him a rub intellectually. . . . After dinner when the coffee and cigars had been finished, we all went into the school-room and the boys read compositions. The subject of the compositions was a book that Mr. Olmsted had recently read to the boys, each boy being allowed to take some incident from the book. With the exception of John and one other boy, they all hit on the same incident. . . . After the reading of the compositions, every one was given a piece of paper and we all voted who we thought was best. John won. This is the third time that his composition was voted as the best. I thought Laurance did extremely well because it is quite difficult for him to express himself on paper, so I voted for him. Big John thought that Little John was the best but being a man did not vote for him. . . . Then they had a spelling match, at the end of which both of the Rockefellers were at the foot, Laurance at the very foot and John next to him. I am afraid they inherited the Aldrich lack of ability to spell, but Mr. Olmsted assured me that by the end of the season they would be admirable spellers—that he thought they showed lack of proper preparation.[9]

In the deep of winter, melancholy returned and John 3rd began reminiscing in his diary about the Browning School and how much he loved it. He wrote that he liked Mr. Olmstead, but that Mrs. Olmstead wasn't very nice—she had breakfast in bed. Still, "the boys here are all pretty good." In the spring, spirits revived. The boys practiced almost every day with their horses for a gymkhana. They played tennis and baseball, dug charcoal pits, boxed, played marbles ("Great fun. I won lots of them"), took long rides through beautiful country. John and his classmate Kenneth Jenkins always won at tennis doubles, and so called themselves "the Invincibles." During spring vacation, a momentous day came when John was taken to DePinna's to be fitted for long trousers ("All my suits will have long trousers from now on"). John added new hobbies, collecting coins and books about the Great War. For the gymkhana on April 30, about fifty people attended, including Father, Nelson, and Winthrop. Laurance won three of the seven events and John two.

By this time, it had become clear to Junior that a suitable prep school had to be found. John had progressed, but not enough, and while it was clear from the Olmstead experience that a small school was best, Olmstead's was *too* small. Junior sought advice in a letter to Charles Eliot:

We are looking for a relatively small country boarding school for our oldest son, John, for this coming year. He has grown rapidly, is under weight, not very rugged and inclined to be nervous. He is now and has been for the past year at the Olmstead School at Lakewood, where there are but ten boys and where they lead a healthful outdoor country life; but being the oldest of the ten, it does not seem wise for John to return to this school for another year. We have thought a small school better for John than a large school, hence our choice has been rather limited.[10]

Eliot wrote back that he had heard a lot recently about "vitamines" as being good for "remedying in children a weight disproportionately low in relation to height." He also suggested several schools, two of which Junior and John visited. But in the end they selected yet another, the Loomis Institute at Windsor, Connecticut. On May 6, John and his mother paid it a visit and John took four hours of examination. Two weeks later, he was notified that he would be admitted to Loomis in the fall.

Before John 3rd started at Loomis, there was to be a long, active summer at Seal Harbor, including some experiences that propelled this shy boy of fifteen along the way to the bewilderments of young manhood.

Junior and Abby were to leave in midsummer for a four-month trip to the Orient, the main purpose of which was to attend the dedication of the Peking Union Medical College that had been funded by the Rockefeller Foundation. Junior had been seeking someone who, as he expressed it in a letter to John Browning, "might be suitable as a companion to our boys during the summer months." He found his man in one Zenos R. Miller, by all accounts a most likable and thoughtful youth of twenty-three with a background calculated to appeal strongly to young boys. He had been a flying ace in World War I, first with the British squadrons and then the American 27th Pursuit Squadron. Miller had been credited with seventeen "kills" and had been a prisoner of war during the final four months of the war. He had a free summer before returning for his final year at Harvard Medical School, and he accepted the intriguing assignment of being a sort of surrogate father to the Rockefeller boys for a few months. The one he spent the most time with was John 3rd, the boy who most needed a companion.

At Pocantico before leaving for Seal Harbor, June 4 was a special day for John 3rd, as his diary entry reveals: "Drove Dodge for first time. Never driven a car before; loved it. Mr. Miller, a new red-headed tuter came, pretty nice. Fine day." The boy and his companion got to know each other as they played golf with Grandfather every day (on one morning when they played eight holes, the score was: Miller 57, Grandfather 51, John 42). That afternoon it rained, and John had his first automobile accident while taking Winthrop for a ride, only one week after his first driving lesson: "The car skidded into the gutter & lay on its side. Nobody hurt. Lots of nice men came and writted the car & we drove off as nothing was hurt except the mudguards. Very lucky accident." Apparently, the "nice men" and Miller kept quiet about it because there is no record of any punishment by Junior for this mishap.

Junior had a surprise for the boys at Seal Harbor that summer, a new thirty-six-foot Marconi-rigged sloop, the *Jack Tar*. With the assistance of Miller and a Captain Breacy ("who always goes along"), young John became an accomplished sailor, taking others out often, entering races and often winning them, and spending much time "polishing the brass." John and Miller played squash together, went riding, bowled, and became doubles partners in tennis.

A major activity was finishing the construction of the log cabin that had been started the previous summer. The work was done by John and Laurance after Nelson went off to summer camp, escorted there by Miller. The boys cut down cedar trees for logs, skinned them ("because they last a lot longer that way"), made doors and windows, shingled the roof, and filled the cracks with moss. At the end of the summer, Miller wrote Abby in an amused way about "finally being admitted" to this sanctum in the woods.

There was an active social life among the many families who summered in the area. Junior's complex at the Eyrie included a "playhouse," a harbinger of greater things to come at Pocantico. Among other amenities, the playhouse had a squash court, a bowling alley, and a large room where a Miss Covington conducted a dancing class for the Rockefellers and neighboring children—some ten boys and a dozen girls. Every several weeks, the dancers and other invited guests would have a party that, John 3rd reported to his diary, was always "a great success." After the last such party, he wrote: "I am beginning to really enjoy dancing with girls." It was a premature judgment—John was a long way from feeling socially at ease.

There was no indication that John was attracted to any particular girl. Romance that summer swirled mainly about Babs, who was the object of attention on the part of a number of young men (including possibly Zenos Miller, judging by his description of the "pall" that settled on Seal Harbor when Babs left to join her parents on the trip to China). But the man with the inside track seemed to be David Milton, a Williams graduate who now attended Columbia Law School. His family were friends of the Rockefellers, living near Pocantico in Westchester County. David and Babs had known each other a long time.

Miller escorted John home to Pocantico early in September, because school at Loomis was due to start at midmonth. There was more driving of the Dodge, shopping for school, and playing games that Miller had taught John, notably the "Chinese game" (mah-jongg) and Five Hundred Rummy. It was clear that a strong bond had developed between the boy and his companion. One Saturday they were away for the entire day, going first to the Aero Club in Manhattan and then to Forest Hills in Queens to watch the Americans (including Bill Tilden) defeat the Japanese in a Davis Cup match ("Had wonderful day").

In his last report to Abby, Miller took the opportunity to give Junior some indirect advice about the role of a father. Miller's father was a missionary in China, and Miller felt deeply about the subject, because he had seen so little of him since the age of fifteen. He wrote:

John, I think, has grown in manliness this summer. He has reached the age when boys grow up very rapidly. You will notice a big difference in him when you get back from China. I believe that Mr. Rockefeller should try to recall his own youth and as far as his time permits try to be with John as much as he can.

For the next three years John will consciously imitate men he meets. All boys do at this age. If Mr. Rockefeller visits Loomis occasionally and takes an interest in John's activities it will be a fine thing for John and he will get in the habit of bringing his questions to his own father.[11]

Ten months later, in July 1922, Miller was flying an airplane with two passengers aboard, coming in for a landing at Framingham, Massachusetts, on a rainy afternoon. The passengers were his younger brother, Ralph, also a student at the Harvard Medical School, and Clarence Gamble, a 1920 graduate of the same school. They were on the first leg of a transcontinental trip to Pasadena, California, to visit Gamble's relatives. Gamble, an heir to the Procter & Gamble fortune, was about to begin graduate studies at Princeton in biochemistry. Interestingly, he later became active and controversial in the field—population control—that would come to dominate much of John 3rd's adult life.

The plane, which Gamble had purchased from the Italian government, was loaded with luggage for the trip. Something went wrong, and it dove three hundred feet into a quagmire near the airfield. Zenos Miller was buried under the wreckage and died almost instantly from a broken neck and fractured skull. Gamble was severely injured and Ralph Miller escaped with bruises and cuts.

There was no mention of this accident in John's diary. But he took up a new hobby, compiling scrapbooks. The first clipping in the first scrapbook was a lengthy account of the accident in the *Boston Sunday Post* of July 23, 1922.

12

LOOMIS DAYS

NATHANIEL HORTON BATCHELDER was very much the schoolmaster of his times. The winds of change were blowing generally in educational circles in the early decades of the century, and Batchelder was a firm believer in progress and in bringing a wholesome and democratic experience to the privileged boys who attended private preparatory schools. The objective of the school he presided over, the Loomis Institute, was to "train youth in habits of vigor and self-reliance" and thereby prepare them to lead responsible lives as leaders and citizens of a great democratic nation.

Although at the core Loomis was a traditional prep school, it had some characteristics that distinguished it from its larger, better-known, and longer-established counterparts such as Groton and St. Paul's. For one thing, tuition was free, as specified in the bequests of various members of the Loomis family and in the charter of the school, which opened its doors in 1914 with Batchelder as the first headmaster.[1] Free tuition had the effect of attracting many more applicants than spaces in a school designed for 180 boys; it was, moreover, a source of great pride to the headmaster and trustees of Loomis that family wealth was not a precondition to accepting an applicant.

Loomis offered two courses of study apart from the standard college preparatory program—a "business" course and an agricultural course. The latter utilized a hundred-acre farm on the fertile bottomland that had been the ancestral home of the Loomis family since 1639. It stood six miles north of Hartford, very near Windsor and so near the confluence of the Farmington and Connecticut rivers that every spring there was fear of flooding. The literature of the Loomis Institute naturally extolled the virtues of "the unusual combination of life in the country with all the advantages of close proximity to a considerable city."

Aside from providing some produce for the tables of Loomis, the farm also helped fulfill the objective of training youths in the "habits of vigor." The boys supplied an instant source of labor when occasion demanded, as in bringing in the corn harvest. They also took on other chores, such as shoveling snow, preparing the athletic grounds, and waiting on tables. In addition, of course, there was strong emphasis on a full program of all the sports of the day.

Participation in these activities also contributed to the other objective of "self-reliance," but more important in this regard was the Student Council, whose members were all elected by the boys. The council had a substantial measure of authority in self-government, yet this presented no danger to the school administration: there were no student radicals on hand, nor were there likely to be.

These characteristics of the Loomis Institute made up the "democratic" experience that was of such importance to Junior as a parent. In other respects, the place was, as noted, quite traditional. From Batchelder (Harvard '01) on down, the eighteen-member faculty was drawn almost exclusively from those northeastern colleges later to be known as the "Ivy League," and the great majority of Loomis graduates attended the same colleges. Most boys took the college prep course, which required Latin. And there was the customary emphasis on a good moral and religious environment. The boys attended chapel regularly. Any boy caught smoking was likely to be expelled (although the council would make the final decision).

Clearly, it was not free tuition that made Loomis an attractive school to Junior for his oldest son. The school seemed made to order for what he was seeking—small, but not too small; not nearly as Spartan as the Olmstead School, yet with an emphasis on making use of the healthy physical environment; it had a good moral atmosphere; and it had a strong faculty and program.

It might be argued that it was selfish or thoughtless for a Rockefeller to send a son to Loomis when the effect might be to deny a place to another boy whose family could not afford the tuition elsewhere. But there is another way of looking at the matter. For Junior to yield to this objection would be to accept the idea of rigid class stratification. Besides, it was not the Loomis policy to populate the school to any great extent with boys from underprivileged families. It wanted to be competitive with the well-established private schools in matters of class, image, and status, so that having a Rockefeller in the student body was all to the good. Evidence that Junior did give thought to the bonus of free tuition was the fact that he made a $50,000 grant to Loomis when his son neared graduation. And as was to be expected, Loomis benefited substantially over the years from the annual contributions of its distinguished alumnus.[2]

By the time John 3rd entered Loomis, his sister was already a lost cause as far as formal education was concerned. She would take an occasional course, in French or in dancing, but directed her real energies to as active a social life as the chaperones would allow. Babs' penchant for evading their protection was one reason her parents and her Aunt Lucy took her along on lengthy trips to the Orient. Junior was determined that his sons would do much better in school than Babs, and so John entered Loomis earnestly mindful of his father's goals for him—that he do well in studies, participate in sports, engage in school activities, keep clean and temperate habits, and be financially responsible.

He was a stripling in that September of 1921, standing five feet, seven inches, but weighing only ninety-five pounds. His trepidation over entering a boarding school where he knew no one was soon eased. He helped the boys fix up the tennis courts, and he played tennis every day he could. The food, he found, was "fair," though the meat was "tough." He liked his single room with a fireplace on the ground floor of Taylor dormitory. After only a week at school, he wrote in his diary: "For some reason, I don't know why, I am having a great time. The fellows are all awfully nice to me." And a few days later: "I think the school is a great place to be." He planned to practice hard to make the tennis team the following spring, and he signed up to sell advertising for the *Loomis Log* (the "weakly" newspaper).

He found even the infirmary to be "very nice" when he spent a night there with a bad cough in late September. However, his frail health made this a decidedly premature judgment. He came to dread the place, his diary over four years being peppered with hopes and prayers that he could either avoid it or get out of it. Only a month after his first infirmary visit he had an earache while playing tennis. He went to Windsor to see a doctor, and then had to go to the infirmary. The ache grew worse, accompanied by pain over his eyes. The school brought in a special nurse. Miss Scales came up from New York to attend him. His diary records: "Hundreds of doctors (it seems that way to me) come to see me." The next day, two more doctors from New York arrived, and he was put under gas to have the ear punctured.

There followed a prolonged series of ups and downs, recovery and classes followed by relapses. Home for Christmas vacation, the ear improved, John experienced a rise in spirits when he was given an Evans power cycle for Christmas. But back at school the ear infection flared up again, filling his sinuses and giving him headaches. By late January, Junior and Abby had had enough. John was brought home, where a doctor came to treat him three times a day. Old John Browning came from his retirement to tutor the boy during his illness. During this time, there was a poignant diary entry revealing how little John saw his father: "Nelson and I had supper with Father tonight." The ear was better, but the decision had been made: John would spend the winter with Grandfather at Ormond Beach. A tutor was hired, a Mr. G. de Lagerburg, who was to follow the Loomis curriculum in the hope that John could pass the examinations at the end of the semester.

On February 1, he wrote: "Ear less deaf. No pain. Feel fine." Ten days later, he was on the train for his "first trip south." To his delight, the power cycle was shipped down and he taught his tutor to ride it. The family thoughtfully provided another power cycle so John would not be off riding alone. He noted: "Hot weather does make you feel lazy." And indeed John and the tutor spent much time riding power cycles, trading postage stamps, and playing pinochle, with occasional bouts of studying to catch up.

In March, Junior came down for ten days to visit his father and his son, and the rare experience of being with his father every day made it a wonderful time for the boy. He taught his father to ride the power cycle. They went horseback riding, took automobile and boat trips, "heard darkies singing in the evening," watched baseball games, "saw President Harding at the Ormond Golf Course," played golf and tennis. But the visit ended on a typical note: on the last evening, John had to "go over his accounts" with his father.

The other noteworthy event in Florida was John's first faint stirring of adolescent romance. He went swimming in the ocean for the first time and learned the lesson that he was very susceptible to sunburn, something he had not discovered in the cool mists of Maine. But it was worth it because he was able to meet Dorothy Johnson, who went swimming every day. She was the daughter of the manager of the Ormond Beach Hotel, where the tutor stayed. John and Dorothy went swimming together daily, John with a towel draped over his shoulders, the ear problem forgotten. He wrote in his diary that he had been "waiting a long time to meet her," and that he was "awfully strong" for her, but also, "Am awfully bashful . . . decided Dorothy doesn't dislike me."

In April, Senior, with John in tow, made his annual trek north to Lakewood and the cooler golfing weather in New Jersey. Here John played golf every day ("I can't improve"), enjoying the droll company of his grandfather. He was feeling fine now and weighed 108 pounds. "My voice is almost all changed. I am glad." At the end of May, he went to Loomis for the semester examinations in a pessimistic mood: "I almost bet I don't get to Loomis in the fall." He was doubtless still too young to appreciate that Headmaster Batchelder would do his best to keep this particular student in the fold. Indeed, Batchelder soon arranged with Junior for a young Loomis faculty member, Ralph Stevens, to serve as John's tutor for the summer.

That July at Pocantico (as John reported fully in his diary), Nelson shot himself in the leg with BB shot that he had glued to a .22 blank and fired in a toy pistol. He was taken to the hospital, where the pellets were removed under gas. The result of his experiment was dependence on crutches for several days.

Just as John 3rd's health had its ups and downs, so it was with other aspects of these school years, that long stretch of adolescence that is so painful and bittersweet for many people. John had his share of suffering because of his shy and sensitive nature, because of the burden of his name and his father's expectations, and because he took very seriously the moral values he had been taught. In short, he was extremely self-conscious and very inhibited. He wanted desperately to participate, to be popular and accepted by others, but he would not try to achieve this by smoking, drinking, swearing, violating the Sabbath, or seeking sexual activity. And he was really comfortable only with others who felt the same way, invariably a small percentage of any given group. There is no doubt that his principles sustained him, but they often resulted in bleak and lonely sustenance.

Like most boys of his age, John was attracted to girls, but the puzzle of how to deal with the opposite sex without really dealing with it was a constant frustration. His heart took a jolt during that summer of 1922 at Seal Harbor when he met Catherine Robb of Concord, Massachusetts, a very pretty blond girl, made all the more attractive by her sweet and thoughtful nature. They went sailing, for rides in the red Willys his father let him use, and to the social affairs where, for once, John enjoyed dancing—as long as it was with Catherine. She later wrote to him that he should get over feeling he was not a good dancer: he was "as good as most boys."

Catherine became one of John's more faithful correspondents, over a period of some six years. Their relationship was sweet, but essentially long-distance in nature. For years they kept inviting each other to dances at their respective schools, but something almost always kept them apart. Catherine's dances always came on the weekends that John could not leave school. For her, the train connections from Providence (where she attended the Wheeler School) to Hartford were all but unworkable. One time she had to be a bridesmaid at a cousin's wedding on the big weekend at Loomis. She managed a visit to Loomis only once, at the end of John's junior year. Perhaps it was the long wait, but he somehow managed to act "dumb," as he told his diary. Catherine's follow-up letter, though, was typically generous and warm. Even this occasion had been threatened when the prospective chaperone, Abby, came down with tonsillitis, but at the last minute Catherine's mother was able to enlist a family friend as substitute.

John did go to Concord for a few days as a houseguest of the Robbs, and Catherine almost reciprocated one Christmas vacation in a trip to Manhattan, but had to return home abruptly because of her grandfather's impending death. The best opportunities for John and Catherine to see each other were at Seal Harbor, but even there the fates were unkind. In the summer of 1923, Junior and Abby took their children on a tour of Europe while the Robb family was in Maine. The following year, the Robbs went to Europe while the Rockefellers traveled in the United States.

Although John and Catherine were pen pals more than anything else, her image, the stream of letters, and the fact that his schoolmates knew he had a girlfriend (even though she never seemed to materialize), helped to cheer him during the lonely years at boarding school. Yet it may also have reinforced his shyness. He was uncomfortable in company when he did not know anyone as well as he felt he knew Catherine. Because there was no other such person, he tended to avoid social occasions when he could, and when he did attend, he often would make an entry in his diary such as: "CR should have been there. She is the nicest and prettiest girl I know." The names of other girls popped up occasionally—Mary Clark (who later married Nelson), Marion "Molly" Angell (who later married Billy McAlpin, John's cousin from Baltimore), Lydia Garrison, Mildred Vanderpool, Anne Colby. During one Christmas vacation, John attended his first house party in Orange, New Jersey, at Anne Colby's home, where he had "a really nice time." He was much attracted to Anne, but then, so was everyone else. He told his diary that being with her was like "being one in 100."

Christmas vacation always brought a joyous release, a chance to be with the family again after the loneliness of school. These holiday weeks were packed with activities—attending the automobile show, the boat show, and plays or movies almost every matinee or evening (as well as the inevitable appointments with doctors and dentists). On one occasion, John was taken to a performance of *Tosca*, and the future developer of Lincoln Center for the Performing Arts wrote in his diary: "Can't say I like opera much." There was time with Father—playing squash, visiting his office, meeting his associates, visiting the Stock Exchange, having dinner at the Whitehall Club. And there were the social invitations that mounted every year for each of the boys. Nelson would gleefully tote his up as if they were merit badges, but for John they were a source of anxiety. One year his mother wrote to him at Loomis that unless he objected she would accept an invitation to a major dance that had come for him. He objected. She dutifully declined on his behalf and wrote gently: "Of course I don't want you to go anywhere unless you want to, but I am afraid that if you put off too long going out socially that it may be hard for you when you begin."

Bringing one's cousin or sister to a dance at a boarding school for boys was by no means a social disgrace, given all the logistical problems involved in securing a true date. On one occasion, Abby brought up one of John's many cousins, Madeline Spelman. It was her first dance, and although John was properly attentive, his diary reveals that his mind was on "CR." On another occasion, John was dateless and did not attend a dance; had he done so, he might have met his future wife. Kenneth Ward Hooker, a classmate John did not know well, brought his cousin to the dance. She was Blanchette Ferry Hooker, youngest of four daughters in a family that had recently moved to Manhattan and was to be very much involved in the 1920s social whirl. One time Babs was scheduled to be John's "date" at a Loomis dance. She wrote to him that she would try to persuade "the family" to allow David Milton to drive her there, but if they refused, she and David would do it anyway. She cautioned John not to tell. He would not—he kept confidences well even when he did not approve of the behavior. But he may have found another answer: he ended up in the infirmary, and Babs had to give up her plot.

Much of John 3rd's career at Loomis was a struggle. He developed quite a habit of self-depreciation with such diary entries as: "I have no personal attraction. Nobody wants to sit next to me at the table or anything" . . . "I have no real friends here at school" . . . "Wish I was more popular." There was always the contrast offered by his brother, Nelson, who was fast becoming a social dynamo, cutting quite a figure with the girls. On one occasion John wrote: "Nelson dances very well. I am rotten." And later: "Nelson always makes a big hit."

Nelson's ebullience came through in his letters to John, never intentionally cruel, but sometimes thoughtless. He wrote enthusiastically about his girlfriends. Once John nearly had a serious accident when he was stuck climbing a rope at school and had to be helped down. Nelson promptly wrote how he had just set the rope-climbing record at the Lincoln School. Aside from his seemingly inborn self-confidence, Nelson had certain advantages in going to a day school in Manhattan, where social activities abounded and his classmates could be entertained at home. He was able to drive cars much more often than John. Once he stopped to ask a policeman directions in New Haven and had a friendly chat. The policeman told him he should go see the Yale Bowl, but Nelson said he didn't know where it was. The policeman stopped a passing motorcycle cop, and Nelson was given an escort. The future governor of New York State, just turned seventeen years of age, wrote to his brother: "Now if that is not pretty swift I would like to know. Think, when I arrive in a town I have the officer meet me and show me around. That kind of stuff *goes big with me.*"[3]

Abby was concerned over the note of sadness she detected in John's letters, and she tried to cheer him up. But when John was plunged into gloom by failing to be renominated for the Student Council in his junior year, she uncharacteristically lectured him. She told him there must be a reason and that perhaps he could find it out and correct the impression that "the boys find not to their liking." She wrote:

I am deeply grieved to have your feelings hurt but I have felt for some little time that you and Nelson and Babs were assuming a rather superior air about people and places and things that was not justified or becoming. Perhaps the boys [at Loomis] felt this too. I know that this is only a passing phase & that underneath that you are just as fine and good & true as ever but perhaps the boys felt that you were getting to feel a bit "important."[4]

Nelson and Babs may have had this problem, but one hardly finds a hint of snobbery in John's actions, letters, or diary. The truth was that, in addition to the agonies of shyness, he was experiencing the infuriating curse that often attends it—having his quiet and reserved nature, the frequent defense of a shy person, taken for an air of superiority, aloofness, or even arrogance.

John was extremely self-conscious about what he felt was his deformed jaw. Any other person would probably have told him that he was exaggerating the problem, but one cannot doubt the intensity of his feelings. He finally had his hair parted on the left side after years of wearing it straight back, and he felt that this helped a bit in diverting attention from the outline of his jaw. But he kept seeking medical help at every opportunity. One doctor told him his jaw was "out of joint." Another said the muscles were split. He was given heat treatments and a salve to apply. X rays were taken at the Rockefeller Institute. But, in the end, the medical judgment always was the same—nothing could be done about it. And so in group pictures taken at Loomis, John always appeared the same—with a very serious expression and looking slightly to the right so that his jaw would not show in outline. Mrs. Batchelder was able to persuade him to pose for a bas-relief sculpture she wanted to do only after assuring him that it would be in profile (hence not showing the angularity of his jaw). It was a good likeness showing a handsome boy. For years afterward, a photograph of this bas-relief was the only accurate likeness that the newspapers had of the camera-shy John D. Rockefeller 3rd.[5] Ironically, the only other photograph that was identified as him and appeared often during this period was actually a photograph of Nelson. John didn't seem to mind.

Despite his difficulties, John showed a measure of courage, a good deal of resolve, and a lot of hard work during his Loomis years. He took up boxing though he did not like it. He also took up debating for a while although he was "scared stiff." He made the tennis team, moving up from sixth man to fifth to fourth, and winning his share of matches on a regional championship team.[6] He achieved this despite the handicap of a chronically weak ankle. He first sprained it playing hockey at Loomis, and kept on spraining it in tennis; indeed, the only deformity he had in later life was his ankle, not his jaw.

He was active in Junto (a religious club at Loomis) and became president of the French Club. He worked so hard selling ads for the Loomis publications that he became secretary of the Publications Board and president of the *Loomiscellany* (the Loomis yearbook). In his senior year he was reelected to the Student Council, receiving 135 votes out of a possible 162. He called it "a fateful day . . . very happy indeed to get so many."

Nevertheless, John's belief that he was unpopular persisted. "I wish I was different in many ways than I am. Is room for lots of improvement in me," he wrote. Later he showed some insight: "Am much too self-conscious at all times." He was by no means devoid of friends. Those he came to know best were John Ross, who became president of both the council and the senior class; Bob Russell; Dave Swope (whose father was president of General Electric); Doug Robertson; and Milton Bush, who showed spunk by competing in basketball and tennis despite the fact that he had lost an arm as a result of a childhood accident. Ross, Russell, and Swope were all gregarious, but Robertson and Bush, if anything, were more diffident even than John. When Bush spent a week as John's guest at Seal Harbor, John wrote that he "never says anything when any girls [are] around."[7]

John's favorite was Bob Russell, and he was delighted when they became roommates in their junior year: "I really quite like rooming double. Never done it before at school." The two became good friends, frequently inviting each other home during vacation periods. When Russell spent the first semester of the senior year in Europe, John ended up rooming with Doug Robertson. He kept telling his diary that Doug was "very nice," but he was happy to be reunited with Russell halfway through the final semester.[8]

On balance, John scored well on the goals that he knew his father had in mind for him. For moral and temperate behavior, he clearly deserved an A+. He was fully engaged in all of the school activities that he could handle, so he merited an A in this department. For sports and physical activity, another A. He engaged in exercise every day except Sunday. If it was not tennis, it was baseball, hockey, boxing, long hikes in the country, running around the track, or working out in the gym. From the stripling who entered Loomis, he emerged five inches taller and fifty pounds heavier. In his junior and senior years, he and his roommate routinely pulled their beds out to sleep outdoors, even in the middle of winter unless it rained or snowed (their second-floor room in Mason dormitory opened to the roof of the first floor). Perhaps this helped, because John's health seemed to improve generally, and he became a less frequent customer of the infirmary.

As far as financial responsibility was concerned, John merited an A+. His allowance was fifty dollars per week, which was to cover clothing, travel, gifts, charitable contributions, and all other personal expenses. In one early year, he gave more than half of his income to charity, including the Fifth Avenue Baptist Church and the *New York Times* "100 Neediest Cases." In his later years at Loomis, he saved or gave to charity about half his income, prompting Junior to write to him: "To be able to save half of one's income is certainly a fine record, and I congratulate you upon it."[9]

With all his activities (including writing a dozen or more letters a week), John wondered frequently in his diary where he would find the time to do everything. Something had to give, and unfortunately it was the one dimension that cast something of a pall over the fine record in everything else—his grades. Here he earned a C or at best a C+. He did very well in mathematics, not so well in French, and poorly in English, Latin, and history. In physics, he got a midterm E ("Physics makes me sick," he wrote), but he buckled down and managed to pass, and then earned a B the second semester. His average score on the College Boards accurately reflected his overall classroom performance—76 ("not very good," he lamented). This naturally became an item of concern in Abby's letters: she wondered if he was trying to do too many things and whether having a roommate was "too diverting." It also brought on some heart-to-heart talks with Father. After one such talk, John wrote: "F thinks I should get all B's for marks. Admit I would like to but can't say I think it is worth grinding all the time to obtain them."

The high value that Junior always placed on his years at Brown made him especially attentive to the choice of a college for his oldest son. He hoped fervently that John could get into one of the best colleges and do well, and so he began to explore the matter rather early, before John had finished his sophomore year at Loomis. He wrote for advice to Abraham Flexner:

Mrs. Rockefeller favors Princeton first and Harvard next. She does not favor Brown. Personally I have never been greatly interested in Princeton, nor would I ever think of suggesting that any of my sons go to Harvard. Mrs. Rockefeller's interest in Princeton is largely because of Babby's interest, because Mrs. Rockefeller has visited there with Babby a number of times and has come to know a number of Princeton men.

For myself I think John, like his father, would do better in a smaller college rather than a larger one. He is modest, retiring, and self-effacing. In a large college he will not force his way to the front and get into positions of responsibility and leadership, which in a smaller college might be open to him and the educative value of which seem to me very considerable. Since Mrs. Rockefeller is opposed to Brown, I should have in mind Dartmouth, Amherst or Williams. The President at Dartmouth is an extraordinarily fine man and the spirit of the institution progressive and modern.[10]

Flexner also did not think too much of Princeton. In his response he wrote:

I should not myself send a son to Princeton. I confess that I do not know the institution at first hand, though I have spent a few days there at different times, but it does not seem to me to embody a really fine spirit either of scholarship or otherwise. There are some excellent, not to say a few eminent men on the faculty, but the student body is not, I believe, either serious or stimulating.[11]

Of the smaller colleges, Flexner preferred Dartmouth as "the simplest and most democratic," but also praised Amherst and Williams. In responding to another question, Flexner pointed out that all of the colleges except Dartmouth required Latin or Greek for admission of candidates for the B.A. degree. This prompted Junior to think about his four younger sons and whether he had created a problem for himself in sending them to the "progressive" Lincoln School, which did not require the study of classical languages. He asked Flexner, "How are Lincoln School scholars to get into any of these colleges?"[12]

At least one reason why Yale was never mentioned (the same as Junior's for dismissing Harvard, and Abby's opposing Brown) was that both parents thought John should go to college in a small town rather than a city. Abby also thought it would not be good for John to go to college in a city (Providence) where he had many relatives. Junior's dismissal of Princeton is curious, considering that it offered an ideal setting for his purpose and that he knew many distinguished Princeton alumni, including his close and trusted adviser, Raymond Fosdick, and the eminent lawyer Moses T. Pyne, a friend of his father's and a staunch alumnus known as the "Prince of Princetonians." It may be that Junior was perhaps carrying over from his Brown days some bias against the "big three," or he might have thought them too high-powered for John. He added Antioch College and the University of Virginia to his search list. Another mark against Princeton for Junior may have been the fact that the women of his family favored it so strongly.

Junior's ultimate choice was Dartmouth and he wrote its president, Ernest M. Hopkins (a trustee of the Rockefeller Foundation), asking if John could be enrolled in the Class of 1929. He said: "Mrs. Rockefeller agrees with me as to the wisdom of this step, although we have thought best to say nothing to John about the matter at this time, leaving the final decision to be made by him as we confer together about the matter. . . ." Hopkins wrote an intelligent response, saying that he would be delighted to register John, but warning that "I should not want him to come to Dartmouth unless it came to be his own desire to be here."[13]

In September 1924, before beginning his senior year at Loomis, John left Seal Harbor for a series of campus visits. His father let him use "the Cadillac," and John drove throughout New England to visit Bowdoin, Dartmouth, Amherst, Williams, and Brown. He even drove around the campuses of Smith and Mount Holyoke. He dropped the Cadillac at Pocantico and took a train to Philadelphia, where his campus visits were not like those of most prospective students—his tour guides at Haverford, Swarthmore, and Princeton were the presidents of the respective schools. He arrived at Princeton on a Saturday and was shown around by John Grier Hibben, who had succeeded Woodrow Wilson. John had dinner at the Hibbens' that evening. The next morning, he went to church and then had another tour of the campus with Hibben. Back home John wrote in his diary: "Princeton has most attractive buildings and location of all." Princeton was looming as his choice, with the encouragement of Babs and also of Nelson, who wrote that he hoped John would choose Princeton and that he (Nelson) wanted to go there.

By this time, Junior had become so immersed in the subject that he wrote a four-page "Memorandum of the Choice of a College." The points he made under various headings could apply to all of his boys, but it was clear that he had John foremost in mind. The memorandum was undated, but "January 1925" was penciled on a copy in John 3rd's file. Junior wrote that if "health is a consideration, Cambridge, and particularly New Haven, might well be avoided; country life is preferable to city life." On educational opportunities: "The chief purpose for which colleges exist is intellectual development. . . . If a boy goes to college with a desire to get an education and the purpose to work for it, it makes relatively little difference which of the better colleges he goes to. . . ." Similarly, on physical equipment: "In any of the better colleges living conditions are thoroughly wholesome and comfortable." Junior stressed the value of "all-around development . . . thorough participation in the varied experiences of college life—athletic, literary, business, religious, esthetic, social, etc.— which reproduce on a small scale a life in the world at large."

Junior was firm about how he expected his sons to perform:

I covet for my boys scholarly attainment in school and college. By that I do not mean standing at the head of their classes, but being well up in the upper half. They are all of them capable of more than average performance, and should not be satisfied with getting merely pass marks. By natural endowment and through the opportunities open to them they ought to rank well above the average. This I confidently expect. Mediocrity ought not to satisfy them, any more than it does me.

Again, Junior surely had John particularly in mind as he discoursed on the importance of participation:

A boy who is retiring, diffident, slow to make friends and not apt to push himself, however able, may and not infrequently does go through college without getting any of the benefits of participation in college activities. Such a boy will be much helped if he is fortunate enough to go to college having several good friends among his classmates, for it is always easier for a group to get into things than an individual. Fraternity life is another tremendous help to the boy of a retiring disposition. . . . I know of no more helpful single influence in my own college life than that exerted upon me, particularly in my freshman year, by my fellow fraternity members. Sharp distinction should be drawn between those college clubs which take in members only in the junior year . . . and the four year fraternities which take in members of the freshman class.

Here Junior clearly was referring to the always controversial dining clubs that were solidly entrenched at Princeton despite the efforts of several previous presidents (including Woodrow Wilson) to dislodge them. To Junior these clubs were the epitome of the social exclusivity and pretentiousness that he disliked so much. He was not being hypocritical; his fraternity experience at Brown had been so positive that he assumed fraternities were good everywhere. Adherents of the club system, of course, would agree that if anything the fraternities, especially at Dartmouth, were worse than the clubs. Junior was also mindful that although Princeton appeared to have the ideal small-town setting, it had a "fast" reputation, enhanced by F. Scott Fitzgerald's *This Side of Paradise* (1920). Princeton was also conveniently located close to the temptations of both New York City and Philadelphia, while Dartmouth was splendidly isolated. This may be why Junior concluded his memorandum with the injunction that for a boy to get the most out of college he should stay on the campus and avoid "frequent trips home."

However, John soon made up his mind that he wanted to go to Princeton, and Junior somewhat ruefully conveyed the news to President Hopkins of Dartmouth: "I hope John's decision will prove to be a wise one. In any event, it is his own decision and the more assuming of the responsibility in this matter is a good thing for him." Junior offered the consolation that Laurance "says he is going to Dartmouth."[14] As it turned out, Laurance went to Princeton, too, but Nelson, the one who perhaps needed the isolated setting the most, went to Dartmouth.

John finished his career at Loomis on the upbeat—healthier, happier, and doing better in schoolwork than ever before. The big event that spring of 1925 was the wedding of Babs and David Milton on May 14. She had been "introduced to society" on her twenty-first birthday the previous November at an evening reception at No. 10 West 54th. Shortly afterward, the engagement was announced, although Babs and David had been secretly engaged for many months before that. The wedding was the kind of affair the New York press loved, with references to Babs as "rich heiress" and "world's richest bride" and to David as "a penniless law clerk." Typical of the Rockefellers, the list of 1,200 guests for the reception was not taken from the pages of the Social Register. It included politicians (Governor Al Smith, John Davis, Chauncey Depew), businessmen, prominent Jews, members of philanthropic and educational organizations, and all of the Rockefeller servants from both Pocantico and No. 10.

Characteristically for Babs, the wedding was held at No. 10 instead of in church, and the words "obey" and "serve" were dropped from the service. After the wedding, she was quoted as saying that she felt "her first day of freedom." Junior's relief at having Babs married was suggested by his uncharacteristic behavior. After the newlyweds had slipped away, ready to take an ocean liner the next day for a five-month honeymoon in Europe, Junior emerged from No. 10 with a beaming smile. He spotted some "shopgirls" still lingering in front of the house, and invited them in to see the flower-banked ballroom and the rest of the house. Then he reemerged and escorted an "aged Negress with a shopping bag" on the same tour, scoring points in the press for this "democratic" behavior.[15]

Two days after the wedding, the Loomis tennis team competed in the Yale Interscholastic Tournament and won it for the first time. The only match that John lost was to the captain of the New Haven High School team. Commencement came on June 6, and John was chairman of Senior Night, both of his parents being in attendance. In the class voting in the *Loomiscellany*, John was voted "Biggest Grind," but also "Most Gentlemanly" and "Most Dignified." He also received votes for "Most Likely to Succeed," "Done Most for Loomis," "Straightest," "Most Obliging," and "Most Serious."

John had one last Loomis-related experience in which he felt popular for the first time. He agreed to spend a month as an assistant counselor at a summer camp in Maine run by a Loomis faculty member. He slept in a tent with six of the "cute little fellows." His particular role was to teach the boys tennis, but he also took them hiking, fishing, and swimming. When it came time to leave, the entire camp turned out to give him a cheer, and all the campers came down to the dock to see him off. "Really hate to go in some ways," he wrote.

13

THE COLLEGE MAN

IN MID-SEPTEMBER OF 1925, 647 young men descended on the campus of Princeton University. They were the Class of 1929, although only 437 of them were to graduate four years later. Most of the rest were dismissed for academic reasons; a few died, the result of automobile accidents, illness, or suicide.

They came to a campus rich in tradition and history, site of the fourth oldest college in North America, dominated by the stone bulk of Nassau Hall, erected in 1756 and for a time in 1783 the site of the Continental Congress. Across Cannon Green stood the twin Greek temples known as Whig and Clio halls, housing the nation's oldest college literary and debating societies, the American Whig Society and the Cliosophic Society, where such Princeton students as James Madison, Aaron Burr, and Woodrow Wilson developed their forensic skills.

The main campus was a rectangle half a mile across between University Place on the west and Washington Road to the east, and more than a mile in length, bounded on the south by athletic fields and Lake Carnegie and on the north by Nassau Street, the main street and business section of the town of Princeton.

Those were the days before Palmer Square, and some of the shops and buildings on Nassau Street were fairly decrepit. But they did not detract from the charm of the tree-shaded campus, nor from the ardor of alumni who tended to be passionately devoted to the orange and black of Princeton, the Princeton Tiger, their eating clubs, and the worth of all that their degrees represented. Like its counterparts among the elite of American universities, Princeton regularly graduated men who took places of national leadership in business, government, the professions, and the arts.

255

Princeton's previous presidents included such luminaries as Jonathan Dickinson, Aaron Burr, Sr., John Witherspoon, and Woodrow Wilson. The incumbent in 1925, John Grier Hibben, was presiding over an era of peace, stability, and growth following the innovative and stormy years of Wilson's tenure.[1] A minister and philosopher, Hibben was a man John D. Rockefeller, Jr., could not fail to admire once he came to know him. Hibben was distressed by some of the trends of the 1920s, by "the hypocrisy attending the Eighteenth Amendment, by false standards of living growing out of our period of fictitious prosperity and by a skepticism toward old concepts of morals and religion."[2] He did what he could at Princeton to ameliorate the influence of the Roaring Twenties by prohibiting students from having automobiles on campus, enlarging residential capacity by building ten more dormitories, trying (less actively than Wilson) to abate the social dominance of the eating clubs, and drawing up plans for a student center.

His patience and wisdom were evident in his correspondence with Junior once John 3rd decided to go to Princeton. Junior was concerned that John would not know anyone in the large entering class, which raised obvious questions about living quarters and roommates:

John is quite diffident and does not easily make friends. It is for that reason that I personally have felt that he would not be happy, at least the first year, among so large a group of strangers as the Freshman class at Princeton. But he has taken the responsibility of making the decision, and I am hopeful that it will prove to be a wise decision.[3]

There followed a number of letters to Hibben on the subjects of John rooming alone and finding suitable quarters for him, all of this correspondence unknown to John. Junior continued to keep himself informed by writing confidential letters also to the dean of freshmen, Colonel Radcliffe Heermance, and his assistant, John Colt, who was John's adviser. The replies were patient and helpful.

The room problem was finally solved when it turned out that the six Loomis classmates who also entered Princeton included John's former roommate, Doug Robertson. John and Doug agreed to room together, and were assigned to 235 Henry Hall, typically comfortable Princeton accommodations, which included a study with a fireplace, flanked by two small bedrooms. Built in the Collegiate Gothic style of most Princeton buildings, Henry Hall looked ancient although it had been completed only two years before John and Doug moved in.

Being in the southwest corner of the campus, it was convenient to the main hostelry in town, the Princeton Inn, and the terminus of the rail spur to the main line at Princeton Junction.

In 1922 Junior had made a financial contribution to Princeton that had no connection with the possibility that any of his sons might go there. It was a grant of $12,000 annually for five years to support a Library of Industrial Relations in the Department of Economics and Social Institutions.[4] This library turned out to be a handy resource to John 3rd when he came to do his senior thesis. Junior also made two gifts to Princeton after John enrolled, one to the Art Department and the other a $150,000 grant to improve athletic facilities. Junior had visited the campus and found to his surprise that Princeton had no squash courts and that indoor athletic facilities for students were overcrowded during the winter months. The old boiler room was renovated to create a glassed-in but unheated gym, thirteen courts for squash tennis, squash racquets, and handball, a lacrosse practice field, and facilities for visiting teams. These amenities were only some 150 yards from John's room in Henry Hall.

After the renovation, John went over on a Friday to reserve a squash court and found that they were all taken until Monday. "Rather amazing," he told his diary. Later he made an arrangement with the man in charge of the courts to reserve one at the same time every day. His diary comment managed to combine his sense of entitlement with an apologetic note: "Is only decent thing for the University to do though as F. gave the courts," he wrote.

As had been the case at Loomis, John's initial impressions of his new school were good. "Not the least bit homesick," he wrote. "Lots of nice fellows in the Class of '29 it seems to me." He endured the mild hazing by the sophomores ("Seems dumb and petty but I suppose it must be"). The freshmen were made to wear beanies, roll their trousers up to the knee, and walk in lockstep. A ritual was honored when the freshmen had their "flour picture" taken. After running around the campus in old clothes, they gathered on the steps of Clio Hall to be pelted with flour and water before being photographed.

John and Doug were pleased with their rooms after they had scrounged for furniture and stocked up with provisions for late night snacks. They settled down for the adjustment to college studies— "swamped with work," as John put it. He was a candidate for the B.S. degree under the "New Plan," which meant nothing more than avoiding a classical language requirement.[5] His courses were English, French, mathematics, chemistry, and the required survey course in history.

Despite the initial good feelings, the old self-consciousness came back with the lonely grind of study and the difficulty of making new friends. After six weeks, John wrote: "Am terribly nervous. Get all excited over nothing. Can't keep smile on my face which is most embarrassing. Muscles tremble. Give anything to be over it." And later: "Having terrible craving to eat all the time. Am a bottomless pit . . . give anything if I wasn't so nervous." And again: "Wish I was more popular—that is, had more personal attraction. Is a natural gift which I seem to lack, unfortunately."

One possible answer was to lose oneself in activities, and John believed in his father's injunction that this was an important part of college life. He attended a meeting for freshmen given by the Philadelphian Society, the YMCA of the Princeton campus, and heard a lecture about the "immoral conditions of Princeton." He signed up for a program of the society to devote one evening a week to teaching English to foreigners. For three years, he was the most loyal worker in this program, meeting almost every Tuesday evening with small groups of Greek and Italian immigrants at Dorothea House.[6]

The most popular campus jobs were settled by competition, and John was one of eight freshmen who entered the race to become a member of the business side of the *Daily Princetonian*. The object was to sell ads for the paper, and John started off enthusiastically, writing to prospects and trudging around town to solicit the local merchants. But the results were disillusioning:

Am having terrible time getting advertisements for the Princetonian. Makes me sore when the Standard Oil Co. of N.Y. wouldn't even take the trouble to answer my letter. Think they might at least do it on account of name. . . . One fellow in competition has over $500 worth while I have less than $200.

John was enough of a realist to know that he had to employ more "drag." His mother and father visited the campus in January, and he took the opportunity to solicit his father's "advice." The result was a list of some seventy companies prepared by Junior's staff, with asterisks marking those where John was advised to use his father's name specifically. Suddenly, John's prospects began to change as orders came in, including one for a four-hundred-dollar ad from the Standard Oil Company of New York. John commented in his diary on the wonders of "drag," including how he had been turned down by the advertising departments of several companies, but succeeded when he wrote to the presidents mentioning his father's name. He retained a bit of principle, however. When one company wrote that it would place an ad, but did not want to use the company name to avoid solicitation from other college publications, John politely declined.[7]

When the competition ended in March of 1926, John was the only one to be chosen for the *Princetonian* business board. He had written orders for $1,800 worth of ads. His nearest competitor had $1,725 worth, and everyone else was far behind. The victory soured a bit, however, when John learned that the second-place finisher was not taken on the board as well—"sort of a gyp not to take him on I think." He continued to work hard in the *"Prince"* office for several years, selling ads, making up pages, and doing the billing. But before his senior year, he was offered the post of advertising manager rather than the top job, that of business manager, which he thought he had earned, and so he declined.

Scarcely had the advertising competition of 1926 ended when John plunged into two new activities—a bid to make the freshman tennis team and the competition for football manager. He thought his prospects of making the tennis team were poor, but he had a good streak that spring and became sixth man. He played enough in competition to earn his freshman numeral ("Really too good to be true"). He tried to advance his tennis career in his sophomore year, but the ankle problem came back; he sprained it badly enough several times to be forced to use crutches.

In the 1920s, college football was still dominated by the northeastern schools, where the sport had originated, and if one could not play, the next best thing was to manage. Merely to enter the competition, one had to be nominated by two classmates and voted on by the entire class. To his delight, John was one of the eight to be selected. He went to work with this group in spring training and found himself working harder than he ever had before, taking care of the helmets one day, the tackling dummy the next, lugging pails of water, figuring out the schedule for thirty players to have their pictures taken, and so on.

The one sour note was that the managerial candidates had to report to the campus two weeks before the fall semester began. It was two solid weeks of work, and once school started more of the same every afternoon and all day on Saturdays. John endured the "hot swearing" by the coaches, the drudgery of keeping statistics on every game, and the countless errands as the competition intensified. He wrote:

Would give a lot to win the competition as all the family is counting on my doing it. Have never been beaten out in a competition yet. Must get more on the jump and try to anticipate people's wants.

One of the plums was to be among the four candidates chosen to go to Cambridge for the Harvard game in the fall of 1926. John was chosen, and he had a wonderful time: Princeton won and he was able briefly to see Catherine Robb (now attending an art school in Boston) and several of his Loomis classmates who attended Harvard. But about the same time, John learned to his dismay that his more ambitious competitors had been turning up at the field house to work every morning before classes. There was no way he could take more time away from studies, and so he reported matter-of-factly in his diary when "the most ambitious" candidate won the competition as the football season ended.

At Princeton John had to learn to deal with the notoriety of his name much more than he had had to do in the quiet precincts of Loomis. Only a few months after he entered Princeton, he returned to his room one Sunday afternoon to find half a dozen "village boys" waiting to see him. The boys, about ten or eleven years of age, were there to see what "John D." looked like. The object of their curiosity did not record their reactions. Later, as John began to attend dances, he noticed that practically every other fellow would bring his girl over to be introduced to him. He attributed this to "the name," not to any degree of popularity or visible qualities of his own.

Newspaper reporters assumed that the presence of the third "John D." in college must mean "good copy," but they had trouble finding it, so on occasion they invented it. Several times reporters came down from New York to seek out John, attracted by word of his activities, particularly the teaching of foreigners, the selling of ads, and the competition for football manager. The idea of a Rockefeller doing ordinary work was irresistible. John found that his good manners came in conflict with his strong desire to avoid the press. On one occasion, he did not invite several reporters, including a woman, into his room, but chatted briefly with them in the doorway. Afterward, he worried in his diary about this standoffishness. On another occasion, he knew a reporter wanted to make a train back to New York, so he stalled long enough to make the interview unproductive. He would not let his picture be taken, with the result that the bas-relief and the erroneous picture of Nelson were all that the press had for several years, except for one poor candid photo so heavily retouched it looked like a painting. John wrote home to find out if he was handling the press in the right way; murmurs of approval came back from No. 10.

The February 1, 1926, issue of *Time* carried an article about how "John Davison Rockefeller III" had tried to cash a check at "Joe's Lunchroom" on Nassau Street, and Joe declined in colorful fashion, thinking the young man was trying to put one over on him. "Absolutely untrue," John wrote in his diary. "Can't imagine how story started. Is all over college." But the story would not die. Two years later, an article in *Redbook* about John began with a lengthy account of the supposed incident, including remarks by both Joe and John 3rd that were certainly fictitious. Yet John learned that the press was not all bad. Though full of inaccuracies and missing the characterization of its subject by a wide mark, the article was clearly well intentioned in presenting John as a son worthy "to direct and continue the great Rockefeller benevolent trusts."[8]

In contrast to the hearty, gregarious, and relaxed person depicted in the *Redbook* article, John continued to suffer severe self-consciousness. One page in his diary summed up numerous smaller references made throughout his four years at Princeton:

Am afraid I have an inferiority complex—really know I have. Never feel as if people—both boys & girls—wanted to be with me. This, plus nervousness which makes it hard for me to smile, makes life rather difficult and discouraging at times. Feel as if it really was hardly worthwhile at times. Another thing which is bad is that I really don't enjoy things when I do them the way I should. Ought to think am having a good time even if not. Also I worry too much. Am scared of everything always expecting the worst. Must brace up and get more confidence in myself. Will make everything go better & make life much more worth living.[9]

To make matters worse, John's basic nervousness tended to make him irritable and he castigated himself for his "terrible disposition." Or he let out an anguished, plaintive cry over the bleak fruits of his straitlaced behavior:

During the last few years I haven't uttered a swear word, touched a drop of alcohol (ever), smoked a cigarette (ever), studied on Sunday, played tennis (except at Seal and Pocantico with family) or cards on Sunday, done anything I shouldn't with girls, or done anything I didn't think the family wouldn't want me to. The point is, what do I gain by all of this. I am not popular, or especially well or strong, or even half as much in many ways as lots of fellows who do all of the above mentioned things!!!!

Other diary passages suggest the kind of deep depression that, if allowed to worsen, could lead to the mystery of young people away at school committing suicide, even those who outwardly seem to have everything to live for. But this was never a possibility for John, not only for reason of his religious beliefs, but also because he showed signs of developing traits of stubbornness and determination. Much as he criticized himself, he also kept resolving to do better. His New Year's resolutions for 1926 were typical of how he hoped to deal with nervousness, irritability, and unpopularity:

Try to be nice to everyone.
Try not to say mean or disagreeable things about anyone.
Try to like everyone (not have certain people "I can't stand").
Try to do thoughtful things.
Try to always act like a gentleman.
Try to be more sociable (to mix with other fellows in a friendly but not foolish way).
Try not to be so proud (to make apologies and thank people more willingly).
Try not to hold grudge when have been wronged or slighted (to forgive).
Try not to make sharp remarks or lose temper.

Despite his moods of depression and self-deprecation, John gradually began to make friends and lead an active social life. The gloomy diary entries became less frequent, though they never disappeared entirely. He was helped in the first year by his cousin, Billy McAlpin, a senior when John entered Princeton, who did what he could to show the younger boy around, just as John did when his younger cousin, Marcellus Hartley Dodge, entered Princeton in 1927 and when Laurance came in 1928.

At one point, John scanned the *Freshman Herald* to see how many members of his class he recognized, and he counted 380. But the names of boys that appeared more than a few times in his diary, those he would spend time with going to the movies, playing squash or tennis, having a late supper at the Baltimore Dairy (the "Balt") or the Tiger Teapot when the deadline for the Commons was missed, did not number more than a dozen. They were all boys who shared pretty much the same values as John—Doug Robertson; Homer "Huck" Cochran; W. W. Cochran; Joe Quarles from Milwaukee, who was a true "BMOC," a leader in everything; Jim Carey, a popular athlete; Ben Hedges, with whom John spent a long evening discussing the delicate subject of "intercourse." Three friends he particularly liked, all from Baltimore: William F. Cochran, Benson Blake, and Latimer

Stewart, the latter two both graduates of the Gilman Country Day School. John's diary was filled with references to "Bill," "Bense," and "Lat," and he frequently was a guest at the homes of one or another during vacations or long weekends. They went together to the Dempsey-Tunney fight on the Sesquicentennial grounds in Philadelphia and to dances and other social events in Philadelphia or in Baltimore. John reciprocated as host, having his friends to No. 10 or Pocantico and to the special treat of spending a weekend at his grandfather's villa in nearby Lakewood, to meet the old man and play golf.

As his freshman year ended, John longed to room with one of these three friends, and he was able to make an arrangement for the sophomore year with Bense. This meant rejecting the unfortunate Doug Robertson one more time. John frequently told his diary how much he liked Doug, but it bothered him that Doug was just as retiring as he was, only Doug didn't seem to worry about it. John felt he was hampered in meeting new friends when Doug was always following him around—the shy leading the shy.[10]

John and Bense chose their sophomore quarters in 1901 Hall, right next door to Henry Hall. But their windows opened directly onto a particularly boisterous group living in Pyne Hall, so for their junior year they moved back to Henry Hall, facing University Place. Bense comes through as a very solid and dependable fellow, and the pair were entirely congenial. Still, John was not satisfied. The one he was really drawn to the most was Lat, who apparently had a charismatic personality, easygoing, happy, and extremely popular. As a result, he was often busy with other friends and John had difficulty getting as much time with Lat as he wished.

At the end of his junior year, John volunteered to room with Laurance for what would be his last and Laurance's first year at Princeton. The theory was that the older brother would help the younger through the grim first year of college. But Bense thought the plan not particularly good for Laurance, and as it turned out "M. and F." agreed with this assessment. At this juncture, Lat suggested that he and John might room together for their final year, and John leaped at the chance. Bense accepted this, and remained a loyal friend. As seniors, John and Lat had priority in choosing quarters, and they settled on '79 Hall, nearly half a mile across the campus, facing Washington Road. It was a popular dorm for upperclassmen because it looked right down Prospect Avenue where all the eating clubs were, which saved a good deal of time walking to and fro for meals.

From all accounts, the most burning social issue facing Princeton students was that of opting for an eating club and whether or not they would be selected by the "right" one. There were eighteen of these clubs lining Prospect Avenue in great rambling structures with architecture varying from California stucco to English Tudor. The clubs had a definite rank order of desirability and prestige in the minds of those who knew about them and cared. Some were generally regarded as "the best," followed by another group of the "pretty good" and another of the not so good. The tail end numbered a few so low in merit that joining them was hardly better than belonging to no club at all. Some clubs tended to specialize, one catering to athletes, another to those with a literary flair. Among the clubs at or near the top of the heap, Cottage had the "high class party boys," Ivy the "horsy blueblood drinking set," and Cap and Gown was known for having "pious bluebloods."

Advocates of the club system shudder at any comparison to fraternities, but the houses on Prospect Avenue look a great deal like fraternity houses and the process for bringing in new blood resembles fraternity "rushing" in several respects. The differences have to do with terminology, more formalized procedures, the non-residential character of the clubs, and timing. At Princeton the eating clubs are restricted to upperclassmen, so that the selection occurred during the sophomore year. This gave the club members more than a year to begin informally to size up the qualities of the prospects. Their method of learning more was "bicker," the name given to a process resembling the elaborate mating ritual of some primitive tribe. It lasted from early November until the choices were announced in early March. After an initial briefing of the entire class on the system, the candidates would wait in their rooms each night for delegations from the various clubs to pay social calls. When a delegation called, its members would not announce their club affiliation, and the conversation could be about anything but clubs. After they left, the roommates might have to scramble around to figure out which club had called before the next group arrived. Which clubs called, and how often, were matters of intense interest. John gave some idea of the tension involved:

The whole club situation is rather a strain. After the first call in the evening one really can't do any serious work as one can't help thinking a lot about the whole matter. I certainly do pity the poor fellows rooming alone who sit hopefully all evening and don't have a single call. They certainly must worry and think a lot about the matter. If one doesn't get visited it makes one feel as if one was a social failure which isn't true in many cases.

This performance went on to Christmas vacation. It continued when school resumed in January, but then the reverse occurred as well: candidates were invited to visit the clubs. Usually in the company of Bense or Lat, John would call on four or five clubs of an evening, an experience he did not enjoy because he found it "so forced and artificial."

As the process wore on, intelligence-gathering activities by the sophomores and subtle leaks of information by the clubs increased. Networks of friends among the sophomores would huddle to cross-check their prospects. From the point of view of both the clubs and the candidates, the ideal situation would be for an "original" bid from a club to match up with the first choice of a prospect, which was why sub rosa information was filtering around the campus and clues were avidly noted. Given the competition and uncertainty, it was impossible that perfect matches would occur in all or even most cases, so at the proper time "secondary" bids would be issued in an effort to complete the matching game. Straightforward deals were supposed to be illegal; that is, a club could not tell a top prospect that it would give him an "original" bid on the condition that he guaranteed to accept it. Both sides had to take their chances.

John was satisfied that all of the best clubs were calling on him, but then he noted with some concern that the prestigious Ivy Club seemed to taper off. He was not sure he would fit in with this fun-loving crowd, but his concern was that Lat seemed headed there. Then John noted that his other natural choice, Cap and Gown, seemed to drop off. On the day of decision, March 7, the word came from Cap and Gown. "Got original, thank heavens," John wrote. He, Bense, the three Cochrans (Huck, Bill, and W.W.), Joe Quarles, and others spent most of the day at "Cap," cutting their classes. Lat and Jim Carey signed with Ivy. John visited five other clubs he had promised to before signing, only one other an "original" for him, and then signed with Cap. He joined in "arguing about who should get secondaries. Made me awfully sore the way it was run. . . . Went to bed at 8:45 as was completely tired out with all the excitement."

The next hurdle was the "section party" for the recruits. John heard that the Ivy party had been a drunken orgy, so he decided not to attend his. But his club president, George Snowden, came over to tell him he "would not be compelled to take a drop." The party was held at an off-campus site to honor the "gentlemen's agreement" with the Dean not to serve the illegal liquids on club premises. For a time, the Cap and Gown members dropped their "pious" image, as John described the evening:

Main point of party is drinking. Also have ceremony of drinking from silver loving cup. I just put it to my lips but didn't take any. Nine fellows passed out during evening and many pretty tight. Six sophs only took beer. Bense and I only ones didn't take anything. All went off very well. Fellows couldn't have been nicer to me. Didn't have one unpleasant moment. . . . Hadn't anticipated things to go off nearly so well. Was quite worried in fact.

This protracted mating dance took its toll that spring. One sophomore hanged himself in his room. Another was killed and a friend seriously injured in an accident as they were driving home "under the weather." John wrote home to tell how he had handled the loving-cup problem, and again words of approval came back from No. 10.

The critical issue settled, John now had a proper base from which to contemplate his social life over the next few years. He kept up the amiable custom Princeton students had of paying Sunday afternoon social calls on faculty members, university officials, and leading townspeople, all of which he enjoyed. The balls and parties on John's New York–Princeton–Philadelphia–Baltimore social axis threatened to become a social whirlwind. He still felt inadequate about his dancing, not having a true girlfriend (and longing to), his smile, his jaw (with another extensive round of medical consultations, to no avail). But he continued to socialize and at times even to enjoy himself.

Perhaps subsconsciously, he kept becoming attracted to girls who, for one reason or another, were unattainable. It was impossible to break into the crowd around Anne Colby, for example. Catherine Robb became more of a distant image as their correspondence waned, until a "Dear John" letter finally arrived with news that she had eloped with a fellow art student. John grew more interested in Marion "Molly" Angell, daughter of the president of Yale, after he began to suspect that she was secretly engaged to his cousin, Billy McAlpin. Billy finally told him about it, and John became an usher in the wedding party in New Haven, where he kissed the bride but did not join the other ushers in kissing all the bridesmaids; he felt he didn't know them well enough. Then Eleanor Wesley of Baltimore seemed very desirable to John, but she turned out to be Lat's girl, and she and Lat were married soon after his graduation.

John reached nearly the ultimate in the unattainable when he finally fell hard for his second cousin, Faith, the daughter of his father's cousin, Percy Rockefeller. Three years younger than John, Faith was pretty, lively, charming, and the president of her class at the Westover School in Connecticut. She turned eighteen in the summer of 1927, and John began noticing her at Seal Harbor and then at all the New York parties during the following Christmas vacation. They gravitated toward each other, engaging in long, serious talks ("She has really fine ideas"). For the last week of the vacation, Faith invited him to Overhills, a country estate and lodge near Fayetteville, North Carolina, in effect a club "formed by six men from the north," including Percy. Over the next year and a half, John made the long train trip to Overhills a number of times. From his diary, one sees clearly that he was infatuated with Faith. Reality intruded only occasionally, when he lamented: "Wish she wasn't a cousin."

John, of course, continued to see other girls at the many dances he attended, but no one compared to Faith. One year he and Bill Cochran hit on the novel strategy of sharing a date, Edith Joffrey, at the house parties given by the clubs, which were the big event of the spring at Princeton. The following year, he had his own date, Dorothea Villard, and in his senior year Faith was able to join him. In those days, dances did not really get going until around midnight, so that John never got to bed before dawn. When this happened in New York, Junior noticed that his son was missing Bible class and church the next morning, and he voiced his concern.

John was indeed slipping a bit from religion in an organized sense. He remained active in the Philadelphian Society, becoming a member of the board, and he remained true to his moral values. But he began skipping church or chapel, and voted with other students against compulsory chapel at Princeton. He worried about this: "Develop a better religious attitude" was among the resolutions of his twenty-first birthday.

Most of the rest were almost identical with his New Year's resolutions, but there was one newcomer to the list: "Be nice to family and do more for them." Other references also suggest a new appreciation of his family. What was happening was that for the first time John was able to get a sense of what life was like in other families during the many weekends as the guest of his various friends in Baltimore. He particularly enjoyed the Stewarts, and for some years spent the weekend of the Maryland Hunt Cup races with them. These experiences gave him a new estimate of his own family. He felt closer to his brothers, caring very much about Laurance and enjoying his "humorous" letters, worrying about Win's troubles in school. After Nelson started at Dartmouth, John wrote: "Am crazy to see Nel and find out what is going on." He applauded the good news from Dartmouth over the next few years—about Nelson making the soccer team, getting good grades, and being elected vice president of his class. In the summer of 1926, he and Nelson toured France together on bicycles (just as Junior had done with a college classmate), making a low-cost trip home on a freighter to the great interest of the New York press. The following summer, when the entire family went to Europe, John and Nelson took off again together to travel through Switzerland and Germany.

On John's twenty-first birthday, a $1,000 check came from his grandfather (instead of the usual $100), along with a message: "We are all glad to know of your good work and progress at Princeton, and are looking forward with confident hope to your soon being able to begin to relieve your father in the work of looking after family affairs." A loving letter came from his mother, noteworthy for its accurate perception of her son and its prescience about his future:

Dearest Old Johnny,

I am trying hard to think of you as being quite old today but as a matter of fact my mind keeps going back to the time when you were such a big little baby—you were so long and you looked so wise; but you were always just as nice as you could be. I really can't remember you ever having been unreasonable or disagreeable or trying—a little stubborn sometimes but one needs to be firm—a little conservative but that is wise in the eldest son and age will make us all more liberal. You have never been contrary or never jealous and ungenerous in your attitude towards others. I am so thankful that we have you and so happy in you and so proud that you have grown to be such a fine man that this is a day of great rejoicing for me. Being who you are and what you are, life isn't going to be easy or simple for you, but you are starting on the right road, with high ideals, if you don't lose your head, or your heart to the wrong type of woman, or your zeal for the best or your faith that "God is love" and is in all things, then I know that you will carry the honor and respect of your family far. Such is the confidence that your mother has in you. With much love from *her* and birthday greetings.

Relations with Father were somewhat more complex. One Christmas Eve, John recorded how the family "got to talking at supper how F. always has his own way. He was very surprised. Was good for him to hear about it as thought he had always been the one to give in." Another time, John wrote about his father: "He is so wonderfully broad in business relations but so narrow in some of his family ideas. . . . M. certainly is wonderful to him on the details. Lets him always have his own way yet makes him think that he is giving her her way." Part of John's problem was the gap he perceived between his own inadequacies and his image of his father as a towering person, nationally prominent, morally impeccable, seemingly always right, a man who could very nearly work magic in his wise use of his vast resources. One time, after repeating the long litany of his own faults, John wrote: "F. has done so many fine and worthwhile things & is so much liked and respected by all that I am afraid it will be kind of hard for me to fill his place."

Junior took a few opportunities to bring John along during the Princeton years by involving him in discussions and negotiations about various office projects. In John's senior year, Junior put him on the board of the Bureau of Social Hygiene and John was able to attend a few of the meetings. During the family trip to Europe in the summer of 1927, Junior arranged for John to accompany him and Raymond Fosdick to Geneva for discussions of possible grants to the League of Nations. This led to an opportunity for John to work during the summer of 1928 as an assistant in the Information Section of the League, an experience that was to have a profound effect on the young man.

But Junior remained as stilted and pedantic as ever in dealing with his children. In one letter, he invited John to have a frank and open relationship with him in terms that made it seem almost impossible to achieve:

Our relationship will, much to my delight, grow closer as the days go by. We will have many subjects to discuss, and on which to work out some common basis of understanding and agreement. Let us both pledge ourselves in a spirit of complete confidence in the honesty of opinion and loftiness of purpose each of the other, to always speak with absolute frankness, and never let our natural reserve stand in the way of the fullest exchange of view. Such frankness need never be incompatible with full deference to the position, the personality, and the degree of responsibility attaching to the other person.[11]

The difficulty of getting along with Father was shown when John wrote to ask if it would be possible to have the "open Nash car" sent down to Princeton for his use over the weekend of the house parties and prom in 1928. He would drive the car back to Pocantico on Sunday. Junior assented, but in a very cold response, writing, "I could have wished that you had taken this matter up with me a little differently and sufficiently in advance so that we could have had an opportunity to discuss it." He then went on to deliver a long analysis of the problem, citing the fact that "in my own college days I had not had a horse, because I did not want to be different from other boys." The concern, of course, was "the value of the democratic influence you [John 3rd] would have in getting on without a car when others are having them." He mentioned Dartmouth, where cars on a full-time basis were not banned, and where Nelson had made similar requests, including one for the full-time use of a car. Junior had written to President Hopkins for an opinion; Hopkins wrote back politely, but with words to the effect that he couldn't care less. Junior said that he had come to see that it was not unreasonable for Nelson to have a car because Dartmouth was so isolated, and "it was not improbable that I should consent to his having the Dodge at Dartmouth next year." But Nelson had thought the matter over and magnanimously, according to Junior, decided that Father was right all along, that for him to have a car would not be a good "influence on the other men."

Having written a virtual legal brief on the matter, Junior concluded with another call to frankness in their relationship:

You will see from the above lengthy explanation therefore, that there are two sides to this question, just as there were when we originally discussed it before you went to college. Please know that whatever opinion I may hold in regard to any matter of interest to you, I shall always be perfectly open-minded in discussing the question with you, and always ready to reverse my opinion if the facts presented or changing conditions so justify. Therefore, never hesitate to raise with me any question that you would like to discuss, but know always that you can discuss it with me as freely as with any of your contemporaries.[12]

Normally, John's style in dealing with Father was one of elaborate courtesy and deference, often thinking up more reasons than Father did as to why Father was right. But the matter of the car really bothered him. After all, he was twenty-two years of age, finishing his junior year in college, and all he was asking for was to have an old and inexpensive car for one weekend. So this time he took up his father's invitation to frankness, wondering in his response whether an isolated college as against one nearer large cities made any difference if the real issue was "the democratic spirit." He said he was all for "the democratic spirit, which, like you, I feel so important." But, "I feel that there is a limit to the sacrifice we ought to feel it our duty to make." There was no value in not having a car on a special occasion when everyone else would have one. Part of John's plan for the weekend was to take his friends over to visit Grandfather at his villa. John wondered which was more democratic, driving over in an old Nash or being picked up at Princeton by one of Grandfather's chauffeur-driven limousines (which was the usual way to get to Lakewood on a weekend).[13]

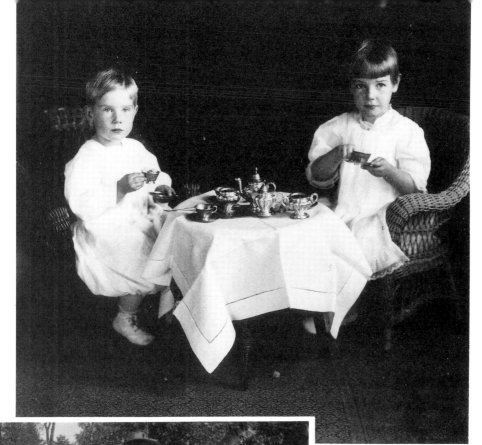

JDR 3rd and Babs at tea
in 1908

The growing family.
Left to right: Laurance, Babs, Nelson,
and John on an outing in Pocantico
in 1911.

Abby with her children at Pocantico,
summer 1912. *Seated on the bench
(left to right):* Babs; Abby, holding
Winthrop; and John. *In the foreground:*
Nelson and Laurance.

Summer at Seal Harbor, 1921. *Left to right:* Laurance, Babs, John, Abby and David, Winthrop, Junior, and Nelson.

Learning to be self-sufficient: baking at Seal Harbor, 1921. *Left to right:* Nelson, Laurance, Pauline Bennett, John, and Winthrop.

(*Left*) John D. Rockefeller 3rd as a teenager at Loomis School, 1922. (*Below*) The John D. Rockefeller dynastic line: Senior, JDR 3rd, and Junior, at Pocantico, 1918.

The aftermath of the "Ludlow massacre." Junior tours the Colorado Fuel and Iron Company coal fields in 1915. *Left to right:* A miner, Dan Morelli (*almost hidden from view*), Rockefeller, and W. L. Mackenzie King.

Tour of Colorado Fuel and Iron Company, September 20–October 9, 1915. Junior poses with Dan Morelli on his front steps in Berwind, Colorado.

Junior discusses working conditions with superintendent Jim O'Neill at the mine head in Frederick, Colorado.

Junior and Starr J. Murphy at the special industrial relations conference convened by President Woodrow Wilson in Washington, D.C., in October 1919

Junior *(right)* poses with Samuel Gompers and John L. Lewis *(center)* at the industrial relations conference in Washington, D.C., in October 1919. The two men at left are unidentified.

Blanchette Ferry Hooker, 1931

John D. Rockefeller 3rd at Princeton
University commencement, 1929. His
classmates voted him "Most Pious" and "Most
Likely to Succeed."

JDR 3rd and Blanchette on their
honeymoon in Bermuda, November 1932
(*International News Photo, Inc.*)

John D. Rockefeller 3rd and Blanchette at
their wedding reception, November 11, 1932

The passing of an era. Junior and his sons await the train bearing the remains of John D. Rockefeller, Sr., Tarrytown, New York, May 1937. *Left to right:* Junior, David, Nelson, Winthrop, Laurance, and John.

The apprentice. Junior and John 3rd conferring at the Fiftieth Anniversary Commencement of the University of Chicago, September 1941.

Junior and Abby at Bassett Hall, their historic home on Francis Street in Williamsburg, Virginia, 1944. *Left to right:* Mrs. Norman Ware, Captain Norman Ware, Jean Chorley, Kenneth Chorley, Abby Rockefeller, and JDR 3rd. Chorley had operational responsibility for the Colonial Williamsburg Restoration.

The postwar years. The clan gathers at Pocantico, 1946. *Left to right:* Mary French Rockefeller, Laurance, John, Peggy McGrath Rockefeller, Junior, Winthrop, Abby, Mary Clark Rockefeller, Nelson, and Blanchette.

Although John ended his letter on a note of apology, this is the only case on record up to this point in which he stood up to his father on an issue. Later on, he was to feel compelled to do this more often on much more important issues, and thus at times in an atmosphere of considerable tension.

If there was one area in which Junior could not fault his son, it was in his academic work. All things considered, John's record at Princeton was outstanding. Princeton had a grade-point system with 1 equivalent to an A, 2 to a B, and so on. In addition, there was a more relative grouping of students according to their performance in each course. Thus, a "1st group" was roughly equivalent to "A" standing, a "2nd" to a "B," and so on. As a freshman, John averaged a "4th," which concerned Junior enough so that he wrote to Dean Heermance, who sent a complete report on the freshman class grades in response. He pointed out that many freshmen had flunked out altogether while John had not failed any courses. Heermance said John's performance was not unusual for a freshman; he saw good signs, and predicted that John would do very well once he found a major subject of interest.[14]

The prediction was accurate. The following year, John moved up to the 3rd group, scoring a 1 in Economics 201. He was stunned with disbelief when he scored the highest test grade in that course among 400 students. In his junior year, he moved up to a low 2nd group, and then to a high 2nd as a senior, graduating with "high honors" and ranking 85th in a class of 437 graduates.

When it came time to choose a major, John recognized that economics was probably most appropriate for him, though he thought it often "deadly dull." He was more intrigued by "politics" and the international scene, but no major was offered in this area at Princeton then.[15] On one of Billy McAlpin's returns to the campus after graduation, he took John over to the Art Department to convince him that he should major in art. John wrote home for advice, and both "M. and F." discouraged him, suggesting that economics was a better choice. So John decided on economics, but concentrated enough electives in art to make the subject equivalent to a "minor."

The Department of Economics and Social Institutions at Princeton was small—nine men—but was headed by a distinguished economist, Frank A. Fetter. An interesting member of the department was George Brinton McClellan, son of the Civil War general and former mayor of New York City. John took all of Fetter's courses and none of McClellan's. He avoided courses in accounting and theory, gravitating toward those having to do with government, international affairs, and labor.

One of President Hibben's innovations at Princeton was the "Four Course Plan," under which upperclassmen took only four courses instead of the standard five, substituting an independent reading course and a senior thesis. John did not look forward to the reading course because he generally found books in his major heavy going. But under the guidance of Professor Fetter, he found the independent reading interesting and rewarding. It was his first introduction to the subject of population, which was to become his major interest throughout life. He read Malthus, two current books on population questions, and one on immigration. Fetter accepted Malthus' theory, and, like many intellectuals of the time, his views on population led him to favor eugenics. He thought that "democracy and opportunity" were favoring the process of "increasing the mediocre and reducing the excellent strains of stock. . . . Progress is threatened unless social institutions can be so adjusted as to reverse this process of multiplying the poorest, and extinguishing the most capable families."[16]

Princeton offered no opportunity for an undergraduate to pursue an interest in population, and John gave no sign that he even thought about the possibility. For his senior thesis he chose the topic of the "new industrial relations plans" in which his father figured so prominently. Junior was very pleased, and they corresponded at length on the subject. John went to interview men in New York whom his father suggested, and Junior read each draft chapter and commented on it. John also went to Washington to interview William Green, head of the American Federation of Labor. He was given a warm reception, and came away very much impressed by Green.

In setting the historical background, John cited the adoption of a shop committee by Colorado Fuel and Iron in 1915 as the first example of an industrial relations plan being introduced into a large corporation. But he did not explore what had brought it about—the 1913–1914 strike and the "Ludlow massacre." John did not say it explicitly, but in reading his diaries one gets the impression that he was somewhat dubious about the paternalism of the industrial relations movement, in contrast to the vitality of the union movement. But he concluded his thesis, "Industrial Relations Plans: A Study," with an evenhanded discussion of the pros and cons of each.

After reading the final draft, Junior wrote in glowing terms:

It has given me unspeakable pleasure to find the extent and breadth of your interest in the industrial relations problem. Your knowledge of the subject is far greater than I had imagined and many times more than mine at your age. It pleased me immensely too to find that you so quickly saw the point of view which I have taken in these matters and were so alive to the necessity for guarded expression and thoughtful consideration, so as to preserve to the fullest extent the friendly relationship which has been established with the unions and with the performance of the industrial plan, also with the leaders of the various companies in which we are interested.[17]

Labor-management relations later became a very tense subject between John and his father, but for the present Junior was euphoric, writing that he was "increasingly eager for the time when we are in frequent, yes, in daily contact in regard to these and a host of other interesting matters which we will have before us." Not until close to John's graduation was a firm understanding reached that he would go to work in his father's office. It had always seemed inevitable to John, but he had entertained other possibilities in the absence of a definite arrangement. John had considered Lat's view that he should go to law school and his mother's opinion that he should go to work in some large company before joining his father. John's performance on his senior thesis apparently mellowed Junior's view of John's desire to go on a round-the-world study trip before going to work. Dubious at first, Junior now wrote that he was "happy" about the plan and thought "the vacation period will be interesting, restful and immensely worthwhile."

The final months at Princeton were a whirlwind of activity—house parties, dances elsewhere, trips home, final exams, preparing for graduation, and trips to Williamsburg, to a YMCA conference, and to Vassar for a "Model Assembly."[18] After the house parties that spring, it seemed that Faith, aware of how much John was attracted to her, thought it necessary to gently point out the realities of the situation. "Know just how things stand between us," John wrote, but he still felt she was the nicest girl he had ever met.

An incident revealing of the times and of John's attitude occurred in his public-speaking class in which the final assignment was "to convince audience of something they did not believe in particularly." John's topic was: "Negroes Should Be Admitted to Princeton." Another occurred when John went car-shopping with his father to select one as a graduation present. He narrowed the choice down to a Lincoln, a Pierce-Arrow, a Cunningham, and a Stutz. He finally chose a green Stutz phaeton. "Feel Lincoln is a better car but is nothing distinctive about it," he wrote.

John had ten guests for the graduation ceremonies, all family members except Mary Clark, who was soon to become one—she and Nelson were all but engaged by this time. On Class Day, humorous presents were awarded to the seniors by a committee of their peers. John was given a shiny new dime to help him on his way to success. The six photographers who followed him around finally got a good candid picture as he accepted the dime with a wry smile, while his classmates roared with laughter in the background.

The gift of the dime was a play not only on his grandfather's habit, but also on the fact that John had been voted by the class as "Most Likely to Succeed." He dismissed this "as just a joke." He thought "the nicest of all" was "Most Thorough Gentleman," which Lat got, or "Most Respected" and "Most Popular," which both went to Jim Carey. The *New Yorker* wrote that it was not possible for a man to succeed with a name like John D. Rockefeller because it would be impossible for him to really be himself, which was the only way to succeed. So the magazine suggested that John change his name to "Amos L. Detweiler." But a number of editorials appeared in which the designation "Most Likely to Succeed" was taken seriously, praising the Rockefeller family for its philanthropies and suggesting that what the Princeton seniors meant was that the young Rockefeller would prove equal to his heavy responsibilities.[19]

Amid all the excitement of graduation, there was room for one last gloomy comment in John's diary: "Guess the reason I am glad to get through college is because have made rather a mess of it; also haven't really made hardly any friends." But this mood soon passed as he began to look forward with genuine excitement to his trip around the world.

14

❧

THE GRAND TOUR

ONE OF THE BENEFICIARIES of Junior's deep interest in foreign affairs was John 3rd. They made a side trip together to the League of Nations in Geneva during the family trip to Europe in the summer of 1927, and were joined there by Raymond Fosdick. One purpose was to work out the details of Junior's gift of $2 million to build a library for the League. John learned that the League hired a handful of American college students during the summer before their senior year, to help cope with the growing number of American tourists. One of the best of these jobs was that of assistant to Arthur Sweetser of Boston, vice director of the Information Section of the League.

Back at Princeton, John was delighted to receive an invitation from Sweetser to be his assistant for the summer of 1928. But John had another opening to consider. His father was keenly interested in the explorers and adventurers who were making headlines in the 1920s. Charles Lindbergh was a guest at No. 10 and Pocantico several times, to the delight of the Rockefeller boys. With Edsel Ford, Junior was one of the main supporters of Richard E. Byrd's polar expeditions, and several times Byrd treated the Rockefeller family to showings of his lantern slides.[1] Junior also supported the International Grenfell Association, formed by Sir Wilfred Grenfell, a British medical missionary who sent his small hospital ship to the coast of Labrador every summer to render medical aid and Christian evangelism to inhabitants of remote areas.

For that same summer of 1928, Sir Wilfred invited John to work aboard the ship. International politics proved the stronger lure and John decided to go to Geneva. Toward the end of the term, he began preparing in earnest, reading everything he could find about the activities of the League and going to Philadelphia to interview Sweetser's previous assistant.

At the end of June, John and Nelson sailed on the *Ile de France*, Nelson to spend the summer improving his French by staying with the family of Mr. Benoit, the current French tutor. Always intrigued by a Rockefeller's earning a salary, the New York newspapers ran stories about John's job: the *New York Telegram* of July 12 said that the heir to an $11 billion fortune would be earning $20 a week for two and a half months.

After stopping to examine the restoration work at the Rheims Cathedral, John met Sweetser in Brussels, and the two went on a leisurely drive to Geneva, traveling some seven hundred kilometers through Belgium, Holland, Germany, and France. John saw the British and French soldiers occupying the Rhineland, and he and Sweetser discussed this and other issues such as German war reparations and Allied war debts. John liked Sweetser, a man in his early thirties and as friendly and thoughtful a boss as could be imagined.

Given the disastrous events of subsequent years, John's diary of that summer in Geneva reads like a fairy tale of a lost and innocent time in a secure and unthreatened world. This was the summer of the Kellogg-Briand Pact renouncing aggressive warfare (without specifying how that was to be enforced).[2]

Sweetser gave John the task of writing articles for *Current History Magazine* and descriptive papers for the throngs of tourists, and had him attend meetings of League bodies such as the "arts and letters subcommittee of the committee on intellectual cooperation." There was also preparatory work for the convening of the League Assembly in September, but little serious business. Most of John's time, and that of everyone else, was taken up by an endless round of luncheons, teas, dinners, dances, with plenty of time left over for tennis, swimming, and sailing.

These affairs took place in the posh hotels and clubs of Geneva, in mountain chalets and in villas in nearby Swiss and French towns. John had rented a Buick for the summer and on one occasion took five visiting Smith College girls for a late afternoon drive to the Castle of Chillon and then to Montreux for dinner. As summer wore on and the meeting of the Assembly neared, John began squiring tourists around and began to feel his life was "talking to one old lady after another." But among the visitors were some of his college friends as well as such family friends as Raymond Fosdick, Ivy Lee, and Harry Emerson Fosdick.

John had a comfortable room at the Carlton Park Hotel, but when the population of Geneva swelled with the opening of the Assembly, he had to move to a smaller room without a bath. On the rare occasion when he was free for lunch, John would go to the Paqui, the place on the Lake Geneva shore where all the young Americans gathered to swim and where lunch could be had for the grand sum of one franc (sixteen cents).

Although there were no exciting international crises to talk about, John learned a great deal. He met foreign ministers, ambassadors, foreign correspondents, and other influential people from a score of countries. Mackenzie King invited him to dine with the Canadian delegation. John attended the dinner of the Foreign Policy Association, given by James G. McDonald, who would play an influential role in his life the following year. He was excited to be asked to meet with Lord Cushendun of the British delegation. Cushendun wanted to explain that his speech in the Assembly criticizing the social affairs program of the League did not apply to projects financed by American donors, but only to the League's own work. John was introduced to Aristide Briand, foreign minister of France, who had already been premier no less than ten times. He found Briand genial, although his speech that morning in the Assembly "really laid into the Germans." Briand told John that he "looked like Lindbergh."

John's summer was made even more interesting by his friendship with another college employee of the League, Elizabeth Peterson, an exuberant and vivacious young lady from Vassar known to everyone as "Pete." John characterized her as "peppy" and as "very pretty and supposedly most attractive girl here for the summer," but "can't say I like to call a girl by a boy's name." John had "a darn nice office" while Pete had a cubbyhole, so she managed to end up sharing his office—"a bit distracting but very agreeable."

John saw a lot of Pete in the evenings as well. Still somewhat naive about girls at the age of twenty-two, he wrote: "Don't know why but we seem to run into each other. . . . For some reason people seem to think that I like her a lot & ask us around together." On at least four occasions, he told his diary that he had not fallen for her, but she was "a peach of a girl" and he enjoyed dancing with her "ever so much." The comments became warmer and the conversations more intimate: "Don't believe I have ever talked so frankly with any girl before—not even Faith. Think [Pete] really quite liked me. Was amusing the way we kept being thrown together at first."

When mid-September came, John "hated to leave Geneva." In particular, it was "awfully hard saying goodbye" to the Sweetsers and their four young children: "They really just made the summer." John and Pete had reservations on different ships, but they were both in Paris for a few days and went dancing each night. On the voyage home, John wrote Pete an eight-page letter, but she topped him— there was a fourteen-page letter from her when he arrived home. "Wonder what she really thinks of me?" he asked his diary.

It was Pete who involved John in the "Model Assembly" at Vassar at the end of February 1929. By then his growing acquaintance with James G. McDonald enabled him to ask the chairman of the Foreign Policy Association to help draft the agenda for the weekend affair and make one of the principal speeches. Several hundred students from northeastern colleges came to Vassar that weekend and were organized into delegations. John played the role of chairman of the Netherlands delegation, and made a speech on the personnel of the League's Secretariat. The highlight of the weekend was his attendance at a Vassar "J" dance at which the more numerous girls cut in on the boys. He found it an unusual and stimulating experience.

True to the protestations of his diary, John did not fall for Pete, though he clearly was intrigued by her. She tried hard to get him to come to the Vassar prom, but he declined on the grounds that his time was committed to his senior thesis. Faith was still his favorite.

Nevertheless, it was clear that John was maturing as he began his last year in college. The shyness and nervousness were by no means gone, as we shall see, but he had become more skillful in managing and repressing these emotional states. He was certainly trying hard, as the resolutions he frequently penned in his diary indicate. For example, as his father had before him John was facing up to his fear of public speaking, never avoiding an opportunity, and while the experience could still be a tormenting one, he was gradually getting better and in time would develop an effective platform style. The summer in Geneva had been good for John, helping him to feel more at ease in the company of highly placed people. In turn, this encouraged in him an inclination that often is effective for a shy person—concentrating more on other people and events and less on oneself.

John's mind was occupied with the question of what he would do after graduating in June and before he took a position in his father's office. He was again invited to serve on the Grenfell expedition to Labrador, but again he declined: Nelson and Laurance were lined up to take his place for the summer of 1929. After his experience in Geneva, John had become thoroughly "hooked" on international affairs. He wanted to take an extensive study trip abroad, possibly around the world.

He began working on the idea in earnest in December. In typically methodical fashion, he wrote letters to a number of senior men to ask their opinion of the wisdom of the idea—to his uncle, Winthrop Aldrich, to President Hopkins of Dartmouth and President Angell of Yale, to Raymond Fosdick and Owen D. Young. A financier and board member of the Rockefeller Foundation, Young was chairman of the committee of experts trying to unravel the knotty problem of German reparations, about which a conference was scheduled at The Hague the following August. All these men approved the idea except Uncle Winthrop. Junior was also cool at first, having foregone the pleasure of the "grand tour" himself and substituting a summer of bicycling in Europe in order to enter his father's office sooner. But he relented and in the end approved the trip. John's plan was to go with a friend: he began soliciting his closest, one at a time—Lat Stewart, Bill Cochran, Bense Blake, Jim Carey. All were interested at first, but for various reasons none could go.

A new opportunity opened up in February when John was invited by Edward C. Carter, secretary of the American Council of the Institute for Pacific Relations, to serve as one of Carter's four assistants at the third biennial conference of the IPR, scheduled for late fall in Kyoto. A YMCA veteran, Carter took over leadership of the council in 1926. He was described as "handsome, free-wheeling, impulsive, and ambitious," and as "a whirlwind of activity for the IPR and a constant source of ideas for new programs."[3] He believed strongly that the IPR should not limit itself to cultural and economic matters as originally intended, but should also grapple with the tough political questions, of which many were brewing in the Far East. Carter was also an accomplished fund-raiser, which may account for his invitation to the Rockefeller scion to work at the conference in Kyoto.

Another bid, stimulated by Arthur Sweetser, came from Merle Davis, secretary-general of the IPR in Honolulu, proposing that John work there for the summer before going on to Kyoto. These were flattering offers, but John wanted a trip that would have more touring and less working in one place. A solution emerged one evening in conversation with James G. McDonald. As chairman of the Foreign Policy Association, McDonald made at least one trip abroad every year, and in 1929 he planned to attend both the Hague and Kyoto conferences. He proposed that he and John travel together, linking the two conferences in a round-the-world trip. This would enable John to arrive in Kyoto in time to accept E. C. Carter's invitation to serve as an assistant secretary. The opportunity for John to travel with a man twenty years his senior who was both a seasoned observer and a congenial companion was not to be missed.

By April 1, the plan was all set, and John and McDonald made their preparations. They agreed to split expenses and to take along a young Frenchman, Adolphe Pervey, whom McDonald knew, to improve their facility with the language. McDonald made a list of statesmen whom he hoped to see, and Ivy Lee gave a number of suggestions. He told John that the most useful and objective sources of information in Moscow were the German and French ambassadors and the correspondent for the *Berliner Tageblatt*. In late June, after John graduated, he and McDonald went to Washington for interviews with State Department officials and with C. C. Wu of China, Count Kabayama of Japan, and the ambassadors of Spain, France, England, Germany, and Poland.

Before the departure, there was time for John to see the restoration work at Williamsburg for the first time and also to spend a few weeks relaxing at Seal Harbor. He joined his mother, father, and brothers Winthrop and David as guests for several days at the home of Commander Byrd's brother, Governor Harry F. Byrd of Virginia, before journeying to Williamsburg to stay in one of the first of the restored houses. The housekeeper, a Mrs. Striker, struck John as "quite a character. She talks all the time and thinks she is part of the family the way she sits around with us. She means well though & is a very good cook." After viewing plans and visiting sites for several days, John reported in his diary: "Was very much disappointed when I first drove in to Williamsburg but feel now that it has great possibilities. Still have a long way to go, though."

Nelson and Laurance were not part of the group because they were already aboard the hospital ship *Maravan* bound for Labrador. That trip was turning out to be grim. Although Laurance was official photographer and acted occasionally as Sir Wilfred's secretary, he and Nelson also served as stevedores, lugging supplies aboard and about the ship, including hundred-pound sacks of coal, and as dishwashers in the galley. Nelson was having his ups and downs, as Laurance wrote to John, at first feeling "strong for Tod" (Mary Todhunter Clark) and then not so sure, starting the trip dreaming of becoming an architect and then changing his mind after he learned he got a B in an architecture course at Dartmouth. Worst of all, the food was bad: Laurance's letter made it sound as if the crew were coming down with scurvy. The boys arrived home on September 1, just in time for Laurance to have his appendix out.

On July 26 John left for his trip around the world on the Italian liner *Roma* bound for Gibraltar. John noted his amusement at the sight the trio made—he and McDonald both six feet two, flanking the much shorter Pervey, five feet six. John switched from his regular diary to a larger notebook, thinking one book would suffice; but he filled nearly three books before the trip was over. These volumes are highly readable in a way that reflects John's growing maturity. The entries mix good travel writing with perceptive comments on political problems and leaders. Although no one could have foreseen the cataclysmic events that would overtake every one of the countries the trio visited, and make casualties of almost all the statesmen they interviewed, one can find in the diaries hints of a world in twilight and drifting toward chaos.

Aside from sightseeing in Tangiers on the North African coast and in Seville[4] and Madrid, the reason for visiting Spain was to meet King Alfonso XIII and the man who had taken power as dictator of the country in 1923, Miguel Primo de Rivera. The two were closely allied and had visited Mussolini in Rome together to express their admiration for fascism. Arrangements had been made by the American ambassador for John and McDonald to have lunch with the king at his summer palace in Santander on the north coast of Spain. It being John's first introduction to royalty, he was quite nervous. The visitors dressed formally in black cutaway coats and striped trousers; they found the king just returned from sailboat racing dressed in "rather sporty clothes." The king, the same age as McDonald (forty-two), was "friendly and cheerful" and spoke excellent English, though his interests seemed limited to sports, tariffs, and whether the General Education Board might help in the building of a new university in Madrid. At lunch with some twenty-five other people, John had difficulty taking his eyes off "the oldest Infanta" (about twenty years old), who sat opposite him and was very attractive. He also committed a faux pas ("inevitable," he wrote) by asking Queen Eugenia where she had learned to speak English so well and then instantly remembering that she was a granddaughter of Queen Victoria and English by birth. He wrote: "Mr. McDonald gets along beautifully at a function like this. I only wish that I could do as well. Of course he has had more practice but just the same he is naturally very good at it. . . . I was never quite sure just what I was expected to do next."

It was a two-day trip by car to Mandariz, the country spa on the northwest coast near Cape Finisterre where Primo de Rivera was staying. Standing at the concierge's desk at the hotel in the morning,

John was astonished to find that the man in line next to him was Primo himself. To their delight, the guests were asked to lunch with Primo and his two daughters at the hotel and then to attend the bullfights in Pontevedra that afternoon. At lunch Primo, who John thought was "just as nice as he could be," explained in French that although as dictator he could do as he pleased and not follow the laws, he was nevertheless working at a new constitution for Spain. John's political sophistication grew steadily as the trip progressed, but here at the beginning it was understandable that he was rather gullible. In actuality, Primo had no such freedom of action; he was in deep trouble and barely hanging on to power.[5]

The bullfights left John "a little shaky," but he found solace in talking with twenty-one-year-old Carmen, Primo's oldest daughter, who was "very pretty and attractive." John wrote: "It certainly was interesting meeting and getting to know a dictator and his family. The impression left couldn't have been more favorable." Even so, John noticed that although people applauded Primo wherever they went, the applause was merely polite.

John and McDonald left Pervey in Paris for a holiday with his family while they went on to their next important stop, The Hague, where they found the International Reparations Conference at an impasse. This had the effect not only of making the principal actors readily available for interviews, but also of putting McDonald in the position of acting as go-between among the parties. The two goals of German foreign policy were to bring about an evacuation of the Rhineland earlier than scheduled and to lower the burden of war reparations. The latter question, as a precondition to the former, was the subject of the "Young Plan," a proposal fashioned by Owen D. Young's committee of experts. Now representatives of all the countries concerned were gathered in The Hague in an attempt to reach agreement on the plan.

The problems were complex and difficult, the product of the clashing policies of France, Great Britian, Germany, and the United States ever since the Treaty of Versailles. The Hague conference was another major attempt to reconcile what seemed fundamentally irreconcilable. The principal causes of conflict were the punitive terms of the Versailles Treaty and the rigidity of the French on the issue of reparations and of the Americans on the issue of war debts, along with British ambivalence on both issues and German resistance to paying. Despite the warnings of John Maynard Keynes and others that reparations would impoverish Germany and retard the economic revival of Europe generally, the final bill submitted by the Allied

Reparations Commission in May 1921 totaled 132 billion gold marks ($33 billion). Inability to pay and deep resentment resulted in German delaying tactics and passive resistance to the point that in 1923 the French occupied the Ruhr, the industrial heartland of Germany, in an effort to force payment. In return, the Germans began devaluing their currency to try to defeat the purpose of the occupation and water down the debt. This set off wildfire inflation, with the mark sinking to the level of 4.2 *trillion* to the dollar.

The war debts were a major complicating factor. Some $10 billion was owed to Britain by various Allied countries, and Britain and other Allied countries owed $10.3 billion to the United States. In 1919 British Prime Minister Lloyd George had offered to cancel the debts owed to Britain if the U.S. would reciprocate. But President Wilson told him it was "highly improbable that either the Congress or popular opinion in this country will ever permit a cancellation of any part of the debt of the British government to the United States."[6] Having declined to ask for any indemnity or compensation from Germany, the United States took the position that the war debts and reparations issues were entirely separate. The United States was just as intent on collecting every cent of war debts as France was on collecting every sou of reparations. The American position was summarized, years later, by President Coolidge's laconic "They hired the money, didn't they."

A further complication was the loans being made to Germany, principally by American banks. In part the Germans used the money to make reparations payments to Allied countries, which in turn used it to make payments on American war debts. This recycled money was serving no productive purpose, and the growing total of the loans was beginning to cause concern in American banking circles.[7]

Tensions were temporarily eased by adoption of the "Dawes Plan," presented by Charles G. Dawes of the United States in 1924 and championed by Austen Chamberlain of England, though actually designed by Owen D. Young. The prominence of such Americans as Dawes and Young in special committees established by the Reparations Commission might seem strange, given the fact that the "isolationist" United States was not officially a member of the League. But it was a symptom of the reality—the United States *was* inextricably involved and the war debts and reparations issues *were* unavoidably related.

The provisions of the Dawes Plan, which the signatories accepted for a five-year period, included an overhaul of the reparations scheme and a new schedule of German payments, the continuation of Allied controls over the German economy, and a plan for new loans. The agreement led to French withdrawal from the Ruhr and German entry into the League of Nations. For this, Dawes and Chamberlain became the co-winners of the Nobel Peace Prize in 1925.

Gustav Stresemann was prominent among the German centrist politicians who labored under formidable burdens to win concessions and stabilize the German economy. He served as prime minister or foreign minister in successive German cabinets. By 1928 he had made significant progress, restoring a measure of prosperity to Germany. But his adroit maneuvers had a bitter taste for many Germans. For example, Stresemann and Aristide Briand of France were the chief architects of the Locarno Pact of 1925, by which Germany renounced the provinces of Alsace and Lorraine, receiving in exchange guarantees of its western border and the first stage of French evacuation from the Rhineland. The two statesmen were rewarded by the joint award of the 1926 Nobel Peace Prize. But German opinion rankled over the loss of the two provinces, as well as the continuing Rhineland occupation and reparations burden that brought the statesmen to The Hague to consider the Young Plan in the year when the terms of the predecessor Dawes Plan were to expire.

The Young Plan asserted the primacy of business over political considerations by recognizing the importance of real market forces in the issues of reparations and war debts. For this Young incurred the displeasure of President Herbert Hoover and Treasury Secretary Andrew W. Mellon, who were against anything that would suggest less than full payment of war debts. The plan called for lowered reparations payments, a new and stretched-out schedule of payments, the removal of controls on the German economy, and a new Bank for International Settlements to facilitate transfer payments.

The conference had come close to agreement on these provisions, but the British were being obstinate on one point. Earlier in the year, Ramsay MacDonald had formed a new Labour government. He believed that Britain had been too subservient to French policy. His chancellor of the exchequer, Philip Snowden, was in The Hague insisting that reparations to England be increased by $12 million, a negligible sum given the totals involved, but this demand had brought the conference to a standstill. When John 3rd and James McDonald met Snowden, he seemed persuasive on the British point of view. Though the chancellor did not use the word, John thought it all came down to "prestige." Snowden wanted the $12 million to be taken out of France's share, not added to the German payments. John wrote:

It isn't the money but to re-establish England's place in European affairs. [Snowden] said that England has been treated like a milch cow in recent years; that she has always been the one to make the sacrifice and give in to meet the demands of France and the rest of Europe. He felt that the English foreign office had been nothing but a subdivision of the French foreign office in the last few years—meaning under Chamberlain. England had been gradually losing her place and her standing in Europe, he said, and it was time that she asserted herself. This seemed like a good opportunity and he was going to take it.

There followed a long meeting with Arthur Henderson, the British foreign secretary. *He* was much more concerned about the Rhineland occupation. England was willing to separate this issue from the reparations, but the French would not. Henderson was sensitive to smoldering German resentment at the occupation and hoped evacuation could begin soon.

McDonald knew and met frequently with newspapermen, and John found in this a confirmation of the lesson he had begun to learn the previous summer in Geneva. Journalists, especially foreign correspondents, could be useful sources of information. They were even likable people, so long as their interest was not focused on him. From reporters he and McDonald learned a great deal about the growing rift between the British and the French and about the delicacies and instabilities of French internal politics.

From Count Zaleski, the Polish foreign minister, a "big fellow" who seemed "rather bored with life and everyone in general," they heard the startling statement that war was not likely before 1935. From junior members of the British delegation they heard misgivings about Snowden's recalcitrance. John described the Japanese as quiet, polite, unvarying in demeanor, and trying to be helpful.

John found Stresemann impressive: "He was fine; has a very friendly face; and is much nicer and better looking than I had expected. He is rather short and heavy set but you forget that due to his friendly, cheery way. He seemed most optimistic—much more so than we could have expected with things as they are. He was very amusing. His English was much better than I had been led to believe." The minister spoke about the growing opposition to him in Germany and about his concern over "big business" getting into the hands of so few people: "He said this wasn't meant against me (thinking of the Standard Oil) as America wasn't a country but a continent."[8]

One of the highlights of John's stay in The Hague was a meeting with Charles Evans Hughes, who was serving a year as a judge in the Permanent Court of International Justice:[9] "I had never met him before and liked him a lot. He has such a nice friendly face with a very winning smile. . . . We talked with him a full hour. . . . He certainly can explain things clearly." Hughes was telling the "inside story" of the 1921–1922 Washington conferences over which he had presided, of his secret agreement with Lord Balfour and the reason why he had been so magnanimous in pledging not to fortify the Philippines and Guam: Senators Henry Cabot Lodge and Oscar Underwood had told him there was no chance of getting appropriations for that purpose in any case.

John and McDonald left The Hague for a prearranged visit with Ramsay MacDonald, creator of the first Labour government in England in 1924 and now prime minister for the second time. He was vacationing at his birthplace, Lossiemouth, on the northeastern coast of Scotland. John described the town as "quaint and unassuming," a fishing village and modest summer resort for "English and Scotch people of moderate means." It struck him that the prime minister's house was indistinguishable from others in the village and that there were no security guards—"quite different from our chief executive of the United States."

They were welcomed by the prime minister's son Malcolm, who was to become a friend of John's and a frequent source of information on foreign affairs. "We saw [the prime minister] up on the second floor in his office which is his bedroom as well. There was no electricity or no running water in the room—just a good old pitcher and bowl." They spent three hours together, including lunch at the local hotel, the conversation ranging over many subjects. The prime minister expressed disappointment at the current state of Anglo-American relations and voiced his backing of Snowden's position at The Hague. MacDonald used the same expression about England having been a "milch cow" and said she had been "left with the baby to hold often enough." The hardened British position was clearly a product of the general election that had brought MacDonald to office.

John censored his diary: "I can't put down much he told us as he talked most frankly and said everything was to be strictly confidential; you never can tell what might happen to this book—at any time my bag might be lost and then picked up by the wrong person. . . . Mr. McDonald and I wondered why we had been told so much unless it was that we were to let it be known where it might do some good."

In London the travelers had further frank talks about British foreign policy with Lord Robert Cecil and Sir Ronald Lindsay of the Foreign Office. They then went to Paris to rejoin Pervey and work out the rest of their itinerary.

They wanted to cross the Soviet Union on the Trans-Siberian Railway, but there was severe tension along the Russian-Chinese border. One reason was that the Chinese had closed down the Chinese Eastern Railway in the belief that the profits were being used to finance Communist propaganda in China. This meant that one had to loop around all of Manchuria to the Russian port of Vladivostok, instead of changing from the Russian to the Chinese Railway and going directly to Mukden. John checked to see if they could go conveniently by passenger ship to Japan, but the schedules were not good and they decided to risk the rail route. First, they spent a week in Geneva for the beginning of the Assembly. Here McDonald discreetly passed on some information and John had a reunion with the Sweetsers. In their honor, he gave a dinner party for thirty-eight people: "I had an awful fight getting the Sweetsers to let me pay for it." Now well more than a month into their trip, the travelers had to forgo stopping in Germany and Poland, and instead went directly by train to Moscow.

The ten days in Moscow and Leningrad were a fascinating experience for John, even though McDonald's hope of seeing Stalin came to naught. In an appointment arranged by Ivy Lee, the one well-known Soviet official they met was Maxim Litvinov, the "Acting Commissar for Foreign Affairs," who was "very friendly and nice and willing to talk but looked very much as if recently he might have been in the clothing business in New York." Litvinov was ominous about the Chinese tension, but said he "was very keen to resume [diplomatic relations] with the U.S. on account of trade and all that [Russia] had to learn from us." But he was not optimistic that this would happen soon. Interviews followed with a whole series of lesser commissars, who spoke zealously about Soviet progress in education, trade, the economy, farm collectivization, and the *Gosplan* (five-year plan). Problems—inflation, unemployment, peasant resistance, and population growth—were minimized. John was interested to hear that rapid population growth was mainly a rural problem, because in the cities abortion and birth control methods were widely practiced.

The only person John debated with a little was the daughter of one Soviet official, a girl who was "very attractive (about 19) and an ardent Communist." John wrote:

She tried to make me understand how in capitalistic countries practically everyone was working for money while in Russia they were working for an idea or an ideal. This ideal was to give everyone from the lowest up an education, decent living conditions, etc. I agreed with her that most men in the U.S. were working for money but couldn't go as far as admitting that communism was the only way in which the poor could be given equal opportunities. I mentioned the Labor party in England as striving for this end but she couldn't see it.

John was well aware of the need to hear from other observers and, as Ivy Lee had promised, the French ambassador (M. Herbeth), the German ambassador (Herr von Dirksen), and the *Berliner Tageblatt* correspondent (Paul Scheffer) proved excellent sources of information. Von Dirksen said there would be no Soviet-Chinese border war, because it would be disastrous for both sides; therefore, traveling on the Trans-Siberian Railway should cause no anxiety. He wired the German consul in Vladivostok to find the best way the party could travel from the Russian port to Manchuria. John had bought some wood carvings for gifts and was worried lest he might not be able to get them out of Russia. Herbeth appointed Pervey a French diplomatic courier on the spot and gave him a diplomatic pouch to deliver to the French ambassador in Japan. The wood carvings went into the pouch.

John found that Scheffer was a much keener analyst of the Soviet economy and society than the British correspondent, Walter Duranty, who wrote for the *New York Times* as well. Scheffer described in detail the big news of the day in Russia: the forced collectivization of Russian agriculture and the conflict between the commissars and the well-to-do peasants (kulaks). He was concerned about "the communistic propaganda being spread in Germany—particularly Berlin— because he didn't feel the government there was on a sure enough footing to be impregnable against it." He said that "Europe and America better watch their step" if the Russians succeeded in mechanizing the urban and rural sectors because they were intent on spreading their system throughout the world. Because of this, he believed war was inevitable some day.

With Trotsky banished, Scheffer said that Stalin was firmly in power as dictator and was bent on the "purification" of the party and of the government and on "reducing" the number of kulaks—delicate terms perhaps appropriate then; the violent purges and mass slaughter of kulaks were in the future.

John filled many pages in his diary with descriptions of the Kremlin, Russian ballet, clothing, customs, the politeness of the people, the banishing of religion. Much of his diary sounds up-to-date for the 1980s—the Russians' fear of being seen with a foreigner, the shortage of consumer goods, the drab clothing, the scarcity of automobiles except for high officials, the "dismal bareness" of offices, the felt presence of the "secret police (G.P.U.)." He was impressed by the status of women ("absolutely equal in all respects to the men"). He found Leningrad, except for the Hermitage and the Winter Palace, to be "dirty, gray, and gloomy": the former capital was being neglected by the Soviets in favor of the new capital of Moscow, where construction was going on in all quarters.

In drawing conclusions, John recalled another comment by Scheffer. "He had said that he now felt that the chances of success [of communism] were much better than ever but that one big factor stood in the way—that was the methods of cold calculation of the officials. . . . Everything is based on paper facts and chart conditions. In short, the human element is left out to a large extent. The country of 12 or 13 million square miles is all run from Moscow on paper five years in advance!" John concluded: "There is a lot in communism, I believe, as there is in socialism, but one wouldn't be too keen about having it forced down one's throat."

The travelers learned that the only way to get to Manchuria from Vladivostok was to take a weekly boat to Japan, another boat from Japan to Korea, and then a train through Korea to Mukden. Even worse was the news that the only reservations they could get on the twice-a-week trains across Siberia was on one that arrived one day after the boat left, which meant a six-day wait in Vladivostok.

John was prepared to be monumentally bored on the ten-day trip across Siberia, but after six days he wrote that he was "enjoying it thoroughly. The food is very good, the car is clean and comfortable, and the porters intelligent and efficient." Outside the windows and at station stops, there was the endless fascination of the changing landscape and the changing ethnicity of the people. John wrote, "I am quite taken by Siberia in the summer." As a diversion, he and Pervey decided to grow mustaches during the ten days, but John's sandy hair yielded meager results in contrast to the jet black hair of Pervey.

The frail youngster, now a young man, was turning out to be a hardy traveler. Whenever the trio went by boat, McDonald and Pervey almost always were laid low by seasickness, but John was unaffected. His companions fell prey several times to the notorious digestive ailments that afflict travelers in primitive places, while John was largely spared.

The low point of the trip was Vladivostok, which John noted was beautiful only when seen from the sea. Of the Golden Horn Hotel, he wrote: "Most of the food isn't edible, the sheets on the beds are really large size towels which don't reach from one end of the bed to the other, there are lots of mosquitoes, there are women hanging around whose occupation is doubtful to say the least (they have rooms on the same floor), the service is poor, etc., etc. I have decided that this is my first and last visit to Vladivostok." Then the water gave out. "The place is dirty and smelly enough with plenty of water so one can imagine what it was like without it." To top it off, he and McDonald discovered that rubles could be purchased legally in Vladivostok at seven to the dollar, about fourteen cents each. In Moscow they had paid the official rate of fifty-two cents each. John figured they had thereby contributed heavily to the Communist experiment and that their trip would have cost one-fourth the amount if it had originated in Vladivostok, without "even the risk of bringing [rubles] across the frontier with us." He wrote: "No wonder the people haven't been more thrilled with the tips we have been giving them."

As it turned out, the travelers were forced to stay only three days in Vladivostok. But they were still glad to rush aboard the *Kagi Maru*, a small Japanese steamer: "It was very clean and neat, the cabins were comfortable, and the food excellent—it certainly tasted good, anyway, after Vladivostok." From this point on, there is a noticeable change in the tempo and descriptive powers of the diary. John wrote of his first two days in "beautiful Japan," the crossing by boat to Pusan and the train trip the length of "wonderfully picturesque Korea" to Mukden. There is a vivid description of the Pei-ling tombs of the Manchu emperors. John clearly was smitten from the outset by Oriental culture; it was to remain for him a lifelong fascination.

The date was September 29, more than two months after the party had left New York. The great complicated mass of China now lay spread before them, nothing about it being more complicated than its political and ideological cross-currents. There were uneasy and shifting patterns of alliance among various warlords and four important forces—the Kuomintang led by Chiang Kai-shek, the indigenous Communist movement with Mao Tse-tung emerging as its political and military leader, the machinations of the Soviet Union, and the heavy influence of Japan.[10]

In 1911 Sun Yat-sen's revolution had overthrown the Manchu dynasty. The Republic of China was proclaimed in 1912, ushering in thirty-eight years of virtually ceaseless warfare, civil and foreign.

Having taken over the Comintern from Trotsky, Stalin failed in his heavy-handed efforts to "convert" the revolution to a Communist victory. In 1927 Chiang Kai-shek purged the Kuomintang of Communists and expelled Mikhail Borodin and other Comintern "advisers." In 1928, with the support of two northern warlords, the "Christian general" (Feng Yu-hsiang) and Yen Hsi-shan, Chiang moved to pacify the northern provinces, changing the name of Peking (Northern Capital) to Peiping (Northern Peace). He then fulfilled Sun Yat-sen's wish by choosing the ancient seat of the Ming dynasty, Nanking, as the new capital of the Nationalist government.

In the fall of 1929 when John and McDonald were touring in China for more than three weeks, the country was relatively quiescent; the Nationalist government was at the zenith of its power. There is no record that McDonald attempted to arrange a meeting with Chiang Kai-shek. In any event, the Generalissimo was busy on a punitive expedition against an errant warlord in the far south. But with a letter of introduction from Sir Wilfred Grenfell, John arranged a meeting with Feng and Yen. Unfortunately, the two warlords were in such a remote area that to visit them would have required two days of travel over treacherous roads exposed to attack by "bandit-soldiers." Moreover, McDonald became ill, so the venture was given up. An ominous sign of the tenuous hold of the Nationalist government and the strains afflicting it was the fact that Feng was now in opposition to Chiang (Russian help was rumored), requiring another punitive expedition by the Generalissimo in 1930.

The only warlord whom the visitors met was twenty-nine-year-old Chang Hsueh-liang of Manchuria, who had succeeded his father, Chang Tso-lin, when he had been killed by a bomb the year before as he withdrew from Peking to allow the Nationalists to enter without a battle. Later research would reveal that the assassins were Japanese agents who believed that the entry of Chinese troops would result in the eventual reduction of Japan's growing influence in Manchuria. Incidents such as this would, in retrospect, signal a profound change in Japanese policy away from the moderation of the early 1920s toward the hardline attitude that led to the annexation of Manchuria in 1931 and the Sino-Japanese War of the late 1930s. At the moment, young Chang was much more worried about Soviet pressure, and he listened eagerly as the visitors told him of their conversation with Maxim Litvinov.

Chang was not the picture of a Chinese warlord that John had imagined. Secure in his heavily protected compound in Mukden and surrounded by older advisers, Chang was "slight in build, quiet, almost timid, very nice looking, well dressed, bright and intelligent." He had given up his "opium habit" in favor of tennis and golf, and lived comfortably with his "wife and several concubines."[11]

Everywhere the visitors went in China, they enjoyed the hospitality, care, and advice of Standard Oil people. The Standard Oil Company of New York (Socony) was still dominant in the massive market of providing "oil for the lamps of China," though now challenged by Shell and Texaco. The company was thoroughly organized into districts and subdistricts throughout the country and had American representatives in every sizable city.

John nearly filled one notebook with impressions of China, alternating lyrical descriptions of Chinese art and architecture with grim portraits of dirty, noisy cities, masses of people, depressing poverty, and armed men everywhere. In Peking he was stunned by the beauty of the Forbidden City, the Ming tombs, and the Great Wall, but was sad to note that many of the antiquities had been seriously neglected. He was cheered, however, by seeing the rooms of the Forbidden City that were being restored with the aid of a grant from his father.

In a country dominated by militarism, John found few examples of positive action in other spheres. One was the Peking Union Medical College, where he was given a tour by the president, Roger Greene, brother of Jerome Greene. Another was the work of the noted educator and land reform expert, James Y. C. (Jimmy) Yen, whom John and McDonald visited at his "model farm and community" in Shansi Province: "Men are to be trained there to be sent around to start similar farms or communities elsewhere, for the whole is entirely practical. Chinese tools and methods are made more modern and efficient instead of importing the foreign things and substituting them for the Chinese."

In Hankow, John took the opportunity to visit the Japanese consul "to explain to him why I couldn't accept the offer of the Japanese Foreign Office to let me use the villa of a certain Baron while we were in Kyoto for the Conference. It was very kind of them to think of it but I couldn't possibly accept it, being only an assistant secretary to the Conference and not really representing Father out here."

Traveling up the Yangtze River, the visitors saw graphic evidence of "gunboat diplomacy" in the surprising number of warships bearing foreign flags, including the American. They passed by "Socony Hill" outside of Nanking, where they stayed the night, famed as the place where the foreign community had gathered under the protection of Western gunboats when the Nationalists had assaulted the city in 1927. In Nanking, John and McDonald had interviews with several ministers of the Nationalist government, and they were unimpressed with most of them. John's notebook began to cite reasons why the Nationalist regime was shaky and might face a grim future.

One exception to the general incompetence he perceived was H. H. Kung, the minister of industry, commerce, and labor. A direct descendant of Confucius and the only minister they met who dressed in Chinese clothes, Kung spoke candidly and intelligently about the problems the government faced. He arranged for the visitors to see T. V. Soong, the minister of finance and to most Americans the best-known figure in the Nationalist government. John described Soong as "friendly and nice and quite willing to talk although he didn't volunteer information like Kung. He seemed very intelligent and able but to lack drive and great force. He might almost be said to be a trifle effeminate." Here John pinpointed one of the many weaknesses of the Nationalist government—nepotism so pervasive that it was "exactly the opposite from America where a man hesitates to appoint a relation no matter how capable he might be." The government was referred to in some quarters as "the Soong dynasty" because the finance minister's sisters had married Sun Yat-sen, Chiang Kai-shek, H. H. Kung, and several lesser officials. John wrote that almost all of the high officials were related.

Increasingly, John began to hear critiques of the Nationalist government. The noted naturalist Roy Chapman Andrews was particularly violent in his criticisms, but he may have been biased because the government had "stopped his fossil gathering." In Shanghai, where the foreign compounds seemed like one giant country club, John heard objective and reasoned analyses from Sir Frederick Whyte of England, adviser to the Nanking government, and Dr. Hu Shih, a brilliant young university president. So penetrating were their analyses that together they read, as recorded in John's diary, like a scholarly treatise on why the Nationalist government failed, though uttered and written long before that fact. The Nationalists were perpetuating the worst of the old ways, notably corruption and nepotism. The government was a dead-hand bureaucracy, inefficient and lacking in vision. The Nationalists also lacked the moral fervor that John discerned in Russian Communist officials and that Whyte and Hu Shih said also characterized the Chinese Communists. Although Chiang Kai-shek himself lived circumspectly, he seemed unable to break out of the prevailing pattern. Hu Shih singled out what he considered to be a fatal weakness—the inability of the government to accept criticism. In fact, because it functioned like a dictatorship, critics were subject to punishment.

Worst of all were the excessive militarism and internecine warfare. Chiang could not reduce his huge army because the warlords and the Communists would not reciprocate. Even if he had been able to, he could have found no jobs for the soldiers. Militarism "is literally the curse of China," John wrote. "The most tragic thing in China is the soldiers."

After the chaos and the fascination of China, the two weeks spent at the Institute for Pacific Relations conference in Kyoto were an anticlimax. For John it was like Geneva revisited. His job was to attend roundtable sessions, take notes, and prepare materials for the delegates. Most afternoons were free for socializing and sightseeing. Malcolm MacDonald was there in a comparable role for the British delegation, and John's friendship with him ripened. At a party given by James McDonald, there was dancing with geisha girls. John wrote: "It was really pretty good fun although I couldn't play with the geishas the way Malcolm did. You just have to let yourself go to enjoy an evening like that. . . . Malcolm liked the geishas so much and got along so well with them that he asked ten of them to lunch."

A significant event that happened to John at the conference, although he did not realize it at the time, was meeting one of the assistant secretaries to the Japanese delegation, Shigeharu Matsumoto, and his wife. John liked the Matsumotos very much. Later their acquaintance would ripen into a unique and firm lifelong friendship.

There were several days for sightseeing in other Japanese cities both before and after the conference. With his Aunt Lucy, who was visiting in Japan, John toured scenic places, temples, shrines and country inns, and his absorption in Oriental culture deepened. He was heartened to see that Japanese antiquities were meticulously cared for in contrast to those in China. One time a Japanese soldier who spoke some English engaged him in conversation. Soon John was surrounded by curious and friendly Japanese, the soldier acting as interpreter. When John was about to leave, the people asked for his autograph.

In Tokyo John inspected the library his father had donated to the Imperial University. He spent an afternoon at Baron Mitsui's villa in the heart of the city to see a No play. The next day he was invited to tea by Emperor Hirohito—along with eight thousand other guests. It was the annual "Imperial Chrysanthemum party." Again he could not have known the special place that Japan was to occupy in his life. The day would come when he and his wife would be the first private citizens invited to luncheon at the Imperial Palace and when the emperor would visit their home in the United States. On this day in 1929, however, John wasn't even able to catch a good glimpse of the emperor. As thousands of people flocked into the palace for tea, John contented himself with touring the gardens with Count Kabayama and his daughter. The beds of chrysanthemums "were perfectly arranged. Till today I never realized that this flower could come in so many different shapes, forms, and colors."

The stay in Japan was not marked by any illuminating interviews or analyses. There seemed no need. Everything was in order with no sense of threat. The "chrysanthemum" side of the Japanese character was then in short-lived ascendancy over the "sword"[12] For John the visit was not a political experience but a cultural one. Several times he wrote that he could not find the words to express the beauty he had seen. In the end, he tried to summarize the four things that stood out in his mind. The words and the thoughts were not profound, but they intimated a deep experience:

First is the loveliness of the kimonos of the women. I don't know why they appealed to me so but they did. The second was the beauty of the Japanese gardens. Some of them are perfectly marvelous. Third is the cleanliness of the people and the towns; and fourth the courtesy and kindness of the people themselves. We were treated in the same polite and friendly way wherever we went whether we were known or not. I hate to think of the contrast when we get back home again.

The next day, John embarked for home at Yokohama aboard the *President Pierce* of the Dollar Line and was reunited with McDonald and Pervey and many of the IPR delegates. John tried to assess his trip, but again words all but failed him. Of his companions, he wrote that there had been "surprisingly little friction among the three of us considering how close we lived under all kinds of circumstances." As a "study trip" it had been an incomparable experience. One of its gains for John was a newfound sense of poise. He had spent more than four months traveling through some of the most interesting countries in the world, meeting and talking with people ranging from kings and prime ministers to peasants and soldiers. And he had had a cultural experience in the Orient that would stay with him the rest of his life.

When the boat docked in San Francisco, reporters thronged around him, but this time he could talk with them freely and easily.

He had committed himself to making a speech about the IPR conference to what he thought was the Junior Chamber of Commerce in San
Francisco: he found that he was the speaker at a large luncheon of the
Senior Chamber. This brought on such anxiety that he vomited in the
men's room shortly before he was due to appear. He screwed up his
courage; although, as usual, he thought he did poorly, the speech was
reported in the papers and McDonald and E. C. Carter congratulated
him on an excellent job.

After a four-day train trip across the country, John finally reached
No. 10 West 54th Street on December 1. The parents' anxiety about
their son during the previous four months had been eased by a
constant stream of letters from McDonald, various U.S. ambassadors,
and John himself.

John returned to a city that was outwardly familiar but had been
the scene of an event that changed the world forever. During the last
days of the IPR conference, panic had set in on Wall Street in New
York City. "Black Thursday" on the stock exchange witnessed a
sickening decline in stock prices and applied the coup de grace to the
unhealthy prosperity of the 1920s. The Great Depression, that unprecedented watershed in American life, had begun to penetrate all
corners of the land even as John and his companions rode eastward.

Americans naturally tend to think of the Depression as primarily
an American disaster, a grim period that brought about profound
political, social, and economic change at home. But, of course, it was a
global disaster as well. In Spain it was one of the factors that resulted
in bloody civil war and the seizure of power by General Franco. In
England the Depression destroyed Ramsay MacDonald's standing
with the Labour Party and very nearly the party itself.[13] In Germany it
ruined the best hope of the Weimar Republic, its modest prosperity,
and led to the rise to power of Adolf Hitler. In Japan the Depression
meant the ascendancy of the "sword" over the "chrysanthemum" and
all that Japanese militarism wrought in the years that followed.

But at the end of 1929, no one, least of all twenty-three-year-old
John D. Rockefeller 3rd, realized the full import of what was happening. He had a much more immediate challenge to face—beginning his
new job in his father's office.

IV

DEPRESSION
AND WAR
1929–1943

15

✁

A CAREER IS
LAUNCHED

JUST AS his father had done some thirty-two years earlier, John D. Rockefeller 3rd showed up at 26 Broadway to begin his career—on Monday, December 2, 1929, one day after returning from his round-the-world trip. But there were some important differences.

In 1897 Junior had found that the family office consisted of several small rooms on the ninth floor of the Standard Oil Building, occupied only by Frederick T. Gates and a few clerks. Senior, having retired, was not there, and Junior was left to make his way under Gates' tutelage. When John arrived at the end of 1929, the office occupied the whole twentieth floor of the building, the Rockefeller Foundation having separate offices up the street at 61 Broadway. The staff had grown to more than a hundred people in management, investment, legal, accounting, real estate, philanthropy, and other functions. The most important difference for John 3rd was that his father's presence dominated the place. The office was oriented entirely to his needs and bore his personal stamp down to the last detail. The employees had been hired by him, and they were organized the way he wanted and doing what he wanted them to do.

Junior introduced his son to the office staff in the morning and then presided over a press conference in the afternoon. Aware that the third successive person bearing the famous name—John D. Rockefeller—was beginning his career, a number of reporters had asked to interview the young man. On the advice of Ivy Lee, Junior decided to handle this economically by inviting all interested reporters at the same time. About twenty showed up, representing all the New York papers and the wire services.

The story in the *New York American* said: "It was a meeting such as would have been inconceivable in the '90s when multimillionaires often eschewed the press." The *Herald Tribune* story described the scene in detail:

The active head of the family passed each reporter along to the son with the words, "My son, John." Seats were drawn up in a semi-circle before Mr. Rockefeller's desk. For about seven minutes the older Rockefeller made a little speech. . . .

Mr. Rockefeller commended his son to the friendly consideration of the press. He declared it a tradition of the family to co-operate with the newspapers in giving the public such news as was properly a matter of public concern. That tradition, he said, would be carried on. With such an introduction, John D. Rockefeller 3rd was submitted to the questioning of interviewers.

The scene was one of democratic simplicity in an atmosphere of wealth and power. There was an oak paneled room, lighted but dimly yet showing old tapestries upon the walls, a bookcase guarded by leaded glass panes through which warm red and brown bindings were discernible, and a massive fireplace in which a small blaze tossed its flames cheerfully.

There were the two Rockefellers, father and son: the older dressed in a grayish cutaway, seated behind his desk with his back to the fireplace. The boy stretched his long legs from a low, deep armchair between his father and the gray windows, across which the evening's snowstorm was falling. The son looked unmistakably what he was, an alumnus just out of college. He was dressed conservatively—a brown sack suit, a stiff white collar, a necktie of blue and gray with a red stripe, just a touch of youthful color.

The two men resemble each other strikingly, but the younger looks even more like his grandfather in some respects than does John D. Rockefeller, Jr. Both show the family aquiline nose. Both have the same high forehead and contour of temples. But the young man's jaw is the grandfather's. He is a lean youth, with a keen eye. He gives the impression of physical fitness.

Both men were cautious in their approach to the public. Twenty minutes of questioning got very little out of John D. Rockefeller 3rd, as to how he feels about going to work, and with what ideas of industry, philanthropy, politics or life he approaches a growing share in the family burdens. He wished to be obliging, but he was modest. His father watched—and helped—the youth's first steps before a critical world with a protective intentness that was almost blazing.

Junior's tendency to dominate the interview was described by the *New York Journal*:

[Reporters] asked [the son] questions and his father answered them, while John passed most of the time trying to tie a knot in his legs and twisting his rather long fingers.

He's twenty-three, well over six feet, inclined to be lanky, with the Rockefeller nose and a shock of light, wavy hair parted on the side. He grins easily, almost bashfully, and when the questions become a trifle rapid and personal he would shift his eyes toward his father before answering. . . .

"Mr. Rockefeller, are you engaged?"

"Now, don't you think that's a little personal. If John ever has an announcement to make on that score he'll make it when the time comes."

John grinned his assent to his father's answer and took up a little slack in his twisted legs.

John was asked how much he would be paid. As the *New York Times* reported, Junior answered by saying it would not be more than any other young man doing the same work: "If you think he is going to get any $5,000 or $10,000 a year, you are guessing way too high."

John was asked what his duties would be. "I am first to be given a chance to look over the whole field of my father's business and get a general picture. If I am particularly interested in one division I will develop my interest there," he said.

Junior interposed: "The idea is for him to just browse around the offices for a while, getting familiar with the work . . . I am not going to urge him to do any work that is not interesting to him, for I think a man succeeds best in what interests him."

Would he don overalls and go out to work in the oil fields? "That would be darned interesting," John said, "but I imagine I can be of more use here helping my father."

The reporters persisted, as the *Herald Tribune* story related:

"How long do you expect it will take you to find the thing you want to do?" the son was asked.

"Maybe a year from now I can tell you," he replied.

"Have you any ideas about philanthropy?" he was asked.

"Only vaguely," he admitted.

"That will take him ten years—or more—to get any knowledge of that," his father suggested.

In responding to more questions about John's job, Junior inadvertently touched on one of the profound differences between his experience and that of his son—the fact that he had been an only son while John was but the first of five: "As a matter of fact, we don't know exactly the right way to start a Rockefeller in business. When we get to the fifth son we'll have a technique developed, I hope."

When John was asked his opinions about the League of Nations and the question of American entry, Junior interjected: "Don't you think he's pretty young to have crystallized his views on so important a subject?"

The lengthy stories that appeared the next day and the many editorials in newspapers across the country were all favorable. John was depicted as modest, obliging, frank, and "not unpoised." Junior's intrusiveness was seen as a pardonable example of parental hope and pride. As the *New York American* said:

Clearly it was a proud moment for the father. The assembled interviewers were permitted that rare thing—a glimpse of the truly human side of a man of enormous wealth.

In the father's eyes shone not only hope, but confident expectation that Rockefeller, 3rd, would carry on the family's finest ideals.

The *New York Sun* reporter wrote perceptively about the end of the interview. Junior was explaining why he had barred photographers from the meeting and why he asked that the press not take pictures of John. He said he felt strongly on the subject, that his children had a right to privacy and freedom from exploitation just like any others:

There was a pause, a break in the interview. The father looked at his boy and then at the others assembled. A smile spread over his features as he seemed to reflect upon what he had just said. He had touched upon something underlying the whole situation—the thing that everyone felt and hesitated to mention.

He was thinking, apparently, of the real problem his son was facing and of the psychological "three strikes" that were already marked up against him. He turned again to his questioners.

"You know," he said, "I really don't want John to be hampered by a lot of publicity and pictures. The fact that he is my son, that he must take over the responsibility of my position, is enough handicap for him."

One result of Junior's caution was that some of the newspapers again made the mistake of running the photo of Nelson to illustrate their stories about John. As for John, he was just glad the interview was over. It was "a little scary," he wrote, but "it went off pretty well on the whole. The resulting articles in the papers weren't half bad. Must get out of the papers for long time now."

The last proved to be no problem at all. John accomplished it by the simple device of doing nothing that was newsworthy for a very long time, his name appearing in the papers only on such occasions as when he served on a jury, when he got married, and when he represented his father at some ceremonial function, like giving certificates of recognition to the workers engaged in building Rockefeller Center.

John's starting salary was $50 a week, and it was not raised to $75 until mid-1931. He turned down his next raise a year later on the grounds that he was not yet earning it. Certainly, he was not suffering. Through gifts and his own purchases, he had built up enough of a portfolio of stocks and bonds to yield earnings of about $2,500 per year. In addition, Junior was paying him an "allowance" of $5,000.

John had passed at least one test in his father's eyes. In his first business communication to John, a letter dated January 2, 1930, Junior confirmed the $5,000 allowance and also absolved John of the requirement of submitting a financial accounting: "Whatever method you may adopt of keeping yourself posted currently on your financial situation to such an extent as seems wise to you will be satisfactory to me." There were still, of course, the familiar expectations:

It is my firm hope and confident belief that the habit which you have formed of both giving and saving is one of which you have come to see the wisdom and propriety and that you would naturally wish to give wisely and generously to worthwhile causes in reasonable proportion to your income, and, at the same time, to lay aside something substantial in a savings account each year.

John needed no prompting to follow these prescriptions; they were by now deeply ingrained habits. Moreover, he was in a good position to both give and save. He was netting over $10,000 a year from his three sources of income, and he had his own car, the green Stutz phaeton that his father had given him as a graduation present. (He now disliked the garish green and resolved to have it painted if it didn't cost too much.) And he was living comfortably at home in his same room and was free to enjoy the family retreats at Pocantico and Seal Harbor. The only others at home were his parents and David, who was still attending the Lincoln School. Nelson was finishing at Dartmouth, Laurance was in his second year at Princeton, and Winthrop was struggling to finish at Loomis, having been transferred there from the Lincoln School in the hope that a boarding school environment would help him straighten out his studies.

Nor was John's social life any serious drain on his finances. The invitations still flowed in, but he did not attend many dances or parties. Occasionally, he would take Faith or Alida Milliken or Betty Pratt to the theater or to a football game or for a drive in the country. He was an usher when his friend, Lat Stewart, married Eleanor Wesley, and he attended the wedding of the popular Anne Colby to "Bill" Vanderbilt, whom he met for the first time and liked very much. "Everybody seems to be getting married," John wrote.

Just like his father, John was obsessed with work, arriving early, staying late, frequently working all day on Saturdays, and coming close to wondering why people didn't work on holidays. He occupied a tiny room next to his father's large office, a most circumspect young man who spent much of his time attending meetings to listen and learn. He tried to spend an hour every day with a staff member to learn bookkeeping and accounting, and he gave himself to the study of his father's philanthropic activities, followed by an equally long study of his business interests.

Many of the faces in the office were familiar. There was Charles Heydt, oldest in point of service, whom Junior had hired as his secretary in 1897, and who in 1908 had become his real estate adviser, and was now heavily involved in Colonial Williamsburg and Rockefeller Center. There was Bertram Cutler, who joined the staff in 1901 as a bookkeeper and now headed the investment department. Willard Richardson, Junior's college chum, was still there as a philanthropic aide. Robert Gumbel could best be described as a general services officer who handled all sorts of chores. The big three were still Debevoise, Woods, and Fosdick.

There were some relatively new faces as well. Most important for John was Arthur W. Packard, a brilliant young man from Boston, five years John's senior, who had graduated from Brown and attended Oxford as a Rhodes scholar. He had worked for a year for the Institute of International Education, and then had been brought over by Junior to work as a philanthropic assistant a few months before John arrived in the office. It seems likely that Junior thought it a good idea to have someone in the office near John's age who could be a friend and mentor as his philanthropic interests developed.

John's time was also taken up by the meetings of the various boards he served on. While he was still at Princeton in 1928, his father had put him on the boards of the Bureau of Social Hygiene and the Dunbar National Bank, managed by blacks in Harlem, which Junior and other financial leaders were supporting. Soon after John entered the office, he was put on the boards of the New York International House, Industrial Relations Counselors, the China Medical Board, and Riverside Church. He served as secretary to the last two organizations, which were thus his most time-consuming responsibilities. John cared little for the work at Riverside, but the China Medical Board was intriguing because of his knowledge of the country and the complicated political situation there. Aside from John, the members included two medical doctors, plus Fosdick, Richardson, Gumbel, and George Vincent as chairman.

By all odds, the most important directorship for John was to be his seat on the Rockefeller Foundation board. In the year he joined the office, 1929, George Vincent retired as Foundation president. The new president was Max Mason, the eminent mathematician, physicist, and inventor who had been president of the University of Chicago before coming to the Foundation in 1928 as director of the Division of Natural Sciences. Well before this time, the Foundation board had achieved the prestigious status that had been the goal of Junior and Gates. Junior recognized the need to avoid unseemly haste in formally taking a brand-new college graduate into the company of such senior and distinguished men. To almost everyone, John was an obvious candidate for membership, the heir apparent to Junior's role. But there would have to be at least the semblance of an apprenticeship.

John began attending board meetings with his father and several times served as a substitute when Junior had to be absent. Through his other office responsibilities and memberships, especially on the China Medical Board, John became well acquainted with key Foundation people, such as President Mason, ex-President Vincent, and Dr. Alan Gregg, the new director of the Medical Science Division. John, of course, was already well known to others, such as Raymond Fosdick. Two years of this process was deemed enough, and John was elected to the board on December 16, 1931. He remained acutely aware of his junior status, content for years merely to get to know the outstanding men among his fellow directors and to observe the fascinating flow of work within the Foundation. Nevertheless, as we shall see, there was some resentment over the election of this untested youth, whose only qualification, some felt, was his name. It took several years for the resentment to come to the surface, and it would continue to haunt John until well after World War II.

John also became an active member of his father's Advisory Committee as soon as he entered the office. This was the nerve center where he could learn things at first hand and work closely with Woods, Fosdick, Debevoise, Richardson, and Packard (who served as secretary).

There were still more directorships for John: in 1931 the General Education Board and in 1932 the Rockefeller Institute and the Community Service Society. In the latter year, he was also given the title of "office manager" at 26 Broadway and made manager of the

Pocantico estate. Here John began applying his interest in industrial relations by studying the men's working conditions, a concern that eventually put him on a collision course with his father.

During these early years, John received a number of invitations to serve on the boards of philanthropic institutions other than his father's. John accepted Junior's advice that he should not spread himself too thin and should avoid additional connections unless he could give time, and perhaps money as well. John was happy to have the excuse to avoid fresh commitments, but in 1933 an invitation came to serve on what was then perhaps the most prestigious institutional board in New York City, that of the American Museum of Natural History. John was tempted to accept, but Junior was against it. After an agonizing period of indecision, John finally made a minor declaration of independence and accepted the bid.

Unlike his father, John did not have to make a difficult career choice between business and philanthropy. As we have seen, Junior made philanthropy his major interest in life, but perforce had to devote a significant share of his time to business affairs because of the requirements of the vast fortune he had taken over. He and his financial staff had to be active in the stock, bond, and real estate markets, and in borrowing or lending money in the form of "call" loans. Junior went deeper than this, into the business affairs of firms or projects, only for motives associated more with his philanthropic outlook than with profit—business ethics in the case of Standard of Indiana, inns and lodges to enhance his conservation and restoration projects (as at the Grand Tetons and Colonial Williamsburg), and civic betterment in the case of several housing and model town developments. As we shall see, Rockefeller Center began as a limited involvement under the "civic betterment" heading; only by accident did it become the dominant business interest of Junior and his family.

As for John, his position as a functionary in his father's office gave him an excellent opportunity to learn about the managing of investments, but for the most part he was content the rest of his life to let the financial experts on the office staff manage his personal portfolio in consultation with him. He did take one early fling in business when he was approached by individuals anxious to exploit the light metallic element, beryllium. Only in 1921 had chemists found electrolytic processes to produce usable quantities of the metal. The organizers, who were considerably ahead of their time, wanted John to take a major financial position and become a director of the new American Beryllium Company. Junior advised against this, and John agreed, but in another minor show of independence he did decide to invest $15,000. For years he was amused when officers of American Beryllium would call every few months to solicit additional funds. It was always the same story, and John refrained from further investment.

John all the while performed many family chores. He made the arrangements for another family trip out west in the summer of 1930. He went up to Loomis several times to help "Winny" through various crises in his struggle to finish prep school. He made loans to his brothers. And he stood up for Nelson when the brand-new Dartmouth graduate got married. During John's round-the-world trip, Nelson had written to tell him of his engagement to Mary Todhunter Clark, daughter of a Philadelphia lawyer who summered every year at Seal Harbor. The engagement came as no surprise—it had seemed imminent for a long time. John served as best man for his handsome and rugged younger brother, and took care of endless details for him.

The wedding, a full-scale affair with ten bridesmaids and ten ushers, was held on June 23, 1930, in Bala, a suburb of Philadelphia, the reception being in nearby Cynwyd where the Clark family lived. At this time, if anything, Nelson was less well known than his older brother. The fact that newspaper editors could still run a photograph of Nelson captioned as John meant that they could not recognize either one of them. Nor did the press know how to deal with the fact that there were five male heirs to the Rockefeller wealth. To make things simple for themselves, editors still operated on the assumption that the oldest son who bore the famous name would be *the* heir, although in fact all five brothers were to be treated well by their father. Therefore, the long stories about the wedding had headlines that did not include the exaggerated phrases about future wealth that were customary whenever a story was run on John. The reporters were content with references to a wedding "of international social importance" and that "linked one of Philadelphia's oldest and most prominent families to one of the richest in the world."[1]

After the wedding, Nelson and Tod spent two weeks at Seal Harbor, where their romance had flourished, and then sailed on a round-the-world honeymoon trip, one of Junior's wedding gifts. The trip lasted more than nine months, until April 1931. During this time abroad, John served as "home base," writing constantly, seeing to arrangements, and making sure that money reached the honeymooners when they needed it. As usual, the representatives of various Standard Oil companies were on hand to help and entertain the pair almost wherever they went. Junior apparently thought that Nelson might be overdoing it. From India, Nelson wrote to John on February 5, 1931:

Tell Pa that I don't think we are spoiling the family name with the company representatives in the Orient and that I don't think all the people wish we hadn't come, after we're gone. He seems to have taken the situation quite to heart, having mentioned it for the fourth time in his last letter.

In the same letter, Nelson waxed enthusiastic about another wedding present:

I'm so thrilled about the new Lincoln that I don't know what to do. Can Mr. Gumbel arrange to have it delivered before we get back so we can have it first thing? We would like the following:

Car—1 Lincoln with *Le Baron convertible roadster body.*
Paint—Black all over with six *chromium plated wire wheels* with an aluminum paint stripe running the length of the body and hood.
Excesories [*sic*]—One trunk behind.
Upholstery—Black leather with a set of covers of lighter color (same for the wheels on the side).
Top—This was to be of a tannish (light) colored cloth.
If you can arrange [this], I'll be a friend of yours for life. I get so excited just writing about it that I don't know what to do. I really think it is going to be the smartest car in New York.
Oh! One more thing! Can you have my initials—just plane [*sic*] in block letters done in the aluminum paint—on both doors. (See large diagram.)

The ebullient Nelson was also very good-hearted. At sea, he wrote:

Dear Johnny,
This is a letter that I've been meaning to write since the day after the wedding, but even tho it is so late in coming the spirit behind it is just the same.
Never did anyone have a better brother. I have always thought you were swell, but since the wedding it's hard to express my feelings. No kidding Johnny, you couldn't have been more thoughtful or efficient. And I can't tell you how grateful and proud I am of you. Everybody speaks of the way you handled things. So quietly, yet always on the spot with whatever had to be done. And not the least bit fussed! . . .
It was so nice to be with you those last two or three nights. I think that's what gave me such confidence.
And then all the work you did on our trip! I promise you that I'm just waiting for the opportunity to start to pay you back. And if I don't do a good job on your wedding, I'm not a married man. Just give me half a chance.

John was also constantly in touch with Laurance at Princeton, on one occasion sending him as his Christmas present a check in early

October to bail his brother out of difficulties in squaring accounts with Father. Laurance was also having problems in his love life. He was dating Polly Rousmaniere of Long Island and Mary French of Greenwich, Connecticut, a Vassar student who was the sister of John French, Nelson's roommate at Dartmouth. Laurance seemed to have his heart set on Mary, but nothing was easy. He wrote to John (September 13, 1930) about having just returned from "a week of active battle in the front line trenches," reporting no gain: "In other words, to sum up Mary's visit here [Seal Harbor] and our return to Woodstock, I can only say the next move is hers; never has she shown greater coolness and indifference towards me."

In the same letter, Laurance tried to console John about his attacks of appendicitis, but his words must have been unsettling: "When I see you I will look forward to telling you all the stories they told me about what a mild operation it is, and I only hope they don't pull the same trick on you as they did on me, as ever since mine was taken out I have had great difficulty in believing any statements made by members of the medical profession." Always the dutiful son, John sought the family's approval before having his appendix removed on September 18. Two months later he was still coming in to the office only half a day. Part of his convalescence included sailing to Europe with his parents in early October, spending thirty-two hours in England, and then sailing home again alone.

The most exciting event in the otherwise uneventful first years of John's working career was his father's highly effective statement on one of the hot political issues of the election year 1932—the effort to repeal the Prohibition Amendment to the Constitution. Junior's statement came in the form of a letter to Nicholas Murray Butler, president of Columbia University, and resulted in front-page headlines across the nation and in hundreds of editorials, almost all soundly approving his stand. After pointing out in his letter that he had been "born a teetotaler," that neither he nor his father "ever tasted a drop of intoxicating liquor," and that they had been lifelong supporters of the Anti-Saloon League, other temperance efforts, and Prohibition, Junior announced his conversion and his support for repeal. His reason was that the result of Prohibition had not been temperance, but an increase in crime and flouting of the law:

When the Eighteenth Amendment was passed I earnestly hoped—with a host of advocates of temperance—that it would be generally supported by public opinion and thus the day be hastened when the value to society of men with minds and bodies free from the undermining effects of alcohol would be generally realized. This has not been the result, but rather that drinking generally has increased; that the speakeasy has replaced the saloon, not only unit for unit, but probably two-fold if not three-fold; that a vast army of lawbreakers has been recruited and financed on a colossal scale; that many of our best citizens, piqued at what they regarded as an infringement of their private rights, have openly and unabashedly disregarded the Eighteenth Amendment; that as an inevitable result respect for all law has been greatly lessened; that crime has increased to an unprecedented degree—I have slowly and reluctantly come to believe.

As a result, Junior wrote, "I shall count it not only a duty but a privilege to support" the effort on behalf of repeal that Butler was generating. The lead story in the *New York Times* presented a typical assessment of the impact of Junior's move:

The wet forces generally accepted the conversion of Mr. Rockefeller as the greatest support that had been given to the repeal movement. Its effect politically was to strengthen the intentions of both parties to adopt liberal planks on prohibition. But perhaps the most significant and far-reaching effect of the unexpected statement by Mr. Rockefeller, whose family had loyally promoted the campaign for adoption of the Eighteenth Amendment, was the impetus given to plans for identical prohibition planks in the platforms of the major parties. This, supporters of this proposal assert, would take a non-political question out of the 1932 campaign, and cause it to turn on the great economic issues of the day.[2]

By the time Junior made this dramatic announcement, the Depression had become a national crisis that seemingly had no end or solution to it. After the stock market crash of October 1929, President Hoover and financial leaders such as Senior and Junior repeatedly expressed confidence in the economic system and voiced the hope that recovery would begin soon. But as the years wore on, it became clear to everyone that this was a financial slump that would dwarf all previous ones in American history. Everything Hoover tried to do seemed to be to no avail, and now he was being challenged at the polls by a strong and attractive Democratic candidate, Franklin D. Roosevelt, the governor of New York.

The Depression made little discernible difference in the life of JDR 3rd. He went to work regularly and took his one-month vacation, falling into a lifelong pattern of taking two or three weeks in mid-summer and saving the rest for a short winter vacation. He began smoking a pipe, having earned the $1,000 promised by Junior if he refrained from smoking until his twenty-first birthday. But the pipe never became a regular habit. He had lunch frequently with his college friends. Bense Blake was with the Hanover Bank and Jim Carey with the Bank of New York. Lat Stewart worked for an insurance brokerage firm in Baltimore, and he and John exchanged visits several times a year. John's financial situation improved considerably when Junior made him a gift of $100,000 worth of securities on the occasion of his twenty-fifth birthday in 1931.

It was at work that the effects of the Depression were visible, in almost everything the Rockefeller family office did. One symptom was a marked increase in the number of "begging" letters—more than a thousand a week. John 3rd kept trying to find better ways to say no as gently as possible, studying the techniques used by the various Rockefeller philanthropic institutions. Clearly, Junior could not become a one-man relief bureau by giving money to those in distress, no matter how heartrending the appeals might be. Even if he gave all his money away, it would provide no more than a few dollars for every person in the United States. And such an idea was technically unworkable, for it would require converting his stocks and bonds to cash, which would only worsen the slump. Systemic means to recovery had to be found, a task that was beyond Junior or any other individual. All he could do was try to help where it seemed workable and sensible.

There were, of course, privately sponsored relief efforts, including those of the Prosser Committee and the Gibson Committee in New York City. Junior contributed a million dollars to an unemployment fund and the Rockefeller Foundation gave half a million. In this enterprise, John 3rd became a "block captain," soliciting all the families living on his block to contribute to the fund. Hardest hit was the construction industry, and John spent long hours studying new ideas for lowering costs and stimulating home construction. He met at length with Max Mason about these ideas, but nothing came of it. As manager of the Pocantico estate, John began to study such ideas as paid annual vacations for day laborers and the forty-hour week, with the thought of extending employment to a larger number of men.

There never was any possibility that Junior would go under as a result of the Depression. Most of his holdings consisted of shares in the companies created as a result of the dissolution order of 1911, and these were "blue-chip" stocks. None of these companies went bankrupt. All continued to pay dividends throughout the 1930s, although these were sharply cut from year to year as the Depression deepened. Junior honored all of the philanthropic pledges he had made, but as his income declined, new commitments were fewer and smaller.

Junior also began a careful review of all the other organizations and causes he was supporting annually, some three hundred of them by 1933, eliminating some and cutting back on others.

One effect of the Depression among the oil companies was to stimulate mergers. Junior did not control any of the companies, but he was a major stockholder, in a few cases the largest single shareholder. This fact, plus the historic family association and the "clout" Junior had shown in the Standard of Indiana proxy fight, placed him in a unique position vis-à-vis the companies. He became a sort of arbiter during the hard times of the 1930s as the companies jockeyed for position in merger schemes. A number of meetings occurred between company officials, Junior, and his key advisers, in which the executives sought his views and influence. John 3rd sat in on these meetings, learning much about high finance and management in the oil industry.

The two most prominent plans proposed to merge Standard of New York (Socony) and the Vacuum Oil Company and the New Jersey and California companies. The oil executives feared that if both mergers were pressed simultaneously the Justice Department would approve neither. Finally, with Junior's blessing, the Socony-Vacuum merger took place while the New Jersey–California idea was abandoned.

Two other notable mergers occurred in the early 1930s that were to have a significant bearing on Rockefeller interests and the work of the Family Office from that time on. In March of 1930 the Equitable Trust Company was merged into the Chase National Bank. The result was the largest bank in the world in terms of total resources, outstripping the Midland Bank and the National City Bank. A year later, the Masten and Nichols law firm merged with Murray, Aldrich, and Webb. The new law firm—Milbank, Tweed, Hope, and Webb— inherited the Rockefeller family as one of its most prominent clients.

The mergers of these banks and law firms were related in that Junior's brother-in-law, Winthrop Aldrich, figured prominently in both. A graduate of Harvard College and Harvard Law School, Aldrich had emerged as a respected member of the New York Bar even before his World War I naval service. During the postwar years, he combined his own innate ability with his personal relationship to Junior to rise to a commanding position within his chosen profession. He joined the Murray firm, utilizing a recommendation from Junior, and soon became a senior partner. This firm had done legal work for the Rockefellers as far back as the 1890s, principally in the acquisition of the Mesabi range and its subsequent sale to United States Steel. Murray and his partners had represented the Equitable Trust ever since its severance from the Equitable Life Assurance Society in 1911. Vanderbilt Webb, another partner, had been involved in Junior's early efforts to expand Grand Teton National Park.

Aldrich, as both counsel to and a board member of the Equitable, had strongly supported the 1929 merger with the Seaboard National Bank, in an effort to provide a domestic counterweight to what he considered to be excessively large foreign loans, especially to Germany. Junior was the largest single shareholder in Equitable, owning slightly less than 10 percent of the stock after the completion of the merger. When the president of the new institution, Chellis Austin, died unexpectedly of a heart attack in late 1929, the board asked Aldrich to cover on an interim basis. He was extremely reluctant to comply, seeing himself as a lawyer and totally inexperienced in the technical side of the business. He talked to his brother-in-law about the dilemma. Both Junior and Tom Debevoise, concerned over the stability of the newly merged bank in the aftermath of the stock market crash, urged him to accept for a period of one year. Aldrich agreed, and, still concerned about Equitable's vulnerability, immediately began the pursuit of a new partner. Within four months, he helped to engineer the Chase merger.

Junior's old Equitable shares were translated into 3.8 percent of the 7.4 million shares of the new Chase National Bank, having a market value of $20,140,000. He was one of 83,000 individuals and institutions that owned stock in the bank. Although his position was significant and allowed him to name a member of the board, Tom Debevoise, his holdings were dwarfed by those of Albert Wiggin, the leading figure in the bank as chairman of the Governing Council. Aldrich was chosen president of the Chase, the only Equitable officer to be given a high post, but he was subordinate to Wiggin, as well as to Charles McCain, chairman of the board, and John McHugh, chairman of the executive committee.

However, Wiggin retired in late 1932, and a year later he and McCain came under intense congressional scrutiny by the Pecora Committee, which uncovered a number of questionable transactions by Chase's top management. Among other things, Wiggin revealed that he had lent himself large sums of money and allowed other officers to do the same, had participated in speculation in Chase stock that included selling short during the period of the October 1929 crash, and had set up a Canadian securities company that allowed him to avoid sizable federal taxes. McCain admitted to similar but much smaller breaches of fiduciary trust and ethics.

Aldrich, in contrast to his former boss and associate, had taken the high road as a leading advocate of banking and securities reform. With the enthusiastic backing of Junior and the intense discomfort of many of his Wall Street colleagues, Aldrich testified in favor of many of the reforms that would be enacted into law through the Glass-Steagall Act of 1933 and the Securities Act of 1933. Among other things, these laws provided for the separation of commercial from investment banking, the strengthening of the Federal Reserve System and the ability of the government to regulate the banking system, the creation of the Federal Deposit Insurance Corporation, and various measures to increase the information available to prospective purchasers of securities.

McCain, after his testimony, found his position at the bank untenable and resigned. As a result of his leadership during this crisis and the sudden and unexpected vacuum at the top of the Chase, Aldrich emerged as the dominant figure. The board selected him as chairman on January 10, 1934.[3]

Because Aldrich's "interim" role in banking became a permanent one by 1931, he had to give up his law partnership for good. This is what triggered the merger of the Murray firm with Masten and Nichols, which had represented the Chase Bank for many years. The leading figure in the firm that resulted from the merger was Albert G. Milbank, Junior's boyhood chum and classmate at the Browning School.

This background is of interest on several accounts. Writers who start from the premise of a Rockefeller conspiracy to control American life have described these events as if Junior had pulled all the strings and Aldrich functioned merely as a tool of his interests. Junior was certainly an influential person in everything he did, but what happened clearly was the result of the luck of circumstance and the ability and character of Winthrop Aldrich. Senior had always tended to distrust banks. As an investment, Junior had accumulated shares in five New York banks in the early 1920s, but by the end of the decade he had come down to interests in only two, Bankers Trust and the Equitable. Aldrich had been asked to take charge of the Equitable temporarily after Austin's death by the board, not through any manipulation by Junior. And Junior and Debevoise urged Aldrich to accept the interim position for one year to help assure the stability of the bank after the Seaboard merger.[4]

Once the Chase merger occurred and Aldrich rose to the top, it was natural for Junior to do his banking with the Chase. The family identity with the bank grew over the years, three of Junior's sons testing the idea of careers with Uncle Winthrop's bank, and David, the one who stuck with it, eventually becoming its chairman. Although this all happened after the merger and Aldrich's ascendancy, it has been used to suggest that Junior arranged everything.

The long-standing business rivalry between the Chase and the National City Bank, New York City's two largest, and the identification of each with a branch of the Rockefeller family, amounts to a set of curious historical facts with no particular bearing on the matters under discussion. The National City Bank was formed in 1901 by banker James Stillman, aided by William Rockefeller, Senior's brother. Two of William's sons, William and Percy, married two of Stillman's daughters, Sarah and Isabel, and that branch of the family came to be known as the "Stillman Rockefellers." Relations between Senior's and William's branches might best be described as cordial, but not particularly close. Senior and Junior, for example, did not place any significant amount of their banking business with National City.

The rivalry between the two banks, both of which experienced meteoric growth in the 1920s, was intense long before the Chase-Equitable merger. As noted, the merger made the Chase (now the Chase Manhattan) the largest bank in the world, but in the 1970s the National City (now Citibank) became the largest, with the Chase third behind the Bank of America.

For Junior the two mergers were pleasing in that they settled the questions of where he would do most of his banking and where he would get his outside legal advice. As noted, Junior had begun the practice of having at least one seasoned lawyer on his office staff (Starr Murphy at first, and then Thomas Debevoise), but his activities required legal assistance far beyond what they could do. Over the years, Junior had used a number of outside law firms, including the Murray firm, Raymond Fosdick, and Charles Evans Hughes. He had been comfortable with the Murray firm because of his close personal relationship with Aldrich, but now he had become a banker. Junior's congenial relationship with "Bert" Milbank, who had been the head of Masten and Nichols, became the substitute. Thus, Junior's influence—his attractiveness as a client—was a great deal more influential in the merger of the law firms than of the banks. He not only became a client of Milbank, Tweed, but also began the practice after World War II of having a senior member of that firm and one or more junior members located in the family office. This practice was discontinued only in the mid-1980s.

One person who definitely was not involved in all these activities was young John 3rd.[5] Although he, too, would use the services of the Chase Bank and the Milbank law firm the rest of his life, at the time of the mergers he was still very much the apprentice gingerly feeling his way in his father's office. It was not an easy time for him. The excitement of his world trip was in the past, and some of his inhibitions began to return. His work could be varied and interesting at times, but at others it seemed routine and low-level. Junior had started his career during a period of great growth and expansion of opportunities, but John began with the Depression. As Debevoise pointed out to him one day, this meant not only retrenchment in existing programs, but also the impossibility of any bold new initiatives in philanthropy. When Junior began, the overwhelming concentration had been on the problems of the city, and he thought his son should take a like interest in "social work." John was interested in this up to a point, but his real love was "international affairs"—and he saw little prospect of being able to satisfy it.

There was some companionship for a while when Nelson joined the office staff in 1931. But John was the one designated to follow in his father's path, and hence was placed on all the important boards. Left somewhat adrift, Nelson, full of restless energy, thrashed out in several directions on his own. John plodded patiently on, repressing his own restlessness. After two years in the office, on Christmas Eve 1931, he told his diary: "I have not been working on any one thing but doing lots of smaller things. It is all most interesting but does not give one a chance to go to the bottom of anything or get very familiar with anything."

Even though his office was next to Junior's, John did not see his father very often. Junior was as remote and towering a figure as ever, seemingly unapproachable, surrounded by a phalanx of impressive senior advisers who were cordial enough, but rarely had much time for John. Everything seemed settled, even bureaucratic. But there was one great development emerging that soon would offer some excitement and challenge for both John and Nelson—Rockefeller Center.

16

♕

ROCKEFELLER CENTER

WITH THE DEPRESSION barring major new initiatives in the 1930s, the two biggest projects for the Rockefeller family office were ones that Junior had become involved in before the crash—the development of Rockefeller Center and the restoration of Colonial Williamsburg. The Center was by far the more difficult and problematical—the financial stakes were much higher and the design problems infinitely more complex. Moreover, progress was dependent on the decisions of others. In contrast, Williamsburg was all Junior's show. Once the core of the old town was secure, the restoration could proceed at any pace that he desired.

As the Depression wore on, John 3rd became more and more involved in both projects, and Nelson was to play a major role in Rockefeller Center.[1] While still a student at Dartmouth, Nelson took such an avid interest in the Center that Junior made him a director of the Metropolitan Square Corporation, which was set up to manage the development. Soon after he entered his father's office, Nelson displayed political skills and ambition in a single-minded drive to take charge of the Center. Moreover, John 3rd's experience during the development of Rockefeller Center had an important bearing on a project of comparable scale and complexity that he took on some twenty-eight years later—the development of Lincoln Center for the Performing Arts. Given this degree of interest and involvement by the two older sons and the prominence of the Center in the lives and fortune of the Rockefeller family ever since, it is worth taking a closer look at just how Junior became involved and how the project took a turn that no one anticipated.

As noted, it all began with the marriage of two ideas—a new house for the Metropolitan Opera Company and redevelopment of the generally run-down three-block area bounded by 48th and 51st streets and Fifth and Sixth avenues, most of which was owned by Columbia University, its so-called "Upper Estate."[2] A developer was needed, and Junior agreed to play this role because he was attracted by a project combining the arts and civic betterment that seemed low in risk. "Civic betterment" was not an abstraction in this case—this was Junior's neighborhood. And he was not merely the average homeowner concerned only about maintaining the real estate value of his own home. Over the years, he had acquired many lots in the immediate vicinity—six properties on Fifth Avenue between 52nd and 55th streets, and, between Fifth and Sixth avenues, no fewer than fifteen properties on 53rd Street, fifteen on 54th Street, and six on 55th Street.

The lawyers representing Columbia were extremely sharp and, of course, Junior's were no amateurs. As a result, the negotiations lasted for eight months, Junior not finally signing the contract until December 31, 1928. The deal was based primarily on a lease instead of purchase of the land, an arrangement that was congenial to all parties in the beginning, but which became an important issue later on. Ultimately, the way the development turned out made acquisition of the Columbia land highly desirable for Rockefeller Center. Negotiations on this issue began well before the initial twenty-four-year lease period was up, and they continued for many years, not reaching a culmination until 1985.[3]

One might wonder about the original deal: why would corporations want to build skyscrapers on land owned by someone else? But this is by no means an unheard-of practice. For one thing, the corporations do not have to come up with the capital for land purchase, and land values were at a historic high in Manhattan in 1928. An important consideration is the character of the landowner. As a stable community institution, a major university inspires confidence that it would not be interested in gouging or becoming and remaining a real estate manager on a large scale, but would want only a fair return for continuing support of its educational program.

In the beginning, purchase of the entire site was briefly considered, but the university had a strong preference for a lease arrangement. Junior's interest was limited, so a lease was satisfactory to him as well. The agreement included an option for Junior to purchase the middle block for $6 million only if the opera building materialized. If the opera deal was not closed by April 1, 1930, the option would lapse and the block would stay within the lease agreement. The plan called for dividing the middle block into two portions, two-thirds of it for the new opera house and the remaining third, fronting on Fifth Avenue, to be an open plaza. Junior would donate the land for the plaza, valued at $2.4 million, to the city, but counted on the opera to reimburse him $3.6 million for its two-thirds portion. The two side blocks would be cleared and made available to corporations to take over portions of the lease and erect their new office towers.

The lease was a massive document, nearly a foot thick. Over the years, the three blocks had been divided into more than two hundred separate properties, each having its own lease, and all of these had to be identified and collated into the comprehensive lease that Junior signed. In addition to the initial twenty-four-year term, the lease included options for three renewals of twenty-one years each. The annual rent was fixed at $3.3 million.

With one stroke of Junior's pen, the immediate winner was Columbia University. The 1920s had been a boom period for real estate in many parts of the United States, including New York City, but one area that had not benefited at all was the Columbia property. The area was stagnant, poorly served by public transportation. The neighborhoods adjacent to the Pennsylvania and Grand Central railroad stations were booming, as well as others well served by subways. But the Sixth Avenue Elevated was an eyesore that prevented light from reaching the street below. Its patronage was falling off each year. Since 1920 there had been talk of tearing it down and putting in a subway, and the Sixth Avenue Association was promoting this mightily. It seemed inevitable that a subway would come, but in the meantime Sixth Avenue was the shabbiest street in the area. For all these reasons, Columbia was collecting a paltry $300,000 a year in rentals, hardly worth the trouble of administering the two hundred–odd properties. With the new lease, Columbia rid itself of all the headaches of management and increased its income from the property elevenfold.

Never one to waste time, Junior had begun the preparatory work even before the lease was signed. His trusted aide, Colonel Arthur Woods, was designated as his chief administrative person for the project and named president of the Metropolitan Square Corporation. Important to the feasibility of the project was the fact that most of the leases were up for renewal in the period 1928–1931. This meant that the work of clearing the leases could begin immediately, followed by scheduling the razing of the old buildings as they were vacated.

Also important in conditioning the development of the project was the fact that Columbia did not own quite *all* of the three blocks, having sold off some frontage lots over the years. The eastern end of the southern block, fronting on Fifth Avenue, and almost all of the Sixth Avenue frontage was owned by others. These latter properties went back varying distances from the street, but most of them were standard New York lots, a hundred feet five inches in depth. Initially, there was little thought of acquiring these properties; the early design ideas were based on only the Columbia land.

The prospect of redeveloping the tract stimulated the imaginations of architects and urban planners. Ideas and drawings poured in, some solicited, others not. The process began as early as 1926 when the Metropolitan Opera trustees first cast their eyes on the Columbia property. Architect Benjamin Wistar Morris was retained by the opera, and it was he who first envisioned the opera house as the centerpiece with a plaza before its entrance. He stressed the importance of architectural unity for the whole development, a concept followed by all subsequent planners. He proposed three thirty-five-story office buildings in addition to the opera, an emphasis on street-level retailing, with many shops to draw people to the area, and a new north-south street, the "Metropolitan Boulevard," to run from Pennsylvania Station to the opera house.

Among the other ideas considered were a fifty-story tower, apartments and hotels, a three-tier parking garage below the entire development, below-grade concourses and sky walkways to link the buildings, a monorail, roof gardens, and numerous ways to rearrange the proposed buildings on the land. Transportation loomed large in the minds of the planners, including renewed pressure to tear down the Elevated and replace it with a subway, ideas for a midtown tunnel under the Hudson River from New Jersey, for an underground rail terminus to bring direct to the Center the trunk and commuter railroads that stopped at the New Jersey shore of the Hudson (unlike the New York Central and the Pennsylvania, which crossed the river), and for a new transcontinental bus terminal, on the theory that modern buses were going to supplant the railroads.[4]

Out of this chaos of creativity one can begin to see ideas that survived. The El was eventually torn down and replaced by the Sixth Avenue subway line, with a stop at 50th Street linked to Rockefeller Center by underground concourses. The midtown tunnel materialized (the Lincoln Tunnel), but too far south to have any direct bearing on the Center. The grand boulevard envisioned by Morris became the private north-south street bisecting the three-block site and known today as Rockefeller Plaza. The underground concourses and shops of

Rockefeller Center have become world-famous, and the wonderfully extensive public roof gardens were a special delight until they became too expensive to maintain and were gradually closed to all but renters.

But in early 1929 Junior was faced with such a plethora of ideas that he realized he would need additional managerial talent to forge a coherent plan and make it work. Heydt and Debevoise recommended the firm of Todd, Robertson, and Todd. Junior knew the firm; it had done some work at Colonial Williamsburg and had a very good reputation in New York for its unique combination in one firm of expertise in real estate development, management, architecture, and construction, and, through its subsidiary, Todd and Brown, in engineering. The principal figure was John R, Todd, a man past sixty years of age with an austere and commanding presence. Hugh Robertson was an engaging man who was to be effective in lining up tenants. The third member was John Todd's younger brother, James, a physician by training. The principal in the engineering firm was John Todd's son, Webster.

John Todd was invited to Seal Harbor for three days in the summer of 1929. He and Junior got along well, and as a result Junior signed a contract for his company to work exclusively for the development with the title of "managing agents." The compensation was $250,000 per year plus one-third of any profits that would result from the commercial success of the project. In exchange for exclusivity, Junior also agreed to invest in another skyscraper the Todds were committed to develop.[5] The talents of the Todd firm were to prove extremely effective for a number of years, but the situation was made to order for conflict sooner or later. The agents had a direct line to Junior and exerted such power in managing the development that the directors of the Metropolitan Square Corporation began to feel frustrated. And Junior's two oldest sons, especially Nelson, saw the agents as blocking their ambitions.

From the beginning, Junior was emphatic that he expected the project to be both a financial and an artistic success. He expressed this in a memorandum to Todd on August 28, 1929: "While the prime consideration in this enterprise must be its financial success, the importance of a unified and beautiful architectural whole must be constantly kept in mind, and attained, to the fullest extent possible. . . ." The Todd firm had always been motivated to achieve commercial success, and there was an added incentive in the terms of its contract with Junior. The character of the firm was well expressed in a contemporary account: "There is probably no other firm just like Todd, Robertson & Todd anywhere. Its services run the gamut of building . . . there is never any doubt about who is running the job. It is always the two Todds and Robertson."[6]

As one way of maintaining control of such a massive project, John Todd adopted the practice, rare at the time, of "architecture by committee." He first retained the firm of Reinhard and Hofmeister, led by two young architects with a conservative bent who were extremely painstaking and practical in their work. To bring in some creative energy, Todd soon added two other firms: Corbett, Harrison, and MacMurray; and Hood, Godley, and Fouilhoux.[7] Most individual ideas were modified by this group of architects before being accepted, and the arrangement clearly left Todd in control, subject only to pleasing Junior, who stayed intimately involved.

Henry Hofmeister and L. Andrew Reinhard became the "workhorses" of the project. The brilliant Corbett was lost when he became the principal architect for the Century of Progress Exposition in Chicago. Among the others there were two who stood out—Raymond Hood and Wallace K. Harrison. Hood, who had won the international design competition for the Chicago Tribune Tower, was the source of some of the most creative ideas for Rockefeller Center before his death in 1934. Although some of Harrison's ideas were rejected, he was consistently productive for the project for more than a decade. He married the sister of Junior's son-in-law, David Milton, and became an intimate friend of Nelson's. In later years, he was associated with many of Nelson's activities and sat on the boards of a number of Rockefeller organizations. He became the principal architect of the United Nations complex and John 3rd's Lincoln Center project.

Various architects had recommended that the Sixth Avenue frontage properties be purchased if at all possible. Charles Heydt was for this because it would be essential if a railroad terminal were to be built. So Junior formed a corporation with the difficult mission of trying to buy these properties from owners who were eager to get rich. The Sixth Avenue El inspired someone to come up with a whimsical name: the Underel Holding Corporation.

Even as the architects settled down to serious work, trouble arose over the Metropolitan Opera's participation in the project. After the initial flush of enthusiasm, the trustees were confronting some hard realities. The idea that the existing opera house and site could be sold for enough money to pay most of the costs of a new house on the

Columbia land no longer seemed viable to them. The land would cost $3.6 million and the building a projected $8 million. There were also serious problems of timing and coordination. Selling the existing property to finance a new one meant that the opera would have to be dark for at least a year, possibly two. The delaying tactics of the opera had been evident for months before the stock market crash of late October. When that happened, of course, it made the situation all the worse. Junior began to get a whiff of genteel blackmail. Word came to him that the opera trustees now felt the only way the project could go forward would be if Junior paid half the costs of the new building. From Junior's perspective, this smacked of the trustees thinking they had him "on the hook," that he had no real choice but to agree. Junior was not a man who took kindly to being pressured in this way.

Back when the idea of building an opera house on the Columbia land had first been discussed, there had been skepticism that any person could be found who would pay for the plaza, but Junior had committed himself to this at a cost of $2.4 million. Moreover, he had accepted the risk of developing the whole site in order to make the project possible and provide a proper setting for the opera house. Now he was being asked to come up with something on the order of $6 million more for the opera, quite apart from the fact that developing the rest of the land now seemed much more risky than before. Nearly a year had passed since Junior had signed the lease. During that time, the opera trustees had done nothing to firm up their commitment and further their plans. Precious time was being lost and costs were mounting. Planning could not go forward until it was known for certain whether or not the opera would be the centerpiece of the project. Among other considerations, Junior recognized that if he agreed to the "genteel blackmail" there would be no end to it. He would truly be "on the hook" and the opera would be an endless drain on his resources. He felt he had done his part in contributing to the opera and that the trustees were now trying to change the terms of an unmistakably clear agreement in principle.

Winthrop Aldrich, at the time serving as vice president of the Metropolitan Square Corporation, was the intermediary. He attended a meeting of the opera's trustees on December 6, 1929, to say that the time had come for the opera to make a firm commitment under the existing agreement. Otherwise, planning would have to go ahead without them. He then came back to tell Junior the bad news. The "whole attitude" of the trustees was: "You've got the money and therefore there's no reason why you shouldn't do this [pay half the cost of the new opera house]." Junior paused and then said: "Winthrop, go back and tell them I am not interested."[8]

The opera trustees had erred not only regarding Junior's reaction to being pressured, but also to the indispensability of the opera to the project. Junior had always thought it *was* important as the centerpiece and raison d'être for the whole enterprise. But he was also willing, indeed he felt compelled, to proceed without the opera if necessary.

In an address to Rockefeller Center employees a decade later, he said he had signed the lease "never thinking for a moment but that I would shortly sublet the remaining property to various corporations, which, without further investment on my part, would develop and finance their own building programs as the Opera proposed to do." In the same speech, he referred to the grim prospect of going forward with the project "in the definite knowledge that I myself would have to finance it alone, without the immense impetus that the new Opera House would have given, and with no escape from the fact that under the changed conditions it would be necessary to improve all the land in order to lease it, thus involving immense capital outlays never contemplated."[9]

For nearly two more years, Junior kept the door open, trying to find a way for the opera to come into the project, even as planning and construction began on another basis. John Todd, for one, did not share Junior's view of the importance of the opera. He wrote to Winthrop Aldrich: "The Opera House would be a dead spot and greatly reduce shopping values in all property facing it. I am saying this because I am hoping so keenly that the matter will not be re-opened."[10]

Going it alone was a grim prospect indeed. By the spring of 1930, Junior had already spent nearly $10 million on the project—for fees, licenses, rent, salaries, taxes, the costs of clearing leases and razing some buildings and of acquiring others through Underel. Meanwhile, his assets were rapidly eroding under the force of the Depression. From a high of nearly a billion dollars in 1928, Junior's net worth had already shrunk by several hundred million—and the end was nowhere in sight.

To Junior a deal was a deal. There is no evidence that he ever thought of going back to Columbia and saying, in effect, now that the opera has dropped out and the economy has plummeted, let's just cancel this lease and forget the whole thing. That would have been a humbling experience because Junior and his advisers knew full well that Columbia could not agree. What had been merely a financial coup for the university now seemed like salvation—a dramatic increase in income at the time that its other assets were being eroded by the Depression.

Not only had the opera dropped out, but the delay and uncertainty had prevented the lining up of any corporate clients. Now, with the economy in a tailspin, that prospect began to appear remote. Junior seemingly had only two choices. One would have been to freeze everything to stop the financial drain (other than the Columbia lease) and wait for the economy to recover. It should be remembered that in 1930 no one had an inkling that the economic bad times would last throughout the decade. Past experience suggested a recovery within a few years.

The second choice was for Junior to go ahead and develop the project on his own by providing the capital to erect the new buildings and by lining up corporate tenants as they became available. Over the twenty-four-year period of the lease, Junior's basic liability was more than $90 million in rent and taxes, with only $7 million or $8 million coming back in existing rentals over that span of time. If he developed the project himself, his liability would increase to the extent of the construction costs, variously estimated at between $120 and $160 million. As Junior analyzed his dilemma, he concluded that he had only one choice. He could not stand still; he would have to go ahead alone. He and his father several times had publicly expressed confidence in the recovery of the American economy. Junior decided to back his convictions by taking the much larger risk of proceeding with the development. When his biographer, Raymond Fosdick, asked if it did not take considerable courage to do this at such an unpropitious time, Junior replied: "I don't know whether it is courage or not. Often a man gets into a situation where there is just one thing to do. There is no alternative. He wants to run, but there is no place to run to. So he goes ahead with the only course that's open, and people call it courage."[11]

Just as prospects seemed at their lowest ebb, a marvelous turn of fortune developed that gave the project not only its first major corporate client, but also one that provided a new focus for the development in place of the opera. The idea apparently came from architect Raymond Hood, who had designed several studios for the National Broadcasting Company elsewhere in Manhattan. Hood suggested NBC's parent company, the Radio Corporation of America, as a prospective corporate client. RCA also controlled Radio-Keith-Orpheum, one of the major producers of motion pictures. To Hood, Harrison, and the Todds, this opened up a dazzling prospect. The opera looked to the past; the adolescent and glamorous broadcasting and motion picture industries had the look of the future about them. Both had grown dramatically during the 1920s. RCA could give the project new life: an office tower for its corporate headquarters, studios for NBC, and theaters for RKO.[12]

Through a mutual friend, Hood and Harrison got in touch with Edward Walker Harden, a director of RCA and chairman of its real estate and locations committee. Intrigued by the idea, Harden wrote to Junior on December 27, 1929. During the early months of 1930, negotiations proceeded in earnest with Owen D. Young, chairman of General Electric, which at that time held a controlling interest in RCA, and David Sarnoff, president of RCA. Sarnoff was excited by the idea and almost immediately began to speak of the project as "Radio City."

To provide a basis for agreement, Todd rallied his architects to produce an entirely new design. Instead of the low-rise opera building flanked by office towers on either side, the new plan put the tallest structure—the RCA Building—at the center of the project. Initially planned at fifty stories, it ultimately was increased to seventy. The remaining buildings would step down in size, giving the project a more open prospect to the east and north. Junior was pleased with this. Instead of having the area where he owned all of his property walled off by office towers, the line of sight would rise to the RCA Building. In front of the RCA Building would be a small sunken plaza (where the skating rink is now located) with a broad promenade, flanked by two low-rise buildings, leading to Fifth Avenue. Four theaters were planned, the two largest to front on Sixth Avenue on the two blocks on either side of the RCA Building. Office buildings of various sizes would complete the project. The Sixth Avenue location would place the major theaters as close as possible to the entertainment district of the city, only a few blocks to the west and south. The theaters would require entrances and marquees on Sixth Avenue, but no windows. The facade of the RCA Building West would front directly on Sixth Avenue, having the effect of walling off some of the unsightliness and dirt of the Elevated to those inside the buildings.

Agreement was reached with RCA in June 1930, and all leases were signed by early 1931. RCA agreed to lease 1 million square feet of office and studio space at $2.75 a square foot and to pay an annual rental of $1.5 million for the four theaters. This agreement, the lining up of other tenants, and the success of Underel in acquiring and clearing almost all of the missing properties (at a cost to Junior of more than $10 million) moved the project into high gear for both design and construction.

Hugh Robertson came up with the idea of trying to interest foreign governments and commercial interests in leasing buildings. This resulted in a number of trips to Europe for the managing agents and architects for negotiations and the study of theaters and building decoration. It also produced the British Empire Building and La Maison Française, the two low-rise buildings flanking the promenade leading to Fifth Avenue, and the International Building, fronting on Fifth Avenue on the northern block with the bronze statue of Atlas before it. The U.S. Passport Office located its New York headquarters in the latter building, serving to draw renters associated with foreign governments, trade, and tourism.

Junior was influential in bringing in a number of tenants—Standard of New Jersey (Esso), Consolidated Oil, Sinclair Oil, the Rockefeller Foundation, and three branches of the Chase National Bank. Agreements were soon reached to erect buildings to be leased by the Associated Press and Time, Inc.

With commitments in hand for the construction of eight buildings, it was time for Junior to concern himself with the financing of the project. He concluded an agreement with the Metropolitan Life Insurance Company for $65 million worth of gold mortgage bonds, at the time the largest single financial commitment by a life insurance company. This, in effect, was a line of credit, but with specific amounts designated for each building.[13] Just as the Columbia University lawyers had done, Metropolitan Life insisted that Junior be personally liable, so that two sets of documents were required, one to be signed by officers of the Metropolitan Square Corporation and the other by Junior. This requirement did not end until 1947.

No longer in the impossible position of not knowing what to build or for whom, Junior and his planners could now proceed with zest. The principle of architectural unity, in place from the earliest thinking, was maintained. Although the buildings would vary considerably in size and shape, all would be sheathed in Indiana limestone and designed in a style to complement one another.

To make up for the loss of the magic and charm of an opera house as the centerpiece, Junior and the architects were determined to bring as much imagination and flair to the project as possible. They decided on the clean, vertical look of European modernism for the exteriors, but for exterior details and interior decoration they adopted the Art Deco motif so popular in the period 1925–1935. Raymond Hood designed a lobby for the RCA Building that would be much grander than normally found in office buildings. These decisions, together with the underground concourses, shops, sunken plaza, and roof gardens planned for every setback up to the sixteenth floor, began to give the development a unique ambience. Most impressive was the RCA Building itself as it began to take shape, rising like a blade to its seventy-story height and dominating the surroundings.

There were two holdouts among the Sixth Avenue property owners, identical small buildings on either corner of the block where the RCA Building was being constructed. One was a bar-restaurant and the other a store. Junior refused to pay the inflated prices, so the architects simply indented the new building around the two obstructions.[14]

With construction of the RCA Building well under way, General Electric and its subsidiary companies began to feel the severe effects of the Depression. The RKO subsidiary was particularly hard hit and soon went into receivership. This forced RCA to petition Junior for a revision of the lease, and he agreed to halve the commitment, down from four theaters to two and from 1 million square feet of office space to 500,000.

To help assure the success of the two theaters, the radio group retained S. L. Rothafel, a colorful impresario known as "Roxy," who had fulfilled one of his life's dreams two years earlier by building the Roxy Theater only two blocks from Junior's new development. But Roxy happily agreed to sever his connection with his partners to accomplish even bigger things in the new project. Roxy was given a free hand, and he dominated the designing and building of the Radio City Music Hall, an extravagant 6,200-seat entertainment palace, and the 3,500-seat New Roxy Theater only a block to the south on the other side of the RCA Building. A name change was forced when the owners of the original Roxy Theater threatened to sue, so the New Roxy Theater became the Center Theater.

The Music Hall in particular was regarded by many as one of the modern wonders of the world, having the world's largest proscenium arch, the largest organ, movable stages, stage elevators, elaborate backstage facilities, a huge lobby and salons, and an immense grand staircase. Roxy also included in the plans for the Music Hall building an elegant apartment for himself, which still exists today as a virtual Art Deco museumpiece.[15]

Although the opportunity for a new opera house to be the centerpiece had passed, a large parcel of land on the southernmost block had been reserved against the possibility that it still might be possible to bring the Metropolitan Opera back into the project. Owen D. Young had made a new attempt to find a basis for this, but by 1932 it was clear that there no longer was any hope. This raised the question of the name of the development. The Metropolitan Square name would have been fine under ordinary circumstances, but it had been so visibly associated with the presence of the opera that Junior and his colleagues decided that a new name was needed. Informally, the project was being called Rockefeller Center by many people and Radio City by others as the first two buildings, the RCA Building and the Radio City Music Hall, neared completion. Junior's associates banded together to persuade him to formally adopt the name Rockefeller Center. According to Raymond Fosdick, Junior demurred at first, but he was led to agree by the consideration that this was a business project, not a philanthropic one, and that using the family name would be good for business, helping to restore some of the "rank and standing" that had been lost with the withdrawal of the Met.[16] General Sarnoff of RCA agreed that there should be one formal name for the project and that it should be Rockefeller Center, although the western end of the project continued to be known as Radio City.

As construction of the buildings progressed, plans were drawn and redrawn to keep pace with new ideas. There were frequent disagreements among the architects and between the architects and the builders. As always, Junior was the arbiter. He thoroughly enjoyed the planning and supervision of new construction. With Colonial Williamsburg and Rockefeller Center going on both at once, he was in his element. Fosdick reports one associate describing Junior as "living knee-deep in blueprints" and loving every minute of it.[17]

High-speed elevators had just been approved under the city's building code, which made possible the grouping of elevators in the central core of an office tower. The RCA Building became the first structure in which this was done. When Westinghouse took rental space in the building, its elevators were chosen over Otis. Junior took care that design and amenities were of the most advanced sort possible for the benefit of office workers. For example, a rigid requirement was that no desk be more than $27\frac{1}{2}$ feet from a window, the maximum distance thought suitable for natural light and ventilation.

Air-conditioning was not then sufficiently advanced, but the design included ducts and blowers for air-cooling. This was useful when it became necessary to convert to air-conditioning after World War II in order to stay competitive with newer buildings, but the conversion still cost a staggering sum. The shops lining the sunken plaza in front of the RCA Building did not succeed commercially, but one of the architects had come across a new process for freezing open-air skating surfaces even in mild weather. A skating rink in the plaza was tried as a one-year experiment in 1936, and it was so successful that it has been a winter fixture ever since. The area serves as an open-air restaurant the rest of the year. The custom of erecting a giant Christmas tree every year on Rockefeller Plaza, near Paul Manship's large golden statue of Prometheus, was begun by workmen in 1933.

Late in 1932, Junior, John, and Nelson visited the nearly completed RCA Building to choose space for the new family office. The first stop for the highest bank of elevators was the fifty-third floor. RCA had chosen this as the topmost of its executive floors. The Rockefellers took the fifty-sixth floor, thus exchanging 26 Broadway, often referred to by newspapers as "the most famous address in the world," for a subtle and low-key designation—"Room 5600." The RCA Building was opened in May 1933, and the first day of business for the Rockefellers in their new headquarters was October 2. The eastern half of the fifty-sixth floor was reserved for the Rockefeller Foundation while Junior and his staff took the western half. Not until after World War II would the family office and small related institutions expand to take over the fifty-fourth and fifty-fifth floors as well, all still with the same low-key address, Room 5600.

Ten years earlier, Junior had redecorated his office at 26 Broadway. Using the services of a renowned antique and furnishings dealer, Charles of London, Junior had spent $70,000 to secure sixteenth-century English Tudor oak paneling, complete with bookcases with leaded glass panes and a fireplace mantel. His purchases had also included an Elizabethan hand-carved conference table, a Jacobean refectory table and chairs of the early seventeenth century, and a Queen Anne desk of the early eighteenth century. These were the warm, dark, and luxurious surroundings so well described by the *Herald Tribune* reporter on the occasion of the press conference during John 3rd's first day at work in 1929. Junior had all these furnishings removed and transported to Rockefeller Center, where they were installed in his spacious office and anteroom at the southwest corner of the fifty-sixth floor. He did not like any form of artificial ventilation, so the air-cooling ducts in his office were covered by paneling. But he did want his fireplace to work, so a special chimney flue was built to vent outside at the fifty-sixth-floor level, the only working fireplace in the RCA Building.

The building of Rockefeller Center was an enormous boon to tens of thousands of workingmen in the hard times of the 1930s, not only those directly involved on the site, but also many employed by the suppliers of building materials, as well as those employed by the Center, a sizable and well-trained force in line with Junior's insistence that maintenance and management of the Center be first-class in every respect. This enhanced the already positive image of the Rockefeller family with trade unions and blue-collar people, and resulted, for example, in the absence of strikes until after World War II.[18] As worthy as the project was from this point of view, it also benefited from the effects of the Depression in that wages and costs were held down. There were bargains to be had in building materials, and this was reflected in the final price tags of the new structures: $8.6 million for the Center Theater and its associated building, $8.8 for the Music Hall, $25 million for the International Building, $3 million for the British Building, $2.8 for La Maison Française, and $57.5 million for the RCA Building.

During the design and construction phases, the architectural critics began their evaluations. With the notable exception of the most influential critic of the time, Lewis Mumford of the *New Yorker*, the reviews were almost all scathingly critical, so much so that the architects and managers began to fear that Junior would become enraged and fire them. But Junior was a veteran of criticism and the vacillations of the press, and he simply ignored the bad reviews. He also knew that bold innovations often went through a cycle of disapproval before their worth became evident. This is precisely what happened to Rockefeller Center. Before long, the criticism dissolved into almost universal praise of the Center for its innovations in urban design, its accomplishment in completely turning around a run-down commercial area of the nation's largest city, and its surprising value as a tourist attraction. One of the most persistent critics was the *New York Times*. An early editorial wrote of "architectural aberrations and monstrosities," and said: "From every source of intelligent appreciation . . . has come a perfect stream of objection, protest, and, one may say, wondering malediction."[19] By late 1933, however, the newspaper's editor in chief, John H. Finley, had a change of heart and was gracious enough to write to Junior about it:

I wish you could have seen your high tower as I saw it from a Times window in the late afternoon light on Thanksgiving Day—a shaft of rose color rising from the gray buildings in the foreground. I have since found this line which describes it better than any words of mine: "a rose red city half as old as time." It turned to a deeper color as the light changed and it was ever more impressive. I am now quite reconciled and grateful.[20]

The proximity, scale, challenge, and potential of Rockefeller Center quite naturally engrossed the minds of Junior's sons as they entered his office. Much of the work of managing the complex development was carried out by some sixteen committees set up by the managing agents and the board of Rockefeller Center, Inc., the successor to the Metropolitan Square Corporation.[21] By 1933 Nelson was serving on seven of these committees and John on six. John's energies were directed mainly to the finance, foreign buildings, and theater committees, especially the last-named. He, of course, had all of his other roles in the family office as the eldest son; foreclosed from these, Nelson tried a number of things, but seems from an early date to have set his mind on ultimately becoming the leading figure in Rockefeller Center. It will be recalled that Junior had placed Nelson on the board of the development in 1929 while he was still at Dartmouth; John did not become a director until 1932.

During his senior year at college, Nelson had been made a Senior Fellow, which freed him from the routine of classes and allowed him to choose his own activities. His choices reflected the strong interest he had developed in modern art, an interest that his mother encouraged. In 1928 she had written to him: "My mind is full of ideas for a new Museum of Modern Art for New York. I have great hopes for it. Wouldn't it be splendid if it would be ready for you to be interested in when you get back to New York to live."[22] Once in New York, Nelson followed up this interest by accepting a seat on the board of the Metropolitan Museum of Art. In 1932 Nelson became a member of the Museum of Modern Art's board and in 1935 was elected treasurer. In this capacity he headed a successful fund-raising drive to finance a new building for the museum. That led to his becoming president of the museum in 1939.

With this background, it was not surprising that Nelson plunged zestfully into the work of the art and architecture committee of Rockefeller Center. Art was a major consideration for the development; several dozen artists had been recruited to produce a wide variety of decorative murals and statuary. It was one of Nelson's recommendations that led to a celebrated fiasco. Contracts had already been let with two artists, Frank Brangwyn and José María Sert, to paint sepia murals to decorate the large lobby of the RCA Building—on the ceiling, inside the front entrance, and on the south wall of the elevator banks. Nelson proposed that the famous Mexican artist Diego Rivera be commissioned to execute the most important of the murals, the one that would be opposite the main entrance to the lobby at the eastern end of the building. The fee was $21,500, and Nelson secured the approval of the managing agents to Rivera's request to do the mural in color. Rivera submitted a plan for the mural, which would cover an area sixty-three by seventeen feet, and it also was approved. But he proceeded to use the opportunity to make a propaganda statement on behalf of the Communist Party. The unpublished history of Rockefeller Center described what happened: "Señor Rivera's mural, entitled 'Man at the Crossroads,' included a likeness of Lenin as the leader of the masses in opposition to the decadent capitalists featured and symbolized by, among other things, objects which appeared to be the germs of social diseases."[23]

In correspondence and in a meeting with Rivera, Nelson tried sweet reason to get him to return to his original plan, but Rivera said that rather than "mutilate" the work he would prefer its "physical destruction."[24] When he proceeded to add even more pro-Communist symbolism to his work in vivid color, the managing agents took over. Hugh Robertson summoned Rivera to his office, handed him a check for payment in full, and told him that he was dismissed from the project. Rivera made an obscene gesture and left.

Nelson made a futile attempt to preserve the fresco for the Museum of Modern Art by removing the plaster wall on which it was painted. When this failed, the mural was destroyed. José María Sert was retained for $28,000 to paint a new and inoffensive mural in its place. The incident caused a storm of controversy over the right of an artist to free expression. It was a decision that could be argued on both sides, but prevailing opinion at the time was in Nelson's favor. Amusing approbation came from Will Rogers in his newspaper column:

Santa Monica, Cal., May 15
    I am hereby entering this argument between young Rockefeller and the Mexican artist, for there are two things that a dumb guy knows as much about as a smart one, and that's art and inflation.

I string with Rockefeller. This artist was selling some art and sneaking in some propaganda. Rockefeller had ordered a plain ham sandwich, but the cook put some onions on it. Rockefeller says, "I will pay you for it, but I won't eat the onions."

Now the above is said in no disparagement of the Mexican artist, for he is the best in the world, but you should never try to fool a Rockefeller in oils.

Yours,
WILL ROGERS[25]

Nelson also threw himself into the labor relations, promotional, and rental activities of Rockefeller Center. He made good friends with union leaders, among them George Meany, head of the plumbers' union, who was already becoming a power in the American Federation of Labor. In promotional work, Nelson was everywhere at once—arranging for bands or choral groups to perform in the plaza, opening new garden displays along the promenade, presenting medals to workingmen. There were many such activities, leading one historian to say that Rockefeller Center invented real estate public relations in its need to court tenants for the huge project during hard times.[26]

Nelson worked hard on securing tenants, in fact forming his own private firm for this purpose, which he called Special Work, Inc. He contracted for 300,000 square feet of the 5.5 million available in the Rockefeller Center buildings. So zealous was he in cutting rates and picking up the unexpired leases of new clients that August Heckscher, who had lost some tenants from his large office building, sued Rockefeller Center for $10 million, charging unfair competition and coercion of tenants. The suit was eventually dropped after Heckscher's death.

To fulfill his ambition of taking leadership of Rockefeller Center, Nelson needed better luck than he had experienced with Diego Rivera and August Heckscher. Ousting the managing agents would not be an easy matter. To do this and win his father's approval, Nelson would also need a good deal of cunning and some allies. There was also the problem of John 3rd. Would he have a prior claim on Rockefeller Center as he seemed to have on everything else? Clearly, the first ally Nelson would need was John, and he began to work on this in earnest. Meanwhile, a marvelous preoccupation intervened in John's life—genuine romance, as he came to know, and eventually marry, Blanchette Ferry Hooker.

17

━━━━━━━

ᵂ

THE MARRIED MAN

IT HAPPENED at a "Pierrot" dance at the Hotel Pierre in Manhattan on the evening of December 23, 1931. John D. Rockefeller 3rd and Blanchette Ferry Hooker found themselves together alone for the first time, and serious romance was set in motion.

They had met several times before, but only momentarily and in a crowd. John's diary records that he attended a "Hooker family party" in the winter of 1927–1928, which in fact was Blanchette's "coming out" party. And at the Model Assembly at Vassar in 1929, Blanchette was one of the many students John met just to shake hands with. He was therefore vaguely aware of her as he was of scores of postdebutantes on the eastern seaboard. Given his work habits and natural reserve, John had not been scouting the social scene very energetically.

The Rockefellers, of course, were in a social class by themselves, given the family history, Junior's national prominence and enormous wealth, and the coming of age of five sons. The roots of the Hooker family were in Detroit, upstate New York, and Greenwich, Connecticut. The family did not summer in Maine or Newport, and did not establish a Manhattan base until the early 1920s. However, with two extraordinary parents, four daughters, and considerable wealth, the Hookers became socially prominent very quickly. Blanchette thus was like other young women of Manhattan society, all of whom knew the Rockefeller boys or at least felt they did, having seen them often at large parties or dances. Blanchette's earliest memory of the Rockefeller boys was seeing the five heads bobbing up and down during Sunday services at the Park Avenue Baptist Church. "Everybody knew who they were," she said. The Rockefellers sat toward the front of the church, while the Hookers were toward the rear. The reason was that they normally attended Henry Sloane Coffin's Madison

Avenue Presbyterian Church, but were often late, so they would instead stop to catch Harry Emerson Fosdick's sermon at the Park Avenue church.

Because she grew up in Greenwich as a friend of Mary French and of Faith Rockefeller, Blanchette *did* know Nelson and Laurance, both of whom were more socially active than John. Most parties in Manhattan centered on the debutantes, so that postdebs had a bit of a problem staying in the limelight. Blanchette decided to stir things up for the postdebs by hosting a party at her family's Manhattan apartment in November 1931. She invited Nelson and Laurance, both of whom accepted. On impulse, she also invited John. He sent his regrets.

The "Pierrot" series of three dinner dances was a social convention aimed at helping the postdebs. Abby was listed among the five "patronesses" of the series, and Blanchette, Mary, and Faith were among the thirty-four postdeb "members." With his mother and cousin thus involved, John signed up and paid the fifteen dollars for the three dances, escorting Faith to the December affair. His infatuation for her was a thing of the past, but she was still his "favorite cousin" and a convenient date. Toward the end of the evening, John asked Faith if there was anyone else he should dance with. She suggested that if he danced with Blanchette Hooker it would give him a chance to say something about why he had been unable to attend her party. John cut in and had his first conversation with Blanchette on the dance floor. They decided to sit the next one out. For the remaining half hour of the evening, they sat and talked earnestly about social work. Blanchette still laughs when she thinks about how serious and intent they were.[1]

Blanchette was attracted to John, who was a decidedly handsome and clean-cut young man, clearly one who was not frivolous about life. Because the conversation had been all about social work, she was not sure what to make of the encounter. But a spark had been struck. John was definitely drawn to the tall, slender, dark-haired Blanchette, who so obviously was intelligent, thoughtful, lively, and socially at ease— and very attractive. Although the next day was Christmas Eve, it was a working day for John. But he came home that evening and penned a Christmas card to Blanchette. Postmarked Christmas Day, it read:

Dear Blanchette:
    I just tried in vain to get you on the telephone so am writing you this note to ask you, first, if you are a rider, and second (assuming the first to be answered in the affirmative) if you would come up to the country with me on

New Years day for a ride provided the weather is good. Tomorrow afternoon I am going to Baltimore for the weekend but will call you up on Monday when I get back so don't bother to answer this in writing. I enjoyed so much seeing you last night and I hope that you will be able to make it next Friday. We can arrange the details by telephone.

Please excuse this rather informal note but I thought it gave it a rather "Christmassy" touch having it on a Christmas card.

Very sincerely,
John Rockefeller

Blanchette slept with the belated Christmas card under her pillow for the next few nights. She was an accomplished rider, but one suspects that had she never seen a horse she would have learned to ride by the following Friday. Quite naturally, it was a New Year's Day spent in something of a daze for Blanchette. Not sure what to expect, she anticipated the worst—a cold and austere atmosphere with her being raked over by calculating stares. Pocantico was something of a way station for many friends of the Rockefeller boys, so it was not at all unusual or special for John to bring someone there. They arrived in John's Stutz, and Blanchette found there was no ice to break as she was simply swept up in the boisterous goings-on, with the boys milling about, happy and joking, and plenty of activity. For a young woman with no brothers, it was a new and stimulating experience. She remembers Abby as being very warm and Junior as a charming man of great "presence" who reminisced and told stories as they sat at a big table for dinner.

From that point on, it could be said that John and Blanchette were "going steady." There were frequent dates, most often an evening of dinner and the theater. At this time, John's writing in his diary was very much in his businesslike mode—no references at all to the courtship, with Blanchette and the Hooker family not even mentioned until March 21, and then only a laconic entry: "Spent the weekend with the Hookers in Connecticut."

An indication that things were progressing quickly and well was the fact that before the end of January John was addressing his letters to "Dear Hookie," the nickname by which Blanchette was known to her good friends. In February John contrived with Faith to invite Blanchette for a long weekend to Overhills during his ten-day stay there. "You really will love it down there," he wrote to her. "The complete contrast from the New York life makes it wonderful."

A tense occasion occurred later that month when John invited Blanchette to have dinner alone with him and his parents at 10 West

54th Street. She, of course, had already met them, but it was one thing to make an informal visit to Pocantico and quite another to dine with the parents at No. 10. It smacked of the young man bringing his best girl home for approval. Blanchette arrived fifteen minutes early and was ushered into a plush sitting room, very formal and elegant, with blue velvet love seats. She sat staring at the lovely Coptic vases on the mantel and at the clock as the minutes slowly ticked by. Soon John came downstairs to greet her, and she remembers that he "was a little scared, too." There were two butlers to serve the four of them at dinner. As if rising to the occasion, Junior was somewhat formal at first, but Abby was warm and friendly. When it was over, Blanchette went home with the feeling that both of the senior Rockefellers liked her.

In April John sent Blanchette information on how to become a member of the Riverside Church. He also spent his second weekend at the Hookers' elegant country house in Greenwich, "Chelmsford." In his bread-and-butter letter to Mrs. Hooker, John wrote about how relaxing the weekend had been, and then apologized for his own "extremely relaxed condition" on the front lawn on several occasions: "It was, I fear, rather informal for a second visit." John commented on the "extremely interesting" discussion about the Depression at dinner: "Mr. Hooker certainly has been giving the question much careful thought. . . ."

Elon Huntington Hooker was indeed a formidable person, handsome though with a prominent nose, a self-made man of forceful personality and strong opinions, leavened by a gregarious nature. He traced his lineage back to the early colonial days, to the Reverend Thomas Hooker, who in 1636 was a leader in the founding of Hartford and the colony of Connecticut. Born in Rochester, New York, in 1869 where his father, formerly an engineer in the Union Army, had taken up the nursery business, Elon was a young man of energy and ambition. He studied engineering at the University of Rochester, where he played in the new sport of football and was a tennis champion. With funds borrowed from his grandfather, he went on to earn a doctorate in civil engineering at Cornell University and win a fellowship for a year of study abroad in Zurich and Paris. Back home, the talented young man came to the attention of Governor Theodore Roosevelt, who in 1899 appointed him deputy superintendent of public works. Hooker remained devoted to TR, working strenuously in his Bull Moose campaign of 1912. Thereafter, he and the former president often exchanged visits.

In 1901 there were two decisive changes in Hooker's life. He married an attractive and talented heiress, Blanche Ferry, whose family had made their money in Detroit by pioneering the retail sale of seed packets. And Hooker left government employ to become an entrepreneur, the leader of a group that included his two younger brothers and several friends. It was what would be called today a "venture capital" group, the basic idea being to make money by finding ways to apply emerging technologies to industrial needs. Most of the capital was supplied by the new Mrs. Hooker, but there is no doubt that the spectacular success that followed was primarily due to the drive and executive ability of "E.H.," all of whose associates became millionaires. As he somewhat grandiloquently put it, Hooker had been "uplifted to the rare delights of electrolytic research—that shadowy borderland between pure science and commercialized industry where mathematics and chemistry join hands in the Great Unknown."[2]

The Hooker Electrochemical Company was formed in 1905. Other venture capital ideas were forgotten as a vast plant was erected at Niagara Falls (for cheap power) and, several decades later, another in Tacoma, Washington. With the aid of two technical geniuses, Leo Baekeland and Elmer Sperry, Hooker developed electrolytic processes for manufacturing caustic soda, chlorine, and hydrogen in large quantities just at the time when the need for such products was rapidly developing—in water treatment and for use in the soap, paper, and synthetics industries. During the World War, the company was a major supplier of chemicals for explosives.[3]

Hooker had married extremely well, quite apart from any financial consideration. His wife also traced her lineage to seventeenth-century America, the ancestral farm being situated near Unadilla, New York. An ardent feminist, she was at the same time a loyal wife who raised four daughters, yet found time for a wide range of social, educational, and political work, in which she displayed leadership and executive abilities. Blanche and her sister were both alumnae of Vassar, to which they gave a new alumnae house. Like her husband, who was an unsuccessful candidate for the Republican nomination for governor of New York in 1920, Blanche was active in party affairs.[4]

Perhaps because of the overwhelmingly feminine setting of his home life, the virile and energetic Elon Hooker got into the habit of taking long business trips, his whereabouts often unknown. But he became socially ambitious as well, once having the wherewithal to live in the grand manner. With his daughters approaching the age of coming out, he decided to embark on the New York social scene, taking a spacious apartment at 907 Fifth Avenue in the early 1920s and relegating Chelmsford to the status of a "country" place.

The oldest daughter, Barbara, was hampered in life by severe psychological problems, but the two middle daughters, Adelaide and Helen, were typical of the liberated young women of the 1920s. They made a celebrated trip to the Soviet Union in 1930, under the partial sponsorship of *Good Housekeeping*. Adelaide wrote a three-part series for the magazine about their adventures, and Helen illustrated it with her photographs and pen-and-ink drawings. How their father—a businessman, Republican, leader of the National Industrial Conference Board and the National Association of Manufacturers, and president of the highly conservative American Defense Society—may have felt about his daughters' excursion is suggested by a passage from Adelaide's first article:

After three months in Leningrad and Moscow our life was bounded by two hazards—first, that our father would find out we were in Russia; second, that the G.P.U., or secret police, would find out that Father was president of the American Defense Society. Discovery of the former would make life in the future rather tense at home. Discovery of the latter would make life, in the event of its being allowed to continue, rather tense in Russia. Our reasons for being there at all were curiosity and cussedness. We didn't know much about Marx and Lenin, but from Father's description they were bad enough to be interesting.[5]

Both of these adventurous young women were to have notable marriages. On another overseas trip in 1935, to the Far East, Adelaide managed to meet John P. Marquand and subsequently married him. Marquand then was on the brink of his great success as a novelist. Helen married Cormac "Ernie" O'Malley, who had been a brigadier general and a leader of assassination squads in the Irish Republican Army at the age of eighteen. He had been involved in the "Easter rebellion," and spent years in a British prison. Her parents were shocked, and Helen lived with her husband in Ireland for fifteen years before ever returning home.

The fourth Hooker child was the father's last chance for the son he never had. Blanchette, who was named after her mother, never did anything to alarm her parents. She was a trouble-free child, growing up with a positive attitude toward life, a generally outgoing nature despite the shy side of her personality, no trace of pretentiousness, and a good admixture of common sense and sensitivity. She was born in New York City in 1909, the family having come to the city for the Fulton Centennial. As a result, Blanchette literally spent several of her earliest days in a bureau drawer. She attended Miss Chapin's School and then, like her mother before her, she went to Vassar, where her major interests were music and German, and as a senior was elected president of her class.

Though the youngest of the four daughters by four years, Blanchette was the first to marry. The courtship had been progressing spendidly, so that by the summer of 1932 it seemed likely that John and Blanchette would soon become engaged. It happened at Seal Harbor, although Blanchette's first visit to the Eyrie did not get off to a smooth start. John went up in mid-July with his parents, and he and Blanchette began exchanging enormous letters almost daily. She was to come up by train to join him for the third week of his vacation. The day before her departure, Nelson telephoned to say that he was also going to Seal Harbor to join Tod, and he suggested that Blanchette drive there with him instead of going alone on the train. That seemed like a reasonable idea, but the first surprise came when Nelson drove his car onto the New York–Boston boat. It was to be an overnight trip. When Blanchette and Nelson went into the dining room for dinner, she was mortified to see the entire Winthrop Aldrich family seated at a nearby table.

The next day came the long drive from Boston to Seal Harbor—Blanchette had not realized how long it would be. With the roads under repair, she and Nelson arrived ninety minutes late for dinner, and their reception was a bit frosty. It took John a while to thaw out, but the week that followed seemed like a dream to the young couple. For John it was sheer delight to show Blanchette the natural beauty surrounding the family retreat and the haunts that had been so much a part of his growing up. Each evening they would disappear after dinner for a long walk along one or another of the romantic trails, returning after everyone else was asleep. Blanchette thought it was an encouraging sign when Junior gave John the key to a little cottage that Junior and Abby sometimes used to get away.

In their increasing closeness, John and Blanchette found they had a great deal in common. Though young—twenty-six and twenty-three years old respectively—they both enjoyed getting away from the crowd to simple rural surroundings. They disliked social-climbing and pretentiousness and the superficiality of the "collegiate set." But in one respect, they were different: Blanchette was basically a secure person, happy and buoyant about life; John, of course, was a habitual worrier about what he believed to be his faults and weaknesses, a confirmed self-critic. She was gradually becoming aware of how serious and sensitive a person he was, and how insecure in some respects. In one of her letters before coming to Seal Harbor, she wrote several remarks in an introspective mood. John seized upon them in his reply:

For me it is terribly discouraging to do the kind of introspective thinking which you have been doing but I do feel it is an awfully good idea and exactly what Father had in mind when he was speaking about the benefits of church and prayer. I have been doing some thinking myself along the very same lines and have even gone so far as to use pencil and paper. From previous experience I have found it most helpful to jot down certain points for future reference. It helps one from forgetting too easily which is for me the main difficulty. There are so many things I want to talk to you about along this line and others that I am almost bursting.[6]

He went on to say that he did not "feel quite as much at peace with the world as I probably ought to," that he could not feel cool and calm and contented despite the lovely surroundings and favorable circumstances he was in:

It is nothing new, however. I have been this way for quite a while. Forgive this personal admission of weakness; I didn't mean to get into it. I should love to talk with you about it; I know you can help. That you feel so perfectly happy at the farm is something to be really thankful for. When you dig down into the lives of people by and large (if you could) you would find a very few who are really happy, I believe. Lots think they are—kid themselves into it—but few actually are. That is why Sinclair Lewis's "Arrowsmith" was so interesting to me. It showed a man fighting desperately for peace and contentment and only finding it after a life of false starts. Again apologies; this is all very gloomy and pessimistic. Your letter started me thinking along lines which are interesting but confusing. I will restrain myself till you arrive and we can talk more leisurely on the subject.

What John had in mind was revealed one evening during Blanchette's visit to Seal Harbor. He produced a list of his faults, which he had meticulously compiled, and proceeded to read it to her. It seems likely that he had never been quite so candid with anyone else. He then suggested that she might want to do the same. Blanchette was astonished. A passing mood of introspection was one thing, but the idea of making a list of her faults had never occurred to her. In the main, this difference in temperament was to be complementary rather than divisive—it was part of why John needed Blanchette and one of the ways in which she could help him.

She was undeterred by John's long list of faults, and he was undeterred by her reluctance to try to match him. They became engaged on the day before Blanchette was due to leave Seal Harbor. As often happens, there was no formal proposal; theirs was a mutual coming together—the time was simply right. They then went off for a round of golf with Tod and Nelson, who were overjoyed to hear the news. Blanchette and Tod liked each other and were due to become close friends. In Blanchette's eyes, Tod combined the qualities of a tomboy—full of life and a marvelous sense of humor—with a quiet dignity and intelligence.

The next morning at breakfast, John announced the engagement to the family members present, including Abby and Junior. Abby expressed her delight and Junior's response was a broad grin and the comment: "Well, at last!"

That day Blanchette, still in a daze, went to Woodstock, Vermont, for a visit with Mary French. She telephoned the news to her mother, but her father was on a business trip to Michigan and could not be located. But when John went to Chicago with his parents for a last visit with his Aunt Edith, who was dying of cancer, he was able to meet Mr. Hooker there. The engagement announcement by the Hookers, held up until the end of August because of Edith's death, stated only that the wedding would take place in the fall. The announcement was reported prominently in all of the New York newspapers and many out-of-town ones as well. Most stories featured an especially lovely photo of Blanchette and a handsome profile shot of John. There was the usual hyperbole in some accounts, John being referred to as an "oil prince" and a "billion dollar baby." The *New York Daily News* story was headlined: "John D. 3rd to Marry Social Worker."

From the time of the announcement until the wedding, which eventually was set for November 11, John spent every weekend with Blanchette, once at Unadilla in upstate New York, twice at Seal Harbor with Abby and Junior, and the other times at the Hookers' in Greenwich. John and Blanchette hoped for a four-month honeymoon in Europe, but Junior was having a run of illness and Abby gently suggested to John that his prolonged absence from the office might put too much of a strain on his father. So the young couple settled on a month in Bermuda.

They decided to have the wedding at the Riverside Church, which Blanchette had joined and where her parents frequently attended. The ceremony took place on a beautiful autumn day with the Reverend Harry Emerson Fosdick officiating. Blanchette's sister Helen was maid of honor, and the bridesmaids included sister Adelaide, Mary French, Faith Rockefeller, and other close friends. True to his promise, Nelson was a constant aide to John and served as best man. The ushers included John's other three brothers, his brother-in-law Dave Milton, and five of his best friends from college.

A special police detail arranged by Colonel Arthur Woods handled the throng outside the church. Inside were 2,500 invited guests. Not with them was Senior, now ninety-three years of age, who had planned to attend until his doctors advised against it at the last minute. Senior, however, had sent his standard $20,000 check as a wedding gift. Social columnist Cholly Knickerbocker of the *New York American* described the scene: "It was just the modest assemblage one would expect to discover at a Rockefeller wedding. I did not note a single Astor or Vanderbilt among the guests. Perhaps they were there, hidden among the vast throngs of Greenwichites and men and women identified with the Rockefeller philanthropic works." Knickerbocker also noted an innovation: "'I pledge thee a husband's love and protection.' It was the first time I ever have heard the words used in a wedding service, and they were spoken in stentorian tones by the young bridegroom—leaving no doubt as to his deep love and affection for the pretty young bride at his side."

A rival columnist, Billy Benedick of the *Evening Journal*, described the radiant Blanchette: "To remark that the bride was stately would be but to express one of her moods, for on her walk from the altar on the arm of young Mr. Rockefeller, she was beaming and lilting along with such irrepressible gayety as to make one forget almost her trappings of bridal grandeur."

The reception was held at the Colony Club, a favorite of the Hookers, with 1,000 guests present. Then John and Blanchette slipped away to the St. Moritz Hotel; the next morning, boarding by the crew's gangway and traveling incognito, they sailed for Bermuda.

During her first year of married life, one of Blanchette's few problems was finding new ways to say thank you for Junior's successive acts of generosity. His wedding present to the young couple was a check for $100,000 plus another of $10,000 to cover the cost of the honeymoon. He allowed them to use (and subsequently gave to them) a two-story apartment he owned in the building at One Beekman Place overlooking the East River, and he added a $20,000 check for redecorating and furnishing it. Until their first child was born in 1935, John and Blanchette used only the lower floor, subletting the upper one. Until their apartment was ready they stayed at No. 10, but with their redecorating money and treasure trove of wedding gifts they soon had their own elegant surroundings on Beekman Place.

For several months, Junior made a car and driver available to Blanchette during the day to help her out in shopping for the apartment. And, periodically, eggs and produce and flowers would arrive at One Beekman from the farms at Pocantico. Although Blanchette struggled with her thank-you notes to avoid repeating superlatives, Junior's generosity was not automatic nor was her gratitude merely a formality. Genuine affection grew quickly between John's parents and their new daughter-in-law. In letters to John, Junior wrote of his "unqualified joy" at his son's marriage to Blanchette and of her "charming personality and beautiful spirit." In her letter on the occasion of John's twenty-seventh birthday in 1933, Abby wrote:

You have always been a great comfort to me, I really have worried less about you than any of the other children and I can feel already how much Blanchette's sweet nature, fine character and understanding intelligence is going to mean to me. Already I feel as if I had known her a long time and as if I could depend upon her loyalty and sympathy. I also feel as if you and she were starting upon a wise career. You both have much to contribute to the life of New York. You are both more modest than you need to be, so don't feel that things have to come your way too quickly, patience is a great virtue. Papa and I were very quiet all of the years that our children were young. What is needed most today is sane, normal, upright human beings, people unafraid to do the right thing in spite of the crowd, but, dear, it takes an open mind to recognize the *right thing*, it may not be just what we want it to be.

The implied advice about being "quiet" was scarcely necessary. John and Blanchette were of one mind in avoiding anything that resembled a hectic social life. They had their circle of friends and they enjoyed the occasional weekend with Nelson and Tod at Pocantico, where John and Nelson had each been assigned one of the many houses on the property. But over the years, keeping away from the crowd for John and Blanchette began to mean "from the family" as well—at least to some extent. They did not fall into the habit of going routinely to Seal Harbor every summer, but instead sought out other vacation spots. Their first extended holiday together, in the summer of 1933, was a three-week trip to Ireland and Scotland.

There was, of course, the traditional Rockefeller aversion to publicity, of which John was an exemplar. Thus, when he and Blanchette returned from their honeymoon, the usual mob of reporters and photographers was on hand at the pier to greet them. John tried to prevent pictures being taken of Blanchette, arguing that those allowed at the wedding and in Bermuda were enough. But there was no denying the press, and the couple had to consent to a few quick shots that were published the next day.

Even though shunning publicity, Blanchette found herself appearing in public print several times in 1934. In March her name appeared on the list of enrolled voters of the Socialist Party, and the press had fun with the image of a socialist marrying into the bastion of capitalism. But the news was based on a clerical error. After her marriage, Blanchette had become a board member of the Charity Organization Society, to which she devoted two days a week. As a result, she was asked to be a luncheon speaker at a "Conference on Family Life and National Recovery" sponsored by the Family Welfare Association of America at the Hotel Astor in November. It being her debut as a public speaker, Blanchette worked diligently on the speech, and the results showed. The speech was an intelligent and fresh analysis of the role of the layman in social work. As part of her analysis, Blanchette criticized wealthy people who contribute their names and dollars to worthy causes, but not their time and personal concern. She said:

My interest and belief in social work leads me to desire a justification of the layman's place in it. What one sees of the activities of many citizens along these lines does not tend to offer that justification.

There is much committee-forming and arranging of benefits and along with these a large amount of publicity. There is the use of influential names without much spirit behind them, and continual buying of tickets for one's own or one's friends' so-called "pet charities."

All this leads the conscientious person to wonder whether these things are not done for reasons far removed from the cause at stake. It is a fine thing to be known as a public-spirited citizen and it is pleasant to read of one's activities in the paper. It is also much easier for some people to lend their names and subscribe a few dollars for tickets than to have to give time or thought.

However, this is not the kind of contribution the social worker is primarily looking for, nor the finest type of layman seeking to give.

Her speech received wide coverage in the newspapers and a full column in *Time* magazine. It also sparked controversy in newspaper editorials. Some said, in effect, that charity needs the money no matter what the motive and others applauded her stand. The speech may have been the consideration that prompted Mary Margaret McBride of the NEA syndicate to include Blanchette among her annual list of "10 American women who attained fame in 1934," along with such luminaries as Shirley Temple, Mrs. Floyd Odlum, Evangeline Booth, and Katherine Cornell. The spread in the *New York World-Telegram* of December 26 juxtaposed a photo of the five-year-old Shirley Temple and the familiar studio portrait of Blanchette.

The substance of Blanchette's speech certainly was congruent with Rockefeller traditions of public service and philanthropy. But it attracted a great deal more attention than she had anticipated. She was sensitive enough to recognize the expectations, that her primary role should be the classic one of wife and mother, supportive of her husband's career rather than stepping into the limelight herself. It would not have been John's way to say anything like this to her directly, but the message came through to Blanchette in her new environment.

John, for example, was alive to the problem that David Milton faced in being married to the only Rockefeller daughter. Because of the Depression, David had little chance of earning enough to support his family in more than a moderate style, and the futility of this prospect was benumbing. John wrote a careful, respectful letter to his father (August 21, 1934) with a thoughtful analysis of David's situation, concluding with the suggestion that Junior, in his financial gifts and support to his children, might find a way to make these to both Babs and Dave instead of to Babs alone.[7]

Another reason for Blanchette's muted public presence undoubtedly was her awareness that her husband in the mid-1930s was a troubled person, torn by his great respect and admiration for his father, the difficulties of dealing with him, and deep concern and uncertainty about his own life and identity. Junior was so firmly cast in his patriarchal role, with all manner of decisions relentlessly flowing from him both in the office and within the family, that he came more and more to seem like a one-man Supreme Court, difficult to approach, sitting in remote contemplation, and handing down his decrees with great solemnity. He was often a warm and charming man in relaxed family surroundings, but when it came to acts and opinions, he remained, for the most part, stiff and pedantic, especially in dealing with his children. That three of them were now married and the fourth engaged made no difference. The new engagement was Laurance's. He had won his "battle" and was to marry Mary French in Woodstock, Vermont, in August 1934.

One technique for trying to score a point with Junior was to band together. In 1932 John and Nelson used it in petitioning for six weeks of vacation instead of four; they were rebuffed, as their mother had predicted. Then John and Nelson organized their sister and younger brothers in drafting a four-page letter that they all signed and sent to Junior on May 1, 1933. In part, it was a discussion of the "generation gap," of the "normal but difficult changes" that occurred as the children grew older. And in part it was a petition for a new financial arrangement. The letter pointed out that the children did not see their father very often so that it was difficult to use the time well when they were together:

Very frequently when we are with you we have to talk about personal matters—sometimes important, but more often routine and even vexatious. A week-end's contacts may all concern the details of a trip abroad, the relative merits of one apartment as against another, or the desirability of buying a Chrysler instead of a Buick. Your advice on questions such as these we not only value, but are eager to have. Our regret is, however, that such business matters should occupy such a large proportion of our very limited time with you.

The children reassured their father that they were expressing their views out of a real sense of love for him and concern for family unity, and not because they wanted "to get more for ourselves" or to "cut loose from you and Mother even though all but one of us are of age." However:

Do you not feel that the above mentioned points, which often cause friction, would be avoided if our allowances were to completely cover not only those things at present included, but also such items as apartment rent, hospital expenses at childbirth, moderately priced cars, summer vacation expenses, including trips abroad—in short, all those things which you would be paying for us anyway.

The siblings attempted to use Junior's own reasoning on him: "The older we grow, the more problems we will, of course, have to solve. If while we are still young we can assume the responsibility of final decision in matters such as those mentioned above . . . it will, we feel confident, make us more competent in the years to come."

Junior's immediate response was to raise everyone's allowance by a modest amount. But at the end of the year he acted more decisively by "capitalizing" the allowances of his three oldest children through a gift of 200,000 shares of Socony-Vacuum stock to each of them. Even then he could not forbear from delivering a short homily on thrift:

I want now to capitalize your allowance and the birthday and Christmas presents, and in doing so to provide a sum the income of which will not only be adequate to meet your growing needs, but also to enable you to add each year to your investment account a substantial portion of your income. . . . I should like to feel that it would seem to you wise not to increase your regular expenditures any year by more than five, or, at the outside, ten thousand dollars over the previous year.[8]

By this action, the three oldest children became millionaires. The year-end value of 200,000 shares of Socony-Vacuum was $3,200,000, a value that required Junior to pay $482,000 in gift taxes. Even in the low Depression year of 1934, the stock paid a dividend of 60¢ a share for an income of $120,000.

Thus, John was not only a happily married man, but was also financially secure, as it was always certain he would be. Yet, all the while, the currents of his malaise ran deep. He came close to a nervous breakdown just as his grandfather and father had before him at stressful points in their lives. He was afflicted with what seemed to be a form of agoraphobia, acute self-consciousness and nervousness when out in public or in gatherings of more than a few people. The dizzy spells and fear that he would faint that he had experienced several times at prep school and in college now became commonplace. He consulted a psychologist for a while, but the condition wore on, and for a considerable time John and Blanchette were virtual stay-at-homes.

Whatever the precise causes might have been, it seems clear that John was experiencing severe doubts as to his self-worth and his life's prospects. In short, just as his father had in 1905, John was undergoing an identity crisis, though with some very important differences. Part of Junior's anguish had been the gap he saw between the public attacks on his father and the man he knew in private as a benign, loving, and supportive person, one who had stepped aside to give Junior freedom to grow and develop. For John, it was the opposite. His father was almost universally praised and free of attack, one of the most respected Americans to people of every political persuasion and walk of life. Not only was this a formidable image to live up to, but in private, to John, his father seemed omniscient and was certainly omnipresent, felt everywhere and controlling everything.

Moreover, Junior had come of age at a time of fantastic expansion in the family fortune and of philanthropic opportunities and needs as well. He had been involved in creating all of the institutions and had hired the key people. The contrast for John was the Depression, with the lid clamped down tight and no opportunities for significant initiatives. When John looked around, he saw institutions so mature that they were in danger of becoming tradition-bound and bureaucratic. And he saw legions of older, competent, and self-made men surrounding his father. Though he had been in his father's office for five years, John was still basically a functionary with no chance to be creative in any significant way, to show leadership ability, or even to be an executive in charge of something important. The substance of what passed through the office was interesting and varied, but not John's role in respect to it. And there seemed to be little prospect of changes for the better.

Everything about this situation had the effect of making one basic problem become extremely acute for John—the realization that he was in his father's office because he was his father's son, not because of any innate abilities. He had been perceptive about the customs and effects of nepotism, in China as well as at home; now he had to face the fact himself. Junior had had to live through this problem, too, and he and his son responded similarly, by acting circumspectly and turning down raises in salary. But Junior's salvation had come precisely through what John lacked—wide open opportunities to prove himself.

It was at this most vulnerable point, in 1934, that John suffered an attack in an incident involving policy decisions in regard to the Peking Union Medical College, the China Medical Board, and the Rockefeller Foundation. John had been made a member of the China Medical Board as soon as he entered his father's office, serving first as secretary and then as vice chairman under George Vincent. The other members were Fosdick, Gumbel, Richardson, and two medical doctors. One of the reasons the board had been separated from the Foundation in 1928 was the hope that the Medical College in Peking would gradually become more indigenous—more of a Chinese operation than an American one and less of a financial drain on the Foundation. However, no appreciable progress had been made. The effects of the Depression had been severe in China; for example, the American staff were paid in gold, to ease the problem of a devalued currency and inflation. Meanwhile, the Chinese staff continued to be paid in silver or local currency. In addition, there was a growing sentiment that the Foundation money going to China could be used in more productive ways than in supporting the college. By 1934, the answer to making progress in these directions seemed to lie in relieving Roger Greene as head of the Medical College. Greene was regarded as a competent man, but one who was difficult to work with and for. The decision to fire Greene was taken in a China Medical Board meeting in mid-1934 in which everyone was present except the two medical doctors. The problem was a long-standing one, as the historian of the Medical Board indicates:

> [Roger Greene] had no conception of the intensity of personal antagonism to him that had developed among the officers and members of the China Medical Board and the Foundation with whom he had so often and so vigorously contended for the support which he believed the College deserved. This had not arisen suddenly in response to some specific action of Mr. Greene's, but was rather a smoldering resentment kept alive by each successive altercation, ready to burst into flame at any moment.[9]

Roger's brother, Jerome, was incensed. He had been one of the pioneers in Rockefeller philanthropy, an idealist and a purist, intelligent, honest, and highly opinionated. Indeed, like his younger brother, he was a man of prickly style and personality. He had resigned from the Foundation board in 1917 because he disagreed with the hiring of George Vincent as president; having become a successful investment banker, he had returned to the board in 1928. Greene regarded himself as something of an expert on the Far East—he was a board member of the Institute of Pacific Relations and had become its chairman in 1930.

Before his brother was fired, it happened that Greene had voiced his concern about the performance of the Foundation trustees. Meeting only twice a year, the trustees (so Greene believed) had been reduced to an almost perfunctory role of endorsing dockets prepared by the staff. He was pointing to a genuine problem, one that exists, to a greater or lesser degree, in all boards, especially in nonprofit organizations. Greene further believed that the work of the Foundation was so important that this defect should be removed. The worst blow for Greene in what ensued was the rupturing of his friendship with Fosdick, a man whom he greatly respected. Greene had voiced his concern about the board in a letter to Fosdick on June 29, 1934. He thought Fosdick did not respond adequately, and then that Fosdick had misled him in explaining the firing of Roger.

On the latter issue, Greene expressed his feelings in vitriolic terms, both orally and in writing. He felt the decision was a flagrant example of just the issue he had raised, that of a board being a "rubber stamp." He believed the other two boards, those of the Foundation and the college, should have been consulted in such an important action. It was therefore done "behind the scenes" by agents of the Rockefeller family. As evidence, Greene pointed to the fact that the two Medical Board members he regarded as most knowledgeable about the situation in China and Roger's problems, the two medical doctors, were not present when the action was taken. Of those who *were* present, he had nothing good to say. He dismissed Vincent as a "pensioner" of the Rockefellers, Gumbel and Richardson as "two clerks in Mr. Rockefeller's office" who "do not have independent opinions," and John 3rd as "an inexperienced son" who "can hardly be called independent." In a letter to Fosdick on September 30, Greene wrote: "You I should always have credited with independence, Vincent I should not. Practically every member of the Board was receiving a Rockefeller stipend or retainer."

The affair simmered on throughout most of the second half of 1934, Greene expressing his views loudly and threatening several times to resign as he had done once before. In November he met with Junior on the matter with Debevoise present. Junior at first "bridled" at Greene's accusations, but then heard him out patiently. Greene wrote a memorandum about this meeting in which he repeated his sentiments about John 3rd:

As for Mr. Rockefeller 3rd, I said I thought his appointment as a Trustee of the Foundation premature—that he ought to have won his spurs through experience in affairs, like any other Trustee, whether in the family office or in the world outside. His membership in the Foundation in advance of any demonstration of his ability lent color to the view that the Rockefeller family were in control of the Foundation.[10]

Greene's criticisms naturally deepened John's mood of depression, even though in his own mind he believed that he had acted freely and not as a mere echo of Fosdick and Vincent. He felt he knew something about China, too—and he had worked on China Medical Board affairs for four years. He believed the decision to fire Roger Greene had been the right one and legitimately taken. But he felt defenseless; he had no way to prove that he had acted freely. He was being attacked by a man who had been associated with his father before John was ten years of age. For that reason, any attempt to speak out in his own defense would only have made the situation worse. Except for Blanchette, he felt completely alone.

In his time of trauma, John did not have the kind of safety valve that had been available to Junior in 1905. He could not take a year away from the office, or even a few months, to try to work out his problems. He was so private a person that any such recourse would have been an unbearable public admission of weakness. He could only keep going to the office every day, hanging on and silently fighting his internal struggle.

In due course, he began to pull out of it. He seemed to reach a point where he decided to quit feeling sorry for himself and to stop worrying about things he couldn't change or control—his own fundamental nature, what other people thought of him, and the fact that he was his father's son and had certain advantages in life. He made up his mind not to feel guilty any longer, nor feel apologetic about his station in life. He also seemed to realize that what was a problem for him was a problem for his father as well, which his father couldn't solve for him. He would have to do it himself. He had come independently to certain conclusions about where his career interests in philanthropy lay, and by 1935, for the first time, he was able to stand up to his father on some issues.

There was no instant or miraculous change. There were still difficult years ahead, and it would be a long time before John and the conditions of his life would evolve to the point where he felt in control of his destiny. But his period of depression had served to harden certain traits he had shown before, converting them into strengths that eventually served him well in forging his own unique style of operating. These included perseverance, a rare faculty for being stubborn about what he believed in and yet open-minded at the same time, and above all the quality his mother had written about on his twenty-seventh birthday—patience. He had faced up to the "psychological 'three strikes'" against him that a perceptive journalist had noted on the occasion of the press conference on John's first day in his father's office—and he hadn't struck out.

18

꙳

1934: YEAR OF
DECISION

By 1934 the effects of the Depression forced Junior to make a careful review of his commitments and policies. From this review flowed decisions that were to have far-reaching consequences for the family fortune and the future prospects of his children. Partially as a result of Junior's decisions, his oldest son also made a decision—a philanthropic commitment that was to be the most important and enduring of his career.

More than four years had passed since "Black Thursday" on the New York Stock Exchange in October 1929. The nation was still in the throes of the worst economic battering in its history, and by this time there were few who expected it to end very quickly. The Depression meant personal tragedy for tens of millions of Americans who lost their jobs, their homes, their farms, their savings, and perhaps worst of all, their pride and faith in the future.

So great was the wealth of the Rockefellers that no such personal tragedy ever endangered them. Yet the wealthy could feel a severe pinch as well. Three factors impinged on Junior: enormous financial losses, financial commitments that he felt honor-bound to keep, and steeply rising rates in all categories of taxes, which affected what he had left and what he could do with what remained. The decisions Junior took in 1934 were in two areas. First were those having to do with his fortune; in essence, he began the process of transferring wealth to his heirs. Second, he focused on cutting back, consolidating, and restructuring his main business in life—his philanthropic giving.

The impact of the Depression on Junior's fortune can be seen very quickly. In 1929 his net worth was nearly $1 billion, more than double the $450 million that Senior had transferred to him in the period 1917–1920. By 1934 Junior's net worth had been cut nearly in half. By 1939 it was down to $291.1 million.

Over the years, Junior had diversified to some extent, buying utility, railroad, bank, and manufacturing stocks. He had also acquired close to $50 million worth of real estate, counting his various residences, but not Rockefeller Center.[1] He had large amounts of federal, state, and municipal bonds. But the bulk of his net worth, almost two-thirds, was still in the form of securities of the oil companies that had been formed from the old Standard Oil trust.

Hanging on to these stocks turned out to be a wise policy. Although the market value of the stocks of the six major oil companies declined just like all other stocks, none of the companies went bankrupt and all continued to pay dividends, though at greatly reduced rates. During the 1920s, Junior's income was often in excess of $35 million a year, in one year as high as $56.7 million. By 1934 income was down to $16.5 million; in 1939 and 1940 it declined further to $8.5 million.[2]

It was against this pattern of declining worth and income that Junior's obligations became onerous. For the first time since his father had begun transferring significant wealth to him, Junior's expenses began to equal and then to exceed income. This forced him not only to economize but also to make choices that had never been necessary before.

His obligations fell into four broad categories—personal expenses, philanthropic giving, investments, and taxes. As for the first— the expense of maintaining his family, office, Seal Harbor, and Pocantico—it certainly was no trifle. Junior took every reasonable opportunity to economize, but none of his employees lost his job because of the Depression.

In the 1920s Junior's philanthropic giving had been at the rate of 30 to 40 percent of his income (averaging $11.5 million a year), meaning that he was giving away more money than the Rockefeller Foundation. Almost always, the gifts were out of current income rather than the sale of stocks, bonds, personal property, or real estate. In most Depression years Junior still gave away money at the rate of more than 30 percent of his income, largely because of prior commitments. The major difference now was that his gifts were predominantly in the form of appreciated stock and land. No longer was there an excess of cash, and what came in was needed elsewhere.

As far as investments were concerned, there was only one major and continuing one—the Rockefeller Center development. Junior's total investment in the Center in the 1930s exceeded $120 million for new construction, loan repayments, land acquisition, and operating losses. He stopped drawing down on the $65 million Metropolitan Life line of credit (after having used only $45 million) in 1935 because the repayment schedule began in that year. Junior was responsible for the accelerating repayments, which started out at $4 million in 1935 and rose in stages to $6 million in 1938.

The new tax rates also were a drain on Junior's resources. The gift and estate taxes were especially formidable, and as we shall see, they caused Junior to act in the way the New Deal strategists wanted wealthy people to act. As far as the income tax was concerned, Junior paid an average of approximately twice the percentage that he had in previous years—on an income that was substantially reduced. In the 1920s he was paying at rates that varied from 12.5 percent to 16 percent; in most Depression years, his rate was up to 30 percent or more.[3] This, of course, was the period when the income tax became an extremely important consideration for the well-to-do as the rates soared and the law became ever more complicated, a boon to the professions of tax lawyer and accountant ever since. It was not that the income tax was unimportant before, but it had all been rather straightforward. Now it became a sort of complex game, with every credit and deduction avidly sought.

The steep climb in taxes was not an invention of the New Deal: it began in the last months of the Hoover administration, in the Revenue Act of 1932. Faced with the need for revenue to balance the budget, Congress sharply raised the tax rates at all levels, making the 20 percent maximum rate of previous years look like a "tax holiday" by comparison. The income surtax started at $6,000 and assessed incomes of more than $1 million at 55 percent. Stock distributed as a dividend, although not dividends per se, was made subject to the income tax. The gift tax was reenacted, and the upper limit of the estate tax was raised to 45 percent.[4]

The National Industrial Recovery Act of June 1933, the early effort by the New Deal to stimulate recovery, raised these rates only marginally, but also added a new provision—a 5 percent tax on dividends. The National Recovery Act of the same year, with its emphasis on voluntary industrywide codes regulating competition, prices, and wages, failed to effect recovery, so that by 1934, an election year, pressure mounted for more drastic measures of the "soak the rich" variety. The colorful and demagogic "Kingfish" from Louisiana, Senator Huey Long, organized his "Share Our Wealth" movement in cooperation with the right-wing radical Gerald L. K. Smith. Among other things, Long advocated a redistribution of national wealth through the liquidation of all personal fortunes above a certain amount and the transfer of enough cash to each family in America to enable the purchase of a radio, a house, and an automobile. Joining Long in the attack on the "economic royalists" was a diverse cast of characters including Father Charles Coughlin, the popular radio priest from Detroit, the novelist Upton Sinclair, who was running for governor of California as the candidate of EPIC (End Poverty in California), and Dr. Francis Townsend, who led a powerful organization that demanded two hundred dollars a month for all citizens over the age of sixty to be financed by a 2 percent tax on all business transactions.[5]

These movements were intensely hostile to existing wealth and sought not only solutions to the economic crisis, but punishment and exclusion from power for the men who they believed had caused all the problems. It was a reprise of the denunciations of the rich by the Populists, which Junior remembered so well from his younger days. The attacks perhaps were not as bitterly personal as then, but there was no lack of the Rockefellers' being held up as the epitome of the moneyed class and the symbol of all that was wrong with society. In a nice touch of sarcasm, Huey Long proclaimed in *My First Days in the White House* that he would appoint Junior as the chairman of the National Share Our Wealth Committee.

President Roosevelt and his New Deal advisers had no intention of following crackpot schemes, but sought some measure of redistribution of wealth through the tax power. The Revenue Act of 1934, passed by substantial majorities in both houses of Congress, raised rates in all tax categories. For incomes of more than $1 million, the tax rate went from 55 percent to 63 percent. For estates of more than $50 million, the estate tax was raised from 45 percent to 60 percent. And the gift tax was raised most dramatically in the upper categories— from 33⅓ percent to 45 percent for gifts over $10 million. The estate tax became effective immediately (May 1934), and the other increases on January 1, 1935.[6]

Junior weathered the income tax very well, paying the current rate on his *taxable* income each year, but drastically reducing that income by the many deductions he was entitled to take—charitable gifts, major business expenses for Rockefeller Center, losses on sales and redemptions of securities, and the fact that a substantial part of his income came from tax-exempt interest on government bonds. Rather than the income tax, it was the estate and gift taxes that were worrisome. The reason the estate tax was pegged at 60 percent and the gift tax at 45 percent was to create an incentive that would result in driving money out of the great fortunes. Junior and his advisers responded, being nothing if not rational men. Junior did not reveal his innermost thoughts during this period, but it seems likely that he felt that the situation was forcing him to act prematurely in beginning the process of transferring wealth to his heirs. Junior had passed the age of forty before his father had started to transfer wealth to him in a major way. And Senior had focused this on only one of his children, his only son. In the mid-1930s only one of Junior's six children had passed the age of thirty, and it was too early for Junior to have any reason to do anything other than treat all of them relatively equally.

Yet it seemed that the time to act had come. Everything in the prevailing atmosphere suggested to the wealthy that tax policy would only get more exacting with each passing year. Junior realized that if he acted to transfer some holdings to his heirs before the end of 1934, he would at least save himself the increase in the gift tax. He therefore instructed his financial advisers to study the legal options open to him in the present state of his finances and prepare a plan for his consideration. During that summer, such a plan received his approval. In calling for the creation of seven irrevocable trusts for the benefit of his wife and six children, the plan offered a good solution to Junior's dilemma—taking advantage of the tax incentive and hedging against possible future tax increases by transferring assets out of his hands, yet guarding against his deep fear of irresponsible spending by his heirs in the restrictions that could be placed in the deeds of trust. These became known ever after as the "1934 Trusts," marking an important transition in the history of the Rockefeller family.

Junior received no income from the trusts and retained no control over them. Control was vested in committees of trustees that Junior appointed from among his advisers. The initial members were Raymond Fosdick, Thomas Debevoise, Vanderbilt Webb, Barton Turnbull, and Winthrop Aldrich, all trusted men and able financial managers. The trustees were given the power to appoint their successors as needed. The Trust Department of the Chase National Bank managed the trusts under the supervision of the trustees.

Junior's aim was to provide income from the trusts for his wife and children during their lifetimes, allow the five boys also to draw on the capital in the trusts with the approval of their trustees, and provide a tax-free inheritance for the next generation of Rockefellers—all under controlled conditions that would militate against irresponsible spending by his heirs.

The amounts placed in trust were much smaller than have been estimated in previous written accounts.[7] This was the beginning of a process, not the end—Junior added significant amounts to the trusts for his sons later on, and, of course, all the trusts grew enormously in value when the nation's economy improved. The trust for his wife Abby was the largest, $18.3 million in oil stocks. Babs, John, and Nelson each received exactly the same amount of stock, valued at approximately $12 million in each account. The total was $54.3 million, requiring Junior to pay $18.8 million in gift taxes.[8]

For the three younger boys, each trust consisted of $50,000 worth of stock. Junior explained the reasons in letters to the boys on December 18, 1934, using his inimitable old-fashioned prose:

When I first talked with you about this matter, I had in mind to establish trusts for you three younger boys in the same amounts as for the older children. On further thought, I have come to the conclusion that to do so would be unfair to you and, therefore, wrong on my part although the inducement to make large gifts forthwith, which the government has held out, will terminate with the new year when the gift tax rises twelve and a half points.

To have followed my original thought would be unfair to you, first, because it might result in your being put in a position where you would find yourself bewildered and unprepared because suddenly saddled with heavy and relatively new obligations without having had that longer period of training in the handling of gradually increasing sums of money which has been so helpful to the three older children. Secondly, it would be unfair to you because such a course would necessarily have lessened materially, if not to wholly terminate, that frank exchange of views between yourself and myself on financial subjects which has existed from your early boyhood and seriously to curtail the opportunity for current guidance and advice during your formative years which it is a father's duty to provide for a son and a son's right to have. This relationship no father can cut off permanently with impunity.

One may imagine the three younger boys devoutly wishing that they had received "unfair" treatment from their father in this particular, especially Laurance, who had married and was ready to enter his father's office in 1935. But any anxieties the three younger boys might have felt were eased the following year when Junior found a new reason to act. The 1935 Revenue Act was being debated in Congress with new and steep increases in gift and estate taxes as the centerpiece. "Now we are threatened with another increase in gift taxes that may be almost, if not quite, confiscatory in amount," Junior wrote in letters to the younger boys when he added more than $16 million worth of stocks to each of their trusts.[9] These transactions required Junior to pay $16.9 million in gift taxes. At first glance, it might seem that Junior was being more generous to the younger boys, but in fact he and his advisers strove to make the five trusts as nearly equal as possible in true value. The rationale was that the stocks placed in the trusts for the three older children were of superior quality and earning power, compensating for the higher paper value of those in the younger boys' accounts.

The provisions of Abby's trust gave her complete control of income, but no capability of invading principal. Babs also was prevented from invading principal. The deeds for the boys specified that the full income from the trusts should not be paid to them until they attained the age of thirty (Babs had already passed that age). John would have to wait only a little over a year, Nelson more than three years, and Laurance more than five. Also, the boys could not petition to invade principal until past the age of thirty.

Despite the depressed conditions of the time, the annual income from each of these trusts would be a handsome amount, perhaps as much as $1 million in pre-tax dollars. Junior certainly did not want that kind of money going to his children before they were old enough to handle it properly. Forced to choose, Junior had decided upon the age of thirty. The men he appointed to the Trust Committee were so close to him and knew him so well that he could be confident that they would dole trust income out to the boys under thirty much as he would have done. Thus, for several years David received only about $2,400 a year to handle his expenses at college. The existence of the trusts enabled Junior to cease providing allowances and paying expenses for his children. Junior also knew exactly what to do with the balance of the trust income, which was a very large amount in the case of the younger boys. The deeds instructed the trustees to disburse this income in charitable gifts to certain specified recipients. Junior thus accomplished still another purpose—taking care of a substantial portion of his philanthropic obligations in this manner, at least for a number of years.

All these decisions by Junior were rational—carefully calculated within the context of the time and in consideration of the ages of his children. There are several indications that Junior's obsessive concern about the responsible handling of money by his children was a more important consideration for him than the tax incentive. One certainly was the highly structured nature of the trusts. Another was the fact that if he had acted earlier, before 1932, he would have paid no gift tax at all—but this would have been far too early for him to take up seriously the transferring of wealth to his heirs. It is also true that if he had made the large gifts to the younger boys' trusts in 1934 instead of 1935, he would have paid a lower gift tax. The restrictive clauses in the deeds of trust and his faith in the trustees would seem to have been sufficient protection against irresponsibility by his younger sons. But it appears that the larger tax was worth it to Junior to avoid giving his younger sons even the psychological sense of being independently wealthy before he felt they were ready for that. However, in 1935 the price threatened to be too high, and he felt forced to act.

To understand the trusts, it is important to recognize that Junior's children benefited from them, but did not own them. Upon the death of Junior's children, the deeds specified that the trusts would be divided equally among their legitimate offspring. In turn, when any member of this fourth generation (Junior's grandchildren) died, the trust that person had inherited would finally be terminated, the tax-free proceeds being divided equally among his or her surviving children of the fifth generation.[10]

Having acted as he did, Junior altered the framework of relationships and financial matters for the members of his family. Abby now had the income to pursue her philanthropic interests without having to come to her husband. Babs' financial problems were eased. And the sons now had more than enough financial independence to let them put some psychic distance between themselves and their dominating, if ever-concerned, father. And yet the likelihood that there was more to come from Father was calculated to keep the behavior of the sons within acceptable norms.

What Junior did in 1934 begins to look like a master plan when his philanthropic decisions are ranged alongside the financial ones. For the first few years of the Depression, he tried to continue his giving as if nothing had happened. The number of recipients actually rose, from 278 in 1929 to 304 in 1933. What was happening was that some charitable organizations turned to Junior for help as their other funding sources dried up. He did what he could, but soon realized that he would have to make some changes as his own assets and income declined. In 1933 he asked Arthur Packard and John 3rd to compile a list of all the recipients and the amount of each gift. Junior scanned the completed list, and, with the advice of his assistants, made a notation opposite each entry. The notations—"Pl," "Out," "4," and "OK"—divided the list into four categories and revealed what Junior intended to do. The "Pl" symbol (meaning "pledge") marked the 60 or so recipients that Junior would continue to handle himself, while "Out" identified those to be discontinued entirely, also about 60 in number.

The two cryptic entries, "4" and "OK," related to decisions that Junior executed in 1934. By agreement with Abby, he turned over to her the responsibility for handling 99 of the 300 recipients, those with the notation "4" next to them on the master list. Abby was to do this out of the income she would begin receiving from her 1934 Trust, as well as taking care of any other charitable giving that interested her. The 99 organizations represented the small-scale "citizenship giving" that Junior and Abby had been doing, mostly social service agencies and New York charities of various kinds. In fact, the total given to these 99 recipients in 1933 was only $12,112.50. Clearly, Junior's motive was not to save money, but to pass on the responsibility and detail, and Abby was the perfect answer. With a potential income of more than $1 million a year from her trust, she would have no problem taking care of this, leaving plenty of money for her main interest, the Museum of Modern Art.

In addition to the trusts, Junior also created in 1934 a new organization called the Davison Fund, utilizing the middle name he had inherited from his father and passed on to his oldest son. He gave this charitable fund a start-up grant of stock worth $836,250. The trustees were John 3rd, Raymond Fosdick, Arthur Woods, Willard Richardson, and Arthur Packard as the administrative director. The fund was the new vehicle for Junior's giving, apart from the major projects in which he took a personal interest. To it went responsibility for some of the recipients marked "OK" on Junior's list. The rest, mainly religious organizations, Junior continued to handle personally.

The Davison Fund thus superseded the Advisory Committee on Beneficences that had handled Junior's citizenship giving for the previous fifteen years. It also took over some responsibilities from the Bureau of Social Hygiene. Junior had decided to deactivate the Bureau; it seemed to him to have run its course in some respects, and Arthur Woods was too ill to manage it actively any longer.[11]

Junior never gave money to the Davison Fund after the initial grant, yet the fund disbursed an average of $350,000 a year for the next seven years. The reason was that money came to it every year from the aforementioned trust fund income of Junior's sons who had not yet turned thirty.[12]

These maneuvers left Junior free to concentrate on the causes closest to his heart—Colonial Williamsburg, Riverside Church, the Hudson Palisades, Fort Tryon Park and the Cloisters—and to honor pledges he had made, such as for the French restorations and antiquities projects overseas and the International Houses in Chicago, New York, and Paris. He gave $7.9 million in 1934 and $18.5 million in 1935, more than half of the latter in land to protect the Hudson Palisades. After that, however, the pressure of the times showed—for the rest of the decade Junior gave less than $2 million a year.

Junior's action of setting Abby up as a philanthropist is particularly interesting. In part at least, it appears to have been a roundabout way of supporting her passion in life, the Museum of Modern Art, without Junior having to pose as a convert to modern art himself. But he did occasionally give direct support to MOMA. In 1934 he donated $200,000, on the urgent request of Abby, to help MOMA meet an emergency situation. Lillie Bliss, one of the original trio of "adamantine ladies," had died and left a substantial sum in her will and some fine impressionist paintings to MOMA, but on the condition that her trustees would judge the museum to have enough of an endowment to insure financial stability. Junior's gift was intended to help meet that condition, and, along with the Bliss legacy and Abby's subsequent giving, made it possible for MOMA to survive the dark days of the Depression.

A few years later, Junior helped again in a complicated series of real estate transactions. MOMA was housed in the building at 9 West 53rd Street, paying a small rent to the owner, who was Junior. In 1935 the museum's trustees decided to erect a new building to house the growing collection, but the three lots they owned on the south side of 53rd (Nos. 6, 8, and 10) provided only 75 feet of frontage, too small for the projected building. So Junior traded three lots he owned on the north side of the street (Nos. 9, 11, and 13) for the three MOMA properties and then sold the three adjacent lots (Nos. 15, 17, and 19) to the museum at 40 percent below book value. This gave MOMA 150 feet of frontage, enough to go ahead with the planned building.[13]

MOMA soon was to expand through the block to the south side of 54th Street, thanks again to Junior's generosity. In 1937 he and Abby made a big decision—to give up the family home at 10 West 54th and move to a Park Avenue apartment. Junior announced that No. 10 would be razed, as well as his father's house at No. 4. At the same time he announced the gift of three properties to MOMA, Nos. 12, 14, and 16 West 54th. No mention was made of his plans for Nos. 4 through 10. In 1939, at the time of the New York World's Fair, he allowed MOMA to use these vacant lots for a sculpture garden. Not until 1946 did he give the properties to MOMA, carrying a book value of $922,000.

Like many another aging couple, Junior and Abby had decided to give up the family homestead because the children were no longer living at home, and the parents felt themselves lonely and rattling around in the huge eight-story house. So it seemed to make sense to move to smaller quarters. But they had a lot of personal effects to move, including Junior's overflowing collections of Chinese porcelains, Polonaise rugs, and European tapestries. It was for this reason that "smaller quarters" became a forty-room triplex apartment at 740 Park Avenue![14]

There was one more important item on Junior's 1934 agenda in respect to philanthropy. Knowing that he would be leaving the Rockefeller Foundation chairmanship in 1939 when he reached the mandatory retirement age of sixty-five, Junior wanted to make sure that the Foundation was in the best possible condition to function in the years ahead. Because of the 1928 reorganization, Junior and Raymond Fosdick had the consolidated structure they wanted. But, as noted, it had not worked out quite the way they had expected. Junior saw a need for more change and for paving the way for Fosdick to assume the presidency, replacing Max Mason. The Foundation's program remained unbalanced because public health and medical education still dominated. While Mason did not block the development of the other divisions, he did not provide vigorous leadership to build them up. The grim facts of life of the 1930s reinforced Junior and Fosdick's belief that Foundation policy must shift from gathering knowledge to applying it. By 1934 Fosdick once again was chairman of a Committee on Appraisal and Review, the other two members being James R. Angell and Walter W. Stewart.

Fosdick presented the findings at a board meeting in December 1934. He began with a question: "If the Foundation were now starting with a clean slate, if the capital funds were today placed in our hands for the first time to be used 'for the well-being of mankind throughout the world,' is our present program the program which we as Trustees would adopt?" Not surprisingly, the report answered the question in the negative: "Profound changes in the social and economic situation in this country and abroad" demanded a shift of course. To guarantee the "wisest and most helpful" expenditure of funds, Fosdick urged the application "to concrete problems of our social, political, and industrial life of some of the ideas and data which research all over the world is rapidly developing. This would not mean, of course, the relinquishment of research as a method. It would mean that we have no interest in the promotion of research as an end in itself." In keeping with this view, the report recommended an increase in the funds allocated to the Social Sciences Division and a concomitant decrease for the Divisions of International Health and Medical Sciences. Fosdick went on:

We do not pretend to say that this preponderant interest in health and medicine has been distorted or unbalanced. It is a fair question, however, whether in view of the present outlook this proportion of expenditure would continue to represent the wisest use of funds. Is physical health the outstanding need of the world today? Do we best serve the welfare of mankind by devoting a substantial percentage of our contributions to disease?[15]

By the time the report of the Committee on Appraisal and Review was adopted at the 1934 annual meeting in December, the Foundation was deeply involved in trying to build a new action program in China that would give tangible expression to Fosdick's words. The idea was to shift the Foundation's resources from urban-based medicine to a rural-based program in education, agriculture, land reform, and sanitation. It was, therefore, very much related to the effort to shift support of the Peking Union Medical College to others. Roger Greene's adamant resistance to this was one reason he was fired in 1934, which led to Jerome Greene's outspoken criticism of JDR and others.

Two earlier studies were behind the Foundation's new effort in China. One was the controversial Laymen's Foreign Mission Inquiry. Dr. John R. Mott of the YMCA, a highly respected leader in ecumenical projects, was the stimulus for the inquiry. He returned from a trip in 1929 depressed by the state of missionary work in China. Junior had long been concerned about this, and his conversations with Mott and a growing circle of prominent laymen led to a two-stage project. Junior paid for the first phase, a fact-finding survey by the Institute of Social and Religious Research. In the second phase, a committee of laymen drawn from eight Protestant denominations traveled to China in 1932 and returned home to write and publish their report, *Re-Thinking Missions*. Raymond Fosdick described some of the "startling reforms" proposed in the report:

> . . . a much broader understanding and application of the Christian message; a more sympathetic participation in the culture of the Orient and a deeper appreciation of the kindred elements in other faiths; a greater emphasis on "quiet personal contact and contagion" and upon such social activities as education, medicine, and agriculture, as distinguished from unrelieved evangelistic preaching; a more critical selection of missionaries; a greater concentration of effort among the numerous and overlapping Protestant missions; and a gradual transfer of responsibility to the hands of nationals with a consequent waning of the mission proper and a building up of the indigenous church.[16]

The report became embroiled in the liberal-conservative split in American Protestantism, with Junior at that very time engaged in building Riverside Church. One of the most articulate supporters of the report was the novelist Pearl Buck, whose husband, Lossing Buck, was an agricultural economist at Nanking University in China. After trying unsuccessfully for more than two years to get the Northern Baptist Convention to adopt the report, Junior reluctantly withdrew his financial support of that body in 1935.[17]

While the controversy raged, the Foundation was engaged in its own study, the work of Selskar M. Gunn, vice president for European programs, who spent five months in China during the winter of 1932–1933. His report was entirely consistent with the Laymen's Inquiry. He said that the Foundation's urban-based medical program was good and useful, but did not deal with the real needs of China, which were to be found in the farms and villages of the overwhelmingly rural country. In particular, he cited the need for improvements in agriculture and for beginning to amend the feudal pattern of absentee landlords, holding that the key to the future of China was the welfare of the peasant. Gunn recommended supporting and building up small-scale rural programs already started by the thirteen Christian universities in China and making James Y. C. Yen's "Mass Education Movement" the centerpiece. Yen was working on "rural reconstruction" featuring agriculture, sanitation, and land reform efforts, and on illiteracy through the "thousand character" movement to simplify the Chinese language.[18]

Numerous meetings were held and plans drawn up to implement a program based on Gunn's recommendations. Much of the thinking was reminiscent of the comprehensive program of the General Education Board to help improve impoverished rural areas. Having taken over elements of the GEB's program in 1928, the Foundation's planning for China represented an effort to carry that obligation forward and apply it for the first time overseas. But before concrete steps could be taken, it was already too late. China had become unstable as Chiang Kai-shek battled errant warlords and engaged in his "bandit suppression" campaign against Mao Tse-tung and the Chinese Communists. The Japanese were threatening from newly occupied Manchuria; by 1937 the Sino-Japanese War was under way.

Nevertheless, it seemed certain that the Foundation policy adopted in 1934 would be implemented when its chief author, Raymond Fosdick, became president in 1936, and even more so when his colleague on the Review Committee, Walter Stewart, became chairman in 1939 upon Junior's retirement. As a trustee, JDR had ardently supported the leadership of Fosdick and Stewart. Yet as the years passed, he perceived that nothing in line with the 1934 changes was happening in the Foundation's program. At the end of World War II, JDR himself would begin pressing for a policy of "applied knowledge" and related program innovations. Ironically, his chief opponents would include Fosdick and Stewart.

However, it was not the Rockefeller Foundation, but his personal choices in philanthropy that occupied John 3rd's mind on a clear, crisp Saturday morning in March 1934. He was in his office on the fifty-sixth floor of the RCA Building concentrating on a letter he was writing to his father, spurred by decisions Junior had made. As he gazed out the window, John saw the buildings of lower Manhattan etched cleanly against the sky; below him, the half-finished buildings of Rockefeller Center stood quiet and empty. An occasional gust brought the sounds of keening bagpipes, thudding drums, and the raucous cries of celebrants as New Yorkers enjoyed their first St. Patrick's Day since the repeal of Prohibition.[19]

Composing a letter to Junior was never a simple matter; the subject had to be precisely indicated, facts and opinions placed in logical order, and conclusions and recommended courses of action clearly stated. Moreover, the subject was an unusually important one for John. He thought through what he wanted to say and began to dictate. "Dear Father," he began:

As you of course know, the Bureau of Social Hygiene is terminating its activities on June 30. The two fields to which the Bureau has devoted the major parts of its time and resources are criminology and sex hygiene. It would seem from what Mr. Fosdick says, as if the Rockefeller Foundation might find it possible to assume an interest in the former. As to the latter, which is really the field of birth control and related questions, it would not appear as if it, as a whole, could be taken over by any of the boards in which you are interested, both because of the programs of these boards and the element of propaganda and controversy which so often is attached to endeavors in birth control.

The purpose of this letter is to ask you if you would be interested, through the Advisory Committee, to assume the responsibility for the continuance of the Bureau's support in this important field. I take the liberty of making this suggestion to you because of my great personal interest in birth control and related questions, and because of the fact that from time to time appeals do come to this office which we have previously referred to the Bureau—which procedure, of course, will no longer be possible.

John proceeded to analyze the pattern of assistance that had been given to organizations in the field, and he suggested, for Junior's approval, a level of support for the balance of 1935 and for 1936. He concluded with a solemn statement of personal interest:

. . . may I add one further statement in regard to my interest in birth control. I have come pretty definitely to the conclusion that it is the field in which I will be interested, for the present at least, to concentrate my own giving, as I feel that it is so fundamental and underlying. While I would not, of course, expect to contribute in the amounts that I have suggested for your consideration, if you should feel that it was not wise for you personally to continue the same liberal basis of giving as the Bureau of Social Hygiene has maintained, I would be more than glad to supplement your gifts or make independent ones of my own; or I could confine my financial efforts to individuals, organizations and projects to which you were not giving. In any event I should want very much indeed to coordinate whatever I might be able to do with whatever support you might feel it desirable to lend to this field.[20]

The letter went through several drafts before John allowed his somewhat exasperated secretary to cover her typewriter and hurry downstairs to see the parade as it passed before St. Patrick's Cathedral. Satisfied as he read over the final version, John signed and sent it to his father.

It was a declaration of intent that John followed religiously the rest of his life, to lengths that no one could have imagined in 1934. As a result of the letter, Junior did allow the Advisory Committee to concentrate its reduced budget, about $40,000 a year, in the population field, and John 3rd did follow through as indicated with his gradually increasing capacity to give.[21]

No one can know with any certainty exactly why he made this choice. The question of population was not among the most pressing at the time. Because of the Depression, birth rates were falling in the industrialized world. The science of demography had scarcely come of age. Studies of human sexuality, contraception, and related matters were on a small scale. Birth control was a highly controversial subject, action in regard to it being largely the province of the militant feminists so well typified by the redoubtable Margaret Sanger. For decades the motivation of most people who gave any thought at all to population growth was tinged with racism, prominently so in the field of eugenics and among those viscerally opposed to immigration from southern Europe and the Orient.

Perhaps it was the masses of China that first aroused John's interest. His remark about the field being "so fundamental and underlying" suggests some such insight at least twenty years before it became a generally accepted view. Certainly, he had been exposed to sound thinking about population from the time that he took a reading course in the subject at Princeton, as well as in his experience with the Bureau of Social Hygiene and the Advisory Committee. He was well aware of his father's pioneering support of related projects since the days of the White Slave Grand Jury. Moreover, John was reinforced in his interest in population by the strong views of two men he respected highly, Raymond Fosdick and Arthur Packard.

Whatever the precise reasons for his choice, JDR had found a possible outlet for his philanthropic energies. He was broadly interested in the world of international affairs, and family tradition dictated an involvement in the solution of intractable social problems. Junior had once predicted that it would take his son ten years to learn anything about philanthropy; after less than five years of on-the-job training, JDR felt that he had absorbed enough to make a tentative choice. However, it would be more than fifteen years before major changes in his personal situation and in global perceptions of the dangers of unrestrained population growth would combine to turn an interest into a commitment of major proportions.

19

❧

THE MATURING YEARS

AT THE PRESS CONFERENCE held when John 3rd entered the family office, Junior had answered a question about the nature of his son's duties by saying: "As a matter of fact, we don't know exactly the right way to start a Rockefeller in business. When we get to the fifth son, we'll have a technique developed, I hope."

That never happened. The two youngest sons did not enter the family office, and the three older ones who did each ended up taking a distinctive course. It was during the late 1930s and the ensuing war years that the five Rockefeller sons all came of age and began to show signs of their different orientations—especially John, Nelson, and Laurance.

It was an interesting transitional time for the Rockefeller family, one in which the sons were naturally preoccupied with their evolving relations with one another and with their father, and worked to forge family unity even as each developed independently. The aging father, still in control of a vast fortune and several major enterprises, was concerned with how to deal with five restless and ambitious sons, seeking to walk the fine line between too much help and too little.

Though he was only in his early sixties, Junior found the latter half of the 1930s a difficult time. Both he and Abby seemed to be in failing health. The general diagnosis for Abby, as John 3rd noted in his diary, was that she had a "tired heart." Junior had a succession of migraine headaches and respiratory problems. As it turned out, Abby's condition was serious, while Junior's health, like his father's, lasted to a ripe old age. But, at the time, Junior thought it might well be otherwise.

One consequence was that Junior was away from the office more often than previously. He and Abby would spend most of the summer at Seal Harbor, and during the remainder of the year make frequent trips to such places as Williamsburg, Hot Springs, and Tucson. They also made several trips of two to three months' duration to Europe. One year they rushed back from Europe after only two weeks because Abby was ill.

Junior was thus more remote and difficult to see than ever before; but nothing in his apprehension of failing health caused him to let go the reins over the family fortune and his main enterprises. This set the stage for potential conflict between father and sons, especially John as the one singled out to follow in his father's footsteps. There was, besides, a like possibility of conflict among the sons, especially between John and Nelson, who were so different in personality and temperament. They spent most of the 1930s together in the family office, with Nelson chafing at being preempted from most of the opportunities there by his older brother.

But although there *was* friction at times, no deep division took place. John and Nelson both always placed a high value on family unity, and, at a critical point, John gave way to the ambition of his next younger brother. As for Junior, he worked in his own characteristic way to foster family harmony. He tried to give his sons room to grow without overindulging them, and to treat them as equally as possible, given the fact of John's primogeniture. And he continued to send them homilies, tracts, books, and articles of an uplifting nature.

It also happened at this time that the ranks of Junior's senior advisers were thinned. Colonel Woods was in seriously failing health and by 1935 had retired from the many responsibilities he conducted on behalf of Junior. After Raymond Fosdick's election as president of the Rockefeller Foundation in 1936, he became fully occupied there. Of the original triumvirate, this left only the urbane lawyer, Thomas Debevoise, as a senior associate regularly in the family office. Debevoise had always been a counselor rather than an executive, a neutral and somewhat fatherly figure, a contemporary of Junior to whom John and Nelson often went for information and guidance. With Woods and Fosdick gone and Junior away much of the time, Debevoise by necessity became more of a decision maker just at the time that John and Nelson were seeking more authority. This, too, was a source of friction.

As noted, the managerial arrangements Junior had made for Rockefeller Center seemed destined to come into conflict with the ambitions of his two oldest sons. The expertise of the managing agents was unquestioned in the earlier stages of site clearance and construction, but the project moved into the later stages of leasing, management, and maintenance just at the time that the two older Rockefeller sons were looking for more authority. By 1935 six buildings and two theaters were completed, and four more buildings were either under construction or in the planning stage.[1] Legal authority was vested in the eleven-member board of Rockefeller Center, Inc. Five of the members were on the payroll of the family office—John 3rd, Nelson, Barton P. Turnbull, Colonel Arthur Woods, and Charles Heydt. Woods served as president of the Center and Heydt as vice president and treasurer. Other members included Winthrop Aldrich; Jay Downer, a former Westchester County executive; Albert L. Scott, a civil engineer who served as vice president; and Francis Christy, a recruit from Junior's outside law firm of Milbank, Tweed, who served as secretary.

But this board was so ineffectual that its executive committee, composed of Woods, Aldrich, and Heydt, never even met. The reason was that it was flanked by the two sources of real power—Junior and the managing agents. The latter, in actual control of the budget and the hundreds of employees, made countless daily decisions. The more formal committees of Rockefeller Center, Inc., functioned in an advisory capacity only; the committees would propose and the managing agents would dispose—a situation bound to create discontent. In general, the managing agents were doing a good job and Junior was satisfied. So there was little point in the board's taking action with which the agents might disagree. Junior placed such confidence in the managing agents that an attempt to go over their heads would only irritate him. As a result, decisions that escalated to Junior's level were those that both the board and the agents really did not know how to handle.

Nelson sensed opportunity in this situation. Of the two major projects of the family at the time, he took little interest in Colonial Williamsburg. It dealt with the past, and he cared a great deal more about the future. The obvious plum for the taking was Rockefeller Center. This giant enterprise needed leadership and managerial skill to achieve marketplace success in a difficult economic time. And it offered a unique opportunity to show one's mettle. Nelson was wise enough not to press ahead too fast; he was only twenty-seven years old and the managing agents were solidly entrenched. But nothing was immutable, and Nelson believed he had the ability to do a better job. He began the first step of cultivating his older brother as an ally by talking frequently to John about the shortcomings of the managing agents. He found a ready listener.

John's discontent with the managing agents stemmed from his experience as a member of the Theater Committee. He spent countless hours for several years trying to help make the Radio City Music Hall and the Center Theater profitable, becoming deeply enmeshed in the strange world of show business. The first difficulty was dealing with the engaging and eccentric impresario Roxy. As noted earlier, Roxy held full sway during the construction phase, but when it came to operating the theaters, RKO soon realized that his creative ideas were a recipe for financial disaster. At a "stormy session" in January 1934, Roxy "submitted his resignation . . . for about the tenth time and, much to his surprise, his resignation was accepted."[2]

In the meantime, the fact that RKO had gone into receivership had set off a complicated chain of personnel changes, reorganizations, the creating of new corporations, and litigation. Fortunately for Rockefeller Center, it had favorable terms in the lease agreement if RKO was forced to terminate it. Rockefeller Center was eventually awarded $9.6 million in liquidated damages, but this sum was never paid. The award was susceptible to challenge on appeal, so Rockefeller Center accepted instead 415,000 shares in the reorganized RKO and exercised an option to purchase another 163,629 shares at $3 each, thereby becoming the largest single stockholder in RKO. This settlement and the extra purchase were subjects of prolonged discussion. John 3rd was as leery as his father was of becoming involved in the motion picture business, but Nelson pushed hard for it. In the end, the stock was sold in 1943 and 1945 for $4.6 million.[3]

With the running of the theaters now back in Rockefeller Center's hands, John 3rd's committee was hard-pressed to make a go of them. After some initial failures, a workable formula had been devised for the Music Hall by the producer Leon Leonidoff—the familiar offering of a first-run movie plus a stage show featuring the Rockettes, which prevailed at the theater until it, too, proved uneconomic by the 1970s. Even so, the reduced number of theaters from four to two still proved to be one too many. The Center Theater was a white elephant. As a straight movie house, it competed with the Music Hall only a block away and other nearby theaters—and top-quality pictures were very difficult to obtain because most of the major motion picture companies had their own outlets in Manhattan. The theater was too large for legitimate plays. Several musicals, light operas, and ice shows with Sonja Henie were produced at the Center with indifferent success, and John 3rd was involved in endless discussions and negotiations involving other ideas. Finally, the Center Theater was closed to the public and, in 1954, torn down.[4]

Throughout these tribulations, John 3rd found the managing agents of little help and often a hindrance. To them, the theater situation seemed to be the proverbial "can of worms," best avoided as much as possible. John had to battle alone with W. G. Van Schmus, who had been hired by the agents to succeed Roxy as theater manager.

These facts help to explain why John lent a sympathetic ear whenever Nelson complained and talked about ways to improve the management of Rockefeller Center. An opportunity arose early in 1934 when it became clear that Colonel Woods' failing health would keep him inactive, though he still held the title of president of Rockefeller Center. Nelson realized it was too soon to make a bid for the presidency himself, but he had won the allegiance of a number of board members, including Barton Turnbull, Albert Scott, and Francis Christy. With John's support, Nelson prepared charts detailing the problems of the existing organization and proposing a new one, which he sent with a memorandum to Junior at Seal Harbor on August 6. Nelson proposed a streamlining of the committees and a strong new executive committee composed of himself, John 3rd, and Turnbull. The committee would meet every week with the president when he was able to be present. More to the point, the managing agents would report to the committee every week on all key matters. The proposal completely reversed the flow of decision-making. Instead of the board and the committees functioning as advisers, the executive committee would now decide on what the managing agents proposed.

Nothing happened for two months, and then Colonel Woods formally retired. Making the very large assumption that Junior's silence meant approval, Nelson and John proposed Scott as president, Christy as vice president, and the adoption of Nelson's reorganization scheme. The board approved the measures, but it was a short-lived triumph. John and Nelson had not foreseen that Thomas Debevoise would come down strongly on the side of the agents. He regarded them as partners, not employees, and believed they had done a "stupendous job" in managing the complex development. In his view, the problem was too much backbiting and the endless wasting of time in committee meetings. In a memorandum written on October 29, he said:

There appears to me to be somewhere a fundamental misconception as to the relative importance of the two partners. If Mr. Rockefeller had to choose between them today, it is clear that he could only decide that each and all of the officers and directors of . . . Rockefeller Center, Inc. could be much more readily displaced then the Managing Agents. In fact it would be a comparatively small matter to find others to step into our shoes . . . while to change the Managing Agents would involve endless confusion and loss, the result of which I hate to contemplate.

Voicing his concern about the "upset condition" of the managing agents and their "feeling that they are being punished," Debevoise was clear about what should be done: "It is time that we made the Managing Agents realize that we are with them, that our only object is to do what we can to help them, and that from now on cooperation is to be our first name." The feelings of the agents were reflected in an admonitory letter from the senior member to Turnbull, with a copy to Debevoise:

The Managers find every one trying in some way to take a ride at the expense of the Center. We have to fight it constantly and all these people whom we are trying to hold down to reason, welcome the slightest opportunity to go behind us to some member of the Board or some person on the 56th floor. If they get an audience it makes our job more difficult.[5]

Faced with these strong views, Junior acted decisively. Within a month, Nelson's reorganization was reorganized. Scott was asked to resign and Christy was demoted from what he thought would be the equivalent of "executive manager" of Rockefeller Center to vice president in charge of legal matters. The committees were reduced in number and revamped with a representative of the managing agents on every one. The new executive committee was allowed to stand, but was shorn of the power that Nelson had contemplated. With Woods gone, Debevoise made it clear that there would be no president or chairman of Rockefeller Center and that Heydt would preside at board meetings. In essence, the situation was as before, with the agents having full operational authority.

Somewhat chastened by this turn of events at the very time that their father was executing the 1934 Trusts, John and Nelson coauthored a warm Christmas letter to Junior, which had a strong apologetic flavor:

As we express our mingled feelings of pleasure, satisfaction and appreciation, we cannot help wondering just a little what your reaction has been to our relationship these past few years. We are afraid that at times you have somewhat misunderstood our efforts because of our inability to express ourselves clearly, or possibly because of our enthusiasm coupled with a keenness for action. This subconscious feeling on our part that you may sometimes question the motives which actuate our sayings or doings is our only source of regret. That our relationship should even on occasion be the cause of apprehension and concern to you is something which we feel should not and must not exist. The family's responsibilities are too great and the opportunities for accomplishment too challenging to allow anything of this sort to creep in.

With all due respect, we sincerely request that you have in mind that in our contacts and negotiations your interest is our first thought. From your reactions to our endeavors we are often concerned lest you may think that we suggest this or do that in order directly or indirectly to promote our own ends. However it may appear on the surface, this is the farthest from our thoughts we can assure you.

At times it is no doubt difficult for you to understand our methods due to a certain awkwardness on our part resulting from lack of experience. For this we are most regretful. We do feel, however, that it is the spirit which lies behind the act which really counts, and therefore we respectfully ask that you give us the benefit of any doubt which may exist in your mind. As far as we are concerned the spirit is more than willing although the flesh—our efforts— may be weak.[6]

Junior gladly accepted this olive branch and wrote in return:

Dear John and Nelson:

All the money in the world could not have bought for me a Christmas present as acceptable as your beautiful letter of December 18th. I am grateful and happy beyond expression that you feel as you do about the work in the office, and shall be glad at a convenient time to discuss with you the one or two minor matters that have given you concern.[7]

However, Nelson had only lost a battle, not the war. He and John soon resumed their long heart-to-heart strategy talks. Nelson had counted on John's fair-mindedness, and he was not disappointed. At lunch on January 2, 1935, John cleared the way for his younger brother. John was feeling overburdened with the dozen or more roles he functioned in on behalf of his father. The time was coming, he felt, when he should begin to pick and choose and perhaps pass some of these on to his younger brothers. Still, Rockefeller Center was not easy to pass up. John displayed some ambivalence in his discussion of the division of family responsibilities with Nelson. He reported in his diary what he had told Nelson:

. . . frankly, Rockefeller Center had the more appeal to me at the moment, as its activities were on the firing line, so to speak, while any interest I might have in the [Rockefeller] Foundation would be by necessity at least once or twice removed from the individuals or organizations benefited. Further, that while the position of chief executive officer of Rockefeller Center would have very real appeal to me, probably it would be wiser, everything considered, if I did not assume it, in view of the many other activities which I have besides the Boards, such as the management of the office and the Pocantico Estate, Williamsburg, China Medical Board, Dunbar Bank, and Industrial Relations Counselors. Nel said that very definitely he would be keen to be chief executive officer, and pointed out that he felt this position could best be filled by a member of the family in view of the Managing Agents general attitude as expressed in their relationship with Mr. Scott.

John had developed a habit of being frank and analytical of others in his conversations. He said he was "sympathetic" to Nelson's idea, but he expressed caution because Nelson "changed his opinion so often." He said the head of Rockefeller Center should be someone "who would not move too fast and would give a general feeling of stability and confidence."

Nelson listened good-naturedly to his older brother's advice, as he would often in future years, and proceeded to act very much in his own way. Several months later, John joined his father and Nelson as they were finishing lunch in the Rainbow Room, the elegant Art Deco room on top of the RCA Building that served as a nightclub in the evening and a luncheon club at midday. Nelson had been discussing "certain fundamental Rockefeller Center questions, such as allocation of authority and division of responsibility." John told his diary: "Father seemed to so completely misunderstand our point of view that I really felt as if we were discussing two different questions."

John and Nelson continued to meet frequently to strengthen their alliance. Later in 1935, John reported: "We agreed that it was extremely important that we have . . . an understanding that we can discuss any question together without any form of friction entering in. Spoke particularly of characteristics which we each had which might be annoying to the other. Couldn't have had a nicer talk." In May they discussed "the question of having in the office able advisers. Of course had the future in mind."

The following year, 1936, it was time to negotiate an extension of the managing agents' contract, and John and Nelson won an important concession from Junior—to allow the executive committee to handle the negotiations instead of Junior and Debevoise as before.

The managing agents wanted to change the existing contracts with their two corporations to new contracts for the five principals—John R. Todd, Hugh Robertson, James M. Todd, Webster B. Todd, and Joseph Brown. Nelson negotiated a two-year extension (to the end of 1938) which provided a salary of $80,000 per year for each of the five managers. In return, he won concessions on the profit-sharing arrangement and a clause allowing Junior to pick successors to the managers at his sole discretion.

By 1937 Nelson had won over Debevoise to his side, a considerable accomplishment. There is no record of just how Nelson did this, only the fact that Debevoise suddenly began supporting him. So preeminent and lordly was Debevoise in the family office that the Rockefeller boys had taken to calling him "the prime minister" behind his back. If Debevoise was the "prime minister," then Junior surely was "the king." Probably what happened is that Debevoise, like a good prime minister, realized that the wave of the future lay with the monarch's sons, not the hired hands.

The position of president of Rockefeller Center was still open. John 3rd records a meeting on April 7 (1937) in which he, Debevoise, Turnbull, and Nelson all agreed that Nelson should become president and chief executive officer. There was talk of making Jay Downer chairman at the same time, but Nelson resisted the idea of having someone over him. On May 4, John and Debevoise met with Junior to seek his agreement to Nelson's becoming president. Junior responded that no family member should have that position at the present time, but that it might be possible in the future.

By 1938 Nelson was ready to try again, but he also had become intrigued with several other interests. The solution he worked out, with the support of John and Laurance, was that he would become president and Hugh Robertson would be appointed executive manager under him. Robertson had been the most popular of the five managing agents with the Rockefeller boys, and he had done an outstanding job in leasing Rockefeller Center space. This time Junior offered no resistance. On May 23, the board approved the two appointments. All committees were abolished "with the exception of a larger and revamped Executive Committee, a Finance Committee, and a Renting Committee," as John noted in his diary. The other managing agents were retired with terminal consulting retainers equivalent to one year of their annual salaries.[8] Nelson had worked patiently for four years to win his first important political victory, but, having won, he was soon to move on to the next one.

During the late 1930s, John 3rd's life was more than ever taken up with his membership on various boards of directors. He had become a member of no fewer than twenty boards in addition to service on the Advisory Committee and as manager of the Pocantico estate and the family office. He was also occupied in developing his own philanthropic giving in consultation with Arthur Packard. He joined several clubs, and expressed his interest in international affairs by joining the Council on Foreign Relations, the Foreign Policy Association, and the Institute of Pacific Relations, but carefully avoided any role other than mere membership. By this time, he was routinely turning down outside offers to go on various boards. With the directorships he now held, plus committee assignments, his daily agenda was already overloaded. For the rest of his life, he would struggle to shed old involvements and avoid new ones unless he had a very strong personal interest.

So overwhelming was John's role of relieving his father and following in his footsteps that it could be said of his directorships that only three came of his own choosing—the American Museum of Natural History, Princeton University, and the Community Service Society. Most of the others were taken on in the course of duty. For example, John joined the boards of the Tarrytown Hospital and the Union Church of Pocantico Hills because he felt he should engage in community relations as manager of the Pocantico estate. In other cases, he was clearly a stand-in for his father, as at the Riverside Church, the Sealantic Fund, and the Rockefeller Institute. Although he held a high interest in the future of the Rockefeller Foundation and the role he might play in it, this was a gradual building and stabilizing period under Fosdick, so not much that was exciting was going on. The China Medical Board produced nothing but problems. The Depression so seriously curtailed the bright hopes of the Dunbar Bank that to go on with it would have been an act of philanthropy, uncalled-for in this case. In 1938 it closed down.

Two of the assignments that seemed perfunctory at first soon made impressions on John 3rd that would be important in his future. In 1934 he became the family representative on the board of the Spelman Fund, which had been created out of the old Laura Spelman Rockefeller Memorial to concentrate on the field of public administration. For the first few meetings, John kept recording in his diary how he had told his fellow trustees that he knew nothing on the subject. On one occasion, Charles E. Merriam came to New York to brief John and others about the contents of a report just issued by President Roosevelt's Committee on Administrative Management, Merriam being one of the members together with Louis Brownlow and Luther Gulick. Later John made several visits to the "1313" complex in Chicago, meeting with the heads of the various public administration associations based there. What John 3rd learned about public administration in these experiences proved useful in a program he undertook in the postwar years and in his Washington activities generally.

Work with the General Education Board seemed routine at first, but toward the end of the decade John joined other trustees in three extensive field trips to the South (Georgia, Mississippi, and Arkansas). The GEB program in these areas was a prototype of what the U.S. government foreign assistance programs in underdeveloped countries would be like in the postwar years, a major future area of interest for John. He learned at first hand about race relations, poverty, and the need for education and for integrated agricultural and industrial development. He came home filled with admiration for the courage, stoicism, and capacities of the tenant farmers and other poor people, black and white, whom he met.

John always took pleasure in visiting Williamsburg, where he could see the restoration in progress. He became imbued with the idea that Colonial Williamsburg could greatly serve education, as an aid to understanding and promoting democratic ideals. John displayed a growing and marked interest in the problems of young people, also a major interest of his later life. At Princeton he always met with student groups, and he and Blanchette particularly enjoyed the evening sessions at the New York International House with groups of foreign students. At the Community Service Society, John was chairman of the Committee on Youth and Justice. This committee dealt with the project on juvenile delinquency that he was engaged in when he and Blanchette first met. It involved meetings with youthful offenders, visits to prisons and reform schools, and discussions with experts. All this work resulted in a book, *Youth in the Toils*, published with considerable fanfare in 1938 by Macmillan. John himself had hired the author, Leonard Harrison, and worked closely with him. Thereafter, he continued to work with the American Law Institute and other organizations to promote liberalized and effective laws relating to youthful offenders.

Next to the theater problems of Rockefeller Center, John's most time-consuming duty in the late 1930s was his work with Industrial Relations Counselors (IRC). Here was another involvement inherited from his father, this time with a good deal of natural enthusiasm; for John, it was a continuation of the earlier interest he had expressed in his senior thesis. Industrial relations had changed since Junior's early preoccupation with setting up "industrial plans" as an alternative to unions. It was now an accepted discipline with a solid academic base, particularly at Princeton and Stanford. With the triumph of unionism and New Deal labor legislation, industrial relations had come to be seen as neutral and concerned only with achieving the best possible relations between employers and employees, whether unionized or not. IRC had established an excellent reputation, numbering both employee and employer groups among its clients. It had several former union officials on its staff, and it was frequently consulted by the federal government.

Its board had seven members, but was effectively run by an executive committee composed of John 3rd, Raymond Fosdick, and Clarence J. Hicks, the chairman. Hicks had become perhaps the best-known person in the field. The executive manager was T. H. A. Tiedemann, a fifteen-year veteran of the Industrial Relations Department of Standard of New Jersey. Junior had dropped completely out of the picture, as he had been doing with all of his long-term involvements except those few closest to his heart. Fosdick ended his participation once he took over the presidency of the Rockefeller Foundation. John was left in a position of unique importance. As a nonprofit organization, IRC depended on continuing financial support from Rockefeller sources; for although it charged most of its clients for consultation, it also rendered many free services, supported a large library and much research, and sought to assist university departments. With Junior out, financial support devolved upon John, the Davison Fund, and the trustees of the 1934 Trusts. Efforts to find other donors were largely unsuccessful.

As Tiedemann put it, IRC was concerned with furnishing "authoritative information or advice on employment and personnel practice, wages and hours policy and procedure, accident compensation and safety, sickness and death benefits and group insurance, retirement annuities, unemployment benefits, or collective bargaining."[9] Quite naturally, John wanted to apply the best thought in all these matters to the several organizations where he felt he had some direct responsibility or influence. However, this was limited to occasional suggestions in most cases. He found, for example, that Nelson had preempted the field at Rockefeller Center, bringing in Victor Borella, a man personally loyal to him, as labor relations director. Colonial Williamsburg and Riverside Church were well managed, with little need of help from John. And his father held iron sway at the family office. But at the Pocantico estate, John saw a clear need for some changes, and he was, after all, its manager—or so he thought. He felt that personnel policy at the estate was little better than feudal, no longer acceptable during a time that combined economic hardship with progress in enlightened labor relations.

One incident shows what John faced in opposition from his father as he tried to improve conditions at Pocantico. Junior had a policy of razing the unwanted older houses that existed on parcels of land that had been assembled into the Pocantico estate. Over time, this had the effect of reducing the amount of maintenance work needed. John was trying to avoid letting some men go while the Depression was raging. Many of the maintenance people had been with the estate a very long time. John saw the opportunity for new jobs when Junior let it be known that he wanted more night watchmen at Seal Harbor for the summer—all wealthy families had become acutely conscious of security in the wake of the kidnapping and death of the Lindbergh baby. So John dispatched three men from the estate to Seal Harbor. This brought forth a stream of critical correspondence from Junior to the effect that John could have saved thirty cents an hour if he had hired men in Maine. This attitude may be one reason why John and Blanchette began to appear less and less in Seal Harbor and rented houses on Cape Cod for their summer vacations.

John repeatedly sought Junior's approval for improved working conditions such as the forty-hour week, a pension plan, group insurance, and overtime pay. Only 33 of the 130 Pocantico employees were on salary. John was particularly concerned about the men on hourly wages, who received no pay when they were ill or when the weather prevented outdoor work or when they were for some reason laid off. Only the salaried men received paid vacations. John proposed the same treatment for the hourly men. Making no progress, John wrote Junior a letter in which he began by hinting that it might be best for him to withdraw from the management of Pocantico, and going on to say that he would be glad to continue under a policy by which Junior approved the budget but John had authority for labor policy, making no changes without the advice of Hicks and Tiedemann of IRC.[10]

After several tries, John got no definite response from Junior; so in the summer of 1936 he again made the mistake of thinking that silence meant approval. He arranged for IRC to survey personnel relations at Pocantico under the guidance of Hicks himself. John notified Junior, who shot back a reply from Seal Harbor to call the study off unless it had already started. Following several more letters from John, Junior grudgingly allowed the survey to proceed. The report stated at the outset that working conditions "in general are excellent" and that morale was good. Then it went on to cite numerous deficiencies. It noted that Junior was paying stipends for several widows and retired men and had helped out when serious illness occurred, but it made the case that a regularized policy for all employees would be much superior. It proposed all the measures John 3rd had been urging and a few more.[11]

In several luncheon sessions, John probed to find out why his father was so progressive in industrial relations in the outside world, but seemed considerably less so when his own philanthropic and personal organizations were concerned. Junior maintained that profit organizations had an obligation to the public that did not exist where funds were limited, as in philanthropic and personal ventures. John believed just the opposite—that it was important to be generous and progressive close to home before expecting others to follow suit. Only a month after the IRC report was delivered, John decided to follow his convictions and implement all the recommendations except for the three in which cost was a significant consideration—pension plan, group insurance, and paid vacations; those would be reserved for Junior's decision.

Junior did not countermand John's labor policy decisions at Pocantico, but they clearly did not set well with him. It was a point of friction between the two for over a year, Junior making frequent complaints about the fait accompli. He particularly disliked paying time-and-a-half for overtime. For John it was a period of high tension between him and his father. He recorded that he felt "pressure" every time he met his father in the office. On one occasion, he told Junior candidly that he and Nelson disliked their father's habit of "playing one of us as against the other." Junior said it was the last thing he would want to do and was completely unconscious of it. John replied he "still felt it was definitely the case."

Early in 1938, Junior and John had lunch together, and John reported in his diary: "He indicated rather frankly his disappointment in the way I had handled one or two things for him." At a second luncheon two weeks later, John asked to be relieved as manager of the Pocantico estate. He had two reasons—because he was overloaded with detail work and "because I felt it was a constant source of friction between him and me and that I just hated to see this go on." John said that for eight years he had done everything his father had asked and this was the first time—the most "definite and direct" approach to his father ever—that he wanted to be relieved of a responsibility. But no decision was reached that day.

Once or twice a month, the two met for lunch to hash over their disagreements. John proposed that the estate job be turned over to Nelson or Winthrop. Junior accused John of thinking only of himself in trying to pass the job on. On another occasion, he said that John's position was tantamount to saying that whenever there was friction between them the only solution was resignation. Other points of conflict kept cropping up. They completely miscommunicated on the matter of John's salary. He wanted to keep receiving it because it gave him a formal connection with the office, a sense of rightness about being there. Junior thought he was being selfish after all Junior had done for him financially. Once he learned this, John's psychological point was ruined and he no longer wanted the salary, but now Junior was stubborn and it took John a year to get Junior to discontinue it. John came to believe that relations between the "town" (Tarrytown) and the Pocantico estate were "far from cordial," and several times he proposed that Junior do something special for the community. This only irritated Junior further. He knew much better than John how much the family had done, and he also knew that there would always be a certain amount of griping in the community no matter what the family did. If there was more to be done in the future, he would be the best judge of that.

On the specific issues involved in these disputes, there is something to be said for Junior's point of view. The Hicks report, for example, had pointed out that personnel policy at Pocantico was in every respect at least as good as at other similar estates, and in many cases marginally better. This was the kind of comparison that Junior would deem proper; hence, John's initiatives were tantamount to meddling. On the other hand, one suspects that the owners of those other estates were not nationally known as pioneers in industrial relations, which included among its principles the ending of paternalism. The cost of employee benefits was not an insignificant item, given the times and the demands on Junior. He was doing his best to meet his philanthropic commitments and he was constantly in need of cash to shore up Rockefeller Center. Between 1936 and 1940, he had to put in $17.7 million to cover deficits. During this same period, his annual income from a shrinking asset base fell from $17.4 million to $8.9 million. He was already paying unemployment and Social Security taxes, which had been mandated by law in 1935. In 1938 he finally did implement the costly reforms urged by John and the IRC report for both the office and estate employees—paid vacations, life insurance, and pension plan. The start-up cost for the group annuity covering the last two items was nearly $900,000, and the yearly premium thereafter was about $250,000.

Still, this was done in such a grudging way that it was not unreasonable for John to wonder about the contrast between Junior's outward demeanor and his behavior close to home. In fact, he had been wondering about it for a long time. One recalls, for example, the ridiculously inflated issue Junior had made out of John's simple request for the use of a car for a special weekend at Princeton.

Because of his remarkable career up to this point, Junior was universally respected as a generous, open-minded, principled, and progressive man, one often praised for his "democratic" spirit. Yet in his relations with his children, he was very nearly an autocrat. He was stubborn, stiff, formal, very much the master of his own house, and so obsessed with his own notion of due process that his method of dealing with his children often seemed to be more appropriate to a court of law than the role of a father. Everything about human experience, amply reflected in literature and the findings of the social sciences, tells us that human beings are quite capable of acting consistently in ways that are or seem contradictory. Junior was no exception. In fact, his apparent contradiction presents a familiar image—the man who is seen in his affairs as a fine, decent, and generous fellow, but by his family as an autocrat at the breakfast table. Part of the explanation for Junior is that in his personal behavior he was very much an old-fashioned man, despite his intellectual, emotional, and moral commitment to progressivism in his affairs. He desperately wanted his children to grow up in his own image, and this led him to excessive formalism and moralizing.

The amazing thing is that he succeeded as much as he did with John, who bore the brunt of Junior's autocratic style as the oldest son and was perhaps the one least prepared to deal with it. He was not devious and clever enough to maneuver and manipulate his father in the way that Nelson was to hone into a fine skill. He was not cool and detached like Laurance. And he was unable to rebel in the manner of Babs and Winthrop. These were John's maturing years, and he was accumulating experiences that would gradually lead him to an important realization—that he could never be his own man until he acted independently of his father. Yet he was so respectful and straight, so burdened with the impossible task of living up to Junior's expectations for him, and so doggedly patient that it was to be quite a few years before he would fully accept and act upon that realization.

It is apparent that John and his father both were able to stop short of allowing the friction between them to turn into an open breach. They were, after all, father and son, and each had a very considerable stake in the other. Several times they attempted to work out a modus vivendi for the Pocantico connection, John resolving to carry on after each agreement. At one point, he made a formal inventory of his responsibilities, something he was to do frequently in his life. He presented the detailed list to Junior showing thirty-eight responsibilities in the office and nine personal ones. Junior was becoming persuaded that John's point about being overburdened was valid, and this marked the beginning of a "cooling off" period between the two.

During this same period, John and Blanchette had been producing a family. Their first child, Sandra, was born in 1935, and a son followed in 1937. They named him John, omitting both the familiar middle name of Davison and a numerical designation after the family name, believing that the decision whether or not to adopt these was best left to their son when he came of age.[12] So the boy's name was John Rockefeller, but he became known to everyone thereafter as "Jay." In 1938 a third child, Hope, was born. With their household growing, John and Blanchette began to think about building their own home. One day while out riding, they came across a portion of the Pocantico estate that appealed to both of them. It was a lovely tract in the northwest corner of the estate, about as far from Kykuit and the Park as one could get. It included some high ground that would offer a stunning view of the Hudson River once it was cleared. John wrote to his father and talked with him several times about acquiring it. It took a year of negotiation and uncertainty, but in the end Junior was sympathetic and he generously gave the land. John and Blanchette happily began planning their dream house.

The "cooling off" period was working well. Junior now entirely agreed that John had taken on far too many tasks on his father's behalf and told his son he wanted him to keep only those that genuinely interested him. In May 1939, John was thus able to pass the management of the Pocantico estate to Winthrop, whom he had been grooming for the job. John told his father that his highest interest was in the Rockefeller Foundation and Colonial Williamsburg. Junior said he was ready to retire as chairman of the latter, and that he wanted John to succeed him. This move was to bring on the next surge of friction between the two, though not until the postwar years.

By the end of the decade, the public image and awareness of the Rockefeller family had undergone a change, a product of the passing of time and of the succession of generations.

The change began with the death of Senior. In good health for a man of his age almost to the very end, he died on May 23, 1937, at his home in Ormond Beach, Florida. He was a little over two years short of his final goal of living to be a hundred. Although retired from business for forty years and from active philanthropy for nearly twenty, Senior had been a living legend, an animate chapter in American history. In the public mind, that chapter closed with his death.[13]

Junior was just then in the process of cutting back on his activities because of his own advancing age and concern for his health and that of his wife. When he turned sixty-five in 1939, he retired from several chairmanships, including the Rockefeller Foundation and Colonial Williamsburg. Although Junior had no thought of giving up the management of the fortune and family affairs, the public perception was one of retirement and withdrawal from the limelight.

As a result, public attention naturally turned to the Rockefeller brothers. Perhaps nothing symbolized this shift better than the scene at the Tarrytown railroad station, where the family gathered to await the arrival of the special train bearing Senior's body. The old man was gone, and there was Junior, small and elderly, dwarfed by his five strapping sons, as they appear in the rare photographs of the five adult brothers grouped with their father.

For years the press had not been sure how to deal with the fact that there were five male heirs; it was generally assumed that the eldest would be *the* heir. Now, although John was still apt to be referred to as the "crown prince" from time to time, the press discovered, seemingly overnight, that all five had come of age, all were going to be wealthy and active men, and all were interesting people. In 1939, there was a rash of lengthy stories about the Rockefeller brothers—in the *Saturday Evening Post*, the *New York Times Magazine*, several photo magazines, and in releases by newspaper syndicates. There were more such spreads in the following years, and by and large the depiction of the personalities and interests of the five brothers was accurate. A common theme, as expressed in the *Times* story, was the remarkable fact that all five had turned out so well. None of them were "hellions" or wastrels as many thought inevitable with the sons of rich fathers. They were engaged in diverse activities without blocking each other's ambitions, yet they remained close as brothers.[14]

The first public recognition for something important that John had done came with the publishing of *Youth in the Toils*. The press was intrigued by the fact that he had worked on the problem of juvenile delinquency for six years with no publicity at all. The product was widely praised for its farsighted proposals for the treatment of youthful offenders and for new laws and prison reform. And John was lauded as a worthy successor to his father in managing Rockefeller benefactions and dedicating himself to a difficult project without being self-serving.

Nelson meanwhile was manifesting all the qualities that would make him a consummate politician in later life, but as yet he showed no sign of attempting a career in politics—the *Times* writer thought that Nelson, as the president of Rockefeller Center, had carved out a career for himself in real estate. He had boundless energy and a hearty, charismatic personality, often stopping to chat with tourists in the lobby of the RCA Building, genial, exuberant, slapping people on the back. But he also showed he was not to be taken lightly. He had shrewd instincts and a streak of toughness. He was a hard-driving executive in running Rockefeller Center. Some employees thought he was ruthless, others that he was brilliant.

It was already evident that Rockefeller Center was not enough to contain Nelson's restless energy. He clearly was an unusually talented young man; what was not yet clear was where the talent would take him. At the age of thirty, he appeared on the cover of *Time*, May 22, 1939, the occasion being his election as president of the Museum of Modern Art after four successful years as its treasurer and fund-raiser. He did a six-month stint at the London and Paris branches of the Chase Bank, long enough to find out that banking was not for him. He developed a deep interest in Latin America, traveling there numerous times and learning to speak Spanish. He purchased some stock in Creole Petroleum, a subsidiary of Standard of New Jersey operating in Venezuela, and thus became a minority stockholder on Creole's board. There he soon exerted a powerful liberalizing influence on the company's policies and community relationships in Latin America.

Nelson showed his political skills in his family relations—in his ability to line up his brothers as allies, in becoming a special favorite of his mother because of his zeal for the Museum of Modern Art, and in shrewdly assessing how to deal with his father.

He also showed the politician's knack for accepting defeat, beating a tactical retreat, and preparing for the next campaign, as when he left immediately for his six months in Europe after losing in his first attempt to take power at Rockefeller Center. He perceived the added power that Junior gained from his ring of advisers. Debevoise, Cutler, Heydt, Turnbull, Chorley and others were Junior's men, totally loyal to him. When Junior was away from New York, these men did not turn to John or Nelson for decisions, but continued to deal with Junior by telephone and correspondence. So Nelson developed his own ring of advisers, men such as Beardsley Ruml, architect Wally Harrison, and several young businessmen, bankers, and lawyers. Nelson began referring to them collectively as "the Group." It was the beginning of his ability to attract talented people to him. Never again in his life would Nelson be without a sort of personal "brain trust" surrounding him, although of course the membership changed over the years.

More accurately and quickly than John, Nelson perceived that limiting himself to laboring in Junior's vineyard would be frustrating and too confining. Running Rockefeller Center was good for him; he had a great deal of operational authority because of the sheer volume of decisions to be made. But he knew full well that the real power lay with Junior because of his ownership of the stock and control of finances. And he also knew that Junior was a long time away from giving up any control, despite the public perception. So Nelson was a man in motion, his restless, curious mind constantly spawning new ideas and developing new interests. Almost as soon as he took over the presidency of Rockefeller Center, he stepped up his interest in Latin America. It was this that would soon provide a remarkable launching pad for his career in public life.

About the outlines of Laurance's career, there was no uncertainty once he gave up the law in 1935 after two years at the Harvard Law School. A man of quick intelligence, he wasted no time fretting over his immediate realization that his two older brothers would have first and second choice in adopting sectors of Junior's interests. Fortunately for Laurance, John and Nelson were not attracted to the one major area for which Laurance had a natural affinity—conservation. We have seen the early interest he took in the JY Ranch and the Jackson Hole Preserve. He became a director of the prestigious New York Zoological Society, and formed close friendships with two famous conservationists, Fairfield Osborn and Horace Albright. In 1939, Governor Lehman appointed Laurance a member of the New York State Parks Commission. At one point, John and Laurance talked about going in together to buy the JY Ranch from their father.

Having married Mary French in 1934, Laurance went to work in the family office in 1935, a reasonably prosperous young man by virtue of a handsome wedding gift from his father, plus his salary and allowance. Laurance performed some chores for Rockefeller Center and assisted his father in conservation and housing projects. Very quickly he showed a flair for business, a field that had not been pursued actively by any member of the immediate family since the early years of the century. It was to become Laurance's second major interest. In 1937 he paid $68,000 to take over his grandfather's seat on the New York Stock Exchange, which the old man had never graced with his presence. On one occasion, after a luncheon session with Laurance, John 3rd commented with admiration in his diary upon Laurance's keen knowledge of economic trends and investments. Laurance had his favorite economist, Dr. Lionel Edie, and every few months the brothers would lunch together to hear Edie discourse about the state of the market.

Laurance had the knack of understanding technology and was fascinated by it, especially the aircraft industry. In March 1938, he joined the syndicate that bought Eastern Airlines from General Motors, purchasing 21,000 shares of stock for $267,000. When in 1940 he turned thirty, he wasted no time in petitioning for the right to draw on the capital in his trust fund to increase his financial stake in Eastern. He also invested in a new aircraft firm started in St. Louis by James S. McDonnell, and purchased smaller amounts of other aviation stocks, including United, Pan American, Fairchild Engine, Douglas Aircraft, and the Glenn L. Martin Corporation. He frequently corresponded with his fellow Princetonian, James Forrestal, assistant secretary of the navy, about the nation's aeronautical needs.

Winthrop was the genial giant, six feet three inches tall, weighing 225 pounds, and endowed with a gregarious nature. The press liked him especially because he never avoided reporters and always answered questions with good-natured humor. He had the "common touch," and people could easily identify with him. He smoked, liked to drink, and was linked romantically in the public prints with a succession of beauties, including the actress Mary Martin. In 1935, during his junior year at Yale, Winthrop was thrown out of school. The specific reason was being caught taking a shower with a young lady in his campus room.[15]

None of this behavior was calculated to please Junior. The fact is that from his young manhood on Winthrop was constantly teetering on the brink of becoming the "black sheep" among Junior's sons. Because of this and the fact that he was fourth in line, Winthrop knew that there would not be much for him in the family office. So he decided to try the oil business. He went to work for Standard of New Jersey at $25 a week, in the Bayonne refinery and in industrial relations. Then he worked for several years in the Texas oil fields as a "roughneck" (the actual job title), where he was soon accepted as one of the boys. Back in New York, he joined the foreign department of Socony-Vacuum, now at $88 a week, and made overseas trips to South

America and Egypt. He accompanied Nelson on the latter's first trip to South America, a three-month jaunt.

In 1938 Junior found a constructive use for the Center Theater and an assignment for Winthrop when the Greater New York Fund was founded. Junior was one of the civic leaders who helped bring the fund into existence. A precursor of the United Way, it was intended to increase charitable giving in New York City, which had lagged because of the Depression, and also to provide more centralized efficiency and coordination in organized charity, a long-standing interest of the Rockefellers. Junior made the Center Theater available as the site of a series of rallies and meetings on behalf of the fund. In one of these he described the fund as a "unified program of coordinated planning under which all our charities can move forward in intelligent concert." In the classic fashion of the times, there were to be three vice chairmen of the campaign, a Jew, a Catholic, and a Protestant. Junior tapped Winthrop to serve as the Protestant member. The overly optimistic goal was $10 million; the actual amount raised was $4.4 million.

Two years later, the chairman of Socony-Vacuum, James A. Brown, was named overall chairman of the fund campaign, and he appointed one of his employees, Winthrop, to serve as executive vice chairman of the drive. Winthrop did his best, working out of a seedy office for four months, making several speeches a day, and genially twisting the arm of everyone in sight. Nevertheless, only $3.2 million was raised this time.

As one reporter put it, Winthrop was also the one who "handled all the night life" for the Rockefellers. John got a sample of this one August evening when he was a temporary bachelor. Blanchette and the children were still at the rented summer house at Cape Cod, and so John agreed to the rare experience of a night on the town with Winthrop:

. . . Winny and I had dinner together at "21" on 52nd Street. It seems it used to be a speakeasy but now is run as an expensive restaurant. There was quite an interesting crowd in the place including people like Grover Whalen, Floyd Odlum and his wife, Jacqueline Cochrane, Jock Whitney and Eddie Warburg. After dinner we went down into the basement to see the technique they had developed in prohibition days to protect their wine and liquor supplies. It really was very cleverly done. Winny next took me to the Stork Club, West 53rd Street, and after that to the Cafe Pierre in the Hotel Pierre. The Stork Club really was fixed very attractively and was surprisingly crowded for this season of the year. In all three places we visited Winny knew the proprietors and a number of the head waiters so that it really was quite fun. At the Stork Club we met Ethel Merman.

David, meanwhile, was behaving as the serious and career-oriented young man that he was—the intellectual of the family. He graduated cum laude from Harvard in 1936, doing his senior thesis on Fabian socialism. He did a postgraduate year in economics at Harvard and then a year at the London School of Economics. He earned his Ph.D. in economics at the University of Chicago in 1940. Nelson and Laurance had had brief experiences with the Chase Bank, and David followed suit, working at the London branch a few hours a week during his year at school in England. Unlike the others, David did not mind the staid atmosphere of banking; but before deciding on a career, he wanted to test the world of politics and public life. So he became a clerk in the New York City administration of Fiorello LaGuardia. Although the "Little Flower" insisted to the press that David was just one of sixty interns in the city government, the young man's working space was the vacant office of the deputy mayor.

With the four oldest children married, Junior by this time had twelve grandchildren—Babs' two, John's three, Nelson's five (the twins Michael and Mary having been born in 1938), and Laurance's two. In 1940, David became the fourth son to marry, leaving Winthrop as the only eligible bachelor. On September 8, David married Margaret McGrath of Mt. Kisco in Westchester County, whom he had known for many years.

Even as they developed along distinctive paths, the five brothers concerned themselves with ways to maintain a degree of family unity. As early as 1936, John and Nelson talked with Arthur Packard about ideas for coordinating the philanthropy of their generation, and in 1937 Packard produced a long document proposing procedures and listing fields of activity for a unit he would operate as a central office for the philanthropy of the brothers.[16]

Meanwhile, much of the trust income of the brothers not yet thirty years of age provided the Davison Fund with the bulk of its annual budget. Packard's coordinating effort was working well, but by the end of 1939, with all five brothers present in New York, they began exploring the possibility of a more formal scheme. On the day after Christmas, all five met at John's apartment "to talk about the possibility of the family working more closely together. We discussed the organizational side as well as the more personal aspects."

What emerged after subsequent meetings was the idea of the

brothers incorporating a fund of their own, which would gradually succeed the Davison Fund and stand as a symbol of their unity. Not surprisingly, Nelson was the leader in pressing for the plan. He was also the one who spoke up on one occasion when Junior mused out loud with his sons about his thought of giving all of his stock in Rockefeller Center to the Rockefeller Institute. As president of the Center, it was perhaps appropriate that Nelson should be the spokesman in the attempt to stave off this move. John reported in his diary: "Nelson was raising the question of whether or not it might be better to leave it in trust to the family. Nelson presented his point of view well but did not change Father's point of view." But more than a decade later, Junior did change his mind.

Early in September 1940, the brothers signed a "Rockefeller Brothers partnership agreement," and then invited Junior to lunch to tell him about it. John reported: "He spoke very enthusiastically about it which was gratifying to all of us as he had only known in a general way that we were preparing the statement." On December 28, John recorded:

Today was filed at Albany the certificate of incorporation of the new philanthropic fund which the other boys and I have set up for our own use. It is to be known as the Rockefeller Brothers Fund and is to serve as a convenience for all of us in connection with our personal contributions.

The incorporation was reported in the press, and the phrase "the Rockefeller brothers" came into the public consciousness. It was an auspicious beginning, but before much more could happen, events intervened. Like millions of other young Americans, the Rockefeller brothers went to war.

20

*

POLITICS AND WAR

LIKE THEIR PARENTS AND GRANDPARENTS, the Rockefeller sons
were staunch Republicans. They grew up at a time when young men
almost always followed the political inclinations of their fathers and
party loyalty was largely regarded as a civic virtue. For seventy-two
years, since the election of Abraham Lincoln, only two Democrats had
occupied the White House, Grover Cleveland in two separate terms
and Woodrow Wilson in consecutive terms. And the latter clearly
would not have been president had it not been for the split in the GOP
between the Old Guard and the Progressives. After the World War,
their factional differences seemingly resolved, the Republicans returned to their accustomed role of running the country, electing three
one-term presidents in a row. In the main, the nation basked in
comfortable assumptions about the future of America, taking as
political "normalcy" (Harding's word) the values of businessmen and
the GOP.

All this was shattered as the Depression brought on a period of
profound political change in American history. For Republicans the
election of Franklin Delano Roosevelt and the emergence of the New
Deal heralded a difficult, perplexing time. It is useful to recall the
changed political scene of the 1930s before examining the reactions of
the Rockefellers as loyal Republicans.

At first, there was the honeymoon period of the "first New Deal,"
with FDR's landslide election, his charisma, political skill, bipartisan
approach, and the legislation of the "first hundred days"—all rallying
the nation. The legislation was not radical; similar measures aimed at
recovery had been advocated unsuccessfully by President Hoover late
in his term. These were pre-Keynesian days, with Roosevelt just as
committed to a balanced budget as Hoover.

But in 1934 the honeymoon ended and FDR increasingly came
under attack from both the left and the right. Socialists and Commu-

nists denounced the New Deal as a transparent attempt to restore the power of business, bankers, and trusts at the expense of the common man.[1] Roosevelt had difficulty dealing with such outspoken populists as Senator Huey Long of Louisiana, Father Charles Coughlin, and Dr. Francis E. Townsend, alternately resisting them and allowing himself to be goaded into more liberal actions than he really wanted to undertake, and in the end earning their enmity as they became increasingly radical.[2] From the business community came attacks that amounted to a declaration of war on the president, the U.S. Chamber of Commerce leading the troops. Roosevelt also began to encounter factionalism within his own party: leading Democrats such as John W. Davis and Al Smith joined with prominent businessmen to form the highly conservative American Liberty League. In one speech, Smith accused Roosevelt of stealing all his ideas from the Socialist Party. The growing habit of calling FDR a "red," a radical, or a socialist aroused the ire of a true Socialist, Norman Thomas, who dissected the New Deal piece by piece to show—unfortunately in his view—that it was anything but socialistic.

It was during this period that hatred of Roosevelt became firmly anchored in the breasts of conservative Republicans and many businessmen, a strange phenomenon in that it flowered at a time of mild recovery, when the early New Deal measures seemed to be working. This brought forth one of Roosevelt's favorite stories, that of rescuing a rich old gentleman who had fallen off the end of a pier clad in his tuxedo and top hat. The gentleman was grateful at first, but then became enraged because the rescuer had failed to save his hat.

One of the most astute analysts of the Roosevelt years, James MacGregor Burns, has offered one explanation for the "essentially irrational hatred" of Roosevelt on the part of the business community:

The vehemence of the rightist revolt against Roosevelt can be explained only in terms of feelings of deprivation and insecurity on the part of the business community. Roosevelt had robbed them of something far more important than their clichés and their money—he had sapped their self-esteem. The men who had been the economic lords of creation found themselves in a world where political leaders were masters of headlines, of applause, and of deference. Men who felt that they had shouldered the great tasks of building the economy of the whole nation found themselves saddled with responsibility for the Depression. Men who had stood for Righteousness and Civic Virtue found themselves whipping boys for vote-cadging politicians. And government ceaselessly was becoming more and more dominant.[3]

Most historians agree that Roosevelt was not an ideologue, but a practical politician in the classic American sense, quite capable of taking a zigzag course according to the exigencies of the moment. By 1935 it was clear that the mild recovery had been temporary and that the early New Deal efforts to spur recovery were not succeeding. Goaded by harsh words from business and the actions of the Supreme Court in striking down main parts of the New Deal, FDR counterattacked with his celebrated move to the left. Aided by enlarged congressional majorities resulting from the 1934 off-year election, he introduced the "second New Deal" and the "second hundred days" in 1935 with a rash of legislation including the Wagner Act (National Labor Relations Act), the Social Security Act, the so-called Wealth Tax Act, the creation of the WPA, and a dozen other measures.

Not surprisingly, opposition intensified among businessmen and in the press. Everyone, it seemed, was against FDR—except the voters. In the bitterly contested 1936 election, he won his greatest landslide victory, carrying all but two states. Yet FDR's second term was much less successful than his first. He committed the blunder of attempting to "pack" the Supreme Court, and there occurred the "Roosevelt recession" of 1937, the defection on key issues by conservative Southern Democrats, and growing controversy over foreign policy in the face of rising international tension.

But the basic elements of the New Deal were firmly in place. For most Republicans, the Roosevelt era was one long process of gradually coming to accept measures that once had seemed radical. GOP candidates continued to blast the New Deal in general, but after 1936 there were few sustained efforts to overturn its working elements.

The Rockefellers clearly belonged to the moderate wing of the Republican Party, but Junior was alarmed by some New Deal measures, especially the new tax laws, which seemed to approach confiscatory levels. And yet, as we have seen, Junior was a progressive from almost every conceivable standpoint. In opinion, he normally tried to take a positive view; the negative, slashing attack was not his style. So he did not support the Liberty League or become a Roosevelt-hater. Junior rarely attempted to exert influence on public policy; he made exceptions only when some deep conviction moved him, as in the case of Grand Teton National Park and when he came out for the repeal of Prohibition. He could be called politically active mainly in the sense of loyally supporting his party. As such, of course, he opposed FDR.

Junior's attitude is shown by his warm approval of a letter brought to him by Thomas Debevoise in October 1934, when criticism of FDR was in full swing. The letter, written by Dr. John R. Todd, the senior member of the managing agents of Rockefeller Center, was an impassioned plea (fruitless, as it turned out) to get Republicans to take a positive line in the 1934 off-year election and during the remainder of FDR's term. It reveals the times and illustrates the Republican dilemma:

"The New Deal" is a wonderful slogan and a great platform for these times. Everybody has always wanted a "New Deal" and always will. A new or better deal should be the objective of every government.

Our forebears came to this continent for a "New Deal."

Christ came to the world for a "New Deal."

All the world is waiting for the sunrise.

Do not tell the country it cannot have a "New Deal"! That is, if you want to be heard.

The country doesn't know just what this "New Deal" is, the President doesn't know, we do not know, no one knows accurately because it is in the making—but it sounds good and the people want it.

The Democrats hope to fight this campaign in November and on through 1936—they are for the New Deal and we are against it.

If we fall into that trap, we are sunk. They will beat us to death. We must give them a *"Better New Deal."* Call it what you like, but it must mean just that—A BETTER NEW DEAL. . . . Our New Deal must hold all there has been of good in our national development to date; all there is good in the Democratic New Deal—and it must look for still better things. . . .

The President isn't a Socialist, or a Communist, or a Bolshevik. He has no idea of being a Dictator. He does not want to scrap the Constitution and all we, as a nation, have accomplished. He wants to do well—bring back Prosperity and be re-elected. . . . He needs the full, constant, vigorous cooperation of American business men. . . . Sane Republicans and sound business, for the present, better get mighty busy . . . helping the President get right where he is wrong, rather than by fighting him no matter whether he is right or wrong.[4]

Junior promptly wrote to Todd: "To read this letter has been a real privilege. I regard it as one of the clearest analyses of the present situation and one of the best statements in regard thereto that I have seen. You have rendered a real service in writing it. I wish I could think as searchingly and write as concisely."[5]

As noted, Senior had not been a heavy campaign contributor, but his son did what was expected of a wealthy Republican in the years from 1920 on—he was among the top echelon of contributors to his party. In those years, that usually meant something on the order of $25,000 in a presidential election.[6] Despite putting up a moderate candidate in 1936, Governor Alf Landon of Kansas, Republican sentiments ran so high during the campaign that all the Rockefellers came under intense pressure to increase their normal support of the party. The total family contribution came to $243,000—almost half by Junior, $43,000 by Abby, and $20,500 by Babs. It is worth noting that among the brothers Nelson was the largest contributor ($33,000), with John next ($25,000), and Laurance last ($7,000). Some $103,000 of the total was distributed among state, county, and district committees in New York. After the election results were known, John 3rd commented in his diary on his giving to the campaign.

I did not increase [campaign contributions] beyond $25,000 even though I was urged to do so as I do feel very definitely that in a country such as ours, with its present form of Government, it is a mistake for any small minority to be in such a position that it could be accused of in any sense controlling the outcome of the election. While I feel that it is entirely proper to give a reasonable amount in proportion to one's means, I do think that the support of the political parties should be on a very wide basis.

Obviously, no amount of Republican money would have controlled the outcome of that particular election. In the same diary entry, John ruminated over the crushing defeat of Landon. He voiced the most common Republican criticisms about the Roosevelt administration—fomenting class hatred, too much spending, growing government control over the individual. But he concluded: "Personally I find myself in substantial agreement with the general objectives of the New Deal—social security, higher standards of living, et cetera. I disagree primarily as to the means used to obtain that end rather than in the end itself."

The normal policy of the Rockefellers was to give to party committees, not to individual candidates. But in October 1937, John, Nelson, and Laurance met with Debevoise and agreed that exceptions should be made for Fiorello LaGuardia's reelection campaign as mayor of New York and Thomas E. Dewey's for district attorney of New York County. Dewey's spectacular record as a special prosecutor had made him one of the great young hopefuls of the Republican Party; victory in the 1937 municipal elections of New York City was seen as an essential stepping-stone to higher office.

The family gathers for dinner at Junior's Park Avenue apartment, March 1949. *Left to right, standing:* David, Winthrop, Irving Pardee, JDR 3rd, Junior, and Nelson; *seated:* Barbara Sears ("Bobo") Rockefeller, Mary French Rockefeller, Peggy McGrath Rockefeller, Abby Aldrich Rockefeller, Mary Clark Rockefeller, and Blanchette Hooker Rockefeller.

At the opening of the United Nations headquarters, 1952. Mrs. Trygve Lie, Junior, Martha Baird Rockefeller, Wally Harrison, and Trygve Lie, Secretary-General of the United Nations.

Colonial Williamsburg, 1948. JDR 3rd discusses the restoration of the King's Arms Tavern with Kenneth Chorley and John Green.

JDR 3rd in Tokyo in February 1951 prior to the Dulles Peace Mission.
Left to right: Raitei Tokugawa, Ino Dan, Naokichi Kitazawa, JDR 3rd, Isamu Fukiu, and Masao Maeda.

The Rising Sun on Fifth Avenue. JDR 3rd *(left)* speaks with Ambassador Eikichi Araki, Japan's first postwar ambassador to the United States, and John Foster Dulles, before dinner at the Japan Society, June 1952.

Cultural relations with Asia. JDR 3rd *(left)* and René d'Harnoncourt escort Prime Minister Shigeru Yoshida on a tour of the Japanese House exhibit at the Museum of Modern Art, May 1952.

Frederick T. Gates, the man behind the creation of the Rockefeller philanthropies

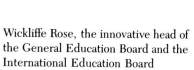

Wallace Buttrick, of the Rockefeller Sanitary Commission and the General Education Board

Wickliffe Rose, the innovative head of the General Education Board and the International Education Board

George E. Vincent, president of the Rockefeller Foundation from 1917 to 1928

Colonel Arthur Woods, Junior's chief of staff from 1918 to 1935

W. L. Mackenzie King, Junior's close friend and adviser on industrial relations, and future prime minister of Canada

Thomas M. Debevoise, the "prime minister," legal counselor to Junior from 1923 to 1955

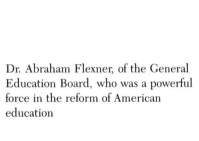

Dr. William A. R. Goodwin, the visionary behind Colonial Williamsburg

Dr. Abraham Flexner, of the General Education Board, who was a powerful force in the reform of American education

Raymond B. Fosdick, president of the
Rockefeller Foundation from 1936 to
1948, and the man responsible for the
reorganization of Rockefeller
philanthropies

Dana S. Creel, the key philanthropic
adviser to the brothers in the
postwar years

Although LaGuardia was a Republican, some of Junior's advisers had previously been cool toward him, seeing him as standing to the left of FDR on many issues. But to Junior he was a "fusionist" and reform candidate in the tradition of Seth Low and John Purroy Mitchel. He and his sons contributed $9,500 to the "Little Flower's" campaign and $11,000 to Dewey's, both crowned with success.

Throughout the decade, the storm clouds gathered that once again presaged world war—the Japanese invasion of Manchuria and then of China proper, the bitter Spanish Civil War, Mussolini's invasion of Ethiopia, Nazi Germany's reoccupation of the Rhineland and annexation of Austria and then Czechoslovakia. The debate soon to rack the nation over American foreign policy proved to be as traumatic for the Republican Party as the battles over domestic issues. Isolationist sentiment was not limited to the Republican Party by any means, but it was conspicuously strong within the GOP, especially in the midwestern heartland where Colonel Robert McCormick's *Chicago Tribune* was a powerful voice for both conservative Republican and isolationist feelings.

Moreover, the GOP had the problem of being in opposition to an enormously popular president whose inclinations seemed obvious at least as early as 1937, when he gave his "quarantine the aggressor" speech in Chicago. FDR moved circumspectly after that, realizing that he was ahead of public opinion in taking sides or seeming to. The antiwar sentiment in the United States was extremely powerful: it had a religious and virtually pacifist base as much as a political one. When war among the European powers became a fact in 1939, Roosevelt could hold much of his administration and party leaders with him as he carefully sought gradual means to help England and France. But the Republicans' opposition to involvement in a European war—especially that of senators from midwestern and western states—was intensified by their role as opposition and their lack of a charismatic party leader to control them. Even more radically than domestic political issues, the struggle between isolationists and internationalists over the war in Europe created a new split in the Republican Party and gave rise to the image of an "eastern liberal establishment."

For the Rockefellers, the character of the Nazi regime became an issue almost immediately. It arose out of the plan to create a series of "foreign nation" buildings in Rockefeller Center. Britain, France,

Germany, and Italy all were thought to have sufficient trade with the United States to supply the tenants and make it appropriate to identify a building with each country. This worked for Britain and France, resulting in the British Empire Building and La Maison Française. For what were to become known as the Axis powers, it was a different story. The difficulty with Italy was not political. The great popularity of Mussolini in the United States—so amazing in retrospect—was at its height. An Italian building failed to materialize because of the ineptness of the Italian promoters and rental agents; however, Rockefeller Center designated a portion of the International Building North as the "Palazzo d'Italia." There were renters available for a German building and the German consul general in New York pushed the idea energetically, but there was a political obstacle.

Nazi oppression of the Jews was a fact from the very beginning of the regime, although it took years for its extent to permeate the public consciousness. Some read the signs early and realized the full seriousness of the situation. One such person was James G. McDonald, John 3rd's mentor on the round-the-world trip of 1929. Late in 1933, the League of Nations offered McDonald the post of high commissioner for refugees, to cope with the growing stream of Jewish refugees leaving Germany. Six months earlier, McDonald had told John 3rd at lunch that the state of affairs in Germany was much worse than the newspapers reported, that there was no excuse for the way the Nazis were treating the Jews, and that he was extremely discouraged and pessimistic.[7]

Colonel Arthur Woods was adamantly against a German building in Rockefeller Center for this same reason and the managing agents were concerned over the possibility of a Jewish boycott if plans for the building went ahead. The decision to be made was the kind that fell to Junior. His first reaction was that he should find out more, principally by seeking the opinions of prominent Jewish friends and associates of many years in philanthropic projects. As chairman of the Center's foreign buildings committee, John 3rd assisted in the research.

As is now well known, even Jews, especially German Jews, had difficulty grasping or believing the true nature of the Nazi persecution. The Jewish leaders John 3rd spoke with in the late summer of 1933 advised postponing the idea of a German building, but did not as yet share McDonald's gloom. For example, Felix Warburg of Kuhn, Loeb told John he "had confidence in the future of Germany" but "hated to see us do anything that would appear to be in support of the Hitler Government." John wrote in his diary: "He was in favor of having a German building, but felt that any action in regard to it should be postponed until feeling in this country should be less anti-German and until the Nazi government should be more modified in its policies."

Only one of the men consulted, Henry Morgenthau, Sr., was despondent. His comments, noted in John's diary, are worth repeating because of the accuracy of his prediction and the effect it may have had on the views of his son, soon to be FDR's secretary of the treasury:

At 11 Monday morning, Father, Blanchette and I went to call on Mr. Henry Morgenthau, Sr. at his house in Bar Harbor to get his reaction to the desirability of proceeding with the German building in Rockefeller Center at the present time. Mr. Morgenthau was very much opposed, not because he particularly feared a boycott of the development, but because of his misgivings as to the future of Germany, as well as on account of public feeling in this country at the moment towards the Hitler government. In Mr. Morgenthau's opinion, the countries of Europe are all lined up against Germany. He fears that a war is inevitable in the near future as a result of which Germany would be dismembered. What would be left would not, he thought, be a world power for many years to come.[8]

John heard another point of view from several young Germans he had come to know at the International House. One of them, Heinz Nixdorf, returned from spending the summer of 1933 in Germany to tell John how "keen" he was about Hitler and that the main purpose of the "Storm Troopers was to break down class distinctions and party lines." Another friend, Leon Transehe, was retained for a time to line up tenants for the German building. He reported that he was making excellent progress, but John had to tell him, in late 1933, that the project was postponed. In the end, of course, it was abandoned.

A considerably more important Rockefeller response to Nazi persecution was just getting under way at the Rockefeller Foundation—the Special Research Aid Fund for Deposed Scholars. The Foundation's emphasis on quality in its programs had put it into frequent contact with the great universities of Europe and many of the best-known scholars. The representatives of the Foundation in Europe were thus well aware of the threat posed by fascist ideology. At first, the program was a rather orderly affair of giving grants to facilitate the relocation of German scholars to European or American universities. These were thought of as temporary relocations until Germany regained its senses. The Foundation gave its grants to other institutions, with the New School for Social Research in New York City serving as the main American conduit. Some scholars ended up on the New School faculty; others were there briefly while a faculty post was arranged at some other American school.

But as the situation in Europe worsened, the Foundation's program changed accordingly. When German expansion endangered scholars from other European countries, they were included in the program. For example, the Austrian economist Oskar Morgenstern was in New York on a trade mission when the *Anschluss* occurred. Morgenstern wisely decided to avail himself of the Rockefeller Foundation's hospitality. He became a particular friend of John 3rd's, who helped him find his post at Princeton. Another famous Austrian economist, Ludwig Von Mises, was also aided by the program, ending up at New York University. Then, when the war began, the Foundation effort became the Emergency Program for European Scholars, with the emphasis shifted from relocation to rescue. A temporary office was set up in Lisbon. With considerable understatement, the writer of a brief unpublished history of the Foundation's program, Thomas Appleget, said that "considerable ingenuity was required" by this staff in extricating scholars from behind German lines. The operation was similar to that of the better-known Emergency Rescue Committee founded by columnist Dorothy Thompson and radio commentator Raymond Gram Swing and funded in part by Rockefeller money. This effort, with its field office in Vichy France at Marseilles, achieved incredible results in rescuing some of the most famed artists, writers, and composers of Europe.[9]

Altogether, the Rockefeller Foundation effort relocated or saved 303 scholars between 1933 and 1945 at an expenditure of $1.4 million. Two-thirds were Germans, with twelve nationalities represented in the total. Among the notable individuals involved in the program were: anthropologist Claude Lévi-Strauss, theologian Paul Tillich, author Thomas Mann, composer Darius Milhaud, philosopher Ernst Cassirer, law professor Max Ascoli (who later published *The Reporter* magazine in the United States), political scientist Karl Polanyi, theoretical physicist Leo Szilard, historian Hajo Holborn, philosopher Karl Mannheim, and political scientist Henri Bonnet (who later became French ambassador to the United States). Almost every conceivable academic field was represented by the refugee scholars, the largest group (35 percent) being social scientists. A significant group was the nineteen theoretical physicists and mathematicians, many of whom were to work on the Manhattan Project.

According to Appleget, the purpose of the program was to aid scholars whose lives were endangered for no other reason than "their race, their religion, or their intellectual integrity." He concluded that the program "not only insured the continuance of important scholarly work; in many cases, it actually saved distinguished, productive lives from destruction." There was another unintended benefit that became evident in the years after Appleget wrote his 1946 report: the work of the refugee scholars was of incalculable value in enriching intellectual life and a score of academic disciplines in the United States.

Decades after the fact, the programs of the Rockefeller Foundation and the Emergency Rescue Committee might seem to be elitist to some—rescuing the famous while millions of unknowns were dying at the hands of the Nazis. There are two important considerations. First, these organizations worked in specific areas that they knew and understood and where they could be effective. Second, large-scale rescue efforts were not possible because of the restrictive immigration laws of the United States. Despite the best efforts of Eleanor Roosevelt and others in Washington, these barriers were not eased until it was far too late.[10]

It was during the 1930s that peace and disarmament movements were springing up in the Western democracies while the Germans were busy rearming. Junior gave $60,000 in grants to half a dozen peace organizations at home and abroad, the largest sums going to support the work of Lord Robert Cecil and Philip Noel-Baker of England, the prime organizers of the "International Peace Campaign." In 1936 John 3rd also gave $5,000 to the campaign. These movements drew their strength from the fervor of men who had seen the terrible slaughter of trench warfare and were determined that it should never happen again. Only by appreciating the depth and sincerity of this feeling can one understand the policies of the British Prime Minister Neville Chamberlain, which soon became labeled as "appeasement."

Unfortunately, the peace movement was one-sided, and the final German provocation—dismembering Poland in 1939 in league with the Soviet Union—brought on the world war that so many had feared. The issue in the United States was no longer peace but neutrality, and the debate over policy began in earnest. Winthrop Aldrich had no doubt where his sympathies lay, and within two months of the fighting abroad he had organized two committees for "medical and civilian aid," one for Britain and one for France. His method of raising the million he wanted as a start was to recruit members of wealthy families for his committees. He enlisted Marshall Field, Harold

Vanderbilt, Jock Whitney, and John D. Rockefeller 3rd. Almost weekly, John 3rd made trips downtown for meetings at Uncle Winthrop's office in the Chase Bank, and he joined his uncle in soliciting $50,000 from Junior to match the first gift by Marshall Field.

Junior complied with some reluctance. Like most Americans, he was ambivalent—his sympathies were with the Allies, but he wanted to avoid American involvement in a war. He reasoned that limited and humanitarian aid was consistent with American neutrality. But any hope that the Allies could prevail without substantial American aid was dashed by the stunning events of the following spring and summer—the German occupation of Norway and Denmark and the blitzkrieg attack through the Low Countries. In a matter of weeks, the British evacuated their troops at Dunkirk, France fell, and Britain stood alone.

In an instant, the debate over United States policy intensified. Junior became a target for requests to use his name and his funds by a host of new organizations covering every shade of the isolationist-interventionist spectrum. For a time, he maintained his own form of "neutrality," still hoping the country could stay out of the conflict. In this he was in the mainstream of public opinion, which gave way grudgingly to President Roosevelt's efforts to prepare the country for war and increase aid to Britain. By the end of 1939 had come the repeal of the arms embargo and the beginning of the "cash and carry" policy. In 1940 came increased defense appropriations, the trading of fifty overage destroyers for British bases in the Caribbean, the first peacetime program of compulsory military service, and the vast step-up in defense production with the Roosevelt proclamation that the United States would become "the great arsenal of democracy."

Still, the controversy raged; stark divergence of views was voiced on the board of the Rockefeller Foundation. A former member, William Allen White, the famed editor of the *Emporia* (Kansas) *Gazette*, had formed the best-known pro-Allied organization late in 1939—the Committee to Defend America by Aiding the Allies. Strongly opposed, although carefully avoiding the label of isolationist, was John Foster Dulles, who had been elected to the board in 1935. Eventually, he was to become chairman of the Foundation and an extremely important person in the life of John 3rd.

A very religious man and a prominent international lawyer, Dulles had become a senior partner of the prestigious New York firm of Sullivan and Cromwell at a relatively young age. Numbering two former secretaries of state among his relatives, he had served on the U.S. delegation to the Paris Peace Conference where he, John Maynard Keynes, and Jean Monnet had formed a trio of young men who believed that the Versailles Treaty was too harshly punitive against Germany. Now he was an outspoken opponent of U.S. involvement, believing that nothing could prevent the European powers from fighting themselves to exhaustion. Dulles did not base his views on the typically simplistic points of the isolationists; he had formed his own intellectualized and densely argued analysis, which he expounded in his book, *War, Peace and Change*, published in 1939.[11]

For several years, Dulles had been sending copies of his speeches and articles to Junior. Early in 1940, when the German army was beginning to overrun Western Europe, an interesting debate by letter occurred between Dulles and two of Junior's friends, his office associate Tom Debevoise and Arthur M. Allen, a lawyer in Providence who had been at Brown with Junior. Debevoise and Allen had crossed the line and were arguing for every possible form of assistance to the Allies short of war. Dulles' response, couched in moderate terms, examined the pitfalls of such a policy.

In a letter to Arthur Allen, written as France was crumbling, Junior surmised that Dulles' "position must have undergone a radical change in the light of recent events."[12] In fact, it had not. Like other strong opponents of the U.S. entry into the war, Dulles did not change his position until the Japanese attack on Pearl Harbor eighteen months later. Dulles' best opportunity to give effect to his views lay in the 1940 presidential election—the American electoral process was in full swing as the German offensive rolled westward. Dulles was Thomas E. Dewey's mentor in foreign policy. Dewey's chief rival for the Republican nomination was Senator Robert A. Taft of Ohio.[13] There was little to choose between the two—both were adamant against involvement. John 3rd reported in his diary on March 21, 1940:

Had lunch at the University Club with Father, Mr. Dewey, John Foster Dulles, Laurance and Mr. Debevoise. Mr. Dulles arranged the luncheon to get Father and Mr. Dewey together. Father asked Mr. Dewey particularly about his feelings as to the international situation, . . . Mr. Dewey felt very strongly that this country should keep out of the European war. He said he drew the line just before extending credits. He thought it was all right to sell war materials on a cash and carry basis but felt we shouldn't go any further. . . . our main job was to serve as the stronghold of democracy and that if we joined the war to save democracy we could not achieve our objective as the country would be so regimented during the war that we would never be able to get back to our present form of government.

John also remarked that Dewey seemed to have thought his answers through very well. The candidate's ideas on foreign policy and those of John Foster Dulles were identical. But the hopes of the pair were dashed three months later at the Republican convention. John wrote about how excited he felt listening to the proceedings on the radio as Dewey and Taft gradually lost strength and the dark horse Wendell Willkie swept to victory on the sixth ballot. Junior and his sons had long been well disposed toward Dewey, but were uncomfortable with his policy of strict neutrality. In Willkie they had a candidate who was not only an able and charismatic New Deal critic, but seemed even more internationalist than FDR. One of Willkie's favorite themes was to criticize Roosevelt for not rearming America fast enough. John wrote:

His nomination really gives the Republican Party a new life and a new hope, not to mention real leadership—something which it has been lacking for a number of years now. Whether he wins the Presidency or not it will be very healthy for our whole democratic form of government to have such a man the head of the opposition party during the campaign.

As for Junior, Willkie's nomination seemed to him "the brightest ray of light . . . for many years . . . national unity is the fundamental thing which needs to be stressed in this country," he thought, and he rejoiced that "Mr. Willkie is so fully aware of that need."[14] Here Junior was expressing a common attitude among moderate Republicans, the view that if the two major parties adopted a similar policy of maximum aid to Britain short of war it would end the divisive wrangle over foreign policy. Already FDR had made a gesture toward unity by appointing two prominent Republicans to his cabinet, Henry L. Stimson of New York as secretary of war and Frank Knox of Illinois as secretary of the navy.

But Willkie's nomination had the opposite effect. It was regarded by many party professionals and isolationist leaders in the GOP as a sellout. Some of these leaders at once formed the America First Committee, whose program was formally announced in September 1940 and which rapidly grew in membership. Until Pearl Harbor settled the issue, it became the champion of isolationism, numbering among its prominent spokesmen an authentic American hero, Charles Lindbergh, as well as several Democratic senators, notably Burton K.

Wheeler of Montana. Under pressure from this group and from a desperate search for popular issues, Willkie was driven to sound like an isolationist during the final weeks of the campaign. He repeatedly accused Roosevelt of being a "warmonger," which forced the incumbent to keep repeating that American boys would not be sent into foreign wars.

Even though Willkie gave FDR a scare before going down to a decisive defeat, all his nomination had achieved was to deepen the conservative-liberal split within his party. A former Democrat and a shrewd New York businessman beneath his homespun midwestern exterior, Willkie was heartily disliked by the conservative core of the GOP. He was what the *Chicago Tribune* called a "me too" candidate, meaning one in the guise of a Republican, but who aped Rooseveltian domestic and foreign policies.[15]

One of the leaders in the very active New York Chapter of the American First Committee was Adelaide Marquand, Blanchette's sister. Adelaide was a speaker at mass meetings in New York on the same platform as Lindbergh, Wheeler, John T. Flynn, and other America First leaders. Her husband, novelist John P. Marquand, did not share her views, though he was tolerant of them. In April 1941 John and Blanchette attended a cocktail party given by the Marquands in honor of a visiting Irish leader, General Frank Aiken, Ireland's minister for coordination of defense measures and a close friend of Ernie O'Malley's. Dinner followed at the apartment upstairs of Mrs. Hooker, the mother of Adelaide and Blanchette. John wrote that Aiken spoke calmly, but that one could feel his "fundamental bitterness . . . and distrust of England." The guests included the Lindberghs, the Flynns, the Archibald Roosevelts, and others prominent in the America First movement. As John wrote: "With the exception of Blanchette and myself the crowd were all pretty much behind the America First Committee. . . . It was interesting to get their slants on things."[16]

John and Blanchette clearly were of another persuasion. He remained active in Uncle Winthrop's committees, which were combined to form the Allied Relief Committee, later renamed the British War Relief Committee. With the Battle of Britain looming, the committee started in 1940 to bring British children to live in safety in the United States with foster parents. John and Blanchette were among the first to subscribe and their household swelled to five children by mid-1940, when Blanchette went to Montreal to meet Benjamin and David Rowntree, the five- and four-year-old sons of

Peter and Bessie Rowntree of London. "We are awfully glad to have them," John wrote.

At the end of the year, John was invited to help in China war relief efforts by Henry Luce, the publisher of *Time*, whose object was to form a United China Relief Fund out of some seven existing organizations. In addition to Luce and John, the board included Wendell Willkie, Pearl Buck, William C. Bullitt, Paul Hoffman, Thomas Lamont, Theodore Roosevelt, Jr., Robert G. Sproul, Artemus Gates, and David O. Selznick. The good work was universally approved. It was not until the postwar years, after the breakdown of the Nationalist government of China and the success of the Communist revolution, that intense controversy started in the United States about what had happened in the Far East. Stirring much of the controversy was the "China lobby," in which Luce played a prominent part.

A foreshadowing of later troubles arising out of the Far East question occurred when John had lunch with Frederick Field early in 1941. This scion of the Vanderbilt family had resigned after a dozen years of service with the American Council of the Institute of Pacific Relations, including six years as secretary. Field had just become executive secretary of American Peace Mobilization, a leftist group that slavishly followed the Communist line.[17]

John did not know that Field, on his "leftward migration," was shortly to become the financial "angel" of numerous Communist-front organizations, a correspondent for the *Daily Worker*, and a prominent figure in the postwar backlash against the Institute of Pacific Relations. At lunch, John wrote, Field "seemed to feel that just about everything is wrong with the set-up in this country at the present time and hence I couldn't find much common ground to start from in our discussion." The objective of Field's new organization—"saving democracy"—was "to be accomplished principally by creating a people's government," Field told John.

By early 1941, Junior was ready to end his public reticence about the war. He had favored all aid to Britain short of war since early 1940, but had not joined any organizations or made public statements. He ended that policy with a letter published in the *New York Times* on April 28, 1941, in which he called for "standing by the British Empire to the limit and at any cost." It was not enough to make munitions and foodstuffs available, they must be laid down "at Britain's door." Writing less than two months before the German invasion of Russia ended the strange Nazi-Soviet pact, Junior called for stamping out the Nazi and Communist "fifth column" machinations that were causing sabotage and work stoppages. He said he would "rather die fighting the brutal, barbarous, inhuman force represented by Hitlerism than live in a world which is dominated by that force." He called for a "united public opinion solidly behind the President in whatever may be necessary to achieve the desired end."

Something about Junior's stature, his husbanding of the use of his name, and his normal reticence about comments on public policy gave special power to his words when he did speak out, as in the case of Prohibition. Now, again, his statement stirred an enormous response, although, of course, the tendencies already ran strongly in the direction he favored. FDR had put through the Lend-Lease Act and was taking action to move the United States toward a belligerent status.

When war finally came on December 7, John analyzed the Japanese attack on Pearl Harbor in his diary. He pointed out that the Japanese had attained a "very great material advantage" from the successful attack, but "they couldn't have gone at a war with us in a worse way from their angle in that it completely rallied the country so that opposition factions such as the America First group are completely out of the picture." He added the prescient comment: "Also, the Japanese methods will remove any reservations which our Government might have had when the time comes for bombing Japan."

A few weeks after Pearl Harbor, John discussed with his father what he might do in the war, and noted in his diary that Junior was "rather keen to have as many of us as possible in uniform." When the draft began more than a year earlier in September 1940, all five Rockefeller sons had registered and then held a meeting to discuss volunteering. Nelson had the lowest draft number, but it was the unmarried brother, Winthrop, who suggested that he should be the one to volunteer. John wrote that Winthrop certainly was "the most likely one . . . although none of us, of course, wanted to be in a position of urging him to do it." John added that "from the public relations angle it would be grand if one member of the family were in military service."

It was unlikely that Nelson would be drafted, because several months earlier he had undertaken a war-related assignment in Washington. He had been appointed by President Roosevelt as the head of a new agency that came to be known as the Office of the Coordinator of Inter-American Affairs. How it happened that FDR chose a rich thirty-two-year-old Republican for this post is a remarkable story that has been often told in various versions.[18] Suffice it to say that Nelson managed to bring his unique Latin American experience and insights to the attention of a president who had a particular interest in that region, where more than ever there was need of American influence. Nelson drew on the thinking of "the Group" to draft a three-page memorandum for the White House. After long interview sessions with Harry Hopkins, James Forrestal, and, finally, FDR himself, Nelson was given the job on June 14, 1940.[19]

Even more remarkable is what Nelson did once he was appointed. A number of factors had made Axis influence extremely strong in Latin America—the presence of more than 3 million persons of German and Italian birth or descent; the existence of several dictatorships; substantial interests in trade, transportation, publishing, and other fields; the belief that the Axis was winning the war; and long-standing resentment of the United States in many quarters. The new coordinator's agency was small by Washington standards—a staff of 1,300 persons and an outlay of $140 million for five years of economic, cultural, and informational work in Latin America. After a few mistakes, the agency by all accounts performed superbly in cutting down Axis influence and reinforcing sentiment for the Allies.[20] It would be called today a "swinging" operation, with a virtually unrestricted mandate, open to fresh thinking and imaginative ideas.

Inevitably, when Nelson first came to Washington, he was regarded as a lightweight. But he soon won respect and a vastly enhanced reputation that set him on his course for public life. The coordinator's office provided a marvelous opportunity for him to display all his talents as a hard-driving and imaginative leader who could inspire loyalty and very often charm the opposition. As if he expected to spend much of his life in Washington, Nelson bought an elegant residence on Foxhall Road in the northwest section. On one occasion John 3rd had dinner there in the company of Walt Disney, Walter Wanger, and James V. Forrestal. At another time, the guests included about a dozen men of Nelson's permanent staff: "Practically all of them were very young," John wrote in admiration, "and they seemed to be very much on their toes." In the group were John Dickey, later to be a Rockefeller Foundation trustee and president of Nelson's alma mater, Dartmouth, and John Lockwood, whom Nelson would successfully back as the successor to Debevoise in the family office.

Several times Nelson expressed concern about not wearing a uniform, but he clearly was too valuable where he was. All his brothers entered the armed forces, John and Laurance in the Navy and Winthrop and David in the Army. True to his word, Winthrop was the first to go, enlisting as a buck private in the infantry almost a full year before Pearl Harbor. He made a distinguished war record during his nearly six years of service, the only one of the brothers to be in combat and wounded in action. He rose to be a gunnery sergeant and then went to Officers Candidate School. He served with the Seventy-seventh Division, achieving the rank of major and participating in assault landings and jungle warfare in the South Pacific before he was wounded when a kamikaze plane struck his troopship near Okinawa.[21]

David also enlisted as a buck private, in May 1942, and also went to OCS, from which he emerged as a lieutenant and was sent for further training in Army Intelligence. He spent two years in a special unit known as "Joint Intelligence Collection Agency—North Africa." David's job and his fluency in French brought him into close contact with members of the French Committee on National Liberation in Algiers, including General DeGaulle. He also served with this unit in Italy and southern France. With the liberation of France, David was assigned to a military attaché's unit in Paris, which for a time functioned as the American embassy. He returned to the United States in November 1945 as a captain, his wartime experience having engendered in him a lifelong interest in foreign affairs.[22]

Because of his knowledge of the aircraft industry. Laurance was able to get a commission as a lieutenant in the Navy, serving in the Bureau of Aeronautics in Washington, but spending much of his wartime service traveling to aircraft plants around the United States to expedite production.

Like Nelson and Laurance, John 3rd also became a "Washington warrior." Nearly overage for the draft, he probably could have avoided military service altogether if he had wished. Early in 1942, he was trying to decide between entering the Navy or going with the Red Cross, which was in dire need of executive manpower. Raymond Fosdick had suggested the latter, and Norman Davis, head of the Red Cross, thought John could be of great help in two areas of his expertise—personnel and liaison with other relief agencies. John's many years of involvement with Industrial Relations Counselors and active work with the wartime relief agencies were obvious qualifications. He soon made his decision, writing in his diary that although the Red Cross "does not have the glamor, so to speak, of a Navy job I feel my background and experience will be much more use there right now than anywhere else I can think of at the moment." Before the end of January 1942, he was on the job in Washington. He and Blanchette lived in a hotel for a while before they were able to rent a small house.

For the next five months John worked hard at setting up programs and recruiting people for Red Cross posts overseas. But he soon decided to switch over to the Navy. He listed several reasons—the "bureaucratic mess" that the Red Cross was in and the fact that he was not able to get into liaison work, but was restricted to personnel because of its heavy demands. The most important reason was probably the lure of the uniform. David Lawrence, the journalist, told him that "unquestionably" he should join up. "He said I would have no peace of mind until I made the change."

Fortunately, John's Uncle Winthrop had been "appointed by the Navy to help in securing officers for specialized jobs." At the same time, unfortunately, the officer whom Uncle Winthrop sent John to see learned that the new candidate's most conspicuous specialization was in personnel work. John was commissioned a lieutenant in the Naval Reserve and assigned to the Bureau of Personnel in Washington where, for the next year, he did find the work to be challenging, at least part of the time. He led a team revising the Officers' Procurement Manual to place the emphasis on civilian skills and worked on methods of recruiting medical personnel and finding men with scientific training for the radar program. But as the tide of war began to turn in 1943, John tried to break away and move toward international affairs and the policy-making that would be required by military occupation and postwar readjustment.

V

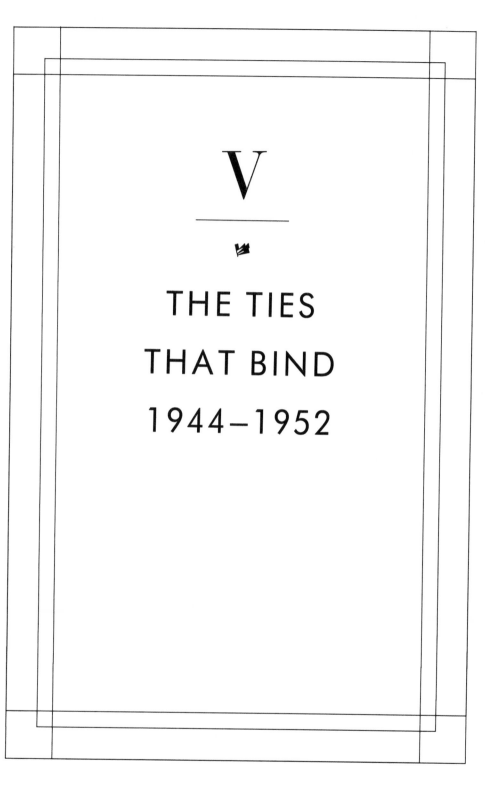

THE TIES
THAT BIND
1944–1952

21

⚑

NEW BEGINNINGS

As it was for so many, World War II was a liberating experience for JDR.[1] It worked a decided change in the pattern of his life. Free from the dominance of his father and the routines of the family office, he found himself in situations where what he could and could not do counted for much more than his famous name and wealth. It was satisfying, because he learned that he could do his assignments well and work with others agreeably. He began to feel an unaccustomed degree of self-confidence. Of course, like other men, he had his ups and downs; he grumbled about bureaucracy and incompetence; but he also felt the exhilaration of discovering how to get things done within large institutions. He learned how a great democratic government functions and what policy issues it has to contend with. All this led to reflection and insights that were to be valuable to him in subsequent years.

After only a year in the Navy, JDR showed some bureaucratic skill in moving out of personnel work and into the job he wanted. First, he surveyed the Navy Department to find the office most likely to be involved in postwar problems—the Office of Occupied Areas. "The next problem," he wrote in his diary, "was to get asked for."[2] He managed to spend weeks working with the men in that office by volunteering to rewrite a personnel program "for the procurement of Military Government officers," which badly needed improving. The result was that the commanding officer requested JDR's transfer to his unit. Suddenly, his old personnel office decided he was too valuable to release and gave him a new assignment. After languishing several months, JDR finally was able to "use a little pressure" to secure his release and take the desired posting with the military government unit. "I dislike very much this method of approach," he wrote, but he realized it was the "recognized" procedure unless he wanted to

415

remain stuck in a routine job. He consoled himself with the thought that he had used "pressure" only to gain release from an unwanted job, not to get a desired one.

Life in Washington was markedly different for Blanchette as well. She and John moved to a larger furnished house on Wyoming Avenue, though not as large as they would have wished, considering their five children. Blanchette could walk around the block with her dog and chat with neighbors. "We have let the children wander around our neighborhood on their own and go to school by themselves, which we would not have felt we could have done in New York," John wrote. "We have really enjoyed a lot living in Washington. It is so attractive with its lovely trees everywhere, has such a friendly atmosphere, and the life is so much simpler and more informal."

JDR became a player and then manager of a softball team in a league drawn from the Navy Department and the British embassy. Even this did not provide enough exercise, so he made sure to walk a good distance every morning before joining up with his "driving squad" (car pool). And he would use his "exercise days" from the Navy to take the train to New York every other weekend to chop wood and build fences on his farm, the property on the northern edge of the Pocantico estate that Junior had given him in 1940.

The "country home" that John and Blanchette built on those 235 acres, later named Fieldwood Farm, was a source of great pleasure. It took several years to complete the attractive, rambling fieldstone structure, which is spacious and comfortable, but by no means palatial. The house takes full advantage of the high elevation that John and Blanchette had chosen after much discussion and changing of minds, offering a sweeping view of rolling fields, forests, and the Hudson River in the distance, and yet the place does not overwhelm the surroundings. The site and landscape planning was done by Frederick Law Olmsted (the younger) and security advice given by an FBI agent dispatched by J. Edgar Hoover. The farm was scarcely ready for occupancy before the family had to move to Washington, hence the weekends spent in Pocantico were a special delight, heightened by the fact that JDR was able to become a gentleman farmer almost immediately: he bought a herd of seventy-five sheep and a dozen of the black Angus cattle that were to be for him a lifelong avocation. He had enough "farm credits" to gain a draft exemption for his farm manager. In addition, he hired a man classified 4-F and several high school boys during the summer, and contributed his own labor to keep the farm going during the war years.

JDR took pains to keep track of the family in his diary. He wrote down what his brothers were doing; he recorded the "sad story" of his sister's trip to Reno to divorce Dave Milton; the return home to England of the Rowntree boys in 1944, after their mother's death of cancer. Of his father, John wrote: "My brothers and I are inclined to feel that he has had quite fun running things with all of us away."

More likely, Junior's emotions were a mix of pride, nostalgia, and loneliness. He was, of course, doing his bit for the war, buying huge amounts of war bonds and playing a leading role in creating and supporting the United Service Organizations, known to everyone as the USO, with its hundreds of rest and recreation centers for American servicemen at home and abroad.

Junior might have felt those emotions most keenly when up at Pocantico, remembering all the family gatherings at Abeyton Lodge and then at Kykuit, which Junior occupied after his father's death. Among the many buildings that now formed the complex at the core of the estate, the area known as "the Park," was one particular extravagance that Junior could not resist building. It is known as the Playhouse, a larger version of the one he had built earlier at the Eyrie in Seal Harbor. A large, rambling French Norman structure that nestles alongside the nine-hole golf course, the Playhouse contains an indoor tennis court, a gymnasium, squash and handball courts, a beautifully tiled indoor swimming pool, a special room for billiard tables, and two bowling alleys, a kitchen, and several dining and living rooms. At the entrance is a large reception room resembling a baronial hall in an English country house, complete with wood paneling, massive fireplaces at either end, and a cathedral ceiling. Tangible evidence of Junior's pride in his sons are the five oil paintings he commissioned during the war, still to be seen hanging on the walls of the great room, showing four of the sons in their military uniforms and the fifth, Nelson, in a navy blue civilian suit befitting the head of a wartime government agency.

There was more evidence of that pride, as for example in the "private and confidential" letter Junior wrote to JDR on September 24, 1943:

Dear John,

More than a year ago you turned aside from all your personal affairs and from that time on have been devoting your entire time to the service of your country in the Navy. That you would have done anything different is, of course, unthinkable, but that you did what you have done has nevertheless been a great satisfaction to me. I have accordingly taken real pleasure in subscribing to $2,500,000 of the New War Loan bonds for you. The office will put them with your securities.

Affectionately,
Father

In December 1944, shortly after JDR was promoted to the rank of lieutenant commander, Junior placed another $3.5 million worth of war bonds in JDR's trust and accompanied the gift with a heartfelt word:

You are the oldest of the boys. Even in your school and college days you gave such evidence of wisdom, sound judgment, frugality and generosity in the use of the monies entrusted to you that I was led to increase the sums put into your hands earlier and more rapidly than in the case of the other boys. With the passing years this evidence has only increased. You have acquitted yourself of these growing responsibilities with ever increasing credit to the family. Your wise example has pointed the way for the others; you have set standards for them to follow. Thus, quite aside from the fact of your seniority, you have established your position as leader in the family in this all important field of the wise use of money. It is, therefore, with a deep sense of confidence, satisfaction and pride in you that I am singling you out as the only one of the boys in whom I am at this time making a further gift.

May these resources that have come to us as a family not only enrich our own lives, but through our wise use of them be made a far-reaching blessing to our fellow men!

From 1943 to 1945, JDR functioned as a Navy representative in what he referred to broadly as "political-military affairs," a bewildering jumble of agencies, offices, and committees that were part of or represented the main centers of power in Washington—the White House and the State, War, and Navy departments. All were trying to plan or coordinate the myriad policies having to do with the occupation of enemy territory, with relief and rehabilitation, with the transfer to civil authority, with democratization and the eventual peace settlement.

In the course of this work, JDR came to know scores of interesting men, some of them already prominent and others to become so, men such as Adlai Stevenson, John J. McCloy, Robert Lovett, Will Clayton, Adolph Berle, Archibald MacLeish, William Benton, Harold Lasswell, Dean Acheson, Harding Bancroft, James Forrestal, Artemus Gates, William C. Bullitt, and Dean Rusk. In serving for a time on the Civil Affairs Committee, an agency of the Combined Chiefs of Staff, JDR met a young lawyer and Army captain named Donald McLean, who later became a close associate in generating some of his most important projects.

There were frustrations along the way, most of them stemming from lack of interest on the part of the Navy Department and the consequent monopoly of the work by the Army. But, on the whole, JDR found the experience stimulating. One highlight for him was a three-week conference in Atlantic City, where he helped draw up the program of the United Nations Relief and Rehabilitation Administration (UNRRA), which had been created by forty-four nations in November 1944.

As victory began to look certain, political problems loomed larger and required better coordination between the military and the State Department. The result was the creation of the State-War-Navy Coordinating Committee (SWNCC) in December 1944; JDR was named one of the three Navy representatives on the secretariat. By that time, he had become officer-in-charge of the General Civil Affairs Branch and had fourteen officers serving under him. The group, in his words, functioned as "the focal point at the working level for all political-military problems in which the Navy was involved." When war ended in Europe, the pace of similar preparations for the Far East increased. With Japanese surrender imminent in the summer of 1945, JDR produced a paper on "the development of a positive policy for the reorientation of the Japanese people," which Artemus Gates, assistant secretary of the Navy, submitted to the State-War-Navy committee.

Throughout this period, leading Americans were thinking about how the peace would be made secure and international affairs conducted thereafter. It was clear to everyone that the United States would emerge from the war in an enormously heightened position of power and would bear a special responsibility for world order. Isolationist sentiment was not absent, but this time it seemed impossible to return to classic American isolationism or to repudiate any international organization that might be created for keeping the peace.

Beyond these points of near-consensus, reactions to the postwar opportunities and responsibilities of the United States varied a good deal. One could discern three points of view, subdivided on single points and at times overlapping: even the best minds were influenced by the events of the moment. One view was chauvinistic: that what was happening was the inevitable extension of America's "manifest destiny." As early as 1941, Henry Luce in *Life* magazine had written an editorial proclaiming "the American Century."[3] More widespread was a revival of Wilsonian idealism, the view that the peace would be kept through international organization and collective security arrangements among nations, based on shared assumptions. The third view was nationalistic, a manifestation of classic *realpolitik*: the assumption that great-power rivalry would continue as ever before and would require a world of preparedness, alliances, and spheres of influence.

Walter Lippmann was perhaps the clearest exponent of the *realpolitik* approach in his two wartime books, *U.S. Foreign Policy* (1943) and *U.S. War Aims* (1944). A good many American leaders were pessimistic about the possibilities of successful postwar cooperation with the Soviet Union.[4] But this point of view was muted, because the overwhelming policy tendency was the Wilsonian approach of seeking postwar security and order through cooperation and a new international organization. Wendell Willkie came out strongly in this direction in *One World* published in 1942, and Sumner Welles, deputy to Secretary of State Cordell Hull, called for a new League of Nations in his book *Time for Decision* (1944). Most Republican leaders were still extremely wary of international entanglements, especially any that might seem to abridge sovereignty; yet John Foster Dulles in 1943 proposed a plan that came close to advocating some form of world government. Under his tutelage, the head of the GOP ticket in 1944, Governor Thomas E. Dewey of New York, moved cautiously toward a more internationalist position.[5]

In a six-week conference held at Dumbarton Oaks in Washington during the early fall of 1944, the four leading Allied powers (the United States, Great Britain, the Soviet Union, and China) forged a plan for a new international organization to maintain peace and security and to be known as the United Nations. Later that year, FDR appointed Edward R. Stettinius, Jr., as secretary of state to succeed the ailing Cordell Hull. One of the many changes made by Stettinius was the appointment of Nelson Rockefeller as assistant secretary for Latin American affairs. This move was made for good reason. Nelson's Coordinator's Office had largely accomplished its wartime goals, but, more important, he had acquired a great deal of influence among the leaders of nearly all the Latin American countries. This could be useful at the much larger international conference scheduled to meet the following spring in San Francisco to ratify a charter for the U.N. The Latin American votes could be crucial for the United States in disputes over issues that had already arisen with the Soviet Union. The following April at San Francisco, Nelson worked successfully with the Latin American delegations, but was also the central figure in

two major controversies arising from his insistence upon including
Juan Perón's Argentina in the U.N. and broadening the reference to
"regional arrangements" in the U.N. Charter so as to include the Act
of Chapultepec (and, incidentally, also making NATO possible later
on). Nelson's aggressive performance resulted in his ouster from the
State Department later in 1945.[6]

During this period, a recrudescence of isolationism was stopped
by the adoption of a nonpartisan approach to foreign policy through
the careful wooing of Arthur Vandenberg, the ranking Republican on
the Senate Foreign Relations Committee. He became a strong advocate of international action, and as a result, approval of the U.N.
Charter was voted overwhelmingly by the Senate on July 28, 1945.[7]

The pace of events and JDR's Washington experience naturally led
him to ponder what role he might play in the postwar world. As his
diary notes make clear, his world view at the time was realistic, so
much so that one might regard it as pessimistic were it not for his
tendency to see every problem as a challenge—to say nothing of the
fact that events turned out even worse than he feared.

He saw a world so filled with vast and complex problems "that one
has concern as to whether the statesmen of the world are up to coping
with them." There could not be "much idea of relaxing or settling
back to the 'good old days' "—future problems "will be more difficult
of solution than those of the war years." Development of the U.N.
"offers real promise," he wrote, but it will be "a long, slow pull"
before it can "effectively handle critical world problems . . . once the
war is over, each country will tend to fight for its own interests and
advancement. No longer will there be the ties of a common enemy
and the forces of patriotism and self-sacrifice."

He went on: "In the new postwar world Russia will be a tremendously important factor and it is essential that our relationship with
her be on a sound basis." But this would be made difficult by
competition, self-interest, and "the underlying complication of the
basic differences between ideologies." On the American side, the
world situation will make "political-military" affairs continuously
urgent and will require the military and the State Department to work
together in hammering out U.S. policy for the next twenty-five or fifty
years.

He wondered about the ability of the U.S. government to meet
those difficulties and found the prospect "not too encouraging." This

was no reflex of distrust toward government as such. He spoke of the educational value of time spent in government service and of his new sense of the need to involve government in the solving of many modern problems. Rather, his worry stemmed from the difficulty of attracting able people to government service. Low salaries, bureaucratic inertia, and uncertain tenure in the higher positions owing to politics were so many barriers to recruiting the ablest:

. . . unless a few people in Government are willing to take the initiative, to "risk sticking their necks out" and to be prepared to do a considerable amount of imaginative follow-up work, not much of a positive, constructive nature gets done. So many career men in Government service, including Army and Navy, just coast along, avoiding trouble and issues, and accepting everything that their superiors tell them, it makes it awfully hard for the few who want to initiate action and have to buck the tide of inertia to get results.

In particular, JDR was concerned about "the weakness of the State Department," which he found "woefully lacking" in men of real talent and stature. He saw State as being without any conception of "a long-range foreign policy" other than as a vague generality. The department merely improvised as each new problem arose.[8] And he expressed the fear that this was true in other parts of the government's activity and responsibility as well: "The only hope for the future in this country, as I see it, is for outstanding younger men to make a career of government."

Given the "weakness in our national government" and his assessment of the future, JDR's conclusion was perhaps inevitable—that the country "is going to need every bit of available creative thinking and intelligent leadership to carry it successfully through the period ahead." Hence, any private agency that could help the government carry its enormous burden is "under obligation to do so." It followed that the Rockefeller Foundation, being one of the "relatively few private agencies or organizations which has the resources, initiative and imaginative leadership," should "be helpful in times such as these."

JDR thought it imperative that the Foundation undertake a basic review of its programs so as to find such ways to "be helpful." As for himself, he resolved to cut down the number of his board memberships and concentrate on the Foundation, Colonial Williamsburg, and the General Education Board. The review by the Foundation would help him in reviewing his own activities. For the present, he would give mind and energy to two general subjects: "One, that of population problems, and the other the fostering of a better understanding and appreciation of democracy in this country."

The concern about population was "new" only in the sense that JDR now saw it as something larger: "a logical broadening of my interest in the birth control problem. . . . Future world stability," he believed, was directly linked to population. And: "I have come to the conclusion that if I am to make a contribution in international affairs it must be through specialization in some one international problem."

For years, as we saw, JDR had thought about the possible educational use of Colonial Williamsburg: could it not be helpful in teaching American history and promoting democratic ideals and values? The political trends of the 1930s throughout the world had reinforced this surmise, and now, after a war for freedom, the opportunity and the need seemed greater than ever before:

> As to the democracy interest, for a long time I have felt that the approach of the average American towards different ideologies of government was very negative in character. He is against militarism, totalitarism [sic], communism, Nazism, etc. but is not really for democracy or anything else. It would seem to me that if there were a positive interest in and support for democracy that we could stop worrying about the other side of the problem. My hope and thought would be to help develop this interest through Williamsburg. I feel that it would be impossible to sell democracy as such but that Williamsburg could be used to dramatize it in a way that would have appeal.

Right after V-E Day, JDR met with Nelson and Laurance in Washington to talk about the postwar directions each would take. The three brothers agreed to act "as if the slate was clean," with each to decide about his own interests and how he could be "most useful and effective. Then, having determined this, we can divide up the family's prewar interests and responsibilities which are of a continuing nature—Rockefeller Center, Williamsburg, The Foundation, The Institute, etc." JDR told his brothers about his own inclinations.

Later in 1945, JDR discussed his pair of choices in a series of meetings with his father, chiefly to see if his special interest in Williamsburg could be pursued without interfering with Junior's "pleasure and enjoyment of the restoration." That they agreed is shown by a letter from Junior saying he "appreciated greatly your coming to talk with me about your plans for the future. Since the war has made such a definite break in what you were doing, I think you are wise to start again with a clean slate. I am deeply gratified that the two things you are most interested to take up again are the Foundation and the Restoration."[9]

JDR had enough "points" to get released from the Navy, provided his job was no longer essential. Most of the action had now gone to General MacArthur's occupation headquarters in Tokyo and JDR felt he could be more valuable in civilian life. Forrestal, secretary of the navy, offered him a post in the administration of the island trust territories in the Pacific, which JDR declined. He did agree to serve as a consultant after his discharge on October 10 to help establish a political-military affairs staff within the Office of the Chief of Naval Operations. With this done, JDR was home by mid-December. Blanchette had returned to New York in September with the children to enroll them in school.

Even before his discharge, JDR had seen signs that making any significant changes in the Foundation's program was not going to be easy. The officers were apparently content with things as they stood. Toward the end of 1944, Raymond Fosdick had circulated to the trustees a document entitled "Report on Future Work," which was a compilation of views from the directors of the five divisions. To deal with "the types of opportunity that will confront us when the war is over," the officers were consistent in advocating the continuation, with minor refinements, of the existing programs. They recommended the extension of research in medicine, the natural sciences, economics, and experimental biology.[10]

Meeting Fosdick in Washington early in 1945, JDR demurred at these conclusions and urged Fosdick to initiate a review of the entire effort at the trustees' meeting of April 4–5. Fosdick later reported:

> Your third point which you made to me in Washington in regard to a study of the whole program of the Foundation—perhaps by a committee of the trustees aided by outsiders—was not considered at any great length. I think the Trustees felt that the present programs were fairly adequate, and they seemed to doubt whether a study at this time would be particularly fruitful. Later on when the present emergency is over and we are operating on a more or less normal routine, I should think that the question might be raised again.[11]

Within six months, the "present emergency" was over and the question of a review was raised again, this time by JDR in person at the annual meeting of the trustees in Williamsburg in December. He had spoken about the idea with half a dozen trustees and he presented his recommendation with a note of urgency. The board approved creation of the Program Review Committee with instructions to report its findings at the next annual meeting in December 1946. The chairman, Walter Stewart, appointed four members—himself, JDR, Chester Barnard, and William I. Myers, dean of the New York State College of Agriculture at Cornell. Fosdick, the president of the Foundation, would meet with the group occasionally. Barnard, president of New Jersey Bell Telephone, was named chairman of the committee.

Pleased with this accomplishment, JDR took Blanchette on a "long anticipated postwar vacation," a six-week trip divided between Arizona and a tour of Mexico, in the company of brother David and his wife, Peggy. Back in New York in February, JDR and David joined Nelson and Laurance in the postwar "invasion" of Room 5600 by the Rockefeller brothers. Only Winthrop, who was touring Army hospitals on special assignment, remained in government service. The staid family office was suddenly filled with restless energy as the four brothers jockeyed for office space, assembled staffs, worked hard on cooperative endeavors, and resumed the development of their own distinctive careers. It was an exciting time for them, but a somewhat puzzling and difficult one for their father and the office staff.

The implicit message for Junior was "Step aside and let our generation take over." Even the "baby" of the family, David, turned thirty in 1945—and Junior had passed the age of seventy. All the old retainers, those who had been with Junior since the 1920s or before, had retired or were on the verge of doing so. The key figures now were those of middling seniority, such as Arthur Packard, Barton Turnbull, and the tax man, Philip Keebler. Then came the more recent employees whom Packard had brought in to strengthen his staff in anticipation of the return of the brothers. Dana Creel and Arthur Jones, hired before the war, had left for service and returned. Doris Goss had been hired during the war and Edgar B. Young was brought on board in 1946. Creel and Young were to serve in the family office until their retirement more than twenty-five years later, Creel as chief philanthropic executive and adviser and Young as JDR's first full-time staff aide.

No overt struggle for power divided the old guard and the new, although at times the frenetic activity generated by the brothers and the bittersweet nostalgia surrounding the figure of Junior and his aides may have given that impression. It was still Junior's office: he paid the bills. And he still controlled the bulk of the family wealth, including sole ownership of the two large and valuable properties, Rockefeller Center and the Pocantico estate. This is not to suggest that money was the only hold Junior had over his sons. His great reputation and experience meant that his counsel and approval were still of importance to them; each son regarded his father with his own particular mix of love, veneration, and fear.

In their collective endeavors, Nelson was the natural leader of the brothers by reason of his qualities, the stature he had achieved in Washington, and the fact that he was the most willing and skillful in manipulating the father. The parents tried to be fair to all five sons, but the special excitement and affection that Nelson kindled in them was still there as it had been when the brothers were children.

To make room for the brothers, the Rockefeller Brothers Fund moved down to the fifty-fifth floor. David staked out office space on the south side of Room 5600, with a view of Lower Manhattan, where he would be spending most of his time working at the Chase Bank. The other three were to be headquartered in Room 5600. JDR chose the northwest corner, next to the antique office in the southwest corner where Junior still reigned. JDR decided on a Colonial decor, with Early American furniture and the walls painted Williamsburg blue. The startling contrast was between Junior and JDR's period motifs and the domain of Nelson and Laurance at the east end of the floor. Their area was done with curving walls, blond wood paneling, and modern furniture, all reflecting the Art Deco style prevailing at Rockefeller Center itself.

The now-risen generation renewed with vigor the institution of "brothers' meetings." They gathered for a long session every other Saturday at Pocantico or at the Manhattan apartment of one or another of them. They were striving for harmonious relations, joint ventures, and cooperation of a kind that would leave each brother plenty of room to follow his particular bent. And they were set on coordinating their efforts to avoid duplication and unintended opposition on projects. Their plan was to jointly use the existing office staff, especially the enlarged philanthropic unit headed by Arthur Packard, and to avoid building up personal staffs except for very specific projects.

To be sure, each of the five had his wartime buddies. For JDR they were two Chicagoans who had worked for him in the Navy, Merrill Shepard and Frank Fowle, and he thought briefly of hiring them instead of relying entirely on the centralized Packard unit. But the Chicagoans formed their own law firm in their home city instead, and JDR gave no more thought to hiring his own people. Winthrop's wartime friend, Frank Newell of Arkansas, turned down an offer to come to New York, but later on he figured in the most important decision of Winthrop's life—his relocation to Arkansas. David's war-time friend was Warren Lindquist, whose long association with him at a later date was largely for real estate matters. Laurance had a specific need in mind almost immediately—setting up a new venture-capital enterprise—and he hired two of his wartime friends, Randolph Marston and T. F. (Teddy) Walkowicz, to run it.

Nelson was by far the most active in bringing in new staff. He had grown accustomed to having his own people around him, first "the Group" before the war and then the bright, eager staff from the heady days as Coordinator of Inter-American Affairs. Nelson sold his father and brothers on the need for a family public relations office, and to run it he recruited two people from the OCIAA, Frank Jamieson as chief and Martha Dalrymple as assistant. Jamieson had won a Pulitzer Prize for his coverage of the Lindbergh kidnapping trial. Like Louis Howe in relation to Franklin D. Roosevelt, Jamieson believed Nelson showed the quality of greatness and foresaw an important political future. Jamieson's office existed to serve the entire family, but his special interest was to further Nelson's career.

Nelson also maneuvered to retain John Lockwood, another OCIAA colleague, to succeed Thomas Debevoise as chief counsel for the family. Debevoise was coming in to the office only part-time and was fully retired by 1952. The choice of Lockwood might look like the overthrow of Junior's regime and total victory for Nelson, but Lockwood was well qualified, having served before the war as the Washington representative for the Milbank, Tweed law firm. In 1945 he returned to that firm in New York and was assigned to the Rockefeller office. By all accounts, he was scrupulously evenhanded in serving the brothers throughout his long association with the family.

Nelson did not stop with filling these jobs in the family office. As soon as he had left the Department of State, he was alive with grandiose plans for new activities in Latin America that he would mount himself as a private citizen, as we shall see in the next chapter. For this he retained a number of his former associates at the OCIAA.

To the extent that any planning had been done for the return of the brothers, it had been the work of Arthur Packard. It will be recalled that as early as 1936 Packard had developed a system for handling and coordinating the philanthropic interests of the five brothers, and had worked with them in 1940 when they established a partnership agreement and created the Rockefeller Brothers Fund. With the office staff reduced during the war, Packard had become the office mainstay, "carrying one hell of a load," in Dana Creel's words. He had become a complete perfectionist, "one of the best minds I ever knew," Creel said, but a man who "drove himself unmercifully."[12] To accommodate the new requirements that he foresaw, Packard enlarged his office and took on new functions, all with Junior's approval. Nelson, who was the first brother to return to the office, contributed his thoughts. He was fond of charts and diagrams, and there were many elaborate tables of Packard's emerging organization.

By the end of 1946, Packard had twenty people working for him, thirteen in the philanthropic office, five in a combined library and research service, including a political analyst, and two in an economic research and reporting unit. The researchers conducted studies of causes, organizations, or problems known to be of interest to one or another of the brothers. The philanthropic staff administered the Brothers Fund and the Sealantic Fund and handled the personal giving of the clan—Junior and Abby, the five brothers, and the wives of the four who were married. It supplied a "personnel service," including a card file on people of "civic or philanthropic interest to members of the family." In 1947 that file held more than seventeen thousand cards. Packard provided staff resources for family members in their roles as trustees, directors, or officers in civic or philanthropic corporations, which in 1947 numbered sixty-eight such commitments.[13]

The staff had in effect three things to do: protect members of the family from the enormous volume of solicitations that came to them; make the proper mix and number of contributions that would constitute the "citizenship giving" expected of any prominent and wealthy person; and work with each Rockefeller on the philanthropic activities of personal interest. The last, of course, was the most demanding of imagination. Working on the citizenship role was mildly interesting, and dealing with the unsolicited requests was a tremendous chore. In 1947, for example, Packard's office logged 5,719 appeals—an average of 22 each business day. Contributions were made to 663 applicants, 950 were ignored as being routine forms, and 4,106 were declined. A substantial portion of the more sizable citizenship gifts of the five brothers was handled through the Brothers Fund—an additional filter and a good coordinating device for contributions of common interest. From its inception in 1941 and for the next ten years, the fund operated solely on money contributed to it annually by the five brothers. It had no endowment. In the postwar years, its total gifts averaged about $250,000 a year, each brother contributing $50,000.

As we saw, JDR at first contemplated setting up his own staff, but as his activities were to be chiefly directed toward philanthropy rather than business, it occurred to him that he could consider the Packard staff as broadly his. He discussed this notion with Nelson in February 1946, saying that "before the war one of the main reasons I had so often felt ineffective and frustrated was because I was in so many things and didn't have any personal assistants to help me with them." His choice was between bringing in a group from the outside or satisfying his own needs from within:

Said that my own immediate preference would be to develop the relationship with Packard's group feeling that if I set up my own organization it would tend to duplicate and confuse Packard's picture as well as having certain other disadvantages. Said that my long range conception of my picture would be that Packard and his group, on the one hand, would be a part of my set-up and on the other, that they would continue to help all of us as a common office service. . . . Nelson was most understanding about the whole situation and agreed entirely.

JDR's view caused no difficulty with any of his brothers. As JDR reported, Nelson was relaxed about it. He had his own people and was fully engaged in promoting his Latin American programs and serving as president of Rockefeller Center. Likewise Laurance was occupied by his conservation and venture-capital work.[14] David was involved in advancing his career at the Chase Bank and in the redevelopment of Morningside Heights around Columbia University. When Winthrop left the Army, he returned to his job at Socony-Vacuum.

JDR's agenda was threefold: finishing the work of the Foundation's Program Review Committee, finding ways to become active in the population field, and moving ahead with his educational plans for Colonial Williamsburg. Of these, the first was the most immediate task.

22

✎

THE POSTWAR CONTEXT

A POWERFUL INFLUENCE in shaping the lives and careers of four of the Rockefeller brothers—as well as innumerable other prominent Americans of their generation—was the Cold War.[1] Historical interpretations of causes and motives vary among traditionalists, revisionists, and postrevisionists, but there can be no doubt of the intensity of emotion that the Cold War generated and its impact on national policies and the course of individual lives and careers.

The hope for peaceful collaboration among the great powers was quickly dispelled by the events of the immediate postwar years— Soviet policy in Eastern Europe and its zone of Germany, pressure on Greece and Turkey, the Czechoslovakian coup, the Berlin blockade, the Soviet Union's development of a nuclear capability, the collapse of the Nationalist Chinese. The American response was swift and varied. The "containment policy" was articulated in the Truman Doctrine of 1947. In the same year, the National Security Act created the unified Department of Defense, the Central Intelligence Agency, and the National Security Council. The Marshall Plan and the North Atlantic Treaty Organization came into existence. The overseas propaganda program was energetically revived by the Smith-Mundt Act of 1948. Large-scale economic assistance to Western Europe was followed by military assistance, authorized by the Mutual Defense Assistance Act of 1949, and the idea of technical assistance to developing nations, first broached by President Truman in "Point Four" of his inaugural address of January 1949. Appropriations for all the instruments of foreign policy rose sharply, and rearmament and new weapons development went on apace.

Laurance's Cold War involvement was not a matter of public leadership, but rather a manifestation of his entrepreneurial drive, especially in high-technology fields, which gave him ties with what

President Eisenhower later would call the "military-industrial complex." David's interest was the product of his career at Chase, where in time he would become one of the most recognizable figures in international banking and an inveterate globetrotter, on close terms with heads of state in a score of countries. In contrast, JDR and Nelson began pursuing their interest in world affairs at war's end, their thinking conditioned by wartime experience. As the Coordinator of Inter-American Affairs, Nelson had trained himself to find ways of neutralizing the enemy and building goodwill for the United States. JDR had immersed himself in the planning for postwar policy and had rubbed shoulders with the men who formed the core of the foreign policy establishment for the next generation.

The two brothers thus might be regarded as among the first of the cold warriors. The interesting fact is that their postwar thoughts and deeds were more positive and creative than the label suggests. Indeed, these acts and attitudes derived from prewar endeavors; they were reshaped or accentuated by the Cold War as much as they were produced by it. Both men were more interested in the underdeveloped countries than in the Soviet bloc, more bent on technical assistance and foreign aid than in confrontation. JDR was consistent in this; Nelson soon changed.

A common background, reinforced by independent experiences, explains their parallel thinking. They had grown up in a family where the support of foreign missionary societies was important. Now they were attempting what could be regarded as a secularized and modernized version of the old impulse. In fact, if one substitutes political goals for religious ones, there was much in the attitude of the two oldest Rockefeller brothers about foreign assistance that is reminiscent of the Laymen's Foreign Mission Inquiry, the fascinating and largely unsuccessful attempt to liberalize the overseas missions of Protestant denominations that Junior had supported in 1931.[2]

Although the two men initially shared the same outlook, they each worked at a vastly different pace and their paths soon diverged. In trying to pursue his interest in international affairs through the Foundation, the population field, and Colonial Williamsburg, JDR for years met with frustration or defeat. Nelson, meanwhile, was a man in constant motion, his motor revving at high speed. His course took him toward a stronger Cold War orientation, while JDR moved away from it.

John and Nelson both figured in the successful effort to secure the permanent home of the United Nations Organization in New York.

Laurance also was involved, and it was Junior who finally provided the wherewithal to make it possible. Early in 1946, Mayor William O'Dwyer appointed Nelson to a committee that tried to interest the U.N. in locating on the 1939 World's Fair grounds in Flushing Meadow, but this was declined. As an interim measure, Nelson had offered the use of the Center Theater to the U.N. This was not a workable idea in any case, and Junior was forced into the embarrassment of overruling his son because of booking commitments at the theater.

The U.N. finally set December 11, 1946, as the deadline for decision, the choice seemingly narrowed down to prospective sites in Philadelphia and San Francisco. Mayor O'Dwyer was still searching for a way to keep New York in the running, and tried to locate Nelson for a last-ditch effort. Parks Commissioner Robert Moses tracked him down in Texas where he was vacationing after attending Miguel Alemán's inauguration as president of Mexico. Nelson returned to New York to find Laurance working on a solution. The latter was prepared to give the 220-acre Rockwood Hall property to the U.N. Less than a year earlier, Junior had given Laurance this far northwest portion of the Pocantico estate. Laurance telephoned JDR at Williamsburg, where he was attending a Rockefeller Foundation board meeting, to suggest that JDR add Fieldwood Farm, or most of it, to the acreage for the U.N. Not happy with the thought of giving up the country estate he had owned only since 1940, JDR nevertheless agreed. He and Laurance also agreed to seek options on adjoining property for purchase and donation so as to further enlarge the site.

Moving in briskly to take over, Nelson telephoned his father to discuss this idea. Junior had already told Laurance and JDR that he was pleased with their generosity and that it was a "beautiful site," but that it got "awfully hot down by the river every summer and the delegates might not like that and the relative isolation from New York." The U.N. had already turned down Flushing Meadow because it was not in Manhattan; the proposed site was much farther away. Nelson gloomily agreed with his father that although this was "the best available site," it was not the "ideal site" and the U.N. would probably turn it down. Junior then wondered aloud whether a seventeen-acre property at Turtle Bay in Manhattan might be a possibility. This site, along the East River between 42nd and 48th streets, had been assembled by the Webb and Knapp real estate firm for a new office complex. The key figure was the well-known realtor

William Zeckendorf, who referred to the project as his "dream city."
Junior asked: could an accommodation be reached with Zeckendorf?

The date was December 10; the U.N. was to decide the next day.
Nelson went to work. His friend, Wally Harrison, was slated to be the
lead architect for the project. Harrison told Nelson that he thought the
right amount to offer was $8.5 million. The two men tracked Zecken-
dorf down in a nightclub at about 10:30 P.M. Harrison spread out a plat
of the area to explain the proposal. Zeckendorf said the land was
worth $25 million. But after more discussion, he penciled an option on
the plat: "$8.5 million—United Nations only. December 10 for 30
days." Nelson telephoned his father, who agreed to put up the
money—and the rest is history.[3]

The chief outlet for Nelson's energy in this period was pursuing his
Latin American interests. His vehicle was a new organization, the
American International Association for Economic and Social Development, a mouthful that inevitably became known simply as AIA. In
some respects, it was a miniaturized private-sector version of Nelson's
wartime OCIAA. But he had contemplated some such device even
before he went to Washington to sell the OCIAA idea and become its
head. So it was not surprising that immediately after he was eased out
of the State Department by the new secretary, James F. Byrnes, in
August 1945, Nelson assembled his advisers to plan the new effort. He
was imbued with the idea that American-style private enterprise and
philanthropy could work wonders in underdeveloped countries if
properly conceived and managed.

The advisers included the familiar faces of Jamieson, Lockwood,
and Harrison, and Nelson also recruited more of his former OCIAA
staff. Prominent among them was Berent Friele, a Norwegian who
was an expert on Brazil. Nelson's idea was that both philanthropic and
business activities could be combined in the same organization, with
the latter supporting the former. In his mind, a dividend would be a
demonstration of the value in the development process of private
enterprise and the market economy. Nelson thought this was important in a region where political trends could veer with alarming
rapidity toward the far left or far right. John Lockwood, as a lawyer,
advised strongly against such a combination, but Nelson went ahead
anyway. Within a year, he was forced to concede that Lockwood had
been right. Among other things, U.S. laws were not amenable.

Nelson's solution was to make AIA strictly a foundation and to create another organization, the International Basic Economy Corporation (IBEC), for business enterprises in Latin America.

Nelson's creative energy was nowhere more in evidence than in raising funds for his new organizations. He put up the first money himself, some $72,000. In September 1946, he wrote a flattering letter to Junior inviting his father to serve as chairman of AIA. Nelson characterized AIA as a "mobile, elastic unit like the Rockefeller Foundation in the early days when it was under your direction." Junior wrote an effusive response, calling Nelson's letter a "master-piece" and saying that he was "deeply touched," but declining the invitation on the grounds of age. He raised the possibility that the Foundation might contribute to some of the work Nelson had in mind for AIA.[4] Junior did, however, purchase $4 million in IBEC stock.

Nelson next turned to his brothers, expounding his grandiose ideas and strong enthusiasm over the prospects for AIA at a brothers' meeting late in 1946. JDR reported in his diary:

These two areas [AIA and IBEC] would take up the full attention of his group for some time to come. He indicated that he was interested in expanding later on to areas outside Latin America and that his objective really was China. He said that he was himself putting up one million dollars as capital and wondered if the four of us would together make up an equal amount. We said that we would. He indicated that things had gone so well in connection with the development program that he was now relatively less interested in getting back into politics.[5]

Nelson then capitalized on the anxieties of American oil execu-tives who were nervous over the Latin American tendency toward expropriation that had been initiated by Mexico in the late 1930s. President Rómulo Betancourt of Venezuela had imposed a 50 percent tax on oil company profits. Nelson's message to the oil executives, in effect, was: "If you want to keep the half of the profits still left to you, you'd be well advised to support the kind of activity that I'm proposing." The oil companies put up approximately half of the $14,524,000 that AIA spent in its twenty-two years of existence, and also invested $12 million in IBEC in return for a nonvoting bloc of stock.[6]

With Nelson as chairman and Wally Harrison as president, AIA proceeded to initiate scores of assistance projects, concentrating on Venezuela and Brazil. The work covered almost every conceivable kind of technical assistance that later would be undertaken by

American foreign aid programs in the 1950s and 1960s. In this respect, AIA was truly a pioneering organization. In fact, the one criticism in a Ford Foundation evaluation report was that AIA tended to spread itself too thin and move to new programs before existing ones were sufficiently advanced, perhaps owing to Nelson's own peripatetic style.[7]

After a shaky start and considerable loss of money, IBEC was reorganized to rid it of its "do good" origins and concentrate more on a businesslike approach in housing, supermarkets, fisheries, and agriculture. Twenty years later, it was on the Fortune 500 list with revenues in excess of $200 million annually and more than 130 subsidiaries in 33 countries.

During Nelson's early efforts to establish AIA and IBEC, JDR was engrossed in his attempt to redirect the Rockefeller Foundation. Arthur Packard helped him with ideas and drafts for the meetings of the Program Review Committee. One of JDR's main points resembled the battle cry that Fosdick had used to bring off the reorganizations of 1928 and 1934—the need to shift from research to applied knowledge. But it soon became clear that the two men understood those terms differently. Deeply worried by the ideological conflict between the superpowers and by the high incidence of poverty, overpopulation, and malnutrition around the world, JDR maintained that the Foundation should take a hand in these problems. He also urged that "the Foundation program be brought into greater overall focus." He thought there was little or no coordination among the programs of the five divisions (international health, medical sciences, natural sciences, social sciences, humanities), with the result that money was wasted on small grants having little or no relation to one another or to any broader objectives.

Indeed, it was the lack of such objectives that mainly bothered JDR. There should be stated "areas of concentration" that would lie between the extremely broad definition in the charter ("the well-being of mankind") and the detailed guidelines within each division. The intermediate "objectives" would give a sense of direction to the whole Foundation and provide the divisions with the means of coordinating their work. At a Review Committee meeting late in June 1946, he offered a draft of three "areas of concentration":

Human Behavior

Support will be given to those projects which promise to make a direct contribution to, or lay the necessary foundation for, an increased understanding of the factors which modify or control human behavior.

Our National Life

Projects of this character will be considered as they promise to make a direct and real contribution towards putting our own house in order; that is, as they make our democracy more effective, our economy more productive and stable and the lives of the people richer and fuller.

International Understanding

In the selection of projects under this heading the governing consideration will be the extent to which the project fosters and develops better relations between countries and makes for a world in which understanding and peace have a better chance to grow.

Most important, JDR wanted to see a shift away from grants to the great universities of Europe and the United States and toward programs in what he called "the backward areas of the world." There, as he told his colleagues, he envisioned a coordinated program across divisional lines:

I pointed out that today the United States was more or less in the position of being a wealthy neighbor in a poor community and that it so happened that the program of the Foundation was mainly concentrated in advanced countries of the world. While we do have certain activities in backward areas—particularly the I.H.D. [International Health Division] work—these are scattered and relatively hit and miss. What I proposed was that we should select a number of carefully selected backward areas and be prepared to render them assistance in health, agriculture, nutrition, and public education, not to mention population problems.[8]

JDR traveled abroad to gather ideas for the review. During the summer, he and Dean Myers spent five weeks in Europe as official representatives of the Foundation. Later they traveled to Mexico to inspect the agricultural research the Foundation itself had started in 1943.

Both trips made a lasting impression on JDR. After returning from Europe, he met with John J. McCloy, a new trustee of the Foundation, who had been assistant secretary of war under Stimson and was to become in 1949 high commissioner in Germany. JDR was seeking McCloy's opinion "as to whether the Foundation should take into account in its programming the basic ideological clash between totalitarianism and democracy which struck me so forcibly in

Europe." JDR said he was not thinking in negative terms such as a boycott of totalitarian states, but was merely asking what consideration the Foundation should give to "this new force in the world." He added that it was "hard not to think in terms of free thought and free expression" when considering the well-being of mankind. The two men discussed the question for a long time, agreeing that it was one that could not be ignored, but coming to no definite conclusions.

Another source of ideas for JDR was brother Nelson. The two frequently discussed their common belief that American private agencies could and should assist developing countries. Nelson wanted to see the Foundation model its program on his OCIAA and the new AIA, helping less-developed countries to deal with poverty, literacy, health, transportation, agriculture, industrialization, and technical training, as well as promoting free enterprise and democracy. JDR's only reservation was that the Foundation lacked resources on the scale that is available to government and should therefore limit its activities to the fields in which it and the General Education Board had particular expertise—health, agriculture, and education. Otherwise, he wrote in his diary, he "was very pleased to find there wasn't too much difference between the program that Nelson had developed in Washington and is so enthusiastic about and what it seemed to me might be practicable for the Rockefeller Foundation."

But soon JDR found himself encountering opposition within the Review Committee. There was polite interest when he first discussed his ideas at a June meeting, but Barnard and Stewart seemed preoccupied with budgetary and staffing matters. At later meetings, JDR found that he had an ally in Dean William Myers, but that Barnard and Stewart were strongly opposed, as was Fosdick when he attended a meeting in October 1946. At that meeting, JDR wrote, "Barnard almost walked out on us," remarking "that Bill [Myers] and I were utterly unrealistic. . . . From that moment on I realized that whatever was written in our report it wouldn't make too much of a difference if the President of an organization, the Chairman of the Board and the Chairman of the Program Review Committee are all fundamentally opposed to certain things being done."

It was indeed a formidable trio for JDR to fight—the chairman of the Institute for Advanced Study, a highly successful businessman, and Junior's closest adviser for many years. Barnard had achieved a reputation for innovative management practices at New Jersey Bell and for his book, *The Functions of the Executive*, which became a classic in the literature of administration.[9] He was also well known to

JDR's father through his service as president of the USO during World War II. The opposition of Fosdick hurt the most; he was a man JDR had always viewed with a respect bordering on reverence. For years JDR had played the subordinate to the wisdom and advice of the great man. Now, the first time that JDR stood up strongly for something, Fosdick was against him.

Before the war, JDR might have given up immediately, but this time he was determined to fight. To help draft his version of the report, he brought in John Lockwood. He sought the views of other trustees when opportunity arose. Uncle Winthrop was enthusiastic, but couldn't be present at the December meeting. John Foster Dulles approved of JDR's intention, but warned that he would face great resistance in trying to persuade the Foundation to come down "out of its ivory tower position." McCloy said it would mean "the Foundation would get its feet wet"; he agreed with the purpose, but as a new trustee he would have to reserve judgment until he heard other arguments.

JDR also tested his ideas on his father, who continued to attend meetings although he had retired, and was still influential. JDR wrote: "He seemed to be entirely with me on my key points although at times I am a little concerned that he somewhat lacks conviction in regard to them."

A few weeks before the annual meeting, Fosdick produced a compromise draft that picked up some of JDR's language, but emphasized the administrative matters that seemed so important to Stewart and Barnard. In his diary, JDR disgustedly dismissed these as "means," whereas the report should deal with "ends." But Packard and Lockwood said he got more than they had expected, and Junior counseled him not to submit a rival report, but to let the points come out in discussion.

Junior and Dulles led off by warmly supporting the first four points of the Fosdick draft, those of JDR's concern, although not stressing the "backward" areas as he would have wished. In due course, the report was adopted, but JDR was under no illusion as to what had happened. Innocuous language about emphasizing the application of knowledge, and the need for regional programs, cooperation among the divisions, and a program in the "field of moral and spiritual values" would not produce the sweeping changes he had advocated to initiate an activist effort dealing directly with postwar problems. He had been defeated and was left to ponder why.

With the benefit of hindsight, one can see a number of reasons. Although JDR had learned something about bureaucracy in the Navy, he failed to understand that the Foundation was subject to bureaucratic ailments as well. His proposals went against the grain of the existing structure and the vested interests of the division heads, all five of whom opposed the change, especially Warren Weaver of the Natural Sciences Division. These men had spent most of the previous decade building and refining their programs. Though open to suggestion and to new ideas from the right quarter, they were nevertheless jealous guardians of their domains. Moreover, so strongly entrenched were the divisions and the president that it was standard practice for the trustees to respond to their initiatives, not the reverse. JDR was considered out of order in pushing so hard for fundamental change.

He did avoid saying that everything the Foundation had done up to that point was somehow less than adequate, but his enthusiasm for a new direction implied it and this rubbed people the wrong way— not only Fosdick and the other officers, but some of the older trustees as well. They knew that any examination of the work done during the previous decade would show a truly extraordinary record of accomplishment. They were not about to make any quick or radical change in direction.

JDR was up against another traditional force as well—inertia. Although it could act with dispatch on occasion, the Foundation was in the main a deliberate and slow-moving body. The earlier reorganizations engineered by Fosdick had taken the better part of a decade. In Fosdick's mind, the surest way to make serious errors was to act precipitately; caution was his motto. As he expressed it in his book on the Foundation:

No one knows better than the writer, much of whose life has been spent with foundations, how profitless some of the research is, how wide the gap between expenditure and product, how often the promising project ends in nothing but intangible or insignificant generalities. Sometimes the fault lies with the research group or institution; just as often, perhaps, it reflects the faulty judgment or misguided enthusiasm of the foundation. One of the great temptations that face foundations is to seek for immediate returns, to judge their activities by standards of quickly maturing results, forgetting that in many fields growth is a slow process which requires a favorable soil. . . . Foundations are particularly exposed to the evils of immediacy, and too often their work is handicapped by what might be called the lack of a sense of depth in time.[10]

Even though JDR used Fosdick's prime argument of 1928 and 1934—the need to move from research to the application of knowledge—the two men clearly were working from different perspectives, priorities, and definitions. JDR perhaps did not realize how galling it must have been for Fosdick to hear his own theme being uttered as if it were a new idea, particularly in view of the fact that he had made a genuine effort in the early 1930s to transform the Foundation's commitment in China from urban-based medicine to a rural-based program that would emphasize agricultural development. True, this had been prevented by instability in China and the outbreak of the Sino-Japanese War, and the Foundation had done little else to pick up on the agricultural experience of the General Education Board. But now the agricultural research program in Mexico had started. Fosdick had a hand in that, and he could certainly point to it as having great potential for the practical results of applying knowledge.

The idea for the program was born during a visit to Mexico by the U.S. secretary of agriculture and vice president–elect, Henry Wallace, in December 1940. He was there to attend the inauguration of Manuel Ávila Camacho as president of Mexico, and he stayed on for a month after the ceremony. During this time, he spoke with Camacho and other Mexican leaders about the sad state of Mexican agriculture and the failure to induce higher crop yields despite years of land reform and redistribution. Indirectly, the Mexicans were sounding out the American agricultural expert on the prospects for some help. Despite his own sympathies and President Roosevelt's "Good Neighbor" policy, Wallace knew that official U.S. government help to Mexico was probably not politically feasible, so strained were relations over the actions of Camacho's predecessor, Lázaro Cárdenas, in nationalizing American oil companies.

Back in Washington, Wallace took the trouble to tell Nelson Rockefeller about his conversations with Camacho. Nelson had then been in his Latin coordinator job in Washington for six months. He relayed the idea to Fosdick in New York with the thought that the Foundation might be interested in undertaking an agricultural project in Mexico. In February 1941, Fosdick came to Washington to discuss the idea with Wallace. The result was that later in the year a team of three experts was dispatched to Mexico to do a feasibility study. Their recommendation that the Foundation undertake a research program in Mexico, focusing on soil management, introduction of improved varieties of corn and wheat, control of plant diseases, and improvement of breeds of animals and poultry, was adopted by the board in

December 1941. The next year was spent in negotiating an agreement with the Mexican Department of Agriculture for a pilot program and in searching for a man to head it. The man chosen was J. George Harrar, a young plant pathologist who had had field experience in Latin America. In 1943 Harrar moved to Mexico to begin the program.[11]

Up to this point, the Foundation had always given grants to others to carry out programs; the Mexican project marked the first instance in which the Foundation operated one directly with its own staff. In due course, the program was to grow and spread and become a phenomenal success, the primary agent in fostering the famous "green revolution" in many parts of the underdeveloped world.

But in 1946, when JDR was pressing the Foundation to engage in multidisciplinary projects, concentrate on applied knowledge, and focus on the underdeveloped world, the Mexican agricultural project was in its infancy—new, small, and with an unknown potential. JDR approved of it heartily, but it represented only a tiny portion of the Foundation's expenditures. He saw the great bulk of the Foundation's efforts going into the same fields as before.

Indeed, Fosdick saw the greatest need in Europe. Acutely aware of the limits of the Foundation's resources in the face of vast postwar problems, his first aim was to help rebuild the war-ravaged scientific institutions of Europe that the Foundation had long supported, not to scatter direct action programs in the "backward" countries as JDR wished to do. Even for Europe, he wrote in his 1946 annual report, "private funds are utterly inadequate in meeting the situation."

Apart from these reasons for the officers' opposition, JDR suffered from another handicap in relation to the board as a whole. He had been on leave of absence and had not attended board meetings for four years. Although he turned forty years of age in 1946 and had been a trustee for seventeen years, he seemed almost like a new member—the only one born in the twentieth century—so that to some of his colleagues his ideas were signs of youthful impetuosity. He was also the only member who lacked independent stature in business, government, the professions, or academia. He was on the board because his name was Rockefeller—JDR was still learning the painful lesson that his presence would not mean much more than that until he achieved independent authority.

At this stage, it is probably not correct to read JDR's attempt to influence the Foundation's policy as a quest for personal control; he was simply motivated by deep conviction. In any case, the Rockefeller

Foundation had long since become an institution with a life of its own, not susceptible to control by any one person. Junior's influence had been due to unique historical circumstances and was not transferable to anyone, including his oldest son. Rockefeller influence had in fact steadily waned as Junior had taken steps to substitute due process for personal direction. We have seen how Junior learned his lesson after the criticism of the hiring of Mackenzie King by the Foundation and how that had made him determined to play an "arm's length" role. The bruising experience of Jerome Greene's criticism of JDR had been another such incident, and Fosdick had explicitly spoken to Junior about the change in his role when he assumed the presidency of the Foundation in 1936, meaning that henceforth he could not be an adviser to Junior in quite the same intimate way he had before.

The sensitivity of the board and staff to any undue family influence, real or imagined, was a subtle force, but a powerful one. Junior was the only member of the family who understood this in 1946, having deliberately done much to bring it about. JDR was still learning it. He would experience that sensitivity again before coming fully to understand it and emerge as the leader of the Foundation, acting with great circumspection as his father had done, and with extraordinary skill. Ironically, his brothers never understood the dynamics involved, to the point that in later years several of them would regard JDR as weak and ineffectual, as having "given away" the Foundation.

For JDR the 1946 experience had been sobering. At this stage of his career, he was not always a tactful person, and he had an instinctive distaste for political maneuvering. On the rare occasions when he employed it, as when he went after a new assignment in the Navy, he always had a fit of conscience afterward. In trying to change the direction of the Foundation, he had made the mistake of the true believer—he was so passionate and certain about what he believed in that he assumed others would see how completely right his ideas were. As a result, he neglected the realities of how to achieve his goal. All he could do now was to accept what had happened and gradually work to build his own stature and influence. He had one strong ally in Dean Myers and had aroused some support in others. He had become chairman of the nominating committee, which meant that he would have some say about who came on the board and who would become president when Fosdick retired in 1948. Beyond that he would have to reconsider whether the Foundation ought to play as central a role in his life as he had counted on, and whether he might try to achieve some of his objectives in other ways.

In the next stage of their respective efforts to play a significant part in international affairs, Nelson and JDR both met with frustration. For Nelson it seemed at first as if he might repeat his remarkable feat of proposing the OCIAA to President Roosevelt and then becoming its head. This time AIA provided the direct inspiration for the Point Four program that President Truman announced in his inaugural address of January 1949, the one memorable portion of the speech. This last-minute improvisation was the work of Ben Hardy of the State Department and Clark Clifford, one of Truman's prominent advisers. Hardy had worked in the press division of OCIAA for Nelson and had stayed in touch with his former mentor's activities in Latin America. Thanks to this experience, he drafted a section for the president's speech proposing a program of sharing American "know-how" with underdeveloped countries to "help raise living standards, encourage worldwide prosperity and peace, and provide an antidote to the spread of Communism."[12] The State Department higher-ups dropped this material from the draft, but when Truman complained that his speech "lacked punch" Clifford remembered what Hardy had written and showed it to the president.

Nelson was as surprised as the State Department leadership when Truman enunciated his "bold, new program." He immediately wrote an enthusiastic letter to Truman and everyone else he could think of and testified several times before congressional committees in support of authorizing legislation. Nelson was pushing the idea of an aid agency that would be independent of the State Department. Legislation was slow in coming, but late in 1950 an International Development Act was passed by Congress providing limited authority for the State Department and creating an advisory board to propose plans for further development of overseas assistance.

As a reward for Nelson's efforts, Truman appointed him chairman of the fourteen-member board, thus ending for Nelson a four-year absence from Washington. Meanwhile, the president had established the Technical Cooperation Administration (TCA) within the State Department. Nelson's group worked for five months on a far-sighted report, entitled "Partners in Progress," which proposed a foreign aid agency and a comprehensive program. His best efforts to sell the report to Secretary of State Dean Acheson and others were unavailing. The concept was too ambitious for the Truman administration, by that time preoccupied with the Korean War. Also opposed to Nelson's report was W. Averell Harriman, who did not want to see a new agency that would take over his Economic Cooperation Administration (ECA). The result was that American foreign assistance continued to be split among at least three agencies (ECA, TCA, and the Mutual Security Agency). Finally giving up, Nelson resigned from the Truman administration for the second time. On his last day in Washington, he ran into Harriman on the steps of the State Department. Despite the fact that they had been opposed, the two men shook hands cordially. It was not to be their last encounter.

JDR, meanwhile, was patiently learning as much as he could about the international scene and awaiting the next step in what he now knew would be a long-term effort to reshape the Rockefeller Foundation. He met scores of influential people and became well informed through study trips abroad—to Europe in 1946, the Far East in 1947, and Africa in 1948, nearly two months on each continent. The careful planning, exhausting itineraries, and high-level briefings can be seen in JDR's diary. In addition, he took several shorter trips to Mexico, Venezuela, and Colombia as a trustee of the Foundation and AIA.

If he had any doubts about the existence of a Cold War, they disappeared after his meetings with high-ranking American envoys, newsmen, and leaders in Germany, France, and England. Traveling with Arthur Packard to the Far East in 1947, JDR came away with an accurate impression of Nationalist China in fatal difficulty, South Korea looming as a "trouble spot," and Japan's sudden emergence as the best hope for a solid anchor in the region. In Nanking with Chiang Kai-shek, he observed: "The Generalissimo was on the tall side for a Chinese, thin, erect, wore a simple uniform, moved slowly, had a nice face, but all the time seemed far away, or maybe I should say out of reach"—no opportunity to talk about substantive issues. JDR was told afterward by the minister of health that the visit gave Chiang "a few pleasant moments among all his worries and problems."

In Seoul, Lieutenant General John R. Hodge, commander of the U.S. forces, described the dilemma of South Korea: if the United States pulled out, the entire peninsula would be taken over by the North Koreans being trained by the Russians. If the United States stayed, Syngman Rhee would run a right-wing dictatorship in South Korea. In Tokyo JDR found General Douglas MacArthur extremely bullish on the future of Japan, asserting that its economy could be self-supporting within a few years and that democracy had been "firmly established." On the latter point, MacArthur said the Japanese were "like twelve-year-olds—adaptable and willing to learn. Germans, on the other hand, [are] like forty-five year-old grownups—too late to change them." MacArthur called the Japanese "the key to the future of the Orient" and "the outstanding race of the Far East." He said China was too divided to assume leadership. JDR recorded MacArthur's further thoughts:

We completely missed the boat in regard to China. Trying to bring the Communists and the National Government together and at the same time reform the National Government an impossible task. Now a year has gone by and the National forces so weakened that there is a real question as to whether or not it will be possible for them to defeat the Communists. The question of reforming the National Government must be treated separately and taken up only after the Communists have been defeated. . . . The State Department seems not to have appreciated the importance of the Far East in the world picture today. . . .

MacArthur was very clear about where he stood in regard to the Soviet Union: "There is a life and death struggle going on between democracy and Communism. U.S. should face realities of situation and fight it on every front even though cannot be certain democracy best form of government. Otherwise we will wake up some morning and find that we have lost out." JDR did not explain or probe MacArthur's remark about not being certain of democracy.

It was on this Far Eastern trip that JDR got the greatest scare of his life. He and Packard were traveling from Seoul to Tokyo on a Northwest Airlines DC-4. The flight was calm and smooth: "As the sun went down the sky to the south was beautiful and a rainbow formed near Mount Fuji. . . . Then the trouble started." Only twenty minutes from the Tokyo airport a typhoon struck, and the plane tossed helplessly for an hour in pitch blackness. Finally, the pilot managed to land safely, and JDR talked with him afterward:

The pilot was in his shirt sleeves and wringing wet with sweat pouring down his face. He said that in all his experience that was the worst flying he had been through. . . . I don't know when I have felt so warmly towards some one as I did to him after we landed. Somehow the experience brought all of us in the plane close together—there were seven of us including the Philippine hostess. She and I were practically holding hands at the end we were so relieved and grateful. A feeling of well-being swept over us after we landed.

One of JDR's main purposes on his trips was to ascertain the current status of the population problem. Throughout the Far East and in some areas of Africa, his observations and interviews yielded ample confirmation of his deep concern: rapid population growth was posing a threat to standards of living and possibilities for progress. After his return from Africa, JDR talked to State Department officials for two hours to present his findings. The senior person present was George Kennan, chairman of the Policy Planning Board. JDR then went to the White House to congratulate President Truman on his recent election ("a triumph of personal courage over seemingly overwhelming odds") and brief him about Africa. Truman was interested in JDR's analyses, and, according to JDR, agreed that "the population problem was the key long range problem of the world today."

On the first of his visits to inspect the Rockefeller Foundation's agricultural program in Mexico, in 1946, JDR noted in his listing of George Harrar's staff one "N. E. Borland," a plant pathologist. This was Norman E. Borlaug, who later won the Nobel Peace Prize for his work in the "green revolution" and the development of the "miracle" strains of wheat and rice. JDR was seeing the other side of the coin—the possibility of increasing agricultural yields to feed increasing numbers of people. Later, the Harrar program was extended to Colombia, which JDR visited in 1951 with Dean Myers and another Foundation trustee, Dr. Thomas Parran. Harrar spoke of a "human ecology approach" in developing societies; it would include, besides agricultural improvement, health, nutrition, social studies, education, and population. JDR noted: "Was very happy at the outcome of the conversation as it was so much along the lines of my own thinking." JDR made a mental note that Harrar might be a good candidate for the presidency of the Foundation, once he had come "to grow a bit more in stature."

JDR was amazed at "the respect and prestige the Foundation has" in Mexico and Colombia. The Colombian minister of agriculture "was pressing the RF to assume responsibility for reorganizing his ministry—he wanted Harrar to do it personally."

At home during these years, JDR's calendar was filled with engagements linked to his interest in foreign affairs—programs at the Council on Foreign Relations and the Foreign Policy Association, conferences at the State Department and the American Assembly of Columbia University, standing in for his father at the cornerstone-laying for the new U.N. Headquarters, meeting foreign dignitaries, and banquet after banquet, at which he might sit next to the Shah of Iran on one occasion and Haile Selassie of Ethiopia on another. He came to know the area experts, including the "China hands" who would be pilloried during the McCarthy years for the "loss" of China—men such as John Carter Vincent and Owen Lattimore, whom JDR praised.

In short, he had become a ranking member of the "leadership group in America [to use the words of Henry Kissinger] that had won the battle against isolationism in the 1940s and sustained a responsible American involvement in the world throughout the postwar period"; the group whose "pre-eminent task . . . is to contribute balanced judgment, long-term perspective and thoughtful analysis to public discussion."[13]

This group was not monolithic. Not all possessed inherited wealth, nor did they all come from the Northeast, go to Ivy League schools, hold identical views on issues, or belong to the same political party. Yet it was in some ways a fraternal group, all men of note through birth or achievement, who shared an intangible sense of responsibility for the conduct of foreign affairs in the interests of the United States. Notable among them was the stratum of "in-and-outers," so-called because they had a secure base in their New York law firms, banks, or brokerage houses, so that they could move back and forth with ease between civilian status and service in Washington when their name was called—men such as Robert Lovett, John J. McCloy, Dean Acheson, John Foster Dulles, C. Douglas Dillon.[14]

These foreign policy regulars generally took a hard line toward the Soviet Union, but they should not be confused with the right-wing reactionaries. After the First World War, there had been a "Red scare," but it was nothing compared to the hysteria unleashed by the fall of Nationalist China, after which a hard-line anti-Communist such as Dean Acheson could be attacked as "soft on Communism."

The intellectual center of the foreign policy establishment was the Council on Foreign Relations and its influential publication, *Foreign Affairs*. And the Rockefeller Foundation served as a kind of incubator, holding ground, and financial resource for the "establishment." This was not a conspiracy of any kind, as frequently alleged by both the right and the left, but a natural convergence. As the role of the United States in the world increased, the Foundation became its reflector as well as a medium for nurturing its leadership. Its location in New York, reputation for excellence, and prior involvement with international issues in both Europe and Asia, made the Foundation a logical center and sponsor of programs and thinking on world affairs.

In his effort to influence the Foundation's course, JDR had been puzzled by Fosdick's opposition to what, after all, was a direction that Fosdick had advocated since the mid-1920s. But soon after his 1946 defeat at the hands of Fosdick, Barnard, and Stewart, JDR saw signs that his views were having some effect—a plan for comprehensive Foundation programs in Germany and Crete and (as we shall shortly see) a mission to study the population problem in the Far East. Now important changes affecting the Foundation's future were imminent—the retirement of Fosdick and Stewart. JDR's colleagues on the nominating committee were Stewart, John Foster Dulles, and Henry Allen Moe, president of the Guggenheim Foundation.

Encouraging progress occurred in 1947 when JDR was able to steer through the committee his own top choices for the first two openings on the board. They were Henry P. Van Dusen, head of Union Theological Seminary, and John S. Dickey, who had become president of Dartmouth shortly after leaving Nelson's OCIAA. JDR held both candidates in extremely high regard. He had known "Pit" Van Dusen since Princeton days, and he thought so highly of Dickey that he made him his first choice for president of the Foundation. The nominating committee agreed, but, as JDR feared, Dickey was forced to decline because he had been at Dartmouth only two years and felt he could not leave.

Among other names under consideration for the presidency, Warren Weaver's had strong support, but JDR expressed reservations "not only because of his health but also because I felt it would be desirable to bring new blood into the Foundation at this time and, further, because I thought it was desirable to have a non-academic President in view of the fact that most of the Staff now was either scientific or academic."

The next man to arouse JDR's enthusiasm was Lester B. Pearson, under secretary for external affairs of Canada, who had been suggested by John Dickey. Dean Acheson and Robert Lovett were also on the short list, but JDR was strong for Pearson. He called on Secretary of State George C. Marshall to get his views on Pearson, and Marshall said his "offhand reaction was favorable . . . but he would like to discuss the matter with Dean Acheson." Marshall made a deep impression on JDR—"Can't think of a finer man to have as Secretary of State in these critical times." Soon a telegram came from Marshall saying he believed "the appointment would have a beneficial effect rather than the contrary."

JDR then went to Ottawa to see his father's old friend, Prime Minister Mackenzie King, to sound him out about Pearson. He told King that if Pearson were regarded as indispensable in Canada the matter would be dropped forthwith. King responded that he thought

Pearson was the ablest of the young men in the Canadian government, that he had a great future in the Liberal Party, but that he should make his own decision. In committee Dulles was opposed at first because Pearson was a "foreigner" and his presidency "might serve British interests," but he later went along with the other three. Not until October was Pearson sounded out. He considered the offer for several weeks and then declined. With the imminent retirement of Prime Minister King, he felt he could not leave Canada.[15]

Time was now pressing. By the normal timetable, the committee would make its recommendation to the annual meeting at Williamsburg in December so that the new president could take office the following June. Just before the meeting, Stewart and Moe pushed hard for a new candidate, Robert Calkins, former dean of the School of Business at Columbia University, who had become president of the General Education Board earlier in 1947. JDR resisted on the ground that he did not know Calkins well enough yet to make a judgment, and so the committee made no report. It so happened that this added to JDR's embarrassment over an incident that occurred after the meeting:

Was amazed and distressed to learn from Mr. Debevoise that there had been some feeling at Williamsburg that there was a family campaign under way to make me president of the Foundation. It seems that it developed from the fact that Nelson had mentioned to Moe at a Modern Museum meeting that [former] President Hopkins of Dartmouth had written Father stating that he thought that I was the person for the job. This coupled with two or three other casual remarks or occurrences led Stewart, Moe and Fosdick to the point where they really seemed very much concerned, sufficiently so that Fosdick asked to see Father on his return to New York. It was all, of course, most distressing to me, having particularly in mind the fact that I didn't know enough about Calkins to support Moe and Stewart in recommending him to the Board at the meeting last week—hence the nomination did not go through and it looked to them as if I were blocking it in terms of my own candidacy.

What hurt JDR the most was the knowledge that these men, especially Fosdick, could seriously believe that he and his father could be conspiring in any such campaign: "Knowing Father as these gentlemen do, not to mention myself, I don't see how the situation ever developed to the point it apparently did."

From that moment on, JDR found himself in a bind. Stewart began urging that the presidency be offered to Chester Barnard, with whom JDR had crossed swords during the Program Review battle. It was now difficult to be in opposition again. Moreover, a great deal of time had been lost in the unsuccessful pursuit of the two candidates he had favored. Stewart said he did not want to go to the April board meeting without a nominee; the staff was on edge, and morale would suffer from the delay. Dulles proposed Dean Rusk, but Stewart held that any man under forty-five could not have been adequately tested for a position of such importance. JDR again brought up the name of Robert Lovett, the current under secretary of state, but Dulles demurred.

Barnard had been proposed as an interim candidate; he had only a little over three years to go before retirement. This, JDR complained, would prevent any long-term program-planning or readjustment. He said nothing more, "realizing that the other members of the Committee knew that I had certain reservations about Mr. Barnard for the job, and I did not want the matter to get on a personal basis."

To break the stalemate, Stewart proposed a double recommendation—Barnard for president and Rusk for vice president, thus filling a position ("overall No. 2 man" as JDR described it) that had been authorized before the war, but had remained vacant. Moe and Dulles approved, so JDR went along "without any further comment." It turned out as JDR surmised—Rusk did not want to leave the State Department for a No. 2 position. The Barnard recommendation went forward and was approved by the board, and Rusk was made a trustee in 1950, with the strong likelihood that he would be the nominee to succeed Barnard.

JDR noted in his diary that there was no question about Barnard's experience and ability as an executive. The problem was that "he and I took opposite positions on what I considered to be fairly basic policy questions." He went on:

My other main concern would be the fact that Fosdick, Stewart and Barnard have been working so closely together in the Foundation picture and that there seems to have developed among them, probably unconsciously, an arm's length attitude towards the family. My own hope had been that it would be possible for me to make a real contribution to the work of the Foundation but this will be appreciably more difficult if this attitude continues. Finally, I would have reservations concerning Barnard's sometimes rather rough handling of individuals with whom he is in disagreement.

With Barnard as president, there would be little chance of policy changes in directions favored by JDR. But the results of the search for a new chairman to replace Stewart amounted to a step forward, as far as JDR was concerned. The nominee presented to the board in December 1949 was John Foster Dulles, and he took office the following June. No spontaneous boom occurred in favor of JDR for the chairmanship. Given the sensitivities aroused by Fosdick's suspicions two years earlier, JDR did not do any canvassing for himself. Although there was some support for him, as we shall see, the time was not yet ripe. Too many older trustees and staff were still on hand, and JDR had not yet passed Stewart's magic age of forty-five. Dulles was a natural choice: he had been a trustee since 1935, was a New Yorker, and, as senior partner of Sullivan and Cromwell, could make time for Foundation affairs. Most important was his prominence in the international field where the work of the Foundation was concentrating.[16]

Dulles and JDR had found how close they were on policy matters when Dulles and Stewart had engaged in an argument during the 1948 search for a president. Following Junior's advice, the Foundation was spending capital at a rate intended to give it a life of no more than fifteen or twenty years. Stewart voiced doubts about this course of action:

. . . Mr. Stewart said that he had been increasingly wondering as to whether these times did offer the Foundation particular opportunities for usefulness. He said he was inclined to feel that until peace was really restored in the world we should limit our program and possibly review the policy as to the use of capital. Mr. Dulles replied that this was a counsel of despair, that there was a head-on clash in the world between two fundamentally different ways of life and that as he saw it the Foundation was in a key position to assist in the strengthening of our way of life because of its unique position and prestige. The conversation was of particular interest to me because it brought out more clearly than ever before Mr. Stewart's feeling as to the Foundation in relation to the current world crisis. . . . it is obvious as to why we had the basic clash in our Program Review Committee.[17]

Of JDR's three postwar goals, he had met with nothing but frustration in one—the effort to redirect the Rockefeller Foundation. By 1950 he knew that it would still be important in his future, but not in the direct way he had counted on. As for the special plans he had in mind for Colonial Williamsburg, they were necessarily delayed because the first priority there was to catch up on the restoration work deferred during the war. His third goal was to become more involved and stimulate activity in the population field.

23

♨

POPULATION:
THE ELUSIVE REFORM

IN THE LATE 1940s, the population question presented a changing, confusing, and controversial picture. This was the time when JDR was struggling to find in it, or make of it, an intelligible pattern. Having reaffirmed at the war's end that population would be one of his major interests, he was now in touch with leaders in the field and trying to understand its exact relevance to the postwar world. In retrospect, one can see that a new perspective on the subject and a measure of coherence in it were emerging and that JDR was instrumental in the process. His work in the end made a marked difference, as well as affecting his life and career. But at the outset hardly any signs of progress could be seen.

Problems and opportunities were mired in the chaotic conditions and unhappy history of the field. It had its mysteries and taboos, its colorful characters, its major theories (half a dozen of them), its alliances and rivalries. For many decades, one of the strongest forces was nativist and racist; this permeated and very nearly poisoned the eugenics movement of the early 1900s and supplied the rationale for most of the immigration legislation in the United States. Simply put, white Anglo-Saxon Protestants became alarmed at the immigration of Jews, Southern Europeans, Irish, and Orientals, and at their fecundity once they had arrived.[1] The great success of Josiah Strong's *Our Country* (1885) crystallized this kind of thinking and produced a line of academic prophets—Homer Lea, who feared the "Yellow Peril"; Lothrop Stoddard, who glorified the Nordic race; and many others.[2] Strong's views infected Junior when he was a student at Brown. As a sophomore in 1894, he wrote an essay entitled "The Dangers to America Arising from Unrestricted Immigration" for a rhetoric course.

He held that the thousands of people arriving daily were "decidedly of the wrong class. They are chiefly the scum of foreign cities; the vagabond, the tramp, the pauper, and the indolent . . . ignorant and hardly better than beasts." Not only was this flood creating problems of disease, crime, and illiteracy in overcrowded cities, but it also tended toward anarchy:

Thus the power of government is passing by degrees from the hands of Americans, whose desire is to cherish and maintain the customs of their ancestors and preserve freedom, into the hands of foreigners who have no respect for our history or our laws, but whose purpose is to turn this land of liberty into a land of unbridled license.[3]

In voicing ideas so offensive to modern ears, Junior was parroting what native, upper-class Americans generally believed. His views were to change dramatically and almost at once. We saw in Chapter 2 the change in his views when he encountered the more enlightened ideas of a series of remarkable teachers in his upperclass years.[4] From them he learned that the causes of vice and poverty were to be found in economic and social conditions, rather than in ethnicity. From E. Benjamin Andrews, Junior learned about the somber demonstration of Malthus, not yet a century old, that population growth inevitably would outdistance the availability of food. Andrews believed that the factors that had held population in check were now disappearing and that disastrous results were imminent. He was, of course, wrong. Apart from immigration, the long-term trend for the American population growth rate was a slow decline, and it would be another half century before world conditions would lend some credibility to the Malthusian prediction.

Junior first was drawn to these issues out of a concern for the social evils so prevalent in New York City—prostitution, venereal disease, illegitimate births, illegal and dangerous abortions. To some, the answer was to halt immigration. To others, such as Anthony Comstock and his New York Society for the Suppression of Vice, the answer was a puritanical crackdown. Since 1873 the Comstock Laws had made illegal the use of the mails for such "obscene matter" as information about contraception as well as contraceptive devices themselves, which Comstock identified with abortion.[5] Although birth control was widely practiced with crude methods, it was a taboo subject in public except for such intrepid radicals as Emma Goldman.

We have seen how Junior's unwanted service as foreman of the White Slave Grand Jury led to his dogged commitment to push for reforms, and hence to creating the Bureau of Social Hygiene in 1913. Junior was moving beyond the simplistic views of the early vice crusaders, who sought to reform society by imposing on the lower classes their own narrow view of morality. They were grappling with symptoms rather than causes. They hoped to redeem the poor, hectoring them to emulate the rich, rather than discovering the links between social conditions and individual behavior.

For a number of years, Junior's policy was eclectic. He supported diverse organizations and methods simultaneously. And for a good reason: he instinctively recognized that questions of population and sexual behavior were extremely complex, interwoven with a congeries of other problems, and he saw that no one had sure knowledge of causal relations or cures. To find answers, one must cast the net wide.

This is why Junior gave money to the Eugenics Records Office and the American Eugenics Society. He was hedging his bets. The society had been formed in 1905, ostensibly as a respectable, scientific organization devoted to the study of heredity as the path to improving the human race. Given the prejudices of the time, it became the bastion of those who held the nativist point of view, most notably the patrician racist Madison Grant. Not until the 1920s did Junior withdraw his support. By that time, he had become convinced that the premise was wrong, a view reinforced by such advisers as Raymond Fosdick and Beardsley Ruml. Moreover, new and promising possibilities had emerged.

Perhaps the best known of these was the crusade led by Margaret Sanger, the daughter of an Irish stonecutter and quasi-socialist, one of eleven children, who at the age of thirty rebelled against her quiet life as a suburban wife and mother to take up first the cause of labor agitation and then birth control. After a flight to Europe to escape prosecution under the Comstock Laws, she returned to the United States to establish her first birth control clinic in 1916. With Sanger's founding of the American Birth Control League, her pressure to keep opening clinics, her ceaseless campaign to overturn repressive laws, her battles with the agents of law enforcement, her will to conquer, and her skill in getting public attention, one may say that the feminist and equal rights attitude to population problems had emerged. The date was 1920.

Sanger was out to free women from "biological slavery" by giving them control of their fertility. She was willing to go to jail if necessary, though she had moved away from her radical beginnings and become an excellent tactician, ready to compromise here and there in order to enlist the support of the medical profession and the well-to-do. In 1923 Sanger created the Birth Control Clinical Research Bureau to attempt to get data on fertility, and in 1929 established the National Committee on Federal Legislation for Birth Control. Besides bringing the term "birth control" fully into the modern lexicon, Sanger was a pioneer in fighting for women's rights and in providing direct social services.[6]

Medical endorsement of contraception was a necessity. But it could only succeed if mounted from within the profession. The prime mover in this labor was a contemporary of Sanger's, Dr. Robert L. Dickinson. He began as her critic, then was her rival, and finally her colleague. One of the three founders of the American Gynecological Society and its president in 1914, Dickinson began devoting his professional career to the study of human sexuality. Convinced that poor sexual adjustment was the major cause of family instability and that effective birth control methods were essential, Dickinson formed the Committee on Maternal Health in 1923. Its purpose was to undertake clinical research into contraception and related issues. But Dickinson's most enduring contributions were to help legitimize contraception and birth control among his fellow doctors and to lay the basis for modern sex education and marriage counseling.

Junior and the Bureau of Social Hygiene became steady supporters of all of these organizations created by Sanger and Dickinson. Raymond Fosdick in particular argued for their support, because "population constitutes one of the great perils of the future" and because these "organizations are doing their best to disseminate knowledge of contraceptive practices, as far as the present somewhat archaic laws allow them to go."[7] Staff work done by Katherine B. Davis of the BSH reinforced Fosdick's views and encouraged Junior to support them financially.

This association was continued by Arthur Packard when he joined the Rockefeller office in 1929 as philanthropic adviser. He pressed the same purpose on others of the family, writing to Abby, for example, about the Clinical Research Bureau:

> I do approve of this organization. . . . Undoubtedly, the Committee on Maternal Health is doing the best scientific work in the field, but this Clinical Research Bureau is doing the best work of its kind, which is of course clinical and therefore essential, practical and direct in its application.[8]

Under Packard's influence, JDR, Nelson, and their wives were all contributors to the cause of birth control before the end of the 1930s.[9]

In the late 1920s, an interesting character, who needed no financial help from the Rockefellers, entered the fray. He was Dr. Clarence J. Gamble, an heir to the Procter & Gamble fortune, the same man who had survived the crash of his airplane in 1922 when the pilot, JDR's summer companion and friend, Zenos Miller, was killed.[10] Concern about the high fertility rate of poor families had begun to lose its racist taint and was more delicately referred to as "differential fertility." It was the plight of the poor that interested Gamble. He believed that the primary need in birth control was developing effective contraceptives that they could understand and would use. It was imperative to reach the poor in remote rural parts and overcrowded slums where medical care was hard to come by. He devoted energy and funds to research, but was drawn more to action, particularly to encourage the manufacture and efficient distribution of contraceptives.[11]

Gradually, the entire field acquired a more scientific basis. Research, necessarily of a limited kind, was part of the efforts of Sanger, Dickinson, and Gamble. Junior and his aides were bent on going much deeper. An effective contraceptive usable by women of all backgrounds presupposed a major research effort into the complexities of the human reproductive system. From the early twenties and continuing for decades, most of the money for such research came from Rockefeller sources. At first, it was funneled mainly through the Bureau of Social Hygiene. After the bureau was terminated in 1934, support came chiefly from the Medical Sciences Division of the Foundation. For many years, this support flowed primarily to the National Research Council's Committee for Research into Problems of Sex, which "virtually paid for the development in American universities of endocrinology, the study of the body's internal system of hormonal regulation, a necessary first step in the understanding of human sexual physiology."[12] Foundation funds also supported research in mammalian biology, human physiology and anatomy, psychology, human heredity, and the pioneering studies of human sexual behavior by Dr. Alfred C. Kinsey of Indiana University.[13]

Yet another interesting character, one who was to be very important to JDR in later years, joined these pioneers in the late 1920s. Frederick Osborn was the son of the investment banker William Church Osborn and the nephew of Henry Fairfield Osborn, the great paleontologist and cofounder of the American Eugenics Society. Having been successful on Wall Street, Frederick Osborn fulfilled his ambition of retiring at forty to devote himself to science. He was interested in anthropology, population trends, and eugenics. For a time, he occupied the room next to Margaret Mead's on the top floor of the American Museum of Natural History, and later coauthored the book, *Dynamics of Population*, that helped to reorient the field. He set out to reform the American Eugenics Society and by the mid-thirties had succeeded in bringing in new leadership and ridding the society of its overtly racist biases.[14]

The Rockefeller and Osborn families had been acquainted since Senior's generation, and Junior, impressed by Frederick Osborn's work on the Hudson River Palisades Commission, asked him to join the board of the Rockefeller Institute. Naturally, JDR came to know Osborn, a man nineteen years his senior, and in April 1938:

> Had lunch with Mr. Frederick Osborn at the Century Club. He told me about his work in the fields of population and eugenics. It was all exceedingly interesting. Do feel that he is doing a good job and should be encouraged. His two fields tie in, of course, very directly with birth control. Told him to feel perfectly free to come to us any time he needed help.

Between the wars, the science of demography was being born and Osborn was one of the midwives. Among other things, he aided its development by helping to further the career of young Frank Notestein, a graduate in economics and statistics from Cornell. Notestein, like Osborn, was to prove an important person in JDR's future.

The beginnings of demography came with the application of statistics (which had been taught for several decades at leading American universities) to questions being asked about population growth and decline. In the 1930s, the major issue was the perception of declining population growth rates in western Europe and the United States, contrasted (by some) with the increasing population of the Far East. Two small foundations provided crucial early support for demographic studies. The newspaper entrepreneur, Edward Scripps, established the Scripps Foundation for Population Research because of his interest in population problems in the Far East. The Milbank Memorial Fund, set up to promote public health, established in 1928 a research division to probe into population questions, and Notestein was one of the young statisticians hired. Impressed by his early demographic studies, Osborn had Notestein in mind when he persuaded the Milbank Fund to help establish population studies in the academic world. This was analogous to Junior's attempt to establish industrial relations as a discipline—the assumption in each case being that a new field would not be generally accepted unless the top universities gave it room.

The first approach was made to Harvard University, but President James Bryant Conant declined. Both Osborn and Alfred Milbank being Princeton graduates, they were glad enough to turn to their alma mater. The result, in 1936, was a five-year grant from the Milbank Fund to set up an Office of Population Research at Princeton. Lodged in the newly created School of Public and International Affairs, the office had Frank Notestein as its head. It started small, with a $12,000 annual budget, one research assistant, and an annual postgraduate fellowship in demography. Notestein's leadership, the research done, the fellowships offered, and the publication of the *Population Index* (providing full bibliographic coverage since 1927) soon constituted a force in the development of demography.[15]

The new demographers quickly documented the decline of the American birth rate that had been going on since the early 1920s and now was below the replacement level for the first time. This fact took urgency away from the efforts to spread the practice of contraception and reinforced the eugenicists' belief that fertility should be increased among "fit" families. This situation caused dissension among the factions of the birth control movement. For some time, Margaret Sanger had dissociated herself from the American Birth Control League, which now had a conservative stance. With prodding by Clarence Gamble and reluctant consent by Sanger, the league and Sanger's Clinical Research Bureau were merged and reborn in 1939 as the Birth Control Federation of America.

One of the agents of the merger was D. Kenneth Rose, a professional fund-raising consultant, who became acting director of the new organization. As such, Rose was in a good position to effect the change in image he had strenuously argued for. He wanted to replace what he considered to be a negative term, "birth control," which was still confused with abortion, with a positive term, "family planning." Three years later, he convinced the membership of the merged organization to change the name from Birth Control Federation of America to Planned Parenthood Federation of America.

Margaret Sanger detested the term "family planning" and the concern with "image," but Rose's moves were undoubtedly effective. They dealt with the awkward element of semantics that afflicts the population field generally—witness the fact that there are hardly any alternatives to using the word "population" either alone or in conjunction with "field" or "studies" or "question" or "issue." "Population" denotes no clear-cut discipline but a wide range of studies, policies, and activities—demography, birth control, biological research, contraceptive research, immigration, migration, sex education, abortion, delivery of services, maternal and child health care, administration of programs, communications, and technical assistance. The increasing pace of biological research and the emergence of demography began to provide a scientific base to "population" and to make it clearer than ever that such terms as "birth control" and "family planning" should be understood as referring to only one branch of knowledge and action under a larger rubric—hence, "population field" or one of the variants noted above.

We can see this semantic transition in JDR's own words, comparing his 1934 letter to his father saying that he intended to devote himself to "the field of birth control" to his ruminations in 1945 about the postwar world in which he wrote that "the population field is a logical broadening of my interest in the birth control problem." The latter statement indicates that JDR was among the relatively few who began to see signs of what would become known within the next decade as the "population explosion." Demographers shifted their attention from declining birth rates in the United States to the remarkable growth in world population that was first perceived in about 1940. Public health measures had begun to take effect in less-developed countries around the world, a result, in part, of the work of the Rockefeller Foundation itself. People were living longer in these countries, giving them a greater chance to have large families and their children a better chance of surviving beyond infancy. And, less noticeable at first, the postwar "baby boom" was beginning in the Western countries.

JDR's early awareness, beyond a spontaneous interest, rested on two sources of information, one impressionistic and the other scientific. The first consisted of a growing volume of reports from the overseas staff of the Foundation's International Health Division. They perceived mounting evidence that success in eradicating disease was leading to population growth and worsening socioeconomic conditions in the less-developed countries. Increasingly, these men came to feel that the mandate of their division should be broadened to include studies and action in the population field. They may also have been preparing a defense against the growing sentiment within other elements of the Foundation that international health had been overemphasized for too long and needed to be cut back if not eliminated. The rising star was the agricultural program in Latin America. Its successes fitted in well with the view of many that population growth could be met adequately by increases in food supply.

The more scientific source of information was the work of demographers, which was steadily enlarging in scope and improving in sophistication. Prominent among them was Frank Notestein and his group at Princeton. During the war years, the office had done a series of demographic surveys of sectors of the world for the League of Nations' Economic, Financial and Transit Section, which had moved from Geneva to Princeton.[16] This led to Notestein's taking a leave of absence in 1946 to become the first head of the Population Division on the staff of the United Nations Secretariat. This office should not be confused with the Population Commission created by the U.N. Economic and Social Council in 1945. Proposed by the British and opposed by the Soviets, the commission became a political hotbed almost at once, in contrast to the Population Division, which was a quiet staff operation in New York City. The political caldron was stirred further by Julian Huxley, the first director-general of the U.N. Educational, Scientific and Cultural Organization, a friend of Margaret Sanger's and a population propagandist since 1926. In his second annual report, Huxley wrote: "Somehow or other population must be balanced against resources or civilization will perish. War is a less inevitable threat to civilization than is population increase."[17]

The battle lines were soon drawn within the U.N. The interest in population came mainly from Western Europeans and Americans. The Communist countries were opposed to any programs of action in the population field (other than those they undertook at home). The idea that population increase was a cause of socioeconomic problems ran counter to Marxist theory; the real culprit was capitalism. Catholic countries, especially those in Latin America, soon began manifesting opposition as well. There also was a division of opinion among the U.N. specialized agencies. The Food and Agriculture Organization believed that increasing food supply was the answer. The World Health Organization thought that any action in the population field properly belonged within its purview. With all this going on, there was no chance for anything except demographic studies being carried on by the U.N., and this Notestein and his small staff in New York were busy doing.

Back at Princeton in 1947, Notestein sponsored more international demographic studies, working with the leading scholars in the field—Kingsley Davis, Frederick Osborn, Clyde V. Kiser, Pascal Whelpton, Philip Hauser, Frank Lorimer, and two members of his own staff, Ansley J. Coale and Irene Taeuber. These studies began to document a rapid rate of growth in world population. But it would be a number of years before this and other work would make enough of an impact to stir Malthusian fears of a "population explosion" in the public mind.

Still another point of view impinging on the question emerged in the late 1940s, that of the conservationists. This was given worldwide scope by the rising worry in many quarters about the continued availability of natural resources and strategic materials. One manifestation of this was the Materials Policy Commission created by President Truman and chaired by William S. Paley of CBS. A concern prominent among conservationists had to do with the effect of rapid population growth on world resources, and this led to some dire pronouncements and extremist views. Examples include the writings of Julian Huxley and two books published in the 1940s, *The Road to Survival* by William Vogt and *Our Plundered Planet* by Fairfield Osborn.[18]

The new views of the late 1940s were promulgated by the demographers, the conservationists, the international health people, and the agriculturists. The earlier motives that had created the population field—race purity, resistance to immigration, linking vice to excess population—had faded, losing their validity. Even the feminist and equal rights point of view waned, though it never disappeared and reemerged as a powerful force several decades later. And the straightforward clinical approach to birth control and planned parenthood lacked dynamism.

In sorting his way through this confusing picture, JDR fastened on two objectives. The first was to find a way to stimulate more activity domestically in the birth control movement; the second was to persuade the Rockefeller Foundation to do something more about population questions on the international scene. Both presented a difficult challenge. A measure of this on the home front was the low level of JDR's personal giving to population causes in the late 1940s. He did not give more than $20,000 a year, usually to Planned Parenthood, although he was capable of giving much more. The reason was not lack of interest, but uncertainty as to what to do effectively. The conviction had grown among advocates of family planning that significant progress could not be made until a breakthrough in contraceptive technique occurred. The contraceptives then in wide use, the condom and the diaphragm, were regarded as not nearly good enough. Margaret Sanger made the point to JDR in 1947 when he first met the famous lady.

Arthur Packard brought in Margaret Sanger for a few minutes. Was very much interested to meet her having heard about her for so many years. She is a very charming person and seemed much younger than I had expected. She felt the real hope for advancing the birth control cause was the discovery of some form of contraceptive which would be so cheap and so simple that it would be available to all on a minimum education basis. If something such as a pill were found there would be no stopping the spread of its use.

About this time, JDR associated himself with an effort to step up the development of new contraceptive techniques. Kenneth Rose, by now the executive director of Planned Parenthood, conceived the idea of reviving the National Committee on Maternal Health, which had become moribund because of Dr. Dickinson's absence due to failing health. The purpose was to make a concerted effort in contraceptive research. Rose, Notestein, and Osborn jointly approached JDR about serving with them on a reconstituted board. JDR, at first uncertain, agreed to do it and then departed on his Far Eastern tour with Arthur Packard. What he observed on that trip so strongly reinforced his concern about population growth that he was considerably more sanguine about the work of the committee when he attended the first meeting at Princeton in November. The prospects looked good, because the National Research Council had appointed a number of scientists to a new Committee on Human Reproduction to advise both Planned Parenthood and the National Committee on Maternal Health in giving grants for research. The next two years were spent in an unsuccessful effort to raise sufficient funds for the research. In 1949 Planned Parenthood withdrew from the project, and a few months later JDR, Osborn, and Notestein all resigned, relinquishing the National Committee to its former moribund state.

Despite the lack of progress, the involvement had been an important step for JDR. He had publicly associated himself with contraception and birth control, a first for a Rockefeller. Junior's support had always been channeled through one or another organization or, when given directly, had been anonymous; he had never actually joined a body concerned with population issues. In December 1947, JDR decided to "go public" on the problem: he discussed it explicitly for the first time at a meeting of the Rockefeller Foundation.

When the International Health Division program was presented I raised the question of its relationship to the population problem in over-populated areas and suggested the desirability of the Officers giving thought to how the Foundation might be helpful in regard to the population problem of the world. The idea was discussed fairly fully and received support from other Trustees. I pointed out how my trip to the Far East made me realize how critical was the population problem in that area of the world.

To reinforce this initial response, JDR sought out Raymond Fosdick soon after the meeting to propose that "a topnotch population man" and a member of the International Health Division staff be sent to the Far East to undertake a survey of the related matters of health and population. Fosdick "seemed prepared to go along," so JDR wasted no time in identifying Frank Notestein as his "topnotch" man on population. To gain Notestein's release, JDR talked to Harold Dodds, president of Princeton and a fellow trustee at the Foundation. With this accomplished, Fosdick had no choice but to appoint *his* man—Marshall Balfour, a public health graduate from Johns Hopkins, who was the Health Division's representative in the Far East, now stationed in India.

In those days, it was still necessary to get official permission to travel to the occupied countries, so JDR went to the Pentagon to ask the new under secretary of war, General William Draper, for approval of what came to be known, to Notestein's annoyance, as "the Balfour mission." Unknown to JDR at the time, he was meeting a man who held pronounced views indeed on population, and would soon be possibly the most vocal of all the proponents of population programs. Draper was enthusiastic about the Balfour mission and promised permission for travel to Japan and Korea, subject to General MacArthur's approval.

The trip was delayed until late 1948 because of Notestein's duties at Princeton. Two more persons were added to the group—Roger Evans of the Foundation's Social Sciences Division and Irene Taeuber of Notestein's office. They toured six Far Eastern countries for three months, meeting with scores of American and local officials and experts. They submitted their report a year later under the title *Public Health and Demography in the Far East*. It supported the view that population growth in the region was an alarming fact and made the case for coordinating efforts toward fertility reduction, public health, education, and assistance in agricultural and industrial development.

Although the report was thus cast in the "human ecology" language that had become something of a catchphrase at the Foundation, there was no mistaking its note of urgency and emphasis on the dangers of rampant growth. Unless means were applied to curb the birth rate, growing numbers would cancel progress in development and keep the region "in a stable equilibrium of poverty and ill health." Of all the problems of the Far East, it said, those of human fertility "are at once the most difficult and important."[19]

JDR was elated by the Balfour mission and its strong report. There had been other encouraging signs since his earlier effort to redirect Foundation policies and programs. A plan had been drawn up for a program in Germany, based on a comprehensive approach across divisional lines. The Foundation had also responded to an invitation from the government of Greece to help plan and effect the rehabilitation and development of the island of Crete. A Foundation team spent more than two years surveying Crete from every conceivable angle. It was perhaps the most detailed and comprehensive study of a discrete population group and geographical entity ever done.[20] These activities pointed in directions JDR had urged on the Foundation.

Unfortunately, the comprehensive plan for Germany remained just that—a plan and nothing more. All of the work in Crete resulted in a survey—and nothing more. And the same fate befell the Balfour Report. In fact, the only special report acted on during this period had a negative purpose—the dismantling of the International Health Division. The two most prominent staff members of the Foundation, Warren Weaver and Alan Gregg, were in agreement that international health programs should no longer receive a major share of the Foundation's attention and funding. Gregg, who had been director of the Medical Sciences Division since 1930, wanted any remaining public health activities to come under his wing to eliminate overlapping and duplication. Weaver, head of the Natural Sciences Division since 1932, wanted to see resources diverted from public health to the agricultural program, which he had nurtured from its inception. In 1950 President Barnard acceded to their demands and created a Commission on Review of the International Health Division. JDR was one of the twenty-two members drawn from the trustees, staff, and outside institutions. A report was adopted a year later that blended public health with the Medical Sciences Division and reconstituted Weaver's division as Natural Sciences and Agriculture.

Perhaps to show that these actions were not meant to disparage the Balfour Report and JDR's views, the report included a favorable reference to the "human ecology" outlook, stressing the need for "integrated" programs and the inclusion of efforts to work on the problem of population.

These were words that JDR wanted to hear, but he realized that they were only words. He had been gently pressing for a follow-through on the Balfour Report. He knew from his earlier failure that he could not press too hard, and at no time did he ask for a program in population control per se, only for work on population under the banner of "human ecology" or an "integrated" approach. But even this was of no avail.

The reason that no action was taken on the initiatives JDR favored was that the normally cautious attitude of the Foundation managers and trustees was intensified by current events. The backlash over the "loss" of China was building up. By 1951 McCarthyism was rampant and congressional committees were mounting witch-hunting investigations. There was a growing tendency to see the major foundations as somehow subversive; they, too, were coming under fire by special congressional committees.

Moreover, in the underdeveloped countries conditions did not seem good for initiating population control. The Balfour Report had pointed out candidly that the priority of political leaders in the Far East was industrialization; they had little interest in population measures. Anticolonial fervor was sweeping the less-developed world, with scores of former colonies becoming new nations. Some of the new leaders saw the American and European interest in population control as another form of imperialism and colonialism. This political spark was assiduously fanned by the Communist bloc.

Even though the Foundation had liberally supported his Office of Population Research, Notestein became contemptuous of the excessive caution he perceived.[21] He regarded John Foster Dulles and Harold Dodds as "sexual Puritans" because they led the move to discontinue Foundation support for Dr. Kinsey's research. He regarded Warren Weaver as a man intent on sabotaging any action in the population field, and he thought that Barnard had knuckled under to pressure from the Catholic Church.[22]

This last point had to do with an incident in 1948, when Barnard took the initiative of testing the opinion of the Church on population issues. He had been surprised to read an account of statements made in Tokyo by Francis Cardinal Spellman of New York City, in which the cardinal seemed to express a broad and tolerant point of view. The newspaper account read in part as follows:

> Asked whether the Catholic Church had any help to offer the Japanese people on their pressing population problem, in view of its stand on birth control, the Cardinal said population was a problem with which statesmen ought to deal.
>
> "Something certainly ought to be done," he said, "so that these people can live and work and raise their families in peace." It was hard to see, he said, how they were going to be able to do it until the statesmen answered this problem.[23]

Barnard, who had just become president of the Foundation, sensed the possibility of a more permissive attitude on the part of the Church toward population programs. From his wartime experience of running the USO, he had become acquainted with the cardinal. He wrote suggesting a meeting to discuss the tentative Foundation interest in population work and to hear the cardinal's "views and the position of the Church with respect to this broad problem." It was a thoughtful letter, registering concern over the prospects of the less-favored nations and reflecting something of the conservationist's point of view, the fear of "an absolute and irremediable loss of resources due to deforestation, erosion, leaching and so forth."[24]

An elaborate exchange of courteous letters resulted in a luncheon meeting at the Archdiocese of New York on September 27. Barnard and three of his division heads met with Cardinal Spellman and nine of his advisers. It was a long and polite discussion, from which it was clear that the cardinal had rethought his Tokyo remarks. As one of the Foundation participants expressed it: "The conversation really never got down to grass roots in regard to the problem but it was quite obvious that the church still holds to its well-known position." Lindsley Kimball, the Foundation vice president closest to Barnard, having worked for him during USO days, did not attend the luncheon, but probably reflected Barnard's own impression in saying that the message from the churchmen was: "Study the population problem all you want, but don't take any action." Kimball said Barnard concluded that "there was no need to challenge the Church in the United States."[25]

Warren Weaver's motives were more complex. Knowing that he had been passed over as a candidate for the Foundation presidency, Weaver was not a devotee of Barnard. In his oral history tapes, Weaver maintained that Barnard's presidency was not nearly as successful as Fosdick's. Barnard's experience in industry (he said) led him to keep emphasizing his own leadership role, which assumed "very definitely that the trustees needed to be told what they ought to do by the CEO [chief executive officer]."[26] This stance was not appreciated by many of the trustees and staff.

Still, like Barnard, Weaver had no difficulty understanding the serious implications of excessive population growth. But, he doubted that "population" was a coherent field adaptable to action overseas. For that reason, he believed that it would be hard to attract good people for any effort in that direction. As head of the Natural Sciences Division, he was in the best position to know that the Foundation was already providing more support for population-related research, both demographic and biological, than any other organization in the world. Perhaps that was all that could reasonably be done. Moreover, Weaver knew what *was* suited to action overseas—the agricultural program—and he wanted to see it greatly expanded.

JDR was much calmer than Notestein about accepting the fact that the Foundation was not going to implement the Balfour Report. After all, in a few years he had become accustomed to inaction in areas that he favored, and he was much more familiar than Notestein with the kind of thinking that permeated the Foundation. It is also likely that by the early 1950s JDR had begun to assimilate that thinking himself, at least with respect to the Foundation. It *was* doing a great deal in research, albeit in noncontroversial areas. Perhaps that was best after all. Perhaps a separate organization was needed. JDR remembered how Junior and his advisers had devised the Bureau of Social Hygiene to work on controversial subjects and take any public heat that developed. JDR began turning that thought over in his mind.

24

♔

FAMILY IN TRANSITION

IN THE HISTORY of every family, one can discern those events, joyous or tragic, that mark the kind of change after which life is never quite the same. For the Rockefellers, there was 1934 when Junior created the trusts, 1937 when Senior died, and 1945 when the brothers came home from wartime duty. In 1948 came another turning point, a sad one that Junior and his children had dreaded for years—the death of Abby.

There had been concern about a "tired heart" for more than a decade. Every winter Junior took Abby out to the warm weather of Tucson for a vacation rest at a small inn they had come to love. After a two-month stay, they returned home on Friday, April 2. Abby enjoyed seeing most of her six children and eighteen grandchildren in family gatherings at Pocantico and in Manhattan over the weekend. JDR wrote in his diary about what happened on Monday:

Early in the morning Mother woke up feeling ill. Her stomach was quite upset but the situation didn't seem particularly different than previous upsets so Father took care of her. Along about seven o'clock Mother was still pretty uncomfortable so Father called the doctor who arrived about eight. While he was talking with Mother about her symptoms her head fell back on the pillow and the doctor listening to her heart said it was all over. Fortunately for Father the doctor was there. It all took place in a matter of a few hours with a minimum of pain and suffering. . . . The wonderful thing was that it happened at home and after Mother had had the weekend with most of the members of the family. . . . Father was terribly hard hit, the end coming so suddenly and so completely out of the blue. . . . Nelson and I stayed for the night.

Abby and Junior were in the forty-seventh year of their marriage, he seventy-four years old, she seventy-three. If success in life for a wife and mother is to be deeply loved and respected by her husband

and children, Abby was uncommonly successful. To this day, it is an emotional experience for David Rockefeller to talk about his mother. Newspaper editorials and Dr. Harry Emerson Fosdick's eulogy all stressed the same attributes: Abby's love of family, her modesty, her gift of warmth and friendship, her moral character, and her great service to the Museum of Modern Art, the Girl Scouts, and the Young Women's Christian Association. The *New York Times* said: "She was a great lady, loved, respected, and consulted by her husband, five sons and one daughter, as few wives and mothers ever are. Hers was the spirit that held them all together."[1]

Though all the family felt the shock of her passing, to Junior it was devastating. He bore up well externally, but his life was now almost unbearably lonely. Everyone tried to ease the pain; most helpful were the eldest daughters-in-law, Tod and Blanchette, who alternated staying with Junior in Williamsburg during spring and fall. Shy in his own way, Junior nevertheless needed companionship and was fond of women, more at ease with them than with men, perhaps a throwback to the days when he was used to having only sisters around him at home. Blanchette recalls the affectionate relation that she and Tod had with him, what a delightful host he was, how he never ran out of conversation.

At other times, the thought of Junior alone with his servants at Kykuit or in his vast Manhattan apartment was a nagging source of guilt for his children. But an event soon occurred that surprised them and filled Junior's remaining years with renewed happiness. He married Martha Baird Allen, the widow of his old friend and college classmate, the lawyer Arthur M. Allen of Providence, Rhode Island. She was an extremely attractive woman of distinction and charm, a former concert pianist of no small reputation, having studied with Artur Schnabel in Berlin. Her London debut occurred in 1926 in the Royal Albert Hall with Sir Thomas Beecham conducting. She retired from the concert stage after her marriage to Allen in 1930.

The Rockefellers and Allens were good friends; they visited frequently in the summer, the Allens also maintaining a summer home in the Seal Harbor area. Arthur died on May 6, 1950. How and when the friendship of the widow and widower blossomed into romance is not known; Junior did not keep a diary and he successfully concealed the romance from journalists until the wedding on August 15, 1951, at the bride's home. JDR served as best man and Nelson and David were also present. Junior was seventy-seven, Martha fifty-six. There was no jealousy or resentment among Junior's children. Their father was happy and the strain of worrying about his loneliness was over. Martha had no children of her own; so gracious, thoughtful, and supportive of Junior's children was she that everyone ended up happy.

During these postwar years, Junior experienced a rebirth of another kind. Compared to his great accomplishments at an earlier stage, he had been relatively inactive during the late 1930s and the war years. But he was still a very wealthy man, in control of the family fortune, and in the 1940s that fortune had rebounded from the ravages of the Depression. The blue-chip stocks of the five major American oil companies grew constantly and dramatically, some tripling and others quadrupling in value.

Between 1940 and the end of 1950, Junior paid $51.1 million in federal income tax on a total income of $173.2 million. He paid $42.2 million in federal gift tax on gifts to his family amounting to $78.9 million. He contributed cash, securities, real estate, and art valued at $76.2 million during this eleven-year period. And yet, after all these and other expenses, his net worth in 1951 was $337 million—$10 million more than in 1940. It was as if he could not give money away or spend it fast enough, so great was the regenerative power of oil stocks.

The net worth and annual income of all of Junior's children also increased substantially during this period, partly through appreciation of the trusts and partly through additional gifts. Under the terms of Abby's 1934 Trust, the beneficiaries were her three oldest children, Babs, JDR, and Nelson.[2] Each received approximately $11.1 million in trust upon her death.

To understand the pattern of Junior's financial gifts to his children, one must isolate the criteria that emerged from his well-developed personal values and see how he believed his children behaved in respect to those values. To begin with, Junior rejected the storied primogeniture of European nobility in which the oldest son inherits the title and all or most of the family wealth. Instead, Junior was guided by the "democratic" values he espoused so much, meaning in this case that his dispensation was to treat all his children relatively equally—*unless* their behavior, in his view, dictated otherwise.

Senior never had to face this choice, having had only one son. Thus, as we have seen, Junior received the great bulk of family wealth, worth nearly half a billion dollars. A combination of factors—

Junior's "democratic" approach to transferring wealth, his generous philanthropic giving, the Depression, the tax laws, and the fact that he had five sons—meant that none of his sons would receive assets worth much more than a tenth of what Junior had been given. Also, the evidence suggests that Junior had advanced beyond the thinking prevalent in his father's day in one respect: he was prepared to treat his only daughter on a par with her five brothers. The reason that Babs was not so treated was not that she was a woman, but that her behavior deviated so widely from Junior's norms.

All six children were treated relatively equally in the first great gift, the 1934 Trusts. Junior recognized full well that this action made his offspring independently wealthy for life. He further assured himself of this by the restrictions he placed on the trusts, guaranteeing that the assets could not be dissipated in a frivolous way.

Having made these basic provisions, Junior's giving to his children from that point on clearly was guided by his perception of their behavior—the values they held as they matured and how well they grew up to their responsibilities in life. In other words, having made his children financially secure, Junior was disposed to give more only when he believed that the gift was merited and would be put to good use. It is not likely that Junior said this in so many words to any of his children, but his direction was unmistakable to them, given all his efforts over the years to inculcate religious and moral values and all his lectures about family responsibilities and the proper use of money.

Junior's approach to transferring wealth thus was subjective and doubtless introduced some tensions into familial relations. His criteria were not all of equal weight, and not often can one discern a single motive for a particular gift. He began the process in 1943, the gifts varying considerably in amount, timing, and form. One reason for this variance was the age of the recipient—no matter how high the marks Junior might give for good behavior, he would not make significant gifts until his children had matured. For him, this meant at least the age of thirty.

Religion was certainly an important consideration. As we have seen, Junior's personal religious beliefs stressed tolerance and engagement with the world, not renunciation. He thus did not necessarily expect his children to be devout churchpeople, but certainly to be religious in the sense of leading upright Christian lives, manifested by a high conception of morality and duty. An immediate corollary of this had to do with family life. Junior expected that his children would exercise due caution in selecting a life mate, as he had done, and that they would have children, rear them properly, and lead a happy family life.

This particular expectation was well expressed by Junior on the occasion of placing $5 million in government bonds in JDR's trust in 1947. He complimented his oldest son for having "developed a pattern of living that is wholesome, simple and well calculated to cultivate in your children those fundamental qualities and aspirations so essential to useful and worthy living."[3] Four years earlier, Junior had established small trusts worth $100,000 each for his thirteen grandchildren. As each new grandchild was born, he created a similar trust.

While Abby and Junior counseled their children from time to time, they did not exert pressure on any of them to adopt a particular career, except to the extent that they influenced JDR to follow in his father's footsteps in the Family Office. Even here, JDR had a wide choice of particular interests that he might adopt. Nevertheless, the parents very much expected that the sons would each find a career path that was meaningful and important, offering possibilities for distinctive service and some measure of leadership.

Beyond career demands, Junior believed that all of his children should devote both time and financial resources to philanthropic activities and public affairs. On no subject was he more clear and consistent than the proper stewardship of wealth. To the extent that his children were given financial assets beyond their own needs, assets they had not earned in a strict sense, they were expected to do more than merely indulge themselves. Indeed, the evidence suggests that this was the most important single criterion in Junior's mind for transferring wealth after the 1934 Trusts were established. He was firmly guided by a favorite maxim: "To whom much is given, much will be expected."

For Junior's children, the choice was clear. They could live up to his precepts and be rewarded with additional gifts. Or they could violate those precepts and do as they pleased if they were willing to settle for what was already theirs by virtue of the 1934 Trusts. Four of the sons had no apparent difficulty in fulfilling the standards that Junior had set. The two children who had great difficulty were Babs and Winthrop.

As the exemplar of giving, JDR received the most, but not by a great margin over Nelson, Laurance, and David. In Junior's first round of transferring wealth to his children (apart from the 1934 Trusts), during the years from 1943 to 1947, JDR received three gifts totaling

$15.1 million and Nelson three gifts worth $12.6 million. In four gifts, Laurance received $14.7 million and David's three gifts were worth $11.87 million. In contrast, Babs' only gift was for $504,000, and Winthrop's two gifts were worth $552,000.[4]

From Junior's point of view, the problem with Winthrop and Babs was that they were rebelling against his strictures, though not in the same way. Winthrop's bad habits seemed to stem from the fact that he was struggling and drifting in life; Junior could cherish the hope that matters might improve. But Babs had been overtly defiant for so long that Junior held out no hope. By her own testimony, Babs had deliberately acted in ways designed to dismay her parents—doing poorly in school, taking up smoking, constantly trying to evade chaperones. She referred to her marriage to David Milton as "liberation" and ceased going to church altogether once she was free of her father's household.

Abby and Junior had not expected Babs to take up some profession or career in any conventional sense, other than the obvious one of wife and mother. But even this was threatened when Babs divorced David Milton in 1943. Divorce was high on Junior's list of transgressions. The divorce surely deepened the rift between Babs and her parents, but there is no evidence that it resulted in a complete break. Abby and Junior accepted the inevitable; it was clear to everyone in the family that the marriage simply had not worked, whatever the reasons. And Babs was soon married again, to Dr. Irving H. Pardee.

Rather, Babs' worst failing in Junior's eyes was that she took no significant interest in giving. She was quite wealthy as a result of the combination of her 1934 Trust and the inheritance of a one-third share of Abby's trust. Given the charitable deductions allowed by the income tax laws, Babs could have had a very active "career" or avocation as a philanthropist without any cost to herself. Junior thus could read as another act of defiance the fact that Babs year after year failed to take charitable deductions to any significant degree, with the result that she paid enormous taxes. Babs' attitude toward giving changed, but not until the 1950s, *after* Junior had completed all the transferring of wealth to his progeny that he was going to do. It was almost as if Babs planned it this way, to make it clear that she was acting for her own good reasons rather than in deference to her father's moralisms.

With Winthrop it was a different story altogether. Despite his exemplary war record, he had habits that Junior heartily disliked, such as smoking, drinking, and acting the playboy role around town. He had done poorly at school; he showed no signs of marrying and settling down to raise a family; he had no discernible career direction. All this raised serious doubts in Junior's mind that Winthrop could handle additional wealth in a responsible manner. However, unlike Babs, Winthrop was active in the field of philanthropy. He was a generous giver to a large number of organizations, participated in the deliberations of the Rockefeller Brothers Fund, and had served effectively in fund-raising for the New York University–Bellevue Medical Center, then rising on the East Side of Manhattan.

When Winthrop finally did marry, it was not quite what Junior had in mind. The surprise wedding took place at the Palm Beach home of Winston Guest on February 14, 1948, with Laurance as the best man. The bride was Barbara "Bobo" Sears, a blond beauty who had been a model and an aspiring starlet under the stage name Eva Paul. But she had been born Jievute Paulekiute, the daughter of Lithuanian immigrants, in a Pennsylvania coal town. This made the Valentine's Day elopement the kind of "Cinderella" romance that the tabloid press loves. Even so, the family did not snub Bobo, not even Junior, who railed against class consciousness all his life. The problem was not Bobo's origins, but the fact that she was a divorcée. Her first husband, Richard Sears, was from a prominent Boston family.

The question now for Junior was whether he should transfer significant wealth to Winthrop, as he had to his other sons. Bobo's divorce was a thing of the past. And Winthrop, after all, *was* Junior's son and he *had* finally married; perhaps it would work and he would settle down. Although serious doubts must have remained in Junior's mind, three months after the wedding he added $6.1 million to Winthrop's 1934 Trust.

When the only child Winthrop was ever to have, Winthrop Paul, was born seven months after the wedding, Junior dutifully created the same $100,000 trust for his latest grandchild as he had for all the others. And in the following year, 1949, Winthrop was included when Junior gave 15,000 shares of Chase National Bank stock (worth nearly $550,000) to each of his sons. At the same time, he made his second and final gift to Babs outside of the trusts—a magnificent strand of pearls that had belonged to Abby, valued at $174,000.[5] But Junior was not yet finished. He was contemplating further gifts to bring Laurance and David up to relative parity with John and Nelson. He was also thinking of doing something more for his grandchildren. And he wanted to observe the progress of Winthrop, who of course still lagged well behind his four brothers in the financial sweepstakes despite the large 1948 gift. All this was reserved for 1952, when Junior would make his final round of gifts to his progeny as well as other major decisions bearing on the disposition of his assets short of his last will and testament.

Once again, from the mid-1940s, Junior's own philanthropic giving was assuming major dimensions. For the most part, his attention dwelt on those projects dearest to his heart, especially Colonial Williamsburg, by far the largest recipient. But special needs also arose and were met—$8.5 million for the U.N. headquarters, several million dollars in land and securities for the Museum of Modern Art, substantial gifts to Brown University, and in 1950 gifts in excess of $5 million each to the United Negro College Fund and the Harvard School of Business Administration.

Junior's interest in ecumenism began to revive, too. For years his support of interdenominational religion had focused on Riverside Church. Now it began to broaden anew, resulting in large gifts to the World Council of Churches and Union Theological Seminary, among others. He used the Sealantic Fund to channel these gifts. Junior established this fund in 1938, with the initial purpose of providing posthumous support for the two small churches he attended in Seal Harbor and Pocantico, hence the name: "Seal" from Seal Harbor and "antic" from Pocantico. He gave the two churches together less than $5,000 a year—minuscule gifts by his standards, but crucial to the churches, and expressive of his special, lifelong affection for them. He was careful to give enough for their survival with their own pastors, but not so much as to discourage other parishioners from contributing.

The Union Church of Pocantico Hills moved into its new building in 1922, after meeting since the 1890s in a small community center, called the Lyceum, that had been built on the Rockefeller estate. The new building was made of simple stone in the Old Dutch style, appropriate in an area that had been a Dutch colony before being taken by the English in 1664. The church was built for $25,000 on land donated by Senior, Junior providing $10,000 and the other parishioners the rest. Junior soon made another gift to pay for a church tower with chimes and a clock as a memorial to his mother. Junior, as the major patron of the small church, was gratified when his six children, following a suggestion made by Nelson in 1949, commissioned Henri Matisse to design a stained-glass window in Abby's memory. Matisse, eighty-four, was confined to his bed in Nice, but he became absorbed in designing the circular window for the small country church, his last major work before his death in 1954. The glass was stained and cut in France and installed in the church in 1956.

Junior first used the Sealantic Fund for gifts other than to the two churches when he made a number of war relief grants. His former general-purpose foundation, the Davison Fund, had been allowed to expire when the Rockefeller Brothers Fund was created in 1940. Thereafter, Junior began using Sealantic as a replacement. The largest project, one that Junior tried to avoid, involved three historical restorations along the Hudson River that eventually were grouped together under the management of a nonprofit corporation, Sleepy Hollow Restorations, Inc.

The story began in 1940 when Junior purchased Philipse Manor, a seven-acre estate located where the Pocantico River flows into the Hudson. The owner was Elsie Janis, a renowned star of musical comedy whose fame had peaked during World War I. She had been pressing Junior to buy the estate since the 1920s, but he resisted until she moved to California and it appeared certain that the property would fall into the hands of a real estate developer. Junior bought it and gave it to the Tarrytown Historical Society. The manor had originally been built by Frederick Philipse, a wealthy Dutch patroon, who at one time owned all the land for twenty-eight miles along the Hudson north of the New York City line.

The story was repeated in 1945 when Sunnyside, Washington Irving's home, came on the market. It was a wonderfully preserved literary shrine on a small peninsula jutting into the Tappan Zee, the widest point of the Hudson, a few miles from Philipse Manor. His hands full with Colonial Williamsburg, Junior acted reluctantly and solely for the purpose of preserving these irreplaceable properties. But it is one thing to buy a historic site (Sunnyside cost only $60,250) and quite another to restore and preserve it the only way Junior could tolerate its being done—perfectly and accurately to the last detail. The Historical Society lacked the money and expertise to do this. When evidence emerged that Philipse Manor had been bastardized by late additions and that errors had been made in the attempt to restore its harbor and mills, Junior was drawn in. He brought in experts from Colonial Williamsburg to advise and to perform the work.

The third property was the Van Cortlandt Manor, ten miles north at Croton-on-Hudson, a treasure house of period furnishings and decor. The two manors provide an interesting historical counterpoint:

during the Revolution, the Philipse family were loyalists and the Van Cortlandts were patriots. Before he was finished, Junior had spent more than $10 million through the Sealantic Fund to fully restore the three properties grouped as the Sleepy Hollow Restorations. Today they remain as marvelous gems of historical preservation.[6]

Beyond all the financial gifts, the most significant by far of the transactions between Junior and his sons was his sale of Rockefeller Center to them in 1948. The price for all the shares of Rockefeller Plaza, Inc.—in other words, 100 percent ownership—was $2,210,000. Each of the five brothers received one-fifth ownership of the Center for $442,000. From the perspective of later years of the immense value of Rockefeller Center, this has the appearance of a "sweetheart" deal. It is not surprising that references to it in print usually imply that this was the case.

When a father sells an asset to a son for something less than its market value, few would find this objectionable if the gap between value and price is not unreasonably large. On the other hand, the sale of a $5,000 automobile to a son for $50, for example, would certainly raise legitimate questions of state sales tax and federal gift tax. But the facts of the sale of the Center point to a very different conclusion. It was approved by the Internal Revenue Service and by two institutions that had a very important stake in any transaction involving the Center—Columbia University and Metropolitan Life. And the price was arrived at on the basis of two independent appraisals.

Without question, the brothers and their heirs ultimately reaped enormous benefits from the purchase. But this eventuality was not at all certain at the time. Five conditions lowered the market value of the Center to its 1948 sale price: (1) extremely tight restrictions on the marketability of the Center that were embedded in the agreements with Columbia and Metropolitan Life; (2) the burden of debt that the Center carried at the time; (3) the fact that it was a leasehold, Junior owning the buildings but not the land; (4) uncertainty about the future, because the original Columbia lease, which had been extended ten years in a 1933 agreement, was due to expire in 1962; and (5) the costly modernization and expansion needed if the Center was to have reasonable prospects for more than temporary economic success.

The most recent books on the Rockefeller family that attempt to be definitive—those by Collier and Horowitz in 1976 and by Alvin Moscow in 1977—treat the 1948 sale briefly and inaccurately. It was easy to miss its significance because it appeared to be a simple matter and some of the pertinent information was not available to researchers until lately. But today, as noted earlier, Rockefeller Center is by far the main repository and wellspring of the family's still very impressive wealth, so it is worth taking a close look at the sale and events that it triggered.

To do this, one must begin with the prewar years, when Junior mused out loud about donating his interest in the Center to the Rockefeller Institute for Medical Research. As reported, Nelson was the leader among the brothers in talking Junior out of this, or, to be more exact, getting him to put the idea on hold. Moscow presents a picture of a bold Nelson confronting his father and laying down an ultimatum:

> Nelson objected strenuously. He had already devoted some nine years of his life to Rockefeller Center, being involved in the architecture of the buildings, the organization of management, financing, renting offices in the depths of the Great Depression, and finally helping to take the operation out of the red and into the black.
>
> "If you give the Center to Rockefeller Institute," he told his father, "I'm out—forget it. I'll step out of the management, because I'm not going to spend my time and energy on something symbolic and I'm not going to work for a philanthropy that already has all the endowment it needs. I'll have nothing further to do with it."[7]

This version of events is marred by illogicality and errors of fact. It is either an apocryphal story told to Moscow by someone else or Nelson's own somewhat self-serving recollection given in an interview some thirty-five years after the event. One cannot tell which, because Moscow and his publisher allowed this lengthy and purportedly definitive book to be published without footnotes or source references of any kind.

We know from much evidence that Nelson was the most skilled of the brothers in manipulating Junior; this was the reason the others were always happy to have him take the lead when they were united on some issue or dispute with their father. Nelson used a variety of techniques—dazzling Junior with a display of energy and vision (as in his Latin American ventures), an exuberant kind of pleading, a sometimes unctuous form of flattery, or a logical presentation usually featuring the turning back on Junior of his own moralisms and favorite ideas. Certainly *not* among Nelson's techniques were confrontation and the issuing of ultimatums; with Junior they never would have worked.

By 1944 Junior had good reasons for beginning to consider how he would dispose of his interest in Rockefeller Center. He was seventy years old and not feeling in the best of health. He and Abby spent so much time away from New York City in various rest spots that Junior no longer felt close to the management of the huge enterprise. He was not eager to bear primary responsibility for the diverse and difficult challenges that lay ahead. The Center was burdened with a debt of about $95 million, two-thirds of it owed to Junior and bearing no interest and the remainder to Metropolitan Life, the latter having precedence over the former. The Center could not be sold without the consent of Columbia University, whose lease took precedence over all indebtedness except the Metropolitan loan. The lease still held Junior liable "in principal and not in surety," as did the Metropolitan loan. All this would present a fearsome tangle for Junior's estate if he were to die suddenly, including the possibility that his heirs would have to sell off their own assets to pay the estate taxes covering the indebtedness and book value of the Center. Junior's legal advisers were telling him that it was too hazardous for him to continue owning the Center while it owed him so much money and while he was liable in principal for all its other debts.[8]

In some respects, the Center appeared to be in good shape when the war ended in 1945. No significant construction had occurred in Manhattan during the war, so the Center was almost fully rented and was by far the largest modern office complex in Manhattan. By this time it had become world-famous as well, a tourist attraction and the site of many patriotic and military displays and rallies during the war. In 1943, moreover, the Center had earned its first modest operating profit of $896,000. This reduced its cumulative operating loss to $47.6 million (representing only a portion of its debt burden). For the years remaining until the expiration of the lease in 1962, the annual profit averaged about $2 million. However, the terms of the lease prohibited any dividends until all debts were retired.[9]

Beneath these promising appearances, there were difficult questions to resolve. For one, plans for new office buildings in New York City were being announced almost daily and construction was beginning on some; all would feature two technologies that now had become feasible—air-conditioning and fluorescent lighting (the latter making every corner of office space usable). To stay competitive, Rockefeller Center would have to install both in all eleven buildings, requiring a multimillion dollar investment. There was not enough time to amortize such an investment before the lease expired in 1962.

Worse, four of the Center's most prestigious clients (NBC and possibly the parent company, RCA, as well; Esso; Time-Life; and Sinclair Oil) had outgrown their space and were contemplating relocation elsewhere. Their leases were up for renewal in 1952. The loss of RCA/NBC would have been devastating, not only economically, but also for the popular "Radio City" image.

Another worrisome fact was that the west side of Sixth Avenue now cried out for development, the El having been torn down in 1939 and replaced by a subway. Rockefeller Center presented a modern front on the east side, making the west side seem all the more tawdry. In an attempt to get rid of the shabby image and promote development, the Sixth Avenue Association managed, with Nelson's enthusiastic backing, to get approval for a new name: Avenue of the Americas (most New Yorkers still avoid this mouthful in favor of "Sixth Avenue.") The obvious candidate for leading the redevelopment charge across the avenue was Rockefeller Center; no one else seemed ready to take the risk.

Further demands were created by the growing success of another technology, television broadcasting. NBC needed much more space for new types of studios, and it took little vision to foresee that television was going to have a damaging effect on movie theater attendance. The Radio City Music Hall seemed safe, but the Center Theater would become even more of a money-loser instead of ever turning a profit.

Junior began to prepare for passing on Rockefeller Center to someone else. His first step was a reorganization to consolidate his ownership in the 1,000 shares of stock of a newly created entity, Rockefeller Plaza, Inc. The second step was to open discussions with Columbia University in an effort to ease some of the restrictions and lay the groundwork for what could happen at lease-renewal time. Junior's immediate goal was to transfer the status of "principal" in the lease from himself to Rockefeller Plaza, Junior assuming the secondary "surety" role.

The negotiations extended over a period of three years, until mid-1947. Columbia released Junior from the status of principal in return for new measures guaranteeing the lease and repayment of the Metropolitan loan. The main provision was that Rockefeller Center would maintain a working capital balance of $30 million, including $14 million in U.S. government bonds placed in an escrow account as security for the performance of the lease. At this point, the Metropolitan loan had ceased to be a major concern; the balance was down to $17.5 million in 1947 and the payment schedule would retire it by the end of 1950. Junior still could not transfer stock without the prior consent of Columbia, and the lease still contained a provision that no more than 20 percent of the stock could be sold outside the Rockefeller family.[10]

Junior had considerable bargaining power with Columbia if he were inclined to use it. As Carol Krinsky points out in her book, he could have done nothing about modernization and expansion and let the ground lease expire in 1962, simply turning over the buildings to Columbia.[11] By that time, the Center would have repaid all of his loans to it. Of course, he would lose his original investment, for which he now held stock. This would have been admitting defeat—twenty difficult years of effort sunk in the great project and nothing to show for it. For Columbia it would have been even worse. It would have faced all the management problems of a somewhat shopworn Center in 1962, with major clients lost and an expensive modernization program looming. Columbia's basic policy was to keep the Rockefeller family enmeshed in Rockefeller Center as the surest guarantee of prosperity.

All the foregoing explains why everyone was happy when Junior came to the solution of selling the Center to his sons. No other option was as good—letting it go to Columbia, selling it to outside interests (which Columbia opposed and could have barred), or giving it to the Rockefeller Institute or any other philanthropy. With a market value of only $2.2 million and laden with burdens, the Center was not a viable gift. Moreover, Junior's sons were eager and willing to take it over. Two of them were very much involved in its management, Nelson having moved up from president to chairman after returning from Washington in 1945, and Laurance serving as chairman of the finance committee. This satisfied Junior's sense of posterity as well: if the Center stayed in the family and his sons made a success of it, all the years of his concern would have gone for something.

The 1,000 shares of stock had a book value of $55.3 million. This was the total that Junior had invested in the project up to 1935 and in return for which he took stock in Midtown Development and Investment Corporation, later converted into shares of Rockefeller Plaza, Inc. Deducting the sale price of $2.2 million left Junior with a loss of $53.1 million. If Junior had sold the Center to anyone but his relatives, he could have taken this sum as a tax loss. However, IRS regulations allowed the five brothers to claim the loss ($10.6 million each) on any future sale to nonfamily members. This was of no immediate use to them, but the time would come when they could claim it.

For the funds that he advanced to Rockefeller Center after 1935, Junior took notes instead of stock. He had put in over $79 million before the Center started making repayments. The balance was down to $60.3 million when the sale was made to the sons. Again, Nelson took the lead in suggesting that perhaps Junior might want to forgive this debt, but that could have been construed as a gift, requiring the payment of tax. Moreover, Junior wanted the transaction to be as businesslike as possible, so the debt remained and he expected it to be repaid.[12]

Meanwhile, Junior, Nelson, and Laurance had already taken steps to deal with the Center's most pressing need—retaining as many of its prestigious clients as possible. The first major move was the erection of a new headquarters building for Esso (Standard of New Jersey). The best site available was on land owned by Junior just north of the original Center, a T-shaped plot through the block, so that it fronted on both 51st and 52nd streets. The thirty-story building designed for the site stands directly facing the northern end of the three-block private street that bisects the original Center, effectively blocking any plans of extending the street northward. Completed in 1947 at a cost of $25.6 million and the first fully air-conditioned office tower in Manhattan, the Esso (now Warner Communications) Building is tied into the Center by its design, its connection with the underground maze of concourses, and the fact that it is managed by the Center. But the Esso Building was independent of the Columbia lease and its restrictions, because Junior owned the land and financed the construction. He could thus proceed with this project unrestrained by any part of his negotiations with the university.

When the Esso staff moved into the new building, space was freed elsewhere in the Center to ease temporarily the expansion needs of other clients; indeed, for a time, as much as 15 percent of Center space was vacant. NBC's requirement of new studio space was eased by converting the Center Theater to television studios. It was a temporary expedient; permanent conversion for this purpose would have been more costly than tearing the building down and erecting a new one.

As soon as the sale had taken place, the Center initiated an $8 million modernization program to introduce air-conditioning and fluorescent lighting into all buildings. And the brothers began looking for new projects that would take care of the expansion needs of other clients, including Time-Life, Sinclair Oil, and U.S. Rubber. Several additional projects for new clients were also under consideration. All of this pointed to a leap across Sixth Avenue and to new negotiations with Columbia for concessions that would make it possible.

During these early postwar years, three of Junior's sons—Nelson, Laurance, and David—were busy and happy in the pursuit of their careers. The other two, John and Winthrop, were floundering, though in very different ways and for different reasons.

Winthrop was struggling both in his career and in his unsuccessful marriage to Bobo. The chance that one of the Rockefeller boys might turn out a success in the oil business, which had a certain plausibility about it, was not to be. Winthrop could find nothing fulfilling, certainly not his job at Socony-Vacuum. By late 1950, Winthrop and Bobo had separated, their troubles becoming grist for the press. Winthrop was more and more being cast as the black sheep of the family—disheartened, aimless, and in deep trouble in his private life.

JDR's difficulties stemmed chiefly from frustration. As we said, he had run into obstacles in the path of each of his three main postwar ambitions. The Rockefeller Foundation was to remain important in his life, but not nearly to the extent he had anticipated. The population field was complex and controversial, resistant to any practical breakthrough. And his plans for Colonial Williamsburg were indefinitely delayed by the financial priorities of the restoration. As a result, JDR turned his attention to consolidating the rest of his business affairs and seeking substitute projects that might be fulfilling for him.

His first step was to shed old involvements as a way of preparing for new ones. In 1946 he resigned as a director of Industrial Relations Counselors, severed his relations with the Youth Committee of the Community Service Society, passed International House on to David, relinquished the presidency of the Sealantic Fund, and notified the leaders of Riverside Church of his intention to retire when his term as trustee was up in 1948. Within the next two years, he also ended his responsibilities vis-à-vis the China Medical Board (that organization received its terminal grant from the Rockefeller Foundation in mid-1947) and the Spelman Fund, when that last autonomous remnant of the philanthropic reorganizations of 1928 and 1934 made its final grant to the "1313" group and passed from the scene in 1948.

JDR naturally received many requests for his participation in nonprofit organizations or causes. From these he chose American Youth Hostels, Inc., which promoted hostels in the United States and encouraged young Americans to enjoy those of Europe, where the system of low-cost, youth-oriented accommodations had originated. JDR remembered his bicycling days in Europe, when he and Nelson had stayed at hostels several times. He now relished having a hand in a scheme that benefited young people and carried with it both a "grass-roots" and an international flavor. It was through the Hostels that JDR renewed his acquaintance with Donald McLean, Jr., whom he had known as an Army captain in his Washington days. McLean had moved from the law firm of Milbank, Tweed to a job with Socony-Vacuum, and he agreed to join the Hostels board with JDR to help monitor progress. Later McLean became a full-time staff aide to JDR. The two stayed with the Hostels for more than five years, working on fund-raising, program policy, and personnel matters until they gave up in despair. The organization never did become a notable success.

Another time-consuming duty that JDR undertook was the chairmanship of the Greater New York Fund for 1949; it proved virtually a full-time job for about nine months. He was determined to bring about an improved showing over the 1948 campaign, which had netted only $5 million of the $8 million goal. The same total was set for 1949, but in strategy sessions JDR was advised not to set his heart on getting more than $6.5 million. He spent long days lining up committees in every major business and trade and in organizing the campaign and the banquets. He concentrated on labor leaders and felt that he had achieved a breakthrough—of sorts—for union participation, which had hitherto been poor. When it was all over, the disappointing total raised came to $5.2 million. In a postmortem, one labor leader made the sensible observation that a quick step-up in one year should not be expected; it would take an educational effort over a longer span. But when JDR was asked if he would like to go on as chairman for 1950, he politely declined.[13]

Edgar B. Young, who had been seconded for work with JDR on the Greater New York Fund, recalls that despite the disappointment the experience was useful to JDR. It made him known in person (and favorably) to a whole set of New York business and labor leaders; they came to see him as a hardworking, dedicated man, instead of merely a member of the idle rich.

A sign of JDR's general frustration at this time was his recourse to counseling, a search for advice in reviewing his career. He consulted Lockwood and Jamieson at times, and made a more systematic effort with Earl Newsom, a successful public relations man who numbered the Ford Motor Company and Standard of New Jersey among his clients. JDR was intent on using Newsom for the Williamsburg project. After several meetings in 1948, JDR became Newsom's client and remained one for the next fifteen years. Newsom thus had a new and prestigious client but not a conventional one. For JDR's purpose was not to gain publicity or recognition for himself. Occasionally, he would ask Newsom to help with public relations for some cause or organization, but usually Newsom's role was to act as his counselor on policy and program decisions.

In a series of sessions in 1949, the two examined all JDR's current commitments and the reasons for them. Then they thought about other endeavors JDR might "wisely consider" if he could free himself sufficiently.

We talked about the field of education with particular reference to a college presidency type of position. . . . about business from the point of view of starting one's own company or becoming associated with an existing one. . . . the field of politics both from the point of view of elective positions as well as those which are appointive. . . . We considered a position of responsibility in other organizations in the philanthropic field such as the Red Cross or a foundation. After a fairly thorough discussion none of these seemed to stand out particularly as "the" thing although much could be said for some of them.

No new direction revealed itself, but the search made JDR feel better about his present responsibilities and his pursuit of the goals he had chosen at the end of the war. He felt "encouraged" by the review, having found "a rather common pattern of interests in spite of diversification."

During these years, John and Blanchette were experiencing all the joys and problems of rearing children. They thought their family was complete with the births of the three children before the war, but in 1949 the "surprise" baby came along—Alida Davison, the fourth and last child. By this time, Sandra was fourteen, Jay was twelve, and Hope eleven. The girls attended the Brearley School and Jay went to Buckley. When it came time for prep school, JDR took his son up to New Hampshire to visit Phillips Exeter Academy, and Jay enrolled there.

Blanchette recalls her husband as an attentive father, although often so busy that his children practically had to make appointments to see him. On one memorable occasion, he took the oldest girls and several of their friends for a tour of the battleship *Missouri* when it visited New York, and to lunch with Captain Robert L. Dennison, the commanding officer—these privileges being granted by Dennison, who had been JDR's boss for a time during the war.

JDR noticed the change that a growing family brought into his life as a country squire. Once in May, he noted that the family had not spent a night at Fieldwood Farm since Christmas: "With the children's Sunday school and weekend social life we have found that we can't very well work the country in." He missed the fresh air and the exercise, the horseback-riding, and the joy of puttering around. But there were compensations. He was taking Sandra to dancing lessons at Arthur Murray's and thought it "quite fun." Jay's passion was baseball—he was a New York Giants fan, an addiction that puzzled his father until Don McLean took JDR and Jay to a night game at Ebbetts Field, where the Dodgers were playing host to the Giants. JDR was at least partially hooked. In the fall of 1949, he took Jay and Hope to the final game of the World Series at Ebbetts Field to see the Yankees beat the Dodgers badly. Once when Jackie Robinson came in to talk about a project of the Harlem YMCA, JDR took Jay out of school so he could be at the family office to meet the Dodger hero.

Seemingly, JDR had every reason to feel happy and satisfied. He had a lovely wife and four healthy children. His financial situation was improving every year because of the gifts from his father and the appreciation of his assets. Yet he knew better than anyone that he had not yet solved the central enigma of his life. He was trying his best to be of service to humanity as his father had so often urged, but he had not found ways to do it that bore his own stamp, that were creative and fulfilling to *him*. Not until 1950 did he finally sense the chance to test the third of his postwar ambitions—the project at Williamsburg that he had dreamed about for so many years.

25

CONFLICT AT

WILLIAMSBURG

FOR NEARLY A QUARTER CENTURY, archaeologists, historians, architects, and craftsmen had come to Williamsburg and labored with loving care and palpable dedication. In 1950 their work was still not finished—in a sense it would never be finished. But the restoration of the historic center of old Williamsburg had passed several milestones and had long since become known as a rare and magnificent undertaking. One could stand in the triangular yard of the College of William and Mary, in the shadow of the restored Wren Building, the oldest academic building in America, and look eastward down Duke of Gloucester Street to the impressive House of Burgesses—the capitol of Colonial Virginia—or north to the Governor's Palace, or between these two landmarks to the Bruton Parish Church, the Public Gaol, the Court House, and the homes and gardens and shops and taverns and streets of Colonial Williamsburg, all restored or rebuilt to the highest possible standards of quality and accurate detail.

The same vista in 1926 had been a depressing one of neglect and decay. The transformation resembled a miracle, and it had happened only because of the imagination and tenacity of John D. Rockefeller, Jr. He had spent millions of dollars on Williamsburg, and lavished on it the passion of true love. Watching the change take place over the long span had been to him a never-ending source of delight and fulfillment. Now seventy-six years old, he was experiencing satisfaction on another score. For the first time, he felt confident that the great project would survive its dependence on him; he believed he had taken the proper steps to enable it to stand on its own feet and prosper after he was gone.

Junior had created two organizations to manage the project. One, a nonprofit, tax-exempt corporation (Colonial Williamsburg, Inc.), owned all the noncommercial property and was responsible for the physical restoration; a subsidiary business corporation (Williamsburg Restorations, Inc.) owned and managed all of the commercial properties, such as stores, restaurants, hotels, and the theater. A trusted executive, Kenneth Chorley, had been president of both corporations since well before World War II, and John 3rd had been chairman of both since 1939.

Late in 1949, Junior felt comfortable enough to announce publicly that his son was fully in charge as chief executive officer—legally and in fact—although Junior meant to continue concerning himself for a while with the actual work of restoration.[1] A few months later, JDR reported to his father that the project had turned the corner financially, registering for 1949 an operating profit of $94,000, compared to a loss of $81,000 the preceding year. Junior told his son that he was gratified "beyond the power of words to express." He wrote:

Clearly, all that was needed was to get the old man out and the young man in. How many hundreds of thousands of dollars my having continued so long in my relation to the Restoration may have cost the Restoration and me, happily we will never know.[2]

Junior believed he had taken care of capital needs. He had donated $6 million in 1949. In 1950 the estimated cost of all the restoration projects approved by Junior and still to be done totaled $9.7 million, and $5.6 million of that was already on hand from the 1949 gift.[3] Then Junior donated another $5.2 million to more than make up the deficit. And there was hope that, in time, operating profits would begin to take care of future restoration needs as well as maintenance and enrichment.

Beyond these practical matters, Junior could take pride in the evidence that his vision had been vindicated by the public response to Colonial Williamsburg. The place was an enormous success—more than half a million visitors each year and the total steadily rising. As restored Williamsburg's twenty-fifth anniversary approached, it was difficult to see what could go wrong. Everything about the restoration seemed encouraging—except that the aims of father and son were about to collide.

As indicated earlier, JDR's relations with his father were never easy. Although they could be effusive in their praise of each other in letters, they were also enough alike to get on each other's nerves. JDR recognized quite soon that Williamsburg was an especially sensitive subject. For Junior the Restoration was not just a project, it was a love affair. Perceiving it as such, JDR in his letters and memoranda to Junior often included a passage to the effect that he realized how important the Restoration was to his father, how much it meant to him, how much pleasure he derived from it.

Despite this mark of sensitivity on JDR's part, the mood between them on this subject was often tense. So obsessive was Junior, so fearful that the undertaking might not be completed in the manner he envisioned, that his nervousness communicated itself to his son. Yet the two men continued in the unstable relation, Junior because it seemed important to have one of the family carry on after he was gone, and JDR because he saw in Williamsburg great possibilities.

It will be remembered that after JDR became a trustee in 1934, he conceived the idea that the Restoration might provide a perfect base for promoting the democratic ideals and values that he felt too many Americans took for granted. He saw Williamsburg as much more than a museum to be visited for its picturesqueness. To him it was a fount of civic education. This fervor presumably resulted from the experience of learning he had himself enjoyed there, coupled with the excitement of the Restoration itself. JDR was moreover aware of the ideological threats to democracy that dominated the temper of the 1930s.

By 1937 he was meeting frequently with leading publicists to discuss his idea—advertising men such as Raymond Rubicam, Fairfax Cone, and William Benton; with publishers and writers such as Henry Luce and Raymond Rich; with radio executives, the producers of "The March of Time," and others. He tried to gear his purpose to the Rockefeller Center theaters: could films about Williamsburg be distributed to movie houses? JDR discussed his ideas with Kenneth Chorley during the latter's visits to New York, and invited him to serve on the Rockefeller Center theater committee. JDR was enthusiastic about the staging at the Center Theater of an operetta with a Williamsburg setting (it was called *Virginia*). Its success was only moderate.

These and other ideas went into limbo during the war, JDR being on leave of absence from all his boards. But the wartime experience only intensified his passion and convictions. He had made up his mind, as we saw, that the "fostering of a better understanding and appreciation of democracy in this country" was to be one of his main postwar purposes.[4]

As early as 1941, after he had become chairman, he had tried out a national radio program to be broadcast from the Restoration. The estimated cost was from $6,000 to $15,000. Junior was against paying this from the operating budget, so JDR put up the money himself. Junior interpreted this as an attempt to force his hand on future commitments, eliciting from JDR a long mollifying letter to explain that he had had no such thought and that he understood his father's position completely.[5]

Junior took pains to make that position as clear as he could when he and his son conferred more than once in 1945 about postwar plans. Junior had long since realized the magnitude of the project if it were to be done as it should be done and had decided that it must, in due time, become self-supporting. Admission would not be charged, but the visiting public would pay its fair share through the income-producing facilities—the Inn and the Lodge, the restaurants, the publications, and the sale of colonial reproductions and tourist items. Moreover, Junior believed that the physical restoration should be completed during his lifetime. As he wrote to Chorley: "The chances of its being completed by succeeding generations [are] small because of lack of funds and also because no one else would be apt to have the same interest in so doing that I have."[6]

Junior's concerns were evident in a written agreement made with his son for the postwar management of the enterprise, detailing "general principles for the expenditure of funds." The four areas for investment were: (1) activities that would produce income; (2) the "enrichment" of the environment and interiors of the buildings; (3) the completion of projects currently approved or to be approved by the trustees; and (4) educational and extension activities. Junior said he was "fully alive" to the need for number 4. He saw that the public should be so attracted to the place that the first three purposes would be served. Beyond that, no gift money or current income should be used for educational and promotional activities "until the physical restoration has been completed . . . lest the larger project . . . fail of completion."[7]

JDR registered his understanding of the agreement as follows:

As a result of our frank and helpful discussions it was agreed that Father would continue an active interest and participation in the handling of all Williamsburg problems having to do with the completion of the physical side of the restoration while I would assume responsibility for the interpretation-educational aspects of the job as well as the business activities. Obviously there are other problems which would fall between but I don't think that there will be any difficulty in regard to their handling. I was very pleased at the outcome of our decisions but realized that Father had come a long way in turning over things to me in order to retain my active interest in the development. My own feeling is that the solution is a very sound and satisfactory one from every angle and that in the long run it will be satisfying to Father.

This sense of harmony proved illusory, though conflict was delayed for several years. Financial needs took precedence over all other things. Despite small surpluses in 1940 and 1943, the effect of the war was to delay steady profits: attendance had declined, work was postponed, new restoration needs were discovered, and costs rose. Chorley wrote to JDR that the trustees had been "floored by the magnitude of the post-war report."[8] JDR's pressing task as chairman was to improve tourist facilities in order to generate income while holding down other costs. JDR did begin to give $50,000 a year to get a small educational and promotional program going, but anything larger would have to wait. Meanwhile, JDR had other things to occupy his mind and his time, especially his efforts at the Rockefeller Foundation and the population program that we described earlier.

Nonetheless, there was good reason for JDR to spend much time at Williamsburg—an average of a week every month. His presence was needed to settle managerial questions, handle ceremonial duties, and attend frequent meetings. The Rockefeller Foundation and the General Education Board, among others, scheduled meetings at Williamsburg every year.

In 1948 John and Blanchette became homeowners in Williamsburg, taking over Bassett Hall, a handsome, historic frame house on Francis Street, near the House of Burgesses. This was the house that Junior and Abby had owned. Abby had left the furnishings to John and Blanchette in her will, and Junior soon followed suit by turning over the deed to the house, subject to his life use.[9]

Colonial Williamsburg was of course linked in the public mind with the name of Rockefeller. For this reason and the fact that he was chairman, it fell to JDR to play a ceremonial role. He had to be on hand when the Virginia Senate and House of Delegates held their opening biennial sessions in the historic capitol, a custom begun in 1934. Dignitaries frequently came, often on state visits, and JDR was expected to be host and preside at special ceremonies.

In March 1946, General Dwight D. Eisenhower and Winston Churchill spent a weekend at the Restoration, arriving by special train. Technically, the wartime prime minister was there as Ike's guest, but the duties of host fell to JDR, who was meeting the two world-famous leaders for the first time. JDR liked Ike, in part for his enthusiasm about the Restoration; Ike "had a spontaneity with the people that was especially appealing." JDR also found Churchill a delight to be with. On the first afternoon, a rest period was scheduled for Churchill while Ike went off to visit Jamestown. JDR tells us what happened after he saw Chorley and Churchill "disappearing down the corridor."

I was informed that they were slipping away for a game of gin rummy, Mr. Churchill being an enthusiastic player having just learned the game on his recent visit to Florida. I decided to join them even though I didn't know the game. For the next hour and a half the three of us sat in the dining room of the private car while Mr. Churchill and Mr. Chorley played. I sat next to Mr. Churchill watching his hand and he explained to me how the game was played. As I became more familiar with the rules he and I worked together on his hand. We couldn't have spent a more enjoyable hour and a half together. It was the nicest possible way to see Mr. Churchill and to get to know him a bit. While we didn't have a chance to talk the way I would have enjoyed doing with him, there was a friendly give and take during the game that was lots of fun. For example when he would discard a king he would comment "Everybody is discarding royalty these days." Then, later on, a remark was made about his picking up a king and he said, "Somebody has got to stand by the aristocracy."

It was an eventful weekend. Photographers' flashbulbs startled a team of horses, spoiling a carriage ride and for a moment endangering the two statesmen. At the banquet, JDR presided and delivered an eloquent toast to Churchill, who responded warmly. So taken was Churchill with such places as the Raleigh Tavern that he summoned the photographers for more pictures.

Another day was made memorable by the visit of President Truman (April 2, 1948), who came to join in honoring Prime Minister W. L. Mackenzie King of Canada and Viscount Alexander, the British wartime hero, newly governor-general of Canada. Unfortunately, all the press attention was on Truman and Governor W. Manton Tuck of Virginia, a staunch segregationist. Truman had taken a strong stand on civil rights in his special message to Congress (February 2, 1948), calling for federal legislation in a number of areas. Southern politicians reacted violently, calling for Truman to withdraw from the presidential race; the seeds were being sown for the "Dixiecrat revolt" if Truman received the Democratic nomination. But nothing went amiss at Williamsburg that day. Truman and Tuck were polite to each other as they and the two visitors from Canada received honorary degrees from the College of William and Mary. Of Truman, JDR wrote:

One cannot help being impressed with his simplicity and seeming genuine friendliness. All who met him were, I believe, drawn to him, particularly when one realizes the terrific load which he carries in these difficult times, not to mention the problems which he is facing in connection with the forthcoming election.

Although JDR's plans for a major educational program at Williamsburg were necessarily in abeyance, the idea never left his mind, and he took every opportunity that arose to discuss it with people whose opinions might count. One such person was General Eisenhower. JDR capitalized on his new acquaintance with him by arranging a second meeting only a month after the March 1946 weekend at Williamsburg. The meeting took place over lunch at the Pentagon, where Ike was stationed before returning to Europe. JDR found Ike so enthusiastic about the idea of promoting citizenship and democracy that he said he would like to retire from the Army to work precisely to that end. He invited JDR back in July to meet with his brother Milton, president of Kansas State College, who was also interested in the subject. Once again, Ike said he would "like to work along the lines we were discussing." JDR made a diary entry that might be regarded as prescient, except that the same idea doubtless was occurring simultaneously to many other persons: "As before was tremendously impressed with the General. Can't help feeling that he would make a great president of the United States in spite of the fact that he is a soldier. In my judgment he is primarily a world statesman and secondly a great soldier."

Among many other conversations that JDR noted, there was only one that might have tempered any excess of zeal on his part. It was with the venerable Henry Stimson, whom JDR encountered during vacation at the Au Sable Club in the Adirondacks in the summer of 1947:

. . . I talked with the Colonel about making democracy a symbol of hope for people in the various troubled areas of the world—something they could look to and live for. He indicated that the only effective way that he knew of was through example in this country or through American activities in other countries. I had thrown out the idea of somehow dramatizing democracy as the totalitarian leaders had so effectively done with their ways of life. He said he just didn't know how this could be done.

In any effort to dramatize democracy, JDR recognized one worrisome problem—the racial situation in Williamsburg. "Jim Crow" practices there made this part of Virginia no different from the Deep South. But change was in the air. President Truman won a stunning reelection victory despite his advocacy of civil rights reforms and the Dixiecrat revolt. Buoyed by that, JDR began in January 1949 to see if there was some way that the segregated dining and housing customs of Virginia could be changed. He wanted to see Colonial Williamsburg take the lead in this regard, making it all the more fit a place for a program to promote democratic ideals. He sought the views of three prominent Southerners: Virginius Dabney, renowned editor of the *Richmond Times-Dispatch*; the historian Douglas Southall Freeman, who was a trustee of the Rockefeller Foundation; and Colgate Darden, former governor of Virginia and president of the University of Virginia. He found Freeman and Darden more liberal in their point of view than Dabney, but in the end all three men agreed that Colonial Williamsburg could feed and house "in a separate wing" Negroes who came as members of a larger group, but that Virginia would not tolerate hotels that accepted Negroes in general.

This was not good enough, so JDR decided to press the issue. He drafted a "Statement of Policy" for Williamsburg that asserted "a strong belief in freedom and equality of opportunity" and urged Americans to be worthy of their "American faith." The passage that directly affected the Restoration read:

> In answer to questions we have been asked by many people, we now therefore say that all who come here to draw inspiration from this Restoration will be welcomed and housed and fed in the facilities of Colonial Williamsburg without regard to race, creed or color.

The problem was an excruciating one for an avowed liberal in racial matters such as Junior. His son's draft might have reminded him of the time in 1902 when he had participated in writing the charter of the General Education Board, which used a similar phrase—"without distinction of race, sex or creed." But now his liberal mind judged that he must pursue a policy that was conservative. He felt he had no choice but to respect the prevailing rules and customs of the host Commonwealth of Virginia. He kept the reference to "equality of opportunity," but made a key change that rendered JDR's draft ineffectual. Junior dropped the final phrase, stating only that all would be welcomed and fed and housed "in so far as that is reasonably possible."[10]

Junior may well have been irritated by JDR's raising of the matter at all, just as his son's initiatives at Pocantico in the prewar days had annoyed him, although this obviously was a far more important matter. There is no record of their discussions on the racial question, but in the end JDR felt he had no choice but to accede to his father's judgment. JDR might have felt that time was on his side, the changes he wanted would occur someday, and the educational program he had in mind might hasten that day.

A hint of some acrimony over the matter can be detected in letters the two men exchanged later in the year, on the occasion of a testimonial luncheon celebrating JDR's tenth anniversary as chairman. Junior wanted to make it clear that he was stepping aside and his son would be fully in charge. JDR agreed, but suggested that Junior should stay involved in the physical restoration work he loved so much. Junior demurred, writing: "If I do not completely sever my relationship now, as I had planned, you will again before long find yourself wondering whether the situation is sufficiently challenging to interest you."[11] But JDR generously pressed the point and Junior agreed. At the luncheon, the two men spoke warmly of each other. JDR followed with a letter praising his father, and Junior's reply seemed to record the relation as clearly as could be:

I was happy to avail of the opportunity afforded by the testimonial luncheon to you to tell the staff that the responsibility for the Restoration had been completely transferred from my shoulders to yours, aside from the one exception temporarily made at your request. I meant every word I uttered of confidence in you, of appreciation of your high purposes and of fatherly pride in your desire and eagerness to assume responsibility for the future destiny of the Restoration. If you found satisfaction in what I said about you, it was because I spoke from the heart. I, in turn, greatly admired your complete self possession and the dignity, simplicity, and appropriateness of your remarks, both in appreciation of the staff's tribute to you and in acknowledgement of what I said.

I am sure, as you say, "that you and I agree completely as to our hopes and aspirations for Williamsburg." Holding always to that common objective, let us forget the tension of past conferences and look to the future with mutual confidence and consideration.[12]

JDR decided that the time had come to begin implementing his long-cherished dream. His leadership role at Williamsburg had just been strongly reaffirmed. The Restoration was now showing a modest profit. And JDR found an added incentive in the fact that the Cold War had become rather warm. He agreed totally with the challenge voiced in April 1950 by President Truman in a speech to the American Society of Newspaper Editors:

Everywhere that the propaganda of Communist totalitarianism is spread, we must meet it and overcome it with honest information about freedom and democracy. . . . We must pool our efforts with those of the other free peoples in a sustained, intensified program to promote the cause of freedom against the propaganda of slavery. We must make ourselves heard around the world in a great campaign of truth.[13]

To JDR the need was obvious for a counterpart program in the private sector that would shore up American values at home. But despite years of thinking, he had not decided on the best way to go about starting to promote democratic values. To devise a plan, he obtained the consent of the Restoration board for setting up a "Special Survey Committee." He doubled his annual contribution to $100,000 to pay for the work of the committee, which consisted of himself as chairman and two Williamsburg staff members, Kershaw Burbank and John C. Goodbody. Originally an employee of the Earl Newsom public relations firm, Burbank had helped to design the Williamsburg public relations program in 1948. Goodbody was already at Williamsburg as director of publications.

The committee began its work in March 1950, the members seeking the information and ideas they needed in order to formulate a rationale for the use of Colonial Williamsburg as a base. They thought they needed to travel abroad to study the Cold War at firsthand, a notion brought home to them by the outbreak of the Korean War. Goodbody traveled to the Far East and South Asia while Burbank toured a dozen countries of Europe during the summer months. Each man wrote back to JDR voluminous reports of impressions and interviews.

Then the two men interviewed scores of prominent Americans along the eastern seaboard. Goodbody spent hours with top people at Time-Life and in Washington with Edward Barrett, assistant secretary of state in charge of the overseas information program, and General Walter Bedell Smith, former ambassador to the Soviet Union. Goodbody also sought out historians. One of them, Kenneth Murdock of Harvard, questioned the recherché or "Marie Antoinette" atmosphere at Colonial Williamsburg, saying that it was a wonderful place to spend a weekend, but that it was difficult to "come away with any particular sense of the association of Williamsburg with the ideas of the American past."[14] This only intensified the belief of JDR and his colleagues that a special program was needed.

Meanwhile, Burbank was developing ideas. His memoranda refer to an "indoctrination" project to be sponsored by the Department of Defense, a "citizen education project" involving Teachers College of Columbia University, and the possibility of Colonial Williamsburg purchasing *American Heritage* magazine. A plan was developed for a series of conferences on international affairs—the "Williamsburg Assembly"—the first timed to coincide, in 1952, with the twenty-fifth anniversary of the Restoration. The New York State Board of Regents, which had a Committee on International Understanding in existence, was planning a variety of programs. Under the label "American history," the board proposed a project for Williamsburg designed to relate the founding values of the United States to the current world situation.

The Special Survey Committee elicited positive responses from a cross-section of leading American intellectuals, academicians, and publicists. One of the most enthusiastic, Elliot E. Cohen, editor of *Commentary* magazine, wrote Burbank long and thoughtful letters filled with ideas, one of them touching the sore nerve of race. Cohen said that times were changing and that Williamsburg was duty-bound "to review carefully and take action on the racial problem" on the spot. His advice was to "follow the law, not the customs" and to "move not to make headlines but to render true service." He suggested consultation with leading liberals in the South such as Virginius Dabney.[15] But JDR had already been down that path. His only hope was that mounting the program he had in mind might in itself help accelerate the pace of change.

After a year, the committee had a mass of materials and began to sift through it to write a program. To keep the work going, JDR contributed another $200,000, bringing his total outlay for educational activities since 1946 to $500,000.

The various drafts of the program might be characterized as Cold War thinking on a fairly sophisticated plane. They dealt with the ideological conflict between communism and democracy, the origins of American ideas, the weaknesses in present-day practice, and the changes necessary to strengthen democracy. Racial discrimination was prominently listed as "the single most widely-criticized aspect of America abroad." Another entry was "confusion in the matter of disloyalty and treason," by which was meant the "intolerance and prejudice bred by McCarthy and others . . . one of the great issues of the day."

In the end, the drafters found it difficult to relate their analytical statement to a program. They were careful to say that there should be no sacrifice of other elements of the Restoration, but "in the light of present world conditions" these must "now give more emphasis to the ideological side of [the] picture." The program "must foster the understanding and appreciation of those concepts of democracy developed in the eighteenth century in such a manner that they will have contemporary meaning in helping to meet today's problems."[16]

The report concluded with the recommendation that provision be made for "the carrying forward on a permanent basis of the work the Committee has done in research, preparation of materials, and the development of ideas." Although discussed, the report was never finished in the sense of being presented to the board for decision. No one had shown much enthusiasm for the draft. JDR did not press for the time being, because he was hearing rumblings about financial problems and newly discovered needs for even more restoration work. The best course, he decided, was to seek outside financing on the basis of the work done so far. Accordingly, he and Burbank met with officials of the Ford Foundation, then headquartered in Pasadena, California. Paul G. Hoffman and Robert M. Hutchins listened politely to JDR's ideas, but were not interested. They already had a surfeit of plans for using the Ford money. Later in 1951, JDR was also turned down by the Carnegie Corporation. The Special Survey Committee was disbanded, and in the fall Burbank was happy to return to New York as part of the family's public relations staff.

As far as JDR was concerned, his vision was by no means a dead issue. He continued to talk about it while waiting for finances at Williamsburg to improve or for other support to materialize. So it came as a surprise at the end of 1951 when a serious breach on the issue occurred between JDR and Junior and between JDR and Chorley. The upshot was that JDR totally abandoned his idea of an educational program at Williamsburg, took a leave of absence from the board, and eventually resigned.

Exactly what happened is unrecorded, but there are clues in a long diary entry for January 11, 1952, and in later letters between JDR and his father. Information had come to JDR "in a roundabout way" that Junior was unhappy about his son's plans. JDR confronted Junior; they met three times between January 6 and 11. Here is the diary entry for the last date:

As a result of these talks it became increasingly clear that Father wasn't happy at the thought of Williamsburg becoming the focal point of a democracy-citizenship program of a broader character, that his conception seemed to be that Williamsburg was an end, not its being a means to an end, as I had conceived it. Father specifically indicated that his thought as to an educational program was limited to two things, first making a visit to Williamsburg as inspirational as possible and, secondly, only carrying on such educational activities outside Williamsburg as would encourage people to visit Williamsburg.

Since my interest in Williamsburg has been primarily on the educational side as against Father's interest in the physical restoration, his viewpoint pretty much cut the ground out from under my work. I realized ever since I came back from Washington following the war that Father had real reservations about the educational program but thought that it had been in terms of the financial side, that he was concerned that money spent for the educational work would be an undue drain on the resources of the undertaking. As a result I had contributed personally towards the educational work.

Our talks together, however, made it clear that his fears were much broader and deeper than I had any conception of before. If I had realized what I now know, I would not have gone back into the Williamsburg picture following the war.

A gentlemanly effort was made to cover up the breach. JDR explained his taking a leave of absence from the board by invoking other activities: "We both agreed it was terribly important not to do anything that would be disrupting to the future of the operation." JDR then had lunch with Chorley to discuss what had been going on: "Indicated that I was very much surprised that Father had stated that both Mr. Chorley and the Board were opposed to my ideas as to an educational program for Williamsburg. Kenneth seemed very much concerned as to the turn of events, as well he might be, I would feel. However, he did not say very much."

From this last remark, it seems likely that JDR believed Chorley had been undermining his position with his father and the other trustees. Other members of the family, including Blanchette and Nelson, had given indications that Chorley and his wife were adopting too proprietary an attitude toward Williamsburg, that they were too aggressive and inclined on occasion to elbow their way past JDR. Without question, Chorley was genuinely alarmed by the trend in JDR's thinking—not necessarily the ideas in themselves but what they might mean if allowed to develop. Williamsburg would become something different, JDR would be in control, and Chorley's power would be reduced. Chorley had played his cards well. He found himself in a position that often is politically fatal—in a squabble between members of a family—but he had survived.

Whatever Chorley may have said to alarm Junior, the decisive fact was the father's long-delayed conclusion that his and his son's views were incompatible. Colonial Williamsburg differed from all of the other organizations that had mattered to Junior in his lifetime. Rockefeller Center, the Rockefeller Foundation, the Rockefeller Institute were no longer dependent upon him in the same way as Williamsburg, no longer absorbing as much of his time and attention. But he still feared that Williamsburg could fail and become an inconsequential village once again. It must be kept on course and made financially viable. Despite the large gifts he had made only a few years earlier, it was now clear that he would have to give much more to cover revised estimates and new needs. This crisis finally brought to the surface his real views about his son's purposes.

Junior was nearing eighty years of age. He realized that practical needs at Williamsburg would continue to appear and must be met. He could not bear the thought of funds being siphoned away for other projects. When death came, Junior wanted to feel confident that his dream would be fulfilled and his obligation discharged. He was prepared to give substantially more money if he could be certain that the Restoration would be managed strictly toward that end. He felt he could trust Chorley and the trustees on this score; he was not sure about his son. However praiseworthy JDR's motives and ideas, Junior thought them a danger to "his" Williamsburg. As a result, first came the break with his son, and second, Junior pledged another $15 million to the enterprise, bringing his total gift to almost $50 million.[17]

The one who, with considerable justice, felt wronged was JDR. He had always been candid about his aspirations for Williamsburg, and he had paid for whatever new activity had taken place. He had always deferred to his father's overriding interest, and he had not pushed hard for a follow-up on the work of the Special Survey Committee when he saw that capital needs were again mounting. Now, suddenly, everything had changed. Men who seemed to approve of what he was doing revealed that they had been against it all along. He believed that Chorley had worked behind his back. His father had put JDR explicitly in charge and then had undercut him. JDR felt he had been made a fool of, that all those years he had merely been indulged.

The measure of the shock is the uncharacteristic abruptness of the actions he took—abandoning and withdrawing, first taking a leave of absence from the board and then resigning at the end of 1952. He kept his composure. He remained correct in his dealings with Chorley, and he worked with his brother Winthrop, who became his successor on the board. Nor could he remain angry at a father who, also uncharacteristically, confessed he had been wrong and couldn't help himself. On June 16, 1952, Junior wrote: "Clearly, I have not kept my part of the agreement . . . I realize more and more that, try as I may, I cannot wholly divorce myself from any aspect of the Restoration." He wrote this "because they say confession is good for the soul."

JDR responded on June 19: "The reason I suggested resigning was because I felt that your confidence in my leadership in Williamsburg had been shaken and this, it seemed to me, would create a situation which would be very difficult for both of us."

It was the final installment in a painful lesson JDR had been learning over a long time. So long as he worked under his father's governing hand, the results were bound to be dissatisfying. He had been trapped into doing this dutifully for too long. As soon as he went beyond the dutiful and brought his own ideas and vision and leadership into something his father had created, there was trouble.

He must liberate himself from his father, begin to accomplish things on his own, as Nelson had done and Laurance and David were beginning to do.

26

⚑

MISSION TO JAPAN

JDR WAS in need of a change. The five years since the end of the war had been frustrating. Little that he attempted had come to pass. Alone, the long study trips abroad (the Far East, Europe, South America, and Africa) had been rewarding. But where was the right outlet for the ideas and enthusiasms that these trips generated? JDR seemed to be drifting and floundering, so visibly that his father and others in the family and on the Rockefeller staff began to form an image of him as somewhat bumbling and ineffectual—a nice and thoughtful and dignified man, but not one who would ever accomplish great things.

At this juncture, a change for the better came about through the unlikely medium of John Foster Dulles, the dour, moralistic, brilliant international lawyer, new chairman of the Rockefeller Foundation and longtime Republican leader in foreign affairs. Dulles had the insight to see qualities in JDR that could be put to good use.

By a strange sequence of events, Dulles in 1950 found himself assigned to lead the American mission to conclude a peace treaty with Japan. Early in December, at the Rockefeller Foundation annual meeting in Williamsburg, Dulles asked JDR if he would be interested in going as a member of the mission charged with responsibility for the cultural, educational, and informational aspects of U.S.-Japanese relations. JDR thought the idea "tremendously appealing," but he demurred because he was under doctor's care for an intestinal ailment.[1] That soon turned out to be no hindrance. But the mission was due to leave for Japan toward the end of January and JDR had been looking forward to working with the Williamsburg Special Survey Committee; he was not sure he could rearrange things on such short notice. But he managed and decided to go. It was one of the most important decisions he ever made.

Like JDR, Dulles in the early postwar years had had difficulties, including a crushing disappointment. Though he was not liked by the

502

Democratic leadership, he benefited from the prevailing bipartisan foreign policy and the support of the moderate Republican leaders, especially Senator Arthur Vandenberg. So Roosevelt put Dulles on the U.S. delegation to the U.N. conference at San Francisco, and Truman did the same for the conferences held in Washington, Paris, and Moscow.

Dulles' stature was further enhanced by the fact that everyone expected him to be the next secretary of state when his man, Governor Thomas E. Dewey of New York, was elected president in 1948. With Dewey the odds-on favorite, Dulles seemed on the verge of occupying the coveted post that his grandfather and uncle had both held. President Truman's stunning victory at the polls crushed this hope.

Dewey was still governor, however, and in July 1949 he appointed Dulles to fill the seat vacated by the ailing Democratic Senator Robert F. Wagner. The timing of the resignation forced a special election in November 1949 to fill out the remaining two years of Wagner's term. Dulles agreed to take on the formidable task of running against the popular former governor, Herbert H. Lehman. Though it appeared that neither man intended it, the campaign turned out to be one of the most vicious in modern times. The Dulles camp alleged that Lehman and his fellow Democrats were soft on communism; Dulles also made some remarks that could be interpreted as anti-Semitic. In their turn, the Lehman campaigners implied that Dulles was anti-Catholic. Dulles came within 200,000 votes of winning, an impressive performance. But his slashing attacks on the Democrats seemed to condemn him to three years in the political wilderness.

Dulles swallowed his pride and asked to be taken back into the policy-making councils of the State Department. This move was at first received as laughable effrontery, but the more it was reflected on, the more sensible it seemed. Bipartisanship had weakened during and since the 1948 election, but was badly needed with the Cold War going strong. Democratic proposals were undergoing rough treatment in Congress. Bringing Dulles back might help to ease the situation and gain cooperation from the Republicans. It took a while to get the approval of Secretary of State Dean Acheson and longer to convince President Truman, who had been outraged by Dulles' allegations against his good friend Herbert Lehman. But in early 1950, Truman gave his consent, on two conditions: Senator Lehman would have to approve, which he did, once Dulles gave assurance that he would not be a candidate again in New York; and Dulles would have to be satisfied with the title of consultant, not ambassador-at-large.[2]

By this time, American policy-makers were thinking seriously about a peace treaty with Japan to formally end the military occupation and the state of war. The occupation had been the most successful in modern history.[3] Each side proved a surprise to the other. The Americans were not brutal conquerors; they acted in a civilized manner, even bringing in their own food instead of ravaging the countryside. The Japanese were not bestial, but docile, polite, and cooperative. With their bureaucracy intact, they were marvelously efficient in dismantling their war machine and following every order that emanated from SCAP (Supreme Commander, Allied Powers), the acronym for General MacArthur's headquarters.

Few among the many Americans who went to Japan during the occupation years possessed any deep appreciation of Japanese culture and history. Yet through a combination of intelligent policies, good intentions, instinct, and luck, the Americans were surprisingly capable victors and occupiers. After some uncertainty, the emperor was maintained, but "demystified." The land reform program was successful. And the effort to "democratize" Japan worked as well as anyone could have hoped, the Constitution of 1947 establishing a democratic political system and providing for civil rights. It also "renounced war," a provision that later proved a troublesome bit of idealism from the American point of view.

The operation was under American control from the beginning, with no occupation zones and no other foreign troops aside from token forces directly under MacArthur's command. In Europe a peace treaty with Germany had been prevented by the outbreak of the Cold War. In Japan the Americans were certainly aware of the interests of their allies, especially those who had suffered Japanese aggression, but nevertheless were determined to keep the occupation free of influence by other powers.

As the Protestant missionaries had done earlier in the Orient, the Americans could try to impose their ideas and values. With their knack of adaptation, the Japanese absorbed what worked for them and in their own way rejected what did not. By 1949 the Japanese were growing restive and American policy-makers had reasons of their own for starting treaty negotiations. Soviet hostility and the Communist takeover in China had drastically altered the political situation. Japan, from a hated enemy only a few years earlier, began to look like the best long-term prospect for a major ally in the Far East.

Acheson decided that Dulles would be the ideal man to lead the peace treaty effort. As he explained:

. . . views within the State Department on broad policy questions were pretty well agreed and had the President's support. The task remaining was essentially one of negotiation both within and without the Government. For this Foster Dulles was well qualified. He was competent, ambitious—particularly to succeed me—close to Vandenberg, and in good standing with both the Dewey and Taft wings of the Republican Party. These qualities would lead him to do a good job and get the treaty through the Senate, if this was possible at all, with the necessary bipartisan support.[4]

This statement is essentially correct, but does not reflect the full difficulty of the task Dulles faced. Truman, his State Department, and the Japanese wanted a peace treaty; others did not, or sought to impose unwanted conditions. The Soviets were opposed and would try to insert the Chinese Communists into the negotiations. The British wanted trade restrictions. Australia, New Zealand, and the Philippines wanted punitive terms and reparations. The most formidable opponent, according to Acheson, was the U.S. Department of Defense, then under the strange and erratic leadership of Louis Johnson. A peace treaty would mean the end of the occupation and of the rationale for having American troops and bases in Japan. The State Department's answer to this was that a peace treaty could be accompanied or followed by a mutual security treaty that would allow an American military presence in Japan under much better conditions than occupation.

By May 1950, Dulles was at work on the assignment; in June he was in the Far East on a preliminary visit with his one assistant, John Allison. Then the Korean War began. Dulles wired home that this made the conclusion of a Japanese peace treaty more, not less, urgent, and Acheson concurred. Back in Washington, Dulles worked through the fall on drafts of treaty provisions based on his findings and State Department policy guidelines. By December, when he asked JDR to join him, he was preparing to leave for Japan for the first round of formal negotiations.

Dulles' invitation did not come out of thin air, nor was it a contrivance to give JDR something useful to do. Overseas information and cultural programs had become accepted instruments of foreign affairs. The United States Information Service (USIS), as it was known overseas, functioned in scores of countries with a broad range of activities—press, publications, film, libraries, radio, cultural and educational exchange programs. Dulles had settled most of the political questions from the American point of view during his work in Washington in the waning months of 1950. But what kind of USIS effort should be established in Japan? How might cultural exchanges help U.S.-Japanese relations over the years? Were there new ideas that might be particularly useful in Japan? The Japanese were avidly interested in things American, and Americans needed to know a great deal more about Japan.

Including in the peace mission an American with stature, who was alive to these needs and understood them, who would study the cultural issues and make recommendations, could be of immense help. There was no precedent for this idea; it was clearly subordinate to the political task. There was no mandate for it either; tangible results would depend on the persuasiveness of the study and its recommendations in generating subsequent support. JDR seemed to Dulles the perfect choice. His interest in the Far East was known and his interest in educational and cultural programs was evident from his plans for Williamsburg.

Dulles was eighteen years JDR's senior, but they had been colleagues since 1935, when Dulles had joined the Rockefeller Foundation board. They were not intimate friends. As JDR noted later in his diary, he had the "highest respect and admiration" for the austere Dulles, but "he is not easy to get to know." Dulles was confident that JDR would work hard and keep within proper bounds. He also thought his manner and style might be effective with the Japanese, and that JDR would be in a good position to develop support from private foundations for programs in Japan. In these assessments, Dulles was exactly right.

For JDR, the invitation fitted perfectly. It rekindled his interest in the Far East, harking back to his 1929 trip, when he had been first captivated by Oriental culture, and to the intense renewal of his interest during his second trip in 1947. JDR was also identified with China through his work on the China Medical Board. He had been one of twenty-five private citizens invited by Secretary Acheson to a State Department conference on China in 1949, after the Communist takeover. But JDR had been most entranced by Japan, and he had played a role in drafting papers in 1945 for the State-War-Navy Coordinating Committee, whose work formed the basis for American postwar policy toward Japan.[5] China seemed closed to Americans indefinitely; Japan was wide open.

With characteristic thoroughness, JDR began to prepare. He went up to Harvard to talk with Edwin O. Reischauer, then associate professor of Far Eastern languages. He consulted Dr. Charles B. Fahs, new director of the Humanities Division of the Rockefeller Foundation, who turned out to be an excellent source of information on Japan. He got in touch with Merrill Shepard, his former Naval colleague, who agreed to take a month's leave from his Chicago law firm to come to New York and work with JDR on the report once the trip was over.

JDR also spent four days in Washington for briefings and meetings with "Foster Dulles each day." He had a sesson with Joseph C. Grew, who had been ambassador to Japan at the time of Pearl Harbor. A key person he consulted was Dean Rusk, assistant secretary of state for Far Eastern affairs, whom he had met during the war.[6] One day Dulles took JDR to lunch with Rusk and Acheson, giving JDR the as yet unforseeable distinction of lunching with three secretaries of state at once. Of Acheson, JDR wrote: "Considering the heavy load [he] is carrying, not to mention all the criticism that has been aimed at him, it really is amazing how calm and cheerful he is."

JDR apparently had some difficulty getting a clear idea of what he was expected to do:

On Monday had a talk with [Dulles] to determine the scope of my assignment in view of the broadness of the cultural field and his reply was, "whatever I wanted to make of it." To that I raised the question of the possible need for follow-up work after the trip and he said the extent of that was entirely what I was interested to do.

He picked up clues in later sessions; Dulles wanted him to study "long-range cultural relations."

He feels that the peace treaty is just the starting point in U.S.-Jap [sic] relations and that it will only have lasting meaning as the basic relationship between the two countries is strengthened and developed. Obviously the cultural relations are an important factor in this connection. . . . A further thought Mr. Dulles had in mind in my participation was to broaden the basis of the Mission—to reduce the emphasis on the military side.

On January 22, JDR and Blanchette joined the official party in Washington for the flight to Tokyo aboard a Military Air Transport Service plane. It was a converted Constellation that had sleeping berths for ten people. The "mission" was quite small. Dulles as leader now held the rank of ambassador and personal representative of the president. The others included JDR, Allison, Assistant Secretary of the Army Earl Johnson, two other Pentagon men, and one other State Department man.[7] Dulles, JDR, and Johnson brought their wives along, and there was one woman secretary.

Always fascinated by the logistics of long-distance plane travel before the jet age simplified things, JDR wrote with wonder of this bizarre flight to Tokyo. It took nearly twelve hours to fly from Washington to McChord Field near Tacoma. Then the flight left for a refueling stop at Shemya in the Aleutian Islands en route to Japan:

We had strong head winds all of the way and the cold was intense—as low as 25 degrees below zero. After a while our heating system went out with the result that it got down to around freezing in the plane. . . . After about 6 or 7 hours of flying it was decided to turn back. Word had come through that there was no gasoline available at Shemya and also that the alternative site, Adak, was pretty much out because of weather conditions.

The group flew back to McChord Field, and then Dulles decided to go to Burbank, California, to the Lockheed plant so that the manufacturer could fix the heater. After this was done, the flight proceeded to Tokyo on a route that required no heater, via Honolulu and Wake Island, bucking hundred-mile-an-hour head winds for the last portion. The elapsed time for the trip was 63 hours, 15 minutes. As JDR put it, "it was like a 2 and ½ day houseparty."

On the first day in Tokyo, the weary travelers plunged right into a heavy schedule of briefings, including two hours with General MacArthur, then at a low point in his career. The entire Dulles mission was played against the backdrop of the erratic fortunes of the Korean War and the dramatic conflict between MacArthur and Truman. After Truman had committed American troops to the defense of South Korea and managed to convert the effort to a United Nations peacekeeping action came the dark days of the "Pusan perimeter," with the U.N. troops nearly pushed into the sea. Then in September 1950, MacArthur pulled off his risky and brilliant landing at Inchon, which culminated in the virtual destruction of the North Korean Army. There followed MacArthur's drive all the way up to the Yalu River, resulting in Chinese Communist troops crossing over and dealing a series of staggering defeats to the U.N. forces. The retreat down the peninsula brought forth erratic behavior on MacArthur's part and the declaration of a national emergency by President Truman. At the end of January, when the Dulles group met MacArthur in Tokyo, the U.N. forces had been pushed down south of Seoul and Inchon. JDR noted MacArthur's words:

He indicated that by the strategic retreat down the peninsula the lines of the enemy supply system had been so lengthened that the number of soldiers he could keep in the front lines was very materially reduced. He indicated that the Communists had somewhat abandoned the initiative and that the U.N. forces were increasingly taking it. . . . we might work our way back to the

38th parallel but beyond that he did not see how we could go [further] with the Chinese hordes that were available to the enemy and with the decision that there should be no bombing of Manchuria, the Chinese "sanctuary" as he called it.

Throughout January worry prevailed at MacArthur's headquarters and in Washington about what to do if the U.N. troops were forced to evacuate Korea. Now General Matthew B. Ridgway had taken command of the Eighth Army and was in the process of rallying the U.N. forces. On March 15, he recaptured Seoul and by early April reached a point slightly north of the 38th parallel. There he stabilized defensive positions for two more years of sporadic warfare, culminating in a truce and the present cease-fire line. Instead of quieting MacArthur's dissidence, Ridgway's success seemed to intensify it. By early April, only a few months after the Dulles mission was in Tokyo, President Truman was forced to dismiss MacArthur because of what Acheson termed his "willful insubordination and incredibly bad judgment" in violently and publicly opposing U.S. policy. Acheson said that the reunification of Korea was not a military goal but a political one.[8]

These dramatic events overshadowed in the public mind the Dulles mission and its progress, but Dulles made rapid strikes in negotiating with Prime Minister Shigeru Yoshida the key points of a peace treaty. Dulles did make headlines around the world when he tested the idea of a mutual security alliance in a speech before the America-Japan Society.[9] If Japan accepted that idea, he said, the United States would consider retaining forces in Japan "as a testimony to the unity between our two countries." The speech was warmly received in Tokyo.

After less than two weeks, Dulles was able to leave for the more difficult part of his trip—to the Philippines, New Zealand, and Australia, where he had to convince those wartime allies to forgo reparations and accept a treaty less punitive than they desired. JDR stayed on in Japan another two weeks, trying to adhere as closely as possible to his professed intention of meeting primarily with the Japanese and doing a lot of listening. By the time he left on February 22, he had consulted with many leaders in virtually every important domain of Japanese life and culture. With the aid of a translator, he spoke to an audience of one thousand Japanese at a "Lincoln Day rally" held at the America-Japan Society. The germination of an important idea came when three Japanese, who as students had lived at International House in New York City, came to call on JDR: they were eager to start an "I House" in Tokyo.

Equally useful was JDR's renewal of acquaintance with Shigeharu Matsumoto, with whom he had served as an "assistant secretary" at the IPR conference in Tokyo in 1929. Matsumoto was to become a great resource to JDR in threading his way through the labyrinth of Japanese customs and sensitivities. A formidable man seven years JDR's senior, Matsumoto was connected by birth and marriage to two important industrial families. He was a law graduate of the University of Tokyo and had studied abroad during the 1920s at Yale, Wisconsin, Geneva, and Vienna. Matsumoto was to become known as a writer, translator, historian, and leader in American studies, being already at that time an accomplished teacher, journalist, and lawyer. From 1936 to 1945, he had been with the Domei News Agency, latterly as its managing director, even though he was a member of a faction regarded as antimilitarist. On this account, he was chosen in 1945 as one of three Japanese to serve on a mission to persuade the Soviet Union to help bring about peace with the United States, but the mission was aborted.

Back home by the end of February, JDR assembled a team to help work his impressions and ideas into a report for submission to Dulles. Merrill Shepard was on hand and U. Alexis Johnson of the Bureau of Far Eastern Affairs sent two people from the State Department, Douglas Overton and Eileen Donovan. Several scholars, including Reischauer, came in to review the draft. By April 9, JDR was able to take it to Washington for preliminary review with senior State Department officials, but Dulles was gone. He had been awakened in the middle of the night by a telephone call from Acheson with instructions to leave immediately for Tokyo. MacArthur had been dismissed and Dulles was needed to calm Japanese fears that this would adversely affect their security or the progress of the treaty.

There followed the spectacle of MacArthur's triumphal return home, his speech to Congress, and the congressional hearings. It was a difficult time for Truman and Acheson, but eventually the old soldier did fade away. In such an atmosphere, JDR's report on cultural recommendations for Japan, formally submitted April 16, obviously did not receive eager attention, and he encountered the notorious State Department caution. In a series of letters, Dulles reported that there was "reluctance" to release the report because some officials felt some passages were too sensitive for the Japanese. Dulles was moreover concerned about releasing the report, "when the draft Treaty is being widely attacked as too lenient upon the Japanese."[10]

Yet the eighty-page document was well written and well balanced.

It analyzed cultural relations and interests, stressing mutuality and the "free and voluntary interchange of ideas and information." In emphasizing the "two-way street" and the need for Americans to learn about Japan, the report said: "If we do not take initiative in this respect, as well as in making our culture available to the Japanese, the loss will be ours." Citing the highly literate nature of Japanese society, the report put quality ahead of quantity and called for "intellectual contacts." It defined "culture" broadly and gave cultural programs a modest role—enriching and contributing to sound relations, but not guaranteeing them.[11]

The recommendations were in two categories: those for government action and the others addressed to the private sector (both Japanese and American). The former dealt with converting the Civil Information and Education program of the Army into a State Department USIS operation in major Japanese cities, including a discussion of objectives and programs. The ideas for the private sector included a "cultural center" in each country, one or more International Houses in Japan, an exchange-of-intellectuals program, and an English-language teaching program in Japan.

Instead of making the report public, the State Department issued a bland press release September 12 without citing any of the recommendations. The report itself was classified "confidential" and remained so. The reason, presumably, was concern as to the possible reaction to a public statement of USIS objectives and programs in Japan. The brief discussion of the "free world" versus "Stalinist imperialism" had the unmistakable stamp of JDR's liking for the positive: "Our problem is that we of the free world too often have a clear conviction as to the things to which we are opposed but lack clarity of thinking as to the things in which we believe." Recommendations apart, the most striking characteristic of the report was its sensitivity to the "unusual cultural and historical development" of Japan and the need to act cooperatively rather than unilaterally.

Probably the main reason for the State Department's reluctance was that the report lacked official status; the bureaucrats did not want to be saddled with responsibility for recommendations made by a private citizen not under their control. Douglas Overton later told JDR's staff aide Ed Young that he had been dispatched to participate in drafting the report because his superiors in Washington were nervous at the thought of what this uncontrolled document might contain; Overton was to try to keep it harmless. He found nothing to worry about and became an enthusiastic supporter of JDR's ideas.

Another sign of the department's caution was Dulles' formal response to the report. Usually, when Dulles wrote to JDR, the message was short and pithy. This one was long and stilted, obviously written by an aide. The point was to distance the department from any responsibility for JDR's private-sector recommendations. The letter asked if he would "be willing to undertake the responsibility of securing the necessary interest and support" for the proposed "Cultural Center and International Houses" that should be "established and operated on a strictly private basis."[12]

During the first week of September, JDR and Blanchette attended the Japanese Peace Conference in San Francisco. Some fifty nations were represented. His diary describes, inter alia, the expected disruptive tactics of the Russians. But "Mr. Acheson, as Presiding Officer, handled the situation extremely well." The peace treaty was signed on September 8. Acheson spoke impressively:

As a result of his statement and the talks by a number of the delegates the Conference really ended in a spirit of unity and high purpose. The whole thing went off much better than had been anticipated by our people—so well that many were concerned as to what the Russians plan next. It was obvious that they did not do an all-out job in their obstructionist tactics, but rather were just making speeches for consumption in the Far East as well as at home.

It had been, as Acheson observed, "the great diplomatic success of 1951,"[13] something of a miracle, given the MacArthur troubles and the rampant paranoia afflicting the nation under McCarthyism. In retrospect, the choice of Dulles for the job was a stroke of genius. So overwhelming were the mindless and withering attacks on Acheson and his department that it is doubtful whether the peace treaty and mutual security pact could have been put through without the counteracting Republican credentials of Dulles. He had been brought in primarily to help smooth relations with Congress and he did exactly that. The treaties were ratified early in the following year.

JDR decided that he needed some evidence of support from the American private sector before scheduling a follow-up trip to Japan. He began canvassing U.S. corporations and foundations. In the meantime, he took an important step regarding his own staff. Anticipating a long-term interest in Japan, JDR decided that he needed a second aide. Ed Young had been adept at managing home base, so JDR thought of him as someone to work on domestic projects; Young accepted this limitation, though he did not agree with it. His sole assignment in planning for Japan was to look up and look into any

American nonprofit organizations specializing in Japanese affairs. For further staff help, JDR tried again without success to get Merrill Shepard. He also talked with Kershaw Burbank about the job, but they jointly concluded that Burbank lacked the overseas experience. So JDR turned to Donald McLean, Jr., who had been abroad during the war and later with the high commissioner in Germany. As will be recalled, McLean had served JDR for several years in the American Youth Hostel program and was a lawyer on the Socony-Vacuum staff. In July 1951, JDR offered him a full-time associate's job, his first assignment being to accompany JDR on his next trip to Japan. After consideration, McLean decided to trade a legal career for a more unorthodox adventure with JDR.

Discussions with the Chase Bank, Socony-Vacuum, and Standard Oil of California about support for cultural projects in Japan showed that help should be available at some point, but probably not until well after the occupation had ended. With backing from Dulles, JDR urged the Ford Foundation to indicate a willingess to make grants for Japanese projects. But Paul G. Hoffman put JDR off again: he said that all the Ford money for overseas projects was tied up in undertakings in India, Pakistan, and the Philippines.[14]

JDR had better luck closer to home. Dulles was chairman of the Rockefeller Foundation and JDR, of course, was an important trustee. As expected, the new president, succeeding Chester Barnard, turned out to be Dean Rusk. He had been sounded out by JDR as early as April 1951. In October, Dulles made the offer, and Rusk consulted with President Truman, who said he would not try to keep Rusk from "taking the best job in the United States."[15] Rusk resigned from the State Department and accepted the post. He was formally elected in December and took office the next June.

JDR hardly needed to wait for Rusk: the existing leadership of the Foundation was favorably inclined. Dr. Fahs had been consulted by JDR from the beginning, and Barnard and his vice president, Lindsley Kimball, readily agreed to support grants for projects in Japan. As early as September 1951, JDR was assured of substantial funds for one or more projects. He thereupon notified Dulles that he would make another trip to Japan to determine the extent of interest there. On October 13, he, Blanchette, and McLean left for Tokyo.

This time JDR was traveling as a private citizen and paying his own way. Given the niggardliness and complexity of State Department expense accounts, it made life simpler—witness this letter from Dulles after the first trip:

Dear John,

I have your letter of March 7th. I am sending you my check for $135, which represents half of the Imperial Hotel bill, less $50, which is half of the provisioning bill and $5 for the steward. The total of the outgoing cost of provisioning was $90, not $180.

I shall try to collect through the State Department the cost of the official reception. If and when I get it back, I shall give you your share.

Sincerely yours,

John Foster Dulles[16]

Still, JDR was frugal and he obtained a small grant from the Foundation to cover McLean's expenses. Without official status and the advantage of bringing peace, the second trip was far different from the first. JDR spent his time in planning sessions with the Japanese leaders he had singled out during his first visit. He also worked with Saxton Bradford and the staff who were to man USIS in Japan. During the busy month, McLean, Matsumoto, and Sterling Fisher (of *Reader's Digest*) all actively supported JDR. After a meeting with two faculty members of the University of Tokyo, JDR confided to his diary: "Don said I talked too much; am afraid he was right. It is difficult to get one's ideas across and at the same time to encourage the development of the other person's thinking."

The visitors noticed that although Japan was changing, traditions were still crucial, few of them likely to change. The importance of status and deference remained, and JDR was learning how things in Japan had to be done: "My problem is to move ahead with our efforts and still be sure the Japanese are really happy with what we are doing together. Is essential in the end that they feel it is their program and not mine." So deferential did JDR become that Fisher warned him to lead more emphatically, or the projects would not get off the ground. JDR enjoyed high status in Japan because of his name and of his part in the peace mission; the Japanese would expect to find this status made full use of if a project were to be taken seriously.

On the Japanese side, "status" was put into play thanks to Matsumoto's suggestion that the former Count Kabayama take part; JDR had met him in 1929. He was now Mr. Aisuke Kabayama, all noble titles except those of Emperor Hirohito's family having been abolished by the Constitution of 1947. But lack of a title in no way lessened the status of this venerable man, who was a confidant of the emperor. Kabayama agreed to be head of a committee to enlist Japanese support for an International House and a cultural center. On November 12, with Matsumoto's guidance, Kabayama chaired a meeting of thirty-five Japanese industrial and intellectual leaders. JDR talked to the group ("it was a good turnout and a good session") and felt he had gone as far as he could: "Will be desirable for us to go away and let the situation develop on its own. Said to the group, however, that I would be glad to come back later if I could be helpful."

Back in the United States, rather impatient to alter the slow pace of things in Japan, JDR moved immediately to establish the first of a series of projects that had emerged from the planning sessions: an exchange of intellectual leaders between the two countries.[17] JDR and McLean first approached Harvard University as a possible home for such a program. Although Edwin Reischauer was enthusiastic, President Conant rejected the idea, for administrative reasons. JDR then turned to Sir George Sansom, the doyen among Japan scholars, who headed the East Asian Institute at Columbia University.

A year-end grant of $101,000 from JDR to Columbia established the Intellectual Interchange Program. In January 1953, Harry J. Carman, professor of history and retired dean of Columbia College, was designated to head the program, assisted by Professor Hugh Borton of the East Asian Institute. JDR made another grant of $25,000 in 1953 and a third, of $103,000, in 1954. Meanwhile, JDR was talking with the Metropolitan Museum of Art in New York about the idea of bringing a Japanese art exhibit to the United States, and Blanchette convinced the Museum of Modern Art to erect a Japanese house in the outdoor area along 54th Street that had been dedicated as the Abby Aldrich Rockefeller Sculpture Garden.[18]

Ed Young had singled out the Japan Society as the most promising organization concerned with Japanese culture and trade in the United States. Founded in 1907, the society had been small and little known, though distinguished for its cultural program. The society had naturally become moribund during World War II. The question was whether to revive the organization or to found a new cultural center. As it happened, a small group of former members and devotees of Japanese culture were trying to revive the society. Prominent among them were two businessmen, the silk importer Paolino Gerli and Raymond Kramer of LaFrance Industries. Kramer was a former colonel who had served on MacArthur's staff in Tokyo. These men were delighted to hear of the possible interest of a Rockefeller. After several meetings, JDR conferred with Dulles, who also consented to be involved. On March 24, 1952, a dozen new members were elected to the board of the Japan Society, including Dulles (chairman), JDR (president), Winthrop Aldrich, and Edwin Reischauer, plus executives of General Electric, the Metropolitan Museum of Art, and the National City Bank. Later that year, Ed Young was appointed secretary and Douglas Overton, who had worked on the JDR report, left the State Department to become executive director of the new Japan Society.

Despite rapid progress in New York, nagging delays continued to keep things from getting started in Japan. JDR had to make a third trip of over a month in April and May 1952. One cause of delay was that Matsumoto was in the hospital with a broken kneecap. Between sessions that tried to get the "cultural center preparatory committee" moving, JDR traveled through the islands and had his first audience with the emperor ("was very favorably impressed by him"), attended the cherry blossom festival with Prime Minister Yoshida, and witnessed a May Day riot of students and workers ("Communist inspired . . . only relatively small number participated"). After this third lengthy visit, JDR had probably become, next to MacArthur, the American best known to the Japanese. And he was probably better known in leadership circles than the general, who had acted with his characteristic remote and imperial quality.

JDR noted on the way home:

The problem as McLean puts it is to get traction on the part of responsible Japanese. They just don't seem to move into gear in the same way we do in this country. It doesn't seem to be any lack of interest or enthusiasm but rather inertia.

Yet he curbed his impatience with this reflection:

As I left Japan was regretful more progress had not been made in connection with the proposed Cultural Center but could not help feeling that it was probably all to the good—that the final product would be a better one due to the delay. That it would be better adapted to Japanese needs and conditions and better received from the Japanese point of view as being more theirs.

JDR was right; in fact, events in Japan were beginning to move quickly. The committee had thought up a new kind of institution, one that would combine several functions. Though the committee decided to call it an International House, it envisaged much more than its American namesake, which is a hostelry for foreign students on a university campus. The Japanese committee had found a two-and-a-half-acre plot (the bombed-out home of a former Japanese baron) in an attractive section of Tokyo, a short distance from the center of the city. The plan was to combine under one roof a hostelry, a cultural center for "men of letters from many lands," and an institute for the study of international relations, something like the American Council on Foreign Relations in New York.[19]

By the end of May, the committee sent a proposal to the Rockefeller Foundation requesting $676,121. The Foundation approved, subject to the committee's raising 100 million yen (about $240,000) by the end of August 1953. The International House of Japan was incorporated, the site acquired, and architects put to work designing the new building. Kabayama and Matsumoto took the lead in the fund-raising and on the deadline date sent a telegram to Dean Rusk announcing success. Contributions had been received from more than 12,000 donors. Less than two months later, Kabayama died at the age of eighty-eight: "It was as if he had been waiting for final assurance of the success of the undertaking to mark the end of a long life of service and usefulness to humanity."[20]

Less than eighteen months after JDR had traveled to Tokyo with the Dulles peace mission, the projects in Japanese-American relations he had been busy generating already had the sweet smell of success about them. This was evident on June 17, 1952, when New Yorkers saw something they had not seen in many years—the Rising Sun flag of Japan proudly displayed along Fifth Avenue. The occasion was the first annual banquet of the Japan Society, taking place only three months after the skillful reorganization of the society's board. More than 750 civic and business leaders attended and heard speakers call for a new era of friendship, trade, and prosperity between the two nations. The speakers were Dulles, JDR, and the new Japanese ambassador to the United States, Eikichi Araki, who had presented his credentials in Washington on June 5. After a half century of rivalry and a bitter war that fanned emotions on both sides to the point of hatred, the two countries indeed were beginning a new era of friendship. Perhaps nothing marked that transition more emphatically than the first public event of the new Japan Society.

Not only the Japan Society, but all the other Japanese-American initiatives that JDR was starting were to flower into remarkable successes as well. After all the frustrating years of working and planning since the war, JDR finally had his new beginning, too. Not in his wildest imaginings could he have anticipated this particular turn of events. He had liberated himself from filial dependency and from his father's overbearing influence and had struck out on his own. Now, suddenly, he had a success on his hands. There would be many more.

27

1952

ANOTHER YEAR of transition for the Rockefeller family came in 1952. Three of the brothers—Winthrop, Nelson, and John—took steps that marked lasting changes in their lives. And their father made decisions concerning Rockefeller Center, the Rockefeller Brothers Fund, the Pocantico estate, his personal philanthropy, and gifts to his heirs that completed the final disposition of his holdings, short of his last will and testament.

It will be recalled that Frederick Gates had written an impassioned letter to Senior in 1905 urging "final disposition" of the great Rockefeller fortune during the lifetimes of Senior and John Jr., lest the fortune "simply pass into the unknown, like some other great fortunes, with unmeasured and perhaps sinister possibilities."[1] Senior played his part, giving half of his assets to philanthropic causes and the other half to his trusted son. We have seen the many ways in which Junior worked hard at giving money to worthwhile causes, how his giving revived after the relative hiatus of the Great Depression, and how in the 1940s he began to pass resources on to his heirs. Junior clearly was concerned with this same question of "final disposition," embarking on a course that reached a peak in 1952. In that year, for example, his charitable contributions reached the astonishing total of $73.4 million.

That total is perhaps a bit misleading, inasmuch as the bulk of it was a paper transaction, accounts receivable worth $57.7 million that Junior gave to the Rockefeller Brothers Fund. It was a gift of the notes owed to him by Rockefeller Center. When the Metropolitan Life loan was retired in 1950, the Center was able to begin a repayment schedule of $2.5 million a year on the $60.2 million owed to Junior at the time he sold the Center to his sons in 1948. One payment was made in 1951, reducing the balance to $57.7 million. It will be remembered that Nelson had made an unsuccessful bid to get Junior to forgive the entire debt to help the Center's financial position. Then he asked his father to waive the next three payments to help the Center pay the costs of its modernization program. Again Junior refused; a debt was a debt. Having lost most of his original investment in the Center when he sold it to his sons, he felt that the outstanding debt at least should be paid.

Why, then, did Junior suddenly decide to give the entire amount to the Brothers Fund? Clearly, it was the move toward final disposition. The debt would not be fully retired until the late 1960s and the odds were great that Junior would die well before that time. In any case, the longer he lived, the less he would be capable of putting the debt repayments to effective use. When he died, the balance of the debt would be part of his estate, subject to estate taxes. It occurred to Junior that the entire matter could be settled at one stroke by giving the claim to the Brothers Fund.

Junior had been pleased when his sons came together in 1940 to create the fund. It was both a symbol of family unity and tangible evidence that all of his exhortations about the value of giving had persuaded his sons. He could show support of both of these laudable ends by substantially increasing the resources of the fund, making it essentially an endowed foundation with a role of its own and no longer merely a device for personal giving, dependent entirely on the amounts the brothers donated each year.

Moreover, Junior was satisfied that the fund was in good professional hands with Dana Creel as its executive head. Although Junior insisted on an accelerated repayment schedule, the money still would not all come at once, enabling the fund and its mission to grow gradually in expertise. And it was a way of helping his sons, not by lining their pockets, but by giving their philanthropic instrument stature in the world of foundations. Recognizing that his sons controlled both the Center and the fund, and wishing to make certain that the debt would actually be paid off in the manner prescribed, Junior insisted that the brothers reaffirm an agreement to that effect.[2]

The balance of Junior's 1952 giving, some $15.7 million, was certainly not insignificant. The major recipients were the Metropolitan Museum of Art ($10.6 million for the Cloisters) and the Museum of Modern Art ($4 million for the endowment fund). In this and later years, Junior continued his postwar pattern of taking care of projects he had started and of manifesting his renewed interest in religion, the arts, conservation, and restoration.

The major gifts in his 1953 total of $13 million were to Colonial Williamsburg ($6 million) and to the Jackson Hole Preserve ($5.2 million) for a variety of conservation purposes. After a dip in 1954 to only $5.2 million, Junior's giving zoomed up again in 1955 to $55.1 million. There was a long list of familiar recipients—Jackson Hole Preserve ($6.3 million), Colonial Williamsburg ($4.7 million for the Abby Aldrich Rockefeller Museum of Folk Arts), Brown University ($5.4 million), Sleepy Hollow Restorations ($3 million), International House at Columbia ($1.3 million for modernization), and gifts of less than a million to Spelman College, Barnard College, the Oriental Institute at the University of Chicago, the Agora project in Athens, the public schools of Tarrytown, and several research hospitals. But most of the giving was in the field of religion, including relatively small gifts to a number of liberal religious institutions and three big ones—$6.3 million to Riverside Church, $4.2 million for a new Interchurch Center next to Riverside, and $20.1 million to "strengthen and develop Protestant theological education."

The Interchurch Center is a seventeen-story office building standing on the block immediately south of Riverside Church. Junior had purchased the block from Barnard College; this and his other gifts resulted in the center being built on Morningside Heights in Manhattan instead of in any one of a number of competing cities. The name of the building comes from the fact that four large denominations make their national headquarters there—the Presbyterians, Methodists, Congregationalists, and Northern Baptists. Many of the floors are rented to religious and secular associations, thus helping to retire the mortgage for the National Council of Churches of Christ in the United States of America, the sponsoring organization of the building. The project obviously was part of Junior's long dream of uniting the Protestant faiths. In fact, the creation of the National Council was something Junior and Charles Evans Hughes had worked on as early as 1900. It finally came into existence in 1948, helped by grants from both Junior and his oldest son.

The major gift for theological education, which Junior had been planning for several years, was administered by the Sealantic Fund.[3] He perceived an accumulation of needs. Earlier, he had frequently aided divinity schools that were interdenominational or strongly ecumenical in character, but he had made no such gifts since the 1930s. Now these schools needed financial help, since by definition they did not have a steady flow of supporting funds from a particular denomination. They also needed upgrading—too many students seeking advanced degrees had to go to European seminaries. And the black ministry needed help—only 10 percent of black preachers had the Bachelor of Divinity degree.

In the classic fashion of other Rockefeller schemes to create "centers of excellence," Sealantic expended $10 million in substantial gifts to five divinity schools in different regions of the country. The remaining $10 million was spent in aiding theological libraries, providing fellowships, and supporting "clusters" of small seminaries in particular areas. This last idea was to link these schools in mutual support. Such clusters were aided in Atlanta, Richmond, San Francisco, Rochester, and Boston. Three of the fellowship programs were for black candidates, many of whom later played leadership roles in the civil rights movement. One notable beneficiary was the Reverend Jesse Jackson, a Sealantic fellow for study at the Chicago Theological Seminary.[4]

Sealantic also continued its activities in the conservation field. One project is noteworthy because it threatened to become a cause célèbre like that of the Grand Teton National Park. It was the preservation of the site of Fort Lee, a cluster of Revolutionary War redoubts perched on the Palisades on the New Jersey side of the Hudson, opposite Fort Washington in Manhattan. The Palisades Interstate Park Commission, which Junior had aided so much, had wanted this historic site and its wooded area for years as part of its preservation plan; Sealantic was acting on behalf of the commission. Leading the opposition was the Borough Council of Fort Lee, New Jersey, which wanted to use the land for commercial development. Sealantic won several court tests, and then made a number of concessions in a search for an amicable relationship. Six of the fifteen acres were given to the borough for development, with the proviso that no building could rise above the tree tops (two-and-a-half stories). Once it got the six acres, the borough rezoned them for a ten-story hotel, but Sealantic won its case before the New Jersey Supreme Court to quash this move. Ironically, the borough's portion was never developed, but was condemned by the state and bought for its "Green Acres" conservation program and became part of the Palisades Park.[5]

Junior also made large gifts to his family in 1952, a total of $63.3 million, requiring him to pay $32.2 million in federal gift taxes. First, he created a new trust for his second wife, Martha, this one worth $10.3 million. The first one, funded with $5 million in securities, had been set up eleven days before their wedding in 1951. Junior wanted his wife to be financially independent from the outset and to know what he regarded as "the joy of giving." Martha reacted to her good fortune by making large gifts in the field she loved, music, and by supporting some of the activities of Junior's sons.

It was at this time that Junior made the final round of gifts to his progeny, completing the process that he had started in 1943. One goal was to bring the younger sons more up to par with the older ones, which he accomplished by giving $2 million to Laurance and $4 million to David. Then there was the special case of Winthrop. His marriage to Bobo had been in deep trouble for several years and by 1952 was clearly on the rocks, with a stormy separation, a bitter divorce battle being waged largely in the press, and huge demands for alimony from Bobo. Everything about this was anathema to Junior, yet he seemed to be understanding and to take pity on Winthrop. It was as if what had happened came as no surprise.

This was a different case from the divorce of Babs and David Milton. In Junior's eyes, Winthrop had made a mistake, and there was no way he could make the marriage work. But Babs' first marriage was one that Junior thought should have worked. He liked David Milton and continued to give him a handsome Christmas gift in the years following the divorce.

Junior's reasoning might have been that the messy divorce might shock Winthrop into a more straight and narrow path. Despite his troubles, Winthrop was continuing to do good work in philanthropic causes. He clearly was going to take a financial loss as a result of the breakup. In the end, Junior decided to make a $1.5 million gift to him and to establish a new trust in the Chase Bank worth $4.3 million, with restrictions that sheltered the trust from any divorce settlement: the income was to be shared by Winthrop and the Rockefeller Institute for Medical Research.

The largest part of Junior's 1952 giving to his family, approximately $42 million, went to fund a new series of trusts managed by the Fidelity Union Trust Company of New Jersey for the benefit of the children of John, Nelson, Laurance, and David. These are commonly referred to as the 1952 Trusts or Fidelity Union Trusts. Junior did not set up trusts of this kind for Babs and her two daughters or for Winthrop and his son. The omission of Winthrop is understandable, given that Junior was in the process of taking care of him (and presumably his son and heir) by other means. As for Babs, the explanation can only be found in Junior's long-standing attitude toward her and his determination not to give her any more income, inasmuch as she had benefited from the share of Abby's trust and her combined net worth was now very formidable indeed.

Always preoccupied with the need to inculcate the values of thrift and stewardship, Junior did not turn over either the income or principal of these trusts to his grandchildren. To his way of thinking, all of them were much too young to be entrusted with this kind of responsibility; the oldest cousin who would benefit from the trust was Rodman, Nelson's eldest son, and he was only nineteen on the date of the gift. Prior to creating the trusts, Junior allowed each of the brothers to determine how the income would be handled for each beneficiary, as well as the precise point in time when full control would pass to them. JDR decided these issues in a straightforward manner. His children would receive an additional 10 percent of the income each year from age twenty-one, meaning that after their thirtieth birthday they would receive all of the income from the trust. Any child past twenty-five who married would receive the full income immediately. In the interim, JDR designated the income of the trust for charitable contributions, rather than taking it as ordinary income, which would be heavily taxed. This was not an insignificant sum— over $600,000 in 1953—and rising each year to well past $1 million, but then gradually declining as each child turned twenty-one and began to receive a growing portion of the income.[6]

One can achieve at least a rough comparison of how each of Junior's six children fared. If all financial transfers from 1934 to 1952 are included—the value of the various trusts as well as personal gifts—and the ranking is made on a scale of 5 to 1, with 5.0 being the highest, the following is a good approximation: John, 5.0; Nelson, Laurance, and David, 4.3; Winthrop, 3.0, and Babs, 2.4. Once again, this comparison holds only when figuring the value of the transactions at the time they were made. All the assets appreciated greatly, and the pattern of use of assets by each individual varied widely, with resulting differences in actual net worth at any given time.

While there is no question that Junior was bent on disposing of his assets in the same two ways that his father had used—gifts to family and to philanthropies—the amounts he gave in the early 1950s would not have been so large had it not been for the value and resilience of the petroleum stocks that still formed the largest portion of his holdings. Oil stocks continued to appreciate greatly due to the general postwar boom and the ever-widening uses for petroleum derivatives. This was especially true of Standard of New Jersey (Esso). A share of

Esso common stock was worth $91.75 at the end of 1950. The company declared a two-for-one stock split in early 1951. Within a matter of months, the value of the new shares had risen from $46 to $76, almost doubling the market value of his original holding and, in fact, doubling his income from this source. Between 1951 and 1955, he gave away 60 percent of his 1.4 million shares of Esso. Yet in the latter year, the value of his much smaller holding was nearly the same as it had been in 1951.[7]

Having sold Rockefeller Center to his sons in 1948, only one major property remained in Junior's hands—the Pocantico estate. He wanted it to stay in the family and knew that it was important to transfer ownership before his death. This is exactly what Senior had done. By the mid-1920s Junior had become the owner of the property, subject to his father's life tenancy. When Senior died in 1937, no estate taxes had to paid. By 1952, the tax legislation passed in the preceding quarter century had radically altered the situation. If Junior wished to avoid both estate and gift taxes, he would have to *sell* the estate to his heirs. The logic was irrefutable, but it still was not easy for him to transfer ownership. With a kind of good-natured grumbling, he wrote to Tom Debevoise in the spring of 1952:

I presume I should make this sale for every reason and that there is really no reason why I should not go forward with it. On the other hand, I still have the foolish feeling that it is pleasant to own the house in which I live. Perhaps by fall I shall have realized the folly of maintaining this position in view of the many advantages a sale would bring.[8]

Anyone who visits the estate will understand Junior's reluctance immediately. The property has an extraordinary natural beauty, with roads and buildings carefully blending into the landscape rather than dominating it. Despite its proximity to New York City and the heavily populated Westchester suburbs, the estate stands in serene isolation from the frenetic growth of the area. This countryside has witnessed the march of history—Henry Hudson's *Half Moon,* the capture of John André, the onset of the age of steam with Fulton's steamboat and Vanderbilt's railroads, and the arrival of the great industrialists seeking estates commensurate with their new wealth and power. The Rockefellers had loved this land since Senior first came to it in the early 1890s, and both Senior and Junior had placed their distinctive imprint on Kykuit and its surrounding acres.

It was very much a rustic area in the late nineteenth century, wooded, the only man-made structures being the old Dutch stone walls here and there, a few roads, some farmhouses, scattered country homes built by affluent New Yorkers, and the tiny village of Pocantico Hills. To the extent that Senior and Junior bought up land in the area, this quiet solitude was preserved. When they were finished, they had accumulated almost 3,500 acres—some six square miles of property— located between the Saw Mill River and the Hudson, the bulk of the estate lying just to the northeast of Tarrytown, but part of it arching over North Tarrytown to the shore of the great river.

Several public roads bisect the estate, as do the tracks of the former New York Central. The village of Pocantico Hills on Bedford Road is entirely surrounded by Rockefeller land. So natural is the setting and so hilly the land that one can drive around the estate and through it without being aware that it is there. Certainly, there is no sign proclaiming it, just as the visitor to Room 5600 in the RCA Building will be puzzled unless aware beforehand that it is the office of the Rockefeller family.

Early in the century, Junior had built Kykuit for his father, on the crest of Kykuit Hill in the southern portion of the property, a relatively modest structure as country houses of the wealthy go. This was in accord with Senior's wishes—he was much more interested in wealth in the form of natural beauty than in structures and ostentatious decoration. The original house was cleverly designed by Delano and Aldrich of New York so as to seem even smaller than it is—forty feet in width and ninety in length. Changes over the years did, however, begin to give Kykuit the aspect of a great country house. At the request of Senior's wife, Laura, a fourth floor and mansard roof were added in 1913. From the upper floors and balconies, one can see fifty miles on a clear day, north toward West Point, west to the Hudson River and the Palisades beyond, south to the spires of Manhattan skyscrapers.

Built of weathered fieldstone, the house has a Georgian character, both in design and in the original furnishings, planned by Ogden Codman. There is a Georgian aspect in the surrounding conceits as well—the formal gardens designed by William Welles Bosworth, a Japanese teahouse with a reflecting pool, a small classical temple with a grotto beneath it of rust-colored granite quarried on the grounds. Gardens stretch away in all directions, each side different in design and content, in some places terraced to take advantage of the ground as it descends from the crest of the hill. To the west is an extraordinarily beautiful Japanese garden with cascading pools that meander down the slope.[9]

The main entrance of the estate is near the center of the property, where Bedford Road passes through the village of Pocantico Hills. One drives through the gate on a tree-lined road. The first structure to be noticed, to the right, is a modern house designed by Marcel Breuer. Exhibited at the Museum of Modern Art, it had been taken apart and shipped to Pocantico to be reassembled as a guest house. Next, to the left, is the Orangerie, a building to house citrus plants, modeled after the original at Versailles. It has extensive greenhouses next to it, where other produce and flowers can be grown off season. Further along, one comes upon the Coach Barn, a brick structure three times the size of Kykuit. One half of the main floor is devoted to well-maintained tack rooms, trophy rooms, stables, and all the carriages the family has owned, now antiques. In the other half are vintage automobiles, some from the estate and others stored there by Nelson.

From the Coach Barn, one approaches Kykuit on its hillcrest, passing through wrought-iron gates eighteen feet high and topped with oxidized copper leaves. The first sight is of the Oceanus Fountain, carved in 1914, a copy of a fountain in the Boboli Gardens in Florence. It has a twenty-foot bowl carved out of one block of granite from Stonington, Maine. Nearby is a statue of Aphrodite, once thought to be by Praxiteles, but actually a seventeenth-century Florentine work. To the right is the broad entrance leading to the circular driveway and the house and grounds. From Kykuit, one can look to the north across the nine-hole golf course to the rambling Playhouse, half a mile away, also three times the size of Kykuit. Across the road from the Playhouse is a stone foundation, all that is left of Abeyton Lodge, the house that Junior and his family used while Senior was still alive.

To Junior all this was truly "home," much more so than his Manhattan residence, Seal Harbor, or even Bassett Hall in his beloved Williamsburg. Kykuit and the surrounding estate was his small kingdom; here he felt most at peace. One can see why the very thought of selling it was disturbing.

To understand the sale and a subsequent transaction in 1954, as well as the enormous complications the estate was to bring to the brothers several decades later, one must remember that the estate is divided into two parts. The core area, described above, is known as the Park. It forms a compact mass of 249.5 acres in the southern portion of the property, entirely fenced in and manicured, though with many carefully preserved trees and copses and outcroppings of rock. The remainder of the estate is known as "the open space." Except for parcels where family members have their houses, its brooks, woods, and riding trails are all accessible to the public for hiking, riding, or cross-country skiing.

During Winthrop's infrequent visits to Pocantico, he stayed in the Breuer house. His four brothers all owned acreage that formerly had been part of the estate, in all cases located in the "open space." JDR 3rd had Fieldwood Farm, 315 acres of the northwestern part of the original estate. Nelson had the 149-acre Hunting Lodge property just east of the Park. Laurance held 262 acres in five locations, the largest being the Rockwood Hall property fronting the Hudson to the west and north of Fieldwood Farm, which Senior had purchased from his brother William's estate in the 1920s. David had the 177-acre Hudson Pines property, just to the north of the Park. He had purchased this from Babs when she decided to distance herself from Junior after her divorce. Though there were whispers that Junior had "banished" her from Pocantico, it seems to have been more a mutual case of the two feeling more comfortable when they were apart. In addition to her Manhattan apartment, Babs bought a house in Oyster Bay, Long Island.[10]

By giving these properties to John, Nelson, Laurance, and Babs, Junior had reduced his own estate by nearly a thousand acres. Only John and David used their properties as country homes. Laurance used the Kent house, a modern steel-frame structure that Junior had allowed him to build in the Park on the site of the original Kent house. Nelson also stayed in the Park, in the Hawes house, one of a dozen houses used for guests or occasional rental to employees or family friends. Whether they lived in the Park or not, all family members had the same rights to use the Playhouse, the golf course, and other facilities.

As usual, Nelson was the leader of the brothers in coaxing Junior along his reluctant path to transferring ownership of the estate. In January 1951, Junior took the first step by turning the estate over to a corporation he created, Hills Realty Company, taking back all of the stock issued by the company, 1,000 shares, which had an assigned value of $700,000. This was some $3 million less than the book value of the remaining Pocantico estate—the 2,500 acres of land, all the buildings and improvements, and the art and furnishings in Kykuit.

The market value presumably would have been much higher, especially if the estate were sold for corporate headquarters or an industrial park, or subdivided for suburban housing. But no such sale was remotely conceivable in the minds of Junior and his heirs. The value of the Hills stock was low because Junior attached the condition of his life tenancy when he "sold" the estate to Hills.

Finally, on October 26, 1952, Junior sold all of the Hills stock to his five sons, each paying $152,059 for one-fifth of the shares, a total of $760,295. The price was further justified by an agreement the brothers executed to sell shares only to each other, thus further diminishing the marketability of the property. In any case, like Rockefeller Center, the transaction once again passed the scrutiny of the tax collectors. Nothing had changed except the legal ownership. Junior retained full control and continued to pay all the bills for the annual maintenance and operation, a total of $1,272,639 in 1953. In 1955 he built next to the Playhouse a $150,000 outdoor swimming pool, which he donated to his sons. Junior continued to make any changes he wished without any reference to the nominal owners—there was no question about who really "owned" the estate.

In 1954 the brothers decided to separate the Park from the rest of the estate by purchasing it from Hills Realty. By this time, Winthrop had moved to Arkansas to make his life and career there. He had never made much use of the estate, so he agreed to the sale without participating in it. The other four brothers paid $311,298 for the Park, leaving the rest in Hills Realty. They divided the Park in unequal amounts, reflecting their current and prospective use of the area. Nelson now owned 38.5 percent of the property, Laurance 30.75 percent, David 23 percent, and John only 7.75 percent. Each brother's payment was proportionate to his share of the land.[11]

Apart from the point about present and anticipated use of the Park, the reasons for this move are not entirely clear, and indeed it was to complicate matters twenty years later when the brothers began to concern themselves with their own problem of final disposition. They may have thought that whatever eventually happened to the estate, they would want to keep the Park in the family, and thus took a step to legally separate it from the rest of the property. There may also have been a consideration of protecting the Park from any involvement in Winthrop's impending divorce. Whatever the reasons, it obviously seemed a good idea to the brothers at the time, and the agreement was reached amicably.

The outcome of this transaction did not indicate, as some writers have inferred, any rearrangement of the hierarchy within the brothers' generation. JDR and his family spent little time in the Park, whereas his brothers either lived there or used the facilities on a regular basis. By this time, JDR's frugal habits had become legendary within the family. He simply was not going to pay for something that he did not use. However, he did want to retain an interest so as to have a voice in determining the future use and ultimate disposition of the property, and that is why he retained a small minority interest. In any case, the new ownership actually changed nothing as far as Junior was concerned. He retained his life tenancy, paid the bills, and ran the show.

28

▚

THE TIES THAT BIND

THE NEW GENERATION had finally arrived. The Rockefeller brothers now had considerably more than familial ties to bind them together— joint ownership of Rockefeller Center and the Pocantico estate, the new prominence and value of their foundation (the Rockefeller Brothers Fund), their joint venture-capital firm (Rockefeller Brothers, Inc., managed by Laurance and his staff), and the family office in Room 5600, where they enjoyed the professional services of the common staff.

In a very real sense, the baton had been passed from the father to the sons. Thanks to Junior's generosity, each of his sons was independently wealthy, though not in the same league as their father, whose net worth, despite all his giving, still exceeded $200 million. Because of his wealth, his special stature in American society, and such mundane considerations as the fact that Junior continued to pay all the general expenses for Room 5600 and Pocantico, he was still important to his sons. But his day had largely passed. He appeared only occasionally in the family office, no longer preoccupied with the affairs of the great philanthropic institutions he had helped to create nor with the business of Rockefeller Center. He was an elderly man who had laid down many of his burdens, at peace with himself and free to enjoy his remaining years with Martha as well as his personal philanthropy.

Now it was the five brothers who were famous collectively, as a sort of unique institution in American society. The course they had agreed upon at the end of World War II was working well: cooperating closely on family matters and common interests and, beyond that, each carving out his own distinctive career. The institution of "brothers' meetings" was in full flower, the five coming together frequently, usually on a Saturday or Sunday, at least once a month, to make numerous decisions on matters of common interest and report on what was going on of note in each brother's life. As the youngest, David was assigned the role of secretary, making notes and reminding his brothers of follow-up action when necessary.[1] It was the high-water mark of communication and cooperation among the five, of thoughtfulness and sensitivity to each brother's concerns. This cama-raderie might be strained occasionally, but it was to be more than twenty years before the ties that bound the brothers would suddenly seem complicated and onerous and lead to dissension.

The biggest business by far for the brotherhood in the early 1950s was the business of Rockefeller Center. It was theirs now, and they faced the challenge of making a success of it. They had good professional talent on the job. Gustav Eyssell had worked his way up from theater management to become president, and Nelson's man, Victor Borella, was also a key figure in the efficient administration of the Center. Nelson was chairman and Laurance head of the finance committee of the board. The real business brain in meeting the challenges of the 1950s was Laurance with his cool judgment and flair for making deals and taking calculated risks. David had also developed business acumen and could provide informed support for Laurance's ideas, but he was involved full-time in his career at Chase. Winthrop and John, for different reasons, made no attempt to match the business zeal of their three brothers and merely went along. Laurance was the man on the spot in Room 5600, analyzing, proposing, and making key deci-sions with the others' advice and support.

The Center went ahead with the modernization program for the existing buildings as a cost of $1 million a year for eight years. The Center Theater was torn down and in its place a nineteen-story addition to the U.S. Rubber Company Building (later the Uniroyal Building and still later the Simon and Schuster Building) was erected. This made space available for a street-level NBC television studio near the midblock underground garage between the Eastern Airlines and U.S. Rubber buildings. Soon pedestrians could gape through plate glass windows at Dave Garroway broadcasting "The Today Show."

Meanwhile, Sinclair Oil moved to a new building at 600 Fifth Avenue built by the Massachusetts Mutual Life Insurance Company, partly on the site formerly occupied by the St. Nicholas (Reformed Protestant) Church. This was at the southeast corner (48th and Fifth) of the original three-block site for the Center. The land was not owned by Columbia University, nor had it been purchased by Underel. The building was financed by the insurance company, but with a financial consideration for the Center, because three plots purchased by Underel were added to give the building an L-shaped site. It was also tied in to the Center's maintenance and amenities.[2]

The moves of Sinclair and Esso to their new buildings made plenty of space available for the expansion of RCA and NBC, and new tenants rapidly filled the leftover space. But David Sarnoff still was not entirely happy, wanting to see brand-new television studios built for NBC. As for Time, Inc., it had long ago outgrown its small building at One Rockefeller Plaza (across the private street from the Eastern Airlines Building). Protracted negotiations with the two companies pointed toward the Center's making the long-delayed leap across Sixth Avenue. For despite many promotional campaigns and inducements, no one had come forth to do this; the conventional wisdom of real estate experts was that it was too much of a risk. Only a combination like the Center, NBC, and Time seemed big enough to attempt it.

The projected NBC-Time Building fell through when Sarnoff changed his mind and renewed the RCA-NBC lease, extending it from 1958 to 1982. But the Center and Time went ahead on a joint venture, Rock-Time, Inc., the Rockefeller interests owning 55 percent. Anticipating the leap, Eyssell had quietly been acquiring lots across Sixth Avenue between 50th and 51st streets, directly across from the Radio City Music Hall. On this site, a modern forty-eight-story office tower was erected, Time taking twenty-one of the floors. The partners shared the revenue from renting the other floors and the tenant roll seemed like a reprise of the Rockefeller-associated enterprises that had first come into the Center in the early 1930s. The Rockefeller Foundation moved from the RCA Building to the Time Building, as did several Esso subsidiaries. And soon there was no difficulty in attracting new tenants. The real estate sages had been wrong; the renewal of the west side of Sixth Avenue was well launched.[3]

Financing these moves required capital and the Center was short of discretionary funds. The brothers could hardly disapprove of their father's action in giving his $57.7 million note to the Brothers Fund, but it did not alleviate the Center's tight capital situation, as would have been done by Junior's forgiving the debt or some of the payments, as Nelson had urged. Indeed, the gift made the capital situation worse, by reason of the accelerated repayment schedule that

Junior had demanded. There were only four ways the brothers could raise capital—borrowing, investing more themselves, seeking concessions from Columbia, or selling stock. They did not want to add to the debt nor put in their own money, so they resorted to the last two choices. The first step was to open new discussions with Columbia in 1950.

For a time, the notion of acquiring the land from Columbia figured in these discussions. The leasehold situation drastically reduced freedom of action and the marketability of the Center, both by the divided ownership and by the many restrictive provisions in the lease. William Zeckendorf suggested a plan for creating a new corporation that would acquire the land from Columbia, paying for it with mortgage money and then leasing it to the Center. When the mortgage was retired by the lease payments, the Center would own the corporation and hence the land, having paid not much more per year than it was already paying to Columbia and freeing itself at the outset from most of the restrictive provisions. Not surprisingly, Columbia balked at this.

Columbia wanted to keep the land and wanted the Rockefeller family to stay involved, even beyond the lease expiration date in 1962. So the brothers were in a good position to negotiate other concessions. One factor was that the original $3.3 million annual rental had been more than market conditions called for in most of the years since 1928. In consideration of this and the modernization now in progress, Columbia agreed to extend the lease period eleven years until 1973 at an increase of only $200,000 per year. This extension allowed ample time to amortize the improvements. Another concession was the withdrawal of the requirement that the $14 million in the Center's escrow account (a fund to guarantee lease payments) had to be in U.S. government bonds. Nelson pressed hard on this point, believing that the country was in a long-term inflationary situation and that investing the escrow fund in common stocks would enhance the Center's financial situation much faster than the bonds would and still serve Columbia's purpose. In this, of course, he was correct. As soon as the agreement was reached, the Center began converting the bonds to common stocks at the rate of $500,000 a month.

An important feature of the agreement relating to the immediate capital need was the sale to Columbia for $5.5 million of the former Underel properties now owned by the Center. This was the land under the U.S. Rubber Building, the RCA Building West, a portion of the Radio City Music Hall, and the Americas Building (formerly the

RKO Building and later the Amax Building). This sale by no means signified that the brothers had given up the goal of acquiring all the land from Columbia some day. In their minds, the sale was a temporary measure that raised capital and straightened out the holdings of the partners, the university now owning all of the land and the Center all of the buildings.

Laurance devised a plan for adding to the recapitalization of Rockefeller Center, based on the idea of the brothers' selling some of their stock in the Center to their 1934 Trusts. Because the trusts were solely for the benefit of family members, this type of sale was permissible under the restrictive provisions of the Columbia lease regarding ownership of the stock. A necessary precondition of Laurance's proposal was the conversion of the existing 1,000 shares of Center stock into 1 million shares so as to increase the flexibility for sales. The stock would be divided into voting and nonvoting classes so that the brothers could retain control. Accordingly, each share was converted into 1,000 shares of new stock at $1 par value each, 600 Class A (nonvoting) and 400 Class B (voting) stock. Each brother received 200,000 shares (120,000 A and 80,000 B) in exchange for his 200 shares of the old stock. The sale of any of these shares would accrue to the brothers personally. To raise capital for the Center, Laurance's plan also called for the issuing of an extra 125,000 shares (75,000 A and 50,000 B). The proceeds for the sale of these shares would go to the Center instead of the brothers.

Laurance had already consulted the Trust Committee, which readily agreed to purchase the Rockefeller Center stock. It was necessary, of course, to set a market value for the Center that would be reflected in the price of its stock, and two independent appraisals yielded a figure of $40 million. This was quite a boost from the $2,210,000 valuation that had formed the basis of the 1948 sale to the brothers, but it was justified on the grounds of the continued profitability of the Center in the intervening six years, the modernization and expansion, the retention of valued tenants, the high occupancy rate, and the concessions granted by Columbia. Laurance suggested that the brothers sell only 40 percent of their shares in order to retain majority control. The Rockefeller Center board approved the plan on March 16, 1955, and each brother sold 80,000 (equal amounts of A and B) of his 200,000 shares to his trust at $40 a share, thus earning $3.2 million. If Columbia University regarded the sale to the trusts as staying within the family, the Internal Revenue Service did not. The result was that each brother could apply a portion of the tax loss he had acquired in the 1948 purchase from Junior, the upshot being that each added $3.2 million to his own portfolio without having to pay any capital gains taxes on the transaction.

There was another wrinkle in Laurance's plan—the 125,000 extra shares, also worth $40 each. He revealed what he had in mind for this in his comprehensive memorandum of December 22, 1954, which laid out the entire plan:

> Nelson has expressed to me an interest in acquiring for his family additional stock. He has expressed a willingness to have his Trust acquire any of the new shares of stock to be issued which any of you do not wish for your Trusts up to the full amount. Having in mind all that Nelson has done for the Center over many years, I for one would like to recommend to you that we all waive any right to acquire any of the additional stock in favor of Nelson's Trust.

This was agreed, and Nelson's trust purchased all 125,000 shares of the additional new stock, bringing $5 million in capital to the Center. The result of the entire transaction was that the brothers retained personal ownership of 600,000 shares of the Center's stock (53.3 percent of the total) and their trusts owned the remaining 525,000 shares (46.7 percent). Of the latter, Nelson's trust owned 205,000 shares and each of the other four trusts owned 80,000.

It is not entirely clear what Nelson expected to gain from having his trust buy the lion's share of the stock. While each brother was $3.2 million richer from the sale—a nice return on the $442,000 paid for one-fifth ownership in 1948—and each still personally owned slightly more than 10 percent of the Center, the counterbalancing fact was that the annual income from their trusts would be reduced because it would be many years before Rockefeller Center stock could pay dividends, at least until the debt to the Rockefeller Brothers Fund was paid. The income from Nelson's trust would be reduced the most because of its larger purchase of stock. Perhaps he was gambling that the Center would have such a glowing economic future that his larger purchase would pay off in the end. But the immediate result for Nelson was that he was to find himself pinched for income because of the large holding his trust had in Center shares.

One can only contemplate with wonderment this series of transactions that began in 1948, which produced so many benefits for the brothers and their heirs. But the fact remains that all the while the brothers were working hard to make the Center the success it eventually became, and that all the transactions were aboveboard and legal, all approved by the IRS, the ruling on the 1955 issue of stock and sale to the trusts coming on February 28 of that year.

The Rockefeller Brothers Fund underwent its first significant transformation in the early 1950s, thanks to Junior's gifts and the growing wealth and prominence of the brothers. From its inception at the end of 1940, the fund had served as a unified device for the citizenship giving of the brothers, each making his annual contribution to provide the wherewithal. This role continued, but by the mid-1950s it was overshadowed by a second role—the fund's use as an important resource for each brother's major philanthropic interests.

By definition, the giving that occurred under this second rubric was not unified in the same manner as the initial function of the fund; that is, the major grants were almost always made to serve the philanthropic interest of a particular brother. Occasionally, there would be a project in which two or three of the brothers shared an interest, but this was the exception, not the rule. The operation of the fund *was* unified, however, in the sense that all of the brothers agreed on this policy and managed to implement it smoothly for many years. No one insisted on an exact division of the grant money that was available each year. The interests of one brother might receive a disproportionate share in a given year, but there were always good reasons and no one raised objections. The brothers were confident that justice and a rough parity would prevail over time, and this indeed was the case. There were no divided votes; differences of opinion were always worked out ahead of time, and the formal record would show that projects had been adopted by unanimous vote.

By the mid-1960s, yet another role emerged, the result of the growth in resources and professional staff of the fund, the presence of more outside directors on the board, and the fact that the brothers were very much preoccupied with their individual careers. While the earlier two roles were maintained, the fund also began to take on the aspect of an independent foundation with a program of its own. True, the grants did not stray from fields the brothers approved of, but they would be made under general headings such as "New York City projects" or "the arts" or "civil rights" as the staff proposed, instead of to particular organizations or causes associated with one of the brothers' interests.

Not until the mid-1970s, when the four surviving brothers were feeling the cold hand of mortality on their shoulders, did the question arise of whether the principal mission of the fund was role no. 2 or role no. 3. The result was acrimonious debate and a sharp division among the four.

In its first full decade of operation (1941–1950), the fund gave to 101 organizations a total of $2,040,000. The giving rose gradually from $54,770 in 1941 to $265,850 in 1950. All the money came from the five brothers, the older ones putting in the most at first, but the five contributing roughly equal amounts from 1946 on—an average of $50,000 a year each. The brothers were the sole trustees, with JDR serving as chairman.

The fund did not have its own staff, but was served by the office unit under Arthur Packard and Dana Creel, his chief aide. The staff soon included Rufus Jones, Gene Setzer, Robert Bates, and Yorke Allen. These men began to take on particular areas of expertise, e.g., Allen in religion and Setzer in conservation. The purpose of the fund in its first phase was clearly stated in its *Ten Year Report*, published in 1951:

> The Fund's viewpoint is essentially that of an individual interested in giving to the needs of the philanthropic agencies to which he believes he has a responsibility as a resident of New York, as a citizen of the United States, and as a member of the international community. For this reason the Fund characterizes its program as a citizenship approach to giving, as distinct from the more typical foundation program directed to research or specialized fields of activity.

This unified citizenship-giving system was pioneered by Arthur Packard; it followed the tradition established by Senior, Frederick Gates, and Junior of seeking to maximize philanthropy through centralization, efficiency, and economy. Packard was a believer in this to the point of being a crusader. In the 1930s and 1940s he worked assiduously to consolidate many of the social service agencies in the New York area and some on the national scene, and with considerable success. The obverse of organizing the recipients was to organize the givers as well, and Packard did this in his work for Junior, in running the family philanthropic office, and in guiding the Brothers Fund.

Junior was immensely pleased with the performance of his sons in their joint giving. Small wonder: the majority of the 101 organizations supported by the Brothers Fund were those that Junior had been aiding, in some cases for thirty years, through the Bureau of Social Hygiene, his benificences committee, the Davison Fund, and the Sealantic Fund. In New York, for example, the recipients of Brothers

Fund grants included the Boy Scouts, Girl Scouts, YMCA, YWCA, Catholic Charities, the Federation of Protestant Welfare Agencies, the Federation of Jewish Philanthropies, the Community Service Society, the Brooklyn Bureau of Charities, Riverside Church, International House, a dozen or more hospitals and medical research centers, and every major cultural organization. On the national level, the recipients included the United Negro College Fund, the National Urban League, the National Council on Alcoholism, the National Conference of Christians and Jews, Planned Parenthood, and the Federal Council of Churches. In addition to war relief and rehabilitation, gifts on the international scene went to such organizations as the Foreign Policy Association, the Institute for Pacific Relations, the American Association for the United Nations, and the international work of the YMCA and YWCA.

With Junior's gifts of 1951–1952, totaling almost $59 million, the stage was set for the fund's expansion and new directions. But in this Arthur Packard was not to play his part: he fell a tragic victim to mental illness. The signs had become manifest in 1949 when Packard's passion for work and addiction to detail began to go beyond rational norms. Soon he had to be institutionalized. He kept trying to return to work, but always had to go back to the sanitarium. He died there in January 1953 during brain surgery. During Packard's long absences, Dana Creel had been acting head of the philanthropic staff; now he became the man the brothers relied upon to guide the growth of their fund.

In the light of the new situation, the brothers soon made three key decisions. The first was to divide the giving of the fund into two programs. The "General Program" was a continuation of the original citizenship giving of the fund; the "Special Program" would consist of grants to projects arising from the particular interest of one or another brother. The second decision was that the General Program would be conducted as before, the gifts being made to a wide range of recipients from monies contributed to the fund annually by the brothers. Thirdly, the Special Program would be operated more as a "foundation" than as a "fund." That is, the large capital sums from Junior's gift would be allowed to accumulate as an endowment and grants would be made under the Special Program from the income of the endowment, not the principal.

Simultaneously, the brothers increased their annual contributions and the endowment began to grow; the first payment of $7.7 million on the Rockefeller Center note was made in 1952 and payments of $5 million were made in each of the three following years. The total outlay of the fund in grants increased from $315,000 in 1951 to $3.6 million in 1956. Slowly, the Special Program began to dominate. Gifts under the General Program rose from $300,000 in 1951 to $733,000 in 1956; during this same span the Special Program grew from $15,000 to $2.9 million.

In 1954, a special three-year report expressed the policy for the Special Program:

> . . . the trustees decided that the program of the Fund should be expanded to include the support or possibly in some instances the direct operation of experimental or new undertakings in areas of special interest to the trustees, which fall generally into the broad fields of human relations, international relations, and development of human and natural resources.[4]

During these early years, the Special Program grants went to organizations identified with one or another of the brothers and sufficiently developed programmatically to need and merit support. Laurance's interests received the largest sum, $1.25 million, to the Jackson Hole Preserve and smaller grants to the Conservation Foundation and the New York Zoological Society. Nelson's American International Association received $900,000 for its nonprofit research operation. And the Museum of Modern Art, in which both Nelson and David were active, received $700,000 for its International Circulating Exhibits Program. Soon, JDR achieved parity as his many philanthropic innovations began to come into being in the 1950s.

A sure sign of the fund's new direction was the addition of two outside directors—the first, though they were not from far outside: the architect Wally Harrison, by now closely identified with Nelson and his activities, and Dr. Detlev W. Bronk, former president of Johns Hopkins, president of the National Academy of Sciences, and president of the Rockefeller Institute for Medical Research. The following year, the brothers' sister, Babs, now Mrs. Jean Mauzé (she had remarried after the death of her second husband, Dr. Pardee), was added to the board. She had begun to take more interest in giving, and began contributing each year to the General Program of the fund as her brothers had been doing.

By 1952, changes were imminent in the lives of John, Nelson, and Winthrop, while Laurance and David were well settled in their careers.

Having worked in the foreign department of the Chase Bank for the previous six years, David in 1952 was promoted to senior vice president and given responsibility for the New York area branches as well as the Economic Research Department. In 1954 he was made chairman of the committee charged with deciding where to build the company's new headquarters. He was also active in the discussions of a merger with the Bank of Manhattan. These were successfully concluded in 1955, giving the bank its present name, the Chase Manhattan Bank. The recommendation for building the new headquarters in the Wall Street area was accepted in October 1955—a decision later credited by many with saving, indeed reviving, New York City's downtown financial district.

Aside from his own philanthropy and service on the Morningside Heights committee, David's public service included membership on the boards of the Carnegie Endowment, the University of Chicago, and the Westchester County Planning Commission, besides the chairmanship of the Rockefeller Institute for Medical Research. His interest in foreign affairs found expression in his work for International House and the Council on Foreign Relations. In May 1954, he was invited to attend the first Bilderberg Conference in Oosterbeek, Holland, sponsored by Prince Bernhard. The Bilderberg model of an international "think tank" was to be used later by David as his prominence in international banking and foreign affairs grew steadily to worldwide recognition.

Laurance differed from his father in his pursuit of his two major interests, business and conservation. It will be recalled that Junior's one entrepreneurial fling, early in life, had resulted in an embarrassing loss of $1 million, which his father had to cover for him. From that point on, Junior handled his investments conservatively, avoiding all business ventures—aside from the chance involvement with Rockefeller Center. Laurance was not only aggressive in managing the affairs of the Center, he was also styling himself quite consciously as a "venture capitalist." There was nothing new about investment banking as such, but the line Laurance took had a distinctly modern flavor to it. In January 1946, he formed Rockefeller Brothers, Inc., one of the first of the postwar venture-capital operations—growth-oriented, taking very measured risks, spreading them by making a large number of relatively small investments, and showing a marked interest in new enterprises, especially those in high technology and business innovation.

The firm started with a capitalization of $1.5 million, $250,000 each from five general partners (the brothers) and one limited partner (their sister, Babs). Aside from investing this capital, the plan was to propose ventures to the partners, each of whom could decide which to invest in and how much. Starting with a staff made up of Laurance's wartime friends Randolph Marston and Teddy Walkowicz, the unit grew to six professionals headed by Harper Woodward. Then the brothers began a search for a senior man who could manage the entire family office for them, including supervision of the venture-capital unit, as well as the more orthodox management of the Rockefeller family portfolios (a function that became known as "Standard Investments"). For a time in the early 1950s, this post was filled by Lewis Strauss, former rear admiral and member of the Atomic Energy Commission. Strauss left in 1953 to become chairman of the commission; he earned notoriety for his part in denying security clearance to the nuclear physicist J. Robert Oppenheimer.[5] The senior Rockefeller post was not filled until 1956, when J. Richardson Dilworth became head of the office.

For quite a few years, the six Rockefellers of the third generation did not have much money to invest. Each had an annual income from their trusts and other sources ranging from $1.4 to $2 million. But the tax bite was enormous—about 60 percent. There were not yet many "tax shelters" and special exemptions made possible by law. After personal expenses, charitable contributions, interest payments, and other taxes, they had only 10 to 20 percent of their income for discretionary investing. In some years this was totally taken up by some special purpose, as in the purchases of Rockefeller Center in 1948 and Pocantico in 1952.

Laurance had pioneered his investment pattern before the war. As we saw, he used every bit of income he could get his hands on (including invading the principal of his 1934 Trust), to invest in the stocks of airlines and aircraft manufacturers, thus gradually building up a major position for himself in Eastern Airlines. After the war, his interests broadened beyond aviation to the aerospace, electronics, and nuclear energy industries. Laurance was neither a compulsive gambler nor a Wall Street plunger. His strong points were cool appraisal of projects, limited investment at the strategic moment, and patient awareness that new enterprises needed time to develop. (Laurance often spoke of a "ten-year risk cycle.") There were failures, such as Island Packers in Samoa, but also many successes. The $159,000 that the firm invested in 1949 in Reaction Motors (later merged with

Thiokol) was worth $1.5 million six years later. The biggest successes were with the Boston-based Itek in electronics and, much later, Apple Computers.

When Harper Woodward retired in 1975, Laurance had his staff analyze the twenty-nine-year record of his venture-capital operation, now renamed Venrock, Inc. He had been the most active of the six partners, investing in seventy-eight companies. Nelson had also been an eager investor, but ceased to participate when he was elected governor of New York in 1958. Winthrop bowed out likewise when he moved to Arkansas. David invested in fifty of the companies and John and Babs in thirty-five. A measure of performance was that Laurance's net profit after twenty-nine years of investing was estimated at $52 million.[6]

There was a venturesome spirit as well in Laurance's work in conservation. He was as much interested as his father in preserving natural beauty and making it accessible to the public under proper conditions, but he went beyond this in creating vacation resorts that satisfied his own standards of taste and quality and harmony with the environment. In the 1950s, tourism increased as Americans generally had more disposable income and as remote spots became accessible thanks to jet travel and lower plane fares. Laurance began developing resorts as a business; it was never a profitable one. At first, he seemed rather to want to show how it should be done; later he undertook projects in Puerto Rico and Hawaii at the request of governing authorities, to help spur tourism and local development.

He gained experience and ideas in setting up and managing tourist facilities at Grand Teton National Park in association with the Park Service, using the large grants his father had made for this purpose to the Jackson Hole Preserve. Laurance's first project on his own was in the Caribbean, where he and his wife, Mary, first cruised in 1949 aboard their motor ship the *Dauntless*. They fell in love with the tropical beauty of the islands, and Laurance began searching for the right spot to build his notion of the ideal Caribbean resort. This he found in 1952 at Caneel Bay, on the mountainous, heavily forested island of Saint John, the most "virgin" of the U.S. Virgin Islands.

Saint John was primitive and unspoiled; it had fewer than four hundred residents, no telephones or electricity or automobiles. Caneel Bay is a unique layout of coves and rocky promontories and pristine beaches within walking distance of a central point on the six hundred acres that Laurance purchased for $350,000. Here he built Caneel Bay Plantation, scattering guest cottages on the property instead of overwhelming it with a high-rise hotel. He took scrupulous pains with every detail in the manner of his father at Williamsburg. The resort opened in 1956 with 40 guest rooms and it has remained virtually at capacity ever since. Today, with 140 rooms, it still sets the standard for Caribbean luxury resorts.

Meanwhile, Laurance accepted an invitation to participate in "Operation Bootstrap" for the economic development of Puerto Rico by building a vacation resort on a site twenty miles west of San Juan. The Dorado Beach Hotel, a series of low-rise buildings in a spectacular tropical setting along two miles of ocean beach, was opened in 1958. Next Laurance restored the Woodstock Inn in Vermont, built the Mauna Kea Hotel on the nearly deserted Kohala coast of Hawaii as a spur to growth in the region, and developed the Little Dix Bay resort on the island of Virgin Gorda in the British Virgin Islands. He created a firm, Rockresorts, Inc., to manage all these properties.

While developing Caneel Bay, Laurance came across a twenty-year-old study proposing that Saint John be made a national park. He talked the idea over with his father and the National Park Service, and, working through Jackson Hole Preserve, began to acquire acreage. One of Junior's large grants to Jackson Hole was made for this very purpose, and so were grants from the Rockefeller Brothers Fund—more than $7 million altogether. In 1956 Laurance turned over 9,500 acres to the National Park Service, and the Virgin Islands National Park—the twenty-ninth in the nation—was opened on December 1 of that year. Since then the Park Service has added 5,600 acres, the total amounting to 85 percent of the land area of Saint John, plus some seven square miles of surrounding water, including nearby Buck Island. The fascinating reefs and underwater vista are thereby protected for snorkeling and scuba trails.[7]

Laurance is an easy target for criticism on the grounds of mixing conservation and business—e.g., protecting his Caneel Bay investment by creating a park around it. The fact that Caneel Bay and the new national park opened on the same day, the proximity of lucrative Eastern Airlines routes and the Caribbean resorts, and other development investments he made in conjunction with building resorts—all point the same way. But if this is a legitimate criticism, it must be coupled with the thought that the world needs many more such profiteers. Everything Laurance did was done with consummate attention to quality and respect for the environment. Most of his resort developments were accompanied by donations for conservation projects and parks. Anyone who cares about the environment of the

Caribbean can only be grateful to Laurance for "protecting" his investment and the sites in this lavish way, keeping Saint John free of the rash and heedless overdevelopment that has blighted Saint Thomas and Saint Croix. What is more, to avoid a conflict of interest, Laurance turned over the ownership of Caneel Bay to the Jackson Hole Preserve, a portion of the profits being assigned to conservation projects in the Virgin Islands National Park. Rockresorts manages Caneel Bay, as well as campgrounds and other tourist facilities for the Park Service.

For Winthrop the early 1950s was a time for working out his troubles. After eighteen months of married life with Bobo, marked by stormy fights and drinking bouts, he desperately wanted release from the marriage. He locked Bobo out of his Park Avenue apartment to force a separation. There followed four years of verbal battling that the gossip columnists loved; Bobo finally demanded a $10 million settlement. The two signed a separation agreement in Reno in 1954, Bobo accepting $5.5 million in cash, trusts, and property. Winthrop got the right to have his son with him on stated weekends and vacations.

Meanwhile, Winthrop had decided to start life over again in another place. His family had stood behind him through his troubles, but he wanted a complete break with New York. His happiest times had been elsewhere, in the Army and the oil fields and on his trips abroad. In 1952 he visited his old wartime buddy Frank Newell in Arkansas. Winthrop stayed there long enough to establish residency and file for divorce, making new friends, enjoying the rugged beauty of the state and its plainspoken people, all so different from the New York environment of his upbringing. His friends showed him Petit Jean Mountain, a wild, primitive plateau overlooking the meandering Arkansas River some sixty miles north of Little Rock. He fell in love with it and began to dream of creating his own version of Pocantico there. In 1953 he announced that he had settled in Arkansas permanently, resigning from almost all his obligations and directorships in the East. At the same time, he added one at the request of his father and oldest brother—the chairmanship of Colonial Williamsburg. This act was a symbol that he was still linked to the family. He turned in a good performance as chairman and helped relieve his father's fears about the future of the Restoration.

Winthrop bought Petit Jean and spent happy years working with his architects and crews to carve out a fabulous spread, Winrock

Farms, where he began to breed Santa Gertrudis cattle. In 1955 Winthrop accepted Governor Orval Faubus' invitation to form the Arkansas Industrial Development Commission and run it, his initial step into public life in his adopted state. It led him eventually to becoming the first Republican governor of Arkansas since Reconstruction.

Throughout, Winthrop maintained cordial ties with his brothers, though from a distance. He was welcomed at brothers' meetings, but rarely attended—only when he happened to be in New York for some other purpose. At first, his move to Arkansas was a flight from Bobo and his unhappy marriage. Divorce was easier there than in New York and the law more protective of property in marital disputes. For the same reason, Winthrop moved the administration of his 1934 Trust from Chase Manhattan to a Little Rock bank, though it still came under the policy guidance of the same Trust Committee that governed all the 1934 Trusts.[8] Winthrop, as we noted, did not join his brothers when they bought the Park from Hills Realty, thereby forfeiting his interest in that portion of the Pocantico estate. But he kept his seat on the boards of Rockefeller Center and the Brothers Fund, the latter making a number of grants over the years to Arkansas projects that Winthrop favored.

He never regretted what began as a flight from his past—he found a home that he loved in Arkansas atop Petit Jean Mountain.

Winthrop's change in the pattern of his life could be called radical; the step that Nelson took in 1953 seemed more like the next move in a predestined path: he returned to public life in Washington as one of the first appointees of the new Eisenhower administration. The Rockefellers had all favored Ike over his chief rival for the GOP nomination, Senator Robert Taft of Ohio. Nelson's uncle Winthrop had been one of those involved in persuading the general to enter politics as a Republican instead of returning to Columbia University as president after his resignation from NATO in May 1952.

Just a few weeks after the November election, Ike named Nelson chairman of the President's Advisory Committee on Government Reorganization. Nelson might have wished for more—his major interests were foreign affairs and defense. But the aim of the Advisory Committee was to revise the structure of the Executive Branch to Republican likings after twenty years of exile from the White House; it therefore offered Nelson the chance to gain visibility and power, to scan the federal establishment in search of targets, and to demonstrate his energy and skill in achieving reorganizations that would meet new needs.

Nelson's job derived from an important power that had been given to the president by the Congress in the Government Reorganization Act of 1945. The act had been passed to speed the dismantling of wartime agencies. It introduced the "negative veto" into government administration—any reorganization proposed by the president would take effect unless it was voted down by both houses of Congress within sixty days. Nelson tackled his assignment with typical zest; he enjoyed the access it gave him to the president and was helped by the fact that he knew Sherman Adams, the White House chief of staff, from their service together on the Dartmouth College board. The reorganization plans had to be sold within the White House, then to the agencies affected, and finally to Congress. Many of them were complex and required an enormous amount of staff work.

One advantage of the new post was that Nelson found he could affect the structure for foreign affairs and defense. Two of his plans separated the overseas information and foreign aid programs from the Department of State and constituted them as independent agencies—the United States Information Agency and the Foreign Operations Administration. It will be recalled that Nelson had promoted the idea of a separate foreign aid agency during his stint in the Truman administration, but had been rebuffed by W. Averell Harriman and Dean Acheson. He succeeded now on the grounds of separating policy and operations, an approach favored by Secretary Dulles, who regarded the State Department as a policy-making agency, not an operational one.[9] Nelson's plan for the Department of Defense was based on the opposite theory, bringing policy and operations closer together.

The most complex reorganization aimed at bringing together numerous federal agencies and programs, most of them the product of New Deal innovations, into a new Department of Health, Education, and Welfare (HEW), perhaps the ultimate vindication of the New Deal by an enlightened Republican leadership. It was a tough job, but Nelson succeeded against the bureaucratic resistance of those who were to be integrated as well as the ideological resistance of conservatives in the Eisenhower administration and the Congress; they disliked the social programs to be integrated and feared that the weight of this new Cabinet "superagency" would inexorably lead to increased expenditures.

Nelson's reward in June 1953 was to be named under secretary of HEW at the request of Mrs. Oveta Culp Hobby of Houston, who had moved from her post as chief of the Federal Security Administration to become secretary of the new department. Rufus Miles, then relatively early in his brilliant career as a federal administrator, was charged with all the details of making the merger work. He recalls vividly the remarkable energy that Nelson brought to the task, the shirt-sleeves atmosphere, the long working days, the quick snacks that Nelson had at his desk instead of leisurely luncheon sojourns at Washington's posh restaurants. Nelson was never happier than when his office and conference room were festooned with charts and he could leap to his feet to sketch with Magic Markers on a newsprint pad propped on an easel his latest brainstorm for structuring the department or making one of its programs more effective. Altogether, it recalled the dynamism of Nelson's days as coordinator of inter-American affairs during the war.

There was heavy pressure in the new administration to cut government spending; its champion was the midwestern conservative George Humphrey, secretary of the treasury. Miles was therefore working under great constraints, especially against creating new jobs or bringing in new staff. He tried to explain this to his new boss when Nelson handed him a list of bright young people whom he wanted to bring in as aides, people he had spotted during his tenure as Advisory Committee chairman. Nelson just leveled a finger at Miles and said: "Do it." Miles, the consummate administrator, made no further argument and found ways to "do it." Given Nelson's later image as a womanizer, Miles recalls with amusement that five of the new aides were attractive young ladies.[10]

After he had helped to generate several programs that resulted in federal aid to public schools (opposition to which was another conservative Republican shibboleth), Nelson felt that he had worked on everything that was of interest to him in HEW and was anxious to move on. Toward the end of 1954, he accordingly jumped at the chance to become special assistant to President Eisenhower in foreign affairs. Technically, Nelson was filling the job vacated by C. D. Jackson, the publisher of *Time* magazine, whose title had been special assistant for psychological strategy. Jackson had resigned from the White House to return to *Time* more than eight months before Nelson's appointment.

There was—and still is—some confusion as to exactly what Nelson's title and responsibilities were. His biographer Joe Alex

Morris uses the title "Special Assistant for Foreign Affairs," but another book refers to Nelson as "Special Assistant for Cold War Strategy." The newspapers variously described the post as "special assistant on psychological warfare and international understanding," "special assistant to coordinate cold war strategy," and "administrative assistant on foreign policy."[11] This uncertainty was due to the state of flux in which the White House management of foreign affairs then stood.

At the time of Jackson's resignation, the Psychological Strategy Board was discontinued. This interagency committee, created in 1951, was a product of the kind of thinking that had prevailed during the war in the Office of War Information with its emphasis on "psychological warfare." The direction of the Eisenhower reorganization in foreign affairs, strongly influenced by Dulles, was to deflate the overblown expectations born of the "psychological warfare" idea and to concentrate on the coordination of overseas operations, with policy-making the exclusive preserve of the State Department. In keeping with this new view, the Operations Coordinating Board was created in September 1954, charged with implementing policy decisions by follow-through coordination of the overseas programs of some forty U.S. government agencies. The chairman was Herbert Hoover, Jr., the new under secretary of state.

To Hoover and his colleagues, Nelson was a loose cannon, with an unclear mandate and the capacity to meddle and strike out in any direction. Nelson had in fact set up a new unit called the Planning Coordination Group, based on a suggestion from the Bureau of the Budget. Hoover naturally saw this as a rival effort and the battle lines were drawn. A series of bitter interdepartmental struggles ensued, most of Nelson's efforts being deflated in the process.

Those were the days before the president's special assistant for national security affairs (the staff chief of the National Security Council) emerged as the White House power in foreign policy, the position held by McGeorge Bundy in the Kennedy administration and successively by W. W. Rostow under Johnson, Henry Kissinger under Nixon, and Zbigniew Brzezinski under Carter. Although Nelson did not head the NSC, what he attempted to do in the White House in his ambiguous position must be regarded as a precursor of the power later held by these men.[12]

Nelson did achieve one success, in a way reminiscent of the circuitous manner by which his ideas emerged as Point Four in President Truman's 1949 inaugural address. In preparations for the

May 1955 summit meeting in Geneva—the first such meeting between the Soviets and Americans since 1945—Nelson perceived that the Russians were gaining the propaganda edge by appearing as the champions of peace. While making rapid progress in the nuclear arms race, they indicated a readiness to consider arms control concessions. Nelson convened a panel of experts at the Quantico Marine Base near Washington to devise a way for the United States to regain the peace initiative. The result was the idea that the president should announce a dramatic "open skies" proposal at the Geneva Summit, calling for unlimited aerial inspection by both countries of each other's territory as a safeguard against secret preparations for atomic war or violations of arms control agreements. Nelson drew on the young Henry Kissinger, then a Harvard professor, for ideas in formulating this proposal.

Eisenhower liked the idea, but it was shot down by the real power in American foreign policy, Secretary of State Dulles, proponent of the doctrine of "massive retaliation." Dulles had been successful in persuading Ike that the president's role should be limited to articulating Cold War issues, leaving everything else to be negotiated by the foreign ministers. However, when it became clear by the second day of the Geneva conference that the Russians were winning the propaganda battle, Ike wanted something dramatic to reverse the trend.

The State Department leadership had seen to it that Nelson was left behind in Paris, but from that city he continued to lobby for the "open skies" proposal through the NATO leadership and Eisenhower's military aide in Geneva. Dulles was cornered and forced to accept Nelson's idea, it being the only "dramatic" one that anyone could think of. The president inserted it in the prepared text of his speech and added: "I only wish that God would give me some means of convincing you of our sincerity and loyalty in making this proposal." As if on cue, a thunderstorm broke outside the hall with a great flash of lightning and the electricity inside failed. Observers were left to ponder whether this was God's response to Ike's plea or some cosmic comment on the "sincerity" of a proposal that had been plucked from obscurity only the day before. In any event, the proposal was rejected, but Ike came away as the hero of the conference in the public eye.[13]

Back home Nelson convened a second Quantico seminar to devise strategy for following up on the advantage gained at Geneva. But Dulles was not a man who took kindly to being upstaged. As the months passed, Nelson found that he was getting less and less access to the president and that his ideas were not being heard. Among them were his arguments for increased defense spending and for the United States to take advantage of its technological capacity to become the first nation to launch an orbiting earth satellite.[14]

By late 1955, Nelson felt that it was useless to stay on and was preparing to resign when Secretary of Defense Charles Wilson sounded him out on the idea of becoming deputy secretary of defense. It seemed a fateful opportunity; it was known that Wilson intended to resign within a year and Nelson imagined himself moving up to inherit one of the two great power positions in the Cabinet. But, by this time, Nelson had too many enemies, not only in the State Department but also in the Treasury Department, where Secretary Humphrey feared that Nelson would be a lavish spender at Defense. Within a week, the crestfallen Wilson had to tell Nelson that the offer was withdrawn.[15]

Nelson was prescient in some of his ideas. In 1957 the Russian launching of *Sputnik* finally galvanized the American space program and the alleged "missile gap" became a much-touted issue in the 1960 presidential campaign. An interesting example of the shifts in political thought is the fact that Nelson was blackballed by the conservatives in the Eisenhower administration in 1955 because they feared he would be too big a spender on defense, whereas decades later, in the conservative Reagan administration, the most sacred of all cows was the defense budget.

When he resigned on December 31, 1955, Nelson was a prophet without much honor in Washington. He had learned a great deal and had gained in a mere three years experience of incalculable value in almost every branch of government administration. The most important lesson was that the surest way to set the agenda and win bureaucratic struggles was to be elected to office rather than appointed. Election was what he set his mind on as he returned to New York.

29

THE PHILANTHROPIST

UNLIKE WINTHROP'S AND NELSON'S, JDR's change in direction in 1952 did not involve physical relocation; it was a psychological change, and all the more powerful for it. In the Williamsburg affair, he had finally liberated himself from the domineering influence of his father. This, combined with the sudden and unexpected success of his Japanese projects, seemed to cast off the blinders and the frustrations of previous years. JDR may have been a late bloomer, but the creative energy he began to display in his forty-sixth year and his achievements from that point on more than made up for lost time.

It also happened that JDR was prepared in both staff and financial resources for his newfound activism. Having hired Don McLean to work on his Japan projects, he now had two trusted associates, McLean and Ed Young. JDR was fortunate in these choices. Both were men of integrity, both highly competent, though in different and complementary ways. Both were Republicans, Young being decidedly the more liberal. McLean, the son of a New Jersey congressman (one of the few Republican freshmen elected in the Roosevelt year 1932), had extensive legal and overseas experience. He was a graduate of Amherst and the Yale Law School. Young graduated from DePauw University and did graduate work at the University of Pennsylvania and the London School of Economics. He had extensive administrative experience—in Washington with the U.S. Employment Service and the Bureau of the Budget and in New York as assistant to Austin Tobin, director of the Port Authority.

Schooled in the ways of bureaucracy and a staff man "with a passion for anonymity," Young was in some ways an extension of JDR—civilized, moral, loyal, polite, self-effacing. McLean provided the contrast, being outgoing, assertive, even a touch flamboyant. He was at ease working with people at any level, an excellent "outside man," a good organizer and negotiator, impatient to get things done.

The family financial transactions of the preceding years, the postwar economic boom, and JDR's unostentatious living and careful management of his financial affairs all combined to put him in a position for the first time in 1952 to undertake significant philanthropic activities of his own. His previous giving had always been to existing organizations; now he had the wherewithal to create his own organizations and programs.

JDR's personal net worth in 1952 was close to $20 million (counting Fieldwood Farm, the Manhattan duplex apartment, and Bassett Hall in Williamsburg, but not his currently unproductive shares of Rockefeller Center and Pocantico). These holdings yielded an income well in excess of $200,000. In addition, he enjoyed the income from three trusts, his own 1934 Trust (worth $64.1 million in 1952), his one-third share of his mother's 1934 Trust (worth $25.6 million), and the 1952 Fidelity Union trust for his children (worth $11.2 million). From all these sources in 1952, his gross income was $5,020,000. He paid $3,104,000 (61.8 percent) in federal income taxes, another $235,000 in state and local income taxes, and gave away $929,000 in charitable contributions. That left him with a disposable income of $752,000 to cover business and living expenses and further investments.[1]

A rough measure of JDR's growing wealth was the steady increase in his charitable giving from year to year. Normally, his target was to contribute at least as much as the maximum deduction allowed by the income tax laws—15 percent in the 1940s, 20 percent in the early 1950s, and then 30 percent until he was able to qualify for the unlimited charitable deduction.[2] In 1946 his giving exceeded $200,000 for the first time, and in 1949 it exceeded $400,000. In 1951 it jumped to $671,586, to nearly $1 million in the next few years, and up to nearly $2 million a year later in the decade.

JDR had other assets in his chosen role as full-time philanthropist. There was the new and growing value of the Rockefeller Brothers Fund as a supplementary source of funding for his projects. At the December 1952 annual meeting, he became chairman of the Rockefeller Foundation, John Foster Dulles having resigned when he at last achieved his life's ambition by becoming secretary of state.

Some of the emotional currents attending the election of the successive chairmen—Dulles in 1949 and JDR in 1952—are found in the correspondence of Douglas Southall Freeman, the famous historian who had been on the board since 1937. Freeman respected the Rockefeller record of philanthropy and entertained warm feelings for both Junior and JDR. He had been disappointed at JDR's being passed over in 1949. When Freeman retired in 1951, JDR wrote him a gracious letter, to which Freeman replied: "As you know, I was profoundly dissatisfied with the action taken by the Board when a new chairman had to be chosen."[3]

About a year later, Junior, writing to Freeman on another matter, said in passing:

The printed reports of Mr. Dulles's selection for Secretary of State suggest the possible necessity of his feeling that he will have to give up for the present at least the Chairmanship of the Rockefeller Foundation. While his successor is no longer a matter for which I have any responsibility, because of my life-long interest in the Foundation, I shall naturally wait with keen interest to see who is appointed to succeed him.[4]

Junior's tone of neutrality on the matter seems overdone, given the fact that JDR was the obvious successor to Dulles. Whether it was this or something else, Freeman's feelings were aroused:

As I am, like yourself, a retired Trustee of the Rockefeller Foundation, I do not know what I can do with respect to Mr. Dulles's successor. Indeed I was so outraged by the election of Mr. Dulles to this post that my ire rises every time I think of it. The ingratitude of some of the members of that Board and the obtuseness of Mr. Dulles himself in accepting an appointment that should have gone to John seemed to me to violate some of the fundamental principles of the society in which we live. There was no excuse whatsoever for failing to elect John. I never felt the same toward some of the Directors afterward. God knows, I cherish no malice toward any man, but ungraciousness and ingratitude are, to my way of thinking, among the basest of vices.[5]

Junior hastened to set Freeman straight about the "facts":

Mr. Dulles has always felt that some member of the Rockefeller family should be on the Board and active in its leadership. When Mr. Stewart retired . . . Mr. Dulles would have been glad to see John succeed him but felt, as I did, that with the makeup of the Board as it then was, an effort to elect John might have split the Board. He, therefore, accepted the position himself, as he frankly told me at the time, that he might prepare the way to insure John's succeeding him which he felt could and should be brought about. . . . For John to have been put in without the whole-hearted backing of the Board would, as I am sure you will agree, have been both unwise and unfortunate. . . . Mr. Dulles has always been very fond of John, and has enjoyed working with him in various relationships.[6]

Freeman rejoined: "Nothing ever pleases me more than to be set right when I am wrong because nothing is so sure a corrective of mental faults." But he still regretted that JDR had not been chairman "during the past two years when important changes in policy were being made."[7] When JDR's election was known, Junior dispatched a final word:

> John will, I know, fill the position . . . with credit and distinction. You express regret that he was not sooner put in that position. Personally, I feel that the timing is just right and that he would not have been as well fitted for it had it been thrust upon him eighteen months earlier.[8]

There is no reference in JDR's letters or diary to an understanding with Dulles at the time of the latter's election, but Blanchette confirms that Dulles told JDR that he regarded himself as an interim chairman, that the Foundation would best fulfill its mission with a family member as leader, and that he believed JDR should succeed him.

On balance, Junior doubtless had the right view of the matter. JDR was probably better off for not having ascended to the chairmanship any earlier than 1952. By then he had passed Walter Stewart's magic age of forty-five, he had psychologically liberated himself from his father, and he had come to understand and accept the circumspect, judicious role that was called for in this particular institution. Almost all of the old guard on the staff and board were gone, and the fact that JDR and Dean Rusk both assumed office in the same year suggested a close working relation between chairman and president. This was to be the case; the two men were contemporaries and friends and shared several interests, especially in Asian affairs.

The two men experienced their baptism of fire almost immediately in confronting the wave of hysteria that gripped the nation following the "loss" of China to the Communists in 1949. A potent force in inflaming the hysteria was a rash of congressional investigations, the most notorious being those of Senator Joseph McCarthy's Government Operations Subcommittee, Senator Pat McCarran's Internal Security Subcommittee, and the House Un-American Activities Committee of Martin Dies and J. Parnell Thomas.[9] The large foundations, always suspected by right-wingers of having radical leanings, did not escape the witch-hunting, guilt by association, and character assassination that attended most of those investigations. Two successive House committees investigated foundations, the first chaired by E. Eugene Cox, Democrat of Georgia, and the second by B. Carroll Reece, Republican of Tennessee. The Rockefeller Foundation was one of those put in the pillory. But Rusk and JDR were steadfast in defending their organization and philanthropy in general.

Ironically, the major foundations that had been wrongly accused of infiltration and subversion from the left had in fact been the objects of attempted infiltration by the U.S. government. Shortly after he became president of the Foundation, Dean Rusk was pressed by Allen Dulles, deputy director of the Central Intelligence Agency, to allow the CIA to see the diaries regularly kept by Foundation officials. These officials were trusted around the world and their diaries contained confidential information based on conversations with foreign leaders. Rusk refused on the ground that the officers would no longer be candid in their entries and the Foundation's integrity and independence would be compromised. This did not satisfy Dulles, and more persuasion was attempted, urging patriotic reasons. Rusk took the matter up with his new chairman; JDR backed him fully, as did two other trustees, Robert Lovett and John J. McCloy, who were consulted because of their eminence in foreign affairs. In the opinion of one staff member, other major foundations similarly pressed by the CIA were emboldened to stand fast thanks to the Rockefeller Foundation's position, and CIA infiltration was averted.[10]

Rusk said that when it came to backing him on matters of policy and principle, JDR was "pure gold." Rusk also said that after he became secretary of state in 1960 he found that Allen Dulles had tried to accomplish his purpose anyway by intercepting Foundation mail![11]

It was at this time—1952—that it can fairly be said that JDR had entered his "takeoff" period as a philanthropist, steadily building a record of leadership and creative endeavor in his chosen work that was to be unparalleled by any other American of his time.

Because his father had been so strong an influence on JDR—*and* because liberating himself from that influence was an indispensable condition for his success—it is interesting to compare the evolution of their careers. Both men served long apprenticeships, not coming into full control as philanthropists until well past the age of forty. But, as we have seen, those apprenticeships were markedly different. Junior's, from 1897 to the end of World War I, was served mostly under the tutelage of the remarkable Frederick Gates, with no competing siblings and with his own father off at a distance, benign and supportive. It was a time of great opportunity, not only for material accomplishments, but also in the realm of ideas. Junior was provided by his father with incredible resources, both institutional and financial, with which to pursue these opportunities. Though he was intelligent enough to develop a cautious and practical method of work, Junior's goals as a philanthropist were suffused with an idealism typical of his time. Junior seemed intent on remaking the world in line with his "liberal vision" of a peaceful, harmonious, cooperative utopia.

In contrast, throughout JDR's long apprenticeship (from 1929 to 1952), he had no mentor other than his father. There is no question that Junior succeeded in inculcating in his oldest son high moral standards, thrift, generosity, openness to change, dedication to good works. It is to JDR's credit that he accepted these values in full and lived by them throughout his life, despite the fact that the rest of Junior's influence was considerably less salutary. For there is equally no question that Junior's behavior for a long time did nothing but repress his son instead of encouraging his development as an independent, self-actualized human being.

In his formative years during the first two decades of this century, Junior had countless opportunities to shape, influence, manage, and create great enterprises, thus steadily developing his abilities as a leader, manager, and decision-maker. He seems never to have been aware that his oldest son had no comparable opportunities, but was cast into a series of preordained roles as agent of his father that very nearly suffocated him. Both father and son were shy and diffident as young men; but the result of their different circumstances and the different behavior of their fathers was that JDR had a much more difficult time than Junior in overcoming his handicaps.

To be sure, the onset of the Depression changed everything: it drastically reduced any possibility of bold, new enterprises. Junior was forced to give up his overambitious plans and to struggle merely to maintain his situation and cope with the burden of Rockefeller Center. Yet, even if this had not happened, one suspects that Junior's posture toward his children would not have been substantially different. There is no easy explanation of why Junior was such a domineering father, in contrast to his own father's attitude of maximum support and minimum interference. Given his high degree of intelligence, love of his father, and gratitude for the way his father behaved toward him, why did Junior not strive to emulate Senior in his own fatherhood?

One clue may be found in the hints that Junior gave of a deep, abiding fear of the dark side of human nature, a fear possibly stemming from the religious fundamentalism of his upbringing, with its stark contrast between the forces of good and evil. This may account for his long agonizing before asking Abby to marry him and even more for his anguished letters to her during the period of his nervous breakdown and prolonged recovery. Junior could well have feared that the combination of the family's great wealth, his father's noninterference, and the dark impulses within himself would lead him to slide into sin instead of keeping to the path of righteousness. He might well conclude that, having had to do battle with temptation, the wise course would be to take no chances with his own children and to try to exert a maximum of influence. The struggles of Babs and Winthrop might have seemed to him to confirm his apprehensions.

Whatever the inner struggle that raged, righteousness clearly won, and Junior went on to fulfill the remarkable career that we know. He did not achieve his ideal goals, yet his accomplishments, taken singly or together, mark him as one of the great figures in two centuries of American history. His work in conservation alone would seem to assure him of that rank. And surely no private citizen ever did more for his hometown than Junior did for New York, notably in his reform efforts even more than in his material triumphs—at Rockefeller Center, Rockefeller University, the United Nations, the Cloisters, the Hudson Palisades, the housing projects, the improvement of entire neighborhoods, the steady support of virtually every cultural and socially useful institution in the city.

This great record of philanthropic accomplishment was in fact another of JDR's problems. One is reminded of the impeccable wisdom in Lord Chesterfield's letters to his son and the irony that the son became a ne'er-do-well, having no chance to live up to his father's ideals. This fate did not befall JDR; his years of relative misery as little more than a highly placed clerk in his father's office somehow served him well by helping to forge within him qualities of perseverance, patience, and far-sighted determination. Despite the accumulated handicaps of a tedious apprenticeship, of a famous father, of an even more famous younger brother Nelson, who saw himself as the real leader of the family, and of his own self-doubts, JDR doggedly kept on the path that life had chosen for him, that of full-time philanthropist, and he succeeded beyond anyone's expectations. Because his financial resources were dwarfed by those available to Junior, JDR could not hope to emulate his father's material accomplishments. Yet he went surprisingly far in this regard, and in other ways his career compares favorably to that of his father and even exceeded it in some respects.

An unmistakable fact is that JDR was more realistic in setting and pursuing his life's goals than his father had been. This perhaps was the result of his apprenticeship and the gritty realities of the Depression and World War II. At the end of the war, he determined that he would devote himself to bolstering American democracy, improving government administration and personnel, working on the worldwide problem of overpopulation, and influencing the programs of the Rockefeller Foundation in the direction of aiding underdeveloped countries. Along the way, he set other goals for himself. His wisdom can be seen not only in the goals themselves, but in his perception of what he could accomplish. His objectives were certainly extraordinarily difficult, requiring sustained, even lifelong, effort, yet not impossible of achievement as some of Junior's were. And JDR approached them with a degree of modesty and humility, believing not that he could *solve* great problems by his own efforts, but that he could make progress and lead in the right direction. Evidence of this is the fact that he thought of his life's work as making progress in four broad fields of activity rather than achieving definite ends. He thought of the four fields as "Asia, the arts, population, and philanthropy," though he engaged, of course, in projects that did not quite fit under these heads.

As we saw, his first great success was in matters associated with Japan—to such an extent that Japan became a second home to him and Blanchette. They came to love the country, its culture and people, and were revered in return. This interest led him to an interest in other Asian countries. He created a cultural center for Asia in New York City that required a lifetime effort to nurture. And he sponsored an agricultural development program in Asia that became recognized as the finest of its kind.

In population, JDR went against prevailing advice by creating a scientific and technical assistance organization that became the world's leading resource in its field. In this, and in his personal commitment and activities at home and abroad, JDR became the acknowledged world leader in combating overpopulation.

In the arts, JDR devoted thirteen years to creating Lincoln Center, a great cultural oasis in New York City that rivaled Rockefeller Center in its scope, cost, and significance for the city. He amassed great collections of Asian art and American paintings, and in the end bequeathed them to the public. He created a gem of a program in supporting the arts in Asia. In all of his overseas activities—in population, agriculture, the arts, and other fields—JDR scrupulously avoided heavy-handed Cold War attitudes and cultural imperialism; they were the "purest" programs to be found because of their dedication to their stated function without ulterior motives and their focus on the genuine needs of the host countries.

Nor do these accomplishments exhaust the list; others were: an innovative program in urban housing for low-income families; activities in support of youth, blacks, and women; support of the arts and sex education in the schools; an awards program that became the badge of distinction for civil servants and that led directly to important administrative reforms in Washington. In leading the Rockefeller Foundation, JDR gradually succeeded in moving that institution in the directions he had articulated at the end of the war, but with such even-handed patience and regard for due process that he won the unanimous respect of all the people who served on the board and on the staff during his long tenure.

It was in his fourth field—"philanthropy"—that JDR made a unique contribution that his father never had any reason to give thought to. By philanthropy, JDR was not referring to his own or anybody else's role as a practicing philanthropist, but to philanthropy as a social phenomenon, a unique historical force that he regarded as indispensable to the continued health and success of American pluralistic democracy. He saw it as threatened by modern trends, in particular the great growth of government and business and the seeming indifference in those sectors to the welfare of what JDR called "the third sector" (a term that he favored instead of the seeming pretentiousness of "philanthropy"). He thus became the great champion of preserving, enhancing, and democratizing the third sector.

Despite his dislike of the word, JDR unquestionably was the major philanthropist of his time, the principal carrier of the tradition pioneered by his grandfather and carried on by his father. Against odds, he lived up to their standards, even if he, his father, and his brothers never quite realized it. Because of changing times, he was also the last of the great philanthropists in this tradition, and his death marked the effective end of the dynasty.

APPENDIX A

John D. Rockefeller, Jr.'s Net Worth, 1928, 1938, 1950

(MILLIONS OF DOLLARS)

	1928	1938	1950
Real Estate	41.7	26.4	5.4
Receivables	33.6	40.0	63.0
Cash	29.1	.1	.2
Securities	875.8	313.0	267.4
Stocks	724.8	181.8	151.6
Bonds	151.0	130.8	115.8
Other	14.8	.1	.5
Total	995.0	379.6	336.5

Note: In 1928 the Receivables category includes money advanced to that point for Rockefeller Center, Colonial Williamsburg, and land purchases in Wyoming. The large cash balance reflects money out on call loans. The lower 1938 total reflects the erosion of values due to the 1929 Crash and its aftermath and also the creation of the 1934 Trust and the gift taxes paid on them that totaled almost $150 million. In 1938 and 1950 the Receivables category is composed almost exclusively of debt owed by Rockefeller Center to Junior.

All of the amounts shown above are given in market value for the years in question. To reach current dollars, these figures need to be multiplied by different factors; approximately 6.5 for 1928 and 1938 and 5 for 1950. Using this formula, JDR, Jr.'s total assets in 1928 would be worth approximately 6.5 billion in 1988 dollars. SOURCE: JDR, Jr., Accounting Files.

APPENDIX B

Charitable Contributions, 1856–1960

(MILLIONS OF DOLLARS)

JOHN D. ROCKEFELLER

The Rockefeller Foundation	$182.9
The General Education Board	129.2
Laura Spelman Rockefeller Memorial	74.0
Rockefeller Institute for Medical Research	60.7
Baptist Churches and Organizations	50.0
American Colleges and Universities—principally, the University of Chicago	35.0
Miscellaneous	8.2
Total	$540.0

During his lifetime, Senior made approximately $540 million in charitable contributions. In addition, he made gifts to his family totaling approximately $500 million.

JOHN D. ROCKEFELLER, JR.

General and Operating Foundations—RBF, IEB, Sealantic, BSH	$192.2
Churches and Religious Organizations—Riverside, Baptist Organizations, YMCAs, YWCAs, Ecumenical Groups	71.7
American Restorations—Williamsburg and Sleepy Hollow	63.3
American Colleges and Universities	58.4
Parks and Conservation	44.4
Libraries and Museums	35.1
Foreign Universities and Institutes	13.2

Cultural Organizations	$12.1
Hospitals	11.8
Relief Agencies	9.5
French Restorations	2.5
Miscellaneous	22.8
	———
Total	$537.0

During his lifetime and through his estate, JDR, Jr., made approximately $537 million in charitable contributions and made gifts of approximately $261 million to his family.

APPENDIX C Genealogical Chart of the Rockefeller Family

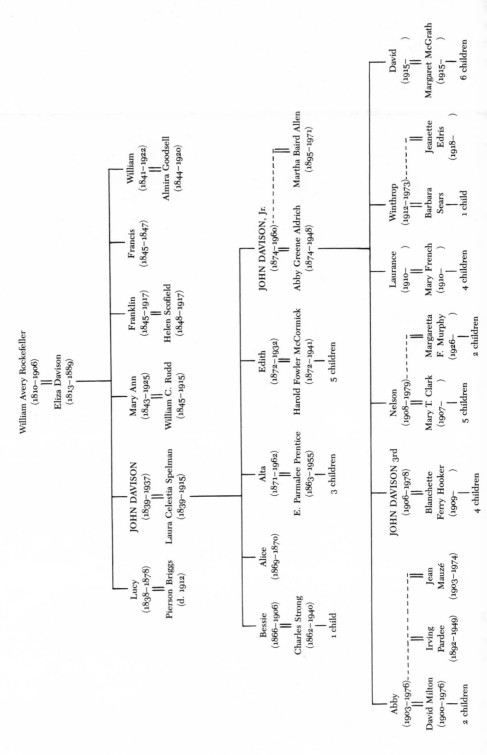

BIBLIOGRAPHIC NOTE

In their study of the Rockefeller Family published more than a decade ago, Peter Collier and David Horowitz noted that ". . . the serious student of the family is handicapped not only by the tight control of primary sources, but also by the paucity of secondary material." Happily, this situation has improved dramatically in the intervening years as more material has been processed and transferred from the Family Archives in Manhattan to the Rockefeller Archive Center in Pocantico Hills, New York. This book, in fact, is only one example of a number of studies completed in recent years that have utilized the primary source material now available to scholars at this location.

The Center is the repository for the collected Papers of the Rockefeller Family and many of its affiliated organizations, including, but not limited to, the Rockefeller Foundation, the General Education Board, Rockefeller University, the Laura Spelman Rockefeller Memorial, and the Rockefeller Brothers Fund. The Collection spans more than a century and is a rich and relatively untapped resource for scholarly investigations of many areas of late-nineteenth- and twentieth-century life.

As of this writing, the Center houses more than 20,000 cubic feet of documents—approximately forty million items ranging from Senior's famous "Ledger A" to the most recent minutes of the Rockefeller University Council. Most of this source material is available for research, and additional files are being opened as time passes.

We do not claim to have examined more than a fraction of this enormous collection. The Papers of John D. Rockefeller constitute a separate record group and we used them in only a limited way. We focused on those files most directly related to the lives and careers of John D. Rockefeller, Jr., and John D. Rockefeller 3rd, the vast majority of which can be found in the record group entitled "Office of the Messrs. Rockefeller." This covers the period from 1890 to 1961 and also contains the personal papers of other family members active during these years and a number of sub-record groups, or subject files, dealing with areas of special interest to Junior or his children.

These subject files are divided into fourteen areas, of which nine are open for research. Among the files that are open for research, we found the material in Housing Reform, Economic Reform, Civic Interests, Medical, Colonial Williamsburg, and Rockefeller Boards particularly useful and rich in historical detail. Among the subject files that are currently closed (they may be used with the permission of the Director of the Center) the documents in the Business, Cultural, Education, Religion, and World Affairs sections were extremely informative and will reward the attention of scholars. Of the more than 450 cubic feet of material in these files, we read every document at least once prior to their transfer to the Archive Center in the early 1980s.

Additional material relating to the career of John D. Rockefeller 3rd, covering the years from 1906 to 1961, can also be found at the Archive Center in a separate record group. In general terms, the documents in this record group are concerned with projects and institutions initiated and developed by JDR 3rd rather than by his father. Therefore, in addition to a substantial and very important personal correspondence, essential documentary material on the birth control movement, the Population Council, the Japan Society, and the Rockefeller Foundation can be found in this collection.

Quite often leads uncovered in these two record groups led us to exciting discoveries in other areas of the archives. We found the material in the Rockefeller Foundation, General Education Board, China Medical Board, Laura Spelman Rockefeller Memorial, Davison Fund, and Spelman Fund files extremely useful and comprehensive, even though we were able to examine these files in only a random fashion.

In addition to material held at the Archive Center, Mrs. John D. Rockefeller 3rd and the executors of her husband's estate granted us access to other material that does not yet form part of any archival collection. This enabled us to examine the full series of John D. Rockefeller, Jr.'s financial records from 1918 to 1960 and similar documents from his eldest son's files for the years 1925 to 1961. This analysis enabled us to trace accurately the size, distribution, and eventual transfer of the Rockefeller fortune for the first time and also allowed us to assess the real significance and impact of Rockefeller Center, philanthropy, and federal tax law on the family's financial situation over time. This financial analysis was paralleled by an examination of the federal income tax returns of Junior and JDR 3rd that corroborated the amounts devoted to investment, philanthropy, and other purposes. Therefore, all financial data in this study have been derived from at least two distinct sources and can be considered definitive. We have found all previous estimates of the Rockefeller fortune to be inaccurate because none of them was based upon examination of only the pertinent primary sources.

In addition, we asked for and received special permission to study the 1934 and 1952 Trust Indentures, as well as the files dealing with the sale of Rockefeller Center to the Brothers in 1948, the gift of the Rockefeller Center Note to the RBF in 1952, and the subsequent sale of RCI stock to the Trusts. The documents dealing with the creation of Hills Realty and the later sale of this entity to the Brothers were also placed at our disposal. None of this material is located in the Archive Center and can only be seen by special permission.

Mrs. Rockefeller also made available to us her husband's diaries spanning the years 1917–78 and allowed us to review and quote from her husband's personal correspondence with his parents, siblings, and personal friends that is held privately.

Many members of the Rockefeller Family and staff members of Room 5600, the Rockefeller Group, Inc. (formerly RCI), the RBF, Greenrock Corporation, and the Rockefeller Foundation gave freely of their time, consented to interviews, and helped to find and explain the meaning of obscure documents and events.

We consulted a wide variety of secondary works, including books, articles in learned journals, and newspapers. To list all of them, both those explicitly cited and those that helped to form our view of these events, would be almost a hopeless task and certainly a very pretentious one. Those that were used most often or that we consider to be helpful to others are cited in the notes.

PEOPLE INTERVIEWED FOR THIS STUDY

Hope Aldrich
Robert Bates
Bernard Berelson
Kershaw Burbank
Laura Chasin
Jerome Cohen
Dana Creel
J. Richardson Dilworth
Joan Dunlop
Peggy Dulany
Joseph Ernst

Sandra Ferry
Frederick Fox
Wade Greene
J. George Harrar
James N. Hyde
Neva Kaiser
Lindesley Kimball
Ray Lamontagne
Dave Lelewer
John Lockwood
Elizabeth McCormack

NOTES

CHAPTER 1

1. The meeting is described in the manuscript version of Gates' autobiography (hereinafter referred to as Gates MS), p. 302. Copies of the MS are located in the Rockefeller Archive Center (RAC) in Pocantico and among the Gates papers at the University of Rochester. The Gates MS contains more, and different, material than the published version of his autobiography, *Chapters in My Life* (New York: The Free Press, 1977). See also: Allan Nevins, *Study in Power: John D. Rockefeller, Industrialist and Philanthropist*, Vol. II (New York: Scribners, 1953), pp. 158–78.

2. Quoted in Thomas W. Goodspeed, *The History of the University of Chicago, 1891–1906* (Chicago: University of Chicago Press, 1916), pp. 66–67.

3. Ibid., p. 36.

4. Gates (1977), p. 193.

5. Goodspeed (1916), p. 122. It was the reasoning of Gates and the magnetic influence of Harper that swayed the decision to build up a great Baptist university in Chicago rather than New York or Washington. It would seem likely that Augustus Strong would have had the inside track with Rockefeller, given Strong's eminence, the familial relationship, and the fact that by this time Rockefeller had moved to New York City from Cleveland. But Strong made the tactical error of consistently asking for $20 million all at once, an outrageous demand given what a dollar was worth in those days. Rockefeller managed deftly to delay and avoid his request for years, having no idea, of course, that he would end up giving considerably more than that sum to the University of Chicago. Gates' potent reasoning was that the East was already well endowed with great universities and Washington, as a city of government clerks, did not have the private-sector base to support a great private university over the long term. It was the "West" where a university was truly needed. Once the decision was made, the New York and Washington factions accepted it in good grace.

6. The first major gift in American history was probably the $500,000 that James Smithson willed to the United States to create the Smithsonian, a huge amount considering that it was committed in 1829. There are other examples of large gifts later in the nineteenth century, but none comparable to Senior's commitment to the University of Chicago. Senior thought he was providing a substantial part of the endowment for the university with his initial $600,000 gift in 1889 followed by $1 million in 1890 and $2 million in 1892, but he found himself having to give more in succeeding years to help the university meet operating deficits, as well as buying land and donating it. He finally terminated his general support with a $10 million gift in 1910. The book value of the securities and real estate he gave to the university over this twenty-one-year period was $21 million and the market value was $34.7 million (Goodspeed [1916], pp. 345–46). It is interesting to note that railroad magnate Leland Stanford's commitment to create Stanford University in memory of his deceased son had become known by the time Senior began his support of the University of Chicago. There is no way to compare the two meaningfully because Stanford's death in 1893 meant that the support from his estate was a complicated and drawn-out affair, and consisted mainly of huge tracts of land that carried a low valuation at the time but became extremely valuable many years later. [Roxanne Nilan, "The Tenacious and Courageous Jane L. Stanford," *Sandstone and Tile*, Vol. 9 (Winter 1985), pp. 2–13.]

7. Nevins (1953), Vol. I, p. 1.

8. Ibid., p. 10.

9. The original copy of "Ledger A" is preserved in the RAC.

10. Nevins (1953), Vol. I, p. 18.

11. Ibid., p. 191.

12. For those interested in a detailed account, there is no better source than Nevins, whose Vol. I is devoted almost in its entirety to this story, from Ch. II ("Venture in Oil") through to Ch. XXI ("The First Great Trust").

13. John D. Rockefeller, *Random Reminiscences of Men and Events* (Garden City, N.Y.: Doubleday, Page & Co., 1909), p. 62.

14. Nevins (1953), Vol. I, p. 226.

15. Modern examples include Ferdinand Lundberg, *The Rich and the Super-Rich: A Study in the Power of Money Today* (New York: Lyle Stuart, 1968); Meyer Kutz, *Rockefeller Power* (New York: Pinnacle Books, 1975); Peter Collier and David Horowitz, *The Rockefellers: An American Dynasty* (New York: Holt, Rinehart & Winston, 1976).

16. Nevins (1953), Vol. I, p. 267. Aside from Nevins, an early great book that began to establish the history of business as a scholarly subfield and develop a more balanced perspective on business in the nineteenth century is Adolph Berle, Jr., and Gardiner Means, *The Modern Corporation and Private Property* (New York: Macmillan, 1933). An excellent book on the subject is Alfred D. Chandler, Jr., *The Visible Hand: The Managerial Revolution in American Business* (Cambridge: Harvard University Press, 1977). Also see Melvin G. de Chazeau and Alfred E. Kahn, *Integration and Competition in the Petroleum Industry* (New Haven: Yale University Press, 1959); John H. McLean and Robert W. Haigh, *The Growth of Integrated Oil Companies* (Cambridge: Harvard University Press, 1954); Ralph E. Hidy and Muriel E. Hidy, *Pioneering in Big Business, 1882–1911* [a history of the Standard Oil Company (New Jersey)] (New York: Harper & Bros., 1955); Harold F. Williamson and Arnold R. Drum, *The American Petroleum Industry: The Age of Illumination* (Evanston: Northwestern University Press, 1959), especially Chaps. 14 and 16; Lance E. Davis and Douglas C. North, *Institutional Change and American Economic Growth* (Cambridge: Cambridge University Press, 1971).

17. Ida Tarbell, *The History of the Standard Oil Company*, Vol. II (New York: Macmillan, 1904 [originally published as a series of articles in *McClure's* magazine beginning in November 1902]), pp. 231–32. A great book in its time, Tarbell's work has been placed in its proper historical perspective by modern scholarship. One scholar, for example, comments that her book, "once the standard treatment, has now become a museum piece of historical polemics" (Edward Chase Kirkland, *Industry Comes of Age: Business, Labor and Public Policy, 1860–1897* [Chicago: Quadrangle Books, 1961]).

18. Quoted in John Moody, *The Truth about the Trusts: A Description and Analysis of the American Trust Movement* (New York: Greenwood Press, 1973 [reprint of 1904 ed.]), p. 131.

19. Quoted in Nevins (1953), Vol. I, p. 19.

20. Ibid., p. 97.

21. Nevins (1953), Vol. II, p. 300. See also p. 485 (fn. 2).

22. His only book, *Random Reminiscences* (see no. 13 above), was published in 1909.

23. Robert H. Bremner, *American Philanthropy* (Chicago: University of Chicago Press, 1960), pp. 117–18.

24. There was, for example, the amusing result that occurred in 1904 when Woodrow Wilson, then president of Princeton University, earnestly sought Carnegie's financial help for several purposes, including a new football stadium. Carnegie, who hated football, decided that what Princeton needed most was a lake to promote the sport of rowing. Two years later, a man-made lake was finished at a cost of $400,000, and

Princetonians have enjoyed Lake Carnegie ever since. See Joseph Frazier Wall, *Andrew Carnegie* (New York: Oxford University Press, 1970), pp. 866–69.

25. Quoted in George W. Corner, *A History of the Rockefeller Institute, 1901–1953* (New York: Rockefeller Institute Press, 1964), p. 18.

26. Wall (1970), p. 833.

27. One of the great classics in sociology, Weber's *The Protestant Ethic and the Spirit of Capitalism* was translated by Talcott Parsons and published by Scribners in 1930 as an introduction to Weber's comparative study of religions. Weber began writing *The Protestant Ethic* in sections and publishing it in Germany in 1904 after returning from his trip to the United States. Parsons made extensive use of Weber's ideas in Part III of his *The Structure of Social Action* (New York: McGraw-Hill, 1937).

28. Gates MS, pp. 298–99.

29. Ibid., p. 161.

30. On the dubious administrative practices of the University of Chicago during the early years, see Goodspeed (1916), pp. 273–96, and Gates (1977), pp. 189–97.

31. Nevins (1953), Vol. II, pp. 274–75.

32. Gates (1977), p. 131.

33. As we shall see, it is an interesting coincidence that both Senior's only son and his grandson John 3rd also suffered from severe nervous tension at key transitional points in their lives.

CHAPTER 2

1. The fair proper was held a year late because not enough time had been allowed for construction. There had been a pro forma opening ceremony during the fall of 1892.

2. Albert M. Tannler, "A Perilous Journey to Hyde Park," *University of Chicago Magazine*, Vol. LXXIII, No. 1 (Autumn 1979), pp. 3–11. This article contains an excellent description of the neighborhood of the university and the fair and the "building boom" caused by both. The title is a play on the trepidations of newly recruited faculty members from the East in journeying to the "unknown Western perils" of Chicago. Hyde Park is a neighborhood, not a park, and today is a relatively small section of Chicago, but when it was annexed by the city in 1889 (primarily because Olmsted's park design offered such a good location for the fair), the "village" of Hyde Park was huge, running almost a hundred blocks from 39th Street south to 138th Street.

3. One extraordinary building from the fair still stands on the northern edge of Jackson Park. Originally the Palace of Fine Arts, it was sheathed in permanent limestone in the years 1928 to 1932 to provide 600,000 square feet for a museum, first known as the Rosenwald Museum (after the principal donor) and later renamed the Museum of Science and Industry.

4. There were many more visits to come. Junior served for many years as a trustee of the University of Chicago, and during the years around the turn of the century he acted as his father's agent in buying up parcels of land along both sides of the Midway to donate to the university, in line with his father's belief that a university needed growing space and room around it.

5. Ray Allen Billington, ed., *Frontier and Section: Selected Essays of Frederick Jackson Turner* (Englewood Cliffs, N.J.: Prentice-Hall, 1961), pp. 37, 61.

6. Henry Adams, *The Education of Henry Adams* (Boston: Houghton Mifflin, 1961), pp. 344–45.

7. Ibid., pp. 499–500.

8. Junior to John A. Browning, Sept. 3, 1893. (This and all letters cited hereafter are located in the Rockefeller Archive Center [RAC], unless otherwise noted.)

9. Mrs. McCormick spent a substantial portion of each year in New York City, where

she had come to know the Rockefellers. Her two sons, Stanley and Harold, were classmates of Junior's in New York. Harold and Edith were married in 1895.

10. Senior bought the property, house, and furnishings for "one dollar and other valuable considerations," the latter being nine undeveloped city lots on the northeast corner of Fifth Avenue and 72nd Street, which he had purchased in 1881 for $425,000. Arabella was an adventuress from Virginia who finally was able to marry the aged Collis in 1884, inherited his fortune, and became known for building palaces around the world (see James T. Maher, *The Twilight of Splendor* [Boston: Little, Brown, 1975], pp. 272–75). The furnishings were rather lush and garish, but in perfectly fine shape, so Senior, a practical man, simply kept them intact. Later several rooms of the house with these furnishings were donated to the Museum of the City of New York, where they may still be seen today, giving many people the impression that the Rockefeller taste in interior decorating was rather voluptuous.

11. Kate Simon, *Fifth Avenue* (New York: Harcourt Brace Jovanovich, 1979), p. 13; Lloyd Morris, *Incredible New York* (Salem, N.Y.: Ayer Co., 1975 [facsimile ed. of 1951 publication]), p. 112; *Social Register, 1883–95; New York City Directory, 1883–1900.* The Croton Reservoir was located near 42nd Street on the present site of the New York Public Library.

12. Raymond B. Fosdick, *John D. Rockefeller, Jr.: A Portrait* (New York: Harper & Bros., 1956), p. 39.

13. Ibid., p. 41.

14. In preparing his biography of Junior, Fosdick bound together many of his notes of interviews with Junior in one typewritten manuscript, which is located in the RAC. Substantial portions were not used in the book. This will be referred to subsequently as "Fosdick notes." The reference here is to p. 40 of those notes.

15. Fosdick (1956), p. 11.

16. In 1936 Junior had an exhaustive study and compilation of his father's charitable contributions prepared by Louis Armour, an accountant in the family office. The typescript is available in the RAC, and is referred to hereafter as the Armour Study.

17. "Address on the Fiftieth Anniversary of the Men's Bible Class of the Riverside Church," Feb. 29, 1944 (copy in RAC).

18. Fosdick (1956), pp. 34–35.

19. Fosdick notes, pp. 51, 111–12.

20. Derived from Moses King, *King's Views of New York, 1896–1915, and Brooklyn, 1905* (Salem, N.Y.: Ayer Co., 1980), pp. 15, 24–25.

21. For a record of these contributions, see the Armour Study. Junior followed the example of his father by *not* becoming a heavy contributor to politicians in later life. This might be explained by the fact that although Senior gave to TR's 1886 campaign (and, it seems likely, to his 1898 gubernatorial race), Roosevelt during his presidency became one of the most vociferous critics of Standard Oil and of Senior personally.

22. *Proceedings of the Baptist Congress for the Discussion of Current Questions,* 1892, p. 122 (copy in RAC).

23. William Rainey Harper to Junior, Feb. 11, 1893.

24. W. H. P. Faunce to Junior, Apr. 1, 1893.

25. Fosdick (1956) devotes Chaps. III and IV to a description of Junior's college years, primarily dealing with the socialization process. The Cammarian Society was a prestigious group limited to fifteen seniors who concerned themselves with ethical questions at Brown.

26. Walter C. Bronson, *The History of Brown University, 1764–1914* (Providence: Brown University, 1914), pp. 428–29.

27. Joseph Dorfman, *The Economic Mind in American Civilization*, Vol. 3 (New York: Augustus M. Kelley, 1969), pp. 205–12; Thomas L. Haskell, *The Emergence of Professional Social Science* (Urbana: University of Illinois Press, 1977), pp. 177–89.

28. Before the Brooklyn Ethical Association, Nov. 15, 1892.

29. The businessmen antagonistic to Andrews did not include Senior. He had known Andrews favorably for many years, ever since, as a young Cleveland businessman, he had served as a trustee of Denison University during Andrews' tenure as president. Andrews had also been extensively consulted in the discussions that led to the founding of the University of Chicago.

30. Andrews, "The Economic Law of Monopoly," *Journal of Social Science*, Feb. 1890, p. 6.

31. Bronson (1914), pp. 461–68.

32. Fosdick notes, p. 16.

33. Junior's notebooks from many of his college courses are available in the RAC. Information regarding the content of the courses is taken from them.

34. Junior's annotated copy of Marx is preserved in the RAC. It was published by the Humboldt Publishing Company of New York, an edition that carried no date of publication but was taken from the first English translation, published in 1887 in London by S. Moore and E. Aveling. Junior's copy was Vol. I of a two-volume set entitled *Commodities and Money*. It carried the Engels preface of 1887 and the Marx preface from the second German edition (1873). The first German edition was published in 1867.

CHAPTER 3

1. "Recollections of My Father," speech by Junior before the New York YMCA, Aug. 1920 (RAC).

2. The best sources on the structure and internal functioning of the Standard Oil trust are Nevins (1953), Chaps. XXI (Vol. I) and XXII (Vol. II); Chandler (1977), pp. 416–25; and Ralph and Muriel Hidy (1955), passim.

3. Taken from "Memorial Address for Frederick T. Gates," given by Junior at the Rockefeller Institute, May 15, 1929, and Gates MS (RAC).

4. Fosdick (1956), p. 87.

5. Henry Cooper to Junior, July 14, 1898.

6. A good description of the courtship and wedding can be found in Fosdick (1956), pp. 97–103.

7. On Junior's stock loss, see Fosdick (1956), pp. 90–92; on the negotiations with J. P. Morgan, pp. 105–6.

8. Arthur Link, "What Happened to the Progressive Movement in the 1920s?" *American Historical Review*, LXIV (July 1959), p. 836. This view has been supported in later works, for example Peter G. Filene, "An Obituary for 'The Progressive Movement,'" *American Quarterly*, Vol. 22 (1970), pp. 20–34; John D. Buenker, "The Progressive Era: A Search for Synthesis," *Mid-American*, Vol. 51 (1969), pp. 175–93; William L. O'Neill, *The Progressive Years: America Comes of Age* (New York: Dodd, Mead, 1975).

9. For a thorough account of the attacks on Senior, see Nevins (1953), Ch. XXXV, "Assailants and Defenders," Vol. II, pp. 328–55.

10. Theodore Roosevelt, of course, was a notorious political opportunist; his attacks on Senior constitute merely another example. Because of this political opportunism in part, TR was also a brilliant president, and nothing can detract from his record as a reformer. His performance as president was popular and a valid response to the times, but it did widen the schism in the GOP between liberals and the Old Guard. This, plus TR's erratic behavior after he left office, led to his becoming the candidate of the Progressive (Bull Moose) Party and to the election of a Democrat to the White House in 1912. The liberal-conservative split became a prominent feature of the GOP again in the

years between the Depression and the election of Ronald Reagan in 1980, with Nelson Rockefeller playing an important role. For the more widely accepted view of TR, see George Mowry, *The Era of Theodore Roosevelt* (New York: Harper & Bros., 1958). For a quite different view, see Gabriel Kolko, *The Triumph of Conservatism: A Reinterpretation of American History, 1900–1916* (Chicago: Free Press, 1967).

11. Nevins (1953), Vol. II, pp. 300–301.

12. For details, see the Armour Study and various files (Civics, General Welfare, Religion) in the RAC.

13. Bremner (1960), pp. 117, 121.

14. On the "age of organization," see Robert M. Wiebe, *The Search for Order, 1877–1920* (New York: Hill & Wang, 1967); Louis Galambos, "The Emerging Organizational Synthesis in Modern American History," *Business History Review*, Vol. 44 (1970), pp. 279–90; Jerry Israel, ed., *Building the Organizational Society: Essays on Associational Activity in Modern America* (New York: Free Press, 1972).

15. Wall (1972), pp. 880–84.

16. Bremner (1960), pp. 116–17.

CHAPTER 4

1. Gates (1977), pp. 179–83.

2. Quoted in Fosdick (1956), p. 116.

3. Ibid.

4. Gates MS (quoted in Nevins [1953], Vol. II, p. 217).

5. Fosdick (1956), pp. 111–12 regarding Junior's "salesmanship" role; on his approach to his mother, pp. 113–14.

6. Junior to Dr. L. Emmett Holt, April 29, 1901.

7. For a full account of the Rockefeller Institute, see George W. Corner's highly detailed history (New York: Rockefeller Institute Press, 1964). Two other views of the Rockefeller Institute, the growth of the American medical profession, and the role of Dr. Welch in both are provided by Donald Fleming, *William H. Welch and the Rise of Modern Medicine* (Boston: Little, Brown, 1954); E. Richard Brown, *Rockefeller Medicine Men: Medicine and Capitalism in America* (Berkeley: University of California Press, 1979). The Marxist approach of the last develops the thesis that Rockefeller support of medicine was designed to control and manipulate the masses for the benefit of the capitalists.

8. Biggs had been a medical officer with the Department of Health for a number of years. After the study of the New York City milk supply, he was offered a political appointment as head of the department by the incoming Seth Low, who had been president of Columbia University before his election as mayor. However, Biggs declined and was appointed chief medical officer instead. See Edward T. Devine, "Municipal Reform and Social Welfare in New York," *Review of Reviews*, Vol. XXVIII (Oct. 1903), pp. 433–38; C-E. Winslow, *The Life of Hermann Biggs* (Philadelphia: Lea & Febiger, 1929), pp. 201–34.

9. Corner (1964), pp. 47–48.

10. Quoted in Nevins (1953), Vol. II, p. 310.

11. The GEB technically still exists as a corporate shell, but it ceased operations in 1960.

12. Woodward's book was originally published in 1951 by the Louisiana State University Press as Vol. IX of a series entitled "A History of the South."

13 Ibid., p. 398.

14. For a thorough account of the Rockefeller Sanitary Commission, see John Ettling, *The Germ of Laziness: Rockefeller Philanthropy and Public Health in the New South* (Cambridge: Harvard University Press, 1981).

15. GEB, *Report, 1902–14*, RAC.

16. A good source for detailed information on all of these projects is *Adventures in Giving: The Story of the General Education Board* (New York: Harper & Row, 1962), the best of Raymond B. Fosdick's several books on Rockefeller philanthropies, and also the least-known and scarcest. The bulk of the research had been done and a manuscript prepared by Henry F. Pringle and Katharine Douglas Pringle. After the death of Henry Pringle, Fosdick, who was retired at the time, was asked by the Rockefeller Foundation trustees to edit and revise the manuscript for publication.

17. Quoted in Raymond B. Fosdick, *The Story of the Rockefeller Foundation* (New York: Harper & Bros., 1952), p. 3.

18. Nevins (1953), Vol. II, pp. 367–68.

19. The *New York Times* of July 19, 1909, reported on the sermon of the Rev. Charles D. Williams, Episcopal Bishop of Michigan, in St. Bartholemew's Church in New York in which he called Junior a "young scion of wealth and greed, possessed of more dollars than ideas." The bishop said: "A rose by any other name will smell as sweet, but the odor of that rose to me smacks strongly of crude petroleum." A number of historians, beginning with Richard Hofstadter in *Social Darwinism in American Thought* (Boston: Beacon Press, 1955), have wrongly attributed the "American Beauty Rose" speech to Senior.

20. The subject of Junior's nervous breakdown came up twice in his interviews with Fosdick (see Fosdick notes, pp. 34 and 104), but Fosdick did not mention it in his biography of Junior.

21. At Junior's request, Fosdick affixed a "Confidential" label to the memorandum of his conversation with Junior about the latter's reasons for withdrawing from business. This memo is appended to Fosdick's manuscript of his notes. However, he did quote from the memorandum in his 1956 biography of Junior, presumably with the latter's review and concurrence (see pp. 140–42).

22. Collier and Horowitz (1976). The authors hold that Junior's "dynastic project was a shrewd piece of moral calculation . . . a prolonged exercise in self-justification . . . an extravagant mummery on the theme of the vanity of human wishes," (pp. 622–26). They see it all as a failure: "For more than a hundred years, the Rockefellers have molded their ambition to the imperial course of the nation itself. Now their decline comes into view at the time that the American Century too is ending, over fifty years before its term. Far from what Junior envisioned, in neither fact is there much cause for regret."

CHAPTER 5

1. Among the congratulatory messages that came in after the birth of John 3rd (all presently located in the RAC) was a wire from Andrew Carnegie, dated Mar. 24, 1906. Carnegie, who never had a son and heir, wrote: "Cordial congratulations to Papa and Mama upon advent son and heir. Also to Grandpa and Grandma. Aldrich-Rockefeller combination should count."

Letters from the two grandmothers touched on the fact that the baby was late and rather large. Laura, unable to come to see the baby because of a sore throat, wrote on Mar. 24: "What could be finer than that a *boy* should come in so sensible a manner!" Her piety was evident: "And now another little life is brought into the world and given you to train for immortality. God honors you greatly and you will bring honor to Him by being faithful stewards of the charge entrusted to you. For weal or woe—for good or evil—how many influences enter in. There can be but one result, for if parents are in every least particular what they would have their children to be, the battle is won for God."

From Paris, Abby's mother wrote on Mar. 27: "We were all much pleased to get the welcome news of the birth of your little son and my first grandson. His prosperous condition was obviously an apology for his late arrival, and you are doubtless grateful for the easy time vouchsafed to you, as big boys generally make their arrivals most impressive to the feelings of their mammas. I do not see as you have any drawback now to fulfilling your desire for a large family as all the conditions are in your case most favorable."

This prognosis, of course, was correct, as Abby proceeded to bear four more children to achieve her large family of six. However, the number of births did seem to take a toll. Abby required a prolonged period of rest and recovery after her last child was born, going to Hot Springs, Arkansas, with her husband for that purpose.

2. David Graham Phillips, *The Treason of the Senate,* ed. George A. Mowry and Judson A. Grenier (Chicago: Quadrangle Books, 1964), p. 59.

3. The subpoena had been issued by the State of Missouri in connection with its suit against Standard Oil. The process server missed Senior when he was driven into the city by his chauffeur on Saturday, Mar. 24, to see his new grandson and namesake. The subpoena was never served, and was allowed to lapse after other witnesses made it clear that Senior no longer had an active connection with the business. See Nevins (1953), Vol. II, pp. 361–62.

4. The reference to "Old Uncle Henry Rogers" was to H. H. Rogers, one of the more notorious of the Standard Oil associates of the time, a favorite target of the press. "Rebates" refers to the favored treatment that Standard had been able to exact from the railroads because of its size and power.

5. Senior, of course, had long experience with "crank" letters and used to read some of them aloud at the breakfast table when Junior was a boy (Fosdick notes, p. 49). They seemed somewhat more ominous in the years around the turn of the century, however, as criticism intensified and incidents of violence generally increased in labor disputes and anarchist bombings.

6. Junior made this speech to a group of students at Princeton in 1927 when his son John was enrolled there (copy in RAC).

7. Mary Ellen Chase recounted several examples of this in her slim biography, *Abby Aldrich Rockefeller* (New York: Macmillan, 1950), pp. 26–28, including Abby's refusal to keep a household account book and her warning to Junior that if he ever struck her she would leave him.

8. Fosdick notes, p. 38.

9. Senior still had title to the two houses in Cleveland. The Euclid Avenue house was rented out. Senior's visits to Forest Hill diminished in number over the years as the politicians of Ohio continued to be leaders in animosity toward the Rockefellers. The house burned down in 1917, and after Senior's death the Forest Hill acreage was donated to the cities of Cleveland and East Cleveland.

10. Although Senior had negotiated the purchase of 4 West 54th Street himself, he and Junior soon learned that they would have to deal anonymously, through agents, if they were to pay anything approaching fair market value.

11. A good source on the history of Kykuit is a large unpublished manuscript by Albert I. Berger, which is on file at the RAC. Written circa 1985, the manuscript is entitled "My Father's House at Pocantico Hills," referring obviously to Junior's father, not Berger's. The work was done for the National Trust for Historic Preservation at a time when the trust seemed destined to take over Kykuit. This later fell through. Moscow (1977, pp. 27–33) has a lengthy description of Kykuit. For a more complete description of the Pocantico estate at a later time, see Chapter 27 of this book.

12. No. 13 still stands and the top floor addition can be clearly seen. Junior later acquired No. 15. After the family moved out in 1913, the houses were rented and became something of a problem for a while because the renter used them as rooming houses, another symptom of the decline of the neighborhood. In 1946 Junior deeded both houses to Nelson, who used them later as part of his New York City office when he was

governor of the state. It was in No. 13 that Nelson suffered his fatal heart attack on January 26, 1979. After his death, the two houses were sold to a developer who gutted the interiors for reconstruction as office buildings. However, the facades, protected by a landmark designation, look the same as they did early in the century.

13. The "sale" of No. 13 to Junior occurred in 1909. Senior had not yet begun to transfer substantial wealth to his son (see next chapter), and so was paying certain major expenses (such as the building of a new house) beyond what Junior could cover with his salary and living allowance.

14. Fosdick notes, p. 67.

15. Written by a member of the architectural firm of Delano and Aldrich (RAC).

16. For the interesting story of Abby's important role in developing MOMA, see Ch. 10 of this book.

17. Some of this was eventually fenced in as well, but the Rockefeller family made provision for riding trails to be open to the public.

18. Fosdick notes, pp. 51, 66.

19. Ibid.

20. The authors are grateful to Laura Chasin for making her notes of the interview of Nov. 10, 1973, available to them. A trained family counselor, she had taken an interest in family history and was seeking interviews with members of her father's generation.

21. The slight misshaping of JDR's face probably occurred at birth. His jaw was angular on the right side, slightly concave on the left. By the time that he was a grown man, little evidence of this remained, but until then it was an embarrassment for him.

22. Junior to John Browning, Aug. 1915.

23. Senior to JDR 3rd, Dec. 1921.

CHAPTER 6

1. Roe's typescript report to the "Committee of Three," dated April 3, 1912, is located in the RAC.

2. C. H. Parkhurst, *Our Fight Against Tammany* (New York: Scribners, 1895), p. 59.

3. New York State, *Report and Proceedings of the Senate Committee Appointed to Investigate the Police Department of the City of New York* (Albany, 1895), pp. 1–76 and passim; James F. Richardson, *The New York Police: Colonial Times to 1901* (New York: Oxford University Press, 1970), pp. 235–40.

4. Quoted in August Cerillo, Jr., "The Reform of Municipal Government in New York City: From Seth Low to John Purroy Mitchel," *New York Historical Society Quarterly*, Vol. LVII (Jan. 1973), p. 52.

5. *New York Times*, Jan. 4, 1910; Fosdick notes, p. 3.

6. On such subjects as Taylor, scientific management, and the Bureau of Municipal research, see Dwight Waldo, *The Administrative State* (New York: Ronald Press, 1947); and Samuel Haber, *Efficiency and Uplift: Scientific Management in the Progressive Era, 1890–1920* (Chicago: University of Chicago Press, 1973). On the development of budgeting, see A. E. Buck, "The Development of the Budget Idea in the United States" in Dwight Waldo, ed., *Ideas and Issues in Public Administration* (New York: McGraw-Hill, 1953), pp. 296–304.

7. Prominent among them were E. R. A. Seligman, Jeremiah Jenks, Frank Goodnow, Seth Low, Henry Stimson, William McAdoo, and A. Barton Hepburn.

8. All four of the BSH books mentioned were published by the Century Company in New York from 1915 to 1920. Kneeland may have gotten too close to his subject—he died of syphilis.

9. The best single source on these events is Nevins (1953), Vol. II, Ch. XXXVI, "The Dissolution of the Trust."

10. Quoted in the Hamilton Study, RAC. Like the Armour Study, this was another compendium of Rockefeller gifts and investments done by the office staff.

11. The information in this section was taken from Raymond B. Fosdick, *The Story of the Rockefeller Foundation* (New York: Harper & Bros., 1952). Another good source is Nevins (1953), Vol. II, Ch. XXXVII, "The Well-Being of Mankind."

12. Jerome Greene, "Principles and Policies of Giving," Oct. 22, 1913, RAC.

CHAPTER 7

1 For descriptions of the Colorado strike and the "Ludlow massacre," see George S. McGovern and Leonard Guttridge, *The Great Coalfield War* (Boston: Houghton Mifflin, 1972); Graham Adams, Jr., *The Age of Industrial Violence, 1910–1915* (New York: Columbia University Press, 1966); Irving Bernstein, *The Lean Years: A History of the American Worker* (Boston: Houghton Mifflin, 1960); Collier and Horowitz (1976), Ch. 8; and Fosdick (1956), Chaps. VIII and IX.

2. Fosdick notes, p. 88; Gates to Junior, May 6, 1914.

3. Both Nevins (1953) and Fosdick (1956) erroneously refer to Walsh as a U.S. senator; he was not, although the commission had been created by the Congress and had subpoena powers.

4. See documents in "Economic Reform Interests" file, RAC.

5. "Hearings before House Committee on Mines and Mining," Apr. 6, 1914, pp. 2853, 2874 (copy in RAC).

6. Ray Eldon Hiebert, *Courtier to the Crowd* (Ames, Iowa: Iowa State University Press, 1966), pp. 4–5.

7. Ivy Lee to Junior, Aug. 1914.

8. Labor had been combined with the Post Office Department before that.

9. F. A. McGregor, *The Fall and Rise of Mackenzie King* (Toronto: Macmillan, 1962).

10. Ibid., p. 96.

11. Greene to King, June 9, 1914.

12. Fosdick (1956), p. 154.

13. McGregor (1962), p. 190.

14. All quotations in this section are from ibid., Ch. 10, "A Friendship for Life."

15. All quotations in this section from ibid., Ch. 4, "A Heaven-Sent Deliverance."

16. Fosdick (1956), p. 157.

17. "Testimony of John D. Rockefeller, Jr., before U.S. Industrial Commission," January 5, 1915, p. 7764. Despite the ferocity of Walsh's attack, Junior later told Raymond Fosdick: "Oddly enough, he and I became warm friends. When my mother died he wrote a letter of sympathy that was the most beautiful one I had." Fosdick notes, p. 88.

18. King's statements are taken from his diary, as quoted in McGregor (1962), pp. 138–41.

19. Ibid., p. 137 and Ch. 8, "Mackenzie King on the Witness Stand."

20. *New York Times*, May 29, 1915.

21. Fosdick (1956), pp. 158–59.

22. McGregor (1962), p. 139.

23. Fosdick (1956), p. 162.

24. For a thorough description of the plan, see Ben M. Selekman and Mary Von Kleeck, *Employee Representation in Coal Mines: A Study of the Industrial Representation Plan of the Colorado Fuel and Iron Company* (New York: Russell Sage Foundation, 1924), pp. 59–69; and Stuart D. Brandes, *American Welfare Capitalism, 1880–1940* (Chicago: University of Chicago Press, 1976).

25. McGregor (1962), p. 221.

26. Ibid., pp. 195–96.

27. Ibid., pp. 273–74.

28. Letter of gift, Mar. 3, 1914, RAC.

29. In 1875 John Heyl Vincent, later Bishop of the Methodist Episcopal Church, cofounded (with industrialist Lewis Miller) the summer encampment in the upstate New York village of Chautauqua, which became renowned for well more than half a century for its adult education activities and its attraction for, and sponsorship of, the orators of the time.

For a full listing of all Rockefeller Foundation board members up to 1950, see Fosdick (1952), pp. 309–10.

CHAPTER 8

1. For insights into this fascinating period in U.S. foreign affairs, see Betty Glad, *Charles Evans Hughes and the Illusions of Innocence* (Urbana: University of Illinois Press, 1966); Akira Iryie, *After Imperialism* (New York: Atheneum, 1966); and Carl Parrini, *Heir to Empire* (Pittsburgh: University of Pittsburgh Press, 1969).

2. These were the so-called "irreconcilables"—Senators William Borah, Hiram Johnson, and Robert La Follette, who totally opposed the League. Senator Henry Cabot Lodge appeared to be seeking a compromise but was in fact the most effective opponent of Wilson.

3. See Elisabeth Jakab, "The Council on Foreign Relations," *Book Forum*, Vol. III, No. 4, pp. 418–57; Whitney H. Shepardson, *Early History of the Council on Foreign Relations* (Stamford, Conn.: Overbrook Press, 1960).

4. For information on these financial transactions, see: *Nomination of Nelson A. Rockefeller to Be Vice President of the United States* (Washington, D.C.: GPO, 1974). This corroborates the figure of $465 million transferred to Junior, although it must be pointed out that the difference in book and market values of shares brings some uncertainty into the assigning of exact dollar figures to such transfers. In contrast, Junior's two surviving sisters received considerably less. Edith Rockefeller McCormick received 45,000 shares of Jersey Standard and 14,886 shares of Indiana Standard, worth about $13 million, plus some real estate and a few thousand dollars in cash. Alta Rockefeller Prentice received 26,000 shares of Jersey Standard and 12,000 shares of Indiana Standard, worth about $10.4 million, plus real estate in New York and New Jersey and $200,000 in cash. No other member of the family or friend received more than $1 million, most considerably less.

Other sources on Rockefeller holdings during this period may be found in the RAC, the Hamilton and Armour studies and "John D. Rockefeller, Jr., Financial Statement and Balance Sheet," Room 5600 Tax and Accounting Files.

5. The rates rose steeply during the war with the addition of an income tax surcharge. For example, in 1917 Senior paid a tax of $20.8 million on an income of $33 million, and in 1918 he paid the full 65 percent—$22.8 million on an income of $35 million.

Given the importance that many attach to the charitable deduction as a motivation for philanthropic giving, it is interesting to note that the law exempting "gifts to charitable corporations" did not take effect until February 24, 1919. During the six years from the beginning of the income tax (March 1, 1913) until it became possible to deduct charitable gifts, Senior gave almost a quarter of a billion dollars to charity! Sources: *Standard Federal Tax Reporter* (Chicago: Commerce Clearing House, 1986); Hamilton Study; Room 5600 Tax and Accounting Files.

6. In fact, Lee tried without success during the remaining years of his life to find the "right" biographer for Senior. His first attempt was the hiring of William O. Inglis, a

reporter for the *New York World*, at a salary of $8,000 per year. Out of deference to his son's wishes, Senior was tolerant of this effort, but never really interested in it. Over a period of years, Inglis made notes of his conversations with Senior, and he interviewed others who had known Senior earlier in his life. This part of the effort worked because Inglis, an affable man and a golfer, was a good companion for Senior. The material compiled by Inglis is a valuable record, but the manuscript he delivered in 1925, after ten years on the job, was not objective and not of the quality that Junior and Lee had in mind. So his effort was shelved. Lee kept looking for a writer of stature to do the job. Emil Ludwig turned him down. Winston Churchill agreed to do the project for a fee of $250,000. Lee wanted to go ahead, but Junior thought the sum was exorbitant and rejected the bid. The problem was not solved until after Lee's death in 1934 when John D. Rockefeller 3rd came up with the name of Allan Nevins, professor of history at Columbia and a prolific writer whose biography of Grover Cleveland had won a Pulitzer Prize. Nevins demurred at first, but then agreed, asking for no financial help other than provision of a research assistant on the grounds that royalties from the scholarly and definitive work that he contemplated could not compensate him for the time he would have to spend on research. It should also be noted that Nevins was well known for assigning research topics that would be useful in his next book to the students in his graduate seminar. Nevins was wrong on one count—the book was successful and became his best-known work. It was published in 1940 and again, in a major new edition, in 1953.

A ten-page "bibliographic note" in the Collier and Horowitz book (1976) tells in detail about the search for a biographer of Senior and also critiques the Raymond Fosdick biography of Junior—all by way of making the case that the only really good book about the Rockefellers is the one by Collier and Horowitz.

7. Raymond B. Fosdick, *Chronicle of a Generation* (New York: Harper & Bros., 1958), pp. 173–74.

8. Ibid., Ch. IX, "The League of Nations," pp. 187–213.

9. Ibid., pp. 220–24.

10. Ibid., p. 215.

11. Fosdick (1952), p. 1.

12. Nevins (1953), Vol. II, pp. 399–400.

13. Fosdick (1956) tells the story of Edmonds' work, pp. 390–93.

14. For an account of how the Peking Union Medical College has fared in recent years under Communist rule, see the *New York Times*, June 9, 1985.

15. For more detailed accounts of the accomplishments of the Rockefeller Foundation in public health, see Fosdick (1952), Chaps. III, IV, V, and VI; also, Ettling (1981).

16. "A Scheme for Promotion of Education on an International Scale," memorandum from Wickliffe Rose to the trustees of the IEB. See also: Fosdick (1952), pp. 148–52 and 182–84; also the files of the IEB at the RAC for complete information.

17. Junior to Premier Poincaré, May 3, 1924.

18. Ambassador Jusserand to Junior, May 18, 1927.

19. Fosdick (1956), p. 356.

20. For this quotation and more detailed information on Junior's restoration projects overseas, see Fosdick (1956), Ch. XVIII, pp. 349–68.

21. Junior to Abraham Flexner, Nov. 15, 1932.

22. Junior made this explanation in a letter to Jerome Greene, Sept. 30, 1932.

23. Junior to Dr. Yoshinao Kozai, Dec. 31, 1924.

CHAPTER 9

1. The text was published in the Feb. 9, 1918, edition of the *Saturday Evening Post*.

2. H. Richard Niebuhr, "Modernism," in *The Encyclopedia of the Social Sciences* (New York: Macmillan, 1933), p. 1066.

3. Gates (1977), p. 131.

4. Quoted in Fosdick (1956), p. 207. Fosdick's Ch. XI is devoted to the story of Junior's efforts in religion during the 1920s.

5. Junior's "support" in the solution of this inordinately complex problem consisted of contributing an extra $1 million and putting pressure on the various denominations to take a share of the debt out of the monies they had raised.

6. For accounts of the development of Fosdick's career, see his autobiography, *The Living of These Days* (New York: Harper & Row, 1956), and an excellent new biography: Robert Moats Miller, *Harry Emerson Fosdick: Preacher, Pastor, Prophet* (New York: Oxford University Press, 1985).

7. Cited in Fosdick (1956), p. 221.

8. Miller (1985), pp. 154–55. By "Taylorization," Miller is referring to the "scientific management school" and stress on economy and efficiency in the work of Frederick Winslow Taylor.

9. Located in the RAC. Ivy Lee thought this draft would make another good *Saturday Evening Post* article, but Junior decided against it.

10. David Brody, "The Rise and Decline of Welfare Capitalism," in John Braeman et al., eds., *Change and Continuity in Twentieth Century America: The 1920s* (Columbus: Ohio State University Press, 1968), p. 154.

11. Junior reported Judge Gary's viewpoint in a letter to Mackenzie King, Sept. 18, 1919, RAC.

12. Issue of Oct. 25, 1919, p. 36.

13. *New York Times*, Oct. 23, 1919.

14. Feb. 23, 1923.

15. Fosdick (1956), pp. 180–81. No record can be found of this sale, but it should be noted that some financial records of the early 1920s are missing. In a flash of liberalism in 1911, U.S. Steel had given up the seven-day week under intense public pressure but had kept the twelve-hour day. Not until 1925 did Judge Gary yield on the latter, under pressure from public opinion and Secretary of Commerce Herbert Hoover.

16. Fosdick (1956) devotes a chapter to the Stewart case (Ch. XII).

17. Brody (1968), p. 177.

18. Martin Bulmer and Joan Bulmer, "Philanthropy and Social Science in the 1920s: Beardsley Ruml and the Laura Spelman Rockefeller Memorial, 1922–1929," *Minerva*, Vol. XIX, No. 3 (Autumn 1981), p. 353. Also, the files of the Memorial are located in the RAC.

19. Ibid., p. 354.

20. Ibid., p. 355.

21. Fosdick (1952), p. 193.

22. The Bulmers examine Ruml's Memorandum in detail, pp. 361–71.

23. Quoted in Fosdick (1952), p. 200. Fosdick devotes two chapters (XVI and XVII) to the functioning of the social sciences in the Memorial and the Rockefeller Foundation.

24. For a good account of the development of the birth control movement, see James Reed, *From Private Vice to Public Virtue* (New York: Basic Books, 1978). On Sanger's career, see pp. 67–139.

25. Martin and Joan Bulmer, *op. cit.*, p. 397. The Bulmers mistakenly exaggerate Ruml's opposition to the reorganization.

26. May 4, 1926.

27. In his book on the Rockefeller Foundation (1952), Fosdick downplays his own role, but there is no doubt that he was the chief figure in forging the reorganization. He discusses the subject in his Ch. XI, "The Foundation Enters New Fields."

28. Junior to Fosdick, Dec. 28, 1925.

29. Fosdick to Junior, Oct. 6, 1927.

30. Fosdick (1952), pp. 137–38.

31. Hadley died before attending his first board meeting.

CHAPTER 10

1. Cited in Fosdick (1956), p. 302.

2. Original documents detailing Junior's involvement in the creation and development of Acadia National Park may be found in the RAC.

3. Samuel P. Hayes, *Conservation and the Gospel of Efficiency* (New York: Atheneum, 1969), pp. 265–66.

4. Robert W. Righter, *Crucible for Conservation: The Creation of Grand Teton National Park* (Boulder: Colorado Associated University Press, 1982), p. 141. Much of the description of the Grand Tetons project is based on this excellent source as well as on documents in the RAC.

5. Righter (1982), pp. 29, 66–67.

6. Fosdick (1956), p. 308.

7. Ibid., p. 311.

8. Righter (1982), pp. 41–42.

9. Ibid., p. 130.

10. Ibid., p. 63.

11. Ibid., p. 77.

12. Ibid., p. 84.

13. Junior to Arno Cammerer, Aug. 31, 1937.

14. Junior to Ickes, Sept. 27, 1942.

15. Ickes to Junior, Dec. 4, 1942.

16. *New York World-Telegram*, June 16, 1943.

17. Righter (1982), p. 110.

18. *New York Times*, Sept. 16, 1944.

19. Righter (1982), p. 106.

20. Ibid., pp. 107–8.

21. Ibid., pp. 108–9.

22. Ibid., pp. 151–52.

23. With the notable exception of Righter's case study of the Grand Tetons, the available references do not begin to do justice to Junior's work in parks and conservation. A good visual overview may be obtained in a beautifully illustrated book, *A Contribution to the Heritage of Every American: The Conservation Activities of John D. Rockefeller, Jr.* (New York: Knopf, 1957), though the text is superficial. For a description of Junior's work on the Palisades, see Chapter XVI in Fosdick (1956) and source documents in the RAC.

24. John F. Horan, "Will Carson and the Virginia Conservation Commission," *Virginia Magazine of History and Biography*, Vol. 92 (Oct. 1984), p. 395.

25. Fosdick (1956), pp. 300–301.

26. Russell Lynes, *Good Old Modern* (New York: Atheneum, 1973), pp. 3–4. Abby's key role is suggested by the title of Lynes' first chapter, "Mrs. Rockefeller's Wild Oat."

27. Frank Crowninshield, "Art and Mr. Rockefeller," *Vogue*, Aug. 1, 1938, p. 85.

28. Lynes (1973), p. 378.

29. Junior to Senior, Feb. 1, 1915.

30. Cited in Fosdick (1956), pp. 335–56.

31. Barnard to Junior, Apr. 1916.

32. Bosworth to Junior, Apr. 1916 and Feb. 1917.

33. Fosdick (1956), p. 344. Fosdick's Chapter XVII, "Beauty in the Well-Rounded Life," discusses Junior's interests in the arts and the creation of the Cloisters.

CHAPTER 11

1. Junior to John A. Browning, Aug. 17, 1915.

2. John A. Browning to Junior, Aug. 25, 1915.

3. Junior to John A. Browning, June 7, 1917.

4. Junior to David H. Morris, Apr. 22, 1941.

5. Report on the Lincoln School to Junior, 1919 (RAC). Based on Flexner's experience in a private school he had started in Louisville and also on Dewey's laboratory schools of the turn of the century, the Lincoln School curriculum organized units of work through the twelve grades in four basic areas of study—civics, aesthetics, science, and industry—in line with Flexner's purpose to cut back on the traditional and emphasize the utilitarian. See Lawrence A. Cremin, *The Transformation of the School* (New York: Knopf, 1961), pp. 280–91. Also, there is a full chapter on the Lincoln School in Fosdick (1958), pp. 212–25.

6. These personal diaries, a priceless source, have been made available to the authors through the generosity of Mrs. John D. Rockefeller 3rd.

We assume that John 3rd began his diary-writing habit in Jan. 1920 because no earlier diary has been found. The 1920 diary has the earmarks of a beginning effort for a thirteen-year-old boy. It had, as noted, sparse entries, and the booklet is quite small, akin to a datebook, with space for four days on each page. The following year, John began keeping a five-year "comparative" diary in a slightly larger book. Each page had space for five days—the same date in each of five consecutive years. John's skill and interest in keeping a diary obviously increased, with every bit of the cramped space painstakingly occupied and the diary becoming more informative and personal. It was quite a job, and several times John wondered in his diary whether the effort was worth it, but he kept at it, rather convincing evidence of how methodical and organized he was.

After the five-year diary, John moved to a more standard format, larger books and one for each year, with each day given a full page. Rarely does one find a date for which the page is not completely filled. These were the college years, and along with the inevitable trivia one finds intense personal revelations. Often John would fall behind a week or so, but he would always backtrack and fill out the earlier pages from memory.

Once out of school and into his working career, John 3rd's diary changed dramatically, at once less compulsive, less personal, and more businesslike. The length of daily entries changed according to the time pressures on the author and what he felt was worth reporting, rather than his feeling that he had to fill up a page. Also, the "office" diaries were typewritten on standard paper and bound in looseleaf notebooks, one for each year. The contents varied over the years, dry and factual for years on end, and then suddenly intense and analytical for a while, but in general much more attuned to "business" than personal life.

7. Alvin Moscow (1977) describes Winthrop's recollection of his bitterness at being left behind (pp. 53–54). He apparently felt he had recovered enough from the measles to join the trip, but that the real reason his parents had kept him home was so that David would not be left alone.

8. The spelling errors are shown as they appeared in the original, a practice followed in later quotations from diaries and letters. In due course, the boys' errors disappeared.

9. Abby to Lucy Aldrich, Oct. 26, 1920. The assurance of Mr. Olmstead (not Olmsted) on the matter of spelling was somewhat premature.

10. Junior to Charles Eliot, Mar. 29, 1921.

11. Zenos Miller to Abby, Sept. 11, 1921.

Chapter 12

1. See the Loomis Class Announcement for 1926, the *Loomis Bulletin* for Mar. 1964 (a special edition devoted to the history of the first fifty years of the school, entitled "The Harvest of Our Lives"), and other sources. The Loomis family bequests had been made in the 1870s and amounted to over $2 million in value when the last of the donors died and the money could be used to open the school. The free tuition, of course, could not

be sustained indefinitely, and today Loomis charges normal tuition. The founders wished that the school be coeducational, but this was not deemed practical by the trustees. To honor the wish, however, they started a girl's school in a house in Windsor (numbering only half a dozen students at the time John 3rd was at Loomis) and named it the Chaffee School after the maternal side of the donors' family. This grew over the years, and today the institution is known as Loomis-Chaffee. This material was made available by Loomis-Chaffee, for which the authors would like to express their thanks.

2. The grant was unsolicited in the sense that Junior made the first move, telling Batchelder that he was prepared to contribute from $25,000 to $50,000 for things that might need doing at Loomis. Batchelder found $50,000 worth of things to do.

3. Nelson to John 3rd, July 14, 1925. Italics in original.

4. Abby to John 3rd, Jan. 1924.

5. The photograph of the bas-relief was credited in newspapers and magazines to Evelyn B. Longman, Mrs. Batchelder's maiden name, which she used professionally.

6. In the *Loomis Bulletin* of Mar. 1964, this was called a "remarkable" tennis team, "the strongest team in New England."

7. Several years later, John had a reference in his diary to the effect that Milton Bush was unaware that Abby was paying his college expenses at Cornell. There is no record of how this happened, but presumably Abby admired the spunky nature of the one-armed boy and became aware that his family could not afford to send him to college, so she decided to make an anonymous gift.

8. For this to happen, John had to face up to the unpleasant task of asking Doug Robertson to vacate, presumably on the basis that he had a prior understanding with Bob Russell. However, Doug ended up rooming with the very popular John Ross.

9. Junior to John 3rd, Jan. 19, 1924. During this period, John 3rd began to learn about investing. With the advice of people in his father's office, he began to buy shares of stock in Manhattan Railway, U.S. Steel, and Standard Oil of New Jersey.

10. Junior to Flexner, Mar. 20, 1923.

11. Flexner to Junior, Mar. 25, 1923.

12. Junior to Flexner, Apr. 2, 1923.

13. Junior to Hopkins, Oct. 16, 1923; Hopkins to Junior, Oct. 20, 1923.

14. Junior to Hopkins, Dec. 1, 1924.

15. All of these points about the wedding were repeated for days by the New York newspapers.

CHAPTER 13

1. Wilson's great gifts as an orator, leader, and administrator came into full evidence during his tenure at Princeton (1902–1910), where he undertook a wide range of measures to pull the school out of the doldrums and make it a full-fledged and top-ranking university. Two issues were particularly controversial. In one Wilson attempted to replace the eating clubs, which he regarded as socially unhealthy, with clusters of residential quadrangles or "colleges" within the campus. The trustees agreed, but then bowed to relentless pressure by club advocates. Interestingly, Wilson's idea was adopted by Harvard and Yale; it is now being attempted again at Princeton, aided by a grant of western lands, valued at $15 million, made by the alumnus and trustee Laurance Rockefeller in 1979.

The other matter was a long battle between Wilson and Andrew West, dean of the graduate school, over the location of a new graduate school complex. Wilson lost on both issues but continued to press, refusing to compromise, and historians have seen this as an early indication of the one flaw in Wilson, one that plagued him during his tragic struggle to have U.S. entry into the League of Nations approved by the Senate.

One historical judgment is that if Wilson had agreed to compromise, the Senate would have ratified and the U.S. would have entered the League. See, for example: John Morton Blum, *Woodrow Wilson* (Boston: Little, Brown, 1956). Discussion of the Princeton controversies is on pp. 27–36. Wilson left Princeton in 1910 to become the Democratic candidate for governor of New Jersey, where he was so successful with his progressive reforms that he became the Democratic candidate for president of the United States in 1912. Hibben was made acting president of Princeton upon Wilson's departure and was confirmed in the job in 1912.

2. "Princeton's Presidents: An Historical Sketch of the University," Princeton University Publications Office, 1980.

3. Junior to Hibben, Nov. 24, 1924.

4. *Daily Princetonian*, Nov. 16, 1922. The grant was made on the advice of Raymond Fosdick, one of Junior's main counselors in industrial relations. The reason was probably not so much the fact that Fosdick was a Princeton alumnus as that this type of grant to a university is a familiar strategem whenever proponents of a cause are trying to have it accepted as a legitimate academic field. Quite apart from the later support given by the two Rockefeller sons who were Princeton alumni, gifts to the university from Rockefeller sources that were the result of Junior's decisions eventually totaled well over $1 million.

5. By this time, many colleges and universities had adopted the "New Plan," which specified that only students who took classical languages would qualify for the B.A. degree; others would earn the B.S. This was the only difference in the two degrees in most cases. Before long, of course, this distinction and classical languages as a requirement for any degree were dropped.

6. In those days, the YMCA was much more overtly religious than now; it had in fact a fairly strong missionary flavor. The Philadelphian Society was active at Princeton in a broad program of "good works," including running the Princeton summer camp, visiting settlement houses, raising funds for worthwhile causes, working with Boy Scout troops, and teaching English to foreigners.

7. When making personal calls to solicit ads, John never used his name. It is not clear whether this was due to principle, shyness, or fear that it could be counterproductive.

8. John K. Winkler, "The Third John D. Rockefeller," *Redbook*, Aug. 1928.

9. On diary "memoranda" page opposite date of Sept. 30, 1927.

10. This switch was probably just as well from John's point of view because Doug flunked out of Princeton during the first semester of his sophomore year. At John's request, Junior intervened on Doug's behalf, but he was not reinstated. Doug, however, seemed to do very well thereafter, finishing college at Columbia, discovering a love for the sea, and pursuing it by running a marine business on Eastern Long Island.

11. Junior to John 3rd, Jan. 1, 1929.

12. Junior to John 3rd, Apr. 24, 1928.

13. John 3rd to Junior, Apr. 30, 1928.

14. Heermance to Junior, Aug. 30, 1926.

15. By this time, "political economy" as a discipline had faded out and "political science" was yet to come. At Princeton courses in "politics" were offered within the History Department.

16. Dorfman (1948), p. 364.

17. Junior to John 3rd, Apr. 15, 1929. John's thesis is on file at Mudd Library, Princeton University.

18. John's participation in the Model Assembly at Vassar was a direct result of his experience at the League of Nations in Geneva the preceding summer. See next chapter.

19. Among editorials of this sort were those that appeared in the *St. Paul Dispatch* and the *Tampa Tribune* of June 17, 1929.

Chapter 14

1. Junior contributed approximately $200,000, about one-third the costs of Commander (later Admiral) Richard Byrd's early expeditions to the Arctic and Antarctic. In honor of his patrons, Byrd gave their names to areas that he was the first to see in Antarctica—the Rockefeller Mountains, the Rockefeller Plateau, and the Edsel Ford Range.

2. Also known as the Pact of Paris, the Kellogg-Briand Pact was signed in Paris on Aug. 27, 1928, by the U.S., Japan, and most European nations, the major exception being the USSR. The League of Nations accepted the pact by passing an act in September requiring conciliation and arbitration of all international disputes—also with no means of enforcement.

3. Thomas (1974), pp. 4–5.

4. John wrote a poignant comment on the "Ibero-Americana Exposition," which he visited in Seville: "I have never seen an exposition that was better laid out or executed." The only problem was "that there was no one there to see it." The theme, the art of Spain and the Americas, was not "of the type to attract the ordinary person" and Seville was an "out of the way place" for tourists in Europe. John came away depressed because there were more guards than visitors.

5. Primo seized power in a coup d'état in 1923 and began modeling himself on Benito Mussolini, but he had much less success than the Italian dictator. Initially, Primo's strength had been based on his ability to quell trouble in Spain's African colonies and hold back the Catalan and Basque irredentists. But trouble arose in these regions again, as well as considerable civil discontent throughout Spain and unrest in the Army. In talking to John, Primo was exaggerating his power; in fact, he had been forced to end martial law and reconstitute the Cortes several years earlier. His political ineffectuality and ailing health forced him out, and he died in Paris in 1930.

6. Alexander De Conde, *A History of American Foreign Policy* (New York: Scribners, 1963), p. 556.

7. The concern about German loans had some relevance to the Rockefellers. The Equitable Trust Company had taken a major position in German loans. While the total, $50 million, was small by today's international banking standards, it was a significant amount for a bank with assets of about $1 billion. Junior owned less than 10 percent of Equitable's stock, but this made him the largest single shareholder. His brother-in-law, lawyer Winthrop Aldrich, was a member of the Equitable board, and he pressed the bank's officers to seek suitable merger partners to provide some domestic strength as a counterweight to the foreign loans. This resulted in the merger of the Equitable and the Seaboard National Bank in 1929 and the larger Chase-Equitable merger in 1930. As a result of the merger, the Chase National Bank became the largest in the world in terms of total resources. In the following years, Rockfeller interests increasingly did their banking with Chase.

8. On Oct. 3, 1929, Stresemann died, less than two months after John had met him. The Hague conference had ended with the issues unresolved, but, expecting that progress would soon be made, Stresemann had introduced enabling legislation in the Reichstag. At a second conference in Jan. 1930, the powers settled the issues and the Young Plan was adopted. Its benefit was slight because of the Depression.

9. The fact that the United States was not a member of the World Court did not prevent the occasional appointment of an American jurist to a term on the court. Hughes was respected because he had supported American participation, on the basis of four "reservations," when he was secretary of state. It seemed that these would have been acceptable to the court, but when the U.S. Senate approved a treaty in 1926, it added a "fifth reservation" that was unacceptable—that the court could not entertain any

request for an opinion on a dispute in which the U.S. had an interest without prior American approval. After his service at The Hague, Hughes became chief justice of the U.S. Supreme Court.

10. Among the several excellent accounts of this period of Chinese history is William Morwood, *Duel for the Middle Kingdom: The Struggle Between Chiang Kai-shek and Mao Tse-tung for Control of China* (New York: Everest House, 1980).

11. The "timid" Chang, known as the "Young Marshal," took a bold step in 1936 when he took Chiang Kai-shek prisoner for two weeks in order to press his demand that Chiang join in a united front with the Communists against the Japanese invader. The Xian Incident, as it was called, was glossed over and the Young Marshal accepted technical punishment. Chiang Kai-shek ultimately followed his advice. But the Young Marshal had to pay for his indiscretion later. When the Nationalists fled to Taiwan, he was placed in detention for the rest of his life, though he outlived Chiang Kai-shek and became in his old age a scholar of the Ming dynasty. See Morwood, Ch. 16, pp. 227–43.

12. This imagery was employed by the sociologist Ruth Benedict in her study of the Japanese character, *The Chrysthanthemum and the Sword* (New York: New American Library, 1967). The "chrysanthemum" symbolized the peaceful and polite side of the Japanese character as typified by the emperor and the diplomatic service; the "sword," the samurai side, the militarists who dominated from 1931 to 1945.

13. In the midst of the financial crisis in 1931, MacDonald went to Buckingham Palace to resign, but to general astonishment he acceded to George V's request to remain as prime minister over a coalition government. Although MacDonald held office for three more years, power gravitated to Stanley Baldwin. Labour Party leaders felt they had been betrayed by MacDonald.

Chapter 15

1. *New York Herald Tribune* and *New York Evening World* of June 24, 1930.

2. Both the text of Junior's letter and the lead story were printed in the *New York Times* of June 7, 1932.

3. The Glass-Steagall Act (Banking Act of 1933), passed during FDR's famous "first hundred days," introduced important changes that brought banking into its modern phase. It broadened and strengthened the Federal Reserve System, permitted branch banking, divorced investment and deposit functions, and created the Federal Bank Deposit Insurance Corporation. For an account of the reform effort, Wiggin's downfall, and the career of Winthrop Aldrich, see Arthur M. Johnson, *Winthrop W. Aldrich: Lawyer, Banker, Diplomat* (Cambridge: Harvard University Press, 1968). After Aldrich retired as chairman of the Chase, he was named U.S. ambassador to the Court of St. James's by President Eisenhower.

4. The view of Junior as conspirator is told in Collier and Horowitz (1976), pp. 158–62, and in Ferdinand Lundberg, *Sixty Families* (New York: Vanguard Press, 1937). A more balanced picture is presented in Johnson, *Winthrop W. Aldrich*, pp. 95–106, 122–61. Financial informatiobn is from JDR, Jr., Room 5600, Tax and Accounting Files. Rockefeller Family Office.

5. John 3rd was a director of the Equitable Trust (as indicated on his standard biography released to the press) from 1930 to 1934, but this was not the same company that was merged with the Chase. It was a new company that was a subsidiary of the Chase Securities Company, created to keep the old corporate name and handle certain residual and contractual estate matters. It is likely that Junior arranged for John to sit on this comparatively unimportant board as a way of acquainting him with aspects of the banking business.

CHAPTER 16

1. Aside from the Rockefeller Archives, JDR's diary, and Fosdick's (1956) Chap. XIV, the main sources of information on Rockefeller Center for this and subsequent chapters are one published book and an unpublished manuscript. The book is Carol Herselle Krinsky, *Rockefeller Center* (New York: Oxford University Press, 1978). The typeset manuscript is a detailed account of the development that was commissioned by the Rockefeller Center management in 1948 and never published. A copy, available in the RAC, is slugged "Third Draft—Nov. 7, 1949," and is referred to hereinafter as "RC Manuscript." It contains detailed legal, financial, and personnel information, but also some interesting and amusing sidelights.

2. The history of the land is interesting. It was first developed by Dr. David Hosack between 1797 and 1804. He purchased part of the area and leased the rest from the Common Lands of the City of New York for the purpose of developing a "public Botanic Garden." The area was more than three miles north of the settled portions of New York City. An eminent physician and botanist, Dr. Hosack cultivated more than 700 species of plants in his garden. But the cost of maintaining it proved too much for him, and in 1811 he sold the garden to the State of New York for $75,000. In 1814 the state granted the land to Columbia in compensation for lands in Gloucester County, which the college lost when Vermont was admitted to the Union. Columbia leased the land to various tenants over the years, beginning at $400 a year for the entire tract. It became known as the Columbia Upper Estate to distinguish it from the "Lower Estate," the college land farther south on Park Avenue. About 1912 the college sold the frontage on the three Sixth Avenue blocks and one Fifth Avenue block to help finance its move to Morningside Heights.

3. Rockefeller Center was finally able to purchase the land in 1985 for $411 million. If the land was worth $18 million in 1928 (extrapolating from the $6 million Junior had agreed to pay for one of the three blocks), this means that it grew in value about twenty-one times in the intervening fifty-seven years. Rockefeller Center, Inc., was paying $11 million a year in rent in 1985, up from the original $3.3 million (the reason the rent was not higher was that the times for renegotiating the lease had happened to coincide with real estate slumps in New York). In effect, Rockefeller Center bought out the current lease, which extended well into the next century; as for Columbia, it could earn considerably more return on $411 million in capital than the $11 million annual rent.

4. The architectural and planning history of Rockefeller Center is extremely complicated. The best source on this is Krinsky (1978).

5. Junior's commitment of $5 million in capital for the other Todd skyscraper project, in exchange for which he would have received notes and a stock bonus, was canceled in 1934 when the Todds abandoned the project. In return for this loss to them, Junior upped their annual Rockefeller Center compensation to $450,000.

6. Quoted in Krinsky (1978), p. 30.

7. All three firms had participated in an earlier "symposium" of planners that Col. Wood and Heydt had organized. The Reinhard and Hofmeister firm had done so on behalf of the Todd firm.

8. Johnson (1968) tells this story, citing an interview with Kenneth Chorley (p. 59).

9. This speech was delivered on Sept. 30, 1939. A text is in the RAC.

10. John Todd to Winthrop Aldrich, Dec. 4, 1929.

11. Fosdick (1956), p. 266.

12. The idea is attributed to Hood in Krinsky (1978), p. 50, with no source. Others claimed credit for the idea, including Harrison, Sarnoff, and Young.

13. The interest was 5 percent. Junior used only $45 million, providing all the remaining financing of Rockefeller Center himself.

14. In the 1970s, Rockefeller Center finally acquired both of these small buildings, renovating and leasing them as restaurants.

15. A description of the apartment and a photograph of one room may be found in Krinsky (1978), p. 168.

16. Fosdick (1956) recalls having attended the conference at which the decision was made (p. 269). He attributes the comment about "rank and standing" to John Todd.

17. Ibid., p. 266.

18. Speaking at a ceremony on Nov. 1, 1939, celebrating the driving of the "last rivet" in the buildings of Rockefeller Center (although many more were to come), Thomas A. Murray, president of the Building and Construction Trades Council of New York City, warmly praised the developers of Rockefeller Center for providing work for 75,000 New York tradesmen "at union wages and under union conditions." Murray referred to "friendly labor relations" and the fact that there were no strikes. Cited in Fosdick (1956), p. 270.

19. Apr. 3, 1931.

20. John H. Finney to Junior, Dec. 4, 1933.

21. In addition to Rockefeller Center, Inc., and Underel, there was another corporation, Midtown Development and Investment, which Junior organized in 1930 as a New Jersey corporation through which to channel his investments in the project. This corporation was later changed to Rockefeller Plaza, Inc. For the complex trail of debits and assets, see the RC Manuscript, Ch. XIII, "Financing the Development."

22. For the text of this letter and other background on Nelson's art interests in college, see Joe Alex Morris, *Nelson Rockefeller: A Biography* (New York: Harper & Bros., 1960), pp. 52–56 and 72–76.

23. Ibid., p. 76.

24. Diego Rivera to Hugh Robertson, May 14, 1933.

25. RC Manuscript, p. 76.

26. Krinsky (1978), p. 71.

CHAPTER 17

1. Source material for this chapter includes interviews with Mrs. John D. Rockefeller 3rd, correspondence, diary accounts, and newspaper articles.

At the time that John and Blanchette met at the "Pierrot" dance, she was spending two days a week working for the Charity Organization Society (COS) where she was an assistant to a caseworker, checking out the work records of those in need of aid. At the same time, John was chairman of a four-man committee making a study of juvenile delinquency on behalf of the Boys Bureau, a joint department of the COS and the Association for Improving the Condition of the Poor (the two organizations later merged to create the Community Services Society). The report of the committee was eventually published: Leonard V. Harrison and Pryor McNeill Grant, *Youth in the Toils* (New York: Macmillan, 1938).

2. The quotation and other information about Elon H. Hooker are taken from a testimonial book about his life published after his death in 1938 by the Hooker Electrochemical Company.

3. The renamed Hooker Chemical Company later was acquired by the entrepreneur Armand Hammer and his Occidental Petroleum Corporation.

4. Mabel Ward, ed., *The Bibliographical Cyclopedia of American Women* (New York: Halvord Publishing Co., 1924), Vol. I, pp. 74–75.

5. Adelaide Hooker, "A High Time in Red Russia," *Good Housekeeping*, July 1930, p. 32.

6. John to Blanchette, July 26, 1932.

7. Junior was well aware of the sensitivity of the issue John was raising, and the fact that he did not respond to his son's letter suggests that he might have been irritated by what he regarded as unneccessary and unwanted advice. The pattern of his assistance to Babs and David indicates that Junior was trying to find a way to resolve the delicate problem. As the oldest child and the first to marry and have children, Babs received more support in the early years than her brothers. In 1925 Junior began giving her an "allowance" of $10,000 per year, gradually increasing this to $25,000 by the early 1930s. He also gave Babs and David small monetary gifts each year and loaned them some money. In 1931 he gave Babs stock, cash, and gifts worth $425,000, but this sum included cancellation of a loan of $125,000 made to her in 1929. At the same time, Junior gave David $170,000 in value, including cancellation of a $75,000 loan. From this point on, as John 3rd's letter suggests, significant gifts from Junior were made to Babs, not David.

8. Junior to John, Dec. 20, 1933. The same paragraph appeared in the letters to all three recipients. Prior to this gift, Nelson's allowance had been $17,000 per year, up from the $4,000 he had been receiving before his wedding. John 3rd's allowance was $8,000, up from the original $5,000. but John was better off financially than either Babs or Nelson, both because of his frugal nature and the fact that he had benefited more than they had from special gifts—$100,000 on his twenty-fifth birthday and $110,000 at the time of his wedding (compared to wedding gifts of $11,000 to Babs and $40,000 to Nelson).

The next of Junior's children to benefit from the "capitalizing" of allowances was Laurance, though not as handsomely as the three older children. When Laurance married Mary French in 1934, Junior gave him stock and cash valued at $835,000.

9. Mary E. Ferguson, *China Medical Board and Peking Union Medical College*, (New York: China Medical Board of New York, 1970), p. 82.

10. Unpublished memorandum by Jerome Greene, Nov. 17, 1934, RAC. Greene did not resign from the Foundation board until he reached the retirement age of sixty-five in 1939. After his meeting with Junior, Greene voiced his criticisms in more temperate ways and, as a result, was made chairman of a small committee to recommend ways to improve the proceedings of the Foundation's board. He subsequently delivered a report which, in essence, repeated the points he had made in his letter to Fosdick of June 29, 1934.

CHAPTER 18

1. In effect, Junior was stockpiling land during the 1920s. In addition to land purchases in Manhattan, Westchester County, Cleveland, and Chicago, his main acquisitions were for Acadia National Park in Maine, the future Grand Teton National Park, Fort Tryon, and the Hudson Palisades. Thus, these acquisitions were not made for investment purposes, but for personal or philanthropic use. Land accounted for a major share of Junior's philanthropic giving in the 1930s. The only significant commercial possibility had to do with the many lots Junior acquired in the area to the immediate north of Rockefeller Center. Several times serious consideration was given to grand strategies for expanding the Center northward, but this did not happen until after World War II and then involved only two buildings (Sperry-Rand and Esso, later the Warner Communications Building) on the next northward block, between 51st and 52nd streets. There was also postwar expansion to the west and north on the other side of Sixth Avenue. Any further expansion directly north had been blocked by the refusal of the owners of the "21 Club" (21 W. 52nd Street) to sell. In the end, Junior gave away or sold all of his acquisitions in the neighborhood.

2. Data on Junior's net worth, income, taxes, contributions, and holdings in oil stocks, market value at specific times, dividend rates, and overall performance were

derived from a study of his balance sheets and financial statements for each year from 1918 to 1959. Additional information came from a variety of sources in the RAC. The details about basic holdings assigned to Junior by his father were derived from the Lybrand, Ross study, *Gifts Made by John D. Rockefeller During His Lifetime*; these details were then compared to memoranda that listed Junior's holdings at various times, the most important of which are Houston to Junior, Apr. 4, 1923; Cutler to Junior, Jan. 30, 1933 and Feb. 26, 1934. Information on stock prices and dividends was taken from the *New York Times*. One of the better secondary sources on the performance of the oil companies is George S. Gibb and Evelyn H. Knowlton, *History of the Standard Oil Company, 1911–1927: The Resurgent Years* (New York: Harper & Bros., 1956), pp. 666–71.

In 1928 the oil stocks owned by Junior were valued at $606.2 million and accounted for 61 percent of his total holdings. Following are the number of shares and value for the six major oil companies, both shown in the millions: Standard of New Jersey—2.9, $157.4; Standard of California—1.9, $140.0; Socony—2.7, $120.0; Vacuum—1.2, $130.1; Standard of Indiana—.4, $36.2; Standard of Ohio—.3, $22.6. By 1936 the value of his holdings in the five major companies (Socony and Vacuum had merged) had declined to $236.7 million.

3. The percentage of income that Junior paid in taxes in the 1930s does not show a neat linear pattern for several reasons. In 1934, for example, he paid only 5.4 percent, lower than in any year in the 1920s, because of large tax losses he had accumulated. In another year (1938) he paid at the rate of 67 percent, but this included back taxes for the previous two years. In most "normal" years, his rate was about 30 percent, and this in fact is what the average turns out to be for the ten-year period 1932–1941.

4. Roy G. and Gladys C. Blakey, *The Federal Income Tax* (New York: Longmans, Green & Co., 1940), pp. 185–88, 246–50, 320–25; Randolph E. Paul, *Federal Estate and Gift Taxation* (Boston: Little, Brown, 1942), Vol. I, pp. 152–53, Vol. II, p. 988. It was at this time that depletion allowances were created, 27½ percent for oil and 5 percent for coal.

5. William E. Leuchtenberg, *Franklin D. Roosevelt and the New Deal* (New York: Harper Torchbooks, 1963), pp. 64–71, 95–117; Ellis W. Hawley, *The New Deal and the Problem of Monopoly* (Princeton: Princeton University Press, 1966), pp. 53–72.

6. *Congressional Record*, 74th Cong., 1st Sess., p. 12328; Blakey (1940), pp. 381–82.

7. Collier and Horowitz (1976) state on p. 204: "In December of 1934, Junior wrote each of his sons a letter to inform them that he was settling most of what was left of his fortune on them in the form of trusts composed primarily of Standard Oil stock and amounting to about $40 million each." Not only is this wrong about the amount in the trusts and the impact on Junior's fortune, but there is no mention of the trusts for Abby and Babs, of the different conditions for the trusts, and the gift tax incentive. Moscow's (1977) description of the trusts (pp. 110–11) is better, although he, too, misstates the amount, estimating it at $20 million for each of the seven trusts. He also fails to mention the tax incentive.

8. Junior to Abby, Dec. 18, 1934; Junior to JDR 3rd, Dec. 18, 1934; Junior to Chase National Bank, Dec. 18, 1934; "Deed of Trust, John D. Rockefeller 3rd Trust."

9. Junior to Winthrop, June 28, 1935.

10. JDR 3rd Deed of Trust, RAC. The best explanation in print of how the trusts function from generation to generation may be found in a *Fortune* magazine article, "The Rockefellers: End of a Dynasty?" by Carol J. Loomis, Aug. 4, 1986, pp. 26–38.

11. The BSH technically continued to exist until 1940 to fulfill its commitments. The Social Sciences Division of the Rockefeller Foundation took over some of the bureau's areas of interest. The Davison Fund gradually cut down the number of religious organizations receiving grants to about ten.

12. In this the trustees were following Junior's stipluations in the deeds, which

specified such charitable recipients as Colonial Williamsburg, the Rockefeller Institute, and the Davison Fund.

13. Junior was not being entirely altruistic in the trade. Acquiring the three MOMA lots on the south side of 53rd Street gave him uninterrupted ownership of two-thirds of the block, from Fifth Avenue west. This would have come in handy in the event of Rockefeller Center expansion, but the "21 Club" still blocked the way.

14. Junior paid $40,000 a year in rent for this triplex. After World War II, he purchased it. Many of the rooms were given over entirely to displaying Oriental art and tapestries.

15. Rockefeller Foundation, "Report of the Committee on Appraisal and Review," Dec. 11, 1934, RAC.

16. Fosdick (1956), p. 216.

17. Both Junior and his father had been major financial supporters of the Northern Baptist Convention and its missionary programs for decades. On Nov. 29, 1935, Junior wrote to his father, then in his ninety-sixth year, to explain what he had done, making the point that he would continue giving "directly to those missionary efforts—whether Baptist, or other denominations, interdenominational or non-denominational—that have proved themselves to us as vital, effective, Christian agencies."

18. Gunn's report, "The Rockefeller Foundation in China," with the notation "prepared and submitted January 1934," may be found in the RAC. Two good sources on the Foundation's activities in China are Peter Buck, *American Science and Modern China* (Cambridge: Cambridge University Press, 1980); and James C. Thomson, Jr., *While China Faced West: American Reformers in Nationalist China, 1928–37* (Cambridge: Harvard University Press, 1969).

19. *New York Times*, Mar. 18, 1934. Although Prohibition had ended almost a year earlier in New York, alcohol still was not available in taverns, restaurants, and nightclubs because the state legislature had not yet established the conditions for its sale and distribution. The Rockefeller family office followed the general practice of working half a day on Saturday until after World War II.

20. JDR 3rd to Junior, Mar. 17, 1934.

21. The spending of $40,000 annually in support of birth control and related activities might seem small, but it was critically important to those struggling in the field. It is also noteworthy in view of the fact that contributions to the birth control movement did not become tax-exempt until 1941.

CHAPTER 19

1. The buildings completed by 1935 were the Center Theater, the Music Hall, 1270 Sixth Avenue, the British Building, the RCA Building, the French Building, the International Building, and the International Building North. The next four were to be the Time, Associated Press, Eastern Airlines, and U.S. Rubber Company buildings.

2. RC Manuscript, p. 105.

3. Ibid., p. 57.

4. After the Center Theater was closed, it was used for a time by NBC as a studio. It was torn down in 1954 to make way for an addition to the U.S. Rubber Company Building, now known as the Simon & Schuster Building.

5. John R. Todd to Barton P. Turnbull, Nov. 9, 1934.

6. John and Nelson to Junior, Dec. 18, 1934.

7. Junior to John and Nelson, Dec. 20, 1934.

8. The terminal consulting payments were made in lieu of the provision that the managing agents would be entitled to one-third of Rockefeller Center's profits. Negotiating this agreement was difficult because the managing agents believed, quite

rightly, that Rockefeller Center would become profitable some day, even after accumulated operating losses plus interest and amortization of capital were figured in the formula. However, at the time, prospects were exceedingly dim and profitability was a long way off, so the agents yielded. See RC Manuscript, pp. 42–43.

9. William A. McGarry, "The Oldest Trouble in the World," *Rockefeller Center Weekly*, May 2, 1935.

10. John to Junior, Dec. 30, 1935.

11. Industrial Relations Counselors, Inc., "Report on Personnel Relations at Pocantico Hills Estate," Feb. 5, 1937.

12. Jay subsequently did adopt both the middle name and the numerical designation, in Roman rather than the Arabic designation his father favored: John Davison Rockefeller IV.

13. The press coverage after Senior's death attested to the importance of his career and the fascination with his life. Some major newspapers devoted half a dozen full pages and more to the Rockefeller story. It would seem that Senior died simply of the effects of old age. The body lay in state at Kykuit and then was taken by special train to Cleveland for burial in the family plot next to Laura. Senior's estate, estimated at $25 million, was left in trust to his niece, Mrs. Margaret Strong de Cuevas (his sister Bessie's daughter), the only one of his descendants who did not receive substantial gifts during his lifetime.

14. Samuel Williamson, "The Rockefeller Boys," *New York Times Magazine*, Apr. 9, 1939.

15. The story was told to the authors by a staff aide who asked to remain unidentified. He was with Winthrop at Winrock Farms one morning when the ex-governor of Arkansas was opening his mail. One letter was an appeal for funds from Yale. As he tossed it in the wastebasket, Winthrop said, "They should've thought of this before they threw me out." He described the circumstances of his eviction.

16. The twenty-two page document ("Report on the Philanthropies of the Messrs. Rockefeller") was distributed to all five brothers, and for each brother Packard added another section devoted to that person's specific situation. In addition to providing counsel, Packard's operation relieved the brothers of the tedium of grant-making, screened them from many solicitors, and cut down on duplication.

Chapter 20

1. This sort of criticism soon ceased when the American Communist Party made its first sharp about-face on orders from Moscow. That was when Stalin, fearful of the rising menace of fascism in Europe, called a halt to international revolutionary activity in favor of a "united front" policy. The second sharp turn occurred at the time of the signing of the Nazi-Soviet pact in 1939. On the zigzags of the party line in the 1930s, see Harvey Klehr, *The Heyday of American Communism: The Depression Decade* (New York: Basic Books, 1983).

2. A good source on the populists of the 1930s is Alan Brinkley, *Voices of Protest: Huey Long, Father Coughlin, and the Great Depression* (New York: Knopf, 1982).

3. James MacGregor Burns, *Roosevelt: The Lion and the Fox* (New York: Harcourt, Brace & Co., 1956), p. 240.

4. Dr. John R. Todd to Hon. Warren H. Barbour, Oct. 2, 1934.

5. Junior to Todd, Oct. 10, 1934.

6. The GOP, of course, was in good shape financially, having hundreds of wealthy members like Junior who formed their upper echelon of financial supporters. Unlike the Democrats, the GOP did not have to ask any one individual to contribute a very large amount. Every so often, a wealthy liberal would have to come to the rescue of the

Democratic Party, as when Thomas Fortune Ryan paid off its debt ($350,000) in 1904 or when John J. Raskob ($360,000) and Herbert Lehman ($250,000) financed Al Smith in 1928. A good source is Louise Overacker, *Money in Elections* (New York: Macmillan, 1932). Information on Rockefeller contributions may be found in the RAC.

7. McDonald accepted the League of Nations post even though John counseled against it on the grounds that McDonald could be more useful at home. McDonald's work on behalf of Jewish refugees led to his appointment by President Truman as the first U.S. ambassador to Israel in 1948. He died while holding that post in 1951.

8. This meeting was held in Maine over the Labor Day weekend. The elder Morgenthau was correct about the outbreak of war and the eventual dismemberment of Germany. His son became the leading proponent of the plan that would have left Germany little more than an agricultural nation after World War II.

9. Appleget's document, dated Mar. 5, 1946, may be found in the RAC. Appleget was a vice president of the Foundation from 1929 to 1949. The field operation of the Emergency Rescue Committee, managed by Varian Fry from Sept. 1940 to the end of 1941, succeeded in bringing out hundreds of refugees, including such luminaries as Heinrich Mann (brother of Thomas Mann), political scientist Hannah Arendt, poet Franz Werfel, novelist Lion Feuchtwanger, musician Wanda Landowska, and artists Marc Chagall, Jacques Lipschitz, and Max Ernst. See Varian Fry, *Surrender on Demand* (New York: Random House, 1945).

10. The only reason the programs of the Foundation and the Emergency Rescue Committee could function at all was the existence of a clause in the U.S. immigration law that made possible the granting of visas to persons of career distinction under special circumstances.

11. See Leonard Mosely, *Dulles* (New York: Dial Press, 1978), pp. 97–100, regarding Foster Dulles' strong stance against U.S. involvement. Allen Dulles, later to be head of the CIA, felt just the opposite, but muted his views in deference to his older brother.

12. Junior to Arthur M. Allen, June 20, 1940.

13. After his election as Manhattan district attorney in 1937, Dewey a year later ran for governor of New York against the incumbent Democrat, Herbert H. Lehman. He came so close to defeating Lehman that it boosted his stock as a prospective head of the ticket for the GOP in 1940.

14. Junior to Arthur M. Allen, June 3, 1940.

15. On the dilemmas Willkie faced, the evasive manner in which both candidates dealt with the war issue, the scare in the FDR camp, and other features of the 1940 campaign, see Burns (1956), pp. 432–55; and George H. Mayer, *The Republican Party* (New York: Oxford University Press, 1964), pp. 454–60.

16. Blanche Hooker had moved to One Beekman to be near her two daughters after the death of her husband in 1938. In addition to the Marquands and Mrs. Hooker, other interesting neighbors at One Beekman included William Paley of CBS and Colonel William "Wild Bill" Donovan, soon to be head of the OSS during World War II. John 3rd and Donovan often played squash together. For a discussion of Adelaide's involvement in the America First Committee and her husband's reactions, see Millicent Bell, *Marquand: An American Life* (Boston: Little, Brown, 1979), pp. 293–98. Frank Aiken, who died in 1983, took part in the 1916 "Easter Rebellion" against British rule. With Eamon De Valera, he was a cofounder of Fianna Fáil, the Irish Republic's largest political party, and from 1951 to 1969 he served as deputy prime minister and foreign minister.

17. On Field's career and "leftward migration," see his autobiography, *From Right to Left* (Westport, Conn.: Lawrence Hill & Co., 1983); also, John N. Thomas (1974), pp. 8–10.

18. See Moscow (1977), pp. 154–60; Collier and Horowitz (1976), pp. 211–14; and Joe Alex Morris (1960), pp. 128–35. The best single source on the OCIAA is still the official

history: *History of the Office of the Coordinator of Inter-American Affairs* (Washington, D.C.: GPO, 1947).

19. By this time, Hopkins had become FDR's intimate adviser. Forrestal was to be the head of the OCIAA, but instead was tapped for the post of under secretary of the navy, making room for Nelson, who accepted only after consulting his father and the GOP candidate, Wendell Willkie.

20. Jacques Barzun to the authors: "Having been assigned one small task by the Agency, I remember one of the mistakes (not mine)—an ad to appear in all South American newspapers, including Brazil's, in *Spanish*."

21. Most of the senior officers of the division were killed in the attack, and Winthrop was lucky to survive with face and hand burns that responded readily to treatment (Moscow [1977], pp. 200–204). Probably more serious for Winthrop was a later case of hepatitis, after which he was discharged in Oct. 1946.

22. Interviews with David Rockefeller. His reports during his two-year period in intelligence work may be found in the Allied Forces Headquarters (AFHQ) Papers, stored at the National Archives in Suitland, Maryland.

CHAPTER 21

1. At this juncture, it seems appropriate to the authors to abandon the youthful nomenclature of "John 3rd" in favor of "JDR," which is how they addressed him (his older associates called him "John").

2. The use of the past tense is indicative of the fact that JDR had to handle his diary in a different way during his naval service. Naval regulations prohibited the keeping of diaries during wartime. JDR circumvented this by writing a lengthy account every six months or so about what had happened during that time. The essays covering the years 1942 through 1945 were all placed in one looseleaf notebook with a copy of the order prohibiting diaries as the frontispiece.

3. Issue of Feb. 17, 1941.

4. For a discussion of Lippmann's views and the two wartime books, see Ronald Steel, *Walter Lippmann and the American Century* (Boston: Little, Brown, 1980), Ch. 32, "Realpolitik," pp. 404–17. Latent feelings of skepticism about the Soviet Union did not become manifest until after the death of President Roosevelt, when the collapse of Germany seemed only weeks away. The American ambassador to Moscow, W. Averell Harriman, was one of the strongest of the skeptics, along with the secretaries of state, navy, and war—Stettinius, Forrestal, and Stimson. See the interesting discussion of the views they pressed upon President Truman in Gar Alperovitz, *Atomic Diplomacy: Hiroshima and Potsdam* (New York: Vintage Books, 1965), pp. 22–33.

5. The Dulles plan, entitled *The Six Pillars of Peace*, was published by the Federal Council of Churches. Having narrowly missed being elected governor of New York in 1938 and having failed to get the GOP presidential nomination in 1940, Dewey finally had better luck and was elected governor in 1942. But he paid a price—he could not avoid the GOP assignment to run against FDR in 1944. For an account of the Dulles plan for a "United Nations" and how it was used in the 1944 election, see Mosely (1978), pp. 150–54.

6. Nelson was among those who were deeply skeptical about the Soviet Union. His performance in San Francisco was disliked not only by the Soviet bloc, but also by some members of the U.S. delegation and other State Department colleagues who were still idealistic about the possibilities of postwar cooperation with the Soviet Union. See Joe Alex Morris (1960), Ch. 10, "San Francisco—World Politics," and Ch. 11, "New Regional Framework."

7. For a discussion of the emergence of "nonpartisan foreign policy," see Dean

Acheson, *Present at the Creation* (New York: Norton, 1969), pp. 95–99. Regarding the conversion of Senator Vandenberg, see Steel (1980), pp. 418–20.

8. Here JDR was expressing a widely held view that had some basis in fact. The State Department had been undernourished during the war in contrast to the huge buildup of the War and Navy departments. All recruitment had ceased for the duration, and State was placed in even more of a backseat position because of the distant relation between Roosevelt and Cordell Hull.

9. Junior to JDR, Dec. 26, 1945.

10. A copy of "Report on Future Work" (dated Nov. 16, 1944) may be found in the RAC.

11. Fosdick to JDR, Apr. 18, 1945.

12. Much of the information on the operation of the family office during this period comes from interviews with Dana Creel and Edgar B. Young.

13. Packard turned in detailed annual reports. Information taken from "Mr. Packard's Department—Annual Report for the Year 1947," RAC.

14. Laurance's four brothers were also investing in the venture-capital operation. Originally set up as a partnership, it was changed to a corporation (Rockefeller Brothers, Inc.) late in 1946 to limit liability and give each brother more say over how much he would invest in any given project.

CHAPTER 22

1. Because of his permanent move to Arkansas, Winthrop was never to be involved in Cold War activities to an extent comparable to the four brothers who remained in New York.

2. Supra, Ch. 19.

3. This is the true story of Rockefeller involvement in helping the U.N. to find a home. It is told in some detail because previous printed versions are erroneous. Although Nelson clearly played an important role, it is exaggerated in previous versions, which also say that Nelson persuaded his father to donate the entire Pocantico estate to the U.N. See, for example, Morris (1960), pp. 280–83, and Collier and Horowitz (1976), pp. 246–47. The inference in the latter book that the Rockefellers were motivated to purchase the East River tract and donate it to the U.N. because it would mean "wiping out a potentially serious rival to Rockefeller Center" is a good example of the way these authors frequently strain for an unfavorable implication when none is warranted. The statement that the Center was only 60 percent rented is wrong; its records show that it was more than 85 percent rented at the time.

The sources from which the account in this book was drawn include: Fosdick, "Conversations with JDR, Jr.," RAC; interview with David Rockefeller, Nov. 14, 1986; James Monahan, "How the U.N. Found Its Home at Last," *Reader's Digest*, May 1947; Samuel E. Bleecker, *The Politics of Architecture: A Perspective on Nelson A. Rockefeller* (New York: Rutledge Press, 1982). Most useful is the Fosdick manuscript. Junior told his recollection of the episode in detail to Fosdick only six years after the event.

At the time Junior's gift of $8.5 million to the U.N. was made, it did not qualify as a charitable deduction from his income tax (all of his gifts to the League of Nations had also not been tax-exempt). However, a special bill was passed in Congress to make the $8.5 million gift deductible. Junior had asked for city support in seeking this; he also set the condition that the city make concessions (mainly the city streets on the site) before his donation would be made. Prodded by Robert Moses, the city agreed in the amazingly short time of three days.

4. Nelson to Junior, Sept. 6, 1946; Junior to Nelson, Sept. 9, 1946, RAC. There is no record that Nelson attempted to get Rockefeller Foundation grants. Junior did join with his sons in contributing modestly to AIA and buying IBEC stock.

5. JDR was using the word "politics" loosely to refer to any government position in Washington, not elective office. For Nelson that would come later.

6. Source material is limited on AIA and IBEC. The best available are Martha Dalrymple's history, *The AIA Story*, published in 1968 by AIA, and Morris (1960), Chaps. 12 and 13.

7. Authors' interview with Arthur Mosher (Mar. 31, 1983), who made the study and wrote the Ford Foundation evaluation of the AIA. Mosher later was to become the extremely successful president of JDR's own agricultural development organization.

8. JDR recorded his views at length in his 1946 diary, in particular the entry for June 22–23.

9. Barnard's book was published by the Harvard University Press in 1938. One scholar termed it the "ultimate pre-World War II expression of the concept of administration." [William G. Scott, *Organization Theory: A Behavioral Analysis for Management* (Homewood, Ill.: Richard D. Irwin, 1962), p. 36].

10. Fosdick (1952), pp. 301–2.

11. An unpublished manuscript in the RAC, "The Beginnings of the Mexican Agricultural Program" by William C. Cobb, is a good source. See also E. C. Stakman et al., *Campaign Against Hunger* (Cambridge: Belknap Press of Harvard University Press, 1967), pp. 19–71. Unaccountably, Fosdick (1952, pp. 184–85) fails to tell the interesting story of how the program got started, saying only that "its genesis was a casual comment" to him by Wallace.

12. Morris (1960), pp. 270–72.

13. *Time*, Mar. 8, 1982, p. 45. This was the magazine version of Vol. II of Kissinger's memoirs, *Years of Upheaval* (Boston: Little, Brown, 1982). The context for Kissinger's description of the foreign policy establishment is what he holds to be its demoralization and failure over the issue of the Vietnam War.

14. These men, of course, were leading members of the American foreign policy "establishment" of the time that Kissinger was referring to. An interesting attempt to analyze this phenomenon is *The Wise Men* by Walter Isaacson and Evan Thomas (New York: Simon & Schuster, 1986). Isaacson is quoted in the *New York Times Book Review* (Nov. 2, 1986) as saying: "We found that the Establishment was a very nebulous idea, and the best way to get at it was a biographical treatment of men who were at the core of that idea." The six men covered in the book are Acheson, Bohlen, Harriman, Kennan, Lovett, and McCloy. It is interesting to note the frequency with which John and Nelson Rockefeller interacted with these and other establishmentarians.

15. The parallel between Junior recruiting Mackenzie King and JDR consulting King in an attempt to recruit Pearson is striking. Pearson, born in 1897, went on to an illustrious career, of course, winning the 1957 Nobel Peace Prize for his role in resolving the Suez crisis of 1956 and serving as Canadian prime minister from 1963 to 1968.

16. John Dickey believed that the Foundation should concentrate exclusively on international projects; JDR did not want to go quite that far. One reason JDR was uncertain about Robert Calkins as a candidate for the presidency was that he had had little foreign affairs experience. Calkins went on to the presidency of the Brookings Institution in Washington, a post he held for many years.

17. Two factors aborted the possibility that the Foundation might spend itself out of existence in fifteen or twenty years. One was that the resolution requiring that it must spend out of capital was relaxed. The other was that the value of its portfolio grew enormously during the boom years of the 1950s and 1960s, at one point coming close to $1 billion.

CHAPTER 23

1. Those who held this view were wrong, however, about the Jews and the Japanese, whose birthrate was lower than U.S. norms.

2. The best discussion of racist thinking regarding immigration may be found in John Higham, *Strangers in the Land* (New York: Atheneum, 1974).

3. A copy of Junior's essay is in the RAC.

4. Supra, Ch. 2.

5. Numerous state laws were patterned after the federal law that Comstock was able to push through Congress in 1873. For an account of this rare example of censorship, see James Reed, *From Private Vice to Public Virtue: The Birth Control Movement and American Society Since 1830* (New York: Basic Books, 1978), pp. 38–39.

6. For the story of Margaret Sanger's remarkable career, see David M. Kennedy, *Birth Control in America: The Career of Margaret Sanger* (New Haven: Yale University Press, 1970). See also Reed (1978), Pt. II, Chaps. 6 through 10.

7. Raymond Fosdick to Junior, June 13, 1924.

8. Arthur Packard to Abby Aldrich Rockefeller, Nov. 14, 1933.

9. Family contributions to this cause averaged about $25,000 a year in the 1930s. JDR and Junior contributed $8,000 to Sanger's National Committee on Federal Legislation for Birth Control. The Comstock Laws were effectively weakened by the 1936 decision in *United States* vs. *One Package of Japanese Pessaries* in which Judge Augustus Hand ruled that birth control information was not "obscene" and could be transmitted through the mails to licensed physicians.

10. Supra, Ch. 9.

11. For a good description of Gamble's activities, see Reed (1978), Pt. V, Chaps. 17 through 20; also, Dagne and Greer Williams, *Every Child a Wanted Child* (Cambridge: Harvard University Press, 1938). Unlike JDR, Gamble thought of himself as a professional in the field and not just a philanthropist, with the result that he was regarded as excessively meddlesome by many of the professionals.

12. Reed (1978), p. 283.

13. Fosdick (1952), p. 126.

14. Osborn's coauthor for the book, which was published in 1934, was Frank Lorimer, one of the half dozen architects of the science of demography. Eugenics nearly suffered a mortal blow from its misuse by the Nazis, not regaining respectability until the postwar days of molecular biology and the cracking of the genetic code.

15. Much of the information in this section was obtained in personal interviews with Frank Notestein (May 1979) and Frederick Osborn (June 1979).

16. Frank W. Notestein, "Demography in the United States: A Partial View of the Development of the Field to the Mid-1970s," unpublished monograph, RAC.

17. Richard Symonds and Michael Carder, *The United Nations and the Population Question* (New York: McGraw-Hill, 1973), p. 54.

18. Osborne's book was published by Little, Brown, Vogt's by Sloane.

19. The Rockefeller Foundation, *Public Health and Demography in the Far East* (New York, 1950), p. 111.

20. *Crete: A Case of an Under-developed Area* (Princeton: Princeton University Press, 1953).

21. In 1944 the Foundation made a $200,000 ten-year grant in support of the Office of Population Research, and in 1948 made a supplemental grant of $100,000.

22. Interview with Frank Notestein (May 1979).

23. *New York Herald Tribune*, June 10, 1949.

24. Chester Barnard to Cardinal Spellman, June 21, 1948.

25. The report on the luncheon was written by George K. Strode, head of the Foundation's International Health Division, in his 1948 diary, p. 132, RAC. Kimball's views were voiced in an interview in September 1982.

26. *The Reminiscences of Warren Weaver*, Columbia Oral History Collection, 1962, p. 299.

CHAPTER 24

1. *New York Times*, Apr. 4, 1948; *New York Herald Tribune*, Apr. 11, 1948. Memorial services for Abby, at which Fosdick delivered his eulogy, took place at Riverside Church on May 23.

2. Abby's 1934 Trust, originally worth $18.3 million, sank in value like everything else in the Depression, but the oil stocks that comprised the trust recovered very well in the 1940s, to the level of $33.3 million upon her death.

3. Junior to JDR, May 26, 1947.

4. The information on Junior's gifts was taken from: JDR, Jr., Financial Records, Accounting Files, Rockefeller Family Office. The gifts were made variously in stocks, bonds, or cash. Some gifts were made personally to the recipients; others were placed in their 1934 Trusts. It is not possible to arrive at an exact figure for the total of the gifts Junior made to any of his six children for several reasons. For one, the value of the gifts cited in the text is the value at the time the transfer was made; all of these assets appreciated considerably in the following years. For another, there is an important distinction between personal gifts and those placed in the Trusts. The former went entirely into the portfolio of the recipient, while the latter increased the value of the Trusts from which the six children received the annual income. Another complication in trying to estimate total value is that the five brothers could invade the principal of their 1934 Trusts for purposes approved by their Trust Committees; Babs was the only one of the six who could not do this. Thus, the net worth of the brothers would vary considerably over the years depending on how much each brother took out of his Trust for other investments and how well the investments did. The limitation on Babs may have been a factor in her rebellion against her father. Yet the value of her 1934 Trust at the time it was established ($12 million) plus the value of her one-third share of Abby's Trust ($11.1 million), the whole growing steadily in value, made her quite wealthy just in terms of the income yielded.

5. JDR, Jr., Financial Records, Rockefeller Family Office.

6. The best source of information on the Sealantic Fund is a lengthy unpublished manuscript entitled "John D. Rockefeller, Jr., and the Sealantic Fund" by William G. Wing, a staff member of the Rockefeller Brothers Fund in the 1960s and 1970s. The manuscript, written at some point after 1973, is on file at the Rockefeller Brothers Fund office. Hereinafter cited as Wing MS.

7. Moscow (1977), p. 166.

8. Financial data in this section is derived from the annual statements of Midtown Development and Investment Corporation and accompanying correspondence, RAC.

9. Profit-and-loss data provided by Rockefeller Center, Inc.

10. Christy Manuscript, p. 16, RAC.

11. Krinsky (1978), pp. 106–7.

12. Midtown Development and Investment files, RAC.

13. Information on the progress of the Greater New York Fund campaign is taken from JDR 3rd's diary and the pages of the *New York Times*.

Chapter 25

1. Among many other places, Junior stressed this in a letter to JDR dated Nov. 15, 1949, specifically noting that a copy was being sent to Chorley. Kenneth Chorley was born in Bournemouth, England, in 1893 and emigrated to the U.S. with his parents in 1900. In 1923, after an early career in railroading, he became an assistant to Arthur Woods and Beardsley Ruml at the Laura Spelman Rockefeller Memorial and the Spelman Fund. He then worked on conservation projects for Junior. In 1930 he became vice president of Colonial Williamsburg, and served as president from 1935 to 1960.

2. Junior to JDR, Feb. 23, 1950.

3. These facts were set forth in a detailed report transmitted to Junior by Chorley on Jan. 1, 1950.

4. Supra, Ch. 22.

5. JDR to Junior, Mar. 25, 1941.

6. Junior to Chorley, Nov. 27, 1945.

7. Ibid. A memo listing the four points was attached to the letter. Also see Junior to JDR of Dec. 26, 1945.

8. Chorley to JDR, Nov. 27, 1945.

9. Bassett Hall was built by Col. Philip Johnson between 1753 and 1766. In 1800 it was purchased by Burwell Bassett, a nephew of Martha Washington, who lived in the house for approximately forty years. Although the house is only one block from Duke of Gloucester Street, it sat on a 250-acre site when Junior purchased it in the early 1930s, and he deeded the entire property to JDR.

10. The edited draft is in the RAC in a file entitled "Racial Question—Williamsburg—1946–51."

11. Junior to JDR, Aug. 31, 1949.

12. Junior to JDR, Nov. 30, 1949.

13. *New York Times*, Apr. 21, 1950, p. 1.

14. Special Survey Committee memorandum by John C. Goodbody, Mar. 30, 1950, RAC.

15. Kershaw Burbank memo of Apr. 8, 1950, with attached letter from Elliot C. Cohen to Burbank dated Apr. 4. Some of the information in this chapter is based on an interview with Kershaw Burbank on April 28, 1982.

16. Untitled draft of Mar. 28, 1951, RAC.

17. Letter from Junior to trustees of Colonial Williamsburg, Apr. 10, 1952. Five years later, Junior made still another grant to Colonial Williamsburg, again for $15 million. It was his last grant, so that his total giving was nearly $65 million over a thirty-year period.

Chapter 26

1. JDR to Dulles, Dec. 21, 1950.

2. On Dulles' return to State, see Mosely (1978), pp. 248–52.

3. For an excellent description of the occupation, see Ch. 15 ("Supine Japan") in James C. Thomson, Jr., Peter W. Stanley, and John Curtis Perry, *Sentimental Imperialists* (New York: Harper & Row, 1981), pp. 203–16. For a contemporary account, see Robert A. Fearey, *Occupation of Japan: Second Phase* (New York: Macmillan, 1950).

4. Dean Acheson, *Present at the Creation* (New York: Norton, 1969), p. 432.

5. Ibid., p. 426.

6. Acheson (1969, pp. 431–32) tells the story of how Rusk asked for demotion from the post of deputy under secretary of state to take over the Far Eastern Bureau at a critical time, a move that won Acheson's "high respect and gratitude" and caused him to put

Rusk's name "very high on the list" when President-elect Kennedy asked for recommendations for the post of secretary of state in 1960.

7. The other State Department man, who traveled ahead of the main party, was Robert A. Fearey, the author of the 1950 book about the occupation.

8. Acheson (1969), p. 526.

9. "U.S. Offers to Defend Japan Against Russia," *New York Herald Tribune*, Feb. 2, 1951, p. 1.

10. Dulles to JDR, Apr. 25, July 13, and July 31, 1951.

11. "United States-Japanese Cultural Relations: Report to Ambassador Dulles," Apr. 16, 1951, RAC.

12. Dulles to JDR, July 30, 1951. Some of the information in this section is based on an interview with Edgar B. Young in March 1982.

13. Acheson (1969), p. 538.

14. Paul G. Hoffman to JDR, Sept. 30, 1951.

15. Interview with Dean Rusk, Mar. 1979.

16. Dulles to JDR, Mar. 8, 1951 (one of two letters bearing the same date).

17. The idea for this project came out of a discussion JDR had with Matsumoto and Yasaka Takagi, a prominent scholar of American history and constitutional law at the University of Tokyo. Like Matsumoto, Takagi became an important counselor to JDR in his Japanese projects.

18. The Japanese art exhibit, a "major" one in Douglas Overton's view, appeared at the National Gallery in Washington and the Metropolitan Museum in New York in early 1953. For a photo story about the great success of the Japanese house in the MOMA garden, see *Life* magazine, August 23, 1954. For the story of the dedication of the Abby Aldrich Rockefeller Sculpture Garden, see the *New York Times* of April 29, 1953.

19. *The International House of Japan, Inc.: Challenge, Response, Progress—1952–1962*, 2 Toriizaka-machi, Azabu, Minato-ku, Tokyo, June 1963, p. 14.

20. Ibid., p. 22.

CHAPTER 27

1. Supra, Ch. 5.

2. Evidence of Junior's approval of the Brothers Fund was the fact that he donated $1 million to it in 1951. Junior and his sons signed the agreement concerning the $57.7 million gift on May 21, 1952 (RAC). The debt repayment schedule that Junior imposed called for Rockefeller Center to make its first payment of $7.7 million in 1952 and then to pay $5 million in each of the next three years. Following that, the payments would be $2.5 million a year, finally retiring the debt in 1969. Otherwise, the agreement was a reaffirmation of the terms of the 1948 sale to the brothers.

The discussion of Junior's gift in Collier and Horowitz (1976) is erroneous in almost every detail and omits pertinent information such as the relation of the gift to Rockefeller Center and Junior's tax incentive. The statement that "none of his sons with the possible exception of JDR3 seemed as interested in giving as he hoped they would be" (p. 253) is clearly wrong. All five were active in charitable giving and public service at the time, which pleased Junior immensely. The reason the Brothers Fund was created and the motive for Junior's gift are both incorrectly stated. And the statement that the gift catapulted the Fund "overnight" into national prominence is wrong. The gift came in installments and the Fund did not become nationally prominent until the 1960s, after it had received another large gift from Junior's estate.

3. Wing MS, Ch. III, "The Churches Come Together."

4. The theological education program of Sealantic is described in Wing's Chaps. V and VI.

5. Motorists crossing the George Washington Bridge today can see the cliff and extensive wooded area saved by this series of maneuvers. After years of negotiating and court cases, Sealantic bought the property in 1956 for $308,000. The opposition of the borough is explained by the fact that Fort Lee had been technically bankrupt as a result of the Depression and the move of the infant movie industry from Fort Lee to Hollywood. So much of the borough's land was taken by Palisades Park and the roads leading to the George Washington Bridge that the borough was zealous about getting "ratables." Today Fort Lee is prosperous, with many high-rise buildings.

6. The four Fidelity Union trusts had slightly different values—$11.2 million for JDR's four children; $9.3 million for Nelson's five; $9.2 million for Laurance's four; and $11.1 million for David's six. These were per capita trusts, meaning that they would be divided among the children living at the time of the indenture and *en ventre sa mère* (this legal term served to include the last of David's six children—his wife, Peggy, was pregnant at the time). The fathers could not invade the principal, but the children could petition the trust committee to do so once they were of age and were receiving the full income of their portion of the trust.

The authors have been able to see only JDR's 1952 Trust indenture. Indications are that the specific provisions for each trust differ, the brothers making choices appropriate to their own needs. In at least one other case, the process of transferring income to the children did not begin until age thirty and was completed by age thirty-five.

Another effect of the "per capita" nature of the trusts (as contrasted to the "per stirpes" 1934 Trusts) is that the 1952 Trusts will terminate upon the death of the youngest of Junior's descendants alive at the time the trusts were created, at which point the trusts will be divided equally among *all* of Junior's descendants. Ironically, the individual upon whom that eventuality is fixed is the first of Babs' grandchildren, none of whom benefited from the 1952 Trusts because Junior did not create one for Babs. Nelson's two youngest children, born long after the trusts were created, are also not covered by them.

Another difference is that spouses of beneficiaries of the 1952 Trusts can inherit both income and principal, up to 50 percent, if the beneficiary so stipulates in a last will and testament.

Alone among the brothers, JDR was appointed to the five-member trust committee for the 1952 Trusts.

Collier and Horowitz (1976) say that Junior funded the 1952 Trusts with 120,000 shares of Standard of New Jersey stock (p. 560 and note on p. 726). This is way off the mark. He actually put in more than 440,000 shares of New Jersey stock and nearly 150,000 shares of Standard of California. JDR, Jr., Balance Sheet and Financial Statement 1951 and 1952, Accounting Files, Rockefeller Family Office. JDR 3rd, 1952 Trust Indenture.

7. The Esso stock split three for one in 1956 and two for one in both 1976 and 1981. The 1.4 million shares of Esso that Junior owned in 1951, then worth $105.1 million, would in 1985 have been more than 17 million shares worth approximately $900 million. *Wall Street Journal*, Jan. 1, 1986.

8. Quoted in Collier and Horowitz (1976), p. 252.

9. Moscow (1977) has a detailed description of Kykuit, pp. 27–33.

10. The acreage cited here refers to the holdings of each of the brothers in the early 1970s. Junior's gift to JDR of 240 acres from the original estate in 1940 for Fieldwood Farm was augmented by him with a later gift of 28 more acres. JDR then rounded his property to the final 315 acres by making purchases of small adjoining parcels as they became available. When David bought Hudson Pines from Babs in the mid-1940s, the property was only 28 acres in size. Junior made up the balance by additional gifts in later years.

11. Again, Collier and Horowitz (1976) are in error on the Pocantico estate sale,

having confused the 1952 sale by Junior to his sons with the subsequent transaction among the brothers themselves in 1954, even though they cite the Hills Realty Files (RAC) where the information is contained.

CHAPTER 28

1. David's notes would make excellent source material, but it is likely to be a long time before they are made available to researchers, if ever.

2. The complicated history of Rockefeller Center makes it difficult to clarify what is and is not "part" of the Center. Which buildings are on the original Columbia land is clear enough, but there are other buildings in which the Center has a partial financial interest and still others in which it has no financial interest but which are managed by the Center and tied into its underground concourses. The best sources for untangling this are Krinsky (1978) and the Center files at the RAC. For some of the information in this chapter, the authors are grateful to the public relations department of Rockefeller Center, Inc.

3. Because of the lengthy negotiations, the Time Building was not completed and occupied until 1959. Its total cost was $83.3 million, partially secured by a mortgage. It and later buildings across Sixth Avenue are tied into the Center's undergound concourses and services.

4. Rockefeller Brothers Fund, *Three Year Report (1951–1953)*, 1954, RAC. From 1954 on, the fund published annual reports, one of the relatively few foundations to do so until this was made a legal requirement.

5. For an itinerant shoe salesman from West Virginia who never graduated from college, Strauss had a remarkable career. He became Herbert Hoover's private secretary in 1917 when Hoover was running the War Relief Administration. There Strauss came to the attention of Mortimer Schiff, who offered the bright, ambitious young man a position with Kuhn, Loeb. Strauss entered the Navy in World War II as a lieutenant commander and came out as a rear admiral. He had taken a deep interest in atomic energy, which led to his appointment to the AEC by President Truman. Strauss was brought into the family office by Laurance in Apr. 1950. See *Time* cover story, "U. S. Atom Boss," issue of Dec. 23, 1953.

6. Moscow (1977), pp. 314–15.

7. Ibid., pp. 299–311.

8. Technically, there was a committee for each trust, but since the five members were the same in every case, it was, for all practical purposes, a single committee. The original trustees were all closely connected to the family—Vanderbilt Webb, Winthrop Aldrich, Thomas Debevoise, Barton Turnbull, Raymond Fosdick. The members were empowered to fill vacancies, and over the years the members had less direct connections with the family, such as the former Federal Reserve Chairman William McChesney Martin; the president of Harvard, Nathan Pusey; and the chairman of New York Life, Devereux Josephs.

9. Most of the reorganization plans followed recommendations of the Hoover Commission, as noted in press reports of the time (*Christian Science Monitor*, Dec. 1, 1952). It is interesting to note that, at the time, Nelson was serving as the president of the Citizen's Committee for the Hoover Commission Report.

The perennial presidential candidate Harold Stassen was named administrator of the Foreign Operations Administration. Within a few years, the independent FOA was brought back into State and renamed the International Cooperation Administration— and then was taken out again in the Kennedy administration and renamed the Agency for International Development (AID).

10. Interview with Rufus Miles, Sept. 1982.

11. Morris (1960), p. 291; Collier and Horowitz (1976), p. 272; and the Dec. 17, 1954, issues of the *Washington Post*, the *New York Herald Tribune*, and the *New York Times*.

12. For a good discussion of the reorganization of this period, see I. M. Destler, *Presidents, Bureaucrats, and Foreign Policy* (Princeton: Princeton University Press, 1972).

13. Collier and Horowitz (1976) give a good description of the Geneva "open skies" story, pp. 273–76. For the timely thunderstorm, see Walter A. McDougall, *The Heavens and the Earth: A Political History of the Space Age* (New York: Basic Books, 1985), p. 127.

14. For a good analysis of the origins of the space program, including Nelson's urgings that the U.S. take leadership, see McDougall (1985), pp. 120–22.

15. Morris (1960), pp. 303–4.

Chapter 29

1. JDR 3rd, Financial Records, Accounting Files, Rockefeller Family Office.

2. The "unlimited charitable deduction" was a feature of the tax code until 1969; it meant just what the name implies—that the taxpayer had no limit on the amount that could be deducted for charitable giving. The catch was that to qualify for it one had to have paid at least 90 percent of taxable income in any combination of charitable contributions and taxes for nine of the ten previous years.

3. Douglas Southall Freeman to JDR, Dec. 8, 1951.

4. Junior to Freeman, Nov. 25, 1952.

5. Freeman to Junior, Nov. 26, 1952.

6. Junior to Freeman, Nov. 28, 1952.

7. Freeman to Junior, Dec. 4, 1952.

8. Junior to Freeman, Dec. 9, 1952.

9. For an excellent book on this era, see David Caute, *The Great Fear: The Anti-Communist Purge Under Truman and Eisenhower* (New York: Simon & Schuster, 1978).

10. Interview with Chadbourne Gilpatric, Sept. 1982.

11. Interview with Dean Rusk, Sept. 1979.

INDEX